INTRODUCTION TO THE PHILOSOPHIES OF RESEARCH AND CRITICISM IN EDUCATION AND THE SOCIAL SCIENCES

James L. Paul
University of South Florida

PEARSON

Merrill
Prentice Hall

Upper Saddle River, New Jersey
Columbus, Ohio

Library of Congress Cataloging in Publication Data

Introduction to the philosophies of research and criticism in education and the social
  sciences / [edited by] James Paul.
      p. cm.
  Includes bibliographical references and index.
  ISBN 0-13-042253-3
    1. Education—Philosophy. 2. Social sciences—Philosophy.
  3. Education—Research—Methodology. 4. Social sciences—Research—Methodology. I. Paul,
  James L.

  LB14.7.I58 2005
  370'.7'2—dc22

2004049914

Vice President and Executive Publisher: Jeffery W. Johnston
Publisher: Kevin M. Davis
Editorial Assistant: Margaret Bowen
Production Editor: Mary Harlan
Production Coordinator: Jolynn Feller, Carlisle Publishers Services
Design Coordinator: Diane C. Lorenzo
Text Design and Illustrations: Carlisle Publishers Services
Cover Design: Jason Moore
Cover Image: SuperStock
Production Manager: Laura Messerly
Director of Marketing: Ann Castel Davis
Marketing Manager: Autumn Purdy
Marketing Coordinator: Tyra Poole

This book was set in Berkeley Book by Carlisle Communications, Ltd. It was printed and bound by Phoenix Color
Book Group. The cover was printed by Phoenix Color Corp.

Pearson Education Ltd.
Pearson Education Singapore Pte. Ltd.
Pearson Education Canada, Ltd.
Pearson Education–Japan

Pearson Education Australia Pty. Limited
Pearson Education North Asia Ltd.
Pearson Educación de Mexico, S.A. de C.V.
Pearson Education Malaysia Pte. Ltd.

10 9 8 7 6 5 4 3 2 1
ISBN: 0-13-042253-3

Preface

During the last half of the 20th century, public life changed in fundamental ways that reflected, among other things, different social values, global consciousness, and new visions of the human community. Changes in concepts of communication, economics, space, time, transportation, human development, and intelligence are but a few of the life-altering changes that occurred during this time. The world we inhabit now and the values and systems of thought we use in making meaning of our lives stand in stark contrast to the world as it was before the 1960s. A part of this change was a radical transformation of thinking about knowledge. New perspectives on knowledge and approaches to acquiring or creating knowledge emerged, creating a diverse literature filled with vigorous debates about what is, and what is not, research. This book presents nine of those perspectives that now support different approaches to research and the implications of those perspectives for how we understand and critically appreciate the new pluralism in research that now exists.

Generally, students are not expected to know enough about all or even most of the different perspectives to be sophisticated in using the methods derived from those views. However, in order to read the literature and participate as a member of critical research communities, students need to have some knowledge of different perspectives and be able to think critically about the implications of the multiple discourses on knowledge and knowing that now exist.

Learning to value different approaches and to accord respect to those who hold views different from our own is an ethical matter as well as a necessary attitude for participating constructively in the conversation about the nature of research. This in no way suggests that students and researchers must believe all approaches to be equally valid or must agree with views that do not make sense to them. That, too, is an ethical matter. Rather, it suggests the need for a positive regard for those whose work is guided by different lights and for vigilance in keeping the conversation fair. Rapprochement may or may not be possible in some instances, and agreeing on basic research issues is not necessarily a goal. However, there should be a credible space where diverse scholarly perspectives are shared and valued and where an ethic of positive regard for diversity in scholarship sustains a pluralistic discourse about knowledge and ethics.

This book is intended for those who are learning to read education and related research literature as well as those preparing to become education researchers. It is intended to help students read and think critically about alternative approaches to research. The focus is not on research methods in different approaches but on the perspectives that provide the justifying reasons for those approaches.

The book begins with two chapters, both of which are essentially preamble to Parts Two and Three. In Chapter 1, I discuss some of the historical and political influences shaping the current conversations about different perspectives on research. In Chapter 2, Lynda Stone prepares those readers with a limited background in philosophy for reading and understanding Parts Two and Three. She provides foundational concepts and vocabularies related to the nature and history of philosophical arguments related to knowledge and method. Part Two includes nine research perspectives, each written by a senior scholar whose expertise in the perspective is widely known and respected. Part Three provides a "guided tour" of criticism, with the scholars introduced in Part Two demonstrating the use of critical method in applying their perspectives in critiquing six studies selected as exemplars of different research approaches or methods. In both Parts Two and Three, readers will learn the basic concepts and vocabularies of the perspectives and methods of criticism. In Chapter 11, I discuss central issues raised by a pluralistic view of research and the likely influence of critical perspectives on the future of education research.

Before the journey begins, however, a brief word about "perspectives" is needed. Throughout this text the emphasis is on different perspectives. Other words such as lens, worldview, or paradigm are used interchangeably with perspective. Although the nature of a particular perspective can be complex, it is essentially a coherent, systematic view of what is believed to be true, real, and of value. These perspectives and their use in critiquing different approaches to research form the core of this text.

The idea of perspectivism, or perspectivalism, is that there are different legitimate ways of understanding reality, different truths, and different ways of knowing the truth. This concept, associated with the work of Nietzsche in the last quarter of the 19th century, became significant in criticism of all forms of research in education and the social sciences during the last part of the 20th century. The implication of perspectivism, that knowledge is relative to the knower and the view of truth he or she holds, has divided the research community that had traditionally grounded its work in pursuit of universal truths and understandings. At issue here is whether reality is regarded as external and independent of an observer, the traditional positivist view, or a product of the mind of the observer. What may appear at first blush to be a "common sense" matter turns out to be a serious philosophical problem that, in the last quarter of the 20th century, generated a considerable literature on the nature of research and how it should be conducted.

This literature now includes multiple discourses about knowledge, each with its own vocabulary, history, worldview, and priorities. So, what is research? Or, what is "good" research? Although peer review is a mainstay for the research community in validating a researcher's work, such reviews are usually conducted within the perspective of the work being reviewed. Criticism, however, includes but also extends beyond the perspective in which the research is conducted. Perspective-based critique involves employing a point of view, a set of values, and assumptions that may be different from those of the study. For example, a quantitative study can be critiqued through a race-based, or a gender-based, lens or perspective. Such a critique yields a different view of the work. It raises questions and offers insights that are not a part of the logics and conventions of the perspective that guided the research. Some may question whether it is fair to raise questions that are outside the worldview reflected in the study. As you will see, this issue is raised in the text. However, the view here is that all authoritative texts are strengthened by critique from different perspectives. For example, Biblical texts are investigated and critiqued by archaeologists, historians, linguists, and individuals with different theological perspectives, each of whom brings a particular point of view, assumptions, and knowledge to the criticism. Similarly, published research is a text that has the authority of a particular approach or method and the academic community supporting the publication. All research should be examined and critiqued from any perspective that adds information and value with respect to the methods, claims, and implications of the research. The politics of research and the ethical quandaries that can arise in the methods and substance of different approaches to research can pose great difficulty for anyone reading and interpreting the texts who does not understand the perspectives involved and the nature of criticism.

The perspectives described in this text include postpositivism; pragmatism; constructivism; ethics and deliberative democracy; criticism; interpretivism; race, ethnicity, and gender; arts based educational research; and poststructuralism. Each perspective reflects a point of view and assumptions about the nature of research. Each has its own constructs and poses particular dilemmas when applied to other perspectives. Each tends to privilege one or more methods or approaches to research. And, finally, each has its own utilities with respect to applications in practice.

Why these perspectives? There are other perspectives that could have been included. Conversely, it could be argued that the differences could have been illustrated by focusing on a smaller number of more distinct perspectives. For example, postpositivism places a high premium on objectivity while others, such as interpretivism, prize subjectivity. Certainly, the perspectives selected are not mutually exclusive. Critical theory and race, ethnicity, and gender perspectives are similar and the similarities and differences depend, in part, on the scholar describing and interpreting the perspective. However, I selected these nine perspectives because, in my view, they are among the most prominent perspectives guiding research and framing criticism in the current research literature. Debates about different approaches to research are filled with concepts drawn from one or more of these perspectives. I chose to include what I consider to be a sufficiently broad sample of perspectives from several fields to enable students preparing to be researchers and those learning to read the research literature to see the similarities and differences in vocabularies, core concepts, and values of the different perspectives.

The studies critiqued are experimental, correlational, ethnographic, autoethnography, narrative, and arts based. Why these studies? Again, they do not reflect all possible approaches to research. They do, however, span a wide range of approaches in education and related research and provide critics with an opportunity to make rather clear discriminations with respect to different perspectives. Selecting an exemplar for any approach to research can be problematic. Researchers who share the same general perspective do not necessarily agree on exemplars. I consulted researchers within the different traditions and made decisions based on their advice and, in my opinion, the potential for the studies selected to serve the purpose of the text.

There is no presumption of endorsing or privileging a particular view in this text, but it would be naïve to assume that preferences will not surface. Indeed, it could not be otherwise. Although the purpose here is to appreciate the nature and values of different perspectives providing the justifying reasons for different approaches to research and the complexity of the increasingly diverse cultures of inquiry, my own perspective is clearly present in the construction of this text. I believe different kinds of research approaches are needed to answer different kinds of questions. This should not be confused with an eclectic view suggesting that anything can count for research and that any critique is as good as another.

Research is a systematic approach to knowledge that leads to understanding and it should conform to the rules and reflect the values of a particular perspective. Whether or not the research is "good" should be determined by the canons of the perspective. However, there is much more to be known about the research than is revealed in the findings or the product of a study. All approaches to research should be critiqued with respect to their implicit values and applications as well as the more typical peer review that focuses on the logic of the methods consistent with the perspective guiding the research. The critic should also work within a perspective. Just as the researcher is guided by a perspective and is held accountable by an academic community of peers, so the critic should be informed by a perspective that is anchored in a set of values and has its own integrity. An art critic, for example, has knowledge of the culture and art of the period in which a work was done and brings an informed view to his or her critique of a painting. Similarly, a postpositivist, poststructuralist, or critical theorist, for example, works within a perspective, the substance of which guides the critique of any work.

Most perspectives do not leave the person of the critic out of the critique. Although the perspective guides the critique, the critic is a thinking, valuing, cultural being whose voice in the critique should not be lost. Herein lies one of the conundrums of criticism. How much of criticism is personal beliefs and values? How much of it involves applying the standards and values of a particular perspective and how much of it is a personal construction based on the critic's beliefs, values, and cultural identity? Is such a distinction artificial? Scholars differ in their responses to these questions. My own view is that the individual is always in his or her work, whether planning, conducting, and sharing the findings of a study or in critiquing the work of another researcher. Determining where and how the "personal" voice of the researcher and critic is situated is a perspective-based issue. Postpositivist researchers, for example, seek to minimize the influence of their personal values and identity on their research while interpretivists emphasize the centrality of their personal voice.

Reasonable arguments have been advanced by some that a distinction needs to be made between research and inquiry, associating research more with basic science and inquiry more with applied studies. I did not make that distinction in this text because of the complexity and diversity of the various perspectives described here. Research and inquiry are, therefore, used interchangeably as are the terms researcher and scholar.

Although the book is written primarily for those interested in education research, the focus extends beyond education into the social sciences. My decision to broaden the focus was based on the fact that education researchers are continuing to explore and use new approaches to research in the social sciences and there is, therefore, a need to understand the perspectives grounding those approaches. The narrative perspective included in Part Two is an example of a view of research that is beginning to be used by some education researchers. Also, autoethnography, included as one of the studies in Part Three, has gained the interest of education researchers focusing their work more on individual students and teachers. Research approaches in education have had limited success in helping educators know more about the emotional lives and emotional capacities of their students. Although the focus of the narrative study included here is not directly related to education as it is typically framed in the research literature, it is an example of, among other things, an approach to examining qualities of the emotional life which is of concern to educators.

Finally, with respect to the purpose of this text, different genres of inquiry now are part of the educational research landscape and researchers need to be able to interpret and negotiate that landscape. Some will require statistical tools, others facility in creating and interpreting texts, and still others, paints, a canvas, and brushes. The purpose here is not to elevate the relative value of what one can come to know in the laboratory, library, writer's office, or studio but to provide the basis for visiting these different sites of inquiry with informed respect.

Acknowledgments

Any work of the scope and complexity of this text usually involves many participants. I have been most fortunate to work with competent and generous scholars who shared my commitment to a more credible pluralistic and respectful discourse on epistemology and method in research. The extent to which this text advances this agenda is a credit to those who provided the professional and personal support in making this project a reality.

It has been an extraordinarily satisfying experience to work with nine exceptional scholars in writing this text. Although they are deeply divided on their views of research, they all share the belief that researchers should be informed about the philosophical and historical foundations of knowledge and have respect for the different traditions of inquiry. Their individual and collective voices create the true value of this book.

In addition to the time commitment each of them made to write the perspectives and critiques of six studies, several provided additional support that was invaluable. Nel Noddings, a leading philosopher of education, is a mentor who provided guidance and encouragement without which this would have been a very difficult project to complete. George Noblit, a long-time friend and colleague who has a deep grasp of critical issues in research, gave me the courage to begin the work and support to see it through to the end. Lynda Stone, a gifted scholar, believed in this project and helped shape the focus of the book. Denis Phillips, a generous and thoughtful philosopher, provided candid and helpful criticism. He and Margaret Eisenhart, members of the NRC panel on the definition of research, provided unpublished materials and feedback on drafts that helped guide my interpretation of the history, intent, and perspective reflected in the panel's report.

I appreciate the scholarship and careful reading by those who reviewed the total manuscript. John Creswell, University of Nebraska–Lincoln; Patrick Dilley, Southern Illinois University; Helen Harrington, The University of Michigan; Mirka Koro-Ljungberg, University of Florida; Sandra Mathison, University of Louisville; George Noblit, University of North Carolina–Chapel Hill; and Amira Proweller, DePaul University, offered insightful commentaries. As can be expected when scholars with differing perspectives read and provide feedback on a book about perspectives, they had different views of the strengths of the work and areas they thought could be improved. Their insights were helpful to me in writing the final draft of the book.

Kevin Davis, publisher at Merrill/Prentice Hall, was committed to this project from the beginning and provided strong support and wise guidance in all phases of its development. His wisdom about what makes a useful textbook and his enabling style made this an enjoyable as well as an engaging project. I also appreciate the remarkable competence and assistance of all of the editorial and production staff at Merrill/Prentice Hall. Their professionalism and the technical quality of their support were consistently outstanding.

I am especially grateful for the contributions that Ben Graffam and Kathleen Fowler, two of my doctoral students, and Patricia Parrish, a former doctoral student, made to this book. They provided major assistance with all phases of the work, including substantive feedback and edits on various drafts of the manuscript. Their competence and enthusiasm for scholarly work are sources of inspiration and personal satisfaction.

Doctoral students in the philosophies of research and criticism seminar I have taught for the past 10 years contributed to the development of my thinking about the kind of text needed in this area. The readings for the seminar changed over time as students helped me appreciate the kind of material needed to assist them in understanding and respecting different philosophies of research.

William Rhodes and William Morse, emeritus professors of psychology at the University of Michigan, have been sources of inspiration and support. Rhodes, who started his career as a behaviorist, has written extensively about his intellectual journey into postmodern social theory, especially involving understandings of research on disability. His ideas have challenged my thinking about knowledge and knowing. Morse, a pragmatist and humanist with views akin to my own, is an astute critic with a discerning mind and a very generous spirit. His values as a scholar and mentor have become markers for me in thinking about multiple perspectives and criticism in research.

The development of this text has extended over a period of several years and I have benefited from the counsel of colleagues in different disciplines. I was given generous assistance that ranged from advice about exemplar studies in different genres of research to reviews of drafts of manuscripts. Although it would not be possible to name all who added value to this text, I do wish to acknowledge and express my appreciation to several colleagues who made special contributions. They include Betty Epanchin, Ann Cranston-Gingras, Wayne Sailor, Elliot Eisner, Scot Danforth, Kofi Marfo, Robert Dedrick, Carolyn Ellis, Scott Paul, and Glen Dunlap.

Finally, I am grateful to my wife, Maria, for her continued support of my work. This meant, among other things, tolerating my being "away from home" for many hours, even while I was in my study. It meant being willing to explore Istanbul while I remained on a balcony overlooking the Bosphorus to write. It meant spending time alone on the beach at Angelino's Sea Lodge while I remained in the room working on this manuscript. It also meant giving me access to her considerable editorial skills.

My hope is that the text will justify the confidence of all who contributed to this work. It will if the purpose of the text, i.e. providing basic understandings of research perspectives and criticism for graduate students learning about research, is realized.

James L. Paul

Brief Contents

PART ONE

RESEARCH IN EDUCATION AND
THE SOCIAL SCIENCES   1

CHAPTER 1
Historical and Philosophical Influences
Shaping Perspectives on Knowledge   1

CHAPTER 2
Philosophy for Educational
Research   21

PART TWO

PERSPECTIVES IN EDUCATIONAL
RESEARCH   43

CHAPTER 3
Perspectivism and Critique of Research:
An Overview   43

CHAPTER 4
Nine Perspectives of Research   49

PART THREE

THE PERSPECTIVES AS CRITIQUES   90

CHAPTER 5
The Carr et al. Study   92

CHAPTER 6
The Heath Study   135

CHAPTER 7
The Alexander Study   171

CHAPTER 8
The Raudenbush et al. Study   206

CHAPTER 9
The Ellis Study   250

CHAPTER 10
The Sullivan Study   284

CHAPTER 11
Challenges Facing Researchers
and Scholars in the 21st Century   315

AFTERWORD
A Metacritique of the Text   327

GLOSSARY   329

AUTHOR INDEX   331

SUBJECT INDEX   333

Contents

PART ONE

RESEARCH IN EDUCATION
AND THE SOCIAL SCIENCES   1

CHAPTER 1

Historical and Philosophical Influences
Shaping Perspectives on Knowledge   1

James L. Paul

The Positivist Legacy   1
   The Tenets of Logical Positivism   2
   Defeat of Positivism   2
   Remnants of the Positivist Legacy   3
Changing Perspectives of Knowledge   4
Perspectival Issues Dividing Researchers   5
   Logics in Use   5
   Culture, Identity, and Research from the Margins   6
   Utility and Application of Research Products   7
   Politics and Self-Interest   8
   Postmodern Social Theory   8
The Nature of Debates About Perspectives
of Knowledge   9
Twenty-First Century Markers for the Interactions
of Research, Public Policy, and Values
in Education and the Social Sciences   11
   Education Science and Public Policy   11
   Education Science and the Law   13
   Science and Social Values   14
   Concluding Perspective on the Interaction of Science,
    Public Policy, and Social Values   16

Summary: Basic Concepts   17
A Concluding Perspective   17

CHAPTER 2

Philosophy for Educational Research   21

Lynda Stone

Philosophy   23
Modern Philosophy   25
Sub-Traditions   26
Twentieth Century   28
Knowledge   30
Science   32
History   34
Language   36
Conclusion   38

PART TWO

PERSPECTIVES IN EDUCATIONAL
RESEARCH   43

CHAPTER 3

Perspectivism and Critique of Research:
An Overview   43

James L. Paul, Ben Graffam, and Kathleen Fowler

Nine Critics   44
Basic Topics Comprising the Perspectives   45
Conclusion   48

CHAPTER 4

Nine Perspectives of Research   49

Perspective 1: A Postpositivist, Scientifically
Oriented Approach to Educational
Inquiry   49
D. C. Phillips

Perspective 2: Pragmatism   57
Nel Noddings

Perspective 3: Constructivism as a Theoretical and
Interpretive Stance   60
Yvonna S. Lincoln

Perspective 4: Interpretive
and Narrative   65
Arthur P. Bochner

Perspective 5: Arts Based Educational
Research   68
Tom Barone

Perspective 6: Race, Ethnicity,
and Gender   72
Beth Harry

Perspective 7: Critical Theory   76
George Noblit

Perspective 8: Ethics, Methodology,
and Democracy   79
Kenneth R. Howe

Perspective 9: Poststructuralism   83
Lynda Stone

PART THREE

THE PERSPECTIVES AS CRITIQUES   90

CHAPTER 5

The Carr et al. Study   92

READING: "Comprehesive Multisituational
Intervention for Problem Behavior in the
Community: Long-Term Maintenance and
Social Validation"   92
Edward Carr et al.

Perspective 1: Postpositivism
on the Carr et al. Study   114
D. C. Phillips

Perspective 2: Pragmatism
on the Carr et al. Study   116
Nel Noddings

Perspective 3: Constructivism
on the Carr et al. Study   118
Yvonna S. Lincoln

Perspective 4: Interpretive and Narrative
on the Carr et al. Study   120
Arthur P. Bochner

Perspective 6: Race, Ethnicity, and Gender
on the Carr et al. Study   125
Beth Harry

Perspective 7: Critical Theory
on the Carr et al. Study   126
George Noblit

Perspective 8: Ethics, Methodology,
and Democracy on the Carr et al. Study   130
Kenneth R. Howe

Perspective 9: Poststructuralism
on the Carr et al. Study   132
Lynda Stone

CHAPTER 6

The Heath Study   135

READING: "Questioning at Home and at School:
A Comparative Study"   135
Shirley Brice Heath

Perspective 1: Postpositivism
on the Heath Study   151
D. C. Phillips

Perspective 2: Pragmatism
on the Heath Study   153
Nel Noddings

Perspective 3: Constructivism
on the Heath Study   155
Yvonna S. Lincoln

Perspective 4: Interpretive and Narrative
on the Heath Study   156
Arthur P. Bochner

Perspective 6: Race, Ethnicity, and Gender
on the Heath Study   160
Beth Harry

Perspective 7: Critical Theory
on the Heath Study   162
George Noblit

Perspective 8: Ethics, Methodology,
and Democracy on the Heath Study   166
Kenneth R. Howe

Perspective 9: Poststructuralism
on the Heath Study   167
Lynda Stone

CHAPTER 7

The Alexander Study   171

READING: "Performing Culture in the
Classroom: An Instructional
(Auto)Ethnography"   171
Bryant Keith Alexander
Perspective 1: Postpositivism
on the Alexander Study   188
D. C. Phillips
Perspective 2: Pragmatism
on the Alexander Study   190
Nel Noddings
Perspective 3: Constructivism
on the Alexander Study   192
Yvonna S. Lincoln
Perspective 4: Interpretive and Narrative on the
Alexander Study   193
Arthur P. Bochner
Perspective 6: Race, Ethnicity, and Gender
on the Alexander Study   197
Beth Harry
Perspective 7: Critical Theory
on the Alexander Study   198
George Noblit
Perspective 8: Ethics, Methodology, and
Democracy on the Alexander Study   202
Kenneth R. Howe
Perspective 9: Poststructuralism
on the Alexander Study   203
Lynda Stone

CHAPTER 8

The Raudenbush et al. Study   206

READING: "Higher Order Instructional Goals in
Secondary Schools; Class, Teacher, and School
Influences"   206
Stephen Raudenbush et al.
Perspective 1: Postpositivism on the Raudenbush
et al. Study   226
D. C. Phillips

Perspective 2: Pragmatism on the Raudenbush
et al. Study   229
Nel Noddings
Perspective 3: Constructivism on the Raudenbush
et al. Study   231
Yvonna S. Lincoln
Perspective 4: Interpretive and Narrative
on the Raudenbush et al. Study   234
Arthur P. Bochner
Perspective 6: Race, Ethnicity, and Gender
on the Raudenbush et al. Study   238
Beth Harry
Perspective 7: Critical Theory on the Raudenbush
et al. Study   240
George Noblit
Perspective 8: Ethics, Methodology, and Democracy
on the Raudenbush et al. Study   244
Kenneth R. Howe
Perspective 9: Poststructuralism
on the Raudenbush et al. Study   246
Lynda Stone

CHAPTER 9

The Ellis Study   250

READING: "'There Are Survivors':
Telling a Story of Sudden Death"   250
Carolyn Ellis
Perspective 1: Postpositivism
on the Ellis Study   263
D. C. Phillips
Perspective 2: Pragmatism
on the Ellis Study   265
Nel Noddings
Perspective 3: Constructivism
on the Ellis Study   267
Yvonna S. Lincoln
Perspective 4: Interpretive and Narrative
on the Ellis Study   268
Arthur P. Bochner
Perspective 6: Race, Ethnicity, and Gender
on the Ellis Study   273
Beth Harry
Perspective 7: Critical Theory
on the Ellis Study   276
George Noblit

Perspective 8: Ethics, Methodology,
   and Democracy on the Ellis Study   279
   Kenneth R. Howe
Perspective 9: Poststructuralism
   on the Ellis Study   281
   Lynda Stone

CHAPTER 10

The Sullivan Study   284
   READING: "Voices Inside Schools: Notes from a
   Marine Biologist's Daughter: On the Art and
   Science of Attention"   284
   Anne McCrary Sullivan
Perspective 1: Postpositivism
   on the Sullivan Study   292
   D. C. Phillips
Perspective 2: Pragmatism
   on the Sullivan Study   294
   Nel Noddings
Perspective 3: Constructivism
   on the Sullivan Study   296
   Yvonna S. Lincoln
Perspective 4: Interpretive and Narrative
   on the Sullivan Study   298
   Arthur P. Bochner
Perspective 5: Arts Based Educational Research
   on the Sullivan Study   301
   Tom Barone
Perspective 6: Race, Ethnicity, and Gender
   on the Sullivan Study   305
   Beth Harry
Perspective 7: Critical Theory
   on the Sullivan Study   307
   George Noblit

Perspective 8: Ethics, Methodology, and
   Democracy on the Sullivan Study   310
   Kenneth R. Howe
Perspective 9: Poststructuralism
   on the Sullivan Study   311
   Lynda Stone

CHAPTER 11

Challenges Facing Researchers
and Scholars in the 21st Century   315
James L. Paul
Challenges in Defining Research   316
The Wall: Coming Down or
Being Repaired   318
Critical Philosophical Issues
Dividing Scholars   319
Educational Researcher's Identity
in the Academy   322
Preparing Researchers and Scholars
for the 21st Century   323
A Concluding Perspective   324

Afterword: A Metacritique
of the Text   327
James L. Paul

Glossary   329

Author Index   331

Subject Index   333

NOTE: Every effort has been made to provide accurate and current Internet information in this book. However, the Internet and information posted on it are constantly changing, so it is inevitable that some of the Internet addresses listed in this textbook will change.

CHAPTER 1

Historical and Philosophical Influences Shaping Perspectives on Knowledge

James L. Paul

Educational researchers at the beginning of the 21st century work in an intellectual environment in which there are many views of research, each of which is supported by an academic community. This was not true 40 or so years earlier. Until sometime after the middle of the 20th century education researchers were guided by a single perspective or philosophy of science, logical positivism. In this perspective, the definition of research was clear, the standards well specified, and the methods agreed upon. Whether writing a dissertation proposal, applying for research funding, submitting a manuscript for publication, presenting a research paper at a professional meeting, or compiling a portfolio to support academic promotion and tenure, the norms were well established. So what changed? When and why did it change? Why are there now many views and so much controversy among researchers about the nature of research? Are all of the various perspectives equally valid? How can those learning to read the research literature make sense out of the different perspectives and discriminating judgments about their relative qualities and values in research?

In this chapter, I describe some of the cultural, professional, and political contributions to the rather dramatic changes that have occurred in thinking about research over the past several decades and the current context of the pluralistic discourse on knowledge and method. I discuss the background of the emergence of postpositive views of science, including the positivist legacy, changing perspectives of knowledge differences, and the kinds of issues that continue to divide researchers in their views of knowledge and method. I then examine the nature and functions of debates in addressing perspective-based differences, recent legal and political markers for what may be interpreted as a mainstream philosophy of science in an environment of multiple possibilities, and a concluding discussion of the interaction of science, public policy, and social values.

THE POSITIVIST LEGACY

For a half a century, more or less, we have been in a post-positivist world, i.e. a world after positivism. This means that positivism, the view that provided the philosophical foundation for research methods in education and the social sciences since the latter part of the 19th century, is no longer accepted as a philosophy of science. In order to understand and appreciate the history and complexity of current research perspectives, it is useful to have some understanding of the nature of positivism, the reasons for its defeat, and the significant remnants that continue to be a part of research cultures.

Michael Friedman (1999), a historian and philosopher of science, describes logical positivism as one of the most influential intellectual movements in the 20th century. It is, he asserted, "not too much to say . . . that twentieth century intellectual life would be simply unrecognizable without the deep and pervasive current of logical positivist thought" (p. xii). The nine perspectives presented in this text emerged as alternatives and, to some extent, as resistance to logical positivism. Understanding the positivist legacy provides a basis for interpreting some of the ongoing controversies about the nature of legitimate research. Although an extensive discussion would go beyond the purpose here, the following discussion will center on three issues: (1) the tenets of logical positivism, (2) the defeat of logical positivism, and (3) the remnants of positivism.

The Tenets of Logical Positivism

Logical positivism, or logical empiricism, refers to philosophical ideas developed by the Vienna Circle, a group of mathematicians, philosophers, physicists, a historian, and a sociologist that convened at the University of Vienna during the 1920s and 1930s under the leadership of Moritz Schlick, a professor of philosophy. The Vienna Circle was committed to ridding philosophy of science of the influences of metaphysics, idealism, and phenomenology that had dominated European philosophy during the 19th century. Michael Scriven colorfully captures their rather extraordinary character and success in this regard:

> The Vienna Circle or *Wiener Kreis* was a band of cutthroats that went after the fat burghers of Continental metaphysics who had become intolerably inbred and pompously verbose. The *kris* is a Malaysian knife, and the Wiener *Kreis* employed a kind of Occam's Razor called the Verifiability Principle. It performed a tracheotomy that made it possible for philosophy to breathe again. (Scriven, 1969, p. 195–209)

Although there were philosophical differences among members of the Vienna Circle, the argument that, for purposes of science, only verifiable statements have meaning, became the centerpiece of their position (Phillips, 1987). Statements that are neither verifiable nor tautological, i.e., such that the truth arises entirely from the meaning of its terms, are simply meaningless. The line between science and nonscience, such as metaphysics, ethics, aesthetics, and religion, was clearly established by the Vienna Circle's definition of true statements.

Defeat of Logical Positivism

Friedman (1999) points out that the "logical positivists" who migrated to the United States became associated with a simplistic view of radical empiricism that led to an understanding of natural science as ". . . elaborate devices for recording and systematizing our sensory experiences (and a belief that natural science is) . . . the continuous accumulation of more and more observable facts" (p. xiv). Viewed in this way, Friedman suggests the extreme and "one might even say violent" reaction within professional philosophy and the humanities more generally was to be expected.

Phillips (1987) offers another view of the confusion that has resulted from researchers discussing the demise of positivism without being clear about what, exactly, had died. He suggests that scholars, ostensibly debating positivism, have not been very discerning regarding the different perspectives brought into the line of rhetorical fire. He lists positivism, developed by Comte, a French philosopher; logical positivism, developed by the Vienna Circle; behaviorism, developed by Watson and others; and empiricism, referring to several epistemological positions, as the perspectives that have unwittingly been represented in various debates as "positivism."

The loss of a single authoritative voice in the definition of knowledge and the standard for method that occurred after the middle of the 20th century created a context of controversy among scholars and researchers in education and the social sciences. Late 20th century understandings of language, self, and the nature and sociology of different kinds of knowledge juxtaposed with behaviorism, for example, have been predictably confusing and resisted attempts at rapprochement among scholars. In fact, debates between positivist and nonpositivist scholars have been difficult and, at times, rancorous (Sailor & Paul, 2004). There have been various levels of sophistication in the debates, and it is prudent to maintain a degree of skepticism about claims or counterclaims concerning all perspectives. If a perspective developed by professional scholars of whatever stripe is reduced by critics to something that appears ridiculous, one is well advised to look at least as carefully at the arguments used in reaching such a conclusion as at the conclusion itself.

As penetrating as logical positivism was in philosophy and the sciences, it was defeated both politically and philosophically. The political interests of positivists were defeated when the Nazi regime came to power, and when Moritz Schlick, the leader of the Vienna Circle, was shot and killed by a deranged student at the University of Vienna in 1936.

There are two general accounts of what defeated the logical positivism as a philosophy of science. One is the work of W. V. O. Quine, an American philosopher and logician, in *Two Dogmas of Empiricism* (1951) in which he successfully challenged the validity of the positivist distinction between analytic and synthetic statements. The other account is the work of Karl Popper (1959) who articulated the principle of falsification as an alternative to the principle of verification. Popper, in his *Logik der Forschung* (1935; *The Logic of Scientific Discovery,* 1959), held that a criterion of demarcation between empirical, or scientific, statements and metaphysical statements should replace the meaning criterion employed in the verification principle. He argued that the demarcation criterion should be falsifiability, or refutability, not verifiability. In making his case, Popper used psychoanalytic theories as examples of claims that could be supported with "evidence" but still not be true. On the other hand, theories, which he viewed as "bold conjectures" that could emanate from almost any place, including metaphysics, should be stated such that it is possible to provide evidence through criticism and experiments that could refute the theory if it were not true. From Popper's perspective, knowledge comes from the elimination of error. Unlike the theory of verification, in which you never have all of the case required to be absolutely certain that a proposition is true, a single case can be used to render a proposition false.

Some scholars have continued to be interested in logical positivism and its influence on 20th century philosophy of science. There are even different accounts of the nature of logical positivism as developed by the Vienna Circle (Friedman, 1999). Nevertheless, the current status of logical positivism as a defeated philosophy of science remains the same.

Remnants of the Positivist Legacy

Phillips (1987) points out that there are several important and enduring remnants of the positivist legacy, three of which deserve attention here. First, although the verifiability principle became a "contorted monstrosity that choked to death under its own weight" (Phillips, 1987, p. 42), the rejection of metaphysics as having any valid explanatory status in research is still embraced by most researchers. Second, although early behaviorism was defeated by philosophical and linguistic arguments, several variations of behavioral theory are now reflected in well-developed social science programs such as positive behavior support, cognitive behaviorism, and social learning theory. Third, notwithstanding the predilection of nonempiricists celebrating the demise of positivism to throw the baby out with the bathwater (Phillips, 1987, p. 43), the role of empirical data in the growth of human knowledge continues to be recognized and valued.

However, when one explains the ultimate defeat of positivism, three conclusions appear warranted. First, positivism is no longer regarded as a tenable philosophy of science. Second, alternative perspectives on knowledge were developed and, to some extent, were defined as reactions against positivism. Third, many basic positivist principles have survived and continue to be reflected in research in education and the social sciences.

A basic question arises, then, as to how knowledge is developed, critiqued, and extended in a systematic way within diverse communities of scholars and researchers. In the following section I address some of the political issues and institutional consequences involved in the changing views of research.

CHANGING PERSPECTIVES OF KNOWLEDGE

The development of the social sciences was dramatic during the first half of the 20th century. Most of the disciplines accepted the positivist view that empirical knowledge was the *sine qua non* of science and that a precondition for the development of a social science was the adoption of empirical research methods for describing and discovering the lawful regularities of phenomena such as human behavior, learning, communities, and social institutions.

Guided by a positivist epistemology, researchers in education and the social sciences produced sophisticated bodies of knowledge and practices during the 20th century. Whereas philosophers had traditionally occupied a significant role in the critique of knowledge and research methods, many social scientists, following the lead of the physical scientists, came to believe that the method for discovering and knowing the truth, i.e., the scientific method, was sufficient and there was no need for a critique of method. In general, the focus in education research and the social sciences was on the judicious employment of the right methods, with relatively little social, moral, political, or epistemological critique of those methods. There were, of course, notable exceptions (see Chapter 4, pp. 72–76).

The defeat of positivism around the middle of the 20th century had profound effects on thinking about what we know, what we can know, and how we can know it. This unsettling of the epistemological foundation of science, combined with the uprooting of basic social institutions and public policies, created an unstable and turbulent intellectual environment for scholars during the latter part of the 20th century. Precedent and tradition in approaches to research no longer trumped reasoned alternatives ethically and/or epistemologically. Research in the social sciences and education strained, mostly unsuccessfully, to contain or, in some instances, to negate new discourses addressing issues of power, privilege, and voice, confounded with gender, race, ethnicity, and ideology. An inability of positivist conceptions of knowledge and method to address some of the most salient social issues during and following the 1960s formed the backdrop for the philosophical debates about knowledge and knowing. It was in this context that the perspectives discussed in this text were developed and debated. For example, the results of "objective" tests of achievement and of intelligence created a negative image of minority students in schools. The objectivist tradition was limited to what could be observed and measured. The cultural bias in tests made them invalid for students whose ethnic culture was different than students on whom tests were normed. Needed was not only a different norming of tests but a perspective to enable educators and policymakers to understand more about the complex and culturally variable lives of all students.

Issues such as this informed the critiques of the dominant research perspective. The debates that ensued were not on a level academic playing field. They never are. The politics of science are coextensive with the systems of interests and the structures of authority in the academy in which scientists and scholars are educated and trained and in which many do their work. The contrasting voices of those who uphold the canons of tradition, often referred to as conservatives or mainstream thinkers, and those who challenge the traditions, often called liberals, dissenters, radicals, or worse, form necessary tensions among the perspectives needed for the growth and survival of intellectual traditions. When the canons, i.e., the beliefs about knowledge and knowing in a perspective, become indefensible to those in the mainstream of a discipline, major shifts in the perspective occur. (See Kuhn, 1970, for an extensive discussion of paradigm changes in science.) This is what happened when logical positivism/empiricism was defeated and alternative perspectives, such as those later discussed in Part Two, emerged.

This rather linear sounding change can be misleading, especially in education and the social sciences. Mainstream perspectives change slowly and are accompanied by changes in research funding, publications criteria, and so forth. An example in education research was the slow acceptance of single subject research designs in the late 1970s and early 1980s. Prior to this time research funding was generally not available and publication outlets were limited. Now most education researchers accept this view of research and the methods associated with it. At the present time, the "arts based" perspective is not widely accepted by mainstream education researchers. This may change. The reality is that there are always contending perspectives, alternatives that reflect different worldviews and interests. That, in my opinion, is desirable and necessary for the growth of understanding within and among groups of researchers embracing different views of the nature and purpose of their work. In the following section, I discuss some of what may arguably be considered the more basic issues dividing research perspectives.

PERSPECTIVAL ISSUES DIVIDING RESEARCHERS

Many perspective-based issues divide researchers and those differences are described in the literature from different disciplines. I will describe five of the issues that figure prominently in the continuing debates: (1) the nature of the logic used; (2) identity, culture and research from the margins; (3) the utility and application of products of inquiry; (4) the role of politics and self-interest; and (5) the bold challenge of postmodern social theory and poststructuralism.

Logics in Use

Abraham Kaplan (1964) wrote *The Conduct of Inquiry* when the shifts in the vocabulary and philosophical underpinning of research methods were only beginning. His text, in many ways, anticipated the discussion to follow over the next several decades and his analysis continues to be useful in examining the nature of arguments.

Kaplan (1964) distinguishes between the cognitive styles of scientists and philosophers, or what he called their "logics in use," and the explicit formulation of logic or, "reconstructed logic." "Logics in use" are to reality what a physician's explanation is to a patient's fever. Many logics in use are evident in fields of inquiry, but Kaplan observes,

> What is objectionable is only the claim to proprietorship, the implication that criticism is inadmissible unless the soundness of the criticized method is first granted. The policy is objectionable, equally in science and in politics, that what's mine is mine and what's yours is negotiable. (p. 8)

Kaplan (1964) argues that the concept of a "natural logic," or universal rationality, is a myth, as linguists and anthropologists have demonstrated. Language, culture, the state of knowledge, the stage of inquiry, and the particular problem under consideration affect the logics in use.

Following the work of Carnap, one of the leaders of the Vienna Circle, and Reichenbach, a member of the Berlin group of logical positivists (although he preferred the term "logical empiricist"), one of the most widely accepted reconstructed logics was the "hypothetico-deductive method." According to this reconstruction, Kaplan (1964) observes, "The scientist, by a combination of careful observation, shrewd guesses, and scientific intuition arrives at a set of postulates governing the phenomena in which he (sic) is interested; from these he (sic) deduces observable consequences; he (sic) then tests these consequences by experiment, and so confirms or disconfirms the postulates, replacing them, where necessary, by others, and so continuing" (p. 10).

Kaplan (1964) notes that a reconstructed logic is, essentially, a hypothesis although it has been accorded extra logical status and has been useful in advanced physics and, to a lesser extent, in the biological and behavioral sciences. Kaplan does not argue against the hypothetico-deductive reconstruction. Rather, he challenges its usefulness in revealing logics in use that do not fit the reconstruction. He recounts the well-known example of an inebriated man looking for his lost car keys under a street light because the area around the light was the only area where he could see. That is, we are guided by the lights of the logic we use but those lights are of little help in seeing other possible constructions. Kaplan's argument four decades ago remains useful in thinking about the self-limiting, or logically contained, nature of all perspectives.

Culture, Identity, and Research from the Margins

A rich and diverse research literature is coming from persons who have been marginalized. A central argument is that research is situated in time and cultural space and this has profound implications for what is studied, how it is studied, who studies it, and how it is interpreted. Sleeter (1999) emphasizes culture, history, and a cosmological frame of reference as grounding research. Research from the margins, in her view, is distinguished epistemologically by

> . . . its interrogation of the position of the knower within a stratified society, and the implications of that position for knowledge construction. . . . [Knowledge is] bound with one one's viewpoint, which in turn is influenced by one's life experience and social position in a stratified society. . . . Afrocentricism rests on the premise that people of African descent should be their own subjects of their own history rather than someone else's objects of study, and that the place of people of African descent in the knowledge production process matters epistemologically. (pp. 16, 17)

This general view is reflected in new fields of inquiry such as Africana studies, feminist studies, womanist studies, gay and lesbian studies, neo-Marxist studies, and disability studies that emerged with considerable force during the last quarter of the 20th century, some earlier.

Is all knowledge subjective?

Emphasizing the socially constructed and value-laden nature of knowledge, each of these areas of research and scholarship seeks to reclaim and to rescue their identity from social constructions by researchers who have been disproportionately middle class, able bodied, white men. They have an implicit goal of improving the lives of persons from marginalized groups with an emphasis on emancipation and an action agenda.

The values reflected in these areas of scholarship were nurtured and, to a large extent, grew out of the advocacy movement in the late 1960s and early 1970s that gave a great deal of attention to the issue of voice, i.e., "Who speaks for whom?" Questions of agency, identity, and values became primary concerns in framing human rights. They also helped refocus research approaches that had been unable to address issues of lived experience and meaning. This was the political and cultural context within which qualitative and interpretive research methods from anthropology, sociology, and the humanities began to gain support in education research.

The civil rights movement and the litigation that followed impacted education research programs in the academy. Enclaves of researchers gathered and new departments, institutes and centers were formed. Further, the Western canon included in the undergraduate liberal arts curriculum of universities was challenged and the critics of the canon and the research that had established and informed it gained a niche for critiquing and informing the curriculum.

In summary, research from the margins is research that emerged in resistance to, or rejection of, the epistemology and values implicit in an objectivist, or positivist, perspective. At issue is the very nature of knowing as creating rather than observing; for example, gender, ethnicity, and racial identities. Knowledge is the product of social construction, formed out of the values and insidious forces of culture. Research from the margins, then, has focused on the politics of knowledge and the pretense of objectivity in discourses on truth, validity, and value.

Utility and Application of Research Products

One of the significant issues dividing researchers is their different views of, and emphasis on, the applied or practical value of their work. All researchers want their research to be relevant and meaningful. They differ, however, in their views of the nature and terms of the relevance and meaning of their research. Federal research funding agencies and many private sources of support for research are now specific about their expectations that research dollars have specific, quantifiable returns in improving practice, which is an important issue with implications for the research culture. For example, some approaches to research, such as the study of positive behavior support, have clear and specific applications in schools. The empirical methods commonly associated with postpositivism are generally more easily applied to practice in the way we typically think about the curriculum, student learning, and achievement. The implications for interventions may not be as clear, however, for other approaches such as narrative, or arts based research. These approaches have different utilities. The issue here is not the epistemology of the perspective of the approach but where the perspective leads in terms of practice.

This concern arises in the context of the current school reform movement and the focus on measurable student outcomes and the practical knowledge needs of teachers and policy makers. This has been interpreted as specific interventions or methods and, therefore, tended to devalue theory. Noddings makes a strong point about this issue in her discussion of pragmatism in Chapter 4. She comments, "Thinking and acting work together as one process. Both theory (to guide thinking and acting) and practice (to test the suggestions of theory) are important; they are *equally* important".

Politics and Self-Interest

Complex issues motivate challenges to the prevailing view of science at any point in time and equally complex issues motivate resistance to change. As suggested earlier, some of the issues are philosophical, involving concerns about the nature of knowledge and assumptions about objectivity, truth, certainty, and self. Others are more blatantly political, involving the self-interest of those resisting change and the self-interest of those advocating it. Throughout most of the 20th century, the hegemony of positivist science made it difficult to publish articles that addressed voice and privilege in appropriate narrative and interpretive forms. The hegemony extended beyond criteria for publications to research funding, and criteria for promotion and tenure. The interaction of these philosophical and political issues created an intellectual environment for researchers, and for advanced graduate students learning how to understand and conduct research, that became contentious and difficult. Intense struggles in academic departments and professional associations between and among those from different research traditions ensued. This is not new, of course. John Dewey (1910) describes the process well:

> Certain men or classes of men come to be the accepted guardians and transmitters—instructors— of established doctrines. To question the beliefs is to question their authority; to accept the beliefs is evidence of loyalty to the powers that be, a proof of good citizenship. Passivity, docility, acquiescence, come to be primal intellectual virtues. Facts and events presenting novelty and variety are slighted, or are sheared down till they fit into the Procrustean bed of habitual belief. Inquiry and doubt are silenced by citation of ancient laws of a multitude of miscellaneous and unsifted cases. This attitude of mind generates dislike of change, and the resulting aversion to novelty is fatal to progress. What will not fit into the established canons is outlawed; men who make new discoveries are objects of suspicion and even of persecution. (p. 149)

More recently, in similar spirit, Page (2000) observes,

> If "questions authority" and "question everything" are apt watchwords for recent developments in qualitative research, the momentum they signal has not operated in isolation, but has evolved in tension with conserving tendencies that have sought to blunt or discredit critique. . . . (p. 100)

Identifying an issue as self-interest does not, or should not, in any way diminish its importance or validity. Self-interest, whether referring to an individual, a professional organization, an academic department, or adherents to a philosophy of research, is a part of any progress or regress. The issue here is that we work in human and political contexts with many interests, some of which are in conflict. Some of the conflicts are about technical or philosophical issues. Others are more about territoriality or personality. It is important to recognize and respect the difference and to be aware that some are amenable to reasoned argument and some are not. It is not infrequent that ethical dilemmas are created by the conflicts. These too must be recognized and addressed.

Postmodern Social Theory

Both positivists and postmodernists have been reduced to caricatures in debates, with positivism being portrayed as simplistic and postmodernism as nonsense. Neither of these portrayals, in my opinion, is even close to the truth.

Postmodernism, discussed by Stone in Chapter 2, means after the modern period. Modernity is a broad concept referring to major cultural changes and shifts in thinking about the material world reflected in science, art, architecture, and religion that started roughly in the 17th century and ended around the middle of the 20th century. Just as there was no single positivist view, neither is there one postmodern view. This has been confusing for those trying to understand literature and it has contributed to the difficulties in critiques of postmodern theory.

Like most significant intellectual shifts, the postmodern movement has had a pervasive impact on discourses in virtually every area of the humanities and the social sciences. The impact on the academy and on professional and scientific associations and literature has been extensive. Not all of what is argued is, in my view, of value; neither is all without value. Eagleton (1996) comments,

> Postmodernist culture has produced, in its brief existence, a rich, bold, exhilarating body of work. . . . It has also generated more than its share of execrable kitsch. It has put the skids under a number of complacent certainties, prises [sic] open some paranoid totalities, contaminated some jealously protected purities, bent some oppressive norms and shaken some rather frail-looking foundations. . . . It is [sic] produced in the same breath an invigorating and paralysing [sic] scepticism [sic], and unseated the sovereignty of Western Man, in theory at least, by means of a full-blooded cultural relativism. (p. 27)

Smith (1989) asserts that a new epoch of human thought emerged quietly and irrevocably, with the triumph of Christianity in the fourth century and the dawn of modern science in the seventeenth century serving as key radical turning points in the understanding of self and the world. John Dewey despaired of any integrated outlook and attitude (as) the chief intellectual characteristic of an age and, Smith (1989) observes, "every succeeding decade has borne him out" (p. 2).

This view can be instructive in the present context of competing perspectives on knowledge. Whether one takes a postmodern view in challenging the prospect of any integrated outlook, there is certainly reason for concern when any perspective is represented as sufficiently inclusive to negate the need for, or reality of, alternative views.

THE NATURE OF DEBATES ABOUT PERSPECTIVES OF KNOWLEDGE

Debates are a method for taking the measure of the strength of arguments. They help keep intellectual diversity alive. They also serve an important political purpose in leveraging interests in particular points of view. Debates typically take more the form of arguments found in courtrooms, where attorneys amass evidence to support a claim, than the form of investigation found in a medical clinic, where physicians, guided by theory, collect data to discover the most accurate diagnosis for an illness. That is, debates are not necessarily designed to gain a rapprochement or deeper understandings, although those are desirable ends, so much as they are to provide space for arguments and counter arguments. Indeed, they could not be otherwise because the perspectival differences exist at the level of assumptions that are, by definition, givens and less likely to be debated. Facts can be used to refute assumptions but assumptions are not fully supported by facts or they would not be assumptions. Scholars frame their arguments in the context of perspectives such as those later discussed in Part Two. Interest is usually in extending the rationality or applicability of a perspective with coherent arguments and, often, with data.

There was a great deal of contentious debate about research perspectives in education and social science literature during the last quarter of the 20th century. As Page (2000) suggests, the focus and qualities of the debates varied widely:

Whether questioning authority or insisting on it, exchanges about research methodologies have sometimes been heated and, at other times, studiously indifferent. Both incarnations have prompted periodic calls for détente . . . . Détente is not aimed at consensus, but, rather, seeks to configure a space for public deliberation where just criticism can be accommodated and excel and unnecessary rupture be avoided. Such a space is easily closed by ideological sniping, even in such seemingly abstract debates as those over research methodologies. (p. 100)

The early debates about quantitative versus qualitative research in the late 1970s and 1980s were in some instances incoherent, with neither a shared vocabulary nor agreement about basic concepts needed to gain common understanding. K. Howe, in his "Two Dogmas of Educational Research" (1985) provided a perceptive and timely analysis of the major dimensions of the quantitative-qualitative debate, suggesting the arguments should be less dichotomous. Guba's *Paradigm Dialog* (1990), among other works during the late 1980s and early 1990s, was helpful in bringing some conceptual coherence to the debates by delineating the broad dimensions of systems of thought, or paradigms, that were at issue in the debates. Several scholars sought to lessen the contrasts and to articulate views that, while not reconciling the differences, constitute more inclusive arguments (Garrison, 1994; Howe, 1998; Howe & Eisenhart, 1990; Martin & Sugarman, 2001; Paul, 2002; Sailor & Paul, 2004). Other scholars found a rapprochement to be untenable (Heshusius, 2002). They argued that views with incompatible assumptions cannot be reconciled and that attempts to do so do not take seriously the depth of the disagreements. Nevertheless, the foci, vocabularies, and qualities of the debates have changed since the 1970s and 1980s when the legitimacy of qualitative or nonpositivist perspectives were broadly challenged by scholars representing a quantitative, or positivist, perspective. Deeper paradigmatic analyses and denser rhetoric in debates about the nature of research in education and the social sciences in the 1990s drew all perspectives and approaches to research into the sites of critics. This literature grew and now constitutes a new era in criticism for education research.

Some of the perspectival debates during the 1990s were especially interesting and even dramatic, with senior scholars arguing opposing views. One of the most illuminating was the debate between Elliot Eisner and Howard Gardner (1996) at the American Education Research Association meeting. The issue was whether a novel could count as a dissertation in education. Gardner rejected the idea, arguing, "the essence of research is effort . . . to find out as carefully as you can what's happening and then to report it accurately" (Donmoyer et al., 1996, p. 403). Eisner, on the other hand, supported the idea arguing that the issue has to do with "the form in which one has learned to write, the virtues of that form for addressing the particular problem that one wants to address, and the kind of understanding that one wants to foster" (Donmoyer, et al., 1996, p. 407).

In summary, students of research and scholarship are challenged to understand the substantive terms of the debates and the histories and dynamics of forces that attempt to "hold the line," those that seek to blur the line, and those that seek to rid discourses on knowledge of lines altogether. The spirit of debates challenging the traditional line of research is to obtain freedom and legitimacy in exploring alternative venues. The challenge has been, and remains, to create and sustain a valued space for expressing differences about important matters (Sailor & Paul, 2004). A major purpose of this text is to provide knowledge of the perspectives and critical methods that will help secure that space in negotiating perspectival differences about knowledge.

TWENTY-FIRST CENTURY MARKERS FOR THE INTERACTIONS OF RESEARCH, PUBLIC POLICY, AND VALUES IN EDUCATION AND THE SOCIAL SCIENCES

In an environment of change in research perspectives such as occurred during the last part of the 20th century, there are typically markers for what is considered to be the consensus or prevailing view. The markers remind the field that all is not up for grabs, all views are not of equal value, and that a mainstream opinion exists. Such markers give stability and ballast to a discipline so that the assumptions, definitions, and preferred methods can be specified. This is part of the political process that sustains the work of discipline-based researchers.

In this section, I discuss three current markers for what constitutes "good" science and a deepening concern about ethical issues in research. Each marker reflects the typically complex interactions of social science, public policy, and values. Together, they make visible some of the critical issues facing researchers and students of research at the beginning of the 21st century.

The first marker, the publication of *Scientific Research in Education* (2002) by the National Research Council, illustrates the deep coherence of education science and public policy. The second, the No Child Left Behind Act of 2001, clearly depicts the interaction of education science and law. The third, "the political storm in psychology" (Garrison, & Kobor, 2002) that was created by the publication of a scientific study in the *Psychological Bulletin,* a prestigious research journal in psychology, is a compelling example of the complex interaction of science and social values. These markers provide vivid illustrations of the epistemological issues and the political and ethical conundrums created by the complex interface of the society's values and moral perspectives and the work of science.

Education Science and Public Policy

The publication of *Scientific Research in Education* (2002) is a useful marker for beginning a discussion of the nature of science and the debates about knowledge and methods that have ensued since the middle of the 20th century. Sponsored by the National Academy of Sciences (NAS), the view of research described by the distinguished panel convened by the National Research Council (NRC) that wrote the report, some might view as the "official education science." Although most scientists and scholars may take offense at the idea of an "official" view of science in the liberal tradition of the academy and the free market of ideas, it is not likely that many would deny the special importance of a NAS report in shaping the concepts and vocabularies of inquiry and influencing the allocation of research funds as well as the culture of inquiry. The government sponsorship of the report, together with the senior professional status of the panel members, gives the report an authoritative voice in the research community.

The panel, convened late in 2000, was charged with responding to a bill proposed by Mike Castle, a Republican Representative from Delaware. (Note: My discussion of the background of the Panel's report is informed by personal communication with M. Eisenhart and D. Phillips (2003), both of whom were members of the panel, although I take full responsibility for my interpretation of the information they provided.) The Castle bill would have considered only "scientifically based quantitative research" and "scientifically based qualitative research." Scientifically based quantitative research referred to experimental studies with hypothesis testing and random assignments. Scientifically based qualitative research, on the other hand, was described ". . . quite incomprehensively—as a list of methods and a preliminary form of investigation requiring additional assessment of the 'experimental knowledge' derived from the methods" (Eisenhart & Towne, 2003, p. 32). This legislation would have specified that this definition of research be used in all programs applying for federal funding. The intent of this rather restrictive view of research was to address what Congress and many policy makers considered to be a somewhat bleak picture of educational research. Concerns included, among other things, the paucity of evidence that educational research had improved educational outcomes for students and the lack of standards to evaluate educational research.

In the presence of the kinds of questions raised about the nature and value of the research, it is not uncommon for the federal government to turn to the National Research Council (NRC) for guidance. The NRC is the operating arm of the National Academies of Science, Medicine, and Engineering which provides review and oversight functions for research that has implications for national policy. The NRC (2002) commissioned a distinguished panel of scholars to ". . . review and synthesize recent literature on the science and practice of scientific educational research and consider how to support high quality science in a federal educational research agency" (p. 1). The panel consisted of researchers from different disciplines in the social sciences and two from the physical sciences. The panel's report, *Scientific Research in Education,* was published in 2002. Bruce Alberts, President of the National Academy of Sciences, captured the spirit of the work of the panel:

> [The panel] was assembled amid vibrant debate about quality and rigor in scientific education research. In the course of its work, the committee revisited long-standing philosophies about the nature of science, so as to place them in the context of modern education research. [The panel] applied rigorous reasoning to its scrutiny of evidence and ideas, considered alternative perspectives, and presented its findings and conclusions in a language that invites constructive discussion. (NRC, 2002, p. vii)

Scientific knowledge progresses as a result of a "not-so-invisible hand of professional skepticism and criticism" (NRC, 2002, p. 2). With this view in mind, the thrust of the panel's work was to "help transform education into an increasingly evidence-based-field . . . " (NRC, 2002, p. viii). The panel defined scientific research as

> . . . whether in education, physics, anthropology, molecular biology, or economics, [scientific research] is a continual process of rigorous reasoning supported by a dynamic interplay among methods, theories, and findings. It builds understandings in the form of models or theories that can be tested. Advances in scientific knowledge are achieved by the self-regulating norms of the scientific community over time, not, as sometimes believed, by the mechanistic application of a particular scientific method to a static set of questions". (NRC, 2002, p. 2)

The panel of scholars described six principles that should guide researchers and underlie all scientific inquiry, including education research. According to these principles, researchers should (1) pose significant questions that can be investigated empirically; (2) link research to relevant theory; (3) use methods that permit direct investigation of the question; (4) provide a coherent and explicit chain of reasoning; (5) replicate and generalize across studies; and (6) disclose research to encourage professional scrutiny and critique.

The report generated considerable discussion when it was presented and distributed at the American Education Research Association meeting in 2002. As can be expected when vested interests in particular perspectives are present in debates, there was some distortion of the panel's position. Although the principles of research articulated by the panel were understood to apply across the social and physical sciences, the panel did not view research as necessarily always involving a search for universal laws or causal explanations. It did not suggest that research is neutral or value free, that knowledge is cumulative, or that the methods are infallible. Illustrations of research were included from a wide range of fields such as geophysics, political science, anthropology, and education to indicate the "context-dependence, value-ladenness, partiality, and messiness that characterize—in practice—all of scientific research." (M. Eisenhart, personal communication, 2003).

The panel suggested that scientific education research, "whether it is aimed primarily at uncovering new knowledge or meeting the dual goals of generating knowledge and informing practice, is influenced by the unique configuration of characteristic features of the educational enterprise" (Shavelson & Towne, 2002, p. 84). They described these features as values and politics, human volition, variability of educational programs, organization of education, and diversity. Further, they delineated three features of educational research: (1) its multidisciplinary nature; (2) ethical considerations; and (3) its reliance on relationships with educational practitioners.

When examined within the context of multiple frameworks for knowing, the report is situated within a post positivist perspective. It rescued the view of research from the narrow positivist tradition suggested in the Castle bill. Notwithstanding what can be accurately viewed as a move away from logical positivism, those who have critiqued the positivist tradition as the former overarching epistemology for the social sciences, including many education researchers, are concerned that the imprimatur of the NAS in general and the NRC in particular could serve to limit the view of what constitutes research. This has implications for the kinds of research that will be funded and published in the future and the curriculum in research training programs. Although the panel obviously worked very hard to be clear in its opposition to logical positivism, one can question whether it enhanced the conversation among those holding nonpositivist views of knowledge and knowing. Quite apart from what may or may not have been the intent of the panel is whether or not the report will effectively silence some of the debates about knowledge that raged during the last part of the 20th and the beginning of the 21st centuries. This remains to be seen. What can now be seen, however, is postpositivism serving as a marker for the contemporary understanding of knowledge and research.

Education Science and the Law

The No Child Left Behind (NCLB) Act of 2001 provides, among other things, more choices for parents and students, greater flexibility for states, school districts, and schools, and an emphasis on reading as a top priority. The Act has strong accountability provisions with an emphasis on high stakes tests in reading, science, and mathematics as measures of student achievement and the success of schools. It targets funding to research-based education programs that have been proven to be effective with most children. For example, federal funding will be available only to those programs that use "scientifically proven" ways of teaching children to read.

Section 1208 of the Act, which provides definitions, defines "scientifically based reading research" as research that applies rigorous, systematic, and objective procedures to obtain valid knowledge relevant to reading development, reading instruction, and reading difficulties. More specifically, it includes research that

1. Employs systematic, empirical methods that draw on observation or experiment;
2. Involves rigorous data analyses that are adequate to test the stated hypotheses and justify the general conclusions drawn;
3. Relies on measurements or observational methods that provide valid data across evaluators and observers and across multiple measurements and observations, and

4. Has been accepted by a peer-reviewed journal or approved by a panel of independent experts through a comparably rigorous, objective, and scientific review.

The view of research and useful knowledge described here is rather specific and reflects the increasing focus on evidence-based practices across different fields of education. The Act assumes that we can specify and measure what all children should know and learn in reading, mathematics, and science, and the grade level at which they should know it. Further, it assumes that accountability for assuring that children will have the expected grade-level knowledge and skills can be established on the basis of these measures. Scholars in education have challenged both of these assumptions. (See Noddings, 2002, for an excellent discussion of the challenges of high stakes testing.)

Whether or not one agrees with the standards movement and the high stakes testing policies and practices that accompany it, it is difficult to deny the shift in thinking about accountability in education and the science supporting it that has occurred during the past decade. The conflation of law and a particular view of education science, as reflected in the accountability provisions of NCLB Act of 2001, has created a political conundrum for those who have a different view of research and the educational interests of a diverse group of students. Resources are tied to a specific view of research that discourages approaches reflecting other views and could reduce the relevance of some voices in the important debate about knowledge in education science and the kinds of issues that should concern us in educating children.

Eisenhart and Towne (2003) provide an excellent discussion of the definition of "scientifically based research in education" in the NCLB Act of 2001 and the NRC report on *Scientific Research in Education* (2002). As participants in the development of some of these policy documents, they point out that neither the definitions contained in these documents nor their purposes are the same. Eisenhart and Towne (2003) make a well-reasoned argument that ". . . the various definitions, together with public input about them, can provide leverage for altering the meanings of scientifically based research and education research that are being operationalized in current public policy" (p. 31). This view is both helpful and illustrative of the interaction of research, public policy, and the policy making process.

Science and Social Values

A significant development in social sciences arose in psychology over the publication of controversial research related to the long-term effects of child abuse. The controversy was characterized by the Public Policy Office of the American Psychological Association (APA) as "the political storm of the century for the field of Psychology" (Garrison, E.G., & Kobor, P.C. 2002, p. 165). The issue arose in the spring of 1999 in response to a study by Rind, Tromovitch, and Bauserman published in 1998 in the *Psychological Bulletin* on the long-term effects of child sexual abuse. Authors of the study concluded that, contrary to public opinion, child sexual abuse "does not cause intense harm on a pervasive basis regardless of gender in the college population" (p. 46). The public outcry against the publication of these findings created a crisis in the APA and the scientific community at large.

The authors used a meta-analysis, an accepted statistical tool, to examine and integrate empirical findings across studies. The *Psychological Bulletin,* a highly respected journal in psychology, is peer reviewed and this process, involving the judgment of members of the scientific community, is the standard of choice for determining the quality of research before it is accepted for publication. The science and its safeguards were intact. The resistance came, however, as a result of the deep conflict between the study's findings of little or no harm from child sexual abuse and social values that condemn the abuse as abhorrent and *prima facie* harmful.

Social scientists, the media, and Congress condemned the study. Although some researchers in psychology challenged the method employed in the research, the credibility of the method being the only defense for publishing the study, the overarching concern was the ethical justification for publishing a study with findings that so obviously run counter to deeply held values. Fundamental concerns were raised about the proprietorship of knowledge, i.e., who "owns" it and has a right to it, and the prerogatives of scientists, e.g., the right and even the obligation to publish research that has been judged to be methodologically sound. The argument generally holds that a scientist has a duty to share her or his research findings and the scientific community and the public have a right to know.

Concerns about the potential harm in publishing the findings were weighed against the issue of academic freedom and the integrity of the quality control measure in place for publishing research, i.e., peer review. Criteria for suppressing research, which would be the net effect of not publishing work that had received a positive peer review, are not easily specified but rest, presumably, on some determination of the "public's interest." The difficulty of balancing the public's interest and the interest of science is well illustrated in this case as suggested by the different perspectives of the social scientists described below.

Lilienfeld (2002), in the same issue, supported the right of scientists to "explore controversial research questions, draw conclusions that are potentially unpopular, or both" (p. 183). He pointed out that the APA Council of Representatives (2002) "unequivocally affirmed [the] importance of protecting scientists' rights to report controversial or unpopular findings and journal editors' rights to publish them without interference" (p. 183).

The issues in this controversy serve to illuminate the power of science in public opinion and serious ethical dilemmas created when the interests of science, the scientist, and society are in conflict. The adjudication of these interests can be complex.

In the aftermath of the storm, George Albee, a distinguished psychologist, served as guest editor of a special issue of the *American Psychologist: Interactions Among Scientists and Policymakers: Challenges and Opportunities* (2002). Referencing the 500 years it took for the Catholic Church to admit its error in opposing Galileo's findings, Albee commented,

> . . . science ultimately wins out. Scientific findings may elicit passionate opposition, censorship, and official (religious and secular) condemnation, but scientific findings that are valid and reliable persist, whereas their critics do not. (Albee, 2002, p. 312)

Newcombe (2002), in the same issue, described five commandments for publishing scientific studies:

> (a) Scientific articles should be judged only by their logic and the strength of their evidence; (b) the results of a competent peer review should be accepted; (c) disagreements with scientific articles should be aired in peer reviewed commentaries; (d) efforts to judge scientific articles on the basis of political concerns should be resisted; and (e) the explicit rules and normative expectations of peer review should not be arbitrarily altered. (p. 202)

Sher and Eisenberg (2002), editors of the *Psychological Bulletin* in which the Rind et al. study was published, commented,

> Neither of us would attest to the ultimate scientific validity of this or any article that we have published. The state of knowledge in psychology is a moving target; what is state of the art one day can become obsolete and dated in light of new data and revised theory. The question is not whether the conclusions will stand the test of time but whether the article advances knowledge at present and helps to define a new research agenda based on a synthesis of what is known. Our opinion is that Rind et al. (1998) made the type of contribution that we look for in a *Psychological Bulletin* review. (pp. 206–207)

They also argue that the findings and conclusions of the study were mischaracterized:

> . . . [things] began spinning out of control when the venue for the scientific discussion of the article moved from the pages of scholarly journals and the meeting rooms of scientific conferences into advocacy-oriented Web sites, radio talk shows, political fundraising groups, and the halls of state legislatures and the United States Congress. (Sher and Eisenberg, 2002, p. 290)

The publication of this study, then, raised several fundamental questions: Does a finding that something is true trump a social value that declares that finding to be harmful? Must, as Albee suggests, science ultimately win? Is there an authorizing ethical principle that guarantees that any validated research, i.e., peer reviewed, can be published? How are the interactions of the interests of society and science best understood and managed? These are complex and interesting questions, especially at the beginning of the 21st century when, on the one hand, knowledge has been problematized both epistemologically and ethically, and, on the other hand, the strong voice of science is able to presume an amoral stance with respect to knowledge, even knowledge of the long term effects of the sexual abuse of children.

Concluding Perspective on the Interaction of Science, Public Policy, and Social Values

The scientific publication and laws discussed here mark significant and substantive direction or, depending on your point of view, redirection in education science at the beginning of the 21st century. Together, they suggest a coalescence of commitment to some of the remnants of the positivist legacy as well as postpositivist principles of research that may well reduce the intensity of the debates about knowledge that characterized the 1980s and 1990s. This does not mean, of course, that there is a uniformity of perspective among scholars in education and the social sciences. There is not. Even members of the panel that authored the NAS report were not of one mind about the philosophy of research. As will become clear in the discussion of perspectives in Part Two, prominent perspectives embrace some of the concepts rooted in the positivist legacy. It may well mean, however, that the positivist legacy has been somewhat embolden in its resistance to relativism, radical subjectivity, self-referenced constructions of knowledge, narrative understandings of truth, and the multiple literary and philosophical critiques of method included in Parts Two and Three.

Questions can be raised about the view of research presented in the NRC report by researchers and scholars whose scholarship is anchored primarily in postpositivist views of research. On the other hand, the NRC report, if read carefully, does accommodate some of the more critical issues raised by nonpositivist scholars (Eisenhart, 2002).

SUMMARY: BASIC CONCEPTS

The basic concepts discussed in the chapter are the following:

- Questions of the nature of reality, truth, value, and method in the social sciences were re-opened to the humanities in the 20th century and a rather exciting and complex pluralistic discourse about different perspectives of knowledge and method has followed.
- After positivism, several research perspectives were developed, all of which are supported by productive academic communities that transcend disciplinary boundaries and whose work is published in the literature on philosophies of research.
- Basic questions about the nature of knowledge and defensible methods continue to be reflected in debates among researchers who embrace different perspectives.

- Logics in use, views of the role of culture and personal identity, the perceived purpose and value of research, and the politics of self-interest are some of the critical differences among the perspectives.
- Some researchers embrace the notion of pluralism as a positive quality, some see possibilities or rapprochement, and others strive for supremacy of the perspective within which they work.
- Political influences on research are illustrated by recent Federal law (NCLB) and the NAS report on the nature of research that specify criteria, however disputable and varied, for what will count as research.
- The role of philosophy, especially ethics, has become more important as critique of method has become a more essential tool in a pluralistic research environment.

A CONCLUDING PERSPECTIVE

Perspectival shifts, or "turns," in the justifying reasons for different approaches to research radically altered the discursive practices and methods of researchers in education and the social sciences during the last half of the 20th century. What had been presumed to be objective, amoral, and, under specifiable conditions, universal was drawn under the lights of new physics and critiques of the confluence of mind, culture, and the representation of knowledge. Normative standards and procedures for adjudicating the trustworthiness of knowledge through peer review were challenged by critiques of the interactions of power, self-interest, and science. Critical interest in the nature and roles of mind, self, and language grew within and between different disciplines contributing to the development of widely varying perspectives of knowledge and knowing. Discourse communities with shared perspectives grew to create a complex and diverse intellectual environment for scholars and researchers.

The stakes are high and include such basic issues as the presumptive claims about the nature of reality, truth, and virtue, and material interest in the research industry. Not surprisingly, the debates in the social sciences about such basic issues range over an uneven terrain marked by self-interest and confusion over terms and concepts that have often mitigated open and reasoned arguments. The literature is vast and the analyses of knowledge and knowing can be dense and esoteric as well as erudite. Saul Bellow commented in his 1976 Nobel Laureate Lecture,

> The intelligent public is waiting to hear from Art what it does not hear from Theology, Philosophy, Social Theory, and what it cannot hear from pure science: a broader, fuller, more coherent, more comprehensive account of what we human beings are, who we are, and what this life is for. If writers do not come into the center it will not be because the center is preempted. It is not. (Quoted in Smith, 1989, p. 2)

The threats to the development of more productive and relevant educational research programs in the future may not be, as often assumed, the unyielding retrenchment of positivist researchers or, as also often assumed, the forceful entrenchment of those advocating radical nonpositivist epistemologies that challenge the traditional canons of educational research. The deeper threat, and one that will require vigilant resistance, is the possibility that the dynamics of intellectual battle, where political advantage is used to leverage outcomes of arguments about truth and value, will prevail over thoughtful and respectful argument. The most desirable future is most likely to be realized if researchers, guided by different lights, are committed to creating a valued space for different epistemological perspectives rather than subverting the interests of those who embrace different perspectives.

Different research perspectives are presented and applied in an analysis of different kinds of research in this text. Both the reality of multiple approaches to inquiry and the critical value each can have to the others are appreciated. The implicit argument is that different approaches to research have heuristic and critical value in advancing our understandings of our lives and our work, whether we are developing a theory of learning, performing culture in a classroom, attempting to improve the social skills of a child, or coping with our own grief.

QUESTIONS

1. What are some distinguishing characteristics of positivism, postpositivism, and nonpositivism as systems of inquiry?
2. Where do the worlds of science and social policy meet? What do the three examples discussed in the chapter tell us of that meeting?
3. How do the spaces in between disciplines affect inquiry's power and direction?
4. What has changed over the last half century in the nature of discourse about knowledge and knowing?
5. How do language, culture, knowledge, and inquiry affect the logics in use?
6. How might we define the margins of inquiry?
7. In what ways does the postmodern construct of self affect inquiry in the humanities and social sciences?

REFERENCES

Albee, George W. (2002). Exploring A Controversy. *The American Psychologist, 57*(3): 161–164.

Asantre, M. K. (1990). *Kemet, Afrocentricity, and knowledge.* Trenton, NJ: Africa World Press.

Banks, J. A. (1993). The canon debate, knowledge construction, and multicultural education. *Educational Researcher, 22*(5), 4–14.

Carter, K. (1993). The place of story in the study of teaching and teacher education. *Educational Researcher, 22*(1), 5–12.

Cizek, G. J. (1995). Crunchy granola and the hegemony of the narrative. *Educational Researcher, 24*(2), 26–28.

Connelly, F. M. & Clandinin, D. J. (1990). Stories of experience and narrative inquiry. *Educational Researcher, 19*(5), 2–14.

Creswell, J. W. (1998). *Qualitative inquiry and research design: Choosing among five traditions.* Thousand Oaks, CA: Sage Publications.

Dewey, J. (1910). *How we think.* Boston, MA: D.D. Heath and Co.

Donmoyer, R., Eisner, E., Gardner, H., Stotsky, S., Wasley, P., Tillman, L., et al. (1996). Viewpoints: Should novels count as dissertations in education? *Research In Teaching of English, 30,* 403–427.

Eagleton, T. (1996). Literary theory: An introduction. Minneapolis, MN: Minnesota University Press.

Eisenhart, M. (2002). Unpublished materials presented at the American Association of Colleges for Teacher Education Conference.

Eisenhart, M. (2003). Personal communication.

Eisenhart, M., & Towne, L. (2003). Contestation and change in national policy on 'scientifically based' education research. *Educational Researcher, 32*(7), 31–38.

Eisenhart, M., & Phillips, D. (2003). Personal communication on the National Academy of Sciences.

Eisner, E. W. (1991). *The enlightened eye: Qualitative inquiry and the enhancement of educational practice.* New York: Macmillan Publishing Company.

Foucault, M. (1980). *Power/knowledge: Selected interviews and other writings 1972–1977.* New York: Pantheon Books.

Friedman, M. (1999). *Reconsidering logical positivism.* Cambridge, MA: Cambridge University Press.

Gage, N. L. (1989). The paradigm wars and their aftermath: "A historical sketch of research on teaching since 1989." *Educational Researcher, 18*(7), 4–10.

Garrison, E. G., & Kobor, P. C. (2002). Weathering a political storm: A contextual perspective on a psychological research controversy. *American Psychologist, 57*(3), 165.

Garrison, J. (1994). Realism, Deweyan pragmatism, and educational research. *Educational Researcher, 23*(1), 5–14.

Geertz, C. (1988). *Works and lives: The anthropologist as author.* Stanford, CA: Stanford University Press.

Gieryn, T. F. (1999). *Cultural boundaries of science: Credibility on the line.* Chicago, IL: University of Chicago Press.

Giroux, H. A. (1992). *Border crossings: Cultural workers and the politics of education.* New York: Routledge.

Guba, E. (Ed.). (1990). *The paradigm dialogue.* Newbury Park, CA: Sage Publications.

Heshusius, L. (2002). More than the (merely) rational: Imagining ability diversity. *Disability, Culture and Education, 1*(2) 95–118.

Howe, K. (1985). Two dogmas of educational research. *Educational Researcher, 14*(8), 10–18.

Howe, K. (1988). Against the quantitative-qualitative incompatibility thesis (or Dogmas die hard). *Educational Researcher, 17*(8), 10–16.

Howe, K., & Eisenhart, M. (1990). Standards for qualitative (and quantitative) research: A prolegomenon. *Educational Reseacher, 19*(4), 2–9.

Howe, K. R. (1998). The interpretive turn and the new debate in education. *Educational Researcher, 27*(8), 13–20.

Jaeger, R. M. (1997). *Contemporary methods for research in education.* Washington, DC: AERA

Kaplan, A. (1964). *The conduct of inquiry.* San Francisco, CA: Chandler Publishing Company.

Kuhn, T. S. (1970). *The structure of scientific revolutions.* Chicago: University of Chicago Press.

Lagemann, E. (1988). The plural worlds of educational research. *History of Education Quarterly, 29*(2), 184–214.

Lagemann, E. C., & Shulman, L. S. (Eds.). (1999). *Issues in education research: Problems and possibilities.* San Francisco, CA: Jossey-Bass Publishers.

Leary, D. E. (2001). One big idea, one ultimate concern: Sigmund Koch's critique of psychology and hope for the future. *American Psychologist, 56*(5): 425–432.

Lilienfeld, S. O. (2000). Everything you need to know to understand the current controversies you learned from psychological research: A comment on the Rind and Lilienfeld controversies. *American Pschcologist, 57*(3), 193–197.

Lilienfeld, S. O. (2002). When worlds collide: Social science, politics, and the Rind et al. (1998) child sexual abuse meta-analysis. *American Psychologist, 57,* 176–188. — USE 2002.

Loflund, J., & Loflund, L. H. (1995). *Analyzing social settings: A guide to qualitative observation and analysis* (3rd ed.). Belmont, CA: Wadsworth.

Lyons, N. (1990). Dilemmas of knowing: Ethical and epistemological dimensions of teachers' work and development. *Harvard Educational Review, 60*(2), 159–180.

Martin, J., & Sugarman, J. (2001). Modernity, postmodernity, and psychology. *American Psychologist, 56*(4) 370–371.

Metz, M. H. (2000). Sociology and qualitative methodologies in educational research. *Harvard Educational Review, 70*(1), 60–74.

Mills, W. W. (1959). Philosophies of science. In *Sociological Imagination* (pp. 119–131). New York: Oxford University Press.

National Research Council. (2002). Scientific research in education. R. J. Shavelson & L. Towne (Eds.). National Academy Press: Washington, DC.

Newcombe, N. S. (2002). Five commandments for APA. *American Psychologist, 57*(3): 202–205.

No Child Left Behind Act of 2001, Pub. L., 107–110, 20 U.S.C. 6301 et. seq. (2002).

Noddings, N. (2002). Educating moral people: A caring alternative to character education. New York: Teacher's College Press.

Page, R. N. (2000). Future directions in qualitative research. *Harvard Educational Review, 70*(1), 100–108.

Paul, J. L. (2002). Perspectival and discursive discontinuities in special education research. *Disability, Culture, and Education, 1*(2), 73–93.

Peshkin, A. (1993). The goodness of qualitative research. *Educational Researcher, 22*(2), 23–29.

Phillips, D. C. (1987). *Philosophy, science and social inquiry: Contemporary methodological controversies in social science and related applied fields of research.* New York: Pergamon Press.

Popkewitz, F. S. (1991). *A political sociology of educational reform.* New York: Teachers College Press.

Popper, K. (1959). *The Logic of Scientific Discovery.* University of Toronto Press: Toronto.

Quine, W. V. O. (1951). Two dogmas of empiricism. *Philosophical Review, 60*: 20–43.

Rind, B., Tromovitch, P., & Bauserman, R. (1998). A meta-analytic examination of assumed properties of child sexual abuse using college samples. *Psychological Bulletin, 124, 22–53.*

Rogers, A. G. (2000). When methods matter: Qualitative research issues in psychology. *Harvard Educational Review, 70*(1), 75–85.

Sailor, W., & Paul, J. L. (2004). Framing positive behavior support in the ongoing discourse concerning the politics of knowledge. *Journal of Positive Behavior Interventions, 6*(1), 37–49.

Scheurich, J. J., & Young, M. D. (1997). Coloring epistemologies: Are our research epistemologies racially biased? *Educational Research, 26*(4), 4–17.

Scriven, M. (1969). Logical positivism and the behavioral sciences. In P. Achinstein & F. Barker (Eds.), *The legacy of logical positivism.* Baltimore, MD: The John Hopkins Press, (pp. 195–209).

Shavelson, R. J., & Towne, L. (Eds.) (2002). *Scientific research in education.* National Research Council. Washington, DC: National Academy Press.

Sher, K. J., & Eisenberg, N. (2002). Publication of Rind et al. (1998): The editor's perspective. *American Psychologist, 57*(3), 206–210.

Shulman, L. S. (1986). Paradigms and research programs in the study of teaching: A contemporary perspective. In M. C. Wittrock (Ed.), *Handbook of research on teaching* (pp. 3–36). New York: Macmillan Publishing Company.

Sleeter, C. (1999). Toward wisdom through conversation across epistemologies. In J. Raths & A. McAninch, (Eds.), *What counts as knowledge* (pp. 1–29). Stamford, CT: Ablex Publishing Co.

Smith, H. (1989). *Beyond the postmodern mind.* Wheaton, IL: Quest Books.

Snow, C. P. (1959). *The two cultures and the scientific revolution.* New York, NY: Cambridge University Press.

Spendler, G. D. (Ed.). (1955). *Education and anthropology.* Stanford, CA: Stanford University Press.

Stromberg, R. N. (1968). *European intellectual history since 1789.* New York: Appleton-Century-Crofts.

Tetreault, M. K. T. (1993). Classrooms for diversity: Rethinking curriculum and pedagogy. In J. A. Banks & C. A. M. Banks (Eds.), *Multicultural education: Issues and perspectives* (2nd ed., pp. 129–148). Boston, MA: Allyn & Bacon.

Wilson, E. O. (1998). *Consilience: The unity of knowledge.* New York, NY: Vintage Books.

CHAPTER 2

Philosophy for Educational Research

Lynda Stone
University of North Carolina at Chapel Hill

Bertrand Russell, the renowned 20th century English-born philosopher, wrote this in part about philosophy:

> Philosophy is to be studied, not for the sake of any definite answers to its questions, since no definite answers can, as a rule, be known to be true, but rather for the sake of the questions themselves; because these questions enlarge our conception of what is possible, enrich our intellectual imagination and diminish the dogmatic assurance which closes the mind against speculation. (Russell, 1959, p. 161)

This conclusion to Russell's text, *The Problems of Philosophy* (1959), opens a chapter, the purpose of which is to introduce the discipline of philosophy to educational researchers. It serves as an initiation only but can suggest much for further reading. Arguably many researchers pay little if any attention to philosophy: research is about methodology, data, a question. In an Anglo-American context, it is empirical. This chapter poses something more. This is that all inquiry, the asking of questions about life, is premised in philosophical ideas. These questions include what constitutes nature, human being, society, knowledge, truth, science, and the like. From this premise a second premise follows. It is that each researcher operates within a personal belief system of which philosophical ideas are a part and to which any disciplinary position, methodological selection, research stance, and specific research question relate. There is significant value for researchers in reading, studying, and knowing something about philosophy. This chapter offers one perspective, one interpretation on philosophy to assist researchers.[1]

British philosopher Roger Scruton writes this about perspective: "It goes without saying that the description that I . . . give of the nature of philosophy will reflect the particular philosophical standpoint of which I feel persuaded, and its merit in the eyes of the reader must reside in the fact that . . . [we are contemporaries]" (Scruton, 1995, p. 3). Through millennia, philosophers knew that the discipline changed but they largely believed that perennial philosophical truth was possible and that predecessors had not "gotten things right." For example, here is Russell in a later source:

> I do not say that we can here and now give definitive answers to all . . . ancient questions, but I do say that a method has been discovered by which . . . we can make successive approximations to the truth, in which each new stage results from an improvement, not a rejection, of what has gone before. (Russell, 1945, pp. 835–836)

Russell's project for seeking truth is initiation to the 20th century movement in analytical philosophy; a contrasting position from his contemporary, American pragmatist John Dewey. For Dewey, there is no final truth, no end to philosophy; "truth," or warranted assertability as he names it, arises in and is continually tested in on-going inquiry, of consequences of actions, and through consensus. In his *Reconstruction in Philosophy,* he writes, "[The] distinctive office, problems, subject matter of philosophy grow out of stresses and strains in the community life in which a given form of philosophy arises, and that accordingly, its specific problems vary with the changes in human life that are always going on" (Dewey, 1920/1948, Introduction, pp. v–vi). From this contextualist stance, Dewey's method is often a kind of dialectical logic as against Russell's analytical argumentation.

While recognizing the positions of Russell and Dewey, the perspective of this chapter assumes a contemporary contextualism that is stronger than that of Dewey. It posits a "social frame" to all inquiry, a specific location of thought within history. At various points, the writings of Richard Bernstein, Ian Hacking, Richard Rorty, and Stephen Toulmin are influential. Out of this perspective, philosophy today is "situated conversation," and no longer "desituted tradition" (see Toulmin, 2001, pp. 21, 217; Rorty, 1982/1987; 1979). It is historicist. Of these philosophers, Rorty wants to dispense with "Philosophy" altogether; Hacking, Toulmin, Bernstein (and this author) do not go this far. "Philosophy" remains for us (I believe) parasitic on a tradition, located in a present moment but not incommensurable across them, and with much disciplinary modification that yet entails what Toulmin posits as "reasonableness." In general, a paraphrase from Rorty (1967/1992) is useful: philosophy is "opinion" but not just any opinion. This characterization of philosophy for educational researchers is returned to at the close of this chapter.

This chapter is organized by these topical sections:

- Philosophy
- Modern Philosophy
- Sub-Traditions
- Twentieth Century
- Knowledge
- Science
- History
- Language

Before proceeding, a word about reading philosophy. It is an academic disciplinary field with a reputation for difficulty. This is because "questions" are posed that require complex answers at a high level of abstraction. Further, sometimes philosophic discourse is very technical, comprised of step-by-step, logical arguments utilizing discipline-specific words from specialized subfields and traditions. Reading philosophy requires concentration and what American analytical philosophers John Perry and Michael Bratman term an "aggressive" posture; this is imagining oneself "in a dialogue . . . as if the philosopher were . . . [a peer] trying to convince one of a startling new idea" (Perry & Bratman, 1986, p. 813). Two other points are salient: First, today it is well recognized that within the discipline's history, few persons largely wrote for many others—a sociology of intellectual life shared across realms of inquiry. One wants to open up contributions to contemporary thought but to not "throw out the past proverbial baby." Second, locating philosophy from a historicist premise, the perspective introduced earlier, means to be open especially to changing meanings. While the one "right" Plato cannot ever be clearly known, neither is any reading right. Appropriate reading means to locate his texts within his time and at various times down to today. It means gaining sophistication in understanding from various sources such as interpretations, commentaries, and critiques. The point of reading is distinction. In sum, reading appropriately entails always being skeptical about one's understanding—as "a kind of" Popperian falsification (named for British philosopher of science, Karl Popper). This means continually asking not "how right do I have this," but rather "how might I still have this meaning wrong" (see Popper, 1934/1985a).

PHILOSOPHY

Educational research is principally situated in modern philosophy and 20th century formulations. To understand these, a general introduction to the discipline is required. As is well recorded, the term "philosophy" comes from the Greek composite, *philosophia,* meaning love of wisdom and its search. As W. C. Kneale, professor of moral philosophy at Oxford, relates in the *Encyclopaedia Brittanica,* it was first used by ancient historians Herodotus and Thucydides, implying great knowledge, sound judgment, curiosity, and pursuit of mental excellence (see Kneale, 1967). The mathematician, Pythagoras reportedly was the first to call himself a philosopher. Even with texts from the presocratics, initiation of the discipline is usually with the writings of Plato. One recent survey text posits this:

> With Plato . . . we have the complete philosophical perspective . . . a comprehensive epistemology, metaphysics, and ethics, whose centerpiece is an intricately detailed theory of Forms. . . . He has provided . . . [complex] and subtle arguments and defenses . . . [subjecting] them to his own exquisite critical scrutiny. Perhaps it would not be too much of an exaggeration to regard Plato as the Form of a philosopher. (Scott-Kakures et al., 1993, p. 44)

At the dawn of the discipline, three subfields are central and remain so with varying relationships among them through millennia; these are *metaphysics, epistemology,* and *ethics.* If wisdom is entailed in the meaning of philosophy, its historical aim has been truth. Within these subfields and over time, the meaning and method of truth has changed. It has been contemplated, revealed, and proven; it has been sought through thought and "image," through logic and interpretation, and through test. Additionally, the seeking of truth has distinguished philosophy from the history of ideas, however, this distinction blurs for some today. Taken for granted into the 20th century, the philosophical aim of truth has itself become subject to question.

The first subfield of *metaphysics* is characterized, according to John Shand, as "the attempt by reason and argument alone to understand the essential structure of the world" (Shand, 1993, p. x). Its content is the great questions of human life, truth, goodness, and beauty as well as their basic elements such as substance and cause. It also is basic to principal systems-building, of philosophy as foundation, and related to all other inquiry. Over time, philosophy offers distinction with relationships to mathematics, music, astronomy, and later natural philosophy or physics, other natural sciences, and logic. At the outset division between philosophy and rhetoric also establishes a western hierarchy that separates the sciences (based in philosophy) and arts into the relatively late 20th century.

Epistemology, the second subfield of philosophy, concerns knowledge and its relationship to experience, belief, and later language. Importantly, as philosophy, argument and not empirical fact are its methodology. As Shand (1993) comments, epistemological questions, assumptions, and presuppositions underpin those of empirical investigation. Further, epistemology entails not only what can be and is known but also how knowing occurs. As indicated in the next section, if metaphysics is central in the classical period, epistemology assumes primary importance in the modern era.

Finally, the third subfield of *ethics* or moral theory also has ancient roots concerning human conduct and human relationships. Again across time, knowledge is related in varying ways to moral thought and action, as is politics. The latter assumes over millennia its own subdisciplinary distinction with connections to social science. In a turn to and renaissance of interest in ethics, some philosophers see the present 21st century, in late and postmodernism, as initiating an epoch in which ethics rather than metaphysics or epistemology is paramount.

By the 20th century, in philosophy other subfields have been and continue to be added to metaphysics, epistemology, and ethics. A detailed history of thought is interesting here; for now, know that in addition to separation of sciences and arts, separation of empirical and non-empirical disciplines, as just mentioned, is significant as is distinction (or at least attention to the relationship) of the natural and social sciences. One important differentiation in the early decades of the recent century is between philosophy and psychology. Today, a look at university catalogues, reading lists for courses, the proliferation of specialized journals, and the like illustrate present-day subfields. Some are topical, such as philosophy of mind, aesthetics, logic, and language; some are disciplinary and professional, such as philosophy of science, philosophy of biology and physics, and medical and business ethics; and some are interdisciplinary, such as bio-ethics, cognitive science, or artificial intelligence. In general, it is significant that scientists, social scientists, humanities scholars, and artists continue to read philosophy for its relationships to their own work; while status as the "queen of the disciplines" may not remain for philosophy, its significance for all inquiry is well recognized.

Related to a traditional history of ideas, another way to categorize philosophy has been to divide thought into major temporal/cultural epochs relative to changes in life conditions. These periods are Classical (ancient), Scholastic (medieval), and Modern (debatably with recent distinction of Postmodern). They are identified and bounded through the shifting triadic relationship of nature, divinity, and personhood. Here is a simplistic but useful breakdown: In the Classical period from 600 BC approximately to the 11th century AD, philosophers are interested primarily in person-nature distinction with the divine largely assumed. A key question concerns the difference between reality and appearance. Innate ideas from nature and God are perfect, true, and real and human thought is imperfect, not true, and merely appearance. In the Scholastic period, from the 11th to 14th centuries, attention is principally on the person-God relation with nature assumed as given by God. In this epoch, the ideas of God are real and key questions concern what man can know of these ideas. Following a period of non-philosophical dominance during the Renaissance, the conventional beginning of the Modern period, discussed in the next section, is the 17th century continuing into the present or relatively recent time. Modernity is complex as man mediates the relationships between men, asserts "control" over nature and, at least philosophically, separates knowledge from faith in the divine. Questions of reality and truth continue; changes, permutations, and subtleties over them abound or at least it so seems to "we moderns." One notes that in each of the three principal periods, philosophy is most like what today are considered separate disciplines: philosophy to mathematics (with attention to logic), philosophy to theology (with attention to scripture), philosophy to science both broadly and narrowly defined (with attention to language).

MODERN PHILOSOPHY

Philosophy connects to educational research in the 20th century through science; roots and development of this linkage is located in modernity. Manifestation occurs through the dominance of epistemology as the "doing of philosophy" and also in the emergence of a subfield, philosophy of science. Across modernity, too, God is in the picture but presence, it seems, becomes more and more taken for granted or philosophically ignored.

In modernity, science and philosophy are allied in that both seek foundation. Within philosophy, rationality as method is applied in two general approaches: synthesis and speculation. The former is abstraction from the particular to the general; the latter abstraction toward "something beyond," toward universalism, systematization, and teleology (see Scruton, 1995). Two other features typify philosophy across modernity. One is its self-reflective nature; for the first time, a meta-function exists within the discipline in considering its own constitution. The other is self-awareness in the idea that philosophy is written by humans for humans. The modern self is "born."

That modernity comes to be is agreed, but when and why this occurs has been debated. The *Oxford English Dictionary* actually dates the term from the sixth century with a meaning evolving from "existing now or being in this time" to "originating in the current age." What is significant is valuation of the "now" and subsequently the "new"; the latter is returned to shortly. Distinction between modern/modernity, modernism, and modernization is helpful too. Modernism refers to a specific period in late modernity in culture, in the arts, architecture, literature, and film particularly. Modernization has come largely to refer to a political and economic process by which entities not-modern are "made" so.

Modernity and modern philosophy are the present concern. In Toulmin's wonderful *Cosmopolis: The Hidden Agenda of Modernity* (1990), the initiation of the epoch spans from the early 15th to the late 19th centuries, from contributions of Gutenberg to Freud (Toulmin, 1990, p. 5). However, the standard account dates from the early 17th century, from beginnings of nation-states, empirical science and technology, writings of "new philosophers" (p. 9), and different lifestyles.

Lifestyles, forms of societal organization, bound an epoch and are demonstrative of epochal change. Medieval Europe characterized by a feudal order shifts from fiefdoms to nations. Economies based solely on localized agriculture are extended through trade and subsequently through industrialization. Great urban centers develop as do colonies. Events that previously had local impact assume wider significance and here "modern" meaning "new" enters intellectual debate. Canadian sociologist Zigmut Bauman writes, "From the moment of its triumphant entry into public discourse, the idea of the modern tended to recast the old as antiquated, obsolete, out of date, about to be deservedly sunk into oblivion and replaced" (Bauman, 1993, p. 592).

The standard account also has it that everything modern has been revolutionary and "good." Here is Bauman (1993) again: "[The modern was an] expression of a revolution taking place in the European mentality; of the new feeling of self-reliance and self-assurance, readiness to seek and try unorthodox solutions to any current trouble or worry, belief in the ascending tendency of human history and growing trust in human reason" (p. 592). Retrospectively, epochal changes appear to benefit human society and "civilization advances." Not so, Toulmin claims in a recontextualization, when one looks closely both at the record of 17th century events (and across millennia) and when one reconsiders what constitutes modern philosophy. Conflicts in the record indicate three possibilities: either history has been read incorrectly, or the record is mixed, or the desire for modern advancement has colored the view. At the least, the beginning of the modern era in 17th century Europe was not a time of peace and plenty.

As discussed, in modernity that is a complex historical epoch of conflict and change, an epistemological self emerges that is capable of and utilizing cognitive skills of reflexivity and reflectivity. The first, internal awareness of self, makes thought about external others, objects, and persons in a world possible. Physicality and mentality are extended into an environment. Inanimate objects are physical and material, whereas human bodies (special kinds of objects) are mental as well. One "knows" objects through a thought process in which source and outcome of knowing need be manifest. Process is a form of proof that incorporates evidence, justification, or verification of truth. As mentioned, deductive proofs begin with prior premises about data and through logic result in truth; inductive proofs begin with data from perception and through argumentation result in truth (see Hacking, 2002a, p. 168). Superordinate processes of argument include aggregation or association, unification of a single unit into a larger whole, as well as analogy, posing of the one as the same as all others and thus forming a whole. While difference is understood, it is difference "from" and "within" a unity. Basic, too, is a binary logic based in sameness and identity that continues in modernity from ancient times.

By high or late modernity, reflection on knowledge and knowing entails further insight concerning unities, especially as essence or "nature." A set of terms, with meanings that change according to philosophers and over time, is explicative, realist and idealist, and objectivist and subjectivist. The first of each pair asserts that there is something to be right or wrong about, which serves as a framework, as a source for knowledge, and as a possible outcome. The second of each pair asserts that something "in here" as in the self is sacrosanct, serving also as a source or outcome. Each is foundationalist, seeking to locate a ground for knowledge. This ground is truth.

In a present day idiom, earlier philosophies of truth seek correspondence. Evolving from the classical period, appearance gives way to representation. Representation, for some, "has to do" until "the veil of appearances . . . [allows us] to glimpse things as they are in themselves" (Rorty, 1990, p. 2). The language of "things in themselves" is reminiscent of Kant and of modern sub-traditions, which is discussed next. Some in the late modern era believe that there is nothing beyond representations. As one root, Dewey believes that a search for correspondence, for certainty, is wrongheaded (see Dewey, 1929/1988). His own theory of truth is pragmatic, that warranted assertions are made based on the testing of consequences. Still a later theory assumes a semantic form. It is based on the recognition that truth is only "got at" through sentences in which a statement is true as it fits with or is "coherent" to other true statements. Just for information, the roots are from the Polish mathematician Alfred Tarski (1931/1956; Hamlyn, 1987, pp. 308–309). In his own way he searched for the foundation in relations between ordinary and ideal languages; moving to the non-foundation in truth occurred in theory in subsequent times.

SUB-TRADITIONS

In modernity, three philosophical sub-traditions are significant: *rationalism, empiricism,* and *idealism,* with origins respectively in France, Great Britain, and Germany. Constituting a major division across the 17th and 18th centuries, the epistemological debate between the first two is "resolved" in the writings of Kant who initiates the third. Descartes, Spinoza, and Leibniz are named as key philosophers in the first as opposed to Locke, Berkeley, and Hume in the second.

In a recent account, philosopher Peter Markie makes the claim that each side is best understood as having family resemblance—and indeed that the traditions may agree more than disagree (Markie, 1998, p. 76). Nonetheless recognition of a set of basic ideas within each tradition is useful.

Rationalism is initiated in the writings of René Descartes whose interesting cosmopolitan life spanned the early part of the 17th century. One commentator offers this definition: "Rationalism holds that the human mind has the capacity, logically speaking, to establish truths about the nature of reality (including ourselves) by reason alone independently of experience" (Shand, 1993, p. 74). Descartes was a contemporary of Bacon and Galileo, and wrote about a wide range of topics, mathematics, astronomy, physics, and philosophy chief among them. His work ushered in what become known as "the Cartesian Revolution" (see Scruton, 1995), based on his Latin name, *Renatus Cartesius* (Blackburn, 1994, p. 56). In *Meditations on First Philosophy* (Latin 1641)[2] and related texts, Descartes sets out to locate "foundations . . . that are clear, distinct and certain" (Toulmin, 1990, p. 72) and determines two through his method of doubt. These are God and the *cogito,* the latter as mind *a priori* or given. One chief strand of both modern philosophy and science is initiated in this rationalist sub-tradition.

Empiricism is best initiated in the writings of John Locke whose life spanned most of the 17th century; interestingly, Descartes was an early inspiration. Here is the definition: "Empiricists hold that all material for knowledge, our ideas or concepts, and all knowledge of actual matters of fact, as opposed to logical or conceptual truths, must be derived from, or be reducible to, aspects of our experience" (Shand, 1993, p. 114). As Descartes, Locke was interested also in many things including science and politics, and as well, he traveled widely. His *Two Treatises on Government* (1690) is a foundational text for liberal political theory; his epistemology is best found in *An Essay Concerning Human Understanding* (1689). One way to understand Locke's empiricism is to contrast his theory of mind with that of Descartes. For the latter, mind looks in on itself to determine a thought for which no prior thought exists; Descartes is famous for his burning candle and his statement of ego. Locke's mind is the also-famous blank slate upon which "sensa" from external objects implant impressions; his mind too looks inward to determine these "ideas" (see Hacking, 1975). One other contrast is worth noting. If Descartes's limit on knowledge is God, Locke's are the nature of human beings and their knowledge of the external world.

That there is a third strand of modern sub-traditions in philosophy is less evident in standard histories even as the significance of Immanuel Kant is virtually self-evident. *Idealism,* if the term can be said to typify writings of a significant set of German philosophers across nearly a century, begins with Kant and incorporates Fichte, Schelling, and especially Hegel, as well as Schopenhauer, Kierkegaard, and Nietzsche. Marx and his followers write in response to this idealism.

Before turning to Kant and his idealism, one other reference to modern philosophy is important; this is to the 18th century movement of the Enlightenment. As a political "philosophy," it binds together many philosophers across the three strands who, as one commentator puts it, are "committed to liberating mankind from the tyrannies of dead dogma and blind faith" (Wolker, 1998, p. 315). In the 17th and 18th century—and before in Europe—tyrannies were of church and state, comprising and contrasting the darkness of totalitarian authority through dogma as against the light of philosophical reason. Among the best known Enlightenment philosophers are Locke, Montesquieu, Rousseau, and Vico. Kant's comprehensive philosophy and especially his work on political theory extends from Enlightenment thinkers.

Kant's primary work in epistemology is detailed in his *Critique of Pure Reason* (1781). Provincial, obsessive as might be said today, and a late-bloomer, Kant is less known as the father of idealism than as the "father of modern philosophy" (so is Descartes). All his life he read widely and was influenced particularly by Newton, Hume, Leibniz, and Rousseau. Substantively, he set out to reconcile problems in rationalism and empiricism through foundationalist metaphysics; the result is a three part mental architectonic, a formulation for truth, beauty, and goodness. Again a definition: "Kant's basic idea is a distinction between form and content; the form of our experience is knowable *a priori,* the content is given *a posteriori,* and only in combination can these provide knowledge of the world" (Shand, 1993, p. 161). For Kant, knowledge is composed of phenomena and noumena—the knowable sum of experiences and the unknowable "things-in-themselves" behind phenomenal appearances. As a theory of mind, Kant posits a faculty of understanding that actively operates with concepts on intuitions; the latter are particular instantiations of sensations in space/time subject to the former, mental categories of quantity, quality, relation, and modality. Overall, Kant constructs a transcendental idealism in which knowledge is both objective and insubjectively universal. For him, too, the basic model forms knowledge or truth; formulations of ethics or duty and aesthetics or beauty are derivative.

Following Kant, debate within idealism occurs about whether it is necessary to overcome dualisms in his system, among them mind and matter, sensibility and understanding. As Paul Franks outlines in a recent encyclopedia entry, the project is to systematize Kant's work, specifically by focusing on "unbridgeable gaps between elements whose underlying unity must be demonstrated" (Franks, 1998, p. 42). The result—in writings that retain the spirit of Kant if not the letter—is to theorize developmental monisms. Franks sums this significant idea:

> Such systems portray a single, developing principle expressing itself in dualisms whose unstable, conflicting nature necessitates further developments. Thus reality is a developing, organic whole whose principle can be grasped and whose unity can be articulated in a philosophical system. . . . [This process is a] conception of development . . . often called dialectic. (p. 43)

Positing such a unity out of history occurs in the writings of idealist Georg Hegel (perhaps the "father of social theory"). His dialectic of history and reason becomes materialist in the theorizing of Karl Marx, each in his own way attempting to provide "resolution" between thought and existence. In the 20th century, this general dualism is central to epistemology—and thus to philosophy—and is characterized out of the evolving three sub-traditions as between subjectivism and objectivism. Taken up subsequently in the chapter, for now one notes that there is no easy corresponding relationship between the subjective and thought and the objective and existence.

TWENTIETH CENTURY

Turning again to *Cosmopolis,* Toulmin offers a reinterpretation of modernity, setting a transition to postmodernity in the 20th century. His thesis is significant, a recontextualization across several millennia that complements the standard account, the "received view." Recall that modern philosophy generally dates from the 17th century and, with due respect to Toulmin, is characterized as written, universal, general, and timeless. With roots dating from the earlier Renaissance, the second strand is characterized as oral, particular, local, and timely; it becomes postmodernism (Toulmin, 1990, pp. 30–35). A shift in thought, at least a questioning of modernity and at most the dawn of a new epoch, broadly describes 20th century philosophy.

In the past century, western sub-traditions continue, change, and proliferate. Largely but not exclusively, empiricism becomes the basis for an Anglo-American strand of philosophies, arguably identifiable as British/American analysis and American pragmatism. Idealism influences the latter and, more significantly, is transformed into German strands of phenomenology and critical theory; hermeneutics has earlier roots. Rationalism, itself transformed into another idealist strand, contributes to phenomenology and has some connections to critical theory, importantly to French existentialism, structuralism, and poststructuralism. Rationalism also has formalist roots. Some developments across these sub-traditions are "postmodern."

Toulmin's own task is historical, contrasting events and resulting ideas of the standard and now recontextualized accounts of science, knowledge, inquiry, and rationality. This view, out of the Anglo-American tradition, is predated by another, significant one from French philosopher Jean-Francois Lyotard in *The Postmodern Condition* (1984). He begins by acknowledging a "general transformation . . . [in] age and cultures . . . that has been underway since at least the end of the 1950s" (p. 3), which is based in an altered status of knowledge. Presently, different rules operate in language games in the sciences and the arts than in the past. These rules signal a shift in narratives, in general forms of knowledge legitimation that he names "metanarratives". Postmodernism is, in Lyotard's idiom, incredulity toward metanarratives.

Lyotard's (1984) source for positing modern metanarratives is significant, the German idealism of Hegel building from Fichte and Schilling. The central idea is this: "[In] the mechanism of developing a Life . . . [there] is simultaneously Subject . . . a universal 'history' of spirit. . . . But what it produces is a metanarrative, for the story's narrator must not be a people mired in a particular positivity of its traditional knowledge" (p. 34). In the postmodern condition, the metanarrative of history, this totalizing system and all others that follow, are called into question (p. 60). The result is a new condition. Lyotard writes,

> The postmodern would be that which, in the modern, puts forward the unpresentable in presentation itself; that which denies itself the solace of good forms, the consensus of a taste which would make it possible to share collectively . . . that which searches for new presentations, not in order to enjoy them but in order to impart a stronger sense of the unpresentable. (p. 81)

Lyotard's postmodern is a "re-turn" to local narratives, to the particular and the timely. Through the interstices of the unpresentable, these serve as sites for intervention. This is postmodern politics that undercuts modern epistemology.

To sum, postmodern is the label applied to cultural change over the past century. The term has been used to describe material and symbolic culture and specifically as a movement in the arts (see Huyssen, 1990). It has been used to describe a contemporary mood (Noddings, 1995, p. 72) and, much more broadly, an epochal worldview. However, generic, indiscriminate use of "postmodern" to name difference is inappropriate. Since much change may be within the modern, retaining binaries and unities, searches for new syntheses or certainties, and as well incorporate reactionary response along with radical positing, only particular and precise application of postmodernism is useful.

Given this framework, the rest of the chapter takes up specifics in philosophy that entail a move from modern to postmodern. These changes shift in conceptualizing knowledge, in describing science through philosophy of science, in defining the role of history, and in overviewing the significant change in the place of language. Prior to these considerations, brief attention to American philosophy in the 20th century, as exemplar of larger intellectual trends, is in order.

At the beginning of the 20th century, philosophy is still acknowledged as foundational to all inquiry; there are important early trends. In the first decades not only do philosophy and the new empirical discipline of psychology separate, but other distinct social sciences achieve definition and prominence. Pragmatism, America's homegrown western philosophy, develops and is dominant early on, then in the mid-decades the analytic movement is transplanted from Great Britain and becomes superordinate. Notably the writings of the likes of Dewey, James, and Peirce are almost extinct (save for Dewey's place in educational scholarship). Replacing pragmatism, specific and related subfields of logical empiricism/positivism and ordinary language philosophy achieve key importance as philosophy and science become strongly interrelated. In the mid-decades, also, there is some interest in continental traditions, especially in phenomenology, existentialism, and critical theory.

Near century's end, American philosophy is "post-analytic," as a conception from American philosophers John Rajchman and Cornel West is named (see Rajchman & West, 1985). This includes a renaissance of pragmatism as well as an importation of specific continental influences. Rajchman explains that

> [in philosophy, there is a] move to other fields . . . [that] has been more 'dedisciplining' than 'interdisciplinary': less a collaboration between specialized fields than a questioning of basic assumptions. . . . There are . . . post-analytic mergers or amalgamations: philosophy-literary theory, philosophy-history of science, philosophy-public moral debate. . . . The creation of such new fields constitutes a challenge to the great Kantian distinctions between them: the distinction between science . . . [read knowledge], morals and aesthetics. (Rajchman, 1985, p. xiii)

At the turn into the new century, debate continues between adherents of modernity and postmodernity but it seems more muted than in the past several decades (except maybe in education). Within specific intellectual arenas, particular movements occur in two disparate directions: "philosophy" undertaken by those desiring to hold onto disciplinary specificity and continuity as against those reveling in disciplinary sub-tradition and tradition blurrings. Much too simplistic, the first is modern and the second postmodern.

KNOWLEDGE

Across philosophic epochs and traditions, questions of metaphysics, epistemology, and ethics, as indicated earlier, have been paramount. One might well posit that philosophy's beginning concerns questions of metaphysics, or what French poststructuralist philosopher Jacques Derrida has termed the origins of logocentrism (see Derrida, 1973). For him and other poststructuralists and pragmatists inappropriate dualisms have been basic to logocentrism (the issue of presence) and to what have evolved into the modern era as primary matters of knowledge. As discussed, over time person and world are understood as separate and what one knows or can come to know is dichotomized as real and unreal, ideal and non-ideal. The modern epistemological search is to resolve the epistemological problem of dualisms in seeking certainty, for knowledge as justified true belief.

This dualistic logic has cultural effects, A and not-A, conceptually this and that, we and they. Near the end of the 20th century, as already mentioned, the split is between subjective and objective domains. From feminist theorist Evelyn Fox Keller and others, consider the hierarchical relationship of these binaries: body-mind, nature-culture, emotion-cognition, passive-active, procreative-creative, private-public, submission-domination, with the second of each pair hierarchically superior (see Keller, 1983). A first dualism according to Derrida is the relationship of speech and writing, the latter returned to in "language" that itself complicates the male-female dualism.

Turning to late modern binaries, in the 1980s American pragmatist Richard Bernstein offers a useful account of the subjective-objective debate. Evolving to the time of his text, *Beyond Objectivism and Relativism: Science, Hermeneutics, and Praxis* (1983), a "crisis" in philosophy is recognized. As Bernstein reports, "[There] is a growing sense . . . that something is happening that is changing the categorical structure and patterns within which we think and act" (Bernstein, 1983, p. 2). By this time, foundation—that is certainty from source and justification—is "on the line." As Rorty substantiates in his work, *Philosophy and the Mirror of Nature* (1979), a new rationality is posed from the writings of Dewey, Wittgenstein, and Heidegger. For instance, Dewey posits "interaction" or "transaction" to overcome the basic "either-or." He puts it that "the opposite of dualism is not necessarily monism, but a philosophy which regards the distinction in antithetical terms . . . a relative and working, not fixed or absolute, so that they are capable of coming together in a functional unity" (Dewey, 1985, p. 424). This formulation foreshadows later efforts.

Before attending more to Bernstein, situating the modern epistemological crisis in contemporary idiom is helpful. In the 21st century, objectivity usually refers to truth that is independent of the perceiving subject, from person or mind. In an obvious shift across millenia, objectivity is distinct from mind-located idealist/rationalist views. The most straightforward objectivist view, arguably constituting commonsense, entails realism, pertaining to physical/material objects "out there." In contrast, subjectivity refers to person (to personal truth as this now reads) with her or his particular beliefs. Given the search for certainty, it is not surprising that in the 20th century, subjectivity has had to withstand the most criticism—at least in the Anglo-American tradition.

Many philosophers take up the subjective-objective debate, one illustration is British philosopher of science, Karl Popper. Viennese-born, logical positivist and later critic of the movement, Popper builds from German mathematician Gottlob Frege's "objective contents of thought." Best set out in his *Objective Knowledge: An Evolutionary Approach* (1972), Popper poses three worlds, one physical, one of consciousness, and one based in scientific rationality of theories, problems, and arguments. This third world is "independent of anybody's belief, or disposition to assent . . . to assert, or to act . . . or to know" (Popper, 1985b, p. 60). This third world is the aim of knowledge, science, and philosophy; it is autonomous even as humanly constructed since it transcends all men (see Popper, 1972, p. 161).

Now to Bernstein. Attempts at working through the objective-subjective distinction by Popper, Thomas Nagel, and others are unsatisfactory for Bernstein and he turns to the writings of Hannah Arendt, Hans-Georg Gadamer, and Jürgen Habermas as well as Rorty for "social theories," commonly characterized by dualistic resolution through intersubjectivity. Out of these and other late-century sources, for Bernstein the dualistic debate becomes one between objectivism and relativism. His distinction is worth quoting at length:

> By "objectivism," I mean the basic conviction that there is or must be some permanent, ahistorical matrix or framework to which we can ultimately appeal in determining the nature of rationality, knowledge, truth, reality, goodness, or rightness . . . [The] primary task of the philosopher is to discover what it is and to support his or her claims to have discovered such a matrix with the strongest possible reasons. (Bernstein, 1983, p. 8)

In opposition,

> [the] relativist not only denies the positive claims . . . but goes further. In its strongest form, rela-
> tivism is the basic conviction that when we turn to examination of those concepts that philoso-
> phers have taken to be the most fundamental—whether . . . rationality, truth, reality, right, the
> good, or norms—we are forced to recognize that . . . all such concepts must be understood as rel-
> ative to a specific conceptual scheme, theoretical framework, paradigm, form of life, society, or cul-
> ture. (Bernstein, 1983, p. 8)

Assuming a relativist, or relational perspective is transitional in late and postmodern philosophy; a defining feature of the latter, it is still debated. In Rorty's terms, this means the "death" of
tradition, the end of philosophy (for discussion see Baynes, Bohman, & McCarthy, 1987). For
him, philosophy becomes conversation that is anti-foundational, anti-essentialist, and anti-
representational; and Dewey's earlier theorizing that "overcomes" dualism, that argues against a
spectator theory of knowledge and the search for certainty, is "realized." Two aspects of this relativist shift occur in philosophies of history and language. These are taken up following a brief account of 20th century philosophy of science.

SCIENCE

The 20th century is in many respects dominated by the intellectual occupation with science. As
mentioned previously, what constitutes science and its relationship to other forms of inquiry has
been a central philosophical concern leading to the development of a disciplinary subfield. As the
preceding chapter attests, it is this body of thought that has influenced research in education.

In this dominance early on, science, knowledge, and philosophy are named as "one." All are
epistemological disciplines in which the seeking of truth is paramount. At the past century's beginning, the relationship of science to religion is significant and in some but far less intellectually
important quarters remains so across the millenium. Additionally, science and art, just as philosophy and rhetoric are and remain separate for most of the time. Several trends require mention
that in their evolution lead by century's end to the separation of science from philosophy (at least
in some sub-traditions).

A first trend is the refinement of the processes of doing science and the emergence of a modern scientific method. Up until the late 19th and early 20th centuries, truth arrived at deduc-
tively from premise to conclusion was still paramount; then comes the rise of induction. This
process is constituted of the accumulation of facts from observation and testing that leads to conclusion and contributes to scientific concept and theory (see Oldroyd, 1986; Hempel,
1966/1991). Induction is tied to positivism and to the movement of logical positivism with its
marriage of science and philosophy. Discussed more in the section on language, this movement
has its historic origins in the Vienna Circle in the 1920s, with intellectual roots in the empiricism of Hume and Locke, in method through Poincaré and Duhem among others, and in the
mathematics of Peano, Hilbert, and, mentioned subsequently, Frege, Russell, and Whitehead.
Most significant is the early work of Viennese born, complex and controversial, analytical
philosopher Ludwig Wittgenstein in his *Tractatus Logico-Philosophicus* (1983). A common theme
across the work of important philosophers that include Rudolf Carnap, Hans Reichenbach, and
Morris Schlick is the rejection of metaphysics as a foundation to philosophy (and to science; see
Ashby, 1964).

A second trend is the emergence of multiple sciences, some stemming from the latter half of the 19th century and others developing by the latter half of the 20th. As Toulmin (1990) describes in *Cosmopolis*, received science begins with Descartes, Galileo, Newton, and others and develops over several centuries, at least in the Anglo-American tradition, into distinct natural, social, and behavioral sciences. A 20th century "parallel" development in the Continental tradition identifies natural, critical, hermeneutic, or interpretive sciences, and from French philosopher-historian, Michel Foucault in *The Order of Things* (1970), as human sciences. One key and illustrative movement within Anglo-American philosophy asserts a theory of "unified science," subscribed to or at least held with some affinity by those as varied in outlook as Dewey, the logical positivists, Popper, and Thomas Kuhn. Two assertions are central. First, that all sciences devolve in an order of certainty and predictability from mathematical physics, and second, that at some future theoretical point a "superscience" is to be established that incorporates the laws of all sub-sciences.

A third broad trend is the breaking apart of the comprehensive search for certainty within science. While science and its philosophy concerns knowledge, knowledge itself is no longer teleologically "certain." There are many important philosophical debates and contributions to this general change. Perhaps, however, one initiating point is historical, the questioning of science and its consequences with the dropping of the atomic bomb in the 1940s. Significant exemplars of philosophical concepts are these: theoryladenness, theoretical underdetermination, the fallacy of induction, falsificationism, and fallibilism (see Phillips & Burbules, 2000, as an introduction). These ideas call into question processes of science, roles of evidence, and forms of proof—standards for verification. As a result, the meaning of scientific knowledge as justified true belief changes greatly. The further result is that there is no empirical, value-neutral, and objective inquiry, nor should such science be sought (see Hanson, 1958). Rather inquiry is biased and culturally influenced. Further, its predictive value is always subject to methodological maneuverings and even, as from Toulmin, is "timely" and not timeless (Toulmin, 1990, pp. 33–34). Inductive predictions are limited—even with the rise and refinement of statistical tools. Above all, natural science concerns a perhaps definitive physical world but its practice is human with all the fallibility and non-perfection that is entailed.

Given practice by humans, a fourth trend concerns theories of social construction debated in what became known in the late decades as the "science wars" of the 20th century. The classic text, *The Structure of Scientific Revolutions* (1962), from recently deceased historian and philosopher Thomas Kuhn plays a pivotal role. He offers several important contributions. First, scientific discovery is largely the work of communities of inquirers even as key individuals make discoveries. Second, most science is "normal," that is, it is step by step, additive work on focused puzzles. Third, revolutions occur when anomalies within the work of communities build up over time and new concepts, exemplars, and discourse replace those obsolete. Fourth—and this is the most controversial element—incommensurable paradigms of inquiry are identifiable before and after these scientific revolutions. Fifth, and most significant, is a basic insight from the history of science that knowledge and how it is sought and "determined" changes over time. As indicated, Kuhn also proposes that sciences are mature and less mature and thus that there is "progress," (see Hacking, 1999, p. 97) and that unification is possible. In the mid to late decades of the 20th century, responses to Kuhn abound with key work from many, notably Imre Lakatos and Larry Lauden, and from the then-rebel, Paul Feyerabend. Regardless of these challenges, however, the result of the Kuhnian revolution has been an emergence of "a sociology of science." In the latter, the writings of Barry Barnes and David Bloor, Harry Collins and Trevor Pinch, Bruno Latour and his colleagues—and Donna Haraway—among others are important.

A word more about social construction. An excellent source on this broad issue is Hacking's *The Social Construction of What?* (1999). For him, social construction in the natural sciences revolves around three issues: contingency, nominalism, and stability. To uphold the central premise of social construction that "[X] is not inevitable" (p. 6), social constructionists believe the following. First that "actual fit . . . [of results relative to scientific process] is contingent . . . that many robust fits were possible . . . although . . . only one seems conceivable" (p. 73). Second that . . . [current understanding has] . . . "to accommodate, constantly, to the resistance of the material world . . . [in ways that question] experience" (p. 84). Third that scientific belief rests not only on internal process but also on "elements that are external to the professed content . . . [such as] social factors, interests, networks . . . [and so forth]" (p. 92).

HISTORY

Philosophy of history in the 19th century develops under the label of historicism; this concept evolves into the 20th century as a new historicism occurs. What this means, like the linguistic turn discussed next, depends on disciplinary and interdisciplinary connections. In a relatively recent account, one commentator offers this introduction: "The problem does not concern the obvious fact that all knowledge . . . [including philosophy] was produced at some place and time. It is a deeper reflection . . . that the possibility of objective knowledge is itself 'within history'. . . . [Historicism] . . . is a thesis about limits or boundaries of inquiry" (D'Amico, 1989, p. xi; first brackets added). Today, historicism plays a theoretical role in inquiry that includes history, philosophy, literary criticism and literature studies, religious studies, and the social and human sciences.

A useful overview of classic historicism is written by holocaust survivor, Professor Emeritus Georg Iggers. First used by Frederich Schlegel in the late 18th century, historicism names "a 'kind of philosophy' that places the main stress on history" (Iggers, 1973, p. 456). It is explicated by the great German historian Johann Gottfried Herder and then dominates initially as an alternative to the French and British Enlightenment and later, importantly, to Hegel. The writings of Leopold von Ranke is central to the evolution of historicism. His contribution is to locate history in documentary sources, narrations of events "as the reconstruction of the past 'as it essentially was'" (Iggers, 1973, p. 459). For Ranke and his followers, history is the manifestation of spirituality in a state ordained by God. Classic historicism explicitly rejects progress but as Iggers claims, "had been deeply optimistic about the course of history" (p. 461).

By the early decades of the 20th century, German historian Frederich Meinecke posits that historicism is "the highest attained stage in the understanding of things human". Given the cultural crises in Germany, his own move is to reformulate history, formerly relative to specific cultures, into a stance of transcendence. In these same decades, critical responses to classic historicism are written by the Italian philosopher Benedetto Croce, British philosopher and historian R. G. Collingwood, as well as by Popper and the German born, logical positivist, philosopher of science, Carl Hempel. One other tradition is significant, the Annales circle in France, that differs but combines elements that are positivist and historicist. For Annalist members, history is the key to all knowledge and integrative of broad social trends across the human sciences (see Chartier, 1982).

"New historicism" emerges near century's end. Its meaning is relative to historic predecessors and also in comparison to the philosophies of history from Hegel and Marx. To begin, in the Hegelian idiom, as British-trained Canadian philosopher, Charles Taylor writes, "philosophy and the history of philosophy are one" (Taylor, 1984, p. 17; Hegel, 1988). A significant distinction separates Hegel from Kant: for Kant the person is prior, capable of reason with rights and duties as means to freedom, and for Hegel, rational free persons devolve from the state and emerge after great struggle. Hegel's writings on history of philosophy and philosophy of history identify key epochs and civilizations, change in human thought, development of rationality, and movement as progress. This vision is both unitary and totalizing (recall the "grand narrative"); see especially his *Phenomenology of Spirit* (1807). Out of Hegel's idealism, the historical embeddedness of philosophy becomes basic and later problematic to American pragmatism and the several Continental traditions. The impact of Marx's revisioning of Hegel is beyond the scope of this chapter: a class-based, materialist process of dialectical change that undergoes various humanist and existentialist reinterpretations over the 20th century, most notably from the Continental philosophers, Hungarian Georg Lukács and, from France, Jean Paul Sartre (see Young, 1990).

To understand "new historicism," the contributions of Foucault along with those of Americans, Rorty and literary critic Hayden White are central. In an essay from the 1980s and published recently, Hacking considers 20th century philosophy in historical terms, in notions of undoing, progress, and historicism (Hacking, 2002b, p. 59). The first, mentioned at the outset of this chapter, refers to the aspect of philosophical tradition in which predecessors have it wrong, the second relates to beneficial change and development, and the third refers to the idea that "philosophical issues find their place, importance, and definition in a specific cultural milieu" (ibid., p. 53). The last, while simplistic, encapsulates the meaning of new historicism. For Hacking, there is much undoing in the century beginning with the logical positivists—who are not historicists. Historicism characterizes Dewey (recall contextualization), Heidegger, and Rorty. In Rorty, "philosophy," history, and language after the linguistic turn, come together. The result is that philosophy as "Tradition," along with representation and correspondence of truth "dies," and blurs disciplines as cultural conversation characterize intellectual life. Rorty's contribution out of Donald Davidson is to posit vocabularies that are contingent and change when no longer useful (see Rorty, especially 1989).

Hacking is greatly influenced by Foucault and now occupies a chair at the College de France. Arguably the "father of new historicism," Foucault's philosophical-historical writings have been defined as three different historiographic methods that are also the "doing" of philosophy (see Flynn, 1994). Foucault writes, "The object . . . [of a philosophical exercise is] to learn to what extent the effort to think one's own history can free thought from what it silently thinks, and so enable it to think differently" (Foucault, 1990, p. 9). His studies are historicist, through an undercutting historical continuity, by identifying a basic interrelationship of discursive and nondiscursive formations, through stratifying regimes of truth as power-knowledge, and in original, particular, and localized insights of "history of the present." Foucault avoids "presentism" or ethnocentrism entailing as one commentator puts it, "a conjunction of elements inherited from the past and current innovations" (Castel, 1994, p. 238). Unlike classic historicism, in sum, there is no enduring continuity but rather breaks and ruptures in and through thought, and there is no progress.

One other route to new historicism deserves mention; this is through literary criticism and the work of White. White's project has been to bring forth a basic interpretive element of narrative in history, influenced by Hegel and through analysis of tropical prose dimensions of particular historical/cultural epochs. This analysis is the basis of what has become a classic of literary criticism, *Metahistory: The Historical Imagination in Nineteenth-Century Europe* (1973). In an essay from the 1970s, White traces his own historicist roots primarily to the French structuralist anthropologist, Claude Lévi-Strauss. The result is that history, as literature and as criticism, becomes rhetorical (see White, 1973). In her writing about White, American critic Linda Hutcheon makes connections to poststructuralist contributions as part of a general postmodernism. From writers such as Derrida and later Michel De Certeau, a contemporary historicism results in the "equivalence" of history, fiction, and science—and philosophy (see De Certeau, 1986). It is inquiry in which "the past is already . . . encoded, that is, already inscribed in discourse and therefore 'always already' interpreted" (Hutcheon, 1988, p. 97). Lastly, deserving mention at the close, is a specific line of theory in literature studies led by Stephen Greenblatt that has structural and poststructural connections (see Veeser, 1994). Not uninteresting for its own structuralist and poststructuralist elements and developments, it is less central to current educational research than the other movements and contributions just outlined.

LANGUAGE

Philosophy, of course, is concerned with language in a basic sense; it is its medium of expression. In the 20th century, the role of language shifts from medium to focus both in Anglo-American and Continental traditions. At the end of the century, American feminist pragmatist philosopher, Nancy Fraser writes thusly about what becomes known as "the linguistic turn":

> [The linguistic turn] is the most fruitful way of understanding postmodernism: an epochal shift in philosophy and social theory from an epistemological problematic, in which mind is conceived as reflecting or mirroring reality, to a discursive problematic, in which culturally constructed social meanings are accorded density and weight." (Fraser, 1995, p. 157)

To arrive at this point, both traditions evolve through attempts at a "foundation" in language and then a questioning of these. Fodder for debate, a first phase is modernist and a second is postmodern. Across millennia, language is defined as designation, ostension, expression, and signification. It is related to experience, to form, to meaning, to structure, to practice, and to tool. Further, language becomes synonymous with discourse, sign, communicative action, textualism, therapeutic analysis (as well, of course, as traditional linguistic analysis), and performance. Language is central both to disciplinary as well as interdisciplinary studies that have roots in "philosophy" and endemic, through turns especially in history and the social sciences, to social life.

Referred to earlier in his writings on Hegel, Taylor describes the 20th century as preoccupied with language that, among other connections, results from the modern interest in the self. He suggests that across time, human life has been characterized by two forms of language, designative and expressive; the first is central to philosophic Tradition and the second is central to the rhetorical, literary counter-tradition. The first is identified as objectivist and the second as subjectivist (see Taylor, 1985). Taylor's own view is hermeneutic and semiotic, related to textualism and linguistic structure as contemporary expressivism (p. 247). Further his view is another version of a late-modern epistemology, one that while based largely in Continental philosophies takes account of the Anglo-American sub-tradition as well.

In the evolution of Anglo-American philosophy, language matters for a series of philosophical movements, analytical philosophy, linguistic philosophy that includes logical positivism, ordinary language philosophy with interests in ideal languages, and contemporary analytic and post-analytic philosophy (see Rorty, 1992). Classical pragmatists, such as Dewey, pay attention to language but do not manifest the linguistic turn until the dawn of neo-pragmatism. A significant root of the analytic and linguistic movements is the work of the late 19th century German mathematician, Gottlob Frege. Reclusive and reactionary, he nonetheless influences B. Russell and Alfred North Whitehead in their attempts at an epistemological foundation in mathematical logic; their classic text is *Principia Mathematica* (1910–1913). Russell and G.E. Moore are forefathers of the "early Wittgenstein," with whom the term "linguistic turn" is often associated. A helpful essay from Gustav Bergmann written in the 1950s distinguishes their views from the logical positivists (see Bergmann, 1992). Bergmann, aligned with the logical empiricists over unified science, is exemplified by British philosopher, A. J. Ayer. According to Ayer, philosophical focus is on testing the truth and falsity of propositions; the aim, moreover, is to analyze and clarify language and not to determine reality. Central to the movement in ordinary language philosophy are J. L. Austin and the later Wittgenstein. Leaving out so much, moves here are to forms and rules of usage; some even posit ideal languages (recall Tarksi). What is best remembered today is the later Wittgenstein's *Philosophical Investigations* (1958) that posits a theory of language games, practices based in consensually agreed upon rules. Given an openness to language that results, a further idea concerns family resemblances among and between game participants. All too simply, in order to know and to understand, uses of language overlap and are similar and this is all that can be expected; again there is no identity, certainty, or foundation.

Continental philosophies of language are likewise complex with distinct German and French movements. In a recent essay, German critical pragmatist and heir to the early Frankfurt School of Max Horkeimer, Theodor Adorno, and others, Jürgen Habermas locates the roots of the German linguistic turn in the writings of another tradition, German romanticism. In a critique of Kant, in contributions of Herder and Johann Georg Hamann, and specifically from Wilhelm von Humboldt, Habermas identifies the three functions of language that are roots to modern hermeneutics as well as his own critical epistemology. The three are cognitive, expressive, and communicative; in Humboldt's view they constitute the "world-making character of language" (Habermas, 1999, p. 415). Through a romanticist conception of nation, language "[shapes] the totality of concepts and ways of apprehension by which, in some kind of pre-understanding, a space is articulated for everything the members of a community may come upon in the world" (Habermas, 1999). Importantly, Humboldt's semantic theory of language helped found modern neoclassic hermeneutics, especially the writings of Hans Georg Gadamer (who has some disagreement with Humboldt and responds to classic historicism), as well as to those of Heidegger and his phemenological hermeneutics, tied and responding to Husserl (see respectively and retrospectively, *Truth and Method* [1960], *Being and Time* [1927], and *Logical Investigations* [1900–1901]). Habermas's discursive theory, as that of his colleague Kurt Otto Apel, takes a different tact out of Humboldt that is discursive, communicative, and intersubjective. Habermas poses a highly significant egalitarian ideal of speech acts; here there is some affinity with the later Wittgenstein.

Heidegger serves as one root of French theory in the later 20th century; in terms of language more direct importance is located in the structuralist theorizing of the Swiss linguist, Ferdinand de Saussure. His concept of sign, along with contributions from the logic of American pragmatist C. S. Peirce, becomes the basis of modern semiotics. A root that suggests a gap between a term and its utterance, the signifier and signified, evolves into greater ambiguity. The result is that within French poststructuralisms, varieties of language theory and usage abound (see in general Gutting, 2001) and language in Derrida's idiom is dispersed and deferred. First, as already discussed, Foucault develops a vision of power-knowledge consisting of very complex, continuously changing discursive and non-discursive relations. A "structure" of utterative and iterative statements that become stratified and disruptive is theorized and applied specifically to forms of western rationality. Then Derrida writes a text-based deconstruction undermining standard western discourse. His notion of *différance* poses a radical alterity of dualistic western philosophy; this term encapsulates the ambiguity, fluidity, and openness of language. Lastly, Julia Kristeva theorizes a linguistic and psychoanalytic alternative. For her drives found poetic language and ultimately ethics and politics for societal change. Other poststructuralists also posit visions of justice and equity. Three important texts respectively are Foucault's *The Archaeology of Knowledge* (1969), Derrida's *Of Grammatology* (1967), and Kristeva's *Revolution in Poetic Language* (Waller, 1984).

CONCLUSION

Educational researchers have relevant and important reasons to read, study, and know something about the discipline of philosophy, its history, and especially its modern and postmodern formulations. Its significance is found in topics and perhaps in questions that underpin personal, professional, and scholarly beliefs that contribute to research. No research—quantitative, qualitative, historical, narrative—comes "from nowhere." While many do not question their research traditions, viewpoints, and theories, one might posit that good researchers do so question. This book, with its "philosophies of inquiry," represents the best of such questioning. Most significant for today's researchers are philosophical movements of the recent century and their increasing complexity—and according to some their alteration or undermining. This chapter offers a particular perspective on this history, on philosophy for today. It is a rendering largely influenced by a historicist premise, the idea that thought is relative to specific cultural moments and changes over time. In what becomes a 21st century view, philosophy is no longer Tradition in positing perennial views and values, instead it is comprised of changing ideas. Philosophy, adapted from Rorty's language, is opinion but not just any opinion.

In the "opinion" of this chapter, selection is key. What is included assumes prominence but what is not included has importance too, especially for a huge topic reduced to a single chapter. Here are some thoughts on limitation: First, to set a present day stage much more might be made of the predecessor epochs. Just as the scholastics returned to classic roots so too have significant moderns and postmoderns. The human condition indeed may not be developing or progressive, but there do seem some great universal themes whose contents differ in different times. Among these are quests for the meaning of life, abilities to get along with each other, and processes of securing a better existence for those who come after. Philosophy surely has something to say about these and other central human preoccupations. Second, metaphysics gives way to epistemology in the modern era, the latter that might well be giving way to ethics. To give way today, of course, need not be—and surely should not be—to throw out all systematically created thought of yesterday. When considering ideas from the past, distinction as well as skepticism toward meanings are important.

Distinction in and from the near present might well be more difficult than from the distant past and, to contribute to present life, might well be most important. Questions include, What differences in western philosophy have been obtained over the 20th century? What differences are now recognizable in the epochal, intellectual turn from modernism to postmodernism? "Answers" are found in the writings of specific philosophers within particular sub-traditions and movements. To continue with limitations, first the American pragmatists get the short shift—as part of a culture, these roots are found in all of *us*. Second, central philosophers within an American analytic tradition are absent, notably Willard Quine and most interestingly, David-son (Rorty, 1989). Also Nelson Goodman and Hiliary Putnam deserve mention. Third, and connected to American pragmatist and post-analytic philosophies, virtually nothing in the chapter is mentioned of political theory and, related, modern ethics. Here it appears that John Rawls will be historical in centuries to come. Others of importance in this moment include Michael Walzer, Martha Nussbaum, education's own Nel Noddings, as well as the British neo-Kantian, Bernard Williams. Fourth, alternative traditions, those often interdisclinary or multidisciplinary, have not been included. Writings by feminists of all kinds, those in cultural studies, and post-colonial theorists should receive much attention. Finally to bring this chapter to a close, I believe much more should be made of insights from Rorty. What is most significant is not his disdain for philosophy nor his own style but rather his interactions and blurrings of American pragmatism with continent-based sub-traditions.

Before turning to Rorty, attention must be paid to one last philosophical movement that has received much attention in educational scholarship. This is German critical theory. While the work of Habermas and his tradition is referenced near the chapter's close, much more should be said about his and other neo-Marxist, Marxist, and idealist projects, and their critique of Kant that is not well recognized by educational researchers (see Horkheimer & Adorno, [1944/1989]). Again distinction is important even as connections are made to analytical speech act theory from John Searle. There also are connections to Austin and even to Husserl.

Now to Rorty. His basic insight about a neo-pragmatist aim for philosophy, or "conversation"

that includes those philosophical, portends a significant political future. He names this "social hope" and pits it and himself against Tradition and Platonism (see Rorty, 1999). His work is greatly influenced by pragmatist forbears and contemporary French poststructuralists; also influential are literary figures such as Charles Dickens and the father of psychoanalysis, Sigmund Freud. In these connections Rorty recognizes the contemporary importance of language. In the chapter some attention is given to subtraditions and phases of the linguistic turn; however, greater detail is desirable. Rorty asserts that language, self, and community are all contingent. This contingency suggests an openness; even more strongly, others such as French theorists included in this chapter also recognize "the unknown," that "which cannot be known."

At the beginning of the 21st century, contingency, ambiguity, and tentativeness characterize language, the social order, and philosophy. Perhaps the postmodern is not only acknowledgement, but also acceptance of this "condition." Giving up a modern "search for certainty," to use Dewey's idiom, need not be cause for despair. It can, instead, be "liberating," a freeing up to be, to live, to act. Such living, basic to conducting research, I believe, entails a politics, an ethics. This ethics for research can never be reduced to "doing a proper study." It is rather to undertake inquiry recognizing its embeddedness in a historicist moment, its connections to a broader intellectual history that includes philosophy, and its consequences for a time—but not all time—to come. Since *we* cannot know what tomorrow will be like, we "merely" must do our best with today.[3]

QUESTIONS

1. What is meant by the social frame of inquiry?
2. How are the three subfields of philosophy similar and different from each other?
3. How does modernity's view of the self differ from the way it was seen in previous periods?

How does this difference create a new research paradigm?

4. Is knowledge objective or subjective or does it reside somewhere along a continuum that connects both?

5. Science and philosophy have an important relationship. How does that relationship, in some minds, bring about the science wars and social construction?

6. How significant is the shift from medium to focus that language undertakes in the 20th century?

7. Explain and debate the concept of "research from nowhere."

REFERENCES

Ashby, R. (1964). Logical positivism. In D. O'Connor (Ed.) *A critical history of western philosophy* (pp. 492–508). New York: Free Press.

Bauman, Z. (1993). Modernity. In J. Krieger (Ed.), *The Oxford companion to politics of the world* (pp. 592–596). New York: Oxford University Press.

Baynes, K., Bohman, J., & McCarthy, T. (Eds.). (1987). *After philosophy, end or transformation?* Cambridge: The MIT Press.

Bergmann, G. (1992). Logical positivism, language and the reconstruction of metaphysics. In R. Rorty (Ed.), *The linguistic turn: Essays in philosophical method with two retrospective essays* (pp. 63–71). Chicago: The University of Chicago Press. (Original work published 1953)

Bernstein, R. (1983). *Beyond objectivism and relativism: Science, hermeneutics, and praxis.* Philadelphia, PA: University of Pennsylvania Press.

Blackburn, S. (1994). *The Oxford dictionary of philosophy.* Oxford: Oxford University Press.

Castel, R. (1994). "Problematization" as a mode of reading history. In J. Goldstein (Ed.), *Foucault and the writing of history* (P. Wissing, Trans., pp. 237–252). Oxford: Blackwell.

Chartier, R. (1982). Intellectual history or sociocultural history? The French trajectories. In D. LaCapra & S. Kaplan (Eds.), *Modern European intellectual histories: Reappraisals and new perspectives* (J. Kaplan, Trans., pp. 13–46). Ithaca, CT: Cornell University Press. (Original work published 1971)

D'Amico, R. (1989). *Historicism and knowledge.* New York: Routledge.

De Certeau, M. (1986). *Heterologies: Discourse on the other* (pp. 199–221). (B. Massumi, Trans.). Minneapolis, MN: University of Minnesota Press. (Original work published 1983)

Derrida, J. *De la grammatologie*, Minuit, (1967) translation by Gayatri Chakravorty Spivak published as *Of Grammatology*, Johns Hopkins University Press, Baltimore, MD: 1976.

Derrida, J. (1973). *Speech and phenomena and other essays on Husserl's theory of signs.* Evanston, IL: Northwestern University Press. (Original work published 1967)

Dewey, J. (1948). *Reconstruction in philosophy.* Boston, MA: Beacon. (Original work published 1920)

Dewey, J. (1985). Dualism, Contributions to a cyclopedia of education, volumes 1 and 2. In J. Boydston (Ed.), *The middle works, 1899–1924* (Vol. 6, p. 424). Carbondale, IL: Southern Illinois University Press. (Original work published 1911)

Dewey, J. (1988). *The quest for certainty. The later works, 1925–1953* (Vol. 4, J. Boydston, Ed.). Carbondale, IL: Southern Illinois University Press. (Original work published 1929)

Flynn, T. (1994). Foucault's mapping of history. In G. Gutting (Ed.), *The Cambridge companion to Foucault* (pp. 28–46). Cambridge, MA: Cambridge University Press.

Foucault, M. (1969). *The archaeology of knowledge.* New York: Routledge.

Foucault, M. (1970). *The order of things.* London: Tavistock.

Foucault, M. (1990). *The use of pleasure (The history of sexuality,* Volume 2). R. Hurley (Trans.). New York: Vintage. (Original work published 1984)

Franks, P. (1998). German idealism. In E. Craig (Ed.), *Routledge encyclopedia of philosophy* (Vol. 4, pp. 42–45). London: Routledge.

Fraser, N. (1995). Pragmatism, feminism and the linguistic turn. In S. Benhabib, J. Butler, D. Cornell, & N. Fraser, *Feminist contentions: A philosophical exchange* (pp. 157–171). New York, MA: Routledge.

Gadamer, H. (1960) *Wahreit und methode*; English translation as: *Truth and method*. Edited by Garrett Barden and John Cumming, Seabury Press, 1975.

Gutting, G. (2001). *French philosophy in the twentieth century*. Cambridge, MA: Cambridge University Press.

Habermas, J. (1999). Hermeneutic and analytic philosophy. Two complementary versions of the linguistic turn? In A. O'Hear (Ed.), *German philosophy since Kant* (pp. 413–441). Royal Institute of Philosophy Supplement: 44. Cambridge, MA: Cambridge University Press. (Original work published 1997–1998)

Hacking, I. (1975). *Why does language matter to philosophy?* Cambridge, MA: Cambridge University Press.

Hacking, I. (1999). *The social construction of what?* Cambridge, MA: Harvard University Press.

Hacking, I. (2002). Two kinds of new historicism. In *Historical ontology* (pp. 51–72). Cambridge, MA: Harvard University Press. (Original work published 1986)

Hamlyn, D. (1987). *A history of western philosophy*. Harmondsworth, Middlesex, NJ: Viking, Penguin.

Hanson, N. (1958). *Patterns of discovery*. Cambridge, MA: Cambridge University Press.

Hegel, G. (1807). Phenomenology of Spirit; translated by Arnold V. Miller; Jn Findley 1977. Oxford: Clarendon Press.

Hegel, G. (1988). *Introduction to the philosophy of history* (L. Rauch, Trans.). Indianapolis, IN: Hackett. (Original work published 1832–1845)

Heidegger, M. (1927). *Sein und zeit*: Erste Haefre Halle, translated by John Macquarrie and Edward Robinson. Published as *Being and Time*, Harper: 1962.

Hempel, C. (1991). Laws and their role in scientific explanation. In R. Boyd, P. Gasper, & J. Trout (Eds.), *The philosophy of science* (pp. 299–315). Cambridge, MA: The MIT Press. (Original work published 1966)

Horkheimer, M. and Adorno, T. (1989). *Dialectic of enlightenment* (J. Cumming, Trans). New York: Herder and Herder. (Original work published 1944)

Husserl, E. (1970). *Logical investigations*. New York, Humanities Press.

Hutcheon, L. (1988). *A poetics of postmodernism: History, theory, fiction* (pp. 87–101). New York: Routledge.

Huyssen, A. (1990). Mapping the postmodern. In L. Nicholson (Ed.), *Feminism/postmodernism* (pp. 234–277). New York: Routledge. (Original work published 1984)

Iggers, G. (1973). Historicism. In P. Wiener (Ed.), *Dictionary of the history of ideas* (pp. 456–464). New York: Charles Scribner's Sons.

Keller, E. (1983). Gender and science. In S. Harding & M. Hintikka (Eds.), *Discovering reality: Feminist perspectives on epistemology, metaphysics, methodology and philosophy of science* (pp. 187–205). Dordrecht location: D. Reidel.

Kneale, W. C. (1967). Philosophy. In *Encyclopaedia Britannica* (Vol. 17, pp. 864–869). Chicago: Encyclopaedia Brittannica.

Kuhn, T. (1962). *The structure of scientific revolutions*. Chicago, IL: University of Chicago Press.

Lyotard, J. (1984). *The postmodern condition: A report on knowledge* (G. Bennington and B. Masumi, Trans.). Minneapolis, MN: University of Minnesota Press. (Original work published 1979)

Markie, P. (1998). Rationalism. In E. Craig (Ed.), *Routledge encyclopedia of philosophy* (Vol. 8, pp. 75–80). London: Routledge.

Noddings, N. (1995). *Philosophy of education*. Boulder, CO: Westview.

Oldroyd, D. (1986). *The arch of knowledge: An introductory study of the history and methodology of science*. New York: Methuen.

Perry, J., & Bratman, M. (Eds.). (1986). *Introduction to philosophy: Classical and contemporary readings*. New York: Oxford University Press.

Phillips, D., & Burbules, N. (2000). *Postpostivism and educational research*. Lanham: Rowman & Littlefield.

Popper, K. (1972). *Objective knowledge: An evolutionary approach*. Oxford: Clarendon.

Popper, K. (1985a). Falsificationism versus conventionalism. In D. Miller (Ed.), *Popper selections* (pp. 143–151). Princeton: Princeton University Press. (Original work published 1934)

Popper, K. (1985b). Knowledge: Subjective versus objective. In D. Miller (Ed.), *Popper selections* (pp. 58–77). Princeton: Princeton University Press. (Original work published 1967)

Rajchman, J. (1985). Philosophy in America. In J. Rajchman, & C. West (Eds.), *Post-analytic philosophy* (pp. ix–xxx). New York: Columbia University Press.

Rajchman, J., & West, C. (Eds.). (1985). *Post-analytic philosophy*. New York: Columbia University Press.

Rorty, R. (1979). *Philosophy and the mirror of nature*. Princeton: Princeton University Press.

Rorty, R. (1987). Pragmatism and philosophy. In K. Baynes, J. Bohman, & T. McCarthy (Eds.), *After philosophy, end or transformation?* (pp. 26–66). Cambridge, MA: The MIT Press. (Original work published 1982)

Rorty, R. (1989). *Contingency, irony, and solidarity*. Cambridge, MA: Cambridge University Press.

Rorty, R. (1990). Introduction: Pragmatism as anti-representationalism. In J. Murphy, *Pragmatism: From Peirce to Davidson* (pp. 1–6). Boulder, CO: Westview.

Rorty, R. (Ed.). (1992). *The linguistic turn: Essays in philosophical method with two retrospective essays*. Chicago: The University of Chicago Press. (Original work published 1967)

Rorty, R. (1999). *Philosophy and social hope*. London: Penguin.

Russell, B. (1945). *A history of western philosophy*. New York: Clarion.

Russell, B. (1959). *The problems of philosophy*. London: Oxford University Press. (Original work published 1912)

Scott-Kakures, D. Castagnetto, S., Benson, H., Taschek, W., & Hurley, P. (1993). *History of philosophy*. New York: Harper Resource.

Scruton, R. (1995). *A short history of modern philosophy*. London: Routledge. (Original work published 1981)

Shand, J. (1993). *Philosophy and philosophers: An introduction to western philosophy*. London: UCL Press.

Stone, L. (1997). Philosophy: Traditional to postmodern. In J. Paul, H. Rosselli-Kostoryz, W. Morse, K. Marfo, C. Lavely, & D. Thomas (Eds.), *Foundations of special education: Some of the basic knowledge informing research and practice in special education* (pp. 27–48). Pacific Grove, CA: Brooks/Cole (Wadsworth).

Tarski, A. (1956). *Logic, semantics, metamathematics: Papers from 1923 to 1938* (J. Woodger, Trans.). Oxford: Clarendon. (Original work published 1931)

Taylor, C. (1984). Philosophy and its history. In R. Rorty, J. Schneewind, & Q. Skinner (Eds.), *Philosophy in history: Essays on the historiography of philosophy* (pp. 17–30). Cambridge: Cambridge University Press.

Taylor, C. (1985). *Human agency and language, Philosophical Papers I* (pp. 215–247). Cambridge: Cambridge University Press.

Toulmin, S. (1990). *Cosmopolis: The hidden agenda of modernity*. Chicago: The University of Chicago Press.

Toulmin, S. (2001). *Return to reason*. Cambridge: Harvard University Press.

Veeser, A. (Ed.). (1994). *The new historicism reader*. New York: Routledge.

Waller, M. (1984). Revolution in Poetic Language. New York: Columbia University Press.

White, H. (1973). *Metahistory: The historical imagination in nineteenth-century Europe*. Baltimore, MD: Johns Hopkins University Press.

Wittgenstein, L. (1958). Philosophical investigations. Oxford: Blackwell.

Wittgenstein, L. (1983). *Tractatus logico-philosophicus*. London: Routledge and Kegan Paul.

Wolker, R. (1998). Enlightenment, Continental. In E. Craig. (Ed.), *Routledge encyclopedia of philosophy* (Vol. 3, pp. 315–320). London: Routledge.

Young, R. (1990) *White mythologies: Writing history and the west* (pp. 21–27). London: Routledge.

NOTES

1. For an earlier rendering of this topic, see Stone (1997).
2. Given the relevance of modern philosophy, occasional reference to classic texts are included but not referenced. These are available at any library. Readers are encouraged not only to turn to these primary sources but also to writings from key figures in premodernity.
3. Thanks to Aaron Cooley, John Kitchens, and Kathleen Rands for conversation and specific references and to Jim Paul and his graduate students for editing suggestions.

CHAPTER 3

Perspectivism and Critique of Research: An Overview

James L. Paul, Ben Graffam, and Kathleen Fowler

Perspectivism, or perspectivalism, the idea that truth is embedded within a particular perspective, is not new. It is generally associated with the work of Nietzsche in the latter part of the 19th century. In the *Oxford Dictionary of Philosophy*, a perspective is defined as "a general human point of view, set by such things as the nature of our sensory apparatus, or it may be thought to be bound by culture, history, language, class, or gender. Since there may be many perspectives, there also are different families of truths" (Blackburn, p. 284).

Debates about knowledge and method during the latter part of the 20th century centered on different perspectives, each of which was vying for a place in the void created by the defeat of logical positivism, or logical empiricism, the philosophy of science that had guided educational research through most of the 20th century. As discussed in Chapter 1, the dynamics of the debates about perspectives varied widely, ranging from fundamental differences about the logics to cultural and ethical implications to negotiations of political interests. Public officials entered the fray in 2001 by passing the No Child Left Behind legislation and then supporting the work of scholars under the auspices of the National Academy of Sciences, advancing views of research that, in the opinions of some scholars, narrowed the options for what is considered "good" research. Whether focusing on the epistemologies, ethics, or political implications, the debates of the relative qualities of different perspectives have been, and continue to be, significant forces shaping the future of education research. It is important, therefore, to examine individual perspectives that form the substance of many of these debates.

The focus in this section is on nine of those perspectives. The perspectives are not all mutually exclusive, although some represent diametrically opposing views of basic topics such as reality, knowledge, truth, and value. There is no implication here that these nine are the only important perspectives embraced by scholars but they certainly represent a major portion of current thinking about research perspectives.

Each perspective is described by a senior scholar widely recognized for her or his scholarship and contributions in advancing the particular perspective. The descriptions of the perspectives vary in length and format. It was my (Paul) decision not to impose a structure on the descriptions but rather to allow each scholar the space and flexibility needed to convey the basic principles of each perspective.

NINE CRITICS

In the following chapter, distinguished scholars describe perspectives that guide different researchers and scholars in their work. As suggested by a pluralistic stance, these perspectives are not mutually exclusive. Neither do they represent all perspectives found in the current literature. They are, however, among the most common and powerful perspectives, serving as intellectual and heuristic tools for scholars and researchers at the beginning of the 21st century.

 Denis Phillips, professor of philosophy and education at Stanford University, describes the perspective of *postpositivism*. He distinguishes between research, which aims at discovering causal relationships, and inquiry, which is a way of justifying or providing reasons for supporting actions. Competent inquiry, he argues, is a moral issue because it may lead to actions that affect the lives of individuals, e.g., teaching methods and policy decisions.

 Pragmatism is described by Nel Noddings, professor of education and philosophy at Stanford University. Agreeing with Peirce that it is a theory of meaning, Noddings points out the need for pragmatists to devote more attention to the sociology of knowledge, i.e., how knowledge is constructed, questioned, refined, and encoded. She agrees with Gouldner that "Neither abstract, detached theory, nor a mere account of personal experience can yield warranted assertions." Noddings further argues that pragmatism has been weak in considering ethical or moral consequences, asserting that care theory should guide ethical judgment that is consistent with pragmatic insistence on looking at consequences.

 Yvonna Lincoln, professor of educational leadership at Texas A&M University, defines *constructivism* "in its simplest terms as an interpretive stance which attends to the meaning-making activities of active agents and cognizing human beings." It takes many different forms and represents the general views, for example, of scholars who work within specific traditions of phenomenology, symbolic interactionism, philosophical hermeneutics, anthropological interpretivism, and various critical theories (feminist theory, critical theory, queer theory, and race/ethnic theories of knowing).

 Arthur Bochner, professor of communications at the University of South Florida, argues that interpretive social science subverts the dualisms of all traditional categories such as those that separate science and literature, reason and emotion, object and subject, mind and body, and facts and values. Describing the perspective of *interpretivism,* Bochner notes how it shares with constructivism certain assumptions about knowledge and knowing. Interpretivism is self-consciously value-centered rather than pretending to be value free, and being closer to literature than to physics it privileges stories rather than theories.

 Critical theory, according to George Noblit, professor of social foundations at the University of North Carolina, focuses on the dynamics of power and ideology and the emancipation of the less powerful by revealing the dynamics and questioning the justification of power and ideology of the more powerful. It has a value orientation and a critical epistemology. Knowledge is viewed as "a social practice interpenetrated with power," while critical theory and critical ethnography are different ways of viewing and employing the critical perspective.

 Lynda Stone, professor of culture, curriculum, and change at University of North Carolina at Chapel Hill, describes *poststructuralism* as perspectives reflecting the views of, among others, Derrida, Foucault, Kristeva, and Lyotard. Stone points out that poststructuralism is a term referring to several views and is not amenable to one definition, with roots in various structuralisms from linguistics, literary theory, and the social sciences. She also discusses postmodernism and its rejection of grand or metanarratives.

Kenneth Howe, professor of education at the University of Colorado at Boulder, describes *ethics* and democratic deliberation, as well as the deep and pervasive ethical roots of the divisions in the educational research community. The experimental researcher, for example, emphasizes the autonomy of researcher. The interpretivist, on the other hand, focuses more on intimacy with respect to methods and openness in the design of inquiry. A liberal democratic view emphasizes the role of participants and the importance of deliberation.

 Beth Harry describes the perspectives of *race, ethnicity,* and *gender* as specific frames for the critique of research and inquiry. Harry, professor of teaching and learning at the University of Miami, distinguishes between biological categories such as sex and race, and socially constructed categories such as ethnicity and gender. All knowledge, she asserts, must be situated in the "place, time, and perspective of the knower." Central to the race, ethnicity, and gender critique, as with all areas of critical theory, is the insidious nature of power that is manifest in all aspects of research from the technical issues of design and data analysis to the demographics of the researcher and the participants.

 Tom Barone, professor of curriculum and instruction and qualitative methods at Arizona State, describes *arts based educational research* (ABER). Barone references Rorty's view of the two purposes of inquiry, i.e., to enhance certainty and to enhance meaning. These two purposes reflect two very different epistemologies. ABER can be either but is usually understood to be the latter. Barone comments, " . . . a work of art results from a careful reflection upon and recasting of qualities experienced by the artist into a form that is unique." Arts based educational research raises questions that have been hidden by the answers. It provides a different way of experiencing the world.

BASIC TOPICS COMPRISING THE PERSPECTIVES

In order to introduce the discussion of perspectives that follows in Chapter 4, we have provided an advance organizer of the basic topics in philosophy to frame the analyses of each perspectives (see Table 3–1). The topics include: ontology, a branch of metaphysics that is concerned with the study of what is real; epistemology, the study of the nature of knowledge; methodology, the means by which knowledge is acquired; and values, the role of our aesthetic sensibilities and our predispositions toward what is worthy in our judgments of what is true.

This table has been arranged in statement form so that a quick reading horizontally or vertically will allow a snapshot that both isolates and juxtaposes the perspectives. In this way the chart can serve as both an advanced organizer of the perspectives presented by the respective critics as well as an informed, albeit brief, review of the material.

For example, reading vertically down the Ontology column, the reader will find that for constructivism, ethics, critical perspective, and race, ethnicity, and gender, reality is constructed by the knower, who is either, depending upon the perspective, involved in (1) a relationship of power: critical perspective; (2) a set of social or cultural interactions: race, ethnicity, and gender; (3) the interaction of creative social and individual thought: constructivism; or (4) the conflict between professional and social aims: ethics. On the other hand, reality for postpositivists is based on the laws of the natural world and not at all constructed. Somewhere between those views sits pragmatism, which holds that reality is based on justified beliefs and warranted assertions, events, entities, or ideas that have enough supporting evidence—for now—to be called real.

The Methodology column considers the role the inquirer plays within the particular perspective. Here the inquirer seeks evidence (postpositivism), recognizes uncertainty (pragmatism), attempts understanding (constructivism), engages participants (ethics and interpretivism), uncovers power structures (critical perspective and race, ethnicity, and gender), considers her identity (race, ethnicity, and gender), invokes an audience (ABER), and attempts to undermine the status quo (poststructuralism). All here present the act of inquiry as needing a wide range of researchers and interpretations and essentially as working in collaboration with the participants.

Table 3–1
Overview of a philosophical analysis of perspectives.

	Ontology (What is reality?)	Epistemology (What and when is knowledge?)	Methodology (By what manner do we acquire knowledge and truth? How do we know?)	Values (What contributions do our aesthetic sensibilities and our beliefs about what is worthy make towards our knowledge of what is true?)
Postpositivism	Reality is the collection of natural laws and social and social phenomena of our universe; all of these really exist; we can observe (imperfectly) and experience (imperfectly) this reality.	Knowledge is information about the world, constrained by, yet not fully determined by the world. Knowledge is produced through evaluation of evidence and causal events; it cannot, however, be absolutely secure.	The inquirer seeks evidence through rigorous methods that might falsify the knowledge views held; alternative explanations for the same evidence should be sought; there should be an open assessment to a wider community of researchers; the inquirer must win our trust.	Inquiry affects and interacts with the lives of individuals and so it must be trustworthy; it would be immoral to affect those lives without having trustworthy reasons.
Pragmatism	Reality is warranted assertions and justified beliefs; these are held until we have evidence that can make them untrustworthy.	Knowledge is constructed, questioned, refined, and encoded; it is promoted through power structures and contested ideas within social groups; thinking and acting are one process.	The inquirer recognizes that the scientific method is effective but contains inherent uncertainties; knowledge guides method while method also guides knowledge.	Inquiry is not neutral; some benefit from research and some are hurt by it; truth will be applied to society, so a social consequence needs to be a factor. Care theory should be considered.
Constructivism	Reality is constructed through the interaction of the creative and interpretive work of the mind with the physical/temporal world.	Knowledge is a dynamic product of the interactive work of the mind made manifest in social practices and institutions.	The inquirer attempts to understand meaning within a given context, seeking a broad range of inputs and interpretations.	Inquiry is permeated with human values. Because values are inescapable, researchers must make extraordinary efforts to reveal, or uncover, beliefs and values that guide and generate individual and group constructions.
Ethics	Reality is constructed and constrained by the aims societies and professions adopt for themselves.	Knowledge is understood within the context of culture and is negotiated through a democratic process that respects all views.	The inquirer and participants engage each other, searching for collaborative solutions and rationally defensible conclusions.	Inquiry should tie its conclusions to values and include measures to eliminate power imbalances.

	Ontology (What is reality?)	Epistemology (What and when is knowledge?)	Methodology (By what manner do we acquire knowledge and truth? How do we know?)	Values (What contributions do our aesthetic sensibilities and our beliefs about what is worthy make towards our knowledge of what is true?)
Critical Perspective	Reality is constructed; driven by power and power relations.	Knowledge is constructed; theory should be practical, self-reflexive, explanatory, and normative.	The inquirer attempts to uncover the dynamics of ideology and power.	Inquiry employs social and cultural criticism. The goal is to reveal and challenge oppression.
Interpretivism	Reality is mediated by language; because the world does not exist in the shape of our sentences, the mind plays an active role in the construction of reality.	Knowledge and the knower are inextricably linked; events are placed in intelligible frames by a mind that actively engages the world, attaching significance to those events.	The inquirer interacts with participants and the world by using methods closer to literature than to physics; interpretivists probe how meaning is performed and negotiated in the everyday world.	Inquiry is value-centered rather than value-free and strives to recover the moral importance and imagination of the social sciences in order to create change in the world.
Race, Ethnicity, and Gender	Reality is constructed; race, ethnicity, and gender are created by social and cultural interactions.	Knowledge is constructed, situated in the time and place of the knower.	The inquirer must consider aspects of identity (of both the inquirer and the participants) which indicate status and power.	Inquiry is inherently biased and not value neutral.
Arts Based	Reality is reinterpreted and reconfigured through work of art.	Knowledge, represented through a work of art, "results from careful reflection upon and recasting of qualities experienced by the artist into a form that is unique."	The inquirer considers if a particular work invokes the audience to question educational settings, events, and issues.	Inquiry is an "act of personal judgment rather than one of seeking a final truth."
Poststructuralism	Reality in itself is contested. Some poststructuralists deny the concept of reality, while others maintain that language constructs reality.	Knowledge is constructed through signs, governed by the discursive rules for that area of knowledge.	The inquirer attempts to "undermine what has been defined as a present day techno-rational approach to education."	Inquiry is inherently biased and involves a politics and/or an ethic.

Epistemologically, all except postpositivism speak of knowledge as constructed, though occasional different terms arise. For some, knowledge is dynamic and interactive (constructivism and pragmatism); for others it is highly contextual and formed within cultural exchanges and understandings (race, ethnicity, and gender and ethics). Both interpretivism and critical perspective see knowledge as involving the knower in reflexive processes that both explain and engage the world.

Reading the chart horizontally reveals that while some perspectives feel that both reality and knowledge are constructed (critical perspective and race, ethnicity, and gender), others see this differently. Postructuralism, for example, sees reality as contested and knowledge as constructed, while interpretivism sees reality as mediated by language and knowledge and the knower as basically a single set. Some of these apparent disagreements present us with another function of the chart.

Paul (this book) points out that whether or not some knowledge makes sense depends on the assumptions one holds about knowledge. Debating methodology and epistemology without also considering the ontological assumptions creates an incomplete debate. Bringing the perspectives together in this table allows the reader to conflate issues that heretofore may have remained separate. Since one of the goals of this text is to engender an appreciation for the complexity of the interactions of multiple perspectives, the table makes some of the links more apparent in a small space.

For example, Guba (1990) contends that ontology and epistemology should not be seen as separate issues but should be brought together into one category. The table offers a way to experiment with this kind of perspective, putting in front of the reader two "cells" of information that would be conflated into this one view. Taking the constructivist as an example, she brings together the ideas that reality is constructed through interactions of mind and world and that knowledge is a dynamic product of the interactive work of the mind. In short, a constructivist in Guba's frame works from a place where knowledge and reality are one ever-changing process. In a similar frame, we see that an ethical standpoint begins by accepting knowledge and reality as one process constrained by powerful and conflicting negotiations.

CONCLUSION

As demonstrated here, advanced organizers are useful in thinking about some of the basic similarities and differences among the perspectives. As you read each perspective, it will become increasingly clear that the logics do not sort out so easily. What is described as "a perspective" usually is, as pointed out by the scholars writing the chapters, a family of truths. As suggested in the definition of "perspective" earlier in this chapter, some are only loosely connected by culture, history, or language, for example. This should not detract, however, from the fact that the perspectives are useful ways of thinking about broad areas of scholarship and interpreting those areas of scholarship has become a critical tool in understanding the research literature.

REFERENCES

Blackburn, S. (Ed.). (1994). *The Oxford dictionary of philosophy.* Oxford: Oxford University Press.

Guba, E. (Ed.) (1990). *The paradigm dialog.* Thousand Oaks: Sage Publishing.

CHAPTER 4

Nine Perspectives of Research

PERSPECTIVE 1: A POSTPOSITIVIST, SCIENTIFICALLY ORIENTED APPROACH TO EDUCATIONAL INQUIRY

D. C. Phillips   *Stanford University*

KEY WORDS*

Warranted Beliefs   Positivism   Epistemology   Knowledge Claims
Postmodernism

There are vast numbers of people around the globe engaged in one way or another in the educational enterprise—parents, teachers, students, curriculum developers, evaluators, policy analysts and developers, administrators, teacher educators, educational researchers—and many of these (with perhaps the exception of most students) will engage from time-to-time in inquiry *about* education. Teachers may want to improve the effectiveness of their work, or discover the causes of some lesson gone disastrously wrong; two parents may want to identify a program that is suitable for their child who has special needs; evaluators might be trying to determine which of two pilot programs a school district ought to adopt, or what the unintended side-effects of each of the programs happen to be; researchers might be struggling to understand the cognitive demands of a new computer-based educational program, or working on the interaction patterns within multiability groups in a classroom; and a policy group might be weighing the pros and cons of lowering class size in a state, balancing the possible gains in learning and positive attitude changes in students against the considerable drain on taxpayers' dollars that would be involved and the opportunities that would be lost to mount important programs elsewhere.

Educational inquiry can take many forms, and we stand to gain important insights from most (if not all) of them. Historians engage in inquiry, and so do philosophers, psychologists, and sociologists. Curriculum developers inquire, as do policymakers and evaluators. A writer working on the biography of an educational leader probably engages in much inquiry, as do parents who are trying to decide on a suitable school for a child, and as do teachers who are analyzing—as part of a process of self-improvement—why a particular lesson was a success or a failure; and a

*Definitions of Key Words are located in the Glossary at the back of this book.

documentary filmmaker, working on a project such as, for example, the prevalence of bullying in high schools, no doubt also engages in a great deal of inquiry (about bullying, but also about such things as effective levels of lighting and camera angles).

Inquiries, however, are not all equal. Some are shoddy pieces of work—the collection of information may be haphazard, and much of what is collected might be of dubious relevance to the issue at hand; recording of observations might be intermittent; biases may be allowed to intrude; the questions asked of interviewees might be leading ones rather than probing ones, or they might be superficial and fail to reach "below the surface" of events; the way points are thought through might be slipshod, and full of non sequiturs or fallacious reasoning; or the aim of the inquiry might simply be to "confirm" the beliefs that were held prior to the inquiry being initiated. The "inquiry" (in this case a pseudo-inquiry) might merely be a vehicle for allowing an individual to express his or her opinions dressed up, as it were, in disguise. It matters, in short, that the inquiries be—in John Dewey's stark term—"competent." Dewey wrote,

> We know that some methods of inquiry are better than others in just the same way in which we know that some methods of surgery, farming, road-making, navigating, or what-not are better than others. It does not follow in any of these cases that the "better" methods are ideally perfect. (Dewey, 1966, p. 8)

It should be noted that nowhere here has it been insisted that all educational inquiries be "scientific" in some narrowly-defined sense of this term; indeed, the term has not yet been used! Dewey himself used the term in a quite broad sense in which it was equivalent in meaning to "competent or disciplined inquiry," and he did not draw a dividing line between inquiries in the sciences and effective inquiries conducted by lay people in everyday life. The moral to be insisted upon here is that whatever the inquiry, the inquirer seems to be under an obligation to win our trust, to somehow or other make clear how the inquiry was conducted, and to indicate what steps were taken to insure that the conclusions reached are trustworthy (that is, *worthy* of trust by others apart from the individual whose inquiry it was). Some individuals, following Dewey, will want to call such trustworthy inquiries "scientific," but others might balk at using this label.

Dewey said that "**warranted beliefs**" (beliefs that are supported by serious considerations that give us substantive reasons to accept them or at least to take them seriously) come from "competent inquiry"; there seems to be little point in carrying out an inquiry if the aim is to produce *unwarranted* beliefs, or shoddily supported beliefs! After all, as made apparent in the examples used at the outset, *we often want to act on the basis of the findings of our inquiries,* and we want our actions to be efficacious in achieving our goals. Educational issues are important—vitally important—and deserve the best types of inquiry that can be mounted, for we want to foster such things as the intellectual and emotional development of students. Another way to put this is that consequences often follow on the heels of inquiries: A child is sent to a particular school, a teacher adopts a new teaching method that will affect the students in her class, a state-wide policy about school funding is adopted, a local school board issues a policy about punishments for bullying, and so forth. It would be immoral for us to affect the lives of individuals in serious ways, and to use precious public resources that could be well-used for other purposes, without having due reasons—trustworthy ones—for so doing. Acting on mere opinion or belief (no matter how heartfelt), or acting on the basis of an incompetent inquiry, is not good enough.

There are many members of the educational research community who think of themselves as being scientists (or applied scientists), and who aspire to produce work that has the trustworthiness associated with rigorous work in the natural, medical, and social sciences; and there are many legislators and policymakers who, in accord with the line of thinking just outlined, want advice about educational matters that emanates from research that is similar in quality to that influencing policy in health and medical matters. This of course raises the "sixty-four thousand dollar question": What is involved in being a scientist? What are the hallmarks of rigor here, of competence? And there is a deeper question: Can many, or even most, significant educational questions be pursued in a scientific manner, even if "science" is defined—following Dewey—quite broadly? The following brief discussion can only provide the outline of a satisfactory set of answers to these questions. (For more detailed accounts, see Phillips & Burbules, 2000; Phillips, 2000.)

A convenient way to start is by quoting a philosopher who does not believe that the naturalistic approach to the study of human (including educational) affairs is viable; the term "naturalistic" is used here to refer to the view that, in some core way, the "logic" or methodology of the social sciences can be similar to that of the natural sciences. In 1996 Brian Fay, a skeptic about much (but not all) of the naturalistic ideal, wrote as follows:

> Throughout much of its history the basic question in the philosophy of social science has been: is social science scientific, or can it be? Social scientists have historically sought to claim the mantle of science and have modeled their studies on the natural sciences. . . . However, although this approach yielded important insights into the study of human beings, it no longer grips philosophers or practitioners of social science. Some new approach more in touch with current intellectual and cultural concerns is required. (Fay, 1996, p. 1)

In essence, Fay sees us as having a forced choice—either we can accept a **positivistic**, narrow view of science (which he rightly regards as unacceptable), or else we have to adopt a view that is more "**postmodern**" and that stresses that human action and social life have features with which science (as defined) cannot deal. If those indeed are the only two choices, all of us certainly must side with Fay! There is, however, a third alternative to which he gives little weight. For many decades within the philosophical and scientific communities it has been widely recognized that the account of science given by the positivists (and by the behaviorists, who were their fellow travelers in psychology) was flawed; a new, *postpositivist* view has been under development (not to be confused with *postmodernism* that was born about the same time). Thus, there is a third path that we can take, one that is more viable than the two alternatives pointed to by Fay.

The term "**postpositivism**" is not meant to imply that this new view of the nature of science has close links with the positivism of the late 19th and first half or so of the 20th centuries—it is not a kind of "super" positivism! It is merely the position that has developed *post*—that is, *after*—the decline of positivism. Furthermore, it is an exaggeration to call it "*the* position," for it is not one position at all; contemporary (postpositivist) philosophers of science do what all philosophers throughout history have done, namely, they disagree with each other—and often about matters that laypeople are likely to think are arcane. What is described below is merely one version, but (as the saying goes) it is a "vanilla" version that would be acceptable to many contemporary philosophers who work on these issues.

1. Science is no longer seen as being completely undergirded by either a rationalist or empiricist **epistemology**; these epistemologies were (in their different ways) foundationalist views

according to which something could only be accorded the status of knowledge if it could be shown to be fully or absolutely justified in terms of a foundation in either reason or experience. Nowdays it is realized that there is no way in which our knowledge of the physical, biological, and social or human worlds can be made absolutely secure; contemporary epistemology is non-foundationalist in the sense that it is widely recognized that there are no absolutely secure foundations for human knowledge—all so-called "bases" are open to at least the possibility of revision in the light of what future experience (including experience in the laboratory) turns up—a position philosophers label as "fallibilism."

2. It follows from this that science cannot be claimed to establish "**absolute truths**," for we have no way of determining whether the things that today we think are true will be judged to be true tomorrow. Some philosophers see science as progressively getting closer to the truth—this is the point of Popper's idea of the increasing verisimilitude of science, which he sees as taking place not through the *establishment* of anything but rather via the *detection and elimination of error*. Others take a different tack; for example the following represents a position that, in one form or another, enjoys quite wide contemporary support:

> Science does not deliver to us universal truths underlying all natural phenomena; but it does provide models possessing various degrees of scope and adequacy. . . . One goal shared by most scientists is to choose from among the available alternatives the model that best fits the real world. (Giere, 1999, pp. 6–7)

3. It does not follow from the fact that no evidence is sufficient to insulate a scientific "finding" or "conclusion" from the possibility of future revision, that we are free to believe anything at all that takes our fancy about the physical, biological, and social worlds. Our beliefs, fallible though they be, are constrained by what the world is really like—indeed, it is the world that determines whether or not our current beliefs are sound or unsound! Consider this: If the balls that Galileo rolled down his inclined plane actually had behaved differently from the way they consistently did (and still do) behave, physics would have taken on a different shape from what it now has. Whatever Galileo came to believe, as a scientist his beliefs were constrained by the behavior of the things that he studied—but it is important to underscore the point that "constrained" does *not* mean "fully determined by!" Similarly, although it is not absolutely certain that there are only nine planets revolving around our sun, we are not free to believe anything at all about what the solar system is like—our beliefs about it, to be competently formed, must be constrained by the realities that exist out there, rotating around the sun! (And if we were to offer a rival account, we would need to warrant it by offering new evidence, or by presenting some kind of new—and acceptable—argument.)

The same can be said about the social or human realms. People, social institutions, customs and practices, all really exist; and they really do have the characteristics they really have. Thus the claims we make about them, to be well-warranted, need to be constrained by those characteristics. For example, if a political scientist were to claim that the majority of fundamentalist Christians in the United States in 2001 support abortion rights for women, then this claim would seem to be unwarranted, and the inquiry (if any) that led to it would seem to have been incompetently carried out. (This conclusion cannot be voided by suggesting that it all depends how one defines what a "fundamentalist Christian" is. Although there may well be rival definitions, it does not square with accepted usage of this descriptive term to use it in such a way that the majority of those who fall under it currently accept abortion rights; if the term were to be used in this way, the purpose would seem to be deceptive.) An example used earlier also can be taken to illustrate the general point being made here: The parents seeking a suitable school for their child with special needs engage in inquiry to find the characteristics that various candidate schools actually have—they want to place their child in a school that as far as they can tell has the features they find desirable, and their conclusions about the various schools (if those conclusions are going to be well-warranted) will need to have been constrained by the realities that pertain. If they want their child to be well-served, they cannot just believe anything they like about the various schools they investigated.

4. The points already mentioned raise the specter of "reality" and "truth," notions that many turn-of-the-millennium intellectuals of postmodernist disposition find offensive, but which many postpositivist philosophers find essential if we are to maintain clarity of thought. Indeed, the examples used illustrate that these notions are hardly avoidable, either in philosophy or in everyday life. It would seem that a sane person cannot deny the existence of—the reality of—schools, other people, cars and trains, the sun, and so forth. Relatedly, it is not easy to see how we could do away with saying that propositions are true or false; for example, can we easily give up the distinction between the following two propositions, the first of which is false and the second of which is true: (a) "Adolf Hitler was born in the same year as Julius Caesar," (b) "Stanford University is located to the south of San Francisco." We make countless statements each day that are true, and that our hearers take to be true; no doubt we pass on some untruths as well, and we may blush when one of the latter is drawn to our attention—truth in our utterances is pretty central to the successful conduct of everyday social life.

What sometimes confuses the non-philosopher here are the obvious facts that (a) we cannot always, or perhaps even usually, determine what propositions *actually are true,* and (b) we sometimes err in claiming that a particular proposition is true (or false). An example may help here: We cannot tell for sure that there is a tenth planet lying out past the orbit of Pluto, but that does not prevent the proposition that states that there *is* such a planet from being either true or false. As yet we simply cannot *decide* whether it is true or not. If the proposition were *neither* true *or* false, why should we bother with any further inquiry into the matter? And the fact that in the past astronomers claimed that there were only seven planets (i.e., they asserted that this was true), when in fact they were wrong, does not mean that the notion of truth is vacuous. If we could only assert (i.e., put forward as being true) those things that were *absolutely* true, safe from possible future overthrow, then we could assert very little at all! The fact that we are human and prone to make mistakes does not make the notion of truth useless.

When postpositivists deny that absolute truth can be attained in science they are not, then, making the strong—and strange—claim that the word "truth" serves no useful and meaningful purpose; rather, they are making the epistemological point that many of the general propositions (or bodies of propositions) useful in science—such things as laws of nature, theories, conjectures, or models—cannot be known with certainty to be true. For one thing, these laws and theories make universal claims, and as the evidence we have at our disposal is far from being the complete set that in principle exists, any conclusions we reach might well be mistaken. And to seal the case, consider that even if the totality of evidence were available to us we might still be mistaken, for we might have incorrectly explained or conceptualized this evidence; in Giere's terms, we might have produced a model that is compatible with the totality of the evidence but which gets things wrong at the theoretical level—something we would never be able to discover, if in fact all the attainable evidence had been obtained.

Nevertheless, most postpositivists hold that, if we have been careful, we often are warranted in making the truth-claims that we do make on the basis of incomplete evidence (that is, our truth-claims can be rational ones to put forward, given the evidence we have); *but we must always be aware that our claims are never perfectly or fully or absolutely warranted!* Thus (to use an example suggested by Woody Allen's film *Sleeper*), although there is the theoretical possibility that we might be mistaken in believing that eating too many chocolate fudge sundaes is bad for our health, the best evidence currently available suggests that this belief is true, and a wise person will act accordingly and is warranted in so doing. The position outlined by Giere suggests that we need to abandon the quest for "absolute truth," but he still acknowledges that scientists seek models that do justice to the empirical evidence that is available; in common parlance, a model that does this is often said to be true—as far as we can fallibly tell (all judgments of truth in matters pertaining to theories or abstract models of reality are fallible ones)! On the other hand, Brian Fay argues that once we accept the fallible nature of our **knowledge claims** (the position philosophers call "fallibilism," and which has been advocated earlier), while we can in principle cling to a realist philosophy, the better approach is to frankly acknowledge that "the notion of an independently existing pre-formed structure of cosmic order loses its point." (Fay, 1996, p. 210) Many postpositivists dispute whether this is indeed the best approach, and they are dubious about the line of reasoning that led Fay (and others) to this skeptical conclusion.

When we turn to the concept of reality, postpositivists are far from reaching unanimity; the literature abounds with types of realism and types of anti-realism. I wish to take the bull by the horns and suggest that points similar to the ones just discussed about truth also can be made here. A person would not live very long if, in daily life, she acted as if the reality of physical objects was in doubt—she would trip over the first gutter that she ignored, or she would be run over by the first car that came along and whose path she did not vacate! Literally, we bump up against reality every moment of our waking lives. But of course it cannot be denied that there have been many philosophical (metaphysical) controversies about "reality"; however, in the main these are confined to issues involved in ascertaining the status of the entities that theories postulate to exist. There are a couple of standard cases: In the first place, the reality of the objects postulated in certain basic physical theories and laws has long been a topic of debate (the existence of subatomic particles such as electrons and neutrons, or those described in the theory of quarks); and there has been a parallel debate about some entities postulated in cognitive science and philosophy of mind ("Does consciousness exist?" was the title of a famous—and difficult—essay by William James). Second, there has been a debate in the philosophy of social science about the reality of some of the theoretical entities postulated to exist in human affairs; for example, do organizations—which obviously have legal status, and which thus exist in legal theory—actually also exist as real entities in the world apart from the individuals who collectively constitute them? (Does the world contain individuals, or individuals *and* organizations?) But once again in this whole domain we need to be cautious, for it is one thing to claim that there is a reality, and quite another to claim that our current descriptions of that reality are correct!

5. Many postpositivists are not shy of using the concept of causation, and here they also find support in the practice of the scientific community. Researchers in fields such as education are often concerned to identify causal relationships, and much methodological discussion is about the valid ways of pursuing this aim. Knowledge of causal relationships is indispensible for guiding interventions, and for framing policies (for a policy is, in a sense, an intervention in the social realm that takes something like the form "because we want to achieve X, we should do Y," which is based upon the supposition that doing X will *cause or produce* Y). A teacher

adopts a pedagogical practice because she believes it will help students to learn a difficult topic (and "help" is, in this context, a disguised reference to causation). A state legislature might pass a law mandating a reduction in class size in order to produce gains in student learning (and "produce" is another causal notion). It is worth reflecting on the fact that our commitment to the view that educating young people is important is based in part on the causal belief that this will enable them—or at least assist them—to lead productive and fulfilling lives. (Would we educate if we believed that this would have no effect at all—"effect" being, of course, part of causal discourse.)

The postpositivist, then, believes that causal relationships exist in the human and social worlds just as they exist in the physical and biological realms—although it is crucial to note that the *forms* that causes take in these realms are quite different. Rewards and punishments can cause changes in the behavior of children, but not in the behavior of the planets or of volcanoes; the communication of ideas, factual information, and explanations can change the actions of a person but not of a nuclear pile. Consider these cases: If a child understands the notion of injustice, he might decide to oppose a bully who is terrorizing younger children, and a student who understands the corrosive nature of acids will avoid direct bodily contact with them. Parents who know something about the educational practices adopted in a particular school might then choose not to send their child to that institution.

What is at issue here is the theory or model that is adopted of what leads humans to act—are we merely biological machines that react only to physical stimuli, or are we constituted in such a way that our actions are influenced by reason, knowledge, and the like? If we believe that humans can, on occasion at least, act intentionally, then it seems hard to deny the causal role played by such things as meanings, ideas, and reasons. (The issues here are complex; for further discussion, see Phillips & Burbules, 2000, Chapter 4; Phillips, 2000, Chapter 2.) On this general issue Brian Fay's position seems right on the mark:

> Social phenomena . . . are also events and objects which occur in the world. For this reason to understand them requires more than just knowing *what* they mean; we must also know *why* they occurred. . . . Put succinctly, to comprehend intentional acts we need to know more than just their meaning; we also need to know their cause. (Fay, 1996, p. 119)

Fay makes the point that our intentional acts are caused by our reasoning processes (which include, of course, our knowledge and beliefs, our motives, and the like). This provides a neat segue into the final point.

6. The version of postpositivism that I have been outlining is virtually indistinguishable from common sense: We inhabit a real world, in which there are causal interactions; we inquire in order to acquire genuine (warranted) understanding of this world—and to acquire, also, trustworthy knowledge about the mechanisms and causal factors at work so that we can act or intervene to achieve our worthwhile human purposes. The knowledge we acquire may be fallible, but we are justified in believing and acting upon the most rigorously produced knowledge that is available, until something better (more justified or warranted) comes along to replace it.

Postpositivist philosophers are quite reluctant to tell scientific inquirers their business, and to legislate what methods should be used in the quest for reliable knowledge—it is a matter for inquirers, not primarily for philosophers, to develop research methods that are competent. Nevertheless, philosophers do have a few general pieces of advice to offer, and in a sense they can act as the "Jiminy Cricket" of the research community!

Thus—going where angels fear to tread—I can suggest the following items, which are hardly surprising: It is an aid to competence if inquirers avoid what has been called a "confirmatory stance", and instead of looking for evidence that their deeply held views are right, they actively seek for evidence to prove that these beliefs may be wrong. It also helps to make findings more trustworthy if alternative explanations for the available evidence are sought and then tested in an attempt to eliminate them. It is also crucial, for making a piece of inquiry trustworthy, that it has been opened to inspection and criticism from the wider community of researchers. It helps, too, if research reports describe with care the actual steps that were taken during the inquiry, and if research instruments, questions, interview protocols, and the like, are presented for inspection. Above all, clarity and rigor in argumentation are vital—for then the inquirer's train of reasoning can be assessed.

There is much, then, to be said for the view that Karl Popper expressed in this rather poetic passage:

> What we should do, I suggest, is to give up the idea of ultimate sources of knowledge, and admit that all knowledge is human; that it is mixed with our errors, our prejudices, our dreams, and our hopes; that all we can do is to grope for truth even though it be beyond our reach. We may admit that our groping is often inspired, but we must be on our guard against the belief, however deeply felt, that our inspiration carries any authority, divine or otherwise. If we thus admit that there is no authority beyond the reach of criticism to be found within the whole province of our knowledge . . . then we can retain, without danger, the idea that truth is beyond human authority. And we must retain it. For without this idea there can be no objective standards of inquiry; no criticism of our conjectures; no groping for the unknown; no quest for knowledge. (Popper, 1965, pp. 29–30)

QUESTIONS

1. In what ways does postpositivism expand the more common definitions of science?
2. How is a belief that reason and knowledge have a causal effect on truth and reality different from a more biological framework?
3. How does a researcher assert his/her trustworthiness and believability?
4. How is a claim that there is a reality different from the claim that we can know reality?

REFERENCES

Dewey, J. (1966). *Democracy and education: An introduction to the philosophy of education.* New York: The Free Press.

Fay, B. (1996). *Contemporary philosophy of social science.* Oxford: Blackwell.

Giere, R. (1999). *Science without laws.* Chicago: Chicago University Press.

Popper, K. (1965). *Conjectures and refutations* (2nd ed.). New York: Basic Books.

Phillips, D. C. (2000). *The expanded social scientist's bestiary.* Lanham, MD: Rowman and Littlefield.

Phillips, D. C., & Burbules, N. (2000). *Postpositivism and educational research.* Lanham, MD: Rowman and Littlefield.

PERSPECTIVE 2: Pragmatism

Nel Noddings   *Stanford University*

KEY WORDS

Warranted Assertions   Sociology of   Care Theory
                         Knowledge

In their treatment of knowledge, truth, and meaning, pragmatists emphasize effects and consequences. They reject the certainty of first principles, and they deny the infallibility of passive perception. Human beings are active; they have desires and, to satisfy them, they must try things out.
Thinking and acting work together as one process. Both theory (to guide thinking and acting) and
practice (to test the suggestions of theory) are important; they are *equally* important.

Charles Sanders Peirce, the first philosopher to use "pragmatism" as a label for this new philosophy, considered **pragmatism** to be primarily a theory of meaning. In one of his best-known
essays, "How to Make Our Ideas Clear," he said, "What a thing means is simply what habits it involves" or "what habits it produces" (quoted in Thompson, 1963, p. 80). Summing up the pragmatic theory of meaning, Peirce wrote, "Consider what effects, that might conceivably have
practical bearings, we conceive the object of our conception to have. Then, our conception of these
effects is the whole of our conception of the object" (p. 80). As we seek meaning, we are to ask ourselves what observable effects may be associated with the objects of our thinking. We anticipate
certain effects as a result of reflection on past events and, where uncertainty exists, we conjecture.
Meaning so described is dynamic. As we test our conjectures, meaning changes; sometimes it becomes more stable, and at other times, continued uncertainty leads to further testing.

John Dewey developed a pragmatic theory of knowledge. Like Peirce, he insisted on the primary role of consequences in establishing knowledge. We need knowledge to guide activity, but
knowledge is advanced as activity confirms or disconfirms the trial knowledge with which we
started. In an important note, Dewey (1929/1960) wrote, "the essence of pragmatic instrumental-
ism is to conceive of *both* knowledge [theory] and practice as means of making goods—excellencies
of all kinds—secure in experienced existence" (p. 37). Rejecting the traditional reliance on *a priori*
principles, he asserted that "standards and tests of validity are found in the consequences of overt
activity, not in what is fixed prior to it and independently of it" (p. 73).

Another great pragmatist, William James, described pragmatic method this way: It is "the
attitude of looking away from first things, principles, 'categories,' supposed necessities; and of
looking towards last things, fruits, consequence, facts" (1968, p. 380). Complications arise,
however, when we recognize that both false and true ideas have "effects"; we therefore need a
method of testing and, as Peirce advised, a commitment to continued inquiry.

Readers new to pragmatism will not go far astray if they think of pragmatism as a method
that is modeled on scientific practice. Identifying problems, anticipating the consequences of various courses of action, formulating hypotheses, testing them, and reflecting on the consequences
are essential to science and to pragmatism. Because of the inherent uncertainty built into such

methods, Dewey preferred the expression "**warranted assertion**" to "truth." Although we can rarely be sure enough to proclaim having the *truth,* we can make assertions that are warranted— that is, carefully tested and at least partly confirmed. We can, that is, count on a belief justified in this way until something occurs to shake our belief.

In the past two decades, after a long lapse, there has been a revival of interest in pragmatism within philosophical circles. (Interest in Dewey's educational thought never waned in the domain of educational theory.) Richard Rorty (1979) endorses Dewey's notion that "science and philosophy are continuous" (p. 228) and, like Dewey, he rejects the traditional quest for certainty. He points to other prominent philosophers who, without embracing the label, have leaned toward pragmatic approaches—among them, "Sellars, Quine, Davidson, Ryle, Malcolm, Kuhn, and Putnam" (p. 7).

One of the most important features of this renewed interest in pragmatism is an emphasis on the vocabularies we use and how changes in words can affect how we think and act. Rorty (1979) says of such philosophers: "They hammer away at the holistic point that words take their meanings from other words rather than by virtue of their representative character, and the corollary that vocabularies acquire their privileges from the men who use them rather than from their transparency to the real" (p. 368). This comment suggests the necessity of careful attention to the **sociology of knowledge**—that is, to how knowledge is constructed, questioned, refined, and encoded.

Both pragmatism and postmodernism have contributed to the importance of sociology. Instead of looking for the foundations of knowledge or identifiable origins of all knowledge that will guarantee the truth of what is produced from them, we now look at the social history of concepts, the locus of power in which ideas are promoted, and the fruits of contested ideas.

But sociology has itself experienced problems. Thirty years ago, Alvin Gouldner (1970) warned that sociologists must acknowledge their own place in society and its problems. Theory cannot, he said, remain aloof from its social origins and effects without endangering the very life of sociology:

> Any effort to deal with the *extra*-technical sources of theoretical change, if it fails to locate the theorist in society, can only produce a "psychology" of knowledge, overstating the importance of the unique characteristics of the theorist as a person; correspondingly, any such effort that does not relate the theory to the person of the theorist can produce only an unconvincing "sociologism" that fails to explain *how* the society comes to affect theory. (p. 397)

These two extreme traps still threaten sociology and, as we will see in our critiques, sociologists continue to argue over which trap is worse or even whether one or the other should be considered a mistake. Gouldner's statement is very much in the pragmatist tradition. Neither abstract, detached theory nor a mere account of personal experience can yield warranted assertions.

As we examine studies presented for critique in this book, we'll ask pragmatic questions:

What have we learned?

How warranted are the conclusions?

Are further investigations suggested?

Is the field advanced by this study? Is it hurt? How?

Is the chosen method well used?

Is the vocabulary appropriate to the study or does it tend to block change or innovation?

In addition to these questions, we should be interested in ethical questions, such as

Who benefits from this research?

Has anyone been hurt or is anyone likely to be hurt?

Is there a social (as contrasted with scientific) history of the problem?

Has it been discussed?

Should it be?

On this last set questions, I have always found pragmatism a bit weak. When we ask about ethical or moral consequences, we must be ready to evaluate them as ethically acceptable or not acceptable, not simply as predicted or not predicted. What test shall we use for this? Dewey depended heavily on what he called "social" consequences and these are to be counted as favorable when they tend to advance the growth of individuals and strengthen the democratic competence of groups. Much debate has been addressed to the question of whether Dewey's criteria are adequate for the purpose of judging the ethical acceptability of consequences.

Because I think there is a real weakness here (Noddings, 1998), I will use care theory to guide our ethical judgment. This is compatible with the pragmatic insistence on looking at consequences. Using **care theory**, we are directed to look at particular consequences—whether the recipients of our care are hurt or helped and how caring relations are affected. With respect to the latter, we will ask whether caring relations are established, maintained, or enhanced or whether they are damaged. If the research participants feel themselves to have been harmed, then we cannot claim to have maintained or established caring relations.

Research on caring itself can be used to illustrate the concerns of both care theorists and pragmatists (among whom there is considerable overlap). When researchers devise instruments "to measure" caring, the effect can be to trivialize the concept, to reduce it to a set of general indicators instead of describing it in its contextual and relational fullness. Using such methods tends to destroy the possibility of real changes that can follow a significant change in vocabulary, and the new concept can then be assimilated to an old paradigm, its words, and methods. Moreover, if instruments are used to "test" the caring of teachers or administrators, the results may actually damage caring relations. Of course, a devastating "thick description" might also have this effect. The pragmatic test may be applied to the full range of methods used in research, not only to those that fail to do justice to the concepts we favor.

QUESTIONS

1. How is a warranted assertion different from truth?
2. How are thinking and acting one process?
3. What is the role of reflection in pragmatic thinking?
4. How is the link to scientific practice probably a partial cause for the need of care theory to be added to the mix?

REFERENCES

Dewey, J. (1960). *The quest for certainty.* New York: Capricorn. (Original work published 1929)
Gouldner, A. (1970). *The coming crisis of western sociology.* New York: Basic Books.

James, W. (1968). *The writings of William James.* New York: Modern Library.

Noddings, N. (1998). Thoughts on John Dewey's 'Ethical principles underlying education,' *The Elementary School Journal, 98,* 5.

Rorty, R. (1979). *Philosophy and the mirror of nature.* Princeton: Princeton University Press.

Thompson, M. (1963). *The pragmatic philosophy of C. S. Peirce.* Chicago: University of Chicago Press.

PERSPECTIVE 3: CONSTRUCTIVISM AS A THEORETICAL AND INTERPRETIVE STANCE

Yvonna S. Lincoln   *Texas A&M University*

KEY WORDS

Constructivism	Ontology	Methodology or Methodologies	Verstehen
Meaning-Making Activities	Epistemology	Axiology	Bricoleurs

Constructivism covers a fairly large arena in the philosophical literature, an arena too large to permit easy coverage. For purposes of this chapter, however, **constructivism** is defined in its simplest terms as an interpretive stance which attends to the meaning-making activities of active agents and cognizing human beings. These **meaning-making activities** embody both physical and temporal data, acquired through the senses, and the interaction of these physical and temporal data with values, beliefs, opinions, prejudices, hopes, dreams, fears, aspirations, fantasies, attitudes, adopted roles, stereotypes, and other forms of mental processes and received and created knowledge of both individuals and groups. Meaning-making thus engages two dimensions of individual social life: actual events and concrete situations, and the particular and individual mental stances which impute meaning to those events and situations. Constructivists believe *constructions*—the product of meaning-making, sense-making, holism-oriented mental activities of individuals—are critical because they, as much as physical and/or temporal events, determine how individuals (and the groups to which individuals belong) will act toward each other, and toward the physical and temporal events, and how such events will be interpreted and, therefore, frame social performances and cultural space (Guba & Lincoln, 1981, 1989; Lincoln & Guba, 1985, 2000).

Typically, constructivists lay out a metaphysical space which is comprised of (1) an **ontology**, a definition of what will be considered, for the purposes of inquiry, real; (2) an **epistemology**, a model of how an inquirer may relate to and thus come to know about what is considered real; (3) a **methodology or methodologies**, or inquiry design strategies thought most likely to yield information regarded as valuable, truthful, worthy of knowing, or socially useful within this model; and (4) an **axiology**, or a statement about the role(s) values serve in the processes and products of the inquiry process, and what their influence might be on the product of such research or inquiry. Each of these four interactive axioms, or assumptions, is discussed more fully on the preceding pages.

ONTOLOGY

Humans as social beings interact with two realities: a *physical/temporal reality,* composed of houses, streets, offices, carpool groups, children, co-workers, families, desks, mortar and bricks and other tangible objects, and time; and an *enacted,* or *constructed, reality,* composed of the interpretive, meaning-making, sense-ascribing, holism-producing, role-assuming activities which produce meaningfulness and order in human life. These two worlds—or realities—exist in parallel and alongside one another, interacting and influencing each other in ways which are impossible, in theory, to predict, control, or even entirely understand. For 100 years, science has focused on the first, to the exclusion of the latter. This dissociation has occurred to such an extent that David Bakan, former president of the American Psychological Association, commented that love, faith, altruism, will, character, and other important human characteristics had been simply excluded from the study of psychology—which was supposed to be the study of human characteristics (Bakan, 1972)! While not denying for a moment the impact or importance of the physical reality which surrounds us as social beings, constructivists aim to counterbalance the strong behaviorist and measurability foci of experimental social science with a re-emphasis on the immeasurable forms of meaning, and on **verstehen**, deep understanding of the meaning-making processes which permit individuals and groups to *enact* organization (Morgan, 1997; Weick, 1985), to co-create shared knowledge (Heron & Reason, 1997), and to construct meaning within their lives.

Most constructivists come to this theoretical stance and interpretive posture because they have come to understand that we know far less about the *whys* than we originally thought we did. As Terry Denny put it over 20 years ago, if all educational research were translated into human stature, we would have a dwarf slightly over 3 feet high. This is not a stellar record for over 100 years of intensive research on, for instance, schooling processes. Nor do we seem able, with conventional science, to counteract the effects of poverty, motivation, or other human failures on schooling. Consequently, alternatives to conventional science have been sought; constructivism has been posed as one alternative for its ability to see human complexity in its fullness; for its ability to understand unseen human meaning-making forces at work; for its relentless insistence that there is no such thing, in the natural social world, as a "controlled variable"; and for its ability to communicate, in natural language, a variety of portrayals representing the positions of many stakeholders, thus enlarging knowledge and understanding throughout a given community.

Many constructivists also come to this position because they realize that it is less the measurable physical/temporal reality which determines the shape and contours of social life, but rather the meanings which are imputed to, within, and between physical/temporal realities. In short, the meaning-making activities of cognizing humans may be more critical to understanding how social life is organized, how historical structures[1] (e.g., economic oppression) become reified, or how daily life is enacted, performed, and storied.

EPISTEMOLOGY

Constructivists elide the idea of extended and multiple realities with the principle of an extended epistemology, or *multiple epistemologies*. Conventional science frequently falls back on conservative theories of what constitutes scientific knowledge. Such knowledge is considered theoretically appropriate if derived with particular design strategies and methods, organized and treated (analyzed) by particular means thought to be both rigorous and objective, and presented wit particular discursive and rhetorical structure. Data collected and analyzed outside this fairly closed system are suspected of being loose, subjective, unrigorous, theoretically meaningless, and non-contributory to the purposes of prediction and control (and, indeed, constructivist data are neither useful for, nor intended toward, prediction and control).

Extended or multiple epistemologies, however, imply that knowledge derived by conventional (rationalist, experimentalist) methods is not the only knowledge worth having. Other knowledges—feminist, racial, ethnic, cultural, queer, disabled, colonial, marginalized, borderland—grant us insight into the way those different from us construct their own "textured" (Fiske, 1992) realities, their private and public cultural and social milieu, or "habitus." Such knowledges additionally act to resist, undermine, and countermand images of society which are monocultural, majority oriented, or dictated by the interests of powerful elites. Constructivists see as a major responsibility the search for, and representation of, these resistance narratives, wherever they may be found (Lincoln, 1993; McLaughlin & Tierney, 1993). This is done, at its simplest, to recover a fuller and richer description of social life as it is experienced by all research participants. At a more complex level, the search for alternative representations of realities subverts easy "quick fixes" in the policy arenas where dominant interests have long determined images of those for whom social policies are drawn up, and where research portrayals have sometimes been used to "punish" non-mainstream groups (Fine, Weis, Weseen & Wong, 2000). At an even higher level of complexity, the representations of multiple "lived experiences" fosters a richer social imagery from which to build a communitarian ethic of caring and social and distributive justice (Lincoln & Denzin, 2000).

METHODOLOGY

Constructivists are often conflated with those who do solely qualitative research. And indeed, constructivists frequently opt for qualitative methodological strategies because those are the strategies which permit the only entry we have into the "black box" of the human mind, where sense-making and meaning-imputing activities take place. But it would be a mistake to believe that constructivists are solely qualitative researchers, or that those who do qualitative research consider themselves constructivists. These dimensions—qualitative versus quantitative, and constructivist versus non-constructivist—are orthogonal to each other. Many constructivists also utilize, when appropriate to the questions which must be answered, quantitative methods; and many who use qualitative methods are solidly against constructivist forms of interpretation or analysis (Lincoln, in press), preferring instead more "realist" versions of data representation. Constructivists cannot, as a consequence, be called qualitative researchers solely; they are rather **bricoleurs** (Lincoln & Denzin, 2000), choosing and adapting methods which seem to show promise of eliciting the best data for the questions which must be answered.

Nevertheless, all constructivists will have a thorough knowledge of qualitative research methods, and will frequently use design strategies (methodologies) that represent open-ended and rhizomatic (Lather, 1986) stances toward data. Constructivists will also frequently make rhetorical, presentational and narrative choices which refuse closure, and which take problematic and uneven discourses to be a part of the human context being portrayed. Thus, methodology is played out as a part of a much larger set of paradigmatic questions: What problem is chosen? How is it to be framed? What theories (or, conversely, what rejections of theories) will guide the inquiry? Where will the inquiry be conducted—in a laboratory, or in the natural context? What data are deemed most important for answering the inquiry questions? What methods are most likely to

Dissertation structure

uncover those data? What role will the research participants play in the study? Are they simply sources from which data must be "extracted," or are they active agents, suggesting salient issues overlooked in the original design? What form will the research report take? And, what role will values play in the inquiry (Lincoln & Guba, 1985)? Each question presents a set of choices, and each choice acts to either resonate with other choices, or to create dissonance within the inquiry project itself. Thus, methodology, method, and paradigm (model, metaphysic, worldview) interact to reinforce or contradict each other, although rarely in the way presented by naïve researchers who make the assumption that the differences between paradigms are merely "qualitative" and "quantitative."

AXIOLOGY: THE ROLE OF VALUES

The final premise for constructivists revolves around the role of values in the research act. Constructivists are persuaded that because inquiry is a human activity, it is necessarily imbued with human values. Constructivists therefore reject the possibility of a value-free, "objective" human science, arguing that objectivity is a chimera, a fiction which acts only to obscure the values choices of its claimants. That is, the claim of objectivity is itself a particular value position, one which serves the purpose of taking off the table for consideration both the choices about problem definition, and the particular framework within which findings might be interpreted.

Constructivists take an oppositional posture on the role of values. A constructivist will attempt to clarify values which exist in the context, using the various respondents' value positions—as well as the researcher's own—as a way of demonstrating where consensus and conflict exist in ordinary social life. If values are inescapable, argue constructivists, then we should make extraordinary efforts to uncover the value positions which shape, guide, and create individuals' and groups' constructions. It is only when we understand the underlying values of respondents and research participants that we can begin to understand where conflict exists and where negotiation around larger issues might be engaged.

A part of this determination is the inquiry process itself. Another part of the explication of values is the responsibility of the researcher, in a set of activities routinely called reflexivity. Since the researcher is frequently the "instrument" in constructivist inquiries, it is mandatory that this human instrument reflect upon research practices, activities, relationships, decisions, choices, and his or her own values in those arenas. Knowing the self more intimately with each research project means coming to terms with *etic*—or outsider—values, and "coming clean" about those values as a part of the research process.

CONCLUDING REMARKS

Constructivists come in many stripes. Some are persuaded to phenomenology, some to symbolic interactionism, some to philosophical hermeneutics, some to anthropological interpretivism, and some to various critical theories (feminist theory, critical theory, queer theory, race/ethnic theories of knowing). But many would share some of these basic premises, and further, would assert that their end goal is a deep understanding of social processes which might enable and increase social justice, act to increase emancipatory action on the part of citizens, and work toward a communitarian social ethic. Most would argue for a social science which supports positive social change. Many would call themselves liberal, although that term is out of fashion.

All, however, would support an expanded researcher-researched ethic which is far less asymmetrical, and far more egalitarian, inclusive, pluralistic and democratic. These values, as well as the inherent paradigm commitments, are shared values.

QUESTIONS

1. Discuss the role of meaning and meaning-making in the constructivist position.
2. How does the constructivist "vision" of research differ from that of postpositivism?

NOTES

1. The recognition of the historical nature of some social structures (e.g., economic oppression, as previously mentioned, but also racism, class structures, gender discrimination, and the like) is why I continue to emphasize not only physical realities, but also temporal realities.

REFERENCES

Bakan, D. (1972, March). Psychology can now kick the science habit. *Psychology Today, 6,* 26–28, 86–88.

Fine, M., Weis, L., Weseen, S., & Wong, L. (2000). For whom? Qualitative research, representations, and social responsibilities. In N. K. Denzin & Y. S. Lincoln (Eds.), *Handbook of qualitative research,* (2nd ed., pp. 107–132). Thousand Oaks, CA: Sage Publications.

Fiske, J. (1992). Cultural studies and the culture of everyday life. In L. Grossberg, C. Nelson, & Treichler (Eds.), *Cultural studies* (pp. 154–173). New York: Routledge.

Guba, E. G., & Lincoln, Y. S. (1981). *Effective evaluation.* San Francisco: Jossey-Bass.

Guba, E. G., & Lincoln, Y. S. (1989). *Fourth generation evaluation.* Thousand Oaks, CA: Sage Publications.

Heron, J., & Reason, P. (1997). A participatory inquiry paradigm. *Qualitative Inquiry, 3*(3), 274–294.

Lather, P. (1986). Issues of validity in openly ideological research: Between a rock and a soft place. *Interchange, 17*(4), 63–84.

Lincoln, Y. S. (in press). Constructivist knowing, participatory ethics, and responsive evaluation: Family ties and kinship patterns. In D. L. Stufflebeam, T. Kellaghan, & L. Wingate (Eds.), *International encyclopedia of evaluation.* Thousand Oaks, CA: Sage Publications.

Lincoln, Y. S. (1993). I and thou: Method, voice and roles in research with the silenced. In D. McLaughlin & W. G. Tierney (Eds.), *Naming silenced lives: Personal narratives and processes of educational change* (pp. 29–47). New York: Routledge.

Lincoln, Y. S., & Denzin, N. K. (2000). The seventh moment: Out of the past. In N. K. Denzin & Y. S. Lincoln (Eds.), *Handbook of qualitative research* (2nd ed., pp. 1047–1065). Thousand Oaks, CA: Sage Publications.

Lincoln, Y. S., & Guba, E. G. (1985). *Naturalistic inquiry.* Thousand Oaks, CA: Sage Publications.

Lincoln, Y. S., & Guba, E. G. (2000). Paradigmatic controversies, contradictions and emerging confluences. In N. K. Denzin & Y. S. Lincoln (Eds.), *Handbook of qualitative research* (2nd ed., pp. 163–188). Thousand Oaks, CA: Sage Publications.

McLaughlin, D., & Tierney, W. G. (Eds.). (1993). *Naming silenced lives: Personal narratives and the process of educational change.* New York: Routledge.

Morgan, G. (1997). *Images of organization* (2nd ed.). Thousand Oaks, CA: Sage Publications.

Weick, K. E. (1985). Sources of order in underorganized systems: Themes in recent organizational theory. In Y. S. Lincoln (Ed.), *Organizational theory and inquiry* (pp. 106–136). Thousand Oaks, CA: Sage Publications.

PERSPECTIVE 4: INTERPRETIVE AND NARRATIVE

Arthur P. Bochner   *University of South Florida*

KEY WORDS

Contingent   Moral Responsibility   Intelligible Frames

Interpretive perspectives take for granted that all attempts to represent reality are mediated by language. Simply stated, the world does not exist in the shape of the sentences we write when we theorize about it (Rorty, 1989). What we say about the world involves the indistinguishable provocations of the world and the mediations of language by which we make claims about the world. The implication is that we can never completely separate what is being described from the describer. We can never distinguish unequivocally between what is in our minds and what is out there in the world; the mind plays an active role in the construction of knowledge.

If accounts and descriptions of objects are never completely independent of the observer or reporter, then writing and reading scientific (and literary) texts can be understood as activities **contingent** on language, rhetoric, power, gender, and history (Richardson, 1990). No set of procedures can remove the intrusions of the individual knower in order to reflect or mirror nature in an unmediated manner. Knowledge inevitably involves what Steedman (1991) refers to as "attaching significance" by interpreting. From an interpretive perspective, research practices are understood as activities that create value and inscribe meanings and the texts that an investigator crafts can be understood as a site of **moral responsibility** (Richardson, 1990).

The term "interpretive social science" is a generic term covering many different approaches to inquiry: the *verstehen* tradition of Dilthey, Richert, and Weber; the phenomenology of Husserl and Schutz transformed into ethnomethodology by Garfinkel and Sacks; the philosophical hermeneutics of Gadamer; the symbolic interactionism of Mead, Cooley, Blumer, and Goffman among others; the followers of Ryle and the later Wittgenstein who emphasized ordinary language analysis, speech acts, accounts, and justifications; the ethnogenics of Rom Harre; the dramatism of Kenneth Burke; the interpretive ethnographies of Clifford Geertz; the social constructionist, cybernetic, and relational perspectives of Gregory Bateson and Ken Gergen; the standpoint epistemologies of Harding, Trinh, and Behar; the feminist criticism of Clough and

Smith; the performative ethnographies of Turner and Conquergood; the autoethnographies of Ellis and Richardson; the poetic narrativism of Freeman and Bochner; the dialogic pluralism of Bakhtin and Levinas; and the civic minded, post-foundationalism of Norman Denzin among others.

Putting aside the considerable differences among these interpretive perspectives, I often use the term "interpretive social science" to refer to inquiry that attempts to move beyond objects to meanings and, in the process of grappling with meanings, to focus attention on values, thus affording an opportunity to recover and reclaim the moral importance and imagination of the social sciences. To understand and apply social inquiry in this way is to subvert and/or transgress the traditional categories that separate science and literature, reason and emotion, object and subject, mind and body, facts and values. What results is a set of reformed and creative research practices that allow us to consider what social sciences might be and do if they were understood as closer to literature than to physics, if they privileged stories rather than theories, and if they were self-consciously value-centered rather than pretending to be value-free. The causal orientation of empiricism is a restless search for enduring truths and universal generalizations. Conversely, interpretive social science embraces the power of language to create and change the world, to make new and different activities and meanings possible. Interpretivists emphasize how we talk about the world and try to deal with it; they see the goal of triumphing over received or inherited versions of the world and its meanings as heroic. Often, an interpretive vocabulary emphasizes ambiguity, change, improvisation, and chance, and its worldview feeds a hunger for details, meanings, and peace of mind.

Interpretive social science as a collective endeavor has recently been described as a qualitative revolution (Gergen & Gergen, 2000; Schwandt; 2000), which situates its goals as not only intellectual but also political. Certainly, there is a sense in which interpretive social science has flourished by virtue of mounting criticisms of scientism, foundational philosophy, realism, modernism, and the ethics of experiments with human subjects. These repeated criticisms have made it easier to distinguish and legitimate alternatives to mainstream social science. One of the main distinctions I like to make is between description and communication. In traditional approaches to social science we take what the world necessarily causes us to believe as a model for writing about or describing it. In contrast to this orthodox notion of description, interpretivists posit the practices of communication, that is, how meaning is performed and negotiated in the everyday world, as a model for telling about the world. I refer to this as an epistemology of interactive communication that privileges the ways we are part of the world that we investigate, and the ways we make the world and change it. Instead of being spectators, we become agents and participants. This conversational, interactive, or communicative model of inquiry redefines how we see ourselves positioned in our research; that is, who we are in relation to the "others" we study and who they are in relation to us. It also opens us to consider the constraints of various conventional forms of writing and representation, and the intrusive forms of mediation that fall between reality and data, data and text, text and reader.

In shifting the focus of inquiry from objects to meanings, interpretive social science invites a corresponding shift from theories to stories. The primary means that human beings use to attach meaning to experience is to tell stories. Much of social life rests on the fragile activities of human storytelling at least insofar as we make sense of our lives and experiences by placing them in an **intelligible frame**. As a framework for social research, narrative focuses attention on the relationships between author/researcher and subject, on the expressive forms for making sense of lived experience and communicating it to others, on the entanglements that both separate and connect how life is lived and how it is told to others, on the functions of stories and storytelling in creating and managing identity in a social world, and on the cultural stories that circulate through our lives—the processes of "culture-making" that can silence minority voices and shape taken-for-granted assumptions that become scripted ways of acting. Thus we must struggle through difficult and uncertain issues, such as the necessity of problematizing the process of writing about others at least insofar as we can become more reflexive about our own constructions and motives; our accountability as researchers who get to tell the story, encouraging the wider usage of an autobiographical voice; our embeddedness in cultural and disciplinary narrative conventions; our openness to experiment with alternative forms of expression; and what we want from our readers and how we can evoke from them a more collaborative and participatory engagement with our texts.

I will look at the research texts in this book as stories of one sort or another ranging from canonical to counter-narratives and looking at the extent to which they show how people breach canonical conventions and expectations; how they cope with ordinary, exceptional, or difficult circumstances; how they invent new ways of speaking if and when old ways fail them; how they make the absurd sensible and the disastrous manageable; and how they try to turn calamities into gifts or lessons for living. I will also look at these research texts as narrative exemplars that inscribe values and imply moral or ethical ideals, whether they breach or reinforce certain traditions, whether they challenge or underscore traditional or alternative norms of writing and research, what polarities or distinctions they promote or question, and how they contribute to the division or integration of social science and literature.

QUESTIONS

1. What changes occur to our understanding when we accept the contingency of language, power, gender, and history as a factor of scientific and literary texts?
2. Why does the world not exist in the shape of the sentences we write about it?
3. How would research in the social sciences change if we thought of it as closer to literature than to physics?
4. What is the relationship of the described and the describer?

REFERENCES

Gergen, M., & Gergen, K. J. (2000). Qualitative inquiry: Tensions and transformations. In N. K. Denzin & Y. S. Lincoln (Eds.), *Handbook of qualitative research, 2nd edition.* Thousand Oaks, CA: Sage Publications. (pp. 1025–1046).

Rorty, R. (1989). Contingency, irony, and solidarity. Cambridge, MA: Cambridge University Press.

Richardson, L. (1990). Writing strategies: Reaching diverse audiences. Newbury Park, CA: Sage Publications.

Schwandt, T. (2000). Three epistemological stances for qualitative inquiry: Interpretivism, hermeneutics, and social constructionism. In N. K. Denzin & Y. S. Lincoln (Eds.), *Handbook of qualitative research, 2nd edition.* Thousand Oaks, CA: Sage Publications. (pp. 1025–1046).

Steedman, P. H. (1991). On the relations between seeing, interpreting, and knowing. In F. Steier (Ed.), Research and reflexivity. Thousand Oaks, CA: Sage Publications. (pp. 53–62).

PERSPECTIVE 5: ARTS BASED EDUCATIONAL RESEARCH

Tom Barone   *Arizona State*

KEY WORD

Heuristic

ORIGINS AND GROWTH

Art based educational research (ABER) is a relatively new form of educational research, originating in the groundbreaking work of Elliot Eisner of Stanford University in the late 1970s. Eisner was the first to imagine the possibilities of a form of educational research that honors the principles, purposes, and premises of the arts rather than the social sciences. This reliance on the arts as opposed to the social sciences continues to set ABER apart from other kinds of research described in this book.

In the last several decades ABER has grown in legitimacy and acceptance within the field of educational research. Discussions about and examples of ABER have been the focus of many presentations at meetings of professional organizations. ABER is the subject of readings and discussions in courses in schools and colleges of education, especially in qualitative research classes. Six Winter Institutes on ABER have been held under the sponsorship of the American Educational Research Association. In 1996 an AERA Special Interest Group on Arts Based Educational Inquiry was formed, and flourishes to this date. Many professional journals accept articles using or discussing ABER. They include (among others) *International Journal for Qualitative Studies in Education, Curriculum Inquiry, Journal of Curriculum Theorizing* and the online *International Journal of Education and the Arts*. Some journals (e.g., *Teacher Education Quarterly* and *Qualitative Inquiry*) have devoted entire issues to examples of studies employing this approach.

Most arts based researchers have employed the literary arts as modalities for representing their data. Examples of these literary artforms include poetry (Sullivan, 2000), the novel (Saye, 2002; Dunlop, 1999) and novella (Kilbourne, 1998), the life story (Barone, 2000, 2001), ethnodrama (Saldana & Wolcott, 2001), autobiography and "self-narrative" (Buttignol, 1997), and readers theater (Donmoyer & Yennie-Donmoyer, 1995).

Arts based educational researchers have also begun experimenting with non-linguistic forms of the arts for alternative modes of representing research data. Various species of the plastic and performing arts have served as modalities for the representation of research findings at American Educational Research Association (AERA) meetings, in journals, dissertations, and theses (Springgay, 2001), and books (Bagley & Cancienne, 2002; Mirochnik & Sherman, 2002; Diamond & Mullen, 1999).

The introduction and subsequent flourishing of arts based research in the field of education paralleled developments within other areas of the human studies. Indeed, social scientists have long engaged in the creation of research texts that could be characterized as literary or poetic. For example, in *The Children of Sanchez*, anthropologist Oscar Lewis (1961) employed a form of literary nonfiction in portraying the lives of members of one Mexican family. The genre of the ethnographic novel, invented by Bandelier (1890/1971) in the 1890s, was reinvigorated in the 1970s and 1980s (see Tedlock, 2000). In addition to the rise of literary anthropology, the births of an-thropological poetry, ethnopoetics, and literary sociology were evidence of important "turns" in the social sciences. These turns signaled re-orientations of the linguistic, rhetorical, and method-ological proclivities of many scholars in these fields.

Much of this early work appeared during a moment of genre dispersion identified by Den-zin and Lincoln (1998) as the third stage of qualitative research, a time in which "boundaries be-tween the social sciences and the humanities had become blurred" (p. 18). Today researchers who are comfortable with the label of social scientists nevertheless transgress that border with fre-quency. The most adventurous even enter the terrain of imaginative literature, experimenting with the fictionalization of their tests (see Banks & Banks, 1998).

Despite all these encouraging developments, artistic approaches to research in the areas of the human studies, including education, remain somewhat on the margins. Academics who have been professionally socialized into a narrow view of what constitutes legitimate research often find it difficult to imagine the potential utility of alternative research approaches. And when it comes to the acceptance of arts based educational research, a fundamental shift must indeed be made, one that accepts the possibility that there are, not one, but *two* equally important and legitimate *purposes* for doing educational research. I will explain.

INQUIRY PURPOSES

The philosopher Richard Rorty (1989) suggests that there are, indeed, two primary purposes for engaging in human inquiry—a quest for certainty and the enhancement of meanings. These pur-poses reflect different epistemological stances. Converging toward certainty implies movement toward a kind of truth that transcends the individual perspectives of participants in the research. The second purpose suggests that alternative meanings can be construed from human activities, none of which is to be accorded a final, objective status. The first purpose implies the advance-ment of truth claims about educational phenomena; the second purpose implies raising ques-tions about educational practices, discourses, and values that have been taken for granted within the field.

The first important and legitimate purpose for doing educational research purpose is often identified with traditional, or modernist, forms of social science. The modern social scientist moves to uncover findings that are as certain as possible in order to explain phenomena, and sometimes to predict and control future events. Other research projects honor the second im-portant and legitimate goal: they address the various meanings to be found within the multiple dimensions of human life. And which of these two purposes serve to guide projects of arts based educational research (ABER)? The answer to this question will depend upon one's view of the na-ture of art. A few aestheticians might argue that art (and hence ABER) can involve a quest for cer-tainty. For example, ascertaining and conveying a conventional version of the truth about a particular person's actions may be especially important when a decision is to be made that will af-fect the life of that person, decisions that may involve educational matters such as promotion, continuance of employment, and the like. For a story, play, photograph, or film to fulfill this sort of summative purpose, it must function as a kind of mirror that reflects the reality of what has oc-curred. It must accurately represent, with a high degree of certainty, the facts of the matter. To that end, the unique perspective of the researcher must be filtered out of the work lest it be tainted by a bias that reduces certainty.

But most aestheticians hold definitions of art that preclude the possibilities of ABER (if not of other forms of educational research) for performing this sort of service. For them (and me), good art does not merely replicate, through whatever medium, "real" phenomena in an epistemologically neutral fashion. An artist—to the extent that she or he *is* an artist—cannot operate from within a kind of perspectiveless perspective, one that denies his or her own experiential viewpoint. Instead, a work of art results from a careful reflection upon and recasting of qualities experienced by the artist into a form that is unique. The result of this process of reconstructing experience is, as Langer (1957) put it, a "semblance . . . a composed and shaped apparition of a new human experience" (p. 148).

This new experience has the potential for persuading an audience to view the recast phenomena in the bold new light of the work confronted, and thereby to question the usefulness of clinging to a conventional way of seeing the world. Or, in the words of James Baldwin (cited in Sullivan, 2000), art serves the purpose of "raising questions that have been hidden by the answers."

CRITERIA FOR JUDGING

A work of ABER that aims to enhance meaning by suggesting such questions is better suited to recasting qualities within an educational research setting, thereby suggesting significant questions about the familiar ways of viewing educational phenomena. Arts based educational research may thus be **heuristic**, a tool of enlightenment and empowerment, not only for those involved in and affected by the research setting, but in other settings that may be similar to the one in which the research occurs.

From this standpoint, a work of ABER must be judged on its potential for raising such questions. To judge it on the basis of the criteria of traditional social science is to engage in a category error. To critique arts based research using criteria such as validity, reliability, and objectivity is to misunderstand its nature and purpose.

Form is, after all, associated with function. And the criteria used in judging an ABER project must take into account whether the elements of design employed achieve the second inquiry purpose mentioned earlier. *In general, we may ask whether a particular work has the potential to persuade its audience to ask themselves trenchant and important questions about educational settings, events, and issues.*

Specific criteria depend somewhat on the art forms employed in the ABER project. Since the examples in this book are literary in character, I will suggest three questions to be asked about examples of this sort of ABER. Each question, in turn, suggests specific dimensions of literature that are designed to serve its intended purpose. This list of questions and criteria is not meant to be exhaustive. But I do believe these questions can help in assessing usefulness.

1. Does the educational researcher/author/artist create a carefully observed virtual world?

For a reader to be persuaded to ask questions about already familiar educational policies and practices, s/he must be able to imagine alternatives. To this end, the author/researcher must create a virtual world that is (not literally true, but) *possible,* one that is plausible, believable, and credible to the reader, one that to some degree resonates with her/his own experiences. This is more likely if the world is a product of empirical research, based, that is, on careful attention to the particulars of actual educational experiences.

2. Is the virtual world sufficiently inviting to the reader?

If the heuristic purposes of an ABER text are to be achieved, the virtual world within it must not only be believable. It must also be compelling enough for the reader to desire access to it, and to maintain engagement with it. To that end, the researcher/author must effectively employ various formal literary devices. These may include, but are not limited to, the following: strong narrative drive, precise and evocative language, textured characterizations, thematic coherence, and a satisfying emplotment (sequencing) of particular events and observations.

3. Does the recreated world of the text serve as an analogue that prompts questions about educational beliefs and values?

A literary-style ABER text must encourage the reader to see the virtual world that s/he has recreated not only as possible and alluring, but also as an analogue. The text must emit a sense of having been fashioned, of presenting a world that may or may not be fictional (in the usual sense of that word), but one that, even as it is inhabited by the reader, suggests that which is not of itself. If the text is to serve a heuristic purpose, its meanings must be of metaphorical significance, understood as relevant to situations experienced by the reader away from the text.

The researcher may achieve this by avoiding an authorial attitude that signifies a single, close, "correct" textual reading. S/he must instead invite the reader to see the text as open to multiple interpretations. The manner in which an author (often subtly) extends this invitation varies from text to text. But when done successfully, the reader has been coaxed into "pragmatizing the imaginary" (Iser, 1993), using the virtually real to re-think the conventionally real. Serving as an analogue to everyday "reality," the text prompts the reader to question the usefulness of prevailing educational beliefs and practices, to reconfigure meanings that have been taken for granted.

One final note: assessing the quality of an ABER text with a heuristic purpose is itself an act of personal judgment rather than one of convening upon "truth." Because each reader inevitably responds to an ABER text in a different fashion, different critics often arrive at different judgments about the heuristic usefulness of the work. In so doing they may cause readers to confront previously ignored educational issues. And they themselves will be engaged in the second of Rorty's two primary purposes of human inquiry.

QUESTIONS

1. Consider the "value" of ABER. When may utilizing ABER, rather than other forms of inquiry, make sense, or prove beneficial?
2. How may utilizing ABER enhance meaning or understanding of a particular education problem or situation?

REFERENCES

Bagley, C. & Cancienne, M. B. (2002). *Dancing the data.* New York: Peter Lang.

Bandelier, A. F. (1971). *The delight makers: A novel of prehistoric Pueblo Indians.* New York: Harcourt Brace Jovanovich. (Original work published 1890)

Banks, A., & Banks, S. (1998). *Fiction and social research: By ice or fire.* Walnut Creek, CA: Alta Mira Press.

Barone, T. (2000). *Aesthetics, Politics, and Educational Inquiry: Essays and Examples.* New York: Peter Lang.

Barone, T. (2001). *Touching eternity: The enduring outcomes of teaching.* New York: Teachers College Press.

Buttignol. M. (1997). Encountering little Margie, my child as self-artist: Pieces from an arts-based dissertation. In Diamond, C. T. P. & Mullen, C. A. (Eds.), *The postmodern educator: Arts-based inquiries and teacher development.* New York: Peter Lang.

Denzin, N., & Lincoln, Y. (1998). Introduction. In N. Denzin & Y. Lincoln (Eds.), *The landscape of qualitative research: Theories and issues* (pp. 1–34). Thousand Oaks, CA.: Sage Publications.

Diamond, C. T. P., & Mullen, C. (Eds.). (1999). *The postmodern educator: Arts-based inquiries and teacher development.* New York: Peter Lang.

Donmoyer, R., & Yennie-Donmoyer, J. (1995). Data as drama: Reflections on the use of readers theatre as an artistic mode of data display. *Qualitative Inquiry, 1*(4), 402–428.

Dunlop, R. (1999). *Boundary Bay: A novel.* Unpublished doctoral dissertation, Vancouver: The University of British Columbia.

Iser, W. (1993). *The fictive and the imaginary: Charting literary anthropology.* Baltimore, MD: Johns Hopkins University Press.

Kilbourne, B. (1998). *For the love of teaching.* London, Ontario: Althouse Press.

Langer, S. K. (1957). *Problems of art.* New York: Scribner's.

Lewis, O. (1961). *The children of Sanchez: Autobiography of a Mexican family.* New York: Random House.

Mirochnik, E., & Sherman, D. (Eds.). (2002). *Passion and pedagogy: Relation, creation, and transformation in teaching.* New York: Peter Lang.

Rorty, R. (1989). *Contingency, irony, and solidarity.* Cambridge, MD: Cambridge University Press.

Saldana, J., & Wolcott, H. F. (2001) *Finding my place: The Brad trilogy.* A play adapted by Johnny Saldana from the works of, and in collaboration with, Harry F. Wolcott. Performance Draft. Tempe, AZ: Arizona State University Department of Theatre.

Saye, N. (2002). *More than "once upon a time:" Fiction as a bridge to knowing.* Unpublished doctoral dissertation, Georgia Southern University.

Springgay, S. (2001). *The body knowing: A visual art installation as educational research.* Unpublished Masters of Arts Thesis, Vancouver: The University of British Columbia.

Sullivan, A. M. (2000). Notes from a marine biologist's daughter: On the art and science of attention. *Harvard Educational Review, 70*(2), 211–227.

Tedlock, B. (2000). Ethnography and ethnographic representation. In N. Denzin & Y. Lincoln (Eds.), *The landscape of qualitative research: Theories and issues* (pp. 455–486). Thousand Oaks, CA: Sage Publications.

PERSPECTIVE 6: RACE, ETHNICITY, AND GENDER

Beth Harry   *University of Miami*

KEY WORDS

Gender   Ethnicity

To examine educational research from the perspectives of race, ethnicity, and gender is to ask that research take into account key aspects of identity which, in American society, signal both status and power. I would qualify this statement, however, by distinguishing between biological sex identity and racial features on the one hand, and ethnicity and gender on the other. The former are the only visible aspects of identity that belong unequivocally to the individual, since both ethnicity and gender represent constructed meanings determined in different ways by different social groups. It is clear that **gender** roles are culturally and familially defined. **Ethnicity** is negotiable because ethnic affiliation is learned, and is dependent upon the influence of the group in which one finds oneself. Ethnic identity is also a product of political forces that require, for example, racial solidarity in the face of a hegemonic mainstream culture. Thus, sex and race are key physical features that signal how the individual will be treated, taught, and valued according to the group's construction of the meaning of these physical features. Depending also on the extent of indoctrination of these meanings, the individual will internalize the group's definition of this or that gender, of this or that race, of this or that ethnicity. Gender and ethnicity, therefore, can only be defined by the individual himself/herself.

What do gender and ethnicity have to do with knowledge? The scientific paradigm from which the study of education has sought to earn its credibility holds certain premises that require that knowledge eschew considerations of individual identity. The main one of these is the assumption of objectivity. In the positivist paradigm knowledge and the knower have traditionally been thought to be neutral, value-free, and objective. Western science was, theoretically, built upon this premise. Yet numerous scholars have debunked this mythology, showing how, for example, the "science" of the measurement of brain capacity was manipulated to support beliefs about the superiority of male intelligence over female and of White intelligence over Black (Gould, 1981).

Paradoxically, beliefs about racial and gender superiority managed to exist, for many years, side by side with the belief that what was true for the dominant ethnic group should be true for others. This ethnocentric lens resulted in the ignoring, by no less a thinker than Piaget, of the role of culture in children's cognitive and psychomotor development. The paradox, of course, was resolved around the fact that since the dominant culture was accepted as the touchstone for normal development, then differential developmental patterns noted among other groups were taken as indicators of inferior capacities. Only in more recent years has cultural psychology succeeded in foregrounding the role of culture in cognitive development (for a review see Rogoff & Chavajay, 1995).

There is no longer any doubt that education and educational research never have been and cannot be value neutral. A decade ago, Eisner (1991) observed that, "Subjectivity is such a troublesome notion in the educational research community that we have created language norms to reduce its presence. Until quite recently the first-person singular—I, me, my—was proscribed in research reports." (p. 45). The changing stance toward this tradition is evident in the current acceptability of the use of these terms even in reports that rely on the positivistic paradigm. Further, the increasing acceptability of narrative and autobiographical forms have brought the role of the knower to center stage. Awareness of both group and individual identities is considered central to a critical perspective on education and educational research. The study of what is taught, to whom, when, and in what manner has become the subject, indeed the target, of multicultural education and critical pedagogy.

What does it mean, however, to know these identities? Despite apparent physical and cultural markers, neither gender nor race/ethnicity can be treated as essential qualities that are stable across place and time. As McCarthy (1988) has argued, understanding racial identity must take into account both the continuities and the discontinuities—the "nonsynchronous" nature of ethnic identity formation. Despite a common sociohistory and the presence of certain features that have been documented as traditional, African Americans can be expected to be as different from one another as are Americans of European descent. As Morrison (1992) observed in her discussion of the Anita Hill/Clarence Thomas controversy, "It is clear to the most reductionist intellect that Black people think differently from one another; it is also clear that the time for an undiscriminating racial unity has passed" (p. 61). Socioeconomic status, geographical location, language, and ethnic origins (such as West Indian, African, American) all contribute to the individual identities of persons who are called, or call themselves, African American. The same is true for Native Americans. The complexity of ethnic identity is even clearer with Hispanics, who represent not a group, but a conglomeration of racial and ethnic groups who, for sociopolitical reasons, have been clustered under a single, multicultural, multiracial umbrella. The same is true for people referred to as "Asian," a term which, for the West, is merely a geographical convenience.

For all these groups, however, there is one point of commonality, that of being marginalized in American society. In the case of African Americans, Boykin (1994) described ethnic identity as being marked by the "triple quandary" of merging African traditions with the experience of oppression in the new world, and with the cultural norms of the dominant society that has emerged as the United States. By contrast, for Whites in the mainstream of the society, it is perfectly possible to live with only minimal awareness of the traditions, practices, and values of those perceived to be "minorities." The experience of living on the margins allows, as Du Bois (1953) observed, a sense of "double consciousness"—the keen awareness and sometimes competing valorizing of one's own traditions simultaneously with those of another. But the double consciousness based on a perspective from the margins is further particularized by the other aspects of identity mentioned earlier—class, geography, nationality, language. Thus, we think in terms of a "multiple consciousness" operating. For example, Dernersesian (2000) calls for recognition of the "divergent ethnic pluralities" of Chicana/o identities to replace "fixed categories of race and ethnicity" (p. 85). She presents a passionate call for

> a counter discourse that is capable of contesting many dominant cultures, including the ones that are supported by upper-class Latinas/os, who resist being interpolated by Chicanas/os and the new ethnicities they partner, who contest being made to share in the linguistic, social, and economic conditions of campesinos, indocumentados, and factory workers and their children who abhor the presence of a newly hyphenated Chicana/o Latina/o and its forecasting solidarity. (pp. 97–98)

Ladson-Billings (2000) emphasizes that the discussion of multiple consciousness "is not an attempt to impose essentialized concepts of 'Blackness,' 'Latina/ness,' 'Asian Americanness,' or 'Native Americanness' onto specific individuals or groups. Rather, this discussion is about the multiple ways in which epistemological perspectives are developed" (p. 260). In other words, what I know is determined to a great extent by who I am, where I have been in my experience, and who are the others from whom I have learned. While my race/ethnicity and gender are central to my experience, those aspects of my identity must be deconstructed, not essentialized.

The issue of epistemology is at the heart of the critiques offered in this section. The last two decades have seen a confluence of narrative, autobiography, and ethnography in the interests of moving away from the separation of knower and known and in acknowledging that all knowledge is situated in the place, time, and perspective of the knower. In offering my perspectives on the articles in this section, I will begin by briefly outlining my own journey toward the recognition of the importance of race, ethnicity, and gender.

Growing up in Jamaica almost half a century ago, I was, along with my middle class peers, the product of a colonial consciousness that strove to be seen as equal to the masters of that place and time. Like the Apache of Cibeque's "Portraits of the Whiteman" (Basso, 1979), we had an outsider's view of our British masters. But, schooled in their language and indoctrinated with their social system, we had also the advantage of seeing them from the inside. We laughed at the physical awkwardness created, it seemed, by the extreme mind-body dichotomy that dominated their ways of knowing. Yet we craved their knowledge, partly because it would bring us power, and partly because it was also ours.

In addition to my status as both outsider and insider to the ways of the masters, however, so was I both an outsider and an insider to the folk culture of my native land. My mother's "Jamaica White" ethnicity combined with my father's professional education to produce a racial mixture, social status, and cognitive orientation which ensured that the coveted knowledge was in fact accessible to me. The knowledge of the folk, though accessible, was at once loved and reviled by me and by all who sought to replace the colonial master. To speak in Patios, the dialect of Jamaica, to absorb unthinkingly the African rhythms of the traditional mento, which gradually gave way to the ska, then reggae, was to celebrate all that was beautiful about our green, gold, and black island. To read Wordsworth, Jane Austen, and Shakespeare (we did not know that T. S. Eliot existed), was to move into a sphere where the iambic pentametre rolled comfortably off my tongue, although I had never seen a daffodil or felt the chill of winter.

There was, no doubt, a nagging discomfort in being so positioned. In being at that liminal point where I was "other" to two opposing extremes. But I was centered by privilege. I would say that the rest of my life has been a repositioning of myself, a process of altering and revising perspectives learned in that combination of raucus joy and protected elitism. When I submitted my dissertation for publication in book form, my doctoral advisor commented that I had not mentioned my ethnicity in my letter to the editor. Although for my dissertation I had studied ethnicity and disability, and had had the privilege of writing in the first person with the voices of 12 Puerto Rican mothers woven into my narrative, I still did not know that, in America, I must put my race/ethnicity first. (In my home country I would have had to put class first and would have been equally disconcerted in doing so). Really, I still did not believe that it was acceptable to present myself in this personal manner. There were two premises underlying this view: first, that to promote my identity would be self-serving, and, second, I was still imbued with the epistemology that said, "This is academic work. In academic work there is no such thing as personal identity." I write this commentary today with considerable trepidation and know that I will not show it to my mother.

QUESTIONS

1. Discuss the differences between "sex" and "gender"; and "race" and "ethnicity."
2. Consider the statement "ultimately, gender and ethnicity can only be defined by the individual himself/herself." What does Harry mean by this? How may it influence our research, or inquiry?

REFERENCES

Basso, K. H. (1979). *Portraits of "the Whiteman.* New York: Cambridge University Press.

Boykin, W. (1994). The triple quandary and the schooling of Afro-American children. In U. Neisser (Ed.), The school achievement of minority children. Hillsdale, NJ: Lawrence Erlbaum. pp. 57–92.

Dernersesian, A. C. (2000). Chicana! Rican? No, Chicana-Riquena!" Refashioning the transnational connection. In E. M. Duarte & S. Smith (Eds.), *Foundational perspectives in multicultural education.* New York: Longman

Du Bois, W. E. B. (1953). *The souls of Black folk.* New York: Fawcett. (Original work published 1903)

Eisner, E. W. (1991). *The enlightened eye: Qualitative inquiry and the enhancement of educational practice.* New York: Macmillan.

Gould, S. J. (1981). The mismeasure of man. New York: Norton.

Gramsci, A. (1971). Selections from the Prison Notebooks. New York: International Publishers.

Ladson-Billings, G. (2000). Racialized discourses and ethnic epistemologies. In N. K. Denzin & Y. S. Lincoln (Eds.), *Handbook of qualitative research* (2nd ed.). Thousand Oaks, CA: Sage Publications.

McCarthy, C. (1988). Reconsidering liberal and radical perspectives on racial inequality in schooling: Making the case for nonsynchrony. Harvard Educational Review, 58 (2), 265–269.

Morrison, T. (Ed.). (1992). *Race-ing justice, en/gender/ing power: Essays on Anita Hill, Clarence Thomas, and the construction of social reality.* New York: Pantheon Books.

Noddings, N. (1984). Caring: A feminine approach to ethics and moral education. Berkeley, CA: University of California Press.

Rogoff, B., & Chavajay, P. (1995, October). What's become of research on the cultural basis of cognitive development? *American Psychologist,* 859–877.

PERSPECTIVE 7: CRITICAL THEORY

George Noblit   *University of North Carolina, at Chapel Hill*

KEY WORDS

Ideology   Critical Theory   Critical Ethnography

A critical researcher attempts to reveal the dynamics of power and ideology. Critical ethnography is guided by a central idea that social life is constructed in contexts of power that dominate some in serving the interests of others. Critical researchers take as their central task ". . . raising their voice to speak *to* an audience *on behalf* of their subjects as a means of empowering them by giving more authority to the subjects' voice" (Thomas, 1993, p. 4). Thus the critical researcher is expressly working for emancipation of the less powerful by revealing the dynamics of power and **ideology** and questioning the justification of power and ideology.

Becoming the agent of change

Carspecken (1996) argues that critical researchers have both a value orientation and a critical epistemology that characterizes their work. To paraphrase (and quote), the value orientation of critical research includes these characteristics:

1. Research is to be used in cultural and social criticism.
2. Researchers are opposed to inequality in all its forms.
3. Research should be used to reveal oppression and to challenge and change it.
4. "All forms of oppression should be studied."
5. Mainstream research contributes to oppression and thus critical epistemology should presuppose equal power relations. (pp. 6–7)

Carspecken then elaborates central points of critical epistemology. Again paraphrasing (and quoting), he lists

1. critical epistemology must be extremely precise about the relationship of power to research claims, validity claims, culture, and thought;
2. "critical epistemology must make the fact/value distinction very clear and must have a precise understanding of how the two interact"; and
3. critical epistemology must include a theory of how symbols are used to represent reality, how this changes, and how power is implicated in symbolic representation and changes in symbolic representation. (p. 9)

Taken together, then, Carspecken highlights the centrality of working against power and oppression as key elements of the critical approach. For him this acts on two levels. First, the critical researcher works against oppression by revealing and critiquing it. Equally important, though, is that critical researchers understand that knowledge itself is a social practice interpenetrated with power. In this, critical researchers must explicitly consider how their own acts of studying and representing people and situations are acts of domination even as critical researchers reveal the same in what they study. This means Carspecken asks the critical research to turn its value orientation and epistemological understandings back on itself.

The critical approach has multiple origins. It emerged following what was seen as a crisis in social science (Gouldner, 1970) when discipline boundaries were fraying (Geertz, 1973) and when many Western democracies were being challenged by emancipatory social movements. Marxism had been instrumental in challenging dominant social theories, but was in transition itself to a neo-Marxism (and now post-Marxism) that was less deterministic and less associated with the Soviet Union. Stuart Hall (1986) characterized it as "Marxism without guarantees." The critical theory of the Frankfurt School, especially the work of Jurgen Habermas, in many ways, enabled the transition to a less-structuralist neo-Marxism. Yet critical theory was largely philosophical and lacked an empirical methodology to allow it to expand into the social sciences. Similarly, interpretive ethnography was expanding beyond anthropology and symbolic interactionist sociology, and was revitalized by the sociology of knowledge of Berger and Luckmann (1967). Interpretive ethnography, on the other hand, was beleaguered by charges of relativism, and relegated to the status of a "micro" theory. It was seen by many as useful at the level of social interaction but lacking a theoretical base to also be a "macro" institutional and sociocultural approach. What both perspectives shared was an interest in the less powerful and a need for what the other could offer. Critical theory and the sociology of knowledge was first combined in a "new" sociology of education (Giroux, 1983; Wexler, 1987) which gave way to a critical ethnography as educational anthropology joined the synthesis.

The multiple origins of the critical approach means that there are a number of ways to employ the critical perspective: critical theory, critical ethnography, and "science with an attitude" (Ladwig, 1996, p. 161). **Critical theory** is essentially the critique of ideology. Ideologies that concern critical theorists are best understood as ideas that justify differential power that are taken for granted by people. **Critical ethnography** employs philosophical critique as the explanatory theory for ethnographic studies. These studies reveal the dynamics of power and cultural beliefs in stratifying people and in the reproduction of social relations and cultural beliefs. It also demonstrates the contradictions that come to characterize the lives of the less powerful. "*Science with an attitude*" is Ladwig's way of questioning the dominance of critical ethnography within the critical approach. Ladwig argues critical theory's rejection of positivism was a mistake and argues for "strategic methodological stances" (p. 164) that include "poaching mainstream issues" and "poaching mainstream tools" (pp. 165–166). His argument is that if the goal of critical analyses is to defeat mainstream educational research then we should take over their theories and methods. He is strongly influenced by the feminist, postmodern, and poststructural arguments that no research methodology can provide a definitive proof. Given this, he argues for a strategic approach to win the paradigm wars. That is, any methodology that lets critical theory win is appropriate including positivistic methods. However, critical theorists would also point out that Ladwig's interest in the critical approach becoming the dominant paradigm has its own contradictions that have yet to be deliberated.

Critique must be balanced with attempts to construct a better world. The critical approach then has an explicit political and moral stance. It is about revealing how power is hidden and ideas are justified. In doing so, it promotes awareness, political strategy, and, hopefully, emancipation. The critical approach, because it spans philosophy, social theory, and (largely qualitative) methodology, also critiques positivistic and interpretivist approaches as theoretically weak and advancing specific interests (Habermas, 1971). That is to say, the critical perspective reveals the dynamics of power and ideology even in research studies. I will provide examples of this in what follows. Since the articles I will critique exist as texts they can be subjected to a critique that reveals how research itself can be disempowering and dominating.

Using the lenses of critical theory, I will review each of the studies as the other critics will. Yet I will be looking at the studies for different things. I will ask what interests are served by these studies, and how capable are they to reveal power, domination, and the ideologies that articulate and justify power and domination. My reviews, then, are examples of the critical perspective itself. I want to be clear about my view of these articles. I have used many of them in my own courses, and find them instructive in many ways. Thus my critiques should not be taken as rejections of these studies or their authors. Instead, my goal is to point out what a critical perspective demands of research. Moreover I invite the readers to critique my position as well.

QUESTIONS

1. Describe the value orientation, the critical epistemology, and the political and moral stances of critical theory.
2. How does critical ethnography differ from interpretive ethnography?

REFERENCES

Arendt, H. (1968). Introduction: Walter Benjamin: 1892–1940. In H. Arendt (Ed.), *Illuminations: Walter Benjamin* (pp. 1–58). New York: Schocken Books.

Berger, P., & Luckmann, T. (1967). *The social construction of reality.* Garden City, NY: Anchor.

Bowers, C. (1984). *The promise of theory.* New York: Teachers College Press.

Carspecken, P. (1996). *Critical ethnography in educational research.* New York: Routledge.

Conquergood, D. (1983). Communication as performance: Dramaturgical dimensions of everyday life. In J. J. Sisco (Ed.), *Jensen lectures in contemporary studies* (pp. 24–43). Tampa, FL: University of South Florida Press.

Foucault, M. (1979). *Discipline and punish.* New York: Vintage.

Geertz, C. (1973). *The interpretation of cultures.* New York: Basic Books.

Giroux, H. (1983). Theories of Reproduction and Resistance in the New Sociology of Education: A Critical Analysis. *Harvard Educational Review, 53*(3), 257–293.

Gouldner, A. (1970). *The coming crisis of western sociology.* New York: Basic Books, Inc.

Gramsci, A. (1971). *Selections from the prison notebooks* (Q. Hoare & G. Nowell Smith, Eds. and Trans.). New York: International.

Habermas, J. (1970) Toward a theory of communicative competence. In H. P. Dreitzel (Ed.), *Recent sociology no. 2: Patterns of communicative behavior.* Basingstoke, England: Macmillan.

Habermas, J. (1971). *Knowledge and human interests.* Boston: Beacon.

Hall, S. (1986). The problem of ideology-Marxism without guarantees. *Journal of Communication Inquiry, 10*(2), 28–43.

Kuhn, T. (1970). *The Structure of scientific revolutions.* Chicago: the University of Chicago Press.

Ladwig, J. (1996). *Academic distinctions: theory and methodology in the sociology of school knowledge.* New York: Routledge.

Mills, C. W. (1959). *The power elite.* London: Oxford University Press.

Noblit, G. & V. Dempsey (1996). *The social construction of virtue.* Albany, NY: SUNY Press.

Noddings, N. (1984). *Caring.* Berkeley, CA: University of California Press.

Scott, J. (1990). *Domination and the arts of resistance.* New Haven, CT: Yale University Press.

Shujaa, M. (Ed.). (1994). *Too much schooling, too little education.* Trenton, NJ: Africa World Press.

Thomas, J. (1993). *Doing critical ethnography.* Qualitative Research Methods Series. London: Sage Publications.

Wexler, P. (1987). *Social analysis of education: After the new sociology.* New York: Routledge.

PERSPECTIVE 8: ETHICS, METHODOLOGY, AND DEMOCRACY

Kenneth R. Howe   *University of Colorado at Boulder*

KEY WORDS

Expert Approach	Technocratic	Deliberative
Dialogical Approach	Conception	Conception

The spectrum of topics investigated by educational research is broad and so are the conditions under which it must be conducted. Thus, different ethical concerns will come to the foreground or fade into the background, depending on the context and nuances of given studies. The conventional approach to mapping the terrain is to divide it into two areas: research misconduct and the protection of research participants (Howe & Moses, 1999). Research misconduct has to do with how researchers conduct themselves with respect to scientific integrity and relationships with co-workers. It deals with matters such as fabricating or falsifying data, plagiarism, and the abuse of power within research collaborations. The protection of research subjects has to do with how researchers treat research participants. It deals with matters such as informed consent and protecting privacy. The conventional approach is largely silent on broader ethical questions that concern the alignment between research methodology and democracy.

My approach departs significantly from the one just described. I say a little about the protection of research participants, a lot about aligning research methodology and democracy, and nothing about research misconduct. This approach fits best with the emphasis on methodological issues that characterizes this volume. As we shall see, the longstanding divide between the experimentalist-quantitative and the interpretivist-qualitative methodological paradigms is a central issue in the ethics of educational research in the way conceived here (see also Howe, 2003).

My approach also fits better with the studies that serve as the grist for analyses than a more traditional approach to the ethics of research would. Questions concerning the protection of research participants and research misconduct just aren't very prominent among the issues raised.

THE PROTECTION OF RESEARCH PARTICIPANTS

Researchers may adopt two basic approaches toward research participants: *expert* and *dialogical*. The **expert approach** fits most naturally with experimentalist-quantitative research. It emphasizes protecting the autonomy of research participants by ensuring they are provided with the opportunity to give or withhold their informed consent to participate and by ensuring their privacy is not breached. Although it provides more exacting standards for members of "vulnerable populations" whose ability to consent is in doubt—for example, children and prisoners—the expert approach otherwise assumes that consent from mentally competent adults is ethically unproblematic and renders research in which they agree to participate ethically unproblematic as well.

The **dialogical approach** fits most naturally with interpretivist-qualitative research. It emphasizes using dialogue with research participants as the way to deal with the ethical complexities wrought by the "interpretive turn." Compared to experimentalist-quantitative research, interpretive-qualitative research is more "open-ended" in its design and conduct and more "intimate" in the methods it employs (e.g., Howe & Dougherty, 1993).

The feature of open-endedness increases the possibility of unanticipated findings as well as the possibility that new avenues of investigation will emerge over the course of a study. This can prompt researchers to have to wrestle with the question of whether they should seek reaffirmations of consent from research participants. The feature of intimacy increases the possibility of discovering practices of questionable ethicality. This can prompt researchers to have to wrestle with the question of whether they have a duty to breach confidentiality. In a related vein, writing up results with the kind of detail—or "thick description"—often associated with interpretivist research engenders the possibility of unintentionally compromising the confidentiality of research participants.

Neither the dialogical approach nor the expert approach is generally superior with respect to concrete relationships between researchers and research participants. The dialogical approach is well suited to situations in which the research in question is open-ended and intimate, such that risks and benefits unfold unpredictably. By contrast, the more traditional, expert approach is well suited to situations in which the research in question is focused on evaluating well-specified "treatments" or "interventions," such that risks and benefits are much more predictable.

THE ALIGNMENT BETWEEN RESEARCH METHODOLOGY AND DEMOCRACY

Educational researchers must adopt *some* conception of the relationship between their methodology and democratic decision-making in virtue of adopting some stance both toward research participants and toward the use of research results. One conception of this relationship is **technocratic** (which parallels the expert approach to research participants at a higher level of generality). This conception advocates a neutral moral-political stance. Educational research should be confined to "descriptive" work and should take no "prescriptive" position on values. Its conclusions and recommendations should connect to values only *hypothetically:* Policy or practice X should be adopted, *if* value Y is to be promoted. These hypothetical statements are turned over to policy makers who make the value judgments and the related programmatic decisions.

The technocratic conception has been severely criticized, particularly by critical theorists. But care theorists, communitarians, postmodernists have also joined in, as well as contemporary liberal theorists. Although these philosophical perspectives differ in numerous and important ways, each criticizes the technocratic conception's premise that researchers can be morally and politically neutral. Each also criticizes the technocratic conception for its "methodological individualism," such that persons' identities and choices are to be understood and evaluated apart from social and cultural positioning.

That these various critics are *against* the technocratic conception is clear. What they are *for,* however, isn't so clear (postmodernists present special problems in this regard). But sorting through the differences would take me well beyond what I can accomplish here. Below I sketch one alternative to the technocratic conception, the **deliberative conception** (which parallels the dialogical approach to research participants at a higher level of generality).

Deliberative democratic theory is in the liberal tradition (though it also has a strong affinity with certain versions of critical theory). Contemporary liberal philosophers have endeavored to render liberalism more sensitive to the complex social and cultural factors that go into defining "contexts of choice" by acknowledging how these factors facilitate or blunt the exercise of autonomy and thus facilitate or blunt democratic participation (e.g., Kymlicka, 1991). This is linked to rejecting a technocratic conception of democracy in favor of a deliberative conception (e.g., Gutmann & Thompson, 1996).

The deliberative conception holds that there is something to deliberate about when it comes to values, that values are not impervious to rational investigation and dialogue. It holds that the conditions of decision-making should be designed so as to permit free and equal participation. This requires a joint commitment on the part of participants to determine what is truly right, based on argument and evidence, rather than a commitment to a strategy to use the power at their disposal to win assent to what they perceive is in their best interests. Participants can actually see their value commitments change, as new, more adequate positions are "constructed" out of the material of joint deliberation.

On the deliberative conception, educational research should not (and cannot) take a neutral moral-political stance. Its work is "prescriptive." Its conclusions and recommendations should connect to values *categorically:* Adopt policy or practice X *in order to achieve* value Y. And it should incorporate specific measures to eliminate or mitigate power imbalances.

The deliberative conception may be fleshed out in terms of three requirements: *inclusion, dialogue,* and *deliberation* (House & Howe, 1999; Howe, 2003).

Inclusion is both a methodological principle (representative sampling) and a democratic principle (the right to have ones views included in forums that have a bearing on social life). Inclusion ranges from *passive* to *active,* from, say, filling out a fixed response survey instrument to engaging in an open-ended discussion.

Active inclusion shades into dialogue, the second principle. Dialogue also has a range: from *elucidating* (getting the diversity of *emic* perspectives on the table) to *critical* (subjecting *emic* perspectives to critical examination, as appropriate). Dialogue, too, is both a methodological and a democratic requirement. It is a methodological requirement of interpretivist-qualitative research that seeks to ascertain social reality from the point of view of the actors who construct and participate in it. It is a democratic requirement because, like the principle of inclusion, all views should be included in forums that have a bearing on social life. In comparison to (passive) inclusion, however, dialogue is better able to yield *genuine* views.

Deliberation, the third principle, is a species of critical dialogue. It fits with a conception of democratic decision-making that differs not only from the technocratic conception, but also from the conception that restricts dialogue to elucidation. The latter approach— "hyper-egalitarianism" (House & Howe, 1999)—aspires to foster equality in dialogue among research participants, but it perverts the idea of *genuine voice* by not paying attention to the conditions out of which it can emerge. When people enter into dialogue about educational practices and policies, they can be mistaken or misinformed about the attendant harms and benefits, including to themselves. Simply clarifying how they think things work, and ought to work, can be no more than one element of genuine deliberation. Deliberation includes clarifying the views and self-understandings of research participants but also subjecting these views and self-understandings to rational scrutiny. Deliberation is a critical activity in which participants and researchers collaboratively engage, and from which the most rationally defensible conclusions emerge.

Once again, methodological and democratic principles dovetail. Deliberation is required, methodologically, to ensure that the most accurate portrayal of educational practices and policies emerge. Deliberation is required, democratically, to insure that power imbalances, including in knowledge and the resources to garner it, do not tilt—or "distort"—the dialogue so as to advantage the already advantaged. Educational researchers have a fiduciary responsibility in this regard (House & Howe, 1999).

LOOKING AHEAD TO THE COMMENTARIES

None of the studies upon which I will be subsequently commenting are self-conscious supporters (or critics, for that matter) of the deliberative democratic conception of educational research. Thus, this conception cannot be straightforwardly applied in my commentaries. Instead, the deliberative democratic conception will serve as a general backdrop.

Like my fellow contributors', my commentaries will emphasize methodological issues, especially insofar as these overlap with values. However, my commentaries do not provide an additional perspective of the same general kind as postpositivism, critical theory, postmodernism, pragmatism, interpretivism, and constructivism. The deliberative democratic conception of educational research concerns issues that cut across these other perspectives.

QUESTIONS

1. How do ethics differ in each profession?
2. What are the ethical concerns for those researchers of the contemporary approach?
3. Why is the deliberative conception a good fit to contemporary ethics?
4. Is consent from mentally competent adults enough to move research agendas forward?

REFERENCES

Gutmann, A., & Thompson. D. (1996). *Democracy and disagreement.* Cambridge, MA: The Belknap Press.

House, E., & Howe, K. (1999). *Values in evaluation and social research.* Thousand Oaks, CA: Sage Publications.

Howe, K. (2003). *Closing methodological divides: Toward democratic educational research.* Dordrecht, The Netherlands: Kluwer.

Howe, K., & Dougherty, K. (1993). Ethics, IRB's, and the changing face of educational research. *Educational Researcher, 22*(9), 16–21. (Reprinted in *Annual editions: Research Methods,* pp. 16–21, 2000, Guilford, CT: Dushkin.)

Howe, K. & Moses, M. (1999). Ethics in educational research. In A. Iran-Nejad & P. D. Pearson (Eds.), *Review of research in education* (vol. 24, pp. 21–60). Washington, DC: American Educational Research Association.

Kymlicka, W. (1991). *Liberalism, community and culture.* New York: Oxford University Press.

PERSPECTIVE 9: POSTSTRUCTURALISM

Lynda Stone   *University of North Carolina at Chapel Hill*

KEY WORDS

Historicism	Linguistic Turn	Epistemology	Self-Reflexive
Postmodernism			

OVERVIEW

There is no poststructuralism. Better said, the term refers to a group of nearly contemporary scholars—French with international cousins—who form a Wittgensteinian family resemblance.[1] American legal scholar Drucilla Cornell puts it that this is a family of 'chiffonniers,' literally "rag and bone men" (*Mansion's Concise French and English Dictionary*).[2] For her, the writings of this significant group of intellectuals carry no satisfactory definition (Cornell, 1988, p. 1587; Huyssen, 1984/1990, p. 276, note 39); together, however, they do critique, scavenge from, and undermine other more traditional philosophical views. They write "against" humanist, formalist, and structuralist theories and theorists.

For the family, Cornell offers a list of authors and concepts ("catchphrases") of association. The focus of this introductory essay is six of these concepts: *language, relation, subject, practice, aesthetic,* and *ethics/politics.* These function as skeletal terms that are used in diverse ways by these writers, that appear in and in some sense organize their texts. They are variously foregrounded and backgrounded and always specifically interpreted. They are aspects of a theoretical framework necessary for understanding poststructuralisms (note plural). A significant qualification: These are not concepts to be easily lifted and applied to educational research. This is because of the particular theorizing and writing style of each family member. In educational research to date, they are principally presented and analyzed as in this text, even more utilized as inspiration through conceptual adaptation, and are sometimes appropriated as methodological models—with writing in the mode of the original (e.g., see Stone 2000).[3] Finally, one notes that there is danger of inappropriate use in Anglo-American educational research because of differences and complexities of the French intellectual tradition.

What follows overviews philosophical insights of poststructuralists who are well-known to English-speaking audiences: Pierre Bourdieu, Hèléne Cixous, Jacques Derrida, Michel Foucault, Julia Kristeva, and Jean-François Lyotard. Not included are other important family members, Jacques Baudrillard, Michel de Certeau, Gilles Deleuze, and Luce Irigaray. In turn, each of the six serves as an exemplary theorist for separate renderings of the six research examples in this volume, a different one for each. Since the initiating concepts serve as frames, devolving concepts and ideas particular to each theorist are taken up in the critiques. A listing of these is provided at the end of this overview.

ROOTS

Poststructuralists have roots in various formalisms and structuralisms in philosophy, broadly defined. Their family heroes, ironically in many respects and with varying allegiances, include Nietzsche and Freud, Bahktin and Lacan. They share a stance contra Hegel and Marx as well as the phenomenological tradition that includes Husserl and Sartre but not Heidegger. Significantly they are not "critical theorists" in the German tradition—and indeed important philosophical battles of recent decades have pitted the French against the Germans, for example, in the Lyotard-Habermas debate. Although a bit overstated, in the writings one does not find use of nor support for critical ideas such as class, ideology, and state. Moreover, since they also are not "humanists" or "liberals" in the Anglo-American sense, even as their work is ironically part of a broad western tradition of philosophy, one does not either find use of or support for ideas such as experience, democracy, and progress.[4]

Structuralism Roots of the poststructuralists range across disciplines of philosophy, science, social science, literary theory, literature, and art. All, as well-educated European intellectuals, have read their philosophy—and many have returned to the ancients for texts and references. Structuralist fathers are themselves very notable: Claude Lévi-Strauss in social sciences particularly anthropology, Roman Jacobson and then Roland Barthes in literary and cultural studies, Jacques Lacan in psychoanalysis, and arguably Louis Althusser in political theory. Even naming these fathers is problematic since many of the family are and were contemporaries and most if not all have themselves been named structuralists.

One root seems generally clear; this is contribution by Swiss linguist Ferdinand de Saussure, whose theory of the sign initiated structuralism. The basic ideas are these: First, language is form and utterance and they are different. Second, the basic unit of language is the sign, a relation of the signifier or conceptual element and the signified or the acoustic element. This relation entails difference since there is no necessary connection between any signifier and signified and multiple relations are possible. In this structuralist theory every sign forms a unity and is also understood by how it is different from any other. For Saussure language is open but not arbitrary since the places of signs are themselves unique (see Holdcroft, 1998, p. 481).

History   A second kind of root also requires comment. As indicated above, all poststructuralists have read Hegel and respond in some way to his theory of history. Most simply put, they give up a historical teleology but retain forms of **historicism**. This means that as a group they posit a deep significance of history as it relates to living in and making worldly sense, but senses are not only multiple they are also always changing. This means also that as "history" influences thought, such influences are particular and contingent even as they endure for a time. Individual family members' visions of history are characteristically "post-structural."

Postmodernism   Lastly, "poststructuralism" is often rooted in and conflated in Anglo-American scholarship with postmodernism, but they are not the same. It is probably best to say that each theorist is more or less postmodern. Itself difficult to define, **postmodernism** has variously and positively been named an epochal worldview, a historical condition, a contemporary lifestyle, an intellectual tradition, a mood. Less positively it has also been called a mere fad, a spectacle, a phenomenon of advertising. In an excellent discussion from the 1980s, critic Andreas Huyssen offers a general definition as a "slowly emerging cultural transformation in western societies" that entails "shifting sensibilities, practices, and discourse formations" (Huyssen, 1984/1990, p. 234). Initially employed at mid-twentieth century, the term has been applied specifically in architecture and art, in intellectual fields that range from theology to feminist theory, from philosophy of science to literature, and in general cultural production that includes communications, technology, and consumerism. Applications demonstrate a common set of "uncommon" characteristics: eclecticism (some say schizophrenia); mixing of traditions, codes, and symbols; and responses to modernism, modernity, and modernization (see various uses in Huyssen, 1984/1990; Featherstone, 1991; Harvey, 1990; McGowan, 1991; and Sarup, 1988/1993).

Elaboration here is useful. While several of the poststructuralist family have written about postmodernism, the work of Lyotard has been important to an English-speaking audience. For him, the postmodern is a condition "of knowledge in most highly developed societies," of transformations since the end of the nineteenth century in the rules for science, literature, and the arts (Lyotard, 1979/1984, p. xxiii). These rules undermine what in the modern era was a need for and use of grand or metanarratives. In his famous idiom, postmodern is "incredulity" toward these narratives, toward totality, toward emancipation, toward rational consciousness and consensus, and toward the certain aims of western metaphysics.

SHARED CONCEPTS

Cornell's poststructuralist *chiffonniers* are part of a significant contemporary philosophical tradition that is having increasing influence on educational research. The six family members of this account range from those who are most structuralist, Bourdieu, Foucault, Kristeva, to those who are least, Lyotard, Derrida, Cixous. In a gross generalization since many focus on topics and utilize styles that change over time, those on the structuralist end have more in common with social scientists, historians, and psychoanalysts; those on the other are more like essayists, literary critics, and poets. The point of the present analysis is that unique as each philosopher is, they share a framing set of concepts that each has utilized in his or her own way. Again, key concepts are language, relation, subject, practice, aesthetic, and politics/ethics.

Language Already discussed above, language out of structuralism—and more broadly the western philosophical **linguistic turn**—is central to poststructuralisms.[5] Language usage for these theorists is often rhetorical, figurative, performative, and self-reflexive. Building from Saussure, American critic Mark Poster puts it that "[a general] self-referentiality of signs upsets the representational model of language, the assurance of reason to contain meaning, and the confidence in a . . . [traditional logic] to determine the truth" (Poster, 1989, p. 10). A basic point is this: language has a central **epistemological** function for family members; it is basic to sense making and to knowledge. Language takes on various functions and forms and is utilized not only thematically but also stylistically. Among uses are this superficial but illustrative listing: writing for Derrida and Cixous, texts for the former, discourses and discursive practices for Foucault, forms of language games for Lyotard, all kinds of plays like erasures or parallel texts for Derrida and Kristeva, symbolic significance and split texts for Bourdieu, and narratives and poetry for Cixous. Writing from all even looks, ironically sometimes, like typical philosophy.

Relation Relation permeates and is basic to the family of poststructuralist writers and their writings. Elements of discourse, history, culture, and the like are defined by their difference to others. Through difference in language and other structures there is, as indicated earlier, repudiation of traditional philosophical and logical sameness or identity. Something is always distinct from something else. Relations of difference, furthermore, are themselves diffused; they exist perhaps as chains, through links, and are often "of a moment." Thus there is no "resolution" of difference in some kind of new system, no modern unity or essence: structures are worked through one might say. Significantly, as implied in a distinction from critical theory, difference is not part of a dialectical system.

Based in difference rather than sameness, relation also entails difference to itself. To some degree the poststructuralists work with and through difference as radical alterity, for example, the unknown as unconscious and abjection for Kristeva, the unpresentable in Lyotard, and aporias and "excesses" of various forms as theorized by Derrida. Significantly, too, are relations obtained among practices and persons which have no direct agency or simple institutional structure functions.

Subject The subject (person) is central to poststructuralists' writings but negatively since, again, there is no "agency." To begin, of course people act in the world, but thoughts, actions, and their results are not simply desired, conscious, intentional, and consequential. The subject comes to be constituted; how this occurs variously matters to each member of the family. In general, there is no essential self, no unitary person upon which each of *us* can count. Moreover the meanings of our lives—including who we are—are "got at" through language.

One of the most important aspects of the status of *subjects* is that they are related to *others* who are different from them. But here others are not opposites and there is no resolution of otherness:

Everyone is another not only to others but also to themselves. Diversity also characterizes treatment of subjects among family members: Kristeva's subject-in-process has individuality; Bourdieu recognizes a kind of "agency" in power relations; Foucault's subject is self-formed as internalization of external norms. Finally, the poststructuralists recognize hierarchy; in the social order some others count more, have more power and the like. Thus in a spirit of justice, persons on the margins, minorities, foreigners, and strangers receive special attention.

Practice Processes and practices go together for the poststructuralists. Again, there is no agency but, within institutions, ways of being and doing themselves come to be enacted. They are not structures but for unfamiliar readers often seem so; indeed practices do take place within social entities that have their own "histories." The term "practice" best stands for "what gets done"; how this getting done itself is understood, over time and at a time, as having a life of its own. Practices are contextual and iterated, once again got at primarily although not entirely through language.

Each of the poststructuralists conceives of process/practice in unique ways. These range from an emphasis on the discursive/nondiscursive in formations of power/knowledge in Foucault to ones defined in terms of capital for Bourdieu. They concern ways of living that themselves range from the psychological to the societal and combinations of both as in Kristeva. They are primarily linguistic and aesthetic as in Lyotard and textual and writerly in Derrida and Cixous. In this category, significantly, affinity with particular structuralist roots is often indicated. Roots are returned to and transformed—structuralist to poststructuralist.

Aesthetic Use and concern for the aesthetic permeates the work of each poststructuralist writer. Each is, first, **self-reflexively** a writer who—as described earlier—plays with philosophical form and either employs aesthetic/writerly devices or adopts aesthetic genres for theoretical purposes. Each also writes at times about literature and/or the arts. These writings incorporate both analysis and critique of important contributions to a very significant French arts tradition. For example, Foucault and Kristeva write about literature; Cixous and Derrida write in literary forms; Bourdieu and Lyotard analyze the visual arts. Impetus for this aesthetic occupation arises from two premises. The first is a blurring of disciplines with no strong separation of the sciences and arts as in the Anglo-American context. The second is a move away from correspondence and representational truth to a construction of "truth" as a social convention; within the family, not very much is actually written about truth. Commentator Mandan Sarup (1988/1993) sums that for poststructuralists "philosophy, law, and political theory work by metaphor just as poems do, and so are just as fictional" (p. 47). Here metaphor stands for a general and relatively open process of meaning-making that is always aesthetic.

Ethics/Politics Lastly, rebutting a charge by other traditions of conservatism, each writer's project entails a politics and/or an ethics. Foucault and Kristeva either imply or call for revolutionary politics; Lyotard and Derrida write about ethics as justice. Bourdieu inhabits the former camp in his dealings with practices and power and Cixous has affinity with the latter in textual revolts. In conflating the categories two observations are helpful: one is the basic point that a politics/ethics is neither transcendental nor teleological. There is no such congratulatory aim but instead process, a "life-working through" that is always messy. Messiness, as indicated in other categories, arises within ethical/political discursive and other forms of practice that are tentative, ambiguous, complex, always multiple, and with elements that are unknown. The other matter is this—whatever is posed as politics/ethics denies a humanist and a structuralist "consciousness": Persons act and they must. But questions always remain: What in making sense of the world is taken for granted? What warnings are entailed in a philosophical "uncovering"? What is evoked when agency is given up? What does a poststructuralists' de-emphasis of epistemology and an emphasis on aesthetics (or ethics) reveal of cultural life? What does an ethical revolution look like?

CRITIQUES

In considering the exemplars of educational research, each philosopher is turned to as an illustration. Each is briefly introduced given relative non-familiarity in Anglo-American educational research and from each element of a project are presented and "applied." To sum and preview: Six central concepts permeating poststructuralists' writings are language, relation, subject, practice, aesthetic, and politics/ethics. Out of this framework particular conceptions "define" each theorist. (1) Bourdieu describes practices discursively in relational, often aesthetic terms; practices are actions by persons within institutional power structures. A key concept is *habitus*. (2) Cixous's project is one of feminine writing that undermines traditional binary relations; relations are both concrete and textual. For her aesthetic form contributes to politics. (3) In the project of deconstruction, Derrida undermines traditional language, philosophy and other practices of inquiry such as science. His concept *différance* is basic; textual aesthetic plays are methodologically central. (4) For Foucault, traditional relations of knowledge and power in society as in research are reconceived; there is no direct agency or "authority." Instead subjects come to be constituted through constantly shifting discursive/non-discursive formations. (5) Kristeva's subject is one "in process," best got at through poetic language and best recognized in Freudian "structures." Primary is the semiotic, that is, generative, pre-linguistic, and drive-based forces that open up and make symbolic social life ambiguous. (6) Finally in Lyotard, science and art are modern rule-governed practices— language games—that are being transformed within an emerging postmodern condition. Practices, in his idiom—performances—are coming to be justified in new forms of legitimation.

Lastly, a note about the research selections is in order. Considered excellent and even *avant garde* in educational research, they are still largely humanist (with some Marxist or critical representation), and within the greater theoretical realm to which poststructuralisms pose critique. American education (if not by British and other siblings) focuses in practice and most often in research on epistemology, on knowing, learning, truth, on outcome or product. The pieces of this volume in and of themselves seek to undermine what has been defined as a present day techno-rational approach to education. Implication from the critiques that follow, however, is that even with qualitative, narrative, artistic, and more eclectic research forms, the standard western philosophical epistemological traditional remains as basis. From poststructuralisms, the concluding idea is this: unlike fears of "critique-only" and of nihilism that have been expressed, there is a positive aim for education and educational research. It may well be to warn of dangers of reinscription, to see the limits of agentive and institutionally-based panaceas, to emphasize the place of language in educational change, and to move to a basis for change primarily in ethics. Time, theoretical explication, application, and dissemination will tell.[6]

QUESTIONS

1. Why does Stone refer to postructuralisms rather than the singular poststructuralism?
2. To who are poststructuralists aligned and to who are they disaligned?
3. How does the root represented by Saussure grow through all of the postructuralisms?

NOTES

1. The later Ludwig Wittgenstein posited similarities among language games that utilized similar rules. For him and many followers since, these language games form resemblances of sense making and potential for communication.
2. Cornell actually evokes the figure of the *Chiffonnier* chiefly referring to Derrida but generally indicating an ironic role of "salvaging remains" of western mimesis, of identity and sameness as logocentrism (Cornell, 1988, p. 1611). For both Derrida and Cornell, the poststructuralist idea is to undermine in thought the constrictions of mimesis.
3. Various uses and interpretations are found in the excellent work of Gert Biesta, Elizabeth Ellsworth, Patti Lather, James Marshall, Michael Peters, and Thomas Popkewitz. There is a group of younger scholars who are also contributing to a growing Anglo-American/Western European tradition.
4. The American neo-pragmatist, Richard Rorty, along with a few others, writes about affinity between the pragmatist tradition out of Dewey and James and the French writers. There are important differences too.
5. Anglo-American philosophical traditions too underwent the linguistic turn. For all I like to name two phases, the first to locate 'linguistic foundations' and the second to give these up.
6. Thanks to Marianne Bloch, Thomas Popkewitz, and the Wednesday Group at Madison for encouragement and helpful critique.

REFERENCES

Cornell, D. (1988). Post-structuralism, the ethical relation, and the law. *Cardozo Law Review 9*, 1587–1628.

Featherstone, M. (1991). *Consumer culture & postmodernism*. London: Sage Publications.

Harvey, D. (1990). *The condition of postmodernity: An enquiry into the origins of cultural change*. Cambridge, MA: Blackwell.

Holdcroft, D. (1998). Saussure. *Routledge encyclopedia of philosophy* (Vol. 8, pp. 479–482). London: Routledge.

Huyssen, A. (1990). Mapping the postmodern. In L. Nicholson (Ed.), *Feminism/postmodernism* (pp. 234–277). New York: Routledge. (Original work published 1984)

Lyotard, J. (1984). *The postmodern condition: a report on knowledge* (G. Bennington & B. Masumi, Trans.). Minneapolis, MN: University of Minnesota Press. (Original work published 1979)

McGowan, J. (1991). *Postmodernism and its critics*. Ithaca, NY: Cornell University Press.

Poster, M. (1989). *Critical theory and poststructuralism: in search of a context*. Ithaca, NY: Cornell University Press.

Sarup. M. (1993). *An introductory guide to post-structuralism and postmodernism* (2nd ed.). Athens, GA: University of Georgia Press. (Original work published 1988)

Stone, L. (2000). Come again the ghosts: Dewey and democratic education by Derrida. *Journal of Curriculum Theorizing, 16*(1), 41–68.

The Perspectives as Critiques

INTRODUCTION TO CRITIQUES

All research is conducted within a particular perspective. That is, researchers must make assumptions about knowledge and method and those assumptions are framed within a worldview. As we have seen in Part Two, there are many different perspectives, each with its own values and assumptions about knowledge and method. We turn our attention now to the following question: What value does a perspective have in helping us analyze and understand research that was conducted in a different perspective? What, for example, does a postpositivist perspective have to offer in critique of a narrative study? Or, what does a critical perspective have to offer in examining an experimental study?

In this section, each of the nine scholars who wrote the perspectives in Chapter 4 critiques six different types of studies: experimental, correlational, narrative, ethnographic, autoethnographic, and one that combines ethnographic and autoethnographic methods.

It is not likely that this text could have been written 10 years ago, especially this section on criticism. For one thing, some of the perspectives were not as clearly formulated and certainly not as widely recognized outside particular academic communities as they are today. Second, the idea of different perspectives having something of value to contribute in critiques of different kinds of research would not have been accepted by many. One might have argued that the critiques were so predictable that they were pointless. Postpositivist critics had much to be concerned about in nonpositivist research. Similarly, research embracing remnants of positivist philosophy became familiar targets for nonpositivists. Although many of these issues remain, the focus of criticism has changed. Before the early 1990s, the focus was primarily on what was wrong with research guided by assumptions outside a particular perspective. There were territorial struggles as scholars embracing nonpositivist perspectives were seeking legitimacy in the context of a post positivist era.

Criticism became more complex in the 1990s and continues today. Matters are not so straightforward as objective versus subjective criteria or generalizable versus local knowledge although these continue to be substantive issues dividing perspectives. Rather, many critics focus on issues such as the legitimacy of various forms of representation, the assumption that one person, however equipped methodologically, can ever understand and communicate the experience of another, and the nature and role of language. Examples of these kinds of concerns will be found in the critiques that follow. Further, the emergence of new forms of inquiry and increased emphasis on criticism have brought much more attention to critical questions that were, for the most part, not asked when the emphasis during the positivist era was primarily on method. For example: What is the cultural identity of those we study? How are those we study advantaged or disadvantaged by our work? How do our own values and cultural identity interact with what we study and how we interpret and share our findings? These questions direct attention to ethical and political as well as epistemological implications of all aspects of the research process and are more likely to be made explicit now and, often, problematized by critics.

This has created a space for different kinds of scholarship. Of course, postpositivists have not become arts based researchers, traditional research journals have not opened to all forms of scholarship, and federal funding has not become suddenly available to support autoethnographic research. However, critique is more likely to be informed and differences acknowledged respectfully than they were before the late 1990s. The quality of the critiques in this section reflects the higher standard. All of the nine critics seek to find value in works that, in their opinion, do not meet the standards for research in their perspective.

As you read the critiques you will begin to appreciate the complexity of understanding a study that is conceptualized within a perspective that is very different than your own. The challenge is to be intellectually honest, remain faithful to your own values and convictions about the nature of research, and yet become open enough to see that there are other ways of thinking and learning about what is true or meaningful. Some perspectives lead critics to focus primarily on the truth, or trustworthiness, of the findings. Others focus more on the meaning of the findings. All are interested in adding to knowledge, as it is understood within the perspective guiding the research. What follows are models of informed scholars extending their perspectives on research, in some instances, into unfamiliar territory. In some instances they view a study as good research, flawed research, or not research at all. In all instances, however, their reasoning with respect to their own perspective is explicit and respectful.

The lengths of the critiques predictably vary because some perspectives have more to say about some studies than others. Also, as with the chapter describing the perspectives, the authors were not constrained by a common outline or format, leaving them free to write in the voice of their own perspective.

CHAPTER 5

The Carr et al. Study

COMPREHENSIVE MULTISITUATIONAL INTERVENTION FOR PROBLEM BEHAVIOR IN THE COMMUNITY: LONG-TERM MAINTENANCE AND SOCIAL VALIDATION

EDWARD G. CARR, LEN LEVIN, GENE MCCONNACHIE, JANE I. CARLSON, DUANE C. KEMP, CHRISTOPHER E. SMITH, AND DARLENE MAGITO MCLAUGHLIN

State University of New York at Stony Brook and Developmental Disabilities Institute

ABSTRACT: Assessment and intervention approaches for dealing with problem behavior need to be extended so that they can be effectively and comprehensively applied within the community. To meet assessment needs, the authors developed a three-component strategy: description (interview followed by direct observation), categorization (aggregating multiple instances of problem behavior into thematic groups, each characterized by a specific function), and verification (manipulating situational parameters to test the accuracy of the assessment data). To meet intervention needs, the authors employed a five-component, assessment-based, hypothesis-driven strategy consisting of rapport building, functional communication training, tolerance for delay of reinforcement, choice, and embedding. Following intervention, improvements in participants' lifestyle, communication, and problem behavior were noted. The intervention was practical in that parents, teachers, job coaches, and group home staff were able to efficiently implement it without compromising high levels of task engagement. Long-term maintenance of intervention effects (ranging from 1.5 to 2.5 years in duration) was also observed. Finally, 100 group home staff judged the effects to be socially valid in that problem behavior was rated as less severe and less dangerous, and as requiring less restraint following intervention. In light of these results, the authors discuss how future community-based intervention will require additional changes in assessment practices and intervention strategies and a redefinition of successful outcomes to include lifestyle change and life-span perspectives.

Over the past 30 years, behavior analysts have made great strides in the assessment of and intervention for severe problem behavior (Didden, Duker, & Korzilius, 1997; Scotti, Ujcich, Weigle, Holland, & Kirk, 1996). Much of this research has focused on highly controlled experimentation designed to identify and assess the variables controlling the behavior in question (Carr, Robinson, Taylor, & Carlson, 1990). This assessment information has then been used in the design of specific interventions (Carr et al., 1994; Gardner & Sovner, 1994; Koegel, Koegel, & Dunlap, 1996). Generally, research has focused on internal validity concerns that relate to making unambiguous causal statements about problem behavior and its remediation. Data generated from this approach have provided valuable assessment and intervention guidelines, and the field has now evolved to the point of being able to determine how broadly applicable these guidelines are in the natural environment. Specifically, how can we best extend present technology to address external validity concerns?

Three aspects of external validity are of particular interest to stakeholders (including parents, teachers, and job coaches). First, stakeholders want interventions that produce

Originally published in Winter 1999, in The Journal of Positive Behavior Interventions, *1(1), pp. 5–25. Copyright 1999 by Pro Ed Journals. Reprinted with permission.*

comprehensive lifestyle changes (Risley, 1996; Turnbull & Ruef, 1997). Problem behavior reduction per se thus is no longer seen as a sufficient criterion for defining a successful outcome, which instead is now seen as one wherein an individual is able to participate meaningfully in a variety of home, school, community, and work settings from which he or she was previously excluded due to the problem behavior. For example, reduction in aggressive behavior would need to be accompanied by an increase in the frequency with which the individual was able to demonstrate self-care skills, go shopping, have a meal at a restaurant, and hold a job.

Second, stakeholders want interventions that are practical and relevant (Carnine, 1997; Turnbull & Ruef, 1996). With respect to practicality, it means that any competent adult should be able to carry out the intervention. Traditionally, much problem behavior remediation has involved experts and/or researchers as the main intervention agents. What is needed, however, are concrete examples of parents, group home staff, teachers, and job coaches—among others—successfully implementing the kind of multicomponent interventions that are frequently needed to deal with problem behavior in community settings. With respect to relevance, the main issue is whether intervention packages can be implemented across all the contexts in which it is important for the person to function successfully on a daily basis. Much previous research has focused on settings that represent simulations or analogs of the natural environment (Carr et al., 1997). Although this research has helped identify important functional relationships, it does not answer the question of whether information derived from experimental analysis is applicable to all relevant contexts (Wahler & Fox, 1981).

Third, stakeholders want long-term behavior change (Nickels, 1996). A reduction in problem behavior that maintains for a few weeks or even a few months is seen as inadequate. Unfortunately, the published literature to date has provided only a handful of studies where behavior change lasted even 6 months (Carr et al., 1997). Long-term behavior change requires long-term implementation of intervention strategies (Turnbull & Turnbull, 1996; Vandercook, York, & Forest, 1989); therefore, intervention packages that are applicable over a period of years need to be developed.

Some aspects of the external validity criteria we have just noted have been explored in the literature (Carr & Carlson, 1993; R. H. Horner et al., 1996; Kemp & Carr, 1995; Lucyshyn, Olson, & Horner, 1995; Lutzker & Campbell, 1994; Northup et al., 1994; Singer & Irvin, 1989). For example, Carr and Carlson (1993) showed that a multicomponent intervention could successfully ameliorate problem behavior displayed by children in a supermarket shopping situation and, further, could be implemented by group home staff. This research thus met the criteria of lifestyle change and practicality. Similarly, Kemp and Carr (1995) demonstrated that a multicomponent intervention could remediate problem behavior displayed by adults in a greenhouse work situation and also could be implemented by job coaches. This research also met the lifestyle change and practicality criteria previously noted. Typically, most research, including the studies just described, does not comprehensively address the three external validity criteria described previously. Carr and Carlson—and Kemp and Carr—did not demonstrate implementation of interventions across all the contexts relevant for the individuals studied (i.e., the supermarket situation and the greenhouse situation represented only one set of circumstances in which the individuals involved displayed problem behavior). Nor did these studies examine whether the beneficial behavior changes were maintained over a period of years.

In view of what we have just outlined, there is a clear need for a controlled research study that (a) addresses the issue of remediating problem behavior while producing lifestyle change and (b) uses procedures that are practical, relevant, and capable of generating long-term maintenance. The purpose of the present study was to address each of these goals.

METHOD

Participants

Participants were selected on the basis of interviews conducted with group home staff, parents, and classroom teachers working in an agency serving persons with developmental disabilities. Included in the study were the first three people who met the following criteria:

1. The individual was reported to display severe problem behavior in the home, community, and/or school;
2. The individual was currently excluded from participating in community activities because of past displays of problem behavior in the community;
3. The individual's problem behavior included any combination of aggression, self-injury, property destruction, and/or tantrums;
4. The individual's problem behavior was severe, as demonstrated by the need for physical restraint and/or medical attention;

5. The individual was documented to have some communicative abilities in the form of speech, sign language, gestures, or use of picture communication symbols.

The selected participants—Val, Gary, and Juan—were 14, 17, and 38 years old, respectively. Val was diagnosed as having cerebral palsy with ataxia and dyskinesia, as well as mental retardation. Gary and Juan were diagnosed as having mental retardation with autistic features. On the Stanford-Binet (Form L-M), Val, Gary, and Juan received IQ scores of 30, 28, and 12, respectively. With respect to communication skills, Val spoke in short phrases that were poorly articulated, Gary generally spoke in short phrases but occasionally used full sentences, and Juan had a repertoire of 10 poorly articulated spoken words that necessitated his use of picture symbols for effective communication.

Val's problem behavior was characterized by tantrums, property destruction, and aggression (e.g., pulling hair, tearing clothes, kicking, spitting, and slapping). Gary's problem behavior included aggression (punching, spitting, tearing clothing), property destruction, tantrums, and self-injurious behavior (hand biting). Juan's problem behavior consisted of aggression (kicking, slapping, hitting, throwing objects at people), self-injurious behavior (face slapping), property destruction, and tantrums.

Val and Gary lived at home with their parents. Juan had lived in the Willowbrook Developmental Center for 30 years and had just been placed in a group home with three other men.

Procedure

A detailed manual describing the assessment and intervention procedures that we used in the present study has been published (Carr et al., 1994). This manual can be consulted for details; therefore, we will present only an overview of the procedures here. We will mostly use Gary as an example of how procedures were implemented.

Assessment

Assessment consisted of three phases: *describe, categorize,* and *verify.*

Describe. This phase involved an initial interview followed by a period of direct observation. During a 2- to 3-week period, the authors interviewed all relevant informants (e.g., parents, teachers, job coaches, and community residence staff), using a variant of an A-B-C (Antecedent-Behavior-Consequence) assessment format. The published literature has demonstrated the critical role of social variables in most

episodes of problem behavior (Carr & Durand, 1985); therefore, our A-B-C assessment emphasized both interpersonal context (as antecedents) and the social reactions of others to the problem behavior (as consequences). For example, one of the authors interviewed Gary's mother and asked her to list the situations in which Gary displayed problem behavior. Initially, the interviewer asked her to describe the behavior (B) in specific, concrete terms (e.g., "Could you give me some specific examples of Gary's problem behavior?"). Then the interviewer asked Gary's mother to describe an example of the social context (A) that preceded such behavior (e.g., "In what situations does Gary act this way with you?"). Finally, the interviewer asked her to describe her reaction (C) to such behavior (e.g., "When Gary is aggressive, what do you do?").

The interview information was then used to select situations for direct observations, which were subsequently made (i.e., where, when, and with whom). Because the interview process identified so many problem situations, direct observations had to be carried out during significant portions of each participant's normal day. Specifically, observations were made 2 to 4 hours per day (mean = 3 hours), 3 to 5 days per week, including weekends (mean = 4 days), over 2 to 4 weeks (mean = 3 weeks). For example, one of the problem situations identified during the interview with Gary's mother involved lunch preparation; therefore, the assessor visited Gary's home during lunchtime in order to confirm the interview information through observation. Each instance of problem behavior that occurred during the observation period was recorded on an index card using the A-B-C narrative approach illustrated in the top section of Figure 1. This process was repeated for all of the situations identified during the interview, resulting in a large number of index cards for each of the participants.

In the example just given, the results of the direct observation confirmed those obtained from the interview. There also were instances in which direct observation failed to confirm the interview information. For example, during the interview Val's teacher reported that when Val became aggressive during an independent work activity, she (the teacher) would never attend to such behavior. However, during several direct observations, the assessor reported that Val's teacher consistently gave protracted reprimands (i.e., negative attention) in response to problem behavior in that situation. When the results of direct observation contradicted those derived from the interview, only the direct observation results (summarized on an index card) were considered in planning subsequent interventions.

It is important to note that several instances occurred in which direct observation yielded information not mentioned in the interview. For example, no group home staff

NAME: Gary	OBSERVER: Gene	DATE: 04/10
GENERAL CONTEXT: Home chore (making sandwich)		TIME: 12:30 P.M.

(A) INTERPERSONAL CONTEXT: Gary had been making a peanut butter sandwich for the past 5 minutes. His mother was standing nearby. She said, "Gary, you need to clean up the mess you made."

(B) BEHAVIOR PROBLEM: Gary threw the silverware on the floor and bit himself. Then, he screamed "No!" and ran out of the kitchen.

(C) SOCIAL REACTION: His mother jumped out of his way. Three minutes later, she cleaned up the mess herself.

PANEL MEMBERS: Gary's mother, the consulting psychologist, and a doctoral student who worked with Gary's family.

HYPOTHESIS (Purpose): Gary engages in property destruction (throwing silverware) and self-injury (biting himself) to avoid having to clean up the kitchen area (ESCAPE).

Figure 1
Index card format used in the functional assessment of Gary's problem behavior. In addition to A-B-C information, the card shows the composition of the panel used to formulate an hypothesis concerning the function (purpose) of the behavior.

member ever stated in an interview that Juan became aggressive when someone turned the TV off while he was watching his favorite program. (The experienced staff knew not to do this.) During one direct observation, a newly hired staff member did turn the TV off during Juan's program, precipitating an episode of aggression by Juan. That staff member reacted to this behavior by immediately turning the TV on again, thereby calming Juan. When new information was first obtained via direct observation rather than interview, such information was noted on an index card and was also considered in planning subsequent interventions.

This assessment was an ongoing process that took place throughout the 6 years of the study (baseline, intervention, and maintenance), as needed. The following events triggered additional descriptive assessment carried out in the manner just outlined:

1. Any significant change in the person's life situation (i.e., with respect to work, educational activities, staff, living situations, or social relationships);
2. Residual problem behavior that was observed after an otherwise successful intervention had been implemented;
3. Problem behavior that had been under control following intervention but unexpectedly reappeared.

Categorize. The describe phase generated more than 100 index cards per individual. Because this number of problem situations would have made intervention planning cumbersome, we had to develop a method for reducing the array of problem situations to a limited number of functional categories. Our method consisted of three steps: formulate hypotheses about function, group by functional categories, and find common themes within a functional category. These steps were carried out by a panel of three people (example shown in Figure 1, bottom section), two of whom had conducted the earlier describe phase and one of whom was a caregiver (e.g., parent, teacher, job coach).

With respect to the first step (formulate hypotheses), panel members were asked to examine each card independently and formulate an hypothesis about the function (purpose) of the behavior in each situation described (shown in Figure 1, bottom section). All panel members had received information from the authors about the variety of functions served by problem behavior. Hypothesis categories were *Attention, Escape, Tangible,* or *Other.* Specifically, each panel member was told to pay particular attention to the social reaction to the problem behavior (listed on the card), because the research literature has documented that this variable provides the clearest indication of the purpose the problem behavior actually serves (Carr et al., 1990; Reichle & Wacker, 1993). In the three examples described earlier, the social reaction to Gary, Val and Juan's problem behavior was *task removal, contingent lengthy reprimands,* and *reinstitution of TV time,* respectively, leading to hypothesis formulation of *Escape, Attention,* and *Tangible/Activity,* respectively. If two out of three panel members formulated the same hypothesis (e.g., Escape) and one member formulated a different hypothesis (e.g., Attention), the hypothesis chosen for subsequent intervention planning was the one put forth by the majority (i.e., Escape). If the majority hypothesis was Other or if there was no agreement among any of the panel members, the information on the specific index card involved was not used to plan subsequent interventions; instead, the problem behavior was dealt with via crisis management procedures described later. (This situation occurred for less than 1% of the cards.)

In the second step of the categorization method, the index cards were grouped together into the three functional categories (Attention, Escape, Tangibles) based on the majority judgment of the panel. In the third step (find common themes within a category), panel members examined the interpersonal context described on each card and, through discussion, grouped the cards into common themes within each functional category. In other words, themes were stimulus situations that had a defined set of shared features. This step was taken because it is generally not possible to design specific intervention strategies applicable to a wide variety of naturalistic situations based simply on generic hypotheses about functional categories (Carr, 1994; R. H. Horner, 1994). Instead, within a functional category (e.g., Escape), more specific information about the antecedent variables that control problem behavior is needed for intervention planning. This information comes from a detailed examination of interpersonal context. Various interpersonal contexts can be grouped together according to whether they share related stimulus features, giving rise to the concept of a theme. Thus, in the case of Gary, the primary generic functional category was Escape. Within that category, many index cards included information on the interpersonal context in which Gary was performing a task incorrectly and received negative feedback. For example, in a flower-potting task, he put the seeds in too deeply; in making his bed, he put the sheet on top of the blanket; in sweeping the sidewalk, he got dirt on the clean areas. In each case, the negative feedback that he received for poor task performance subsequently evoked aggression and self-injurious behavior. Despite the differences in tasks, people who were present, setting, and type of negative feedback received, the three interpersonal contexts just described for Gary all shared the same critical feature: presence of negative feedback following poor task performance. Therefore, these three cards—and all others that shared the same critical feature—constituted the theme "negative feedback for poor task performance" within the generic functional category of Escape. The same categorization procedure applied to the remaining index cards for Gary produced the themes of "prompted completion of an ongoing series of tasks" (i.e., Gary failed to complete a task in which he was involved and was subsequently prompted to finish up) and "presentation of nonpreferred tasks." Both were associated with self-injury and aggression. The procedure just described was applied across all functional categories for all participants. Space limitations do not permit listing the specific themes associated with each participant or the number of index cards related to each theme; interested readers are referred to Carr et al. (1994).

Verify.   The third assessment phase (verify) was carried out as the baseline. Its purpose was to confirm that the situations represented by the identified themes did indeed evoke problem behavior, thereby corroborating the validity of the data collected and organized during the describe and categorize phases of assessment. Specifically, in this phase the interpersonal context and social reaction were manipulated (rather than passively observed). For example, we used the descriptive data represented in Figure 1 to set up a similar general context, interpersonal context, and social reaction to verify that aggressive and self-injurious behavior did indeed occur for Gary within the situation identified in the descriptive phase. On a given day, we maintained the situation represented in Figure 1 for 15 minutes, during which time, data were collected. Thus, one example (i.e., home chore: sandwich making) drawn from one theme (i.e., prompted completion of an ongoing series of tasks) was used to verify information from the describe and categorize phases. On the same day, the process was repeated two more times: Two more themes from the pool were examined using one specific example of each. Therefore, on a given day, there were three 15-minute theme sessions. Data collected from these sessions were pooled to produce a single baseline probe point of 45 minutes. On the next probe day, three more themes that had not yet been sampled were selected, and one specific example from each was used in the verification process. This process (i.e., sampling without replacement) was continued across probes until all the themes had been sampled. At this point, the themes were recycled with one restriction—the specific example representing a theme could not have been used in any prior probe.

Intervention

The format used in conducting baseline sessions (just described) was repeated during intervention, which was a comprehensive multicomponent approach consisting of building rapport, providing functional communication training (FCT), building tolerance for reinforcement delay, providing choices, and using embedding. All of these approaches were applied continuously throughout the 5 years of the intervention portion of the study, as needed.

Building Rapport. The purpose of this component was to increase positive social interaction between the person with disabilities (the participant) and his or her caregivers because this type of interaction had been infrequent. Increased social interaction was seen as an important initial step in eventually enhancing a communication-based intervention.

First, caregivers provided a wide variety of individualized reinforcers (e.g., foods, games, conversation) to the participant. They thus acted as discriminative stimuli for approach behavior by the person with disabilities. After approach behavior became reliable, caregivers withheld reinforcers until the participant requested them spontaneously or after prompting. Requests made through speech, sign, or gestures were acceptable. As general approach and requesting were being established, steps were taken to enhance the participant's physical appearance (personal hygiene, grooming, clothing) to reduce the possibility of social rejection by caregivers and others. In addition, interests shared between the caregivers and the participant were identified (e.g., jogging, going out for pizza). To further facilitate social interaction, we used these shared interests as one of the bases for programming community-based routines (e.g., daily jogging or weekly visits to the pizzeria). The procedures for building rapport were implemented each time that a new caregiver or support person became involved with the participant.

Functional Communication Training. The increased social interaction that followed successful rapport building provided a useful context for building communicative skills that were directly focused on ameliorating problem behavior. The purpose of the FCT component was to teach the participant a variety of communicative responses that were functionally equivalent to various classes of problem behavior, thereby making further display of such behavior unnecessary. We used the standard FCT procedure reported in the literature (Carr & Durand, 1985). Briefly, this procedure involved matching the function of the communicative response to the function of the problem behavior as identified through the previously described generic

categories of behavioral function: Escape, Attention, and Tangibles/Activities.

The category associated with the greatest number of index cards was addressed first (e.g., for Gary, Escape). Further, the theme associated with the greatest number of index cards within that category (e.g., for Gary, "prompted completion of an ongoing series of tasks") became the initial focus of intervention. For example, Figure 1 shows that the function of Gary's self-injury and property destruction during sandwich making was escape from the prompted task. Therefore, a communicative response that served the same function as the problem behavior (escape) was taught (after a few minutes of sandwich making, Gary was prompted to say, "I need a break," and his request was honored). Over time, the prompts were faded, and Gary's spontaneous communicative acts were honored with a short break prior to his returning to the task.

Because the problem behavior function varied for each participant, many different communicative forms had to be taught. The specific form was determined by the theme that it addressed. In the illustration just given, Gary's self-injury and property destruction were, putatively, escape-motivated behaviors related to the theme of "prompted completion of an ongoing series of tasks." Each index card pertaining to that theme identified an opportunity for teaching Gary to request a break. When Gary had mastered the break request in the situation identified by the first index card (i.e., sandwich making), the FCT procedure was repeated for a second index card for the same theme (home chore: vacuuming). Repetitions of the procedure continued for all the index cards related to that particular theme until spontaneous generalization occurred for three additional cards (e.g., Gary spontaneously requested a break from washing the family car, planting a flowerbed, or making a salad). At this point, a new theme from the Escape category ("negative feedback for poor task performance") was examined in order to create opportunities for teaching the next communicative response ("Help me"). This theme was selected because it was associated with the second greatest number of cards within the generic Escape category. The FCT procedure that had been used to address the first Escape theme was now implemented for the second Escape theme and each succeeding Escape theme. In cases in which there were only a few index cards in a theme, spontaneous generalization sometimes did not occur; therefore, the FCT procedure was applied to all of the situations represented by these cards.

Once training had been completed with respect to the Escape category, the entire FCT procedure just described was repeated for the generic category containing the second greatest number of index cards (in the case of Gary, Tangibles) and then the third greatest (Attention, for Gary).

As noted earlier, if the majority hypothesis of the panel was that problem behavior was a function of variables other than those specifically listed or if a consensus regarding function could not be achieved, no intervention specific to the hypothesis was possible. In these cases, problem behavior was dealt with through the use of crisis management procedures (Carr et al., 1994). We employed five such procedures: *ignore, momentary restraint, protect, remove,* and *introduce cues* (Carr & Carlson, 1993). (For reasons of safety and ethics, these procedures were also employed during the baseline [verify] phase of the study.)

We used the ignore strategy to handle minor problem behavior (e.g., screaming) that had a history of leading to more serious problems if not stopped. For example, when Gary screamed, his mother would sometimes reprimand him, and Gary's screaming would accelerate to self-injury. To avoid this outcome, we taught his mother to simply ignore the screaming; the behavior typically subsided. We used the momentary restraint and introduce cues procedures to handle self-injury. When Gary bit his hand, his mother was taught to hold his hand away from his mouth for a few seconds (momentary restraint) and to present discriminative stimuli (introduce cues) for a highly preferred activity (e.g., putting on a music tape that Gary liked to sing to). These cues typically evoked competing, nonproblem behavior. We used the protect and remove procedures to deal with aggression. If Gary hit his brother, his mother was taught to step between Gary and his brother (protect) and have the brother move to a different room in the house (remove). Often, these procedures were supplemented with introduce cues (e.g., Gary's mother might turn on music following protect and remove, a procedure that resulted in Gary's becoming engaged in singing rather than hitting). Because the hypothesis of "Other" involved only a small number of situations—as was the case for a lack of consensus regarding function—use of crisis management procedures was very rare once intervention had begun. In contrast, during baseline, when problem behaviors were frequent, these procedures had to be used more often. Even after intervention had begun, occasional episodes of problem behavior occurred. These also were dealt with by employing crisis management procedures.

Building Tolerance for Reinforcement Delay. Following successful FCT, there was a strong tendency for each participant to use the newly acquired communicative responses at a very high rate, and caregivers found such responding problematic. Specifically, an individual might (a) ask for so many breaks that little work would be completed, (b) ask for so much attention that the teacher was unable to attend to other students, and (c) ask for tangibles at an inopportune moment or that could not be provided. To address these issues, we built in tolerance for reinforcement delay.

When a participant requested a particular reinforcer, the parent or teacher (for example) acknowledged the request and told the individual that he or she could have the desired item after a specific activity (e.g., chores, independent leisure activity) had been completed. If necessary, the participant was prompted to carry out the activity; these prompts were faded over time. For example, after receiving FCT, Gary made so many requests for breaks that he seldom finished making his sandwich (see Figure 1). A procedure was implemented such that when Gary asked for a break, his mother acknowledged his request ("Sure, Gary, you can have a break") but told him that he could only have a break after he had completed more of the task ("First, you need to spread the peanut butter and jelly on the bread, and then you can take a little break."). Initially, Gary's mother had to help him by physically prompting the extra required work, but over time she was able to fade out these prompts. Now when Gary was told to do the extra work, he readily did so prior to repeating his request for a break. Over many weeks, Gary's mother recycled this procedure so as to gradually increase the duration of the work required prior to having break requests honored. Gary eventually was required to gather all the lunch supplies, make the entire sandwich, pack his drink and snacks, and clean up the food preparation area prior to having his break request honored. At the end of this training, his mother's acknowledgment ("Sure, Gary, you can have a break but first . . . ") became a natural cue for him to complete the entire lunch-making sequence, and the completion of that sequence became a natural cue for him to reiterate his break request. The procedure just described was repeated in all situations in which the too frequent use of communicative responses interfered with task completion and/or a caregiver's need to attend to others. The procedure was also used to deal with excessively high rates of requests for activities and tangibles. If, however, the individual requested an item or activity that could not be provided, a fourth procedure—choice—was used.

Providing Choices. We used a choice strategy to deal with requests that could not be honored and thus might result in problem behavior. Research has demonstrated that providing choices to an individual can be an effective way to reduce problem behavior (Dyer, Dunlap, & Winterling, 1990). For example, Gary once asked to go for a walk during a violent rainstorm. His mother was taught to respond to such requests by encouraging him to choose among several alternative options. Specifically, she began by acknowledging the request (e.g., "Yes, Gary, it would be fun to go for a walk, but it's too dangerous to go outside now."). Then, she offered Gary at least two alternative exercise options (e.g., "Gary, you could use the treadmill in the recreation room, or you could work out with the exercise videotape in the den. Which would you like to do?"). When Gary indicated a preference, his mother honored his request. This procedure was repeated in all situations in which requests for certain tangibles could not be honored for safety reasons or because caregivers were otherwise occupied. The choice procedure just described was also used for attention-seeking problem behavior. For example, Gary might ask to talk with his mother while she was on the phone. If this happened, his mother would respond as follows: "Gary, I know you want to talk, but I'm on the phone. Your brother (Pete) and father are not busy now. Do you want to talk to Dad or Pete?" Depending on the choice made, Gary's mother motioned for the relevant person to approach Gary and speak with him.

Gary sometimes refused the choices. In this case, the caregiver repeated the options; if Gary still refused to state a preference, the caregiver went about his or her business and made no further comments to Gary. If problem behavior arose (this was rare), the appropriate crisis management procedures were carried out.

The choice procedure was also used for escape-motivated problem behavior. Consistent with the literature (Dunlap et al., 1994), we had Gary's family members and teachers offer him choices when appropriate. For example, on various days Gary might prefer one task to another (e.g., vacuuming versus washing the car versus sweeping the floor). We taught Gary's parents to offer him task choices because it was not necessary for him to do all of the tasks each day. Thus, after school and before Gary began his chores, his mother asked him, "Gary, what would you like to do today—vacuum, wash the car, or sweep the floor?" When Gary indicated his preference, his mother allowed him to do the task indicated. Occasionally, Gary refused to choose any option. In this case, a fifth procedure, embedding, was used.

Using Embedding. We used this procedure to deal with escape-motivated behavior in situations in which a participant refused to choose a task option. In the embedding procedure, stimuli that are discriminative for problem behavior (e.g., task demands) are interspersed among stimuli that are discriminative for socially appropriate behavior (e.g., music could be discriminative for singing, dancing, humming, and smiling). Research has demonstrated that

embedding (also referred to as interspersal training and behavioral momentum) can be effective in reducing problem behavior (Carr, Newsom, & Binkoff, 1976; Dunlap & Koegel, 1980; Mace et al., 1988).

For example, Gary's mother might have asked him to choose one of three task options (e.g., "Gary, do you want to vacuum, wash the car, or sweep the floor first?"). If Gary refused to choose, his mother repeated the options. If he still refused to choose, his mother initiated the embedding procedure. Specifically, Gary had a history of responding to his favorite music tapes by humming and singing (socially appropriate behavior). Therefore, after Gary twice refused to make a choice, his mother turned on one of his favorite music tapes. Gary responded by humming and singing. After 2 minutes, his mother turned the music off. Gary immediately requested more music. His mother responded by saying, "Sure, Gary, you can have more music, but first let's do some work. Do you want to vacuum, wash the car, or sweep the floor first?" Typically, Gary then chose one of the options. As he began to work, his mother turned the music on again. In this manner, the demands associated with work were embedded in the music-listening context. If Gary refused to choose one of the options, the procedure was repeated. Following subsequent termination of the music, the stimuli associated with the music were made more salient (e.g., the tape recorder was placed within Gary's field of vision and his mother talked about what a great tune they had just heard and how much she enjoyed singing along with him). This was done in order to help focus Gary's attention on the music stimulus so that it would be more likely to evoke a request for continuation that, in turn, would allow Gary's mother to reintroduce the work options. If at any time Gary responded to the termination of the music by engaging in problem behavior, his mother would initiate the relevant crisis management procedures.

Generalization

We were also concerned with the transfer of intervention success from one specific situation to other situations (generalization). The scope of generalization in terms of the intervention agents, settings, and tasks involved is illustrated in Table 1. Two strategies were employed to enhance generalization: programming generalization and conducting additional descriptive assessments and interventions in situations in which a problem behavior continued or reemerged.

Programming Generalization. Programming generalization involved identifying a successful intervention in one situation and then systematically introducing it into various

Table 1
Multisituational Intervention Implementation: Agents, Settings, and Tasks

Intervention agent	Setting	Task
Parents	Home	Laundry (sort, wash, dry, fold)
Siblings	Parents' home	Exercises/physical education
Group home staff	Group home	Put on makeup
Classroom teachers	School	Wash hands and face
Gym teachers	Class	Brush teeth
Speech therapists	Gym	Shave
Bus drivers	Speech room	Set table
Job coaches	Bus/van	Make sandwiches
Undergraduate clinical assistants	Field trips	Perform academic tasks
	Community	Pack lunch
	Supermarket	Clear and wipe table
	Park	Dry dishes
	Restaurant	Load and empty dishwasher
	Fast-food restaurant	Put dishes/silverware away
	Swimming pool	Sweep floor
	Church	Mop floor
	Hotels	Vacuum
	Trains	Brush hair
	Work	Clean bathroom
	Greenhouse	Clean kitchen
		Wash windows
		Wash car/van
		Ride exercycle
		Make bed

functionally related situations. There is evidence in the literature that successful programming of generalization across a number of situations will evoke spontaneous generalization in other situations (Stokes & Baer, 1977). For example, we previously mentioned that during FCT, Gary's mother had programmed the "I want a break" response for tasks such as sandwich making and vacuuming. After she programmed several more tasks (washing hands and face, making the bed, drying dishes), Gary spontaneously generalized his requests for breaks to several new tasks (washing the car, planting a flowerbed, and making a salad) that were functionally related to the original tasks (i.e., the problem behavior in all situations was escape motivated).

Conducting Descriptive Assessments and Interventions in New Situations. After Gary's mother had produced spontaneous generalization across tasks at home, she decided that Gary was ready to participate in new activities in the community. One situation involved shopping at the supermarket. The first few expeditions were associated with high levels of aggressive behavior; therefore, the descriptive assessment procedure described earlier was repeated in the supermarket. The assessment revealed that Gary's problem behavior in the new situation was motivated not by Escape, but by Tangibles; specifically, when certain favorite snacks (e.g., cookies) were inaccessible (out of reach or prohibited by Gary's mother), Gary became aggressive. Gary's mother used the new assessment information to design a variant of FCT relevant to the function identified for the aggressive behavior: she prompted and reinforced verbal requests for snacks (e.g., "I want the cookies"), combining this strategy with building tolerance for reinforcement delay, as described earlier. Following this intervention, Gary's aggressive behavior decreased.

Maintenance

The procedural distinction between the intervention and maintenance phases was as follows: During intervention, we were present several days a week in the home, school, employment, and community situations to coach and provide feedback to caregivers regarding the design and implementation of intervention strategies. During maintenance, we visited relevant sites one day per month and made phone contact once per month. In addition, we invited caregivers to phone us as needed if questions arose.

Occasionally, problem behavior reemerged during the maintenance phase, typically at low frequencies. When this happened, we repeated the descriptive assessment in the same manner as that just described for generalization, and we built relevant interventions based on the new assessment data.

Social Validity

During this phase, we obtained judgments from direct service providers as to the efficacy of the intervention.

Choice of Judges. A total of 100 group home staff, representing approximately 90% of the total direct care staff in three service agencies on Long Island, were selected as judges based on their availability at the time of validity testing. We selected these individuals as judges because all three study participants were currently in or about to enter group homes; therefore, it was important to know how primary caregivers perceived the seriousness of the problem behavior being addressed.

Choice of Video Segments. We randomly selected one 15-min session from the last day of baseline (pre-intervention segment) and one 15-min session from the last day of intervention (postintervention segment) from the videotapes of each of the three participants (i.e., two for each participant or six segments in all). The viewings were administered to groups of 5 to 10 judges at a time, with the pre- and posttapes randomly selected from across the participants (e.g., the first group of judges saw a 15-min pre-intervention tape for Val, a 15-min postintervention tape for Gary, and a

15-min postintervention tape for Juan). The type of tape shown was counterbalanced across groups of judges (e.g., the second group saw a 15-min postintervention tape for Val, 15-min pre-intervention tape for Gary, and a 15-min pre-intervention tape for Juan). The randomization and counterbalancing procedures were repeated for judging groups until all 100 judges had been tested. We thus avoided having a single judge view the pre- and posttapes for the same participant, which eliminated the potential for biased ratings based on prior exposure. Each of the three pre-intervention tapes was viewed by 50 judges from the pool; each of the three postintervention tapes was viewed by the other 50 judges.

Judges' Ratings. Prior to viewing a 15-min segment, the top paragraph in Figure 2 was read to the judges. After the viewing was completed, the second paragraph in Figure 2 was read, and the judges filled out each of the three 7-point rating scale (7 = *strong agreement with a statement,* and 1 = *strong disagreement*) statements regarding severity, danger, and physical restraint. The latter procedure was repeated for each of the remaining two 15-min segments.

Response Definitions, Recording, and Reliability

Response Definitions

One independent variable was recorded as a measure of intervention integrity. This was defined as the response of the intervention agent to the communicative act displayed by the participant (henceforth referred to as responsivity). Three dependent variables—task engagement, communicative acts, and problem behavior—were recorded for each participant.

Responsivity (intervention integrity) was defined as any of the following three variables: no response, acknowledged, and reinforced. *No response* meant that the intervention agent failed to provide the reinforcer specified in the participant's request and, in addition, failed to comment in any way on the request (e.g., the person with disabilities said, "I want a break," but the intervention agent remained silent or made an unrelated comment such as "You are wearing a nice shirt today"). *Acknowledged* meant that the intervention agent failed to provide the reinforcer but did recognize that a request had been made (e.g., the person with disabilities said, "I want a break," and the intervention agent responded by saying, "Sure, you can have a break, but why don't we finish washing the table first?"). *Reinforced* meant that the

You will be viewing a videotaped session approximately 15 minutes in length. Please watch the session carefully. Afterward you will be asked to respond to the questions below, which will be read aloud for your convenience. Please consider each session separately and answer the questions based solely on the session you have just viewed.

Imagine that the videotaped session you have just seen represents this person's typical daily behavior. To what extent do you agree or disagree with the following statements? Please circle the number that most clearly reflects your response.

1.   This person's problem behavior is severe.

| Agree Strongly | 7 | 6 | 5 | 4 | 3 | 2 | 1 | Disagree Strongly |

2.   This person is a danger to him- or herself or others.

| Agree Strongly | 7 | 6 | 5 | 4 | 3 | 2 | 1 | Disagree Strongly |

3.   This person is likely to require physical restraint at least occasionally.

| Agree Strongly | 7 | 6 | 5 | 4 | 3 | 2 | 1 | Disagree Strongly |

Figure 2
Instructions given to judges who made social validity ratings, and the scales used to make those ratings.

intervention agent provided the specified reinforcer (e.g., the person with disabilities said, "I want a break," and the intervention agent responded, "Okay, why don't you sit down on the couch for a few minutes and relax?").

Problem behavior was defined as the occurrence of any of the following:

1. Aggression toward a person
   - hitting, punching, kicking, biting, or shoving another person;
   - grabbing the clothes, skin, or hair of another person;
   - spitting;
   - taking or attempting to take a tangible reinforcer from another person without permission;
   - hitting another person with an object; and
   - attempting to do any of the preceding behaviors but missing the victim because he or she moved out of the way.

2. Aggression toward an object
   - hitting, punching, or kicking an object;
   - hitting, punching, or kicking the floor, a wall, or a door.

3. Destroying property

4. Injuring one's self (hitting the head with a hand or biting a hand, for example).

A *communicative act* was defined as the occurrence of a spontaneous verbal request (e.g., requesting a tangible item, asking for help when working on a difficult task, requesting a break, calling out a person's name) or non-verbal request (e.g., tapping another person on the shoulder, pointing to a desired object, leading another person by the hand towards a desired object, presenting a picture symbol with the word "break" written on it). To be considered spontaneous, the request could not occur within 5 seconds of a verbal prompt. In addition, at least 3 seconds had to have elapsed between two communicative responses that were not acknowledged or reinforced for each to be scored as a separate response. Thus, if an individual said, "orange" 5 times within a 3-second period, the 5 responses were scored as a single communicative act.

Task engagement was defined as actively participating in an ongoing work, academic, or home chore activity either independently or with prompting from a support person or caregiver. For example, when Gary was washing the family car and he held the hose and sprayed the car with water, his behavior was scored as task engagement. If his brother had had to guide Gary's hands to the hose and help him direct the spray, that activity also would have been scored as task engagement. However, if Gary simply had stood next to the car while his brother filled a bucket with soap and water, Gary's behavior would not have been scored as task engagement.

Response Recording

As noted previously, each baseline, intervention, and maintenance session consisted of three 15-min observation periods conducted on a given day. Each of these periods was videotaped for subsequent reliability analysis. Typically, data were recorded during 3 consecutive or near consecutive days in a row, depending on participant availability. Generally, a set of 3 days was defined as a probe, but this number could vary from 2 to 4 days. During intervention, probes were separated from one another by an average of 3

to 4 months. This interprobe interval was gradually extended so that, by the end of the study, it was as long as 1 year.

Reliability

A psychology doctoral student served as the primary reliability observer. This student viewed each of the videotapes and scored all the variables using the response definitions noted earlier. Responsivity, communicative acts, and problem behavior were all scored as frequency counts summed across the three 15-min observation periods that constituted a session. Task engagement was scored using a time-sampling procedure consisting of continuous 10-sec intervals.

An undergraduate with extensive employment experience in the field of developmental disabilities served as the reliability observer. For frequency data, the reliability index was the percentage of agreement between the two observers, calculated for each probe by dividing the smaller total frequency by the larger. For interval data, observer records were compared on an interval-by-interval basis. Agreement scores were computed as the number of agreements divided by the number of agreements plus disagreements. The percentage of sessions for which reliability was assessed for each class of variable, the mean percentage of interobserver agreement, and the range of agreement for all three participants are given in Table 2.

Table 2
Reliability Data for Each Class of Behavior

Behavior	Participant	% Sessions with reliability	Mean % agreement	Range (%)
Responsivity	Val	40	87	70–100
	Gary	40	89	70–100
	Juan	40	82	64–100
Communicative acts	Val	23	84	70–96
	Gary	19	87	69–98
	Juan	20	83	64–100
Problem behavior	Val	23	96	80–100
	Gary	19	82	60–100
	Juan	20	92	72–100
Task engagement	Val	21	87	75–99
	Gary	26	92	83–96
	Juan	25	95	91–97

The mean percentage of agreement varied from 82% to 96% across the three participants.

Experimental Design

A multiple-baseline probe analysis was carried out within a multiple-baseline-across-participant's design (R. D. Horner & Baer, 1978). Ethical considerations prohibited the use of a standard multiple-baseline design across participants (i.e., continuous data collection) because such a design would have required large numbers of baseline sessions in which participants could have harmed themselves or others due to the severity of their problem behaviors. Because intervention was focused on changing problem behavior and communication per se, the multiple baseline was used to demonstrate experimental control with respect to these two variables. Other variables (e.g., task engagement) were not explicit intervention targets. Data on these variables were not the subject of the controlled experimentation and represent ancillary measures only.

RESULTS

Independent Variable

The data on responsivity are provided in Figure 3. (As noted earlier, intervention agents had three response options: no response, acknowledged, or reinforced.) The data shown in Figure 3 were pooled across each phase of the intervention; thus, the baseline data represent the responses of the intervention agents pooled across all the baseline sessions for a given participant. Likewise, the intervention data represent the responses of the intervention agents pooled across all the sessions for each of the probes that constituted the intervention data set. The total frequency of the three types of intervention agent responses was summed, and the percentage of that total for each type was computed.

No response and acknowledged together constituted the vast majority of responses during baseline, whereas the reinforced response rarely occurred. The type of responses that occurred varied across intervention agents in that Val primarily received no response, but Gary and Juan primarily received acknowledged. The percentage of the total responses representing the reinforced option was 0%, 22%, and 13%, respectively, for Val, Gary, and Juan.

With respect to the intervention data, all three intervention agents showed an immediate and substantial increase in the percentage of their reinforcing responses during the first probe. However, in successive probes the reinforced category diminished from its initially high levels, and the acknowledged category generally increased from initially low

levels so that by the final probe, the percentage of the two types of responses were more comparable. Nonetheless, across all the probes, the level of the reinforced category was substantially higher than that observed during baseline for all three participants and, by the final probe, was 55%, 70%, and 45% for Val, Gary, and Juan, respectively. Additionally, the level of the no response category generally remained low throughout all the intervention probes.

Dependent Variables

The percentages of intervals of task engagement across baseline, intervention, and maintenance probes are shown in Figure 4. As noted previously, task engagement was not directly manipulated in a controlled experimental fashion. For all participants, task engagement occurred at low levels during baseline, increased during intervention, and continued to increase or remained stable during maintenance. Specifically, for Val, task engagement occurred at a mean level as follows:

- 6% of the intervals in baseline (range: 1%–18%),
- 41% in intervention (range: 24%–59%), and
- 69% during maintenance (range: 50%–85%).

For Gary, task engagement occurred as follows:

- baseline level of 36% (range: 23%–49%),
- intervention level of 54% (range: 18%–78%), and
- maintenance level of 70% (range: 52%–80%).

Finally, for Juan, mean levels of task engagement occurred as follows:

- 25% in baseline (range: 1%–52%),
- 35% in intervention (range: 4%–57%), and
- 39% during maintenance (range: 36%–51%).

The frequency of spontaneous (unprompted) communication and problem behavior across baseline, intervention, and maintenance probes is shown in Figure 5. Across all three participants, baseline levels of communication were low and stable across time. In contrast, following intervention, frequency of communication increased in multiple-baseline fashion. During maintenance, there was some diminution in the level of communication for Val and Gary, but none for Juan. Mean frequencies of communication for each participant follow.

1. Val
   - baseline was 23 (range: 20–30),
   - intervention was 61.8 (range: 48–89), and
   - maintenance was 45.4 (range: 25–95).

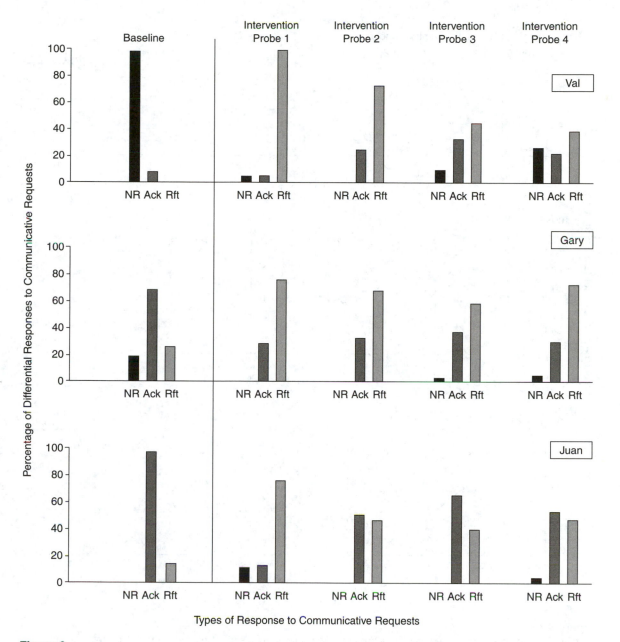

Figure 3

Percentages of different types of intervention agent response to participant's communicative requests. NR = No response; Ack = Acknowledged request; Rft = Reinforced request.

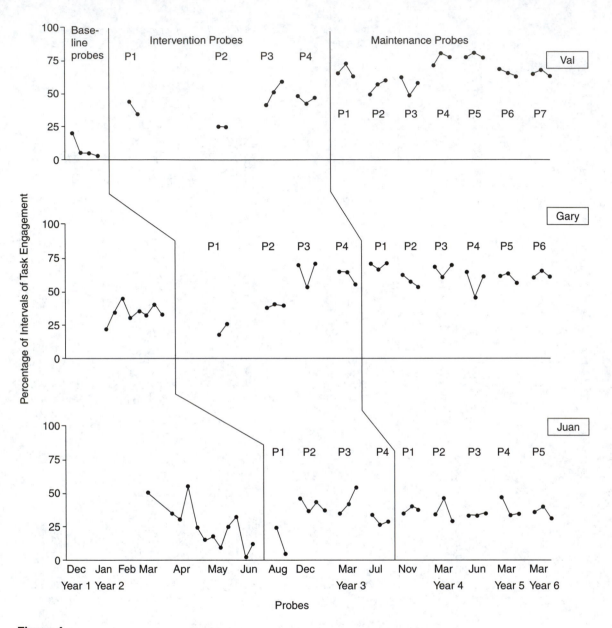

Figure 4

Percentage of intervals of task engagement across baseline, intervention, and maintenance probes. P1 refers to the first probe in a phase, P2 to the second probe, and so on.

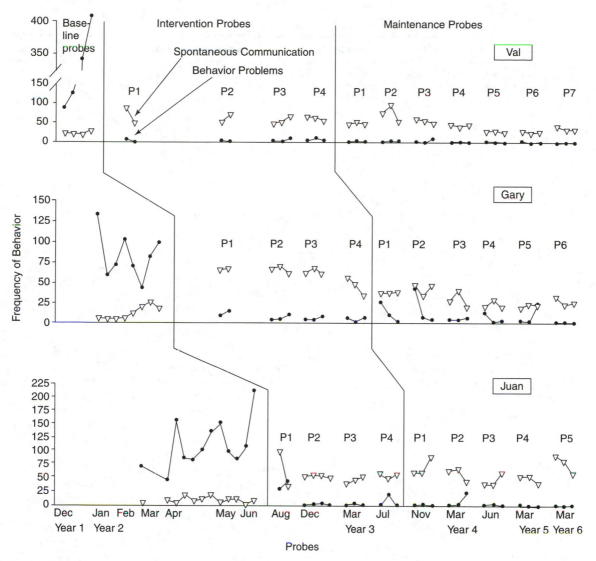

Figure 5

Frequency of spontaneous communicative requests and problem behavior across baseline, intervention, and maintenance probes. P1 refers to the first probe in a phase, P2 to the second probe, and so on.

2. Gary
   - baseline was 9.3 (range: 2–22),
   - intervention was 54.1 (range: 29–64), and
   - maintenance was 25.1 (range: 14–42).
3. Juan
   - baseline was 7.6 (range: 0–17),
   - intervention was 52.5 (range: 32–95), and
   - maintenance was 59.2 (range: 38–92).

Figure 5 also shows a high baseline frequency of problem behavior for all three participants, followed by a dramatic decrease in frequency at the beginning of intervention. This decrease lasted throughout the intervention and maintenance phases. The mean frequencies of problem behavior for each participant follow.

Table 3

Social Validity Ratings for Pre- and Postintervention Videotaped Segments

Behavior characteristic	Intervention for Val		Intervention for Gary		Intervention for Juan	
	Pre-	Post-	Pre-	Post-	Pre-	Post-
Severity	4.06	1.72	4.76	0.56	5.02	1.90
	$t = 5.71$		$t = 17.50$		$t = 9.45$	
Danger	3.66	1.12	4.76	0.52	5.16	1.04
	$t = 7.70$		$t = 17.67$		$t = 15.85$	
Restraint	3.94	1.42	4.40	0.54	4.88	1.40
	$t = 6.81$		$t = 11.70$		$t = 9.94$	

Note: *A 7-point rating scale was used (1 = desirable, 7 = undesirable). All pre-post scores were significant at the* $p < .0005$ *level.*

1. Val
   - baseline was 243 (range: 91–412),
   - intervention was 3.4 (range: 1–8), and
   - maintenance was 1.0 (range: 0–8).
2. Gary
   - baseline was 77.4 (range: 39–128)
   - intervention was 5.5 (range: 0–14),
   - maintenance was 6.4 (range: 0–38).
3. Juan
   - baseline was 110 (range: 44–213),
   - intervention was 9.5 (range 0–23), and
   - maintenance was 1.7 (range: 0–21).

The data on social validity are provided in Table 3. The ratings obtained from judges who viewed pre-intervention segments were significantly different (t test, $p < .005$) than the ratings obtained from judges who viewed postintervention segments; that is, following intervention, problem behavior was judged to be significantly less severe, less dangerous, and requiring less restraint than problem behavior displayed prior to intervention.

DISCUSSION

Intervention

Our study showed the intervention package to be effective and feasible. The five-component intervention package was successful in reducing severe problem behavior in three individuals across many different community-based contexts over a protracted maintenance period (1.5 to 2.5 years). As was the case in previous studies (Bird, Dores, Moniz, &

Robinson, 1989; Carr & Durand, 1985; R. H. Horner & Day, 1991), there was a strong inverse relationship between communicative responding and severe problem behavior. Although the data are consistent with the notion that increased communicative competence has an ameliorative effect on problem behavior, the presence of several other intervention components in this study bars the conclusion that the positive outcomes were due solely to FCT. Indeed, the critical aspect of the present study was its scope: The daily application of multiple intervention procedures across multiple situations over very long periods of time. The data on social validity corroborate the direct observation data pertaining to effectiveness displayed in Figure 5. Specifically, key stakeholders (i.e., group home staff) judged problem behavior to be significantly less severe, less dangerous, and requiring less restraint following intervention. In sum, the intervention package produced long-term maintenance and positive lifestyle changes.

With respect to feasibility, our multicomponent intervention addressed several issues raised in the literature (Carr & Carlson, 1993; Kemp & Carr, 1995). First, given the centrality of communication, there is a legitimate concern that individuals may make increasingly more requests as their communication pays off, thereby dominating the time of their caretakers and relatives. The data shown in Figure 5 contradict this possibility. Specifically, instead of an upward trend in communicative requests, Val and Gary displayed a downward trend and Juan remained stable. Second, the data on responsivity also relate to the issue of feasibility. Specifically, requests were not honored 100% of the time for any of the participants. Indeed, with respect to requests honored, Val and Juan's data showed a downward trend over probes and Gary's data were stable. Third, the data on task engagement (see Figure 4) also relate to the feasibility issue. Specifically, even though parents and teachers honored requests throughout the study, such behavior on their part did not limit active engagement in a variety of academic, work, and household tasks by each of the three participants. The dramatic increase in task engagement from that observed during baseline persisted throughout the intervention period and increased during maintenance. Indeed, one reason for the decrease in frequency of communicative requests noted earlier may be related to the sharp increase in level of task engagement; that is, the participants may have simply been too busy to make requests. Finally, as problem behavior decreased to negligible levels in maintenance, intensive intervention became less and less necessary. Thus, caregivers had fewer intervention demands over time, a factor that also contributed to the long-term feasibility of the approach.

Assessment

As noted earlier, the total assessment took approximately 36 hours per participant. The research literature, on the other hand, reported the use of formal functional analyses that often averaged only 10 to 15 min per session over a small number of sessions (Carr et al., 1997). At first glance, the present assessment may seem overly time consuming. However, functional analyses have typically been carried out in restricted contexts, often as simulations or analogs of natural contexts. Our assessment was multidimensional and involved a large number of problem situations across many intervention agents, settings, and tasks. (Our assessment produced over 100 index cards per participant.) Conducting a formal functional analysis for this many situations is neither feasible nor practical. There are rarely enough people who are trained to do functional analysis, and, in the present case, the need to do multiple analyses in many different situations further exacerbated the problems associated with insufficient expert personnel. Also, the amount of time required to conduct this many functional analyses would be prohibitive. With respect to feasibility, functional analysis requires that problem behavior be evoked repeatedly in order to identify functions unequivocally. Repeated evocation of problem behavior in community settings such as restaurants, supermarkets, and churches is unacceptable because it would provoke other community members to respond strongly and negatively due to fear and/or safety concerns.

We attempted to avoid the problems associated with doing formal functional analysis in the community by using the describe and categorize components of our assessment. Specifically, our assessment method did not involve the repeated evocation of problem behavior and, therefore, was socially acceptable to parents, teachers, and other caregivers. Further, the narrative method associated with the use of index cards could be used by typical members of the community because they did not need the special training required for functional analysis. In other words, the describe and categorize procedures are potentially feasible and practical.

The subjective and qualitative aspects of our assessment method pose some concerns for behavior analysts. Both the interview process and the judgments of the panel members during categorization were clearly subjective in nature. Although not subjective, the direct observation component substituted narrative accounts for quantifiable units and thus was qualitative in nature. Most important, however, subsequent analyses of quantitative data validated and supported the use of our assessment procedures. First, the baseline (verification) procedure generated high rates of problem behavior. As noted previously the baseline situations were derived exclusively from the describe and categorize assessment information; therefore the high rates of baseline problem behaviors confirm the accuracy and utility of this information. Second, most of the intervention components (e.g., FCT, choice, embedding) were based on hypotheses about function derived from our assessment. The fact that the intervention was successful suggests that the hypotheses were useful, and it further validates the utility of our assessment method.

Finally, it should be emphasized that the intensive nature of the initial assessment may reflect the fact that—in general—researchers have less experience investigating comprehensive community-based interventions than analog-style interventions. It is plausible that subsequent research may produce less time-consuming strategies. For example, the systematic assessment packages developed by O'Neill, Horner, Albin, Storey, and Sprague (1997) include several strategies for reducing time demands and enhancing the feasibility of community-based assessment. We should also note that the severity and ubiquitousness of problem behavior for the three participants in the present study may have necessitated a more intensive approach to assessment and intervention. Future research may establish that less effort is needed in the assessment and intervention of individuals exhibiting milder and/or more circumscribed problem behavior. In any case, in clinical practice, where experimental design is not an issue, it may be possible to assess the most problematic situations first and quickly initiate interventions in those situations. Once problem behavior has been reduced to acceptable levels, one may repeat the assessment and intervention protocol for less serious problem situations. In this manner, the demands of assessment would be spread out over a protracted period of time, thereby enhancing feasibility.

FUTURE DIRECTIONS

Carrying out an intervention across multiple community settings that involves natural support persons for protracted periods of time represents the ultimate challenge for current technology. The present study was conceived as a step in the direction of extending our technology to deal with this challenge. Our data raise issues in several different areas relevant for future research: assessment, intervention, outcomes, and measurement related to each of these.

Assessment Practices

Traditionally, the first step in remediating problem behavior involves a functional assessment of such behavior (Carr, 1994; Desrochers, Hile, & Williams-Moseley, 1997). Although this proved useful in the present study, the multicomponent intervention that was built upon it suggested that other assessment foci might also be worth pursuing as we extend applied research efforts into the community. Specifically, the use of rapport building, FCT, choice, and embedding draws attention to the importance of assessing the integrity of living environments and skill repertoires in addition to problem behavior per se. With respect to living environments, because an absence of social relationships or the presence of poor relationships can influence problem behavior, it would be useful to develop instruments that assess rapport. Similarly, low levels of choice are correlated with problem behavior; thus, global assessment instruments that measure the degree of choice and the number of options available in a living situation would likewise be useful. Finally, embedding is only one example of a shift in instructional strategies. More generally, because the quality of instruction can be an important determinant of problem behavior, a variety of assessment instruments that measure different dimensions of instruction (e.g., functionality of the curriculum; facets of instructional presentation such as prompting, pacing, variety, and motivation) would be useful. With respect to skill repertoires, low levels of communicative competence, social skills, and self-management abilities can be correlated with problem behavior; hence, assessment of these types of skills could be useful in subsequent intervention planning.

Clearly, the kinds of assessment we have described for living environments and skill repertoires require measurement practices that are different from those typically used at present. Rapport might be measured sociometrically (e.g., documentation of social preference hierarchies), which is a type of measurement that differs from traditional frequency or time sampling. Even problem behavior requires different types of assessment and measurement in the community. The narrative approach that we carried out was feasible because it did not rely on counting frequencies or time samples of dangerous behavior in public situations. Other forms of naturalistic assessment need to be developed to deal with the various situations that constitute community living.

In sum, because the types of interventions used in the present study were oriented toward changing aspects of living environments and enhancing skill repertoires, future work in assessment could profit from developing new instruments that from the outset measure the living environment quality and the skills that the person with disabilities has for coping with environmental challenges. This shift in assessment practices (from a focus on problem behavior to a focus on living environments and skill repertoires) would in turn produce a shift in intervention practices.

Intervention Practices

Traditionally, intervention has focused on problem behavior reduction per se. A central message of our study is that the scope of intervention needs to be expanded when working in the community. The ultimate goal is not to remediate problem behavior but to remediate problem contexts. Although extensive, Table 1 represents only a sample of all relevant problem contexts because as a person's life circumstances change over time, so will the array of relevant problem contexts. Best practice would demand intervention strategies that address all relevant contexts (Lutzker & Campbell, 1994; Singer & Irvin, 1989). This strategy contrasts with much traditional research in which the goal is to demonstrate definitive causal relationships within a restricted laboratory or analog situation.

The central issue for future research concerns the difference between *static* versus *dynamic* intervention plans. Presently, clinicians will sometimes put in place an intervention plan and modify it only when problem behavior recurs (static plan; Carr et al., 1997). Our research suggests the wisdom of constantly changing intervention plans, even in the absence of problem behavior, as new problem contexts are identified and old ones drop out (dynamic plan). What is needed is a set of guidelines for building dynamic intervention plans that reflect changing assessment information for relevant problem contexts. Clearly, one aspect of these guidelines would be to stress that intervention will almost always be multicomponent in nature. As noted, the unresolved question for the field pertains to how to identify and integrate the constituent elements of a multicomponent intervention.

A second implication of our study is that intervention would have no end point. Circumstances continually arise that produce new problem contexts. These in turn would require modification of the plan. Inevitably significant changes will occur in a person's living situation, and these changes will need to be addressed. In this sense, maintenance is programmed rather than hoped for. Thus, traditional issues related to the maintenance of intervention effects following intervention termination do not apply to our model because there is no termination point. With this perspective in mind, it becomes critical for researchers to develop a set of generic guidelines for building interventions that are sensitive to changes in living circumstances over long periods of time.

A third implication of our study is that problem behavior is best dealt with proactively. All of our interventions took place when problem behavior was not occurring (i.e., both the environmental reorganization and skill-building aspects of our intervention package were oriented toward making positive behaviors more probable, thereby undermining the need for future displays of problem behavior). Therefore, an important research priority for the future concerns the proactive assessment of environmental deficiencies (goodness-of-fit) and deficiencies in coping behaviors (skills) with a view to using this information to build strategies that effectively prevent the display of problem behavior (Albin, Lucyshyn, Horner, & Flannery, 1996).

A fourth study implication relates to the observation that the three individuals with whom we worked still required extensive support from others, even at the end of the study. For example, both FCT and embedding made time demands on parents and group home staff that might not be sustainable indefinitely. This issue pertains to autonomy and independence: We need to structure long-term interventions that permit the individual to achieve his or her goals and satisfy his or her needs without excessive dependence on others. This theme becomes especially important as individuals spend more time in the community, where close supervision and moment-to-moment programming are neither feasible nor normative.

Finally, the future research agenda that we have been outlining calls for the development of new methods of measurement. Frequency and time sampling, so prominent a feature of past research on problem behavior, are often not relevant for dealing with variables such as the ones we have described (Wahler & Fox, 1981). Documenting the salutary effects of environmental reorganization (e.g., changing schedules, matching roommates, building social relationships) may require measurement methods related to sociometrics, consumer satisfaction, and the like that do not lend themselves to traditional microanalytic measurement procedures.

Outcomes

The longitudinal nature of our data suggests two issues related to intervention outcomes that need to be considered: lifestyle change and life-span perspectives.

Lifestyle Change

As noted, traditionally, the main focus of intervention has been on the elimination or management of problem behavior per se. Many advocates and stakeholders have criticized this approach as being too narrow and have pointed out that reduction of problem behavior is only meaningful if it is accompanied by positive changes in the person's lifestyle (Risley, 1996; Turnbull & Ruef, 1997). These changes involve greater inclusion in the community and an improved ability to deal with difficult situations in home, school, and work settings. Our intervention approach documents the necessity of dealing with problem behavior in many different settings, across intervention agents, and across tasks. As a result, the individual's quality of life improves because he or she is now able to take advantage of many community activities. As it becomes clear that successful intervention requires the use of strategies that promote adaptation and integration in various integrated settings, future work will need to focus at the outset on the assessment of barriers to integration with a view to promoting those behaviors that lead to greater inclusion. The identification and measurement of these broader outcomes is one important future research priority. For example, direct and systematic measurement of the outcomes associated with Table 1 would be one important way of extending the research protocol described in the present study. Recent discussions in the literature (Turnbull, Friesen, & Ramirez, in press) pointed to (a) the importance of researchers and stakeholders collaborating in the identification of outcomes and (b) the centrality of stakeholder satisfaction ratings as a key outcome measure.

Life-Span Perspectives

During the 1.5- to 2.5-year maintenance period of the present study, it became clear that many changes occurred in each participant's life situation (e.g., residence, employment status, recreational opportunities). These changes necessitated additional assessments and modification of intervention strategies. Problems associated with transition over the life span (e.g., school to work, living with one's parents versus independent living) are a major concern of stakeholders (e.g., families, teachers) and have become a discussion focus in the literature (Turnbull & Turnbull, 1996). Ultimately, maintenance does not refer even to the time period of our study but, rather, to periods measured in decades as the individual progresses from childhood through adolescence and adulthood. This life-span perspective has become the new measure of maintenance and will require research into methods for identifying and achieving meaningful change over protracted periods of time. In support of this position, we should note that personal futures planning (Vandercook et al., 1989) is one innovation having to do with the identification of life-span goals. This type of identification method will need to drive the construction of systematic approaches for producing intervention strategies that are sensitive to an individual's needs at different stages of development.

ABOUT THE AUTHORS

Edward G. Carr, PhD, is a professor in the Department of Psychology at SUNY–Stony Brook and director of research and continuing education at the Developmental Disabilities Institute in Long Island, New York. His research interests include community integration, systems change, and problem behavior. Len Levin, PhD, is the director of support services at Alpine Learning Group (ALG), a center-based education program for students with autism. Dr. Levin coordinates ALG's supported inclusion program and family consultation services. He has also done extensive work in the area of food selectivity with children with autism. Gene McConnachie, PhD, works as a positive behavior support consultant and trainer for the State of Washington Division of Developmental Disabilities in the Seattle area. He also holds an adjunct faculty position in the Department of Psychiatry and Behavioral Sciences at the University of Washington's medical school. Jane I. Carlson, MA, is the inclusion coordinator at the Developmental Disabilities Institute in Smithtown, New York, and a research associate and doctoral candidate at SUNY–Stony Brook. Duane C. Kemp, PhD, is a coordinator of the Young Autism Program at the Developmental Disabilities Institute and is responsible for curriculum and staff development for preschool students with autism who are subsequently included in general education kindergarten programs. Christopher E. Smith, PhD, is the program coordinator for clinical services in the Children's Residential Program at the Developmental Disabilities Institute. Darlene Magito McLaughlin, MA, is the director of clinical services in the Adult Residential Division at the Developmental Disabilities Institute and is currently a research associate and doctoral candidate at SUNY–Stony Brook. Address: Edward G. Carr, Department of Psychology, State University of New York, Stony Brook, NY 11794–2500.

AUTHORS' NOTES

1. Preparation of this manuscript was supported in part by Grant Nos. G0087C0234 and H133B20004 from the National Institute on Disability and Rehabilitation Research.
2. We thank Joe Pancari, Denise Berotti, Karen Pierce, Julie Soriano, Tracey Vaiano, Sandi Diamond, Lisa Storey, and the members of "Gary's" family for helping to carry out the interventions and for collecting the data.

REFERENCES

Albin, R. W., Lucyshyn, J. M., Horner, R. H., & Flannery, K. B. (1996). Contextual fit for behavior support plans. In L. K. Koegel, R. L. Koegel, & G. Dunlap (Eds.), *Positive behavioral support: Including people with difficult behavior in the community* (pp. 81–98). Baltimore, MD: Brookes.

Bird, F., Dores, P. A., Moniz, D., & Robinson, J. (1989). Reducing severe aggressive and self-injurious behaviors with functional communication training. *American Journal on Mental Retardation, 94,* 37–48.

Carnine, D. (1997). Bridging the research-to-practice gap. *Exceptional Children, 63,* 513–521.

Carr, E. G. (1994). Emerging themes in the functional analysis of problem behavior. *Journal of Applied Behavior Analysis, 27,* 393–399.

Carr, E. G., & Carlson, J. I. (1993). Reduction of severe behavior problems in the community using a multicomponent treatment approach. *Journal of Applied Behavior Analysis, 26,* 157–172.

Carr, E. G., & Durand, V. M. (1985). Reducing behavior problems through functional communication training. *Journal of Applied Behavior Analysis, 18,* 111–126.

Carr, E. G., Horner, R. H., Turnbull, A. P., Marquis, J., Magito McLaughlin, D., McAtee, M. L. Smith, C. E., Anderson Ryan, K., Ruef, M. B., & Doolabh, A. (1997). *Positive behavior support as an approach for dealing with problem behavior in people with developmental disabilities: A research synthesis.* Manuscript submitted for publication.

Carr, E. G., Levin, L, McConnachie, G., Carlson, J. I., Kemp, D. C., & Smith, C. E. (1994). *Communication-based intervention for problem behavior. A user's guide for producing positive change.* Baltimore, MD: Brookes.

Carr, E. G., Newsom, C. D., & Binkoff, J. A. (1976). Stimulus control of self-destructive behavior in a psychotic child. *Journal of Abnormal Child Psychology, 4,* 139–153.

Carr, E. G., Robinson, S., Taylor, J. C., & Carlson, J. I. (Eds.). (1990). Positive approaches to the treatment of severe behavior problems in persons with developmental disabilities: A review and analysis of reinforcement and stimulus-based procedures. *Monograph of The Association for Persons with Severe Handicaps, 4.*

Desrochers, M. N., Hile, M. G., & Williams-Moseley, T. L. (1997). Survey of functional assessment procedures used with individuals who display mental retardation and severe problem behaviors. *American Journal on Mental Retardation, 101,* 535–546.

Didden, R., Duker, P. C., & Korzilius, H. (1997). Meta-analytic study on treatment effectiveness for problem behaviors with individuals who have mental retardation. *American Journal on Mental Retardation, 101,* 387–399.

Dunlap, G., dePerczel, M., Clarke, S., Wilson, D., Wright, S., White, R., & Gomez, A. (1994). Choice making and proactive behavioral support for students with emotional and behavioral challenges. *Journal of Applied Behavior Analysis, 27,* 505–518.

Dunlap, G., & Koegel, R. I., (1980). Motivating autistic children through stimulus variation. *Journal of Applied Behavior Analysis, 13,* 619–627.

Dyer, K., Dunlap, G., & Winterling, V. (1990). Effects of choice making on the serious problem behaviors of students with severe handicaps. *Journal of Applied Behavior Analysis, 23,* 515–524.

Gardner, W. I., & Sovner, R. (1994). *Self-injurious behavior.* Willow Street, PA: VIDA.

Horner, R. D., & Baer, D. M. (1978). Multiple-probe technique: A variation on the multiple baseline. *Journal of Applied Behavior Analysis, 11,* 189–196.

Horner, R. H. (1994). Functional assessment: Contribution and future directions. *Journal of Applied Behavior Analysis, 27,* 401–404.

Horner, R. H., Close, D. W., Fredericks, H. D. B., O'Neill, R. E., Albin, R. W., Sprague, J. R., Kennedy, C. H., Flannery, K. B., & Heathfield, L. T. (1996). Supported living for people with profound disabilities and severe problem behaviors. In D. H. Lehr & F. Brown (Eds.), *People with disabilities who challenge the system* (pp. 209–240). Baltimore, MD: Brookes.

Horner, R. H., & Day, H. M. (1991). The effects of response efficiency on functionally equivalent competing behaviors. *Journal of Applied Behavior Analysis, 24,* 719–732.

Kemp, D. C., & Carr, E. G. (1995). Reduction of severe problem behavior in community employment using an hypothesis-driven multicomponent intervention approach. *Journal of The Association for Persons with Severe Handicaps, 20,* 229–247.

Koegel, L. K., Koegel, R. I., & Dunlap, G. (Eds.). (1996). *Positive behavioral support: Including people with difficult behavior in the community.* Baltimore, MD: Brookes.

Lucyshyn, J. M., Olson, D., & Horner, R. H. (1995). Building an ecology of support: A case study of one woman with severe problem behaviors living in the community. *Journal of The Association for Persons with Severe Handicaps, 20,* 16–30.

Lutzker, J. R., & Campbell, R. V. (1994). *Ecobehavioral family interventions in developmental disabilities.* Pacific Grove, CA: Brooks/Cole.

Mace, F. C., Hock, M. L., Lalli, J. S., West, B. J., Belfiore, P., Pinter, E., & Brown, D. K. (1988). Behavioral momentum in the treatment of noncompliance. *Journal of Applied Behavior Analysis, 21,* 123–141.

Nickels, C. (1996). A gift from Alex—The art of belonging: Strategies for academic and social inclusion. In L. K. Koegel, R. L. Koegel, & G. Dunlap (Eds.), *Positive behavioral support: Including people with difficult behavior in the community* (pp. 123–144). Baltimore, MD: Brookes.

Northup, J., Wacker, D. P., Berg, W. K., Kelly, L., Sasso, G., & DeRaad, A. (1994). The treatment of severe behavior problems in school settings using a technical assistance model. *Journal of Applied Behavior Analysis, 27,* 33–47.

O'Neill, R. E., Horner, R. H., Albin, R. W., Storey, K., & Sprague, J. R. (1997). *Functional assessment and program development for problem behavior.* Pacific Grove, CA: Brooks/Cole.

Reichle, J., & Wacker, D. P. (1993). *Communicative alternatives to challenging behavior.* Baltimore, MD: Brookes.

Risley, T. (1996). Get a life! In L. K. Koegel, R. L. Koegel, & G. Dunlap (Eds.), *Positive behavioral support: Including people with difficult behavior in the community* (pp. 425–437). Baltimore, MD: Brookes.

Scotti, J. R., Ujcich, K. J., Weigle, K. L., Holland, C. M., & Kirk, K. S. (1996). Interventions with challenging behavior of persons with developmental disabilities: A review of current research practices. *Journal of The Association for Persons with Severe Handicaps, 21,* 123–134.

Singer, G. H. S., & Irvin, L. K. (Eds.) (1989). *Support for caregiving families.* Baltimore, MD: Brookes.

Stokes, T. F., & Baer, D. M. (1977). An implicit technology of generalization. *Journal of Applied Behavior Analysis, 10,* 349–367.

Turnbull, A. P., Friesen, B. J., & Ramirez, C. (in press). Participatory Action Research as a model of conducting family research. *Journal of The Association for Persons with Severe Handicaps.*

Turnbull, A. P., & Ruef, M. (1996). Family perspectives on problem behavior. *Mental Retardation, 34,* 280–293.

Turnbull, A. P., & Ruef, M. (1997). Family perspectives on inclusive lifestyle issues for people with problem behavior. *Exceptional Children, 63,* 211–227.

Turnbull, A. P., & Turnbull, H. R. (1996). Group action planning as a strategy for providing comprehensive family support. In L. K. Koegel, R. L. Koegel, & G. Dunlap (Eds.)

Positive behavior support: Including people with difficult behavior in the community (pp. 99–114). Baltimore, MD: Brookes.

Vandercook, T., York, J., & Forest, M. (1989). The McGill action planning systems (MAPS): A strategy for building the vision. *Journal of The Association for Persons with Severe Handicaps, 14,* 205–215.

Wahler, R. G., & Fox, J. J. (1981). Setting events in applied behavior analysis: Toward a conceptual and methodological expansion. *Journal of Applied Behavior Analysis, 14,* 327–338.

PERSPECTIVE 1: POSTPOSITIVISM ON THE CARR ET AL. STUDY

D. C. PHILLIPS   *Stanford University*

I have mixed feelings about both this paper and the study it reports (sometimes the two do not need to be distinguished, but I think that here they do). The paper itself is not well written, in that no clear overview of the study is presented; who did what, to whom, is difficult to fathom; and the purpose of the study is not clearly stated at the outset. A reader has to struggle to piece together what was done, and why. Indeed, the "Abstract" gives one version of what the study is about, in which the expression "external validity" does not appear; yet the opening section is cast in terms of the need to establish external validity. Muddying the waters further, the closing short paragraph of the opening section makes the incautious suggestion that the study is a "controlled research study," where the key term here is being used in at best a loose and nontechnical way. Last, but surely not least, the actual study has some flaws. Nevertheless, the paper (and the study it reports) is useful because it exemplifies a type of work that from time-to-time is found in education—the extended field trial or intervention study—which is important as a genre of scientific inquiry but which faces some daunting difficulties by way of execution.

There is an everpresent temptation to think of randomized, controlled ("true") experiments as setting the standard for rigor and usefulness in educational research, and to believe that other research genres are more defective the more they depart from this standard. Clearly, however, this is a serious mistake; there are many important types of study that have little in common with true experiments, and which can with sufficient care and effort be conducted rigorously so as to produce interpretable—and warranted—results. This being acknowledged, however, there are certain aspects of this present study (which purports to be an "experiment") that could have been greatly strengthened by paying more attention to the tenets of experimental design— apart from not being randomized (in this case not a fatal shortcoming), there was no control group and the treatment (and the deliverers of it) seem to have varied over time. The result is— as it often is when the logic behind the design of a study has been compromised—that the findings are hard if not impossible to interpret. This is not the place to write a monograph on the topic of research design, so my points will need to be somewhat truncated.

1. The discussion needs to start with a description of what seems to have been done in this study (omitting, of course, some nuance). Basically it ran as follows: Three subjects or patients, evidently individuals with severe behavior disorders who lived in group home settings, were selected, using five screening criteria. Over some weeks, their behavior was monitored and the baseline frequency of their problematic behaviors was established, and other documentation secured. Then a multipart, and hence quite complex, intervention was mounted over a number of years

(on my reading there was some inconsistency in reporting the timeline). It was not absolutely clear who carried out this intervention, but it seems that a number of people probably were involved—the parents/caregivers, together perhaps with the researchers themselves, and perhaps also the teachers. (The fact that all this information is not clearly presented is another reason for saying the paper is defective when considered as a scientific document.) Finally, and after a considerable period of time, the degree of change in behavior was assessed; independent but experienced raters scored two short videos of each of the three subjects/patients—one taken during the baseline period and one taken after treatment and maintenance, without the raters knowing which was which. The conclusion was that in all three cases the problem behaviors of the subjects/patients had greatly decreased (the frequency of such behaviors was much lower in the last video than in the first), supposedly establishing the effectiveness of the treatment; in their discussion the authors also state that the study shows that the ultimate goal is not to remediate problem behaviors but to remediate the problem contexts in which this behavior occurs.

2. As was suggested earlier, this genre of study is important in education, especially in the evaluation of educational programs or treatments: a curriculum unit (the treatment) is devised; baseline measurements are taken on a group of students who are then subjected to the curriculum; after which they are assessed again. However, like all research, this type faces a number of *threats to its validity*—these are problems, or potential problems, that arise either from features inherent in the design itself or in its mode of execution that will threaten the validity of the conclusions that are drawn from the study unless the researchers have taken steps to avoid or to nullify them. (One can say that strong research will always have tried to anticipate potential challenges at the outset!) It is instructive to look at some of these.

First, if a program/treatment extends over a considerable time, many things will happen to the students (subjects) involved which makes it difficult to be certain that any changes in behavior that were noted at the end were due solely to the program—life rolls on, and the subjects were all experiencing many other educational inputs, reinforcements, punishments, intellectual stimulus, medical treatment, and so on. Only if a control group is used, which differs from the experimental group *solely in one dimension* (the experimental group gets the treatment, the control doesn't, but otherwise they are treated identically), can we be sure that any difference noted at the end of the study between the control and the experimental groups has been caused by the treatment or program. The control group also allows us to ascertain if developmental or maturational effects were present (this is especially important if the study, as in this case, extends over several years)—people change over time, so the final result might reflect age-related change as much as, or more than, program-related change. In short, a control group is an excellent way of disarming certain threats to validity inherent in this important type of study.

3. There is another important threat to validity that operates here. Technically, the individuals who deliver (teach) a program are part of the treatment, so if there are changes in the members of staff over time (as there almost invariably will be over an extended time period), it will be difficult to disambiguate effects due to the program from effects due to characteristics and actions of the staff. Ideally, an experimental study should have the same individuals delivering the program to the treatment groups and also working with the control groups which, apart from the specified treatment, they would otherwise treat exactly the same. Again, it is a defect of the paper that it gives no information about the staff of the program, and about the degree of changes over time. (The fuller technical report on the program might contain this kind of information, but it should also have been summarized here so that readers could assess the causal claims that are made about the program in this paper.)

4. There is a more subtle threat: In any study in which the effectiveness of a treatment is a major object of attention, it is important that steps be taken to monitor that, in fact, the individuals who are supposed to be delivering the program actually do so, and to document what idiosyncratic changes have been introduced. For it is well-known that teachers often "repair" a treatment by altering it in the light of their own classroom experience with it, and in light of their own intellectual and pedagogical preferences; such deviations from the program or treatment as initially designed are likely to be quite major if the program runs over an extended time period. Why is this important? Simply because, if the treatment has undergone change in the hands of the different individuals who are delivering it to the students, then researchers will not be in a position to say precisely what was responsible for any positive results that were achieved—they will not be able to face policy makers and honestly recommend that *the* program be widely used, for it is not known what *the* program actually is!

In short, because the threats to the validity of this study were not adequately addressed and minimized, the authors were not logically entitled to conclude that "our study showed the intervention package to be effective and feasible"; perhaps the changes that took place in the behavior of the three subjects over the course of a number of years had little, or nothing, to do with the actual "program" that the researchers believed they had instituted at the outset of the study. Nor were the authors able, on the basis of the evidence they presented here, to claim that the aim of intervention should be to remediate contexts rather than individuals, for they did not systematically study different contexts and the effectiveness of changing them! (The design of a project aimed at studying contexts of programs will be different from the design of projects aimed at determining the effectiveness of the interventions.)

PERSPECTIVE 2: PRAGMATISM ON THE CARR ET AL. STUDY

NEL NODDINGS   *Stanford University*

This study exhibits many signs associated with the best social research—carefully defined terms, lengthy periods of observation, validated categories, hypothesis-driven interventions, and well-documented results. That said, some serious concerns arise, not all of them under the authors' control.

We notice, first, that the participants who displayed problem behavior have remarkably low IQ scores. There was a time, not that long ago, when it would have been unthinkable to prepare people with IQ's of 30 and below for anything like full community living. Reasonable people today may be torn between admiration for the attempt and genuine concern for the stress such training induces in both trainees and their caretakers. Indeed, one of the obvious issues in this study is the question: Who is being trained? It is not at all clear that any of the three men would be capable of sustaining their improved behavior in a setting where they would have to communicate with untrained caregivers or fellow workers.

This observation—that it is caregivers who were really trained—is not necessarily a fault of the study. People who, by choice or circumstance, must live in close contact with severely handicapped persons need help, and a comprehensive intervention aimed at helping them to cope might be welcomed. But the authors are not entirely clear about who benefits most and in what ways. They note that "the three individuals with whom we worked still required extensive support from others, even at the end of the study." (p. 111). With that comment, they go on to recommend the formulation of long-term interventions that will increase the autonomy and independence of their subjects.

Is this goal feasible? Thoughtful people may feel conflict over this. On the one hand, we abhor the idea of categorizing people and then consigning them to a form of living prescribed rigidly for their category. The horror of mistaken categorization is only one reason to hesitate in limiting what we do for people who exhibit various problems. On the other hand, the lives and well being of caregivers must be considered. Thousands of parents have sacrificed their own goals (and sometimes those of healthy siblings as well) in order to care for severely handicapped children into adulthood and middle age (Hallum, 1989; Sommers & Shields, 1987). For these people, it might be reasonable to accept some limitations—even enlightened institutionalization—for their children. It is too easy for experts who do not have to live with the situation to urge such parents to "keep trying," "push the boundaries," "reject the limitations."

An alternative to pushing for autonomy and independence for the severely handicapped is to concentrate on the training of caregivers and, insofar as possible, to reduce the strain on their daily lives. This may imply accepting limitations on the participation of the mentally handicapped in community life. It is not necessary, however, to choose one goal or the other. A balanced program should declare its emphasis and help caregivers understand that, if their own well being is emphasized, it is still possible to facilitate the growth of their loved ones. However, failure to overcome the immense difficulties described in this study should not cause caregivers to feel guilty. They are doing a heroic task and need help, not blame.

Although the researchers do not mention it, a conflict seems evident in their methods and discussion. As noted above, they express concern for the autonomy of their handicapped subjects. But, paradoxically, in the verification stage of their study, they actually manipulated situations to bring about problem behaviors. Ethical researchers would not treat "autonomous" subjects this way. On the contrary, subjects are usually asked to give informed consent to the studies in which they participate. Even in the rare cases where an IRB approves research involving deception, researchers are expected to debrief participants and explain the purposes of any deception or manipulation. This was not even a possibility in this study, and that makes talk of autonomy little more than a nod to political correctness. The researchers are thus caught between an ideal (autonomy) that will probably never be accessible to their research subjects and the need to take advantage of their unhappy condition to proceed with the research. Many of us are uncomfortable with methods that manipulate the near-helpless and would much prefer an extended period of naturalistic observation.

Another ethical question arises in the handling of Gary's screaming (p. 98). It may well have been effective to ignore his screaming and even ethically right to do so inasmuch as the method did control his self-injury and made life less difficult for both Gary and his mother. Pragmatists are always concerned with effects, and these positive effects are important. However, generalizing from this incident might be dangerous. There are times when crying or other demands for attention should be met promptly—especially if the goal is greater independence. In the past, behaviorists often advised parents to ignore their infants' crying (after checking to be sure that nothing was obviously wrong) because, they said, responding to such crying would "reinforce" the crying behavior. However, it is not at all clear what is being reinforced when parents respond quickly and cheerfully to a baby's crying. Perhaps it is the child's sense of having some control over its own life that is reinforced. (Notice that a behaviorist might reject this claim on the grounds that such a "sense" is not a behavior and, thus, cannot be reinforced.) Nevertheless, many of us now advise parents to respond quickly and consistently. This does not seem to produce more crying; in fact, it reduces the crying and encourages more relaxed interactions.

Ignoring cries for attention *can* have the effect of reducing such demands, but sometimes a reduction in communicative requests means that the subject has simply given up. Thus, far from becoming more autonomous, the subject has become more apathetic. Such an effect is not unusual in babies who are ignored. We do not know, then, how to interpret the reported reduction in communicative requests. The researchers suggest that the reduction might be a result of increased engagement in tasks, and they present some evidence for this possibility. They may well be right, but other researchers should not automatically assume that a reduction in requests is an unqualified good.

A pragmatic view looks at consequences. In this case, we have to consider not only the study before us but also the whole way of thinking in which the study is embedded. It is a positive sign that our society is now deeply concerned about the growth and welfare of those once considered hopelessly defective. We look for positive effects. But sometimes the goals we hold for the healthy majority may not be suitable for the severely handicapped. Then, we serve neither their best interests nor that of their caregivers by pushing for an impossible ideal.

REFERENCES

Hallum, A. (1989). *An exploratory study of the impact on parents of caring for a physically dependent, severely disabled adult-aged child at home.* Unpublished dissertation, Stanford University.

Sommers, T., & Shields, L. (1987). *Women take care.* Gainesville, FL: Triad.

PERSPECTIVE 3: CONSTRUCTIVISM ON THE CARR ET AL. STUDY

YVONNA S. LINCOLN   *Texas A&M University*

From the perspective of a constructivist, this is a particularly interesting case of research. It catches the interest because while its concerns are frequently positivist—e.g., external validity, generalization, internal validity—and its manner of reporting is exemplary of the technocratic discourse of conventional science—e.g., interventions, problem behavior reduction, discriminative stimuli, and the like—it nevertheless embodies elements of what I choose to call "pre-science." I define pre-science as qualitative inquiry performed in order to "ground" later, more experimental, work (but which I earlier called the "muddy boots syndrome" see Guba & Lincoln, 1981; Lincoln & Guba, 1985). Deep, intensive observations were conducted for three participants in order to discover categories of behaviors which might be amenable to interventions, and after careful analysis of the disruptive behaviors, interventions were designed, taught to caretakers, including parents, group home staff, and others, and then observed for their effects, including the interventions' ability to maintain the desired behavior over a long period of time. One key criterion for the usefulness of the intervention was its practicality and its usability by a wide variety of caretaking stakeholders.

The study likewise violates the common wisdom surrounding most conventional positivist studies in that it was not a short-term, one-shot inquiry. Rather, it unfolded over 5 years (in much the same way as the Heath ethnographic study did), with ongoing observations, and reports from caretakers and other staff. During that time, caretakers were taught techniques for coping with the disruptive behavior of their children/charges, the techniques tried and refined, and the results of interventions carefully observed and recorded.

Two things strike one about this study. First, its discourse and language seem to point to non-constructivist approaches to inquiry. The technocracy of control appears to be at work throughout the intervention stages of the research, and most certainly, one purpose of the research was to control disruptive, dysfunctional, aggressive, and self-injury forms of behavior from several disabled participants. But by the same token, the approach, which appears Pavlovian on its surface, is far more *gestalt*-oriented than it would appear from a first reading. The authors are clearly attempting to change the realities faced by caretakers into realities which are more practical, useful, and functional. Constructivists are first and foremost concerned with the meaning-making activities of research participants, and therefore are deeply concerned with the social realities constructed by various social actors as they attempt to make sense of events, situations, other persons, activities, and communications. With a focus on the lived experiences (and realities) of both participants and caretakers, the study's emphasis is decidedly more phenomenological and praxis-oriented than the typical scientific (positivist) study.

The second thing which strikes the reader, however, was the particularly qualitative way in which the behavioral changes were approached. Rather than simply designing interventions and passing them on to caretakers, the researchers apparently worked with caretakers as *stakeholders* in the process, and continued to do so over a long period of time. In this sense, the research itself took on an action research tone. This level of involvement itself would—in other language, in another journal—have been seen as compromising the study, because of its threat to "objectivity" and the usual distance required for objective scientific study to occur.

Constructivists would also point to the rather explicit role of values in this study, particularly those values which aimed at less aggression from participants, more rapport between caretakers and participants, and enhanced communication skills. While a variety of outcomes might have been chosen, the particular goals chosen for this study seem, at some meta-analytic level, to be less "interventionist" and more aimed at fuller human functioning—a decidedly "liberal" or humanistic set of goals.

None of these worthwhile aspects of the study should deflect the criticisms which one might wish to mount concerning the extent to which induced behavioral changes were considered, quite classically, interventions, or the extent to which the overall emphasis of the research itself was behavior modification. The moving shadows of Skinner's pigeons reflect in different phases of this research. The research, however, cannot escape its decidedly stakeholder-focused emphases, its desire for improved communication and human functioning, and its projected results of better caretaker strategies and diminished numbers of disruptive social behaviors leading to isolation of the participants.

At another level, as technocratic as the discourse of this piece is, it would be easy to miss what has happened here. The researchers, under the guise of a carefully controlled "experiment" which aims for high generalizability, has succeeded in teaching parents and other significant caretakers good parenting skills. What has occurred is that parents and caretakers have acquired new strategies and practiced skills for rapport-building, for increasing communication skills with the participant, for creating the conditions for delayed gratification, for providing choices which lend each of the case participants options and agency, and for what they call "embedding"—surrounding stimuli from which the participant might wish to escape with stimuli toward which the participant is drawn (what we might understand as, "You cannot go out to play with your friends until your bed is made and the trash is taken out to the garbage cans"). These are all skills which high-functioning parents either have or acquire with experience; that they are treated as scientific interventions, and proposed in the language of control and experimentation, is somewhat charming and amusing.

More than amusing, it suggests that at least some of the research undertaken is published under the guise of scientific writing, but which is much less wed to certainty, to objectivity, or to other classical criteria. Even the discussion of generalization which frames the early and last portions of the piece refer to the practicality and usefulness of the strategies by a wide range of stakeholders and parents. As a consequence, this article might be "read" at two levels. At its most superficial, it is a classical positivist, non-constructivist experiment—which just happened to go on a long time, rather than being more time-circumscribed. At a deeper level, however, it is clearly a "transitional" piece of work—in transit between positivist criteria for a study, and genuinely constructivist foci on multiple realities, the alteration of realities, deep observational techniques, and other characteristics which would, in another journal, make it look nearly as phenomenological as it looks experimental and behaviorist.

It makes one begin to wonder just how many other studies such as this—studies which borrow from several different paradigms and from multiple and mixed methods—might be safely hiding in journals which never would have published the pieces had they recognized the dual messages they contained.

REFERENCES

Guba, E. G., & Lincoln, Y. S. (1981). *Effective evaluation.* San Francisco: Jossey-Bass Publishers.

Heath, S. B. (1982). Questioning at home and at school: A comparative study. In G. Spindler (Ed.), *Doing the ethnography of schooling: Education anthropology in action.* Prospect Heights, IL: Waveland Press. pp. 103–127.

Lincoln, Y. S., & Guba, E. G. (1985). *Naturalistic inquiry.* Thousand Oaks, CA: Sage Publications.

PERSPECTIVE 4: INTERPRETIVE AND NARRATIVE ON THE CARR ET AL. STUDY

ARTHUR P. BOCHNER   *University of South Florida*

Interpretive social science shifts the focus of inquiry from objects to meanings. As Charles Taylor (1977) observes, "interpretation . . . is an attempt to make clear, to make sense of an object of study." This shift draws attention to the question of how *people* make sense of their lives as well as what sense they make of them. I emphasize people because we don't normally talk about objects such as rocks or tables as "making sense." If we are going to address meanings, we need a subject for whom these meanings matter; that is, meaning is for a subject, often a particular subject, sometimes a group of subjects. To say that people "make sense" or "have meanings" is to acknowledge the subjective quality of sense-making.

Empiricism, on the other hand, is a theory of knowledge and a body of research practices that attempts to reach beyond subjectivity by emphasizing objectivity, value-neutrality, and intersubjective verifiability. These terms impose certain constraints on inquiry. First, reality is assumed to be independent of the observer and accessible to observations. The objects of observation, therefore, must be treated as things that stand apart from the observer, real things that are likely to remain stable and invariant. Second, facts are presumed to be separable from values. A high priority is assigned to the goal of producing unbiased and verifiable facts. Theory is supposed to mirror or reflect facts, so there must be some assurance that facts have not been prejudiced by the investigator's beliefs or values. Third, claims to knowledge are judged by public deliberation. What counts as knowledge should be publicly decidable. Thus, research procedures and results must be replicable. In short, for empiricists the scientific discovery of truth requires an *objective* method by which the mind can construct accurate representations of nature—truth through method.

One of the major consequences of the empiricist theory of knowledge is *disengagement*. The investigator stands apart from rather than being a part of what is observed. To the empiricist, it makes no practical difference whether we are observing people or rocks. Whenever an objectifying stance is taken, the investigator exerts instrumental control, neutralizing (or controlling) any influence the observed can have on the observer. Empiricists are righteously committed to keeping their distance in order to preserve their objectivity. They believe that disengagement provides the control necessary to carry out the procedures through which knowledge is attained, which they view as the surest road to truth.

Interpretivists do not believe such neutrality is possible. Though we grant that the world view of empiricism promotes a language of neutrality, we believe we can show that terms which appear on the surface to be neutral actually are permeated by values. Thus, when I look at the study conducted by Carr et al., I see a system of meanings that create and promote certain values. I think of these researchers as storytellers and of their research as a story about the problem behavior of three disabled persons, the caretakers, *and the researchers* who engage and connect with them. As storytellers, Carr et al. tell their story to a particular audience (other developmental disability researchers; colleagues; grant agencies) for a particular reason (to increase their standing in the field; to provide new "knowledge" for scholars and practitioners). As a story, the research tale has a plot; and there also is a moral to their story. We can (and should) ask, what's the point? What's the moral to the story?

To be fair, the *narrative/interpretive* perspective I am applying was not what Carr et al. had in mind when they conducted, analyzed, and published this study. Obviously, they see themselves as scientists not storytellers, and they make it clear that they want their work to be judged by such criteria as its rigor, (external) validity, generalizability, replicability, and so on. To the extent that we accept empiricism as our model or standard of judgment, the legitimate grounds for critique are methodological not moral.

As an interpretivist, however, I do not subscribe to the empiricist ideal of a detached observer using neutral language to produce an unmediated mirroring of reality. Rather I see empiricism as a perspective that, like all other perspectives, creates values and inscribes meanings. Empiricism can be especially useful when one's objective is to assess predictions as Carr and his colleagues have done. By rigorously following certain procedures and establishing certain safeguards, one can produce conclusions about the efficacy of one's predictions. Thus, as Carr et al. show, empiricism can be applied usefully to questions on the order of "if we systematically intervene in x ways, can we expect (predict) that y behaviors will result?" Carr and his colleagues show convincingly that when certain interventions are reliably and systematically introduced, problem behaviors can be managed effectively and, in some cases, entirely eliminated. But what empiricism cannot do is tell us whether this is a good thing, whether this is how caretakers *should* act, or whether the outcomes they measure are the ones that *should* be desired.

Empiricists like to say that their work is *value-free,* the implication being that they can only say what is, not what should be. The rub is that all research studies must inevitably be formulated in language. Unfortunately, the terms by which empiricists represent what they see are not the same "thing" as the reality these words represent. Language mediates all attempts to represent reality. In short, the world does not exist in the shape of the sentences we write when we represent or theorize about it (Rorty, 1989). No matter how hard they try not to, Carr et al. must use terms that influence and shape their readers' beliefs and feelings about the world these words represent including the people in it. If we don't interrogate the language used by Carr and his colleagues, we run the risk of tacitly endorsing the *values* that they promote by subjecting these interventions and behaviors to empirical observation and representation in language.

For example, Carr et al. never consider that what may seem good for the caretakers may not be good for the disabled persons for whom they care. Nor do they consider the possibility that their "intervention package" could ultimately become an instrument for domination, a method for controlling and sublimating the desires and emotions of disabled persons. Yet the plot that unfolds in the telling of their research makes this not only possible but likely. Once we have these tools of control—an effective "intervention package"—isn't it likely we will use them? Don't we need to decide, then, whether such a package will do good or do harm and to whom? And isn't this a moral question, one that can't simply be skirted by appeals to neutrality and objectivity? To the extent you see these questions as important issues to address in any research in education, you will agree that it is crucial to look at Carr et al.'s research not merely as an exemplar of technical knowledge but also as a site of moral responsibility.

Let us see what happens when we interrogate some of the language Carr et al. use in order to decide what sorts of values they are inscribing; in other words, as a site of moral responsibility. Did you find it odd (I did) that Carr et al. referred to parents, teachers, and job coaches as **stakeholders?** The term "stakeholder" *is* a gambling metaphor that refers to people who hold money bet by others and then pay it to the winners. A stakeholder usually is a neutral person—someone who merely holds the stake until the outcome of the wager is determined. But these parents and teachers certainly aren't neutral. Thus Carr et al. appear to have appropriated a term from one context and applied it to a different context in which its intended meaning appears to be quite different. Yet it is quite useful to understand how these different contextual meanings may overlap. Carr et al.'s usage of *stakeholder* gives us a hint about how they feel about the persons to whom they apply this term. They empathize with the stakeholders, conceiving them as people who have a lot to lose, who are taking a gamble, risking something valuable. Indeed, the entire study revolves around what the stakeholders want, e.g., interventions that produce lifestyle changes and long-term behavior change that will make their caretaking less of a burden.

The participants in this study are Val, Gary, and Juan, three individuals who display, according to the researchers, a wide range of severe "problem behaviors." The goal of the research is to produce "an intervention package" that can reduce the severity of the participants' problem behavior, making them less dangerous and producing positive lifestyle changes (p. 108). One of the measures of success for Carr et al. is that the stakeholders "should" eventually have fewer intervention demands over time. The goal is to have the participants become less of a burden to their caretakers, in Carr et al.'s words, to not dominate the time of their caretakers and relatives. The more independent the participants become the more the stakeholders win. The stakeholders thus get what they want—a measure of freedom from the perceived burden of caretaking.

But in gambling—to extend the metaphor—there always are winners and losers. We need to ask at whose expense the stakeholders become winners. Carr et al. have a clear and well-documented sense of what the stakeholders want and what it may take to make them winners. I'm afraid the same cannot be said, however, for the view they hold of the participants. Carr et al. begin their paper by describing in detail what the stakeholders want, but they never consider what the participants want (except to identify pleasures—listening to music, watching TV, going for a walk—that can be introduced into the reinforcement schedule as instruments of control). Indeed, as I read this paper, I ached over the neglect that was shown for the desires of Val, Gary, and Juan. Don't they have a lot to gain or lose, too? Why aren't they considered *stakeholders?* How would things be different if Carr et al. considered Val, Gary, and Juan to be the stakeholders, and the caretakers, relatives, and job coaches to be the participants. By not considering what is at stake for Val, Gary, and Juan—what *they* really want, not what the caretakers want them to want—Carr et al. seem to contribute unwittingly to the stigmatization of disabled persons. Apparently, Carr et al. do not construe Val, Gary, and Juan as capable of possessing the kind of subjectivity or power to have a stake. By using the metaphor of a stakeholder to refer to one party but not the other, Carr et al. suggest that it is the parents and the other stakeholders—not Val, Gary, and Juan—who suffer from problem behavior. But what about Val, Gary, and Juan? Do their disabilities make them less than human? Aren't they capable of suffering? Of having something at stake? Or are these participants only the chips to be moved around the board until the stakeholders get what they want. The way the cards have been shuffled by Carr et al., it is unlikely that we will ever turn up an understanding of what it feels like to be as dependent as Val, Gary, and Juan, what it means to be only an object of another more powerful person's desires and "strategies," or what they want out of life. The kind of social engineering that is tacitly promoted in this work, however unwittingly, equates the problem behavior of these disabled human beings with those of pigeons and rats. While we can appreciate the humility of these researchers, we need to question whether the stance they take may create conditions under which cruelty can be exercised in the name of science.

Carr et al.'s study tells a story that teaches how to predict and control the behavior of disabled persons. They do not try to understand their participants or to make sense of how they live in the world. When the goal of their project of social engineering is achieved, that is, when Val, Gary, and Juan have become like everyone else, at least insofar as they can enact prosocial behavior, then the project appears to be finished. The disabled participants are now less of a problem for the rest of us. But does this mean that we now want to get to know them better? Does it mean that we will form closer bonds with them? Will they be more loved, respected, adored, or understood by us?

Carr et al. never ask, what do Val, Gary, and Juan's problem behaviors mean? In the terms of interpretivism, Val, Gary, and Juan have no voice in this research. They do not speak; they are not developed as characters; they have no agency. The researchers aren't concerned about how Val, Gary, and Juan put together their world or about what sense they make of it. Nor are they concerned with achieving a deeper understanding of what aggressive behaviors, self-mutilation, and temper tantrums could mean. What are Val, Gary, and Juan communicating when they act this way? Carr et al. take for granted that such behaviors are not functional and therefore need to be changed. But how do we judge functionality in this context? Functional for whom? Is fitting into a community that stigmatizes disability what Val, Gary, and Juan want? Will it change the force and feeling associated with their stigmatization? Isn't it possible that their "problem behaviors" are an expression of the rage they feel, a response to how they see others seeing them? Couldn't these behaviors tell us something important about the humiliation they may feel? When they mutilate themselves, isn't it possible they are acting out what they perceive others to be doing to them, that is, how they see others acting toward them? When I finished this article I was convinced that the participants had become more manageable and compliant, but I was not convinced that Val, Gary, and Juan were better understood, more satisfied, more interesting, more appealing, more genuinely communicative, or more loveable.

In the context of psychoanalysis, Adam Phillips (1998) says that knowledge should not be promoted as a consolation prize for injustice. Carr et al. make claims to knowledge that seem on the surface impressive and innocent. After 6 years of hard work, and an immense commitment of resources, time, and energy, what do these researchers have to show for it? What we are told—at least what I hear—is a story about stakeholders who have won some release from the emotional burden of caretaking and participants who have been bullied into what the stakeholders believe to be their proper place in the community. But isn't it possible that under a different set of conditions, the caretakers would trade this freedom for a better understanding and appreciation of how exasperating, how frustrating, and how humiliating the experience of being a stigmatized, disabled person can be, especially when your caretaker is trying so hard to be freer from you? What if these researchers expended the same effort to help the stakeholders understand that caretaking was not a burden but a gift. This would be a different story, a different kind of literature, as Phillips (1998) observes, something more like a poem than an intervention manual.

I felt angry when I was reading this paper and when I was trying to turn these feelings into a constructive response to this project. I had to ask myself, what was the source of my anger? I'm not sure, but I think I was reacting to the parts of myself that I don't accept and don't like that much, the parts that have done research that benefited certain groups at the expense of other groups; the parts that conformed to standards of rigor and excellence that gained me a certain status as a social scientist in the eyes of my colleagues, but did not require me to show empathy for the people I was studying; the parts that willingly appropriated data from well-meaning participants for the good of my career but not necessarily for the betterment of their lives; and the parts that convinced me I was only manipulating variables, I wasn't manipulating people.

One of the morals of my story is that we always project parts of ourselves—good and bad—onto the worlds we observe, engage in, and write about. Carr and his colleagues choose not to disclose their self-interests or to let us in on the personal stakes that bring them to research on developmental disabilities. Perhaps they believe that such candor would disqualify them as serious scientists. As an interpretivist, however, I believe it is important to conjure up the emotional and personal investments that connect us to our projects and to make ourselves vulnerable in order to achieve a more complete sense of honesty and integrity in our work. None of us is innocent. As Michael Jackson (1989, p. 17) put it, "our understanding of others can only proceed from within our own experience . . . " If we are to tell meaningful stories, we need to make our own lives and self-interests more evident to our audiences. Some empiricists—presumably Carr and his colleagues—may still see social engineering as a moral exemplar of the best that rationality and method can offer, but most of us recognize that the haunting question of how to live a good and ethical life cannot be circumscribed by appeals to hard facts and objective methods.

REFERENCES

Jackson, M. (1989). *Paths toward a clearing: Radical empiricism and ethnographic inquiry*. Bloomington, IN: Indiana University Press.

Phillips, A. (1998). *The beast in the nursery: On curiosity and other appetites*. New York: Pantheon Books.

Rorty, R. (1989). Contingency, irony, and solidarity. New York: Cambridge University Press.

Taylor, C. (1977). Interpretation of the Sciences of Man. In F. Dallmayr and T. McCarthy (Eds.), *Understanding and social injury*. Notre Dame, IN: Notre Dame University Press. pp. 101–131

PERSPECTIVE 6: RACE, ETHNICITY, AND GENDER ON THE CARR ET AL. STUDY

BETH HARRY   *University of Miami*

This research report is exemplary in its adherence to the basic tenets of applied behavioral analysis. The focus on external validity is admirable when we consider that the main criticism of this genre of research has been its inability to transfer to real life. Thus, the goals of testing an intervention that is practical and relevant, and that targets comprehensive life style change as well as long term behavioral change, is more than welcome in the field. Further to the purpose of practicality and relevance, the researchers used a naturalistic approach to determine the situations described as problematic by primary caregivers.

A key premise of behavioral analysis, however, places its mark indelibly on the research report. This premise holds that human behavior is determined not by individual identities or internal motives, but by the consequences contingent upon behavior. If the consequences of an action are valued by the individual, these consequences will reinforce the behavior, ensuring repetition. This holds regardless of the identity of the actor. In this genre, therefore, it is not important to report the race/ethnicity or gender of the "subjects." Accordingly, this report presents its subjects as human automatons who need to only be prompted, cued, supported, and reinforced in predetermined ways in order to gain the desired behavioral outcomes. We leave the study with no idea of who the three individuals are. Their individual identities do not seem to play any part in the planning or implementation of the intervention, despite the assumption that their behavior is functional, and represent attempts to gain particular outcomes.

Many questions arise regarding these issues: While the researchers display a concern for the social environments of the study participants, there is no mention of whether their ethnicity or gender played a role in the types of activities that they enjoyed and that might have been reinforcing to them. Would some consideration of these aspects of identity have made a difference either to the sorts of reinforcers used, or to the likelihood of the participants' maintaining learned behaviors? Would the gender or ethnicity of the personnel working with them be an important factor for any of these individuals? Could practitioners not learn important lessons by knowing how issues of personal identity might affect the planning of such an intervention?

I believe that a critical perspective on this piece would invoke concerns about the role of power in this kind of research. As a special educator who has worked closely with individuals with the kinds of disabilities and behaviors depicted in this study, I do not necessarily take that critical stance. While acknowledging that there is the potential for undue exertion of power over the lives of these individuals, I also know that, for family members of such individuals, practical issues of how to maintain order in their lives must often take precedence over the ethics of autonomy and personal control. As a mother who has had to face issues of both disability and mental illness, I know that individuals inflicted with these conditions may not, at points in their lives, be capable of making decisions that, under normal circumstances, should be their right. The truth is that, in such circumstances, life and its accustomed rights are not normal.

As a special educator and a mother I appreciate the power of applied behavioral analysis to make important and needed changes in the behavior of individuals like Gary, Juan, and Val. I also believe, however, that the lens of the applied behavioral analyst is too narrow and that a broader perspective on the overall life course of such individuals, and a deeper understanding of the factors that comprise their identities, would allow for even more powerful interventions. A study by Berkman & Meyer (1988), in which self-determination was the focus of a successful behavioral intervention, made the point forcibly that behavior is, indeed, purposive. To understand the true purposes of the behavior, it seems to me, we need to see the whole person.

REFERENCES

Berkman, Karen A. & Meyer, Luanna H. (1988). Alternative strategies and multiple outcomes in the remediation of severe self-injury: Going "all out" nonaversively. *Journal of the Association for Persons with Severe Handicaps, 13* (2), 76–86.

PERSPECTIVE 7: CRITICAL THEORY ON THE CARR ET AL. STUDY

GEORGE NOBLIT   *University of North Carolina*

The critique of ideology and power reframes the study by Carr et al. dramatically. Where the authors see a technical study of effective intervention, a critical theorist would instead see a documentation of the technical efficacy of the exercise of power. The adjective, technical, is important here to both Carr et al. and to critical theorists. Carr et al. justify their study as a contribution to a discourse on how best to intervene with clients with behavior problems. They justify it as a study of external validity, thus situating it in dominant positivist discourse, borrowing legitimacy from the classic positivist distinction between internal and external validity (Campbell & Stanley, 1963) while critiquing the research literature for not addressing external validity. Thus the study is novel, fills in a gap, and enables knowledge to be applicable in the field of education. Yet it is a case of normal science, not revolutionary science (Kuhn, 1970). It fills in gaps, advancing an already established knowledge base and paradigm.

Critical theorists would add that the study is technical in other ways as well. Following Habermas (1971), critical theorists see knowledge as serving interests—different types of knowledge serves different kinds of interests. Habermas argues that critical knowledge serves emancipatory interests, interpretive knowledge serves practical interests, and **positivistic** knowledge serves technical interests. The critique here then is not about the theory, methods, or findings of the study. It is clear that this study is a good example of positivist research. It is depicted as a "controlled" (p. 93) study that assesses whether an intervention can alter problem behavior. It is longitudinal and uses a "narrative" approach to assess change, and with these it could be argued to be a cutting edge study within its paradigm. A critical researcher would recognize that within its genre it is a good study. In fact, because it is a good study, it is especially revealing. Setting aside critiques that emerge from within the positivistic tradition, the focus can be on the type of knowledge it represents. While the authors use the term "practical" (p. 94) to characterize its procedures, a critical researcher would see the study as predominately serving technical interests. That is, the study is ultimately about demonstrating the technical rationality of the intervention approach, which they conclude is "effective and feasible" in "reducing severe problem behavior . . . across many different community-based contexts" (p. 108). It serves the interests of those who wish to alter the behavior of these young men. It accepts the assumption that it is these young men who must be changed without engaging the sources of the stigma that are attached to these men—and furthered by this research. While a critical researcher would not dismiss the significance of the disabilities of these young men, he would point out the irony of requiring those with disabilities to alter their behavior while the fully capable are not responsible for changing theirs, at least towards these young men. This is not to say that working and living with these men would be easy—only that those who have fewer resources and capabilities to change their behavior and environments are required to do so.

A critical researcher would contrast this approach to knowledge with a critical approach designed to create a strategy for societal change as well as for promoting a better understanding of these young men about the situation that has been created for them by social process and forces beyond their control. The goal would be to analyze the ideology and domination present in this situation and change it so that these young men would be less subject to such power. The disabilities would be taken into account in this endeavor but the goal would be to reduce the amount of external control in the lives of the three young men.

In such a critique, it would be necessary to address the assumptions behind disability in this society and in this study. Carr et al. clearly want these young men and others to be able to be maintained in the community and not be institutionalized because of their problem behavior. This laudable stance, however, contains a number of assumptions that show the contradictions in the authors' approach. These young men were selected because they were excluded from community participation. Note that in this statement the power resides in the community not in these young men. The act of community power then made these young men available for "intervention." That is, being powerless in the first case makes them subject to more power in the second. Indeed, the study is justified not by what the young men want but by what "stakeholders" wish, and they wish these young men to conform. The researchers thus accept the current state of politics, cultural values, and fiscal constraints that portray the disabled as a social liability.

Carr et al. assume the idea of a controlled study is good, and thus fail to appreciate how the language of positivistic research reveals its quest for dominance. Not only is there a quest for control within the study, both the assessment and intervention aspects of the study reveal the desire for power over these young men. The authors discuss three phases of assessment (describe, categorize, and verify). The description phase was largely focused on problem behavior with apparently little attention to prosocial behavior. The categorization phase had a panel organize the problem behaviors in "functional categories" (p. 95). However, the assumption about the functionality of problem behaviors is never examined, and a critical researcher would ask if the behavior is functional. Then the most appropriate action would be to alter the social system within which the behavior is functional rather than focus on the problem behavior. Further, the panel is used as an attempt to reduce researcher bias in categorizing. However, the panel constructs its knowledge based on information created by the circumscribed *describe* phase and makes *categories* based on the authors' theory about functional behaviors. Ethnographers, in contrast, would do open-ended description and create inductive, emic categories instead of using the power of the researchers in this way. The *verify* phase is admittedly a manipulation. The authors sought to create similar situations and determine if the behavior was elicited. These data were also used as baseline data for the subsequent intervention. The authors did not consider that the problem behaviors could be in fact be elicited by others exerting power over the young men. Thus their manipulation may be responsible for the results not the context and social reaction variables they posit. In short, the assessment process was indeed powerful. The researchers used their power to focus on the undesirable behaviors of these men and used their power to both create categories and to elicit more undesirable behaviors.

The intervention phase obviously was also an exercise in power and control. However, the critical researcher would move beyond the surface to critique that the term intervention by definition is interjecting something. It presumes power and, in the professional sense used here, intervention also carries with it expert power and the dual presumption that something was wrong and something should be done. The intervention involved building rapport, functional communication training, building tolerance for reinforcement delay, providing choices, and using embedding. "Building rapport" actually recognizes part of our earlier critique, and is directed at changing the behavior of caretakers, increasing their social interaction with the young men, giving new "reinforcers" (Carr et al., p. 97), and developing shared interest. Here the researchers sought to build an expectation of interaction, made caregivers more attractive, and created social activity disingenuously. The sadder part is that even if an authentic relationship were possible in this manipulated environment, it would later be used for another end. That is to say, the primary reason for this social interaction was to control the young men—not to be in a "caring" relationship with them (Noddings, 1984). The "functional communication training" taught "the participant a variety of communicative responses that were functionally equivalent to the various classes of problem behavior, thereby making further display of such behavior unnecessary." (Carr et al., p. 97). This taught the young men a new verbal response to situations they were believed to have trouble with, and were prompted to use this. The young men learned this and used these responses spontaneously.

Education is being used here to teach behavior that others believe is appropriate. Clearly, these young men are capable and do learn. However, these young men are not being educated in any normal sense. They are being trained literally (a prescribed process with little room for student negotiation). Nonetheless, the young men are able to expand upon what they know. It is also important to recognize this training process is backed up with "crisis management procedures" that entailed "ignore, momentary restraint, protect, remove, and introduce cues" (Carr et al., p. 98). The crisis management process involves direct application of power, either socially (denial of interaction and introduce cues) or physically (momentary restraint, protect, remove). The direct application of power was very effective. The number of times the authors thought it was necessary to use this technique more often in the baseline (verify) data collection than subsequently. For the critical researcher, it is clear that the young men can learn, can expand upon what they learn, and have learned the lesson of power, that compliance brings more rewards and less punishment from the powerful. "Building tolerance for reinforcement delay" shows that the young men were able to use what they were taught to actually exercise power on their own, seemingly contesting the power of the caregiver to require things of the young men. When the young men used their new knowledge so that it disrupted organizational routines, the young men were taught that power was personal and possibly arbitrary, as the caregivers delayed the response to what the young men were first taught would be an automatic response to their new communications. By this point, the young men may have learned to resign themselves to this "episteme" (Foucault, 1980) of control and slowly acceded to the demands of caregivers. Ironically, "providing choices" occurred when the young men's choices could not be granted within the situation. If the system provided choices that were not sufficiently attractive the young men were ignored and/or crisis management procedures ensued. That is, the young men learned that they should accept the choices others use to deny a true choice, or that control will be exercised. This is a classic case of forced choice, not free choice. Finally, "using embedding" taught the young men that they could get something else they enjoyed along with a forced choice, but also that if they did not actualize the forced choice when given something else they liked then the something else would be withdrawn. If the young men misbehaved at this point then crisis management ensued. That is, the power of the intervention was universally backed up with social and/or physical coercion.

The investigators were interested to know if the intervention would lead to the young men's generalizing what they learned to other situations, and they developed a procedure to promote generalization and then backed this up with the assessment/intervention cycle. That is, generalization was enforced. Similarly, Carr et al. wished to promote maintenance of the learned patterns after the experts reduced their on-site involvement, and found that the young men continued to comply. Whenever they did not comply, they learned they would be subject to the assessment/intervention cycle once again. Direct service providers validated this in their assessment of the reduced severity of the young men's problem behavior. In short, the investigators seem to have proved that the lessons of power are highly salient and prove to be generalized and maintained over time. This is a working definition of hegemony (Gramsci, 1971).

All of the preceding set up the actual investigation reported by Carr et al. The investigation used a form of experimental design that was in itself an exercise in control over rival explanations. More importantly, however, the data confirm that the intervention did lead to the young men being more compliant, accepting that they were to engage in tasks defined by others, and less likely misbehave, at least as it was defined in this study. To the critical researcher, this would be no surprise. The investigation simply documented power was effective in dominating the young men. The authors' conclusion that the intervention package was "effective and feasible" (p. 108) is, of course, consistent with Habermas' argument that positivistic research serves technical interests. It was assumed that the misbehavior of the young men justified the intervention of experts. In turn, the experts' knowledge served technical interests, using (and justifying) power to effect desired ends. As Carr et al. note, "Indeed, the critical aspect of the present study was its scope: The daily application of multiple intervention procedures over very long periods of time" (p. 108). The technique was the continuing application of multiple forms of power over the young men's life. The authors' closing argument for "dynamic" (p. 108) intervention plans is justified by the need to adapt power to effectively control the agency of those seen as disabled. This in turn leads to the implications that power must be exercised with "no end point" (p. 111); and offering incentives for conformity has benefits over bald coercion.

For the critical researcher, then, the study by Carr et al. reveals the ideology that is embedded in positivistic research. Control is more than a valued characteristic of quantitative research design. Positivism produces a certain kind of knowledge—the knowledge of how control can lead to compliance. Positivism, however, does not create knowledge about agency and/or emancipation. Such knowledge requires a different approach, and necessarily begins with the critique of power and ideology. For disability studies, then, the challenge is to use the above understanding to reconsider the capabilities of the disabled and the limitations of current knowledge to help create the least restrictive environment. Critical theory would ask us to ponder what knowledge is necessary to create the most liberating environment.

REFERENCES

Campbell, D. T. & Stanley, J. (1963). *Experimental and quasi-experimental designs for research.* Boston: Houghton Mifflin Company.

Foucault, M. (1980). *Power and knowledge.* (C. Gordon, Ed.) New York, NY: Pantheon Books.

Gramsci, A. (1971). *Selections from the prison notebooks.* New York: International Publishers.

Habermas, J. (1971). *Knowledge and human interests.* Boston: Beacon Press.

Kuhn, T. (1970). *The Structure of Scientific Revolutions.* Chicago, IL: University of Chicago Press.

Noddings, N. (1984). *Caring: A feminine approach to ethics and moral education.* Berkeley: University of California Press.

PERSPECTIVE 8: ETHICS, METHODOLOGY, AND DEMOCRACY ON THE CARR ET AL. STUDY

KENNETH R. HOWE   *University of Colorado at Boulder*

As I intimated in my general discussion of the ethics of educational research, the particulars of given studies are crucial in ethical analysis. This is certainly true of the Carr et al. study.

At first blush, this study may appear to be a clear instance of the "technocratic" (or "traditional" or "positivist") approach to research, and subject to ethical criticism for that very reason. But matters are more complicated than this.

First, the technocratic approach is ethically objectionable because it foists aims and costs on people that they do not accept and had no role in determining. Research designed to hone certain testing/accountability systems provides one kind of example. Research designed to hone certain language "immersion" programs whose aim is to make all children "mainstream Americans" provides another.

The Carr et al. study differs from these examples. True, "problem behavior," like "mainstream American," is a value-laden concept that guides research. But, as used in the Carr et al. study, "problem behavior" is defined as "aggression, self-injury, property destruction, and/or tantrums." It is not nearly as contentious as "mainstream American," and not nearly as likely to be a tool of oppression. The various problems of Val, Gary, and Juan—cerebral palsy, dyskinesia, mental retardation, and autism, among others—are well-documented disabilities that compromise basic social functioning. That researchers ought to seek "technologies" to eliminate or mitigate the problem behavior that results from these disabilities and, yes, to *normalize* these individuals, seems unobjectionable, both for their own welfare and for the welfare of others whose lives they affect.

Second, Carr et al. employ experimental methods, which have an historical affinity with the technocratic approach to research. But there is no necessary connection between experimental methods and the technocratic approach. Experimental methods can often answer certain kinds of questions more convincingly than non-experimental ones. Provided that *ends* are not in dispute, it makes sense to investigate, experimentally, what *means* can best achieve them. Much medical research proceeds along these lines. The end, say, of a healthy heart, is not in dispute; the question becomes one of the means of preventing heart problems or mitigating those that have already occurred. The rise and fall of "assisted communication" provides a case in point in Carr et al.'s general field of endeavor. The end of enhancing the ability of autistic individuals to communicate was not in dispute, but experimental research countered previous kinds of research and called the means of assisted communication into serious question. For their part, Carr et al. provide experimental evidence for an effective means to the end of eliminating or reducing "problem behavior"—an end that also should not be in dispute.

Third, there are many indications in Carr et al.'s study that they are sensitive to the requirements of the "democratic" approach to research ethics. They make various references to "stakeholders," "context," and "quality of life," all of which signal an alertness on their part to the value-laden nature of their research and the need to engage its participants in dialogue about both means and ends. In a related vein, one of the main objectives of their research is to find means to help integrate Val, Gary, and Juan, and individuals like them, into their local communities. Their aim is to maximize the autonomy of these individuals and, as far as possible, initiate them into the natural, non-coercive form of control exercised by social conditions. An important part of this is helping them to become more communicative in their dealings with others.

In addition to the broad ethical issues I have considered so far, Carr et al.'s study also raises issues within the narrower, more conventional purview of research ethics. In particular, Val, Gary, and Juan's participation is of a different order than the participation of the caregivers. Val, Gary, and Juan are more the *objects* than the *subjects* of the research. Based on the descriptions of their conditions, Val, Gary, and Juan appear incapable of giving their informed consent to participate in research.

This is an instance of a pervasive problem in the ethics of research involving human subjects. It is a common issue in medical research, in studies where the selection criteria includes incompetence, either directly, as in certain mental disorders, or indirectly, as in advanced Altzheimer's disease. The participation of such subjects must be justified on the grounds that the research is in their own best interests.

Val, Gary, and Juan seem to be enjoying an improved quality of life as a result of their participation in Carr et al.'s study, i.e., their best interests seem to have been served. But there is more to the question of the ethics of their participation in the study than this. Although they are incapable of the process of *consent*, they might be capable of the process of *assent* (the criterion used for children), in which they are told what sorts of things will be happening to them and are then permitted to agree or refuse to participate. Carr et al. do not provide the information to determine whether such an assent procedure was employed, or whether it was feasible.

To this point, my discussion of Carr et al.'s study has focused on blunting the criticism that the study is a straightforward instance of technocratic research with all its attendant evils—a criticism that I think is very likely to be advanced from certain quarters. Though I believe such a criticism is too pat and simplistic, Carr et al. have encouraged it in several ways.

First, the study reports virtually nothing regarding Val, Gary, and Juan's perspectives on the intervention. If the aim is other than simply to *control* Val, Gary, and Juan with a "technology," then I would think that the perspectives of these individuals should be included. At least the reader should be told why this is out of the question, if it indeed is.

Second, in my view, Carr et al. are on relatively solid ethical ground so long as they confine their "technology" to the kinds of extreme cases exemplified by Val, Gary, and Juan. But extending this approach to "milder and/or more circumscribed problem behavior", and implicitly expanding what counts as "problem behavior" in the process, is ethically worrisome. Where to draw the lines is not always clear. For example, is the use of Ritalin as the technological fix for problem behavior ethically justified? Some say "yes," and some "no." The burden of proof, however, is on those who would advocate the use of technology to manipulate human lives.

PERSPECTIVE 9: POSTSTRUCTURALISM ON THE CARR ET AL. STUDY

LYNDA STONE   *University of North Carolina at Chapel Hill*

Jacques Derrida (1930–). Recently retired, Derrida is often identified as the chief poststructuralist for his philosophical approach of deconstruction. An Algerian-born Jew, he came to France to study at age nineteen; some 50-plus years later his formal career culminated as Director of Studies at the Ecole Pratique des Hautes Etudes en Sciences Sociales *in Paris and visiting professor in the United States at the University of California, Irvine. Among his notable associations are membership in the avant-garde* Tel Quel *group as well as appointments at Johns Hopkins and Yale universities. He burst upon the international philosophical scene in 1967 with the publication in French of three major texts, among them the introduction to deconstruction,* Of Grammatology.

Carr et al.'s longitudinal case study of three people with developmental disabilities spotlights the realm of "special education" within which a tradition of psychological behaviorism today remains significant. One notes at the outset that this is in contrast to a general behaviorist decline in educational research. Exemplary of the tradition, the study does report fruitful and indeed laudable efforts at long-term learning and personal-social change. There are specific strengths: Unlike earlier work in the behaviorist tradition that appeared too narrowly focused on "treatment-effect," this research is multidimensional in temporality and contexts, behavior characteristics, procedures, interventions, and assessments. While authors judge their efforts as successful in reducing severe problem behavior through increased communicative competence, they also rightly note complications in feasibility. Overall the study reads as viable and its insights valuable for practice.

It is the tradition itself, representative of western metaphysics, that the project of French philosopher Jacques Derrida calls into question. Returning to the overview, Derrida's philosophy is based in and through relations of language in which a unique and always changing aesthetic, his form of practice, is basic to a call for societal justice. As is well known, for him "the text is all there is," a paraphrase often misunderstood in traditions that posit agentive emancipatory ends.[1] Too simply put, texts or writings circulate, are continually reinterpreted and reinvented, and themselves must be "deconstructed" in order to provide a space for ethical "intervention." The following describes one key aspect of all texts is Derrida's "open" relation.

As translator Gayatri Chakravorty Spivak explains, the general problem of western thought is one of "presence." She writes, "Derrida uses the word 'metaphysics' very simply as shorthand for any science of presence" (Spivak, 1976, p. xxi). Here is Derrida: "It could be shown that all the names related to fundamentals, to principles, or the center have always designated an invariable presence . . . essence, existence, substance, subject . . . transcendentality, consciousness, God, man, and so forth" (Derrida, 1967/1978, pp. 279–280). Systems of presence constitute "isms," like behaviorism and logocentrism—the latter Derrida's early favorite. That which is self-evident in "isms" is precisely the problematic, and an approach to this problematic is Derrida's deconstruction.

> *Behaviorism: Seeing, judging "the other," each other? Behavior, behave—"veur," voir, to see, to gaze at those who behave and do not behave, seeing, gazing, looking at, voyeur, looking at, being looked at/objectified, surveillance (sur-dominated), voiler, to veil, obscure, dim . . . to be veiled (to make beyond seeing), alternatively to dim oneself (out of) the gaze/objectivity. Is this desired? Possible?*

This wordplay is illustrative of deconstruction: a takeup on language itself. The basic "ism" is one in which speech dominates writing, western logic dominates any other, and man (literally) controls all; this is logocentrism. As one commentator puts this, "at the heart . . . is the definition of 'man' as that being who can signal his self-presence to himself through language" (Cutrofello, 1998, p. 898). Derrida's point is logically that this is impossible. Pertinently, there are many elements of presence in the play on behaviorism. The "ism" itself suggests foundation and a tradition of inquiry: experiment, science, truth, knowledge, answer, certainty. Equally salient is an egocentric positing of self-essence related to "behavior." There are several aspects: A first is implication of a basic unified self, the self of the researcher and the desired self of the researched. A second is the significance of behavior; herein there is a premise about consciousness that external action manifests internal thought and intention, that such action can be "reinforced" and eventually learned. A third is the position of the researcher, the expert who observes and controls the novice, the one and the "other." And one more is the binary of normal and abnormal behavior. But significantly something more is implied in Derrida's deconstruction; this is the potential for the other to "escape." The play above, itself of course suspect of *logos*, is one such move. More now on deconstruction.

Derrida begins explication by attending to a basic dualism of western logic, a logic of identity (A equals A) and non-contradiction (A does not equal A; see Johnson, 1995, p. 45). As in Cixous's work and many others, these associations have entailed the dominance of one concept over "its" other—and their cultural manifestations. Derrida wants to undermine this dualistic difference but understands that mere reversal retains the invidious relationship.

Given this binary system, an early formulation by Derrida concerns how language functions. The root is Saussure's theory of the sign, of difference inherent *in* terms, of concepts and their utterances. The sign based on difference and not sameness itself undermines the traditional unified relationship of a word to its object. Herein all signs are understood as different from but linked to any possible others. Significantly, Derrida theorizes still another "difference," that of the unknowable, the unpresentable, the radical other. This is his treatment of the shared concept of "relation" from the overview. With respect to the sign, this other "exists" between/within a signifier and its signified. Derrida names this "space/moment/function" *différance*.

Différance is a neologism that encapsulates both the meaning of differ and defer. In *Of Grammatology,* Derrida defines *différance* as "pure trace." His statement is worth quoting at length:

> It does not depend upon any sensible plenitude, audible or visible, phonic or graphic. It is, on the contrary, the condition of such plenitude. Although *it does not exist,* although it is never a *being-present* outside of all plenitude, its possibility is by rights anterior to all one calls sign . . . content or operation, motor or sensory. . . . Of course, the positive *sciences* of signification can only describe the *work* and the *fact* of difference, of determined differences and the presences that they make possible. There cannot be a science of difference . . . as it is impossible to have a science of the origin of presence itself, that is to say of a certain nonorigin. (Derrida, 1967/1976, pp. 62, 63, emphasis in original)

Différance, trace, *chora,* and supplement are several names Derrida assigns to this unknowable difference, this difference from presence. Why, educators may ask, is this idea important for us? One might say that it reminds of what *we* cannot know—as in Freud's unconscious. With this idea, we approach our work not as researchers *who do not know yet,* but by giving up, as what one might put it, an arrogance for a humility. Out of the latter, as Derrida's later work posits, comes justice—justice of which education can be a part. To close, indeed Carr and fellow researchers do desire justice from their research but, according to Derrida, their research tradition contradicts and precludes it.

NOTE

1. This of course is in the tradition of the death of the author.

REFERENCES

Cutrofello, A. (1998). Jacques Derrida. In E. Craig (Ed.), *Routledge encyclopedia of philosophy* (Vol. II, pp. 896–901). London: Routledge.

Derrida, J. (1976). *Of grammatology* (G. Spivak, Trans.). Baltimore, MD: The Johns Hopkins University Press. (Original work published 1967)

Derrida, J. (1978). *Writing and difference* (A. Bass, Trans.). Chicago: The University of Chicago Press. (Original work published 1967)

Johnson, B. (1995). Writing. In F. Lentricchia & T. McLaughlin (Eds.), *Critical terms for literary study* (2nd ed., pp. 39–49). Chicago: The University of Chicago Press.

Spivak, G. (1976). Translator's preface. In J. Derrida, *Of grammatology* (pp. ix–xxxvii). Baltimore, MD: Johns Hopkins University Press.

CHAPTER 6

The Heath Study

QUESTIONING AT HOME AND AT SCHOOL: A COMPARATIVE STUDY

SHIRLEY BRICE HEATH

ABSTRACT: In this chapter Shirley Heath engages with a problem that in one form or another has vexed most classroom teachers where there is a difference between the cultural background of the teacher and that of some or all of the children in the classroom. In the instances with which Heath is concerned, the lack of cultural congruence is between black children and white teachers, where the teachers assumed that the children in their classes would respond to language routines and the uses of language in building knowledge, skills, and dispositions just as other children, including their own, did. The object of her research was to discover why the particular black children in those classrooms she studied in a specific community did not respond "just as the other children did." The focus became the role of questioning in language and socialization. "We don't talk to our children like you folks do" was the response of some Trackton parents to questions put to them about their children's behaviors.

Trackton children are not regarded as information givers or as appropriate conversational partners for adults. But they are by no means excluded from language participation—in a language that is rich in styles, speakers, and topics. The predominant characteristic of teacher questions was to pull attributes of things out of context, particularly out of the context of books, and name them—queens, elves, police, red apples. Trackton parents did not ask the children these kinds of questions, and Trackton children had different techniques for responding to any questions—including deflection of the question itself.

This research required going well beyond the classroom to the interactions in the homes of teachers and of Trackton children. This is a kind of selective holism that we have come to feel is one of the important criteria for a good ethnography of schooling. The ethnographer identifies and moves into whatever context is necessary for an understanding of the phenomena taking place in the classroom.

This research demonstrates the desirability of long-term research. Heath was engaged intermittently in this study for about five years. Much of what she knows could only be learned through long-term exposure. Much of the validity of a good ethnography comes from this kind of exposure.

The study also demonstrates the utility of having a clear frame of reference from and within which to work. In this case the frame of reference is language socialization and the ethnography of communication, both of which are relatively recent developments in cultural anthropology and, by nature, interdisciplinary.

Lastly, it is noteworthy that this research has direct potential for application to the classroom for the improvement of education. Heath discusses this application at the end of the chapter. She stresses interaction of the school and the community and states an important position—that it is a two-way path. She makes the point that the success of such an effort depends on participation on the part of all parties involved. It is not a matter of outside experts telling teachers what to do nor of teachers telling parents how they should talk, but rather a mutual and collaborative effort to discover what the problems are and what can be done about them. This is in the emerging tradition of an applied social science appropriate to a democratic society.

Heath, S.B. (1982). Questioning at home and at school: A comparative study. In G. Spindler (Ed.), Doing the Ethnography of Schooling: Educational Anthropology in Action (pp. 102–127). Prospect Heights, IL: Waveland Press.

INTRODUCTION

"Ain't nobody can talk about things being about their-selves."

A third-grade boy in a community in the Southeastern part of the United States directed this statement to his teacher when she persisted in asking questions about the story just completed in a reading circle.

Teacher:	What is the story about?
Children:	*(silence)*
T	Uh. . . Let's see. . . Who is it the story talks about?
C	*(silence)*
T	Who is the main character? Um . . . What kind of story is it?
Child:	Ain't nobody can talk about things being about theirselves!

The boy was saying: "There's no way anybody can talk (and ask) about things being about themselves." As an ethnographer who had worked in the boy's community and school for more than five years, I was able to place his summative statement about the kinds of questions asked in school into the context of knowledge about those asked of him in his own community.

The boy was reacting to the fact that teachers' questions were so often about things being about themselves; that is, they asked for labels, attributes, and discrete features of objects and events in isolation from the context. Someone—most often the teacher and the brightest kids in class—always had answers for school questions. These answers could usually be given in one word. In the boy's community, people asked questions about whole events or objects and their uses, causes, and effects. Often no one had an answer which was the "right answer." Community members accepted many answers and ways of answering, and their answers almost always involved telling a story, describing a situation, or making comparisons between the event or object being described and another known to the audience.

This paper presents some data on uses of questions in three different situations in a moderate-sized city of the Southeastern United States: a working-class community of black residents, the classrooms attended by children of this community in 1970–1975, and the homes of teachers from these classrooms. We will attempt to show how questions varied in proportion to other types of utterances across the three situations, and we shall look at different uses of questions and the assumptions made by the questioners about the functions of questions. Our aim is to indicate how ethnographic data on verbal strategies in community and home settings can be useful for comparison with data collected in studies of the functions of language in the classroom.

ETHNOGRAPHY IN THE COMMUNITY AND CLASSROOM

The goal of ethnography is to describe the ways of living of a social group, usually one in which there is in-group recognition by the members that they indeed must live and work together to retain group identity. Traditionally, ethnographers have taken up residence in communities made up of one or more of these social groups to record and describe the behaviors, values, and tangible aspects of their culture. More recently, ethnographers have also become participant-observers in settings which do not necessarily have a cross-generational on-going sense of social identity. Anthropologists have studied institutions, such as schools, hospitals, and factories, or short-lived but repetitive group interactions, such as court sessions, conversations, and service encounters. Some anthropologists have made their data available for decision-making by political leadership and institutional management. Anthropologists studying communities in complex societies have also begun to make their studies available to these communities and have offered to provide data about the operations of political/economic institutions through which community members must move in daily interactions outside their own social group.

The fieldwork reported in this paper was carried out over a period of five years in both community and institutional settings. Results of the work were shared with both community and institutional members. One phase of the fieldwork was done in an all-black residential group whose members identified themselves as a community both spatially and in terms of group membership. To distinguish this group from the public community at large, we will hereafter refer to it as Trackton. Over the period of time in which I worked there, its membership declined from 150 to 40, as families moved from the neighborhood into public housing or purchased new homes. Most Trackton households contained one or more members, ages 21 to 45, who worked in jobs providing salaries equal to or above those of beginning public school teachers in the region; however, jobs were seasonal, and work was not always steady. Trackton was located in a Southeastern city with a population of approximately 40,000; in the period from 1970 to 1975, children from the community attended either of two public elementary-level schools. As a volunteer neighborhood service aide, I worked in these schools and with city personnel in a variety of agencies, collecting data on interactions of Trackton residents in institutions with which they came in frequent, if not daily, contact. As a professor at a state teacher-training institution for which the region's citizens had a longstanding respect, I had many of the teachers, their spouses, or other family members in classes, and I worked informally with others on local civic or church-related projects. Over the years, I became colleague, co-author, aide, and associate to many of the classroom teachers, and I had access to not only their classrooms, but also their homes and their activities in the public domain.

I began working in Trackton at the request of some of the older residents who had known me for several years. My initial task, in their view, was to read and talk with the children and explain to adults why their children were not doing better in school. Gradually, I was called on to be a source of information about available services and opportunities for them and their children in public institutions, and I was asked to explain the systems of entry and maintenance which made for success in these institutions. In the late 1960s, numerous policy changes in schools and public systems regulating housing, employment, and preschool educational and medical experiences brought the children of all-black communities into many new situations. Desegregation rulings put black students into formerly all-white classrooms, usually with white teachers. There were many complaints in the first years, but particularly disturbing to older residents was the hatred of their young for school.

> The teachers won't listen.
> My kid, he too scared to talk, 'cause nobody play by the rules he know. At home, I can't shut 'im up.
> Miss Davis, she complain 'bout Ned not answerin' back. He say she asks dumb questions she already know 'bout.

It seemed clear that parents felt there was little meaningful communication going on between teachers and their children in the classroom. When I talked over this view with classroom teachers, they agreed there was relatively little "real" exchange of information, feeling, or imagination between them and many of the black students, especially those in the primary grades.

During this period, much research on language pointed out differences between the structures of Black English and those of standard English, and the effects of these differences on academic performance (Labov 1968; Baratz and Shuy 1969; Wolfram 1969). Many local teachers knew of this research (especially Labov 1970, 1972), and some suggested that perhaps differences between the structures of their language and those of their black students were major reasons for communication breakdowns. Other teachers did not agree; they reasoned that almost daily for many years they had lived and worked with Black English speakers in nearly all institutions except schools and churches. Therefore, the structures of the languages used by teachers and their Black English-speaking students were probably not so different as to cause the almost-total lack of communication which seemed to exist in some classrooms. Their view was that reasons for the breakdown lay in the nature of interactions called for in school. The interactional tasks between teacher and child called for particular kinds of responses from students. These responses depended primarily on two kinds of knowledge: first, the rituals and routines of classroom life, and second, the information and skills acquired in the classroom. It was difficult, however, for teachers to pin down exactly what was called for in these interactions; thus they felt they could not help their students achieve success in these tasks. To be sure, the entry of black students into the schools had caused negative attitudes and bitter prejudices to surface, but there were many well-intentioned teachers who, having accepted the desegregation decision as final, wanted to get on with teaching. They felt a strong need to know more about ways in which they could effectively communicate with all their students.

Of the students with whom they had communication problems, teachers said:

> They don't seem to be able to answer even the simplest questions.
> I would almost think some of them have a hearing problem; it is as though they don't hear me ask a question. I get blank stares to my questions. Yet when I am making statements or telling stories which interest them, they always seem to hear me.
> The simplest questions are the ones they can't answer in the classroom; yet on the playground, they can explain a rule for a ballgame or describe a particular kind of bait with no problem. Therefore, I know they can't be as dumb as they seem in my class.
> I sometimes feel that when I look at them and ask a question, I'm staring at a wall I can't break through. There's something there; yet in spite of all the questions I ask, I'm never sure I've gotten through to what's inside that wall.

Many teachers and administrators felt they were "not asking the right questions" of either the children or their own teaching strategies, and I was asked to help them find ways of helping themselves. As an aide, tutor, traveling librarian, and "visiting fireman" I was occasionally asked to talk about archaeology or show slides of other countries in which I had done fieldwork, I served numerous functions in classrooms across a wide range of grade levels and subject areas for five years. I participated and observed, shared data, and acted as change agent at the request of the institution's members. During this period, some of the teachers enrolled in graduate courses of study which included some anthropology and linguistics courses I taught. They then used techniques of ethnographic fieldwork and data interpretation in their own classes and schools and incorporated into their teaching some of the observation skills associated with anthropology. Some teachers collected data on their own practices in guiding language learning for their preschool children at home; others agreed to allow me to participate and observe in their homes, recording uses of language and language input for their children. Particularly critical to these teachers' understanding and acceptance of ethnography in familiar educational settings—both their classrooms and their homes—was their view that the ethnographic/linguistic research was in response to their felt needs, and they were themselves involved.

During the period of participating and observing in classrooms and some teachers' homes, I continued work in Trackton. A major focus of fieldwork there was the acquisition of uses of language, ways in which children learned to use language to satisfy their needs, ask questions, transmit information, and convince those around them they were competent communicators. Participating and observing with the children and their families and friends intensively over a period of five years, I was able to collect data across a wide range of situations and to follow some children longitudinally as they acquired communicative competence in Trackton and then attempted to take this competence into school settings.[1] Likewise, at various periods during these years, I observed Trackton adults in public service encounters and on their jobs, and I was able to compare their communicative competence in these situations with those inside Trackton. The context of language use, including setting, topic, and participants (both those directly involved in the talk and those who only listened), determined in large part how community members, teachers, public service personnel, and fellow workers judged the communicative competence of Trackton residents. Proper handling of questioning was especially critical, because outsiders often judged the intelligence and general competence of individuals by their responses to questions and by the questions they asked.

In settings outside Trackton, questions had several functions relatively rarely used by residents there. The first situation in which this difference became important for Trackton children came when they entered school. There they had to learn that teachers did not always make the same assumptions about the uses of questions as they did. What follows here provides an indication of the interrogatives teachers used with their own preschoolers at home, questions Trackton adults asked their preschool children, and the conflict and congruence between these differing approaches to questioning as they evolved in classrooms.

QUESTIONS AND LANGUAGE LEARNING

Questions and their uses by children's caretakers have received relatively little attention in studies of language input and acquisition. In general, what emerges from the literature is the view that questions are used for training children to interact verbally with their caretakers and for directing their attention to what it is they should learn (Holzman 1972, 1974; Snow, et al. 1976; Goody 1977). Several studies point out that a large percentage of utterances middle-class mothers direct to their preschool children is made up of questions (Newport, et al. 1977; Snow 1977), and some studies indicate that questions become successively more complex in correspondence with the child's increased language skill (Levelt 1975). Most of these studies consider questions only as they may relate to the child's acquisition of grammatical competence or the structures of his speech community's language system (Ervin-Tripp 1970).

Some attention has also been given to the role of questions in children's acquisition of communicative competence, i.e., how they learn conversational skills (Snow 1977, Ervin-Tripp and Miller 1977) and determine appropriate language uses for different listeners, settings, and topics (Hymes 1962, Blount 1977). Cross-cultural research in child language acquisition has pointed out that the linguistic environment and the language socialization of children vary across cultures. Uses of questions vary in numerous respects. For example, in one society, it may not be the mother or even members of the immediate family who direct the highest proportion of questions to young children, because the language socialization network includes a wide range of participants (Harkness 1977). In another society, questions are not considered highly relevant to learning how to accomplish tasks (Goody 1977); in another, children have very little exposure to *why* or *how* questions (Blank 1975). Among other groups, questions may be intimately linked to imperatives, explaining the reasons for commands or the consequences of not obeying orders (Cook-Gumperz 1973; Sachs, et al. 1976).

The specific characteristics of questions and their uses in socializing young children are highly dependent on the network of those who ask questions. A preschool child who has frequent contacts with individuals of both sexes, different ages, and varying degrees of familiarity with his world will learn very different uses of questions from the child accustomed to a small network of family and close associates. In particular, the assumptions made by questioners about the functions of their questions in the socialization of the child will be very different. The wide variation possible in child language socialization, and especially in the uses of questions, is exemplified in the community of Trackton and the homes of its classroom teachers.

CLASSROOM TEACHERS AND THEIR OWN CHILDREN

Within their homes, children of the classroom teachers involved in this study[2] were socialized into a fairly small network of language users: mother, father, siblings, and maids or grandparents. Children below the age of four rarely communicated with anyone on an extended basis except these primary associates; Visits to Sunday School, the grocery store, shopping centers, and so on provided very limited opportunities for questions addressed to the children by nonintimates. Within the homes, talk to preschool children emphasized questions. In their questioning routines with preverbal as well as verbal children, adults supplied the entire context, giving questions and answering them (cf. Gleason 1973)[3] or giving questions and then pausing to hold conversational space for a hypothetical answer before moving on to the next statement, which assumed information from the hypothetical answer (cf. Snow 1977).

Mother:	(addressing an 8-week-old infant) You want your teddy bear?
Mother:	Yes, you want your bear.
Mother:	(addressing her 2-month-old infant) You don't know what to make of all those lights, do you?
Pause (3 seconds)	
Mother:	That's right, I know you don't like them. Let's move over here. (picks up infant and moves away from lights)
Mother:	(addressing her child age, 2;9) Didja forget your coat?
Mother:	Yes, you did. Let's go back 'n get it.

When parents wanted to teach a politeness formula, such as *thank you* or *please,* they used interrogatives: "Can you say 'thank you'?" "What do you say?" (cf. Gleason and Weintraub 1976). Questions served a wide variety of functions in adult-child interactions. They allowed adults to hold pseudo-conversations with children, to direct their attention to specific events or objects in the array of stimuli about them, and to link formulaic responses to appropriate occasions. Perhaps most important, adults' uses of questions trained children to act as question-answerers, as experts on knowledge about the world, especially the names and attributes of items in their environment and those introduced to them through books.

Mother:	(looking at a family photograph album with Missy, age 2;3) Who's that, Missy?
(The mother has pointed to the family dog in one of the pictures.)	
Missy:	That's Toby.
Mother:	What does Toby say?
Missy:	Woof, woof. (child imitates a whine) grrrrrr, yip.
Mother:	Where does Toby live?
Missy:	My house.

The children seemed to feel compelled to give answers to adults' questions. When they did not know answers (or were bored with the usual routine of expected answers), they sometimes invented fantastic answers.

Adults addressed questions to their children in great numbers and variety. During a period of 48 hours, Missy (age 2;3) was asked 103 questions; 47.9 percent of all utterances (215) directed to her during this period were questions (cf. Sachs et al. 1976).[4] Table 1 contains a description of these questions. Questions designated Q–I are those in which the questioner has the information being requested of the addressee; A–I questions are those in which the addressee has the information being requested. Unanswerable questions (U–I) are those for which neither questioner nor addressee has the information. Of the A–I questions, 25 percent were clarification requests (Corsaro 1977), in which questioners asked the child to clarify, confirm, or repeat a previous utterance. Q–I questions were often used in game-playing, especially games of hide-and-seek or peek-a-boo. These two types, Q–I and A–I, fit the simplicity of syntax expected in utterances directed to children of this age (cf. Newport, et al. 1977), but the U–I questions do not. These were both Why–questions and "I wonder" questions which asked for information neither the child nor the adult was expected to have. The syntax of these and the answers they called for was far more complex than that of other types addressed to the child. For example, a father walking the child outside before putting her to bed would look up at the sky and ask: "I wonder what's up there?" These questions

Table 1
Percentages and Types of Questions (Missy 2;3)

Types	Examples	Total	Percentage
Q–I	What color is that?	46	44.7
A–I	What do you want?	24	23.3
U–I	Why is it things can't be simpler than they are?	18	17.5
Others	(directives, etc.)	15	14.5

The child is taught to expect structured transfer, rather than discovered or guess type answers.

seemed to be self-talk, an out-loud sort of reverie. For these questions, the child was expected to be a passive listener, but a listener nevertheless, thus giving the adult an "excuse" for talking to himself.

Interrogative forms predominated in types of utterances directed to preschoolers. Over a six-month period, a teacher arranged for her child (age 2;8–3;2) and the child (age 3;2–3;8) of another teacher to play in one or the other of the two homes each afternoon from 3 to 5. Adult-children interactions were taped one afternoon each week for six months. Adults who interacted with the children usually included either or both of the teachers (mothers), one grandparent, and two older siblings. In the first month (four sessions), interrogatives made up 58.6 percent of the total utterances (640) directed to the children, imperatives 28.1 percent, exclamations 6.7 percent, declaratives 6.6 percent. In the sixth month (four sessions), interrogatives made up 52.4 percent of the total utterances (770) directed to the children, imperatives 30.3 percent, exclamations 4.4 percent, and declaratives 12.9 percent. Lumping all interrogative forms together in the data masks the uses of questions in behavior correction and accusations of wrong-doing. Many of the interrogatives were, in fact, directives or condemnations of the children's behavior. For example, tag questions attached directly to statements were counted here as interrogatives because of their form, but the speakers usually meant these as declarative or directive. For example, in the utterance "That's a top. You've never seen one of those, have you?" the adult was not calling for a response from the child, but making a declarative statement for the child: "No, I've never seen one of those." In the statement, "You wouldn't do that, would you?" the speaker provides a somewhat softened directive which means "Don't do that." Questions similar in type to tag questions were directives in intent and followed immediately after imperatives in form, extending their force: "Stop it, Jamie. Why can't you behave?" The latter part of this utterance extends the scolding power of the imperative and calls upon

the child to *think* about a response to the question, but not to respond verbally to the condemnation.

Adults and older siblings seemed compelled to communicate to the preschoolers in questions. At the end of the third month, when the strong patterning of questioning was definitive in the data, the teachers agreed to make a conscious effort for one month to reduce their questions and use statements instead. This change evolved out of discussions surrounding analysis of the past three months' tapes. One teacher believed (though she admitted perhaps ideally so) that statements transmitted more information than questions did. Therefore, since she also believed her purpose in holding conversations with her preschoolers was to pass on information, she should make statements, not ask questions. The other teacher was skeptical, believing questions necessary to check on information-transmission. However, both agreed to try to reduce their level of questioning (and that of adults around them) directed to the children for one month to see if their feelings about statements and questions could be borne out in the data in any concrete way. During this period, the percentage of questions dropped to 50.6 percent and the percentage of statements increased to 11.9 percent. However, both teachers reported they were not satisfied with what was happening. They felt they gave more orders, the questions they did ask were scolding in nature, and they were not getting the behavior modifications they expected from their children. They reported they felt they did not involve their children when they used statements. They received no sense of interaction and felt they were "preaching" to a third party; they could not be sure they were being heard. They viewed questions as a way to "share talk" with children of this age. Just "talking *to* them" (interpreted now by both teachers as using statements only) seemed to have no impact; questions allowed adults to "talk *with* children."

Without being aware of any change in their behavior, in the last month of data collected from these adult-children interactions, adults seemed to focus on teaching the children

↳ culturally developed process

to ask the right questions in the right places and not to ask questions which seemed to challenge the authority of adults. The children were told:

> Don't ask why people are sick.
> Don't ask that kind of question.
> Don't ask so many questions.
> Don't ask why.

These corrections seemed to increase dramatically when someone from outside the family circle entered the home. Adults seemed to use correctives to questions to announce they were training their children in the right way. If a child asked an "impertinent" question of a visitor, the adult would reprimand the child and offer an explanatory aside to the visitor. "What do you say?" as a request for politeness formulas such as "please" and "thank you" was an especially favorite question when outsiders were present.

In summary, teachers socializing their own preschoolers to language depended heavily on questions. They used questions to teach their children what they should attend to when looking at a book ("What's that?" "Where's the puppy?" "What does he have in his hand?"). The children were taught to label (Ninio and Bruner 1978), to search out pieces of pictures, to name parts of the whole, and to talk about these out of context. As the children grew older, adults used questions to add power to their directives ("Stop that! Did you hear me?") and to call particular attention to the infraction committed ("Put that back. Don't you know that's not yours?"). Adults saw questions as necessary to train children, to cause them to respond verbally, and to be trained as conversational partners.

LANGUAGE LEARNING IN TRACKTON

In the past decade, linguists have described the structure of Black English, its history, and its particular systems of usage in appropriate contexts. Numerous myths about the language of the black child have been exploded by research, which has shown this language to be rule-governed and as capable of providing an adequate basis for thinking as any other language. Speech acts given particular labels in Black English, such as "signifying," "playing the dozens," and "jiving," have been described in their uses by adolescent and adult members of black communities (Labov, et al. 1968; Mitchell Kernan 1971; Kochman 1972).

Nevertheless, many stereotypes still exist about language learning in black communities. Studies of black communities provide only bits and pieces of evidence on adults interacting with young children for language socialization. Ward (1971) describes a community in Louisiana in which the children have numerous language difficulties in school, but little systematic attention is given to the acquisition of communicative competence by young children in the community. Adult-child interactions described in Young 1970 and Stack 1976 provide few data directly relevant to language socialization. Teachers who participated in the study reported here initially held a variety of stereotypes about how black children learned language: black parents don't care about how their children talk; black children don't have adequate exposure to language, because their parents are probably as nonverbal as the kids are at school; black parents don't spend enough time with their children to train them to talk right. All of these views show that teachers thought black children's language socialization was somehow different from that of other children. Yet in their interactions with black children in the classroom, teachers invariably assumed they would respond to language routines and uses of language in building knowledge, skills, and dispositions just as other children did. Some teachers were aware of this paradox, but felt that since they did not know how language was taught in black communities and how it was used to make children aware of the world around them, they had no basis on which to rethink their views of the language socialization of black children. The teachers could only assume these children were taught language and cognitive skills in the same ways they used to teach their own children.

That was not the case for children in Trackton, as examination of the role of questions in their language socialization indicates. Questions addressed by adults to children occurred far less frequently in Trackton than in the homes of teachers. In Trackton, adults were not observed playing peek a boo games with young children; thus, a major source of Q–1 questions was eliminated. Adults and siblings also did not direct questions to preverbal infants; instead, they made statements about them to someone else which conveyed the same information as questions directed by teachers to their children. Trackton adults would say of a crying preverbal infant: "Sump'n's the matter with that child." The equivalent in the teacher's home would be to direct a question or series of questions to the child: "What's the matter?" "Does something hurt you?" "Are you hungry?" Trackton adults did not attempt to engage children as conversational partners until they were seen as realistic sources of information and competent partners in talk.

It has been suggested that the language used by adults, especially mothers, in speaking to young children has numerous special properties; some of these develop because of the limited range of topics which can be discussed with

Structured learning [handwritten marginal note]

young children (Shatz and Gelman 1977). In addition, most of the research on mother-child interaction has been done in homes where a single child and a single parent were recorded in their interactions (Brown 1973). In this situation, mothers have no one other than their children to talk to or with, and language interactions with their children may thus be intensified over those which would occur if other conversational partners were consistently present. In Trackton, adults almost always had someone else around to talk to; rarely were mothers or other adults left alone in the home with young children (cf. Young 1970, Ward 1971, Stack 1976). The children did not have to be used as conversational partners; others more knowledgeable and more competent as conversants were available. Children were not excluded from activities of adults or from listening to their conversations on any topic. Trackton parents, unlike teachers with their preschoolers, never mentioned the fact that something should not be talked about in the presence of children or that particular words were inappropriate. However, if children used taboo words, they were scolded (cf. Mitchell Kernan's comments in Slobin 1968:15). Young children would often sit on the laps of conversants, at their feet or between them on the sofa, listening. They were rarely addressed directly, however, in an effort to bring them into the conversation. Sometimes they were fondled, their faces and mouths touched, and food offered by community members as well as older siblings. In these cases, the person offering the food would address a comment such as "Hey, he really goes for these!" to someone else in the room. Questions directed by a teacher to her child in similar situations were: "Does that taste good, huh!" "You like that, don't you?"

When weather permitted, the children played on the porch of their home or in the yard within close range of the porch. When intimate associates were present, approximately 10 percent of the utterances conceivably directed to the nearby preschoolers were questions, 75 percent imperatives, 10 percent exclamations, and 5 percent statements (cf. Mitchell Kernan's comments in Slobin 1968:12)[4]. However, Trackton children were exposed to a wide variety of individuals other than their family and neighborhood associates. Friends and kin from other areas of the county came and went often, sometimes temporarily taking up residence in Trackton. These frequent visitors to the community would tease the children, challenging them to particular feats or making statements of fact about the children.

> You ever gonna learn to ride 'at tractor?
> Can you lemme see you go, boy?

> Your momma better come change your pants.
> I betcha momma don't know you got dat.

Children were not expected to respond verbally, but to do what any command clearly addressed to them called for. Children were more talked "at" than "with."

A wide variety of strangers—utility servicemen, taxi drivers, bill collectors, and the like—came to the community. They usually acknowledged preschoolers, addressing questions such as "What's your name?" "Anybody home?" "Are you out here by yourself?" to the children. Most of the time these were met with no verbal responses. Occasionally when older preschoolers answered these questions, they would later be chastised by adults of the community. Children learned very early that it was not appropriate to report on the behavior of their intimates to strangers whose purposes in the community were not known. Likewise, outside the community, when nonintimates asked information about the children's family or living arrangements, they usually got no answer. Thus when school or community service personnel asked questions such as "How many people live in your house?" or "Doesn't James live on your street?" the children would often not respond and would be judged uncooperative, "stupid," or "pathetic."

In Trackton, children did not hold high positions as information-givers or question-answerers, especially in response to questions for which adults already knew the answer. When children were asked questions, they were primarily of five types. Table 2 provides a description of the types of questions used with preschoolers in Trackton. The various uses noted here do not include all those evidenced in Trackton, but they constitute the major types used by adults to young children. Crucial to the flexibility in the uses of interrogative forms is their embeddedness in particular communication and interpersonal contexts. In the analysis of types, it should be evident that there is a distinction between what some of these interrogatives mean and what the speaker means in uttering them. Another way of stating this is to say that the questioner using each of the types has a conception, perhaps unique to this particular communication context, of what the appropriate response by a preschooler to the question asked will be. In other cultures and in other contexts where different age and status relationships might prevail, these question types might not call for the response noted here as appropriate for preschool children. For example, in a classroom, a teacher asking questions similar to "What's that like?" very often has in mind as the answer a specific piece of information assumed to be known to both questioner and addressee.

Table 2
Types of Questions Asked of Children in Trackton

Types	Responses called for	Examples
Analogy	Nonspecific comparison of one item, event, or person with another	What's that like? (referring to a flat tire on a neighbor's car) Doug's car, never fixed.
Story-starter	Question asking for explanation of events leading to first questioner's question	Question 1: Did you see Maggie's dog yesterday? Question 2: What happened to Maggie's dog?
Accusatory	Either nonverbal response and a lowered head or a story creative enough to take the questioner's attention away from the original infraction	What's that all over your face? Do you know 'bout that big mud-puddle. . .
A–1	Specific information known to addressee, but not to questioner	What do you want? Juice.
Q–1	Specific piece of information known to both questioner and addressee	What's your name, huh? Teeg.

Teacher: *(pointing to a small circle used on a map to depict a city of a certain size)* What does that remind you of?

Expected
Response: That set of circles in our book.
                 (the set of circles talked about in the social studies book in the section on reading maps)

culturally structured

Teachers often "answer" questions to themselves as they ask them, and they expect answers from students to conform to those preconceived in the questioner's mind.

It is important to compare these questions with those which called for analogies from Trackton children. These were the closest thing to "training questions" Trackton adults had for young children. Children were not asked "What's that?" but "What's that like?" "Who's he acting like?" Requests that children name objects or list discrete features of objects or events, which appeared in teachers' talk to their preschoolers, were replaced in Trackton by questions asking for analogical comparisons. Adults seemed to assume children knew how to compare events, objects, and persons. Adults' use of these questions, as well as their frequent use of metaphors in conversations in the presence of children, seem to underscore their assumption that listeners understood similarities and differences.

You know, he's the one who's got a car like the one Doug useta have.
She's got eyes like a hawk.

You jump just like a toadfrog.
Sue sound like some cat got its tail caught in the screen door.

Young children noticed likenesses between objects, and even preverbal but mobile children would, on seeing a new object, often go and get another that was similar. Older children also gave great attention to details of objects; this attention was, however, not expressed as questions but as statements: "That thing on your belt look like that flower in your blouse." In parallel situations in teachers' homes, their preschoolers would say "Is that flower like that thing on your blouse?" At early ages, Trackton children recognized situations, scenes, personalities, and items which were similar. However, they never volunteered, nor were they asked by adults, to name the attributes which were similar and added up to one thing's being like another. A grandmother playing with her grandson age 2;4 asked him as he fingered crayons in a box: "Whatcha gonna do with those, huh?" "Ain't dat [color] like your pants?" She then volunteered to me: "We don't talk to our chil'un like you folks do; we don't ask 'em 'bout colors, names, 'n things."

What these speakers meant in asking questions calling for analogical comparisons was very different from what teachers meant in classrooms when they used the same interrogative forms. At home, Trackton children could provide nonspecific comparisons without explanation. Thus, in the classroom, they were likely to respond to questions of "What's that like?" with answers which seemed to teachers too broad or totally unrelated to the lesson at hand.

Teacher:	(pointing to a new sign to be used in arithmetic) What was it we said earlier this sign is like?
Expected Response:	The mouth of an alligator. (an explanation used earlier in the day by the teacher)
Trackton Student's Response:	Dat thing up on da board. (The student looks at a bulletin board for social studies which has yarn linking various cities; the yarn forms a shape like the sign)

Though the gross outlines of the sign's shape have been recognized by the student, he has made the comparison to a temporary and highly specific representation in the room. He has not envisioned the similarity between the open mouth of an alligator (presumably a permanent symbol in the minds of children familiar with this picture from books) and the mathematical symbol. The comparison is valid, but the teacher's response ("Huh? Uh . . . , I guess that's okay") indicated she considered the answer neither as useful nor as relevant as the one proposed in the lesson.

Another type of question used by Trackton residents was a *story-starter*. These questions were addressed to the oldest preschool children as well as to older children and adults. In situations which called for these, a person knew a story, but wanted an audience to ask for the story. However, there had to be some way of letting the audience know the story was there for the telling. A frequent technique was to ask what was ostensibly an A–I question: "Didja hear Miss Sally this morning?" The appropriate response to this question was "Uh-oh, what happened to Miss Sally?" If the respondent (especially an adult) heard the question as an A–I question and replied "No," the questioner would say, "Well, I ain't gonna tell you nut'n."

Accusatory questions were also used by Trackton residents. Similar in form to story-starters, they occurred more frequently than story-starters with children. In these questions, the adult or older child asked a question which was known by all to be a statement of accusation; the addressee, if guilty, had only two appropriate responses. One of these was to bow the head, say nothing, and wait for the verbal diatribe which was sure to follow. The other was to create a story or word play which would so entertain the questioner that the infraction would be forgotten. In these responses, the child was allowed to shift roles, to step out of a submissive role, to exhibit behavior which for older children would be judged as "uppity." One mother exasperated with her son 3;9 years of age, said "Whadja do with that

shoe? You wan me ta tie you up, put you on da railroad track?" The child responded:

> Railroad track
> Train all big 'n black
> On dat track, on dat track, on dat track.
> Ain't no way I can't get back.
> Back from dat track,
> Back from dat train,
> Big'n black, I be back.

All the listeners laughed uproariously at this response, and his mother forgot about the accusation. Older children could use these playful responses to other children or to certain low-status adults in the community, but they dared not do so with high-status adults, either kin or nonkin.

A–I questions were fairly straight-forward, asking the child to express a preference or desire or to give a specific piece of information he was known to have which the questioner either could not or did not have. Q–I questions, so frequent in the homes of teachers, occurred rarely in Trackton. When they occurred, they usually did not have the purpose which dominated teachers' Q–I questions to their own children at home, i.e., requests for confirmation that the children had an objective piece of knowledge (the name of an object, its color, size, use, etc.). In Trackton, Q–I questions were used to confirm subjective knowledge held between the questioner and the addressee. For example, an adult or older child would accost a preschooler with "Whatcha name, huh?" The preschooler would be expected to give as an answer the nickname developed in relations between the questioner and the child, not his given name. In providing the appropriate nickname, the child confirmed the special relationship between him and the questioner.

The creativity of children in language use and their awareness of differences in language use were often displayed in situations where they engaged in self-talk. For example, Mandy, a child 4;1 years of age, was observed playing with a mirror and talking into the mirror. She seemed to run through a sequence of actors, exemplifying ways in which each used questions:

> How ya doin, Miss Sally?
> Ain't so good, how you?
> Got no 'plaints. Ben home?
>
> . . .
>
> What's *your* name, little girl?
> You a pretty little girl.
> You talk to me.
> Where's yo' momma?
> You give her this for me, okay?

When Mandy realized she had been overheard, she said, "I like to play talk. Sometimes I be me, sometimes somebody else." I asked who she was this time; she giggled and said, "You know Miss Sally, but dat other one Mr. Griffin talk." Mr. Griffin was the insurance salesman who came to the community each week to collect on insurance premiums. Mandy had learned that he used questions in ways different from members of her community, and she could imitate his questions. However, in imitation as in reality, she would not answer his questions or give any indication of reception of the messages Mr. Griffin hoped to leave with her.

In summary, children in Trackton were not viewed as information-givers in their interactions with adults, nor were they considered appropriate conversation partners, and thus they did not learn to act as such. They were not excluded from language participation; their linguistic environment was rich with a variety of styles, speakers, and topics. Language input was, however, not especially constructed for them; in particular, they were not engaged as conversationalists through special types of questions addressed to them. Occurrences of Q–I questions were very rare, and frequently involved a focus by an adult on speech etiquette when individuals outside the intimate circle of regulars were present. For example, preschoolers running through the room where a guest was preparing to leave might cause an adult to ask: "Didja say 'goodbye' to Miss Bessie?" Other question types addressed to preschoolers were also used by adults in conversation with other adults and were in no way especially formed for preschoolers. The intent and/or expected response to some of the question types, especially analogy, was sometimes special for preschoolers. (When analogy questions were addressed to adults, they were generally A–I, and the answerer was expected to provide information the questioner did not have, e.g., "What's his new car like?") In general, children were expected to learn to respond to questions which asked them to relate to the whole of incidents and composites of characteristics of persons, objects, and events. Preschoolers were judged as competent communicators if they learned when and how to use the various responses, both verbal and nonverbal, appropriate for the various question types.

INTERROGATIVES IN THE CLASSROOM

Questions teachers used in their homes with their own preschoolers were very similar to those they and their colleagues used in school with their students. Both of these were different from those used in Trackton. Therefore, children enculturated into competence in responding to adults' questions in Trackton had to acquire new uses in the school.

The early nursery-school experiences of Lem, a Trackton 4-year-old, provide one example of the kind of shift which the acquisition of school questioning strategies required.

Before Lem began attending nursery school, he was a very talkative child by community standards. He was the baby of the family and, for several years, the youngest child in the community, and he was on every possible occasion challenged to respond verbally and nonverbally to others in the community. Lem was particularly fascinated by fire trucks, and in the car he would keep up a chain of questions whenever we passed the fire station.

> Dere go a fire truck.
> Where dat fire truck go?
> What dat fire truck do?
> What dat dog do at da fire?
> Whose dog dat is?

As soon as answers were given to this series of questions, he began asking others about the sources of information which the participants had.

> How da firemen know where dey going?
> How come dat dog know to stay on dat truck?

At age 4;3, Lem began attending nursery school. It was his first experience in an institutional setting away from family and primary associates of the community. The nursery school was a cooperative run by middle-class parents and taught by a woman from a local church. During the first few weeks in school, Lem said almost nothing except when cookies and juice were passed out and he felt he was not getting a fair share. At other times, he watched and listened, showed strong preference for manipulative toys, and had little patience for talk-centered tasks directed by adults. At the end of the first 19 days of nursery school, in the car on the way home, he saw a fire truck. His sequence of questions ran as follows:

> What color dat truck?
> What dat truck?
> What color dat truck?
> What color dat coat?
> What color dat car?
> What color . . .

My response was: "What do you mean, 'What color is that truck'? You know what color that truck is. What's the matter with you?" Lem broke into laughter in the back seat, realizing his game had been discovered. During the first weeks of school, he had internalized the kinds of questions which occurred in teacher-talk centered tasks, and he was playing "teacher" with me. In the next few weeks, Lem's game in the car was to ask me the same kinds of questions he had been asked that day in school: "What color dat?" "Dat a square?" "What's dat?"

During those school activities which focused on giving labels to things and naming items and discussing their attributes, Lem did not participate. He listened and often tried to escape these structured sessions to play with trucks, puzzles, and so forth. He had no interest in looking at books and being asked questions about them, and he preferred to be involved in some kind of activity during story-reading time. He enjoyed activities taught to music, and when new activities were taught, he was the first to learn and always showed irritation with the repetitions required for other children to learn. In those learning tasks in which the teacher showed the children how to do things, rather than talked about the things themselves and what one did with them, Lem was enthusiastic and attentive. It is significant that in these tasks, teachers did not ask questions about the things or events themselves, but said instead: "Can you do that?" "Let's try it together. Remember the rope goes this way." (Compare Goody 1977, which discusses cognitive skills in the learning of manipulative tasks and the role of questions in this learning among the Gonja of Africa.) Once Lem began going to school, he had acquired information and had had experiences of which Trackton adults had no knowledge, and many of their questions became information-seeking ones.

> Whadja do today?
> Didja go anywhere?
> Didja have juice?

Lem rarely answered these questions directly, but he volunteered other information he judged relevant.

> Mike got dirty pants.
> Joey go over de swing, and fall off de top. She cried, and her mamma had to come. Mrs. Mason tol us not to go on dat swing like dat anymore.

If questions were directed to Lem about this incident, he would answer; however, if other unrelated questions were continued, he would act as though he had not heard the questions. Adults did not pursue their questioning, and they soon turned their attention to other matters.

The types of questions Lem faced in nursery school were very similar to those used in the first grades of elementary school. At this level, teachers asked questions of children to become acquainted with their students and to assess their level of knowledge of the world.

> What's your name?
> Where do you live?
> Have you ever seen one of these?

> What color's this?
> Can you find the apple in the picture?

These are common and seemingly harmless approaches to acquaintance and judgments of ability. However, children from Trackton either did not respond or gave minimal answers. Increasingly after the first few days of school, when most of the questions were centered around teachers' getting to know their students, the questioning shifted to other topics. Colors, numbers, letters, and elements of pictures in books became the foci of questions. A predominant characteristic of these questions was their requirement that students pull the attributes of objects out of context and name them. The stimuli for such questions were often books or picture cards which represented the item in flat line drawings with no contextual background. Among these items, many of the characters (queens, elves, uniformed policemen) and objects (walnuts, sleds, and wands) were unknown in Trackton. Indeed, to Trackton children, their teachers asked foreign questions about foreign objects.

Research on teacher questions has delineated numerous features of their use in the classroom (for surveys of this literature, see Gall 1970 and Hargie 1978). In studies of classroom language the percentage of questions in comparison to other types of utterances is uniformly shown to be high. Moreover, there are special properties of classroom questions and their use in sequences of units of language arranged to produce interaction (cf. Mehan 1978). In extended interactions, questions consume nearly 60 percent of the classroom talk (Resnick 1972).

Questioning in the classrooms by teachers involved in the study reported here fit the general patterns revealed in research in other classrooms. Questions dominated classroom talk; the predominant type of question used in classroom lessons called for feedback of information included in the lesson; questions which asked for analysis, synthesis, or evaluation of lesson data occurred much less frequently and were used predominantly with top-level reading groups. Of particular importance in this study is attention to types of question used in the classroom as compared with the homes of teachers and students.

In the research literature which attempts to classify question types, little attention is given to questions which do not have directly evident educational objectives, i.e., are not recall, analytic, synthetic, or evaluative questions (Bloom 1956, Gall 1970). In the classrooms of this study, questions which regulated behavior, especially with respect to classroom routines and attention to learning skills, emerged as particularly important (Heath 1978). Many questions asked by teachers were interrogative in form but were imperative or declarative in intent. "Why don't you hang your coat up, Tim?" was intended to be interpreted as "Hang your coat up, Tim." "What's going on here?" was intended to be interpreted as a declarative ("Someone is misbehaving") and a directive ("Stop misbehaving"). The question "Didja forget again?" was to be interpreted as "You forgot again." Teachers used questions with these meanings with their preschoolers at home and continued their use at school. Trackton students had relatively little experience with these indirect directives, viewed by teachers as the "polite way" of controlling the behavior of others. Of the types of questions used in Trackton, the accusatory were closest to these, and neither of the responses used in Trackton (bowing the head or offering a creative answer) was appropriate in the classroom. Trackton students generally ignored these questions and did not alter their behavior until given explicit directives ("Hang your coat up").

In lessons, teachers often asked questions which required confirmation of certain skills necessary to exhibit knowledge. Attention to appropriate stimuli—the person reading, a letter chart, or a specific page of a book—was tested by questions. Teachers used these in extended interactions with single students, small groups, and the entire class. If directed to a specific student, this question type demanded a response, either by display of the skill or by verbal confirmation. If directed to a group of students or the class, these questions were not to be answered, for they were merely forerunners to questions which would require answers.

> Can you point to the short *a*? How do we say it?
> Do you see the silent *e*? What does that make the vowel?

As might be expected, most of the questions used in lessons were Q–I questions, in which teachers asked for information which both they and often many students in class had. Trackton students were unfamiliar with questions which asked for labels ("What's the name of . . . ?") or called for an account of attributes ("How do we know that's a . . . ?") They usually did not respond or would parrot the answer given immediately preceding the question directed to them. Their communicative competence in responding to questions in their own community had very little positive transfer value to these classrooms.

The learning of language uses in Trackton had not prepared children to cope with three major characteristics of the many questions used in classrooms. First, they had not learned how to respond to utterances which were interrogative in form, but directive in pragmatic function (e.g., "Why

don't you use the one on the back shelf?" = "Get the one on the back shelf"). Second, Q–I questions which expected students to feed back information already known to the teacher were outside the general experience of Trackton students. Third, they had little or no experience with questions which asked for display of specific skills and content information acquired primarily from a familiarity with books and ways of talking about books (e.g., "Can you find Tim's name?" "Who will come help Tim find his way home?"). In short, school questions were unfamiliar in their frequency, purposes, and types, and in the domains of content knowledge and skills display they assumed on the part of students.

INTERVENTION: A TWO-WAY PATH

The task of schools is to transmit certain kinds of content and skills, but much of this transmission depends on classroom questions. For Trackton students to succeed academically, therefore, they had to learn to use questions according to the rules of classroom usage. However, intervention did not have to be one-way; teachers could also learn about the rules for community uses of questions. The choice in intervention was therefore not only to change Trackton students, but also to provide an opportunity for alterations in teachers' behaviors and knowledge.

Teachers were dissatisfied with the lack of involvement and the minimal progress of students from Trackton and similar communities. Teachers felt that questions were important to check on pupil learning and students' memory of skills and lessons, and to discover gaps in their knowledge. Yet questions were obviously not working to help teachers achieve these goals. Several agreed to look at the kinds of questions used in Trackton and to incorporate these, when appropriate, into classroom activities. They found that several types of questions used in Trackton could be considered what education textbooks called "probing questions" (cf. Rosenshine 1971). These were questions which followed questions, and questions designed to compare the knowledge questioner and addresses had about situations. Interrogatives modeled on some of the types used in Trackton were therefore justifiable in terms of good pedagogy. If used in classrooms, they would not only benefit students of low achievement; education research had shown these kinds of questions could benefit students across ability levels.

For some portions of the curriculum, teachers adapted some teaching materials and techniques in accordance with what they had learned about questions in Trackton. For example, in early units on social studies, which taught about "our community," teachers began to use photographs of sections of different local communities, public buildings of the town, and scenes from the nearby countryside. Teachers then asked not questions about the identification of specific objects or attributes of the objects in these photographs, but questions such as:

What's happening here?
Have you ever been here?
Tell me what you did when you were there.
What's this like? (pointing to a scene, or an item in a scene)

Responses of children were far different from those given in usual social studies lessons. Trackton children talked, actively and aggressively became involved in the lesson, and offered useful information about their past experiences. For specific lessons, responses of children were taped; after class, teachers then added to the tapes specific questions and statements identifying objects, attributes, and so on. Answers to these questions were provided by children adept at responding to these types of questions. Class members then used these tapes in learning centers. Trackton students were particularly drawn to these, presumably because they could hear themselves in responses similar in type to those used in their own community. In addition, they benefitted from hearing the kinds of questions and answers teachers used when talking about things. On the tapes, they heard appropriate classroom discourse strategies. Learning these strategies from tapes was less threatening than acquiring them in actual classroom activities, where the facility of other students with recall questions enabled them to dominate teacher-student interactions. Gradually, teachers asked specific Trackton students to work with them in preparing recall questions and answers to add to the tapes. Trackton students then began to hear *themselves* in successful classroom responses to questions such as "What is that?" "What kind of community helper works there?"

In addition to using the tapes, teachers openly discussed different types of questions with students, and the class talked about the kinds of answers called for by certain questions. For example, *who, when,* and *what* questions could often be answered orally by single words; other kinds of questions were often answered with many words which made up sentences and paragraphs when put in writing.[5]

Tapes and discussions of types of questions were supplemented by photographed scene sequences showing action in progress. *Why* questions were often the focus of these sequences, because both Trackton students and other students were especially tentative about answering these. Inferencing strategies in reading comprehension depended on the ability to answer *why* questions, making them particularly critical to reading success. The photographed scene sequences depicted a series of events, and students would arrange them in order and explain why they had chosen a particular order. For

example, in picture A, a girl was riding a bicycle; in picture B, the bicycle was on the ground, the girl nearby frowning and inspecting her knee; in picture C, the only details different from those in A were a bandage on the knee and a broad smile on the girl's face.[6] Because workbook exercises in the primary grades frequently called on the children to arrange pictures and later sentences in the proper sequence, children had to be taught to verbalize the characteristics of phenomena in and of themselves and in their relations with other things in the environment in order to complete workbook tasks. Teachers and students came to talk openly about school being a place where people "talked a lot about things being about themselves." Students caught onto the idea that this was a somewhat strange custom, but one which, if learned, led to success in school activities and, perhaps most important, did not threaten their ways of talking about things at home.

The primary rationale behind the research reported here was simple: if change agents (teachers and parents) were willing and involved, knowledge about language use could proceed along a two-way path, from the school to the community, and from the community to the school. Traditionally, education research has emphasized the need to train parents of children who are not successful in school achievement to conform to school practices. Knowledge had proceeded along a one-way path from school to "culturally different" communities. In this research the movement of ideas along that path was made two-way, so that a we-they dichotomy did not develop. In the past decade, research has identified standard English structures and patterns of discourse as "school talk" and non-standard English as "at-home" talk. Prescriptions derived from this dichotomy have found their way into parent education programs, encouraging early home initiation of children to "school talk" and school tasks and ways of thinking. There has been a decided we-they dichotomy, emphasizing how "we" of the school can enrich the background of the "they" of culturally different communities.

Moreover, remediation of language skills in classrooms traditionally followed the pattern of slowing down the process used for teaching "average" children, breaking the pieces of work into smaller and smaller units, presenting them repeatedly, and insisting upon mastery of the skills prescribed for each stage before moving on to the next stages. This breakdown of skills, stages, and units emphasized the use of recall questions, Q–I types for those of low achievement and analytic, evaluative, and synthetic questions with the academically successful. Elaboration and analysis of classroom language, habits leading to academic success, and ways of categorizing knowledge about things often led educators to believe these patterns of behaving had to be transferred to home settings of low-achievers before they could succeed in

Question relating to a lack of solution (handwritten)

Proposed solution (handwritten, left margin)

school. No one, either in teacher training programs or in the daily practice of education, seemed able to tap the uses of language and ways of "talking about things" of the culturally different and to bring these skills into the classroom.

To do so, at least two components were necessary: first, teachers as inquirers and second, credible data from both the classroom and the students' communities. For teachers to be involved in the inquiring process, they had to want to know what and how they and their students learned in language socialization, and they had to take part in collecting the data to answer these questions. In carrying out research on their own families and in their own classrooms—voluntarily and in situations where their job performance was not being evaluated—they acted from their own felt needs. They learned that their own behavior exemplified patterns which were sometimes contrary to their ideals and principles, or, at the very least, unexpected. Taking part in data collection and analysis gave them opportunity to consider how and why data on everyday behavior—their own and that of others—can be useful in bringing about attitude and behavior changes.

Teacher-training activities, whether workshops, graduate courses, or inservice programs, often involve teachers in the inquiry process. Equally necessary, however, in order to bring about change in response to their felt needs, are ethnographic data from their students' communities. Ethnographic data on communities and institutions of the United States can be used in a wide variety of teacher training and curriculum preparation programs. However, such data are rarely available, and of those studies which do exist, many do not provide either the degree or kind of detail and focus on language and learning needed to inform decisions about formal education changes. It is hoped that as anthropologists increasingly turn their attention to the United States, its communities and institutional settings, the ethnographic data needed will become available in formats appropriate for consideration by educators.

Such ethnographic data from communities and schools shared across participants should insure the exchange of information and skills along a two-way path. Ethnographic data which contributed to changes in teaching materials and methods in the classrooms reported here were not collected with the purpose of proving the ways of one group right and another wrong. They were not used to evaluate the practices of teachers. They were not used to prove to school authorities that they should change the ways in which Trackton residents interacted with their children. Data collected by teachers in their own homes and in their own classrooms, combined with data from Trackton, led them to ask questions of their own practices and to admit other practices into their interactions which would not necessarily have emerged otherwise. The long period of time over which these data were

collected, the large number of people involved, and the openness of communication among groups insured that the ethnographic research was not pressuring change. Innovations and adaptations emerged in the educational process in accordance with felt needs of the teachers.

THE AUTHOR

Shirley Brice Heath began her career in education in elementary classrooms, teaching reading, composition, and English as a second language. Helping students learn to use written and spoken language depended not only on the teacher's knowledge of language structures and processes, but also on an understanding of the uses and valuations of language in students' communities. This led her to graduate work in anthropology at Columbia University. Her anthropological fieldwork in Mexico, Guatemala, and communities of the Southeastern United States focused on the language and culture of minorities placed in schools in which success depended on knowledge of a standard language. She has served as consultant for curriculum projects and educational policymaking, and has written curriculum materials for language arts and social studies. She is author of Telling Tongues: Language Policy in Mexico, Colony to a Nation *(1972) and articles on language planning in the United States. Her forthcoming study,* Ways with Words: Ethnography of Communication—Communities and Classrooms, *describes language learning and use in two communities of the Southeastern United States. She is currently professor of education and anthropology at Stanford University and was formerly associate professor of anthropology and educational linguistics in the Graduate School of Education of the University of Pennsylvania.*

NOTES

1. The materials reported here on Trackton, teachers' homes, and classrooms are based on research conducted between 1970 and 1975 by myself and by my graduate students at Winthrop College. A full ethnography of communication study, containing data on Trackton and a Southern Appalachian-oriented community comparable in socioeconomic class, and schools attended by the young of both communities, is in preparation (Heath, forthcoming).

2. The teachers whose children are cited in the study of questioning at home were all primary-level teachers; all either were teaching in local public schools at the time of the study or had taught in the academic year preceding the study.

3. The questions and answers quoted from adults and children in this paper are represented in standard

orthography rather than in phonetic transcription, since our focus is not on pronunciation. Some contractions and other indications of relaxed casual speech are used for the sake of realism, but they are not intended as exact portrayals of speech.

4. Tape recordings were never made in Trackton; all field notes were written either on the scene or immediately after extended stays in the community. Percentages given here are averages based on analysis of field notes recording language use in play periods approximately two hours in length one day a week for eight months of each year, 1973 to 1975.

5. The teachers whose classroom data are reported here include those involved in the study of questioning at home plus the teacher in the nursery school and three additional teachers at the upper primary grades who were familiar with the results of the home questioning study.

6. Based on reading materials prepared by Shirley B. Faile, Rock Hill, South Carolina.

REFERENCES

Baratz, J., & Shuy, R. (Eds.). (1969). *Teaching black children to read*. Washington, DC: Center for Applied Linguistics.

Blank, M. (1975). Mastering the intangible through language, In D. Aaronson & R. W. Rieber, (Eds.) *Developmental psycholinguistics and communication disorder* (44–58). New York: New York Academy of Sciences,

Bloom, B. S., (Ed.) (1956). *Taxonomy of educational objectives handbook I: Cognitive domain*. New York: David McKay.

Blount, B. G. (1977). Ethnography and caretaker-child co. interaction. In C. E. Snow & C. A. Ferguson (Eds.), *Talking to Children: Language Input and Acquisition* (pp. 297–308). London: Cambridge University Press,

Brown, R. (1973). *A first language: The early stages*. London: George Allen and Unwin.

Cook-Gumperz, J. (1973). *Social control and socialization: A study of class difference in the language of maternal control*. London: Routledge & Kegan Paul.

Corsaro, W. A. (1977). The clarification request as a feature of adult interactive styles with young children. *Language and society* 6:183–207.

Ervin-Tripp, S. (1970). Discourse agreement: How children answer questions. In R. Hayes. (Ed.), *Cognition and Language Learning* (79–107), New York: John Wiley and Sons.

Ervin-Tripp, S., & Miller, W. (1977). Early discourse; some questions about questions. In M. Lewis & L. A. Rosenblum. (Eds.), *Interaction, Conversation, and the Development of Language* (pp. 9–25). New York: John Wiley and Sons.

Gall, M. D. (1970). The use of questions in teaching. *Review of Educational Research* 40:707–720.

Gleason, J. B. (1973). Code switching in children's language. In T. E. More. (Ed.), *Cognitive development and the acquisition of language* (159–167). New York: Academic Press.

Gleason, J. B., & Weinlraub, S. (1976). The acquisition of routines in child language. *Language in society* 5:129–136.

Goody, E. (1977). Towards a theory of questions. In E. N. Goody, (Ed.), *Questions and politeness: Strategies in Social interaction* (17–43), London: Cambridge University Press, .

Hargie, O. (1978). The importance of teacher questions in the classroom. *Educational Research* 20:99–102.

Harkness, S. (1977). Aspects of social environment and first language acquisition in rural Africa. In C. E. Snow & C. A. Ferguson, (Eds.), *Talking to children: Language input and acquisition* (309–318), London: Cambridge University Press.

Heath, S. (1978). *Teacher talk: Language in the classroom*. No. 9, Language in Education Series. Washington, D.C.: Center for Applied Linguistics.

Heath, S. (1978). *Ethnography of communication: Communities and classrooms*.

Holzman, M. (1972). The use of interrogative forms in the verbal interaction of three mothers and their children. *Journal of Psycholinguistic Research* 1:311–336.

Holzman, M. (1974). The verbal environment provided by mothers for their very young children. *Merrill Palmer Quarterly* 20:31–42.

Hymes, D. H. (1962). The ethnography of speaking. In T. Gladwin & W. C. Sturrevant. (Eds.), *Anthropology and Human Behavior* (13–53). Washington, DC: Anthropological Society of Washington.

Kochman, T., (Ed.). (1972). *Rappin' and stylin' out*. Urbana: University of Illinois Press.

Labov, W. (1970). *The study of non-standard English*. Champaign. IL.: National Council of Teachers of English.

Labov, W. (1972). The logic of nonstandard English. In *Language in the inner city* (201–240). Philadelphia: University of Pennsylvania, (First published 1969.)

Labov, W., et al. (1968). *A study of the non-standard English of Negro and Puerto Rican speakers in New York City*. Report on Cooperative Research Project 3288. New York: Columbia University.

Levelt, W. J. M. (1975). *What became of LAD?* Peter de Ridder Publications in Cognition I. Lisse, Netherlands: Peter de Ridder Press.

Mehan, H. (1978). Structuring school structure. *Harvard Educational Review* 48:32–65.

Mitchell Kernan, C. (1971). *Language behavior in a black urban community*. Monograph No. 2 of the Language- Behavior Research Laboratory, Berkeley, CA.

Newport, E., Gleitman, H., & Gleitman, L. R. (1977). Mother, I'd rather do it myself: Some effects and non-effects of maternal speech style. In C. E. Snow & C. A. Ferguson, (Eds.), *Talking to children: Language input and acquisition* (109–150), London: Cambridge University Press.

Ninio A., & Bruner, J. (1978). The achievement and antecedents of labelling. *Journal of Child Language* 5:1–15.

Resnick, L. (1972). Teacher behavior in an informal british infant school. *School Review* 81:63–83.

Rosenshine, B. (1971). *Teaching behaviors and student achievement.* Slough National Foundation for Education Research.

Sachs, J., Brown, R. & Solerno, R. A. (1976). Adults' speech to children. In W. von Raffler Engel & Y. Lobruo, (Eds.), *Baby Talk and Infant Speech* (246–252). The Netherlands: Sevets and Zeitlinger.

Shalz, M., & Gelman, R. (1977). Beyond syntax: The influence of conversational constraints on speech modifications. In C. E. Snow & C. A. Ferguson. (Eds.), *Talking in Children: Language Input and Acquisition* (189–198). London: Cambridge University Press. .

Slobin, D. J., (1968). Questions of language development in cross-cultural perspective. In *The structure of linguistic input*

to children. Working Paper No. 14. Berkeley, CA: Language-Behavior Research Laboratory, 1–25.

Snow, C. E. (1977). The development of conversation between mothers and babies. *Journal of Child Language* 4:1–22.

Snow, C., Arlman-Rupp, A., Hassing, Y., Jobse, J., Joosten, J., & Vorster, J. (1976). Mothers' speech in three social classes. *Journal of Psycholinguistic Research* 5:1–20.

Stack, C. (1976). *All our kin.* New York: Harper and Row.

Ward, Martha C. 1971 (reissued 1986). *Them children: A study in language searning.* Prospect Heights, IL.: Waveland Press, Inc.

Wolfram, W. (1969). *A sociolingulstic description of Detroit negro speech.* Urban Language Series, No. 5. Washington, D.C.: Center for Applied Linguistics.

Young, V. H. (1970). Family and childhood in a southern negro community. *American Anthropologist* 72:269–288.

PERSPECTIVE 1: POSTPOSITIVISM ON THE HEATH STUDY

D. C. PHILLIPS   *Stanford University*

I find the ethnographic study reported here to be compelling. Shirley Brice Heath set out, at the request of some concerned parents, to discover why it was that young Black students, who were quite vocal in their home and community environments, often appeared to be unresponsive (or worse) when interacting with teachers in school. Soon she came to focus upon the language of schooling, and the rituals associated with the use of language. Through a careful and long-term comparison of language use (and particularly the use of questions in social interactions) in the homes of Black children and in the homes of the predominantly White teachers, and through a study of language use in schools that helped confirm what she was learning in the other settings (logically, she was doing a type of cross-checking), she builds a strong case that there is a lack of "cultural congruence." In other words, she found that White and Black youngsters were socialized differently at home to the uses of questions, and she showed that at school the practice was overwhelmingly to use the form of questioning that was culturally familiar to White students, but that was essentially quite foreign to the other youngsters.

The work reported here dispels a number of myths about rigorous inquiry. First, it demonstrates that rigorous studies do not have to take the explicit form of hypothesis testing, nor do they have to use a randomized experimental design. This is not to say that hypotheses were not formed or tested; it was probably the case that Heath was constantly making conjectures about what was happening in the verbal interactions she was studying—conjectures that gave guidance to her data-gathering activities—but her study did not take the form of an explicit, large-scale test of a pre-formed hypothesis. But as she went along she seems to have carried out informal tests of her ideas. For example, she tried getting teachers to change the form of the questions they used, to see what would happen; and there is the delightful anecdote that describes her "calling" Lem, whom she was driving home from nursery school, on his parody of the type of questions his teacher asked (the interaction showed that she understood Lem's underlying attitude, so in essence it served as a test of her ideas).

Neither was it the case that Heath carried out the kind of intervention that takes place in an experiment; rather, her work mainly was *naturalistic* in the sense that she studied a natural setting from within, as a participant observer. The individuals she was interacting with were not experimental subjects whom she manipulated, rather they were informants from whom she learned (some writers on ethnographic method suggest that the "subjects" be thought of almost as co-authors!).

Second, the paper illustrates the fact that the distinction between qualitative and quantitative research is artificial. It has often been thought that qualitative researchers—of whom ethnographers are prime examples—do not use numbers, and it also has often been thought that researchers who conduct experiments do not make observations! Yet some of the most compelling parts of Heath's paper are those in which she reports descriptive statistics (the percentage of verbal interactions between mothers and young children that take the form of questions, or the frequency of questions in classroom discourse). A good scientific paper, like Heath's, *makes a case* about an issue or problem, and, like a case made by a good lawyer in a trial, it is a case that draws upon whatever kinds of evidence that are pertinent to the matter at hand and which are judged to be reliable or trustworthy enough to be given credence. Thus, Heath uses these descriptive statistics, but she also fits these into a detailed analytic framework that she presents in the form of tables; she reports her detailed observations (of classrooms, of mother-child interactions, and the like); she draws upon her own conversations with parents, teachers, and children; and she provides clear examples drawn from her field notes.

Third, a little more needs to be said about the method of investigation used by Heath as she built up her case. She says a little about this early in the paper: She worked in classrooms on and off during the period of the study (during which occasions she noted the language practices); she also visited the homes of teachers (to talk with them and to observe how they interacted with their own children), and she visited the homes of Black families in Trackton, where she observed, participated, and asked questions herself about the meaning of what she was seeing or hearing. She followed some children over time, studying the development of their communicative competence at home, in community settings, and at school. She discussed her views in classes she was teaching at a local university, classes in which teachers were enrolled. As discussed above, she carried out some informal tests of her ideas—to check her understanding of the situations she was seeing. She developed classifications of types of questions that were used in various contexts, and she culled the relevant research literatures for insights. Finally, her paper is packed with examples drawn from her years of field observations.

The methodological logic here has been well-described by Michael Agar in his "informal introduction to ethnography," *The Professional Stranger:*

> In many sociological surveys . . . a questionnaire is designed. Then interviewers go out and "collect the data." The data are then coded and keypunched. Only then does "analysis" begin, with the machine-readable data manipulated according to some statistical procedure. In ethnography . . . you learn something ["collect some data"], then you try to make sense out of it ["analysis"], then you go back to see if the interpretation makes sense in light of new experience ["collect more

data"], then you refine your interpretation ["more analysis"], and so on. The process is dialectic, not linear. (Agar, 1996, p. 62)

There seems no reason to deny that this is, in Dewey's terms, a "competent" way to produce warranted knowledge.

REFERENCE

Agar, M. H. (1996). *The professional stranger: An informal introduction to ethnography.* San Diego, CA: Academic Press.

PERSPECTIVE 2: PRAGMATISM ON THE HEATH STUDY

NEL NODDINGS   *Stanford University*

From a pragmatic perspective, this study is in many ways exemplary: "Our aim is to indicate how ethnographic data can be useful for comparison with data collected in studies of the functions of language in the classroom" (p. 136). Further, the study includes an intervention based on what was learned and, finally, the intervention was transactive; that is, teachers learned from students and allowed themselves to be changed as they worked to encourage new language habits in their students.

Like most of the best ethnographies, this one took time—5 years. Today, doctoral students and other young researchers often choose to use ethnographic methods because they allow considerable freedom in terms of analysis and description. The constraints of graduate work, however, or limitations in funding may put severe limits on the time that can be spent in the field. The result is sometimes a weak imitation of ethnography. An important question for every researcher is whether the question to be researched can reasonably be answered in the time that can be allotted.

In this ethnography, the main researcher was well known in the community. She had lived and worked there for years. The research problem—on patterns of questioning at home and at school—emerged gradually in the context of a broader observation of language. Again, many graduate students are attracted to ethnography because one "doesn't need a question" at the outset; the question will disclose itself. But unless the researcher has lived and worked with the social group she plans to study, her time may be up before a researchable question arises.

Another obvious strength of this ethnography is the collaborative nature of the work involved. Heath did not seek admission to a social group in order to study an issue she defined and imposed on the group. Rather, she responded to a problem identified by the two groups involved. White teachers wanted to know why they had such difficulty in getting Black children to respond to their questions, and Black parents wanted to know why their children were not doing well in school. This was research *for* people, not *on* them (Noddings, 1986; Smith, 1987).

Because the research was driven by a pragmatic question, the researchers were careful to use just a few powerful categories for analysis. Q–1 questions include all those teacher-like questions to which adults already know the answer. Their purpose is to find out whether children also know the answer and, if they do not, to teach it—perhaps with another question. "What color is the car?" might be followed by, "It's blue, isn't it?" If you think about the scenes from which the questions are extracted, you can easily imagine getting bogged down in a welter of categories that would shed little light on basic linguistic differences. A powerful computer program of ethnographic analysis might be of little help here. One has to be very well trained in the major topic of analysis—in this case, linguistic patterns. The researcher has to create the categories. Then the computer can look for examples.

Pragmatists are concerned with the social history of problems. In the pragmatist view, culture and science are not separate; problems in science arise in and are deeply influenced by problems and attitudes in the larger society. Approaches to the education of black children have varied over the years, and often the perspectives taken have caused new problems. The so-called deficit model, for example, seems to have damaged the self-esteem and confidence of Black children instead of increasing their resources and opportunities. On the other hand, a more generous theoretical stance that recognizes Black English as a complex system with its own semantic and syntactic rules has sometimes been used as an excuse for failing to help Black children learn standard English. Even the important Supreme Court decision outlawing segregation in schools had its negative effects. In its aftermath, Black children were often separated from their Black teachers and neighborhood schools. Moreover, it seemed as though the society were saying that Black children could not learn well unless they were schooled with White children. Heath gives part of this story but, because it is so important, I wish she had said more. It is vital, especially, for young researchers and teachers in training to be familiar with this social history.

Heath herself is careful to avoid judgmental pitfalls. She describes differences in conversational styles and questioning patterns, but she does not evaluate one way as better than another. Indeed, she even uses different categories to describe the different patterns. However, it is clear that one way is better if we want children to succeed in classrooms as they traditionally operate. Heath suggests that teachers might accommodate different styles instead of operating in the traditional way. Her intervention requires a delicate balance—one that respects and learns from the Black way but also invites Black children to learn the usual White-school way.

There is one, perhaps unavoidable, weakness in this study. We do not learn anything about the long-term effects of the intervention. Did the teachers continue to use powerful transactive methods? Did other teachers adopt these methods? Did the Black children "do better" in school? For how long and in what ways? Today's researchers also need to ask about studies that followed this one. Have other researchers replicated Heath's findings? Did Heath suggest further studies? These questions remind us of the limitations imposed by time. Heath has shown convincingly that communication between school and community can be fruitful, but pragmatists would still like to know more about long-term effects.

REFERENCES

Noddings, N. (1986). Fidelity in teaching, teacher education, and research for teaching. *Harvard Educational Review, 56*(4), 496–510.

Smith, D. E. (1987). *The everyday world as problematic: A feminist sociology.* Boston, MA: Northeastern University Press.

PERSPECTIVE 3: CONSTRUCTIVISM ON THE HEATH STUDY

YVONNA S. LINCOLN   *Texas A&M University*

To paraphrase an old television ad, this is not your father's ethnography. Heath's ongoing focus has been on language acquisition, language use, and the cultural clash evident in the ways in which different children are socialized to deploy language in their everyday activities and in school. This is not a classical ethnographic study, however, because Heath never assumes that there is some single reality which, when properly roped and corralled by words, would provide the lone insightful "key" to the classroom silences of Trackton's Black children. Nor does she assume that there are set categories to be investigated which, when properly described, might bound and frame the issue. Likewise, she never assumes that her answers might be the answers which meet the needs of either children or teachers.

This is, in elegant fashion, the "new" ethnography. The questions are driven as much by the teachers' concerns with the nonresponsiveness of their recently-desegregated pupils as they are by Heath's interests in language acquisition. Teachers themselves, with questions and issues they cannot resolve, become their own inquirers and researchers, recording their own language use at home and in the homes of other teachers and friends with infants, toddlers, and children. Heath acts as a facilitator, analyst, "translator," extra pair of hands in data collection effort, talking with both classroom teachers and the parents of Trackton's children. The inquiry takes on the flavor of a piece of participatory action research, written as a classical ethnography, but with major differences.

The values which undergird this study are clear. The teachers, confronted with desegregation and culturally different pupils in their classroom, now mobilize to be successful at teaching these new children. They want their new charges to be successful at school, and in a vastly different milieu. The central value for Heath is to aid and abet the teachers in finding linguistically and culturally appropriate ways to teach these children. In the openendedness of the new ethnography, there is neither good nor not-good; rather there is a concern for finding answers which can inform practice and classroom teaching.

The multiple ways of knowing—epistemologies—are likewise clear. Trackton parents have their own linguistic and cultural practices with respect to children; Trackton children "are not regarded as information givers or as appropriate conversational partners for adults," unlike the infants and children of non-Trackton (largely White) parents, who question their children constantly, even when it is clear that there is no answer forthcoming. In these questioning strategies lie the clues to teaching in culturally appropriate ways. As the mysteries of conversation, questioning, expected modes of response, and children's understanding of what is expected by adults' conversational styles unfold, it becomes clear to teachers how Trackton children may be taught effectively and engaged in the work of a classroom. Labelling questioning practices of the two different sets of adults—Trackton and non-Trackton—as good and bad is viewed from the start as unuseful. Rather, it is deep understanding which is sought by Heath and the teachers alike. Unpacking the role of questioning in language acquisition, and understanding conversational styles rooted in difference, is the guiding theme of the joint inquiry.

Different ways of "knowing" conversation are viewed as simply that: different conversational strategies. Nowhere is there any effort in this study to label strategies as better or worse. Multiple epistemological structures are recognized to exist alongside each other, and are explored for their implications for classroom teaching and instructional practices.

In the best sense, "Questioning" is a constructivist study. It is ethnographic in intent, largely qualitative in focus—that is, seeking a different kind of understanding from numerate discourses—open to multiple and negotiated values, and admitting of multiple, sometimes competing, frequently overlapping, experiential epistemologies. The study recognizes that community and school/classroom are linked in mutually influencing, rather than casual, ways. Teachers are encouraged and supported in their attempts to deploy several strategies for enticing Trackton children to respond in class, experimenting with working hypotheses until something is found which works, and which elicits answers and engagement from the children.

If there is any criticism to be made of this piece, it is that there is little explication of how Heath worked with and between students, parents, and teachers to arrive at the understandings they all came to share. Clearly, in the schools of this small city, some kind of breakthrough has occurred. Teachers have enriched their capacity for becoming reflective practitioners as well as researchers of their own instructional practices. And just as clearly, the twin communities have arrived at a new level of understanding between White teachers and Black parents which never existed previously. I wish that we knew more about that. Heath's chapter is a lovely example of how research can and should serve a community's felt needs—and at the same time, serve to enlighten other researchers and practitioners via the fairly straightforward research requirement of public inspectability (i.e., publication).

PERSPECTIVE 4: INTERPRETIVE AND NARRATIVE ON THE HEATH STUDY

ARTHUR P. BOCHNER   *University of South Florida*

As a teacher, I often have asked myself, "Why don't I reach more of the students?" "Why aren't more of them touched and inspired?" "What am I missing that causes some students to lose interest or to stay removed?" "Why aren't they more immersed in the process of learning?" When I was younger, I thought it was their problem not mine. My response was similar to the ones I often hear from colleagues: "The students aren't smart enough." "They don't read thoroughly." "They can't write well enough." "They can't think." "They don't care?" "They probably shouldn't be in college." Rarely do I hear these teachers ask themselves how they may be contributing to the circumstances that frustrate and disappoint them. Nor do I hear them question the grounds on which they make these attributions about the abilities, motivation, and commitment of their students. How do we know when our students aren't smart enough, can't think, and don't care? On what basis do we make these attributions?

As I've grown older, I've begun to understand the classroom as a social and relational context for learning. The learning that takes place there is shaped and influenced by the relationships between the students and me, and among the students. My command of the subject matter is not enough; nor are my years of experience as a teacher. Each class poses a different challenge; each emerges as a different community of learners. As I age, the differences between "them" and me grow wider and deeper. My experience has not been theirs; their experience has not been mine. Moreover, as the ethnic, racial, class, and age diversity among students in the same class has expanded, their similarities to each other have contracted. It is not just my differences from them that are notable, it is also their differences from each other.

As teachers, we have to be mindful of the context for learning in which we and our students are embedded. This is where ethnography of teaching and learning enters. The demands of teaching require teachers to become ethnographic practitioners. In this sense, teaching is inquiry.

Shirley Brice Heath provides a definition of ethnography that coincides with the idea of teaching as inquiry. According to Heath, ethnography "describe(s) the ways of living of a social group" and is particularly relevant to groups in which the members "must live and work together to retain group identity" (p. 136). In the community that Heath studied, both the White teachers and the Black parents understood that what was happening in the classrooms had to be changed. The parents felt that communication between their children and the teachers was inadequate, and the teachers wanted to learn how to communicate with these children more effectively. The kids felt their teachers asked dumb questions, while the teachers thought the students were not smart enough to answer even the simplest questions. The parents had to deal with young children who already had developed a fear and hatred of school, while the teachers had to deal with the frustration of feeling as if talking to the children was like talking to a wall. For the parents, the teachers appeared to be poor listeners; for the teachers, the Trackton children were inadequate, inarticulate, and unresponsive students. Collectively, the teachers, parents, and students were people in quandaries.

Conceiving these teachers and parents as willing and involved change agents, Heath proposed a solution that construed change as a reciprocal process between the community and the school. Normally, when children underachieve in school, their parents are encouraged to work on training them to conform to the school's practices. This "one-way" change does not involve alterations in the behavior of the teachers. Moreover, this approach to poor classroom performance implies that the children are to blame because they are doing something wrong that needs to be changed. If the kids change, the learning situation will improve. The burden is placed on the children and their parents rather than on the teachers.

In contrast to this monadic view of change, Heath proposed a two-sided perspective in which it was not only the children who had to change, but also the teachers (and their schools). Eventually, the Trackton students would have to learn to follow the rules of discourse on which successful performance in the schools was contingent, but to make it possible to learn these rules the teachers would need to change their modes of communicating with these students. The teachers had to learn to speak in a manner that would conform more closely to the ways of talking to which the Trackton children were most responsive. They would need to understand that how they talked to the Trackton students had a great deal to do with whether and how these children responded in class. Heath's reciprocal perspective on change meant that the teachers shared the burden of change with the students. It was not a question of which group was to blame. The teachers and students shared responsibility for what was taking place. They were in it together. Thus, both groups—teachers and students (and their parents)—had to be invested in the process of change.

One of the main lessons of Heath's research is that, as teachers, our effectiveness often depends on how well we understand the interactional context of the classroom. The rub is that what happens inside our classrooms is not completely isolated from what takes place outside our classrooms, in the families and communities in which we live our lives. When we do not share the cultural background of our students, we may find it difficult to understand what they mean by what they say and do, or do not say or do not do. And when we don't understand, but do not understand that we do not understand, we may make negative attributions about our students that are

critical position

false and unfair. What Heath seems to be saying is that we should start by understanding that we don't understand, instead of assuming that we do and blaming those who are different from us for the difficulties or conflicts we are experiencing. Heath perceptively advises us to start by examining our assumptions carefully, treating our work as teachers as a process of inquiry, asking penetrating questions about our own practices, collecting data that we can use to address these questions, and altering our practices to accommodate what we learn about ourselves and our students from these data. In short, she wants us to become inquiring teachers.

Enter ethnography. The teachers in Heath's study were both participants (subjects) and co-collaborators in the research project. Over a period of 5 years, Heath gradually developed close ties to the teachers as well as to the Trackton families. On the basis of these relationships, Heath was welcomed into both sets of families, those of the White teachers and those of the Black Trackton students, observing and participating with both groups of parents and their children and friends. Focusing on the functioning of questions in these family contexts, Heath observed that the teachers "did not always make the same assumptions about the uses of questions" (p. 138) that the Trackton children did. The teachers used largely the same style of questioning in their school classrooms as they did in their own homes with their own children. For these teachers, asking questions was a frequent and largely dyadic (one-to-one) activity, a way of training children to become conversational partners, to label, name, and categorize objects in the world. For the Black Trackton families, on the other hand, questioning was a relatively rare communicative exchange. Trackton parents talked "at" their children, more than "with" them and their interaction took place in larger, extended networks, not one-on-one between parent and child. Moreover, the Trackton parents did not normally ask their children to name, categorize, and/or identify objects but rather expected them "to learn to respond to questions which asked them to relate to the whole of incidents and composites of characteristics of persons, objects, and events" (p. 145).

As a result, when they entered school, the Trackton kids were disturbed by the repetitive focus on labeling and categorizing. They wanted "to do things" more than "to talk about them" and they became inattentive and unresponsive when the teachers persisted with this kind of unfamiliar categorical questioning. If the teachers wanted to reach the Trackton students, they would have to change some of their practices of questioning, bringing them closer to what they had learned about the functioning of questions in the Trackton families, e.g., not what is this, but what is happening here?; not what's it called, but what's it like? When the teachers began to do this, writes Heath, the Trackton students became active, involved, and responsive.

In contrast to the studies by Carr, et al. (Chapter 5), and Raudenbush, et al. (Chapter 8), Heath's research is highly context-sensitive. It is doubtful that what she learned about the cultural differences between the White teachers and Black students could have been learned by less context-sensitive research methodologies such as giving questionnaires to the teachers or exerting behavioral (experimental) control over the student's responses to bring them into line with the teacher's expectations. Heath prudently chooses, instead, to study the teachers and their students in their natural environment, at school and at home, taking care not to alter the historical and interactional integrity of the whole setting.

Indeed, the focus of Heath's work centers our attention on the crucial issue of how to bring an interactional integrity to the school setting. In her fieldwork, she discovers that the family communication of the Trackton children is ruptured by the interactional environment of their experience at school. To motivate them, teachers need to make it possible for the Trackton children to have a more seamless transitional experience from home to school.

To her credit, Heath applies a civic and democratic mode of inquiry that involves all of the people who are connected to the learning context she is studying—parents, teachers, and children. Each has a stake in the interventions and outcomes associated with this research and, thus, each is viewed more or less as a partner in the inquiry. While she may not have achieved an optimal balance in voicing the views of each party, she does give us a sense of how each is reacting to the conflicts and irritation they experience. If the changes are to be lasting, each of the parties must have a stake in the plan for change and in its implementation.

As a reader, I felt that Heath's ethnographic mode of representation gave me a space to respond actively to the story she was telling, which I didn't feel when I read the work of Carr et al. and Raudenbush et al. I thought about my life in school, as both a teacher and a student, and about the differences that necessarily divide teachers from students. I thought about the attributions I make about students and questioned how hard I try to understand the basis of the differences that separate us. My personal reactions, however, were inhibited by Heath's discursive style. _interpretive_ She is writing for an academic audience and thus the prose, for the most part, is dry and abstract. Moreover, I never achieved a sense of who Shirley Brice Heath is, what draws her to this work, her political and moral convictions, and what is at stake for her and the community in the outcomes of her research. Like most social scientists, she writes in the third person, not the first. She still constructs me, as a reader, largely as a distant spectator. I never get a sense of her own vulnerability as a researcher or of how heartbreaking it must have been for her to witness the Trackton children struggling to make the transition from home to school without having their cultural premises crushed by the teachers. I get to know her as a researcher, and the children and teachers not as characters but as subjects or participants, though she does provide a few anecdotes that helped me imagine what a fuller portrait might look like. She doesn't try to make me feel what it is like to be a Trackton student or to experience the frustration and pain of the teachers or Trackton students. Hers is a cerebral account, not an embodied performance or suspenseful narrative. Of course, at the time she was conducting this research and writing her monograph, these more personal modes of representation were not options as they are today in the aftermath of postmodernism and poststructuralism.

Heath's is a valuable study that makes us aware of our responsibilities as teachers to examine our assumptions and make our life as teachers an ethnographic life. I am only sorry that, due to the norms of academic writing to which she probably felt she had to conform, she did not have an opportunity to represent her work in a fuller, more embodied, more performative fashion. My point is that the choices one makes (and one has) about how to write a research story have significant consequences. As a research story, Heath's narrative is informative but not evocative. She conforms to the academic norms of distance and neutrality. The story she tells is clean and relatively unproblematic: a problem occurred (Trackton students were underachieving); people wanted to solve the problem (teachers and parents in particular); research was undertaken to discover the source of the problem (an ethnographer did fieldwork in the homes of families of teachers and students and she collaborated on the inquiry with the teachers); and a solution was achieved that produced changes in teaching methods and patterns of communication making life in school a less threatening and more positive experience for the students. For me, then, this research, like so many social science studies during this time period, appears to have been sanitized for publication. As an ethnographer, Heath comes off as the heroine of her story, the person who figured out how to bring the different factions together. She makes the process of intervening into the patterns of the school and the community seem unproblematic, as if there were no power

Cultural bias + Layering

struggles, no racist politics, no emotional vulnerabilities, no resistance to change, no messiness or defensiveness in the research and intervention process.

In the final analysis, then, Heath's portrayal of intervention does not ring true to me. In my experience—over 30 years of teaching—I've seen few teachers who would so readily examine their teaching practices without having their arms twisted or being offered incentives. I believe that there must have been difficult barriers for Heath to break through, including the obvious possibility of institutionalized racism. But this is not the story she tells and we have to ask, "Why not?" When we write the story of our research, we always find that we can't tell everything and we have to make choices about what to tell and what to leave out. Thus, it usually is instructive to ask, what is left out and why? The story Heath tells conforms to the logic and norms of social science writing. In this sense, it achieves an academic sensibility and an anthropological validity. But by sterilizing the story she has to tell, dissolving the characters and the tensions they must have felt in a solution of emotionally neutralizing rationality, Heath risks losing her trustworthiness as a storyteller. What do you think really went on in Trackton and in the schools while she was there? Why did it take 5 years to complete the intervention? What happened after she left?

PERSPECTIVE 6: RACE, ETHNICITY, AND GENDER ON THE HEATH STUDY

BETH HARRY   *University of Miami*

Heath's ethnography of language learning and usage in one Black community offers a radical rendering of child rearing and communication traditions that have long been devalued in American society. One of the problems with research on minority groups, in particular Blacks, is that traditions and practices are interpreted from the perspectives of outsiders whose cultural assumptions may allow them no schema for true understanding. Thus, in the context of the historical devaluing of Black traditions, relying on outsider perspectives is exceedingly dangerous. Yet Heath's research shows that it is not the fact of being an "outsider" or an "insider" that determines the ability to understand. Rather, it is the ability to view knowledge as relative to the knower, and to commit oneself to learning through the eyes of others.

Traditional mainstream reports on Black family practices resulted in innumerable negative stereotypes (e.g., Frazier, 1948), and culminated in the "tangle of pathology" image made official in the U.S. Department of Labor's report of 1965. The language patterns and communication styles of Blacks came to be seen as but one more symptom of deprivation and developmental deviance. Labov's (1972) deconstruction of this belief, followed by other linguists' examination of African-American Vernacular English (AAVE) and other American dialects, began to provide a lens for seeing the linguistic competence of AAVE speakers. Heath's explication of the pragmatic aspects of these patterns goes further, allowing us to see the relationship between language and culture and the impossibility of categorically valuing one form of language over another. Indeed, Heath's portrait is so clear that it provides a lens for a critical analysis of the language patterns promoted in schools and expected of children in classroom settings.

Heath uses the strengths of ethnography to reveal the assumptions and values behind the child-rearing and communicative practices of this Black community. In so doing, she is able to offer the perspectives of insiders to that culture. The portrait reveals the intertwined nature of family structure, community structure, and children's language learning. In contrasting the family structures of the Black group and the "teacher" group, she shows how the presence of several adults in a household can affect communication patterns between adults and children, which are further reinforced by community norms about the roles of adults vis à vis children. The perceptive ethnographer is able to see these relationships, hear and give credence to the explanations of adults, and use the voices of children and adults to illustrate the explanations offered.

In my graduate courses in multicultural education, Heath's portrait is always required reading. Despite the clarity of Heath's analysis, the initial response of most non-Black graduate students is one of shock that the Black adults in the study do not see it as their job to "teach" language to their children. When I give students the responsibility of doing a class presentation on this piece, I know that I run the risk that the tone of the class discussion will be thinly veiled with negativity. A common conclusion of the presenters is that, "these parents hardly even talked to their children but I guess it was okay because the children did learn to talk anyway." Black students also have trouble with the portrait, and often comment that they don't really think this is true because, in their experience, "Black parents do talk to their children."

The reason that students miss the point and need considerable guidance in absorbing the information in the study lies as much in the uncritical nature of their professional training as in their extended experience with only mainstream forms of discourse. Even those Black students who have firsthand knowledge of communicative traditions similar to those in Trackton resist understanding Heath's point, and their denial of any knowledge of such patterns reflects the intense embarrassment felt by minority group members when a devalued practice is presented. What is happening here is that graduate students of all ethnicities, precisely because they have been successful in school, have been socialized into the language patterns of schools. Their professional training furthers this by never requiring them to ask what beliefs and values underlie the teaching strategies they are being taught (see Kalyanpur & Harry, 1999). For them, the way to develop children's knowledge and language is to model, question, and test for correct responses. It is difficult for them to take a critical stance towards their own training and practice.

Teachers' resistance is particularly ironic in the light of Heath's portrait, because it should be clear to any educator that the kinds of questioning to which the Trackton children were accustomed are exactly the kinds of "higher order questions" to which teaching is supposed to aspire. This is easily seen in the contrasting examples of Lem's questions before and after he went to preschool. His untutored questions focused on the why's and wherefore's of the fire truck and its operators: "How da firemen know where dey going?" "How come dat dog know to stay on dat truck?" (p. 145) His mocking imitation of the teachers' style only a few months later make the classroom questions seem simplistic and elementary.

On addressing this piece I am always overwhelmed by the power of ethnography to break through the silences that exist regarding race and ethnicity. In the atmosphere of a liberal philosophy, student teachers find it difficult to discuss issues that may reveal their deeply held biases about Blacks and other minorities. The absence of dialogue reinforces stereotypes, since the negatively valued practice is seen as too unpleasant to be discussed rationally. The power of Heath's research lies in its ability to use the voice of the "other" to explain practices typically seen as pathological. As often happens when these voices are heard, the folk theory being expressed is as clear and as rational as the abstractions offered by scholars. For example, the child who said "Ain't nobody can talk about things being about theirselves!" echoes the literature on cognitive psychology, where studies of learning in non-western societies show how items may be defined in terms of their practical functions, rather than by their physical attributes as would be expected by a western IQ test (Rogoff & Chavajay, 1995.)

Another outcome of this ethnography is the revelation to mainstream members that negative valuing of the practices of "others" is not uni-directional, since the devalued "other" also holds negative views of mainstream practices. The mother who told Heath that "we don't talk to our chil'un like you folks do; we don't ask 'em bout colors, names, 'n things," (p. 143) disturbs the complacency of mainstream members who are unaware of how they are seen by members of minority groups. This view brings to mind Basso's (1979) vivid presentation of how the social interaction style of "the Whiteman" provoked ridicule among the western Apache of Cibeque. Only through the actual voice of such speakers can these important lessons be presented to mainstream teachers.

Heath's recommendation for a "two-way path" of knowledge about language use goes well beyond the issue of language. Teachers will learn from this how limited are the lens by which any one group views the world and ways of knowing.

REFERENCES

Basso, K. H. (1979). *Portraits of "the Whiteman."* New York: Cambridge University Press.

Frazier E. F. (1948). *The Negro family in the United States.* New York: Citadel.

Kalyanpur, M., & Harry, B. (1999). *Culture in special education: Building, reciprocal family-professional relationships.* Baltimore, MD: Brookes.

Labov, W. (1972). *Language in the inner city.* Philadelphia, PA: University of Pennsylvania Press.

Rogoff, B., & Chavajay, P. (1995, October). What's become of research on the cultural basis of cognitive development? *American Psychologist, 50,* 859–877.

U.S. Department of Labor. (1965). *The Negro family: The case for national action.* Washington, DC: U.S. Government Printing Press.

PERSPECTIVE 7: CRITICAL THEORY ON THE HEATH STUDY

GEORGE NOBLIT   *University of North Carolina*

This study is a classic in educational anthropology and one that has spawned a line of research that critiques how Whites teach children of color. This subsequent line of research essentially argues that White children are advantaged in schools because they are being taught in their culture while children of color are being taught in a culture different from their own. This has led to proposals to teach the culture of school explicitly to all students as well as arguments that schools should teach in the children's indigenous culture. This line of research raises contentious issues that will not be resolved easily or soon. Moreover, this line of research also challenged the assumptions of the research that preceded Heath's study. The earlier research argued that it was the Black families and children that needed to change "emphasizing how 'we' of the school can enrich the background of 'they' of culturally different communities" (p. 137) and promoting remediation by "slowing down the process used for teaching 'average' children" (p. 137). Shirley Brice Heath's study started a line of critical inquiry but her study was not guided by critical theory or written as a critical ethnography. Heath's study, like those of Ellis (Chapter 9) and Sullivan

(Chapter 10), is interpretive and serves practical interests (Habermas, 1970). Again practical interests (uncertainty leads people to engage a situation and learn from it in the process) should be
distinguished from technical interests (technical rationality and the control it requires) and emancipatory interests (liberating people from domination). Heath's study promotes the idea that close
attention to lived experience and the interpretations of that experience may lead to better if not
certain courses of action. Her study demonstrates that ethnography, when embedded in a setting
and collaboration, leads all parties to a better understanding of what is going on and potentially
to ways to better teach the Black students who are at a disadvantage in the setting. Since it was
an interpretive study, it did not lead to specific (i.e., technical) pedagogies or to a changed life for
these students. To an interpretivist, either of these outcomes underestimates the complexity and
subjectivity of everyday life.

   As an interpretive study, many of the critiques offered of Ellis' and Sullivan's articles could be
repeated here. Yet there is an additional way to approach this study from the vantage point of critical theory. Heath describes her study as

> Participating and observing with the children and their families and friends intensively over a pe-
> riod of five years, I was able to collect data across a wide range of situations and to follow some
> children longitudinally as they acquired communicative competence in Trackton and then at-
> tempted to take this competence into school settings. Likewise, at various periods during these
> years, I observed Trackton adults in public service encounters and on their jobs, and I was able to
> compare their communicative competence in these situations with those inside of Trackton. The
> context of language use, including setting, topic, and participants (both those directly involved in
> the talk and those who only listened), determined in large part how community members, teach-
> ers, public service personnel, and fellow workers judged the communicative competence of Track-
> ton residents. Proper handling of questioning was especially critical, because outsiders often
> judged the intelligence and general competence of individuals by their responses to questions and
> by the questions they asked. (p. 138)

This passage has much in it worthy of discussion. It highlights that the study was longitudinal
and across a range of participants and contexts. It also establishes how questioning became the
central focus of the study—because questioning was central to being judged communicatively
competent and thus able to effectively participate in school and other White-dominated contexts.
This competence, as the study proceeds to document, is important and does have real consequences for Black children in schools. Yet critical theorists would view this definition of communicative competence to be quite limited. That is, lacking the competence to communicate with
Whites in public institutions has dire consequences but there is another form of communicative
competence that seems lacking as well. Moreover, it is this latter competence that inhibits both
Blacks *and* Whites from transforming the unfortunate state of affairs that Heath documents. Critical theorists define communicative competence the capability to participate in discussions about
the assumptions that make up a culture and to be able to determine what should be maintained
or changed (Bowers, 1984).

   Clearly, this definition encompasses that used by Heath but in effect alters what is important
entirely. Heath is using a definition drawn from linguistics that focuses heavily on language and
verbal interaction, while critical theorists use a definition that involves language but is more directed to the purposes to which language is being used. The critical theorist definition is quite demanding and arguably is achievable in an "ideal speech situation" (Habermas, 1970) that is not
structured by power and ideology or in liminal moments (Bowers, 1984) when people can see
the assumptions that their culture is built upon. Yet it does highlight how different the outcomes

of interpretive and critical studies are likely to be. Achieving communicative competence by Heath's definition allows one to play within the structures of power and ideology while achieving a critical theorist's definition allows you to play with the structures themselves. As I have put it elsewhere (Noblit & Dempsey, 1996), it is the difference between being a pawn (albeit a pawn with more advantages) and a participant in a culture. To be fair, Heath's definition might make Black students more equal to Whites in the competition called schooling but a critical theorist's definition is about having all people participate in what the "power elite" (Mills, 1959) now control as well.

Heath was clearly working to benefit Black children. She was initially invited by older Trackton residents who already knew her to explain "why their children were not doing better in school". Even with her commitments to Trackton, she was also generous in her understanding of White teachers and accepted the educators verbalizations that they were "not asking the right questions" and were "dissatisfied with the lack of involvement and the minimal progress of students from Trackton". A critical researcher would have interrogated desegregation more deeply and engaged racism more seriously. Nevertheless, Heath was able to engage the teachers in a positive program of research and intervention to promote more meaningful communication between teachers and students. Given the power of the teachers, it no doubt was wise to engage them as collaborators in the research. Yet the narrow focus on questioning would seem to a critical researcher too narrow to promote teachers examining the assumptions that undergirded their practice, even if it did change their questioning strategies. Questioning strategies could have been a beachhead to an inquiry into the fuller range of assumptions the teachers employed to justify their power, but it was not. That "[t]hey learned that their own behavior exemplified patterns which were sometimes contrary to their own ideals and principles . . ." was and is important, but changing how they asked questions would not necessarily push them to consider how their Whiteness and social class worked to construct Black students as poor students. Moreover, it is not clear that the White teachers and Black parents had developed a new relationship via this study. There is little sense that these two communities could now work in concert to benefit the children or to work on wider issues of equity in the city or wider society. A critical researcher would say that here was an opportunity missed.

Heath's ethnographic methodology has many of the hallmarks of the best approaches to ethnography. It is longitudinal, collaborative, comparative (across the Trackton and White teachers communities), grounded in the scene and in research on linguistics and education, and so on. Yet the methodology also reproduces differences. A critical researcher would argue that unfortunately the comparative nature of the study highlighted the differences between Trackton and the teachers, between Blacks and Whites. The Black and teacher communities focused on the differences in questioning. In turn the teachers changed because of the difference they came to understand as well as because of their beneficence. The Black community remained different in the eyes of the teachers, and, as well intended as it was, the teachers changed in order to make the Black children find the White-controlled institution to be of benefit to them. This is the essential strategy of colonialism: to have the colonized believe colonialism benefits them. While the critical researcher would want data on how differences were reproduced and the extent to which the colonial analogy was apt, the point here is that the interpretive nature of this study did not consider how it may reinforce perceptions of difference in the community.

Heath was able to move at least some teachers to consider how to help Blacks be successful in school, and this accomplishment should not be underestimated. Yet the critical researcher would lament that this accomplishment was built upon perceptions of difference. The critical researcher would have at least asked for the study to reinforce similarities as well as differences and further would have pushed for both communities to become participants in their culture. It is apparent that neither Trackton residents nor the teachers were, or became, communicatively competent in this sense.

Heath's intervention with the teachers presumed the status quo: "For Trackton students to succeed academically, therefore, they had to learn to use questions according to the rules of classroom usage" (p. 147). She goes on to indicate that the "intervention did not have to be one-way. . . . The choice in intervention was therefore not only to change Trackton students, but also to provide an opportunity for alterations in teachers' behavior and knowledge" (pp. 147–148). The chapter then goes on to discuss how Trackton students responded to changes in the curriculum and instruction the students were receiving. The results were heartening: "Responses of children were far different from those given in usual social studies lessons. Trackton children talked, actively and aggressively became involved in the lesson, and offered useful information about their past experiences" (p. 148). Tapes of the children's responses had teacher questions and answers added so that students could learn the difference between what they did at home and what the school expected: "On the tapes, they heard appropriate classroom discourse strategies" (p. 148), and later "began to hear *themselves* in successful classroom responses to questions . . . " (p. 148). This had important effects: "Students caught onto the idea that this was a somewhat strange custom, but one which, if learned, led to success in school activities and, perhaps most important, did not threaten their ways of talking about things at home" (p. 148). Yet it is important to note that what is discussed is that the goal is to make Black students succeed in the institution of education. The children had to change their cultural patterns. The institution would change only to the extent that these teachers changed some linguistic patterns. The institution was still conceived as dominant and appropriately so, even though Heath's evidence indicates that the school was in fact an institution imposing White culture on all children.

A critical researcher would note that Heath's intervention was primarily at the level of teachers. While it did convince some to change, it surely illustrated the power a teacher has to effect student learning. It also defined productive change for the students to accept the power of the institution to define their success. What was missing to a critical researcher was an attempt to understand how Black students could become part of transforming the institution into one that helped transmit their home culture to others. Similarly, we have little evidence that the Trackton parents were more communicatively competent to negotiate cultural change and maintenance after this study. Teachers did change and presumably learned something about how to change their practice. Yet teachers had their power bolstered, leading critical researchers to be concerned that a study meant to benefit African Americans actually increased the power, communicative competence and capability of middle-class Whites.

From a critical perspective, Heath accomplished much. Yet she was hampered by her limited definition of communicative competence and by not having a critical analysis of how ethnography can promote difference even when it wishes to reduce difference. Interpretive studies are practical but this presumes an acceptance of the ways things are. For Blacks and for White teachers, this is insufficient. They deserve to become participants in their culture rather than pawns of it.

REFERENCES

Bowers, C. A. (1984). *The promise of theory: Education and the politics of cultural change*. New York: Longman.

Habermas, J. (1971). Toward a theory of communicative competence. In H.P. Dreitzel (Ed.) *Recent Sociology no. 2: Patterns of communicative behavior*. Basingstoke: Macmillan. pp. 115–148.

Mills, W. W. (1959). *Philosophies of science in sociological imagination*. New York: Oxford University Press.

Noblit, G., & Dempsey, V. (1996). *The social construction of virtue: The moral life of schools*. Albany: State University of New York Press.

PERSPECTIVE 8: ETHICS, METHODOLOGY, AND DEMOCRACY ON THE HEATH STUDY

KENNETH R. HOWE   *University of Colorado at Boulder*

The foreword to Shirley Brice Heath's study describes it as "in the emerging tradition of an applied social science appropriate in a democratic society" (p. 135). This characterization serves as the point of departure for my commentary.

Heath's commitment to a democratic approach to educational research is exemplified in her "two-way path"—"from the school to the community, and the community to the school" (p. 147). Each of the elements of democratic educational research adumbrated in my general characterization—inclusion, dialogue, and deliberation—are to be found here. Also consistent with my general characterization, Heath contends that "qualitative" research methods (ethnographic methods, in particular) foster such a democratic—or "two-way"—approach.

Regarding methods, compare the way in which Heath goes about her research with the way Raudenbush et al. (Chapter 8) go about theirs. Heath does not take the school behavior of children at face value, to be interpreted in terms of the concepts researchers bring to the situation, such as "higher order thinking skills." If she did, then the Trackton Black children's inability or refusal to engage in the kind of question-answer behavior that typifies U.S. classrooms would serve as evidence that they are defiant or are lacking in some way in intellectual skills. Indeed, the behaviors in question are *lower order,* and Black children's failure to engage in them led certain people to conclude that these children were "stupid" or "pathetic" (p. 142).

My aim here is not to criticize Raudenbush et al.'s study, beyond the limitations I described before. Comparing it to Heath's study in the way I have illustrates an important additional point, however. The relationship between so-called "quantitative" and "qualitative" methods can be the reverse of the way it is often characterized. That is, quantitative methods may be seen as *crude* and *descriptive;* it takes further inquiry with qualitative methods to obtain *precision* and *explanation.* And, because qualitative methods are grounded in the voices of those who are most affected by educational practices and policies, the kind of explanation provided by qualitative methods has important ethical dimensions.

Though Heath does not draw the parallel herself, one can easily draw one between her approach and John Dewey's. Dewey's overarching educational goal was the creation of a truly democratic citizenry. This could best be achieved, he believed, by highly deliberative school communities who constantly engaged in experimenting with subject matter and instructional techniques and who engaged in ongoing dialogue about the results. The peculiarities of the social circumstances, including the make-up of students, were to play a major role in the research activities of such school communities.

As public education is currently structured, educational researchers are rarely school insiders, as they would be if Dewey's vision were realized. Instead, they are usually outsiders, typically university faculty, which includes Heath. Thus, educational researchers unavoidably assume the role of experts, as well as leaders or "change agents." In the case of Heath, she brought her considerable knowledge, experience, and expertise to the situation. Accordingly, her role as educational researcher distinguished her participation from that of others. Appealing to her background in anthropology, she formulated the plan for data collection, directed it, and orchestrated its interpretation. It is highly unlikely that the study she describes would have occurred without her participation or the participation of someone like her.

Interestingly, Heath dodges (or submerges) questions about educational values no less than Raudenbush et al. do. She hangs her hat on the "felt needs" of the teachers with whom she worked. The felt needs in question are based on the thoroughly value-laden ideas that all children, regardless of background, should be given every opportunity to succeed in school and that it is the teacher's responsibility to make every effort to ensure they do. Exploiting these felt needs, Heath conducted her research without in any way "pressuring change" (p. 149).

But one wonders whether *no* teachers felt pressured to change, if only by a ripple effect reaching beyond those committed to Heath's study. One also wonders whether, as Heath intimates, the pressure for change would be a bad thing. Finally, one wonders whether educational researchers have the responsibility to go beyond *responding* to felt needs to include in their endeavors *creating* them. Consider the felt need to eliminate injustice.

Of course, these are large questions about the ethics of educational research that go beyond the particulars of Heath's quite remarkable study.

PERSPECTIVE 9: POSTSTRUCTURALISM ON THE HEATH STUDY

LYNDA STONE   *University of North Carolina at Chapel Hill*

Pierre Bourdieu (1930–2002). Occupying the chair in sociology at the most prestigious French academic institution, the Collège de France, Bourdieu was one of the best known European "social theorists" in the English-speaking world. In addition to his reputation in sociology, he was known both as a philosopher and social scientist. Born in France and educated in traditionally elite institutions, he spent an early period as teacher and researcher in Algeria before taking conventional French academic positions. His work considered French social and cultural life that specifically includes education and ranges from general artistic taste to academic life.

Shirley Heath's classic work on children's literacy has reminded educators at all levels and for several decades of the specific influences culture has on learning and schooling. While the study might be updated today to reflect changes in language use relative to race and class in Trackton, this research has stood better a test of time than much other inquiry. For those of *us* who read the piece some decades ago, questions asked in classroom interactions have never been the same.

Two insights from Heath's contributions about "culture" and the role of language in emergent literacy are initially significant: one is that even as teachers undertake efforts to help "all" children learn, there is much about learning and its contexts that are taken for granted. Moreover, even as most teachers are well-intentioned members of a dominant culture may (often) implement a deficit model of learning; that is, that a sub-group's culture does not fit the dominant discourses and practices of school, that some children come to school "disadvantaged." Heath demonstrates that the first insight must be addressed and that the second is just inappropriate. Both of these core ideas are "poststructural" in spirit, as is a founding third conception of the research: this is to point to the centrality of language (and its specific use) in making sense of and living in the world.

One initial aspect of Heath's study connects to the writing of French sociologist, Pierre Bourdieu. Hers is a "comparative study" of social groups as is often his work; Bourdieu has studied social organization primarily in North Africa and France. Indeed Heath offers two comparisons, home and school as in her title as well as those of White and Black "cultural" worlds. The foci of the study were "the interrogatives . . . [White] teachers used with their own preschoolers at home, questions . . . [Black] Trackton adults asked their preschool children, and the conflict and congruence between these differing approaches to questioning as they evolved in classrooms" (p. 148). Two sub-cultures in effect exist that seemingly continue to play out today.

Bourdieu, who died in 2002, is relatively well known to a group of Anglo-American critical sociologists, specifically for his concept of cultural capital and for early work in education, with Jean Claude Passeron (see Bourdieu, 1991). From the overview, it might be posited that Bourdieu begins with practice and works dialectically across his career to fill it out. This is through particular studies, through the development of characteristic concepts. Practice, as central, is a kind of structure of how people act in the world. Within practices, capital relates language (i.e., discourses) and actions and a second term, *habitus,* relates potential actions to their "context." Practices of politics and ethics result for persons within particular habituses; understanding these practices might portend their change.

Less known than capital, *habitus* first appears in the text, *Outline of a Theory of Practice* (1977) and is refined subsequently in *The Logic of Practice* (1990), Bourdieu's concept of *habitus* is this:

> The conditionings associated with a particular class of conditions of existence produce *habitus,* systems of durable, transposable dispositions . . . as principles which generate and organize practices and representations . . . without presupposing a conscious aiming at ends or an express mastery of the operations necessary in order to obtain them . . . ["Regulated"] and "regular" without being in any way the product of obedience to rules, they can be collectively orchestrated without being the product of the organizing action of a conductor. (Bourdieu, 1980/1990, p. 53, term always in italics by Bourdieu)

"Without being conscious" is central, as response to the *habitus* is "immediately inscribed in the present" in appropriate things to say and do, or not, in relation to "a probable, 'upcoming' future" (ibid.). Indeed response seems necessary and natural, even if it *is* conscious. Bourdieu continues that past experiences produce both an individual and a collective *habitus* with early experiences having special significance, particularly in terms of family. Importantly these dispositions make possible the production of free thoughts and actions within certain conditions: what results is infinite yet limited generative capacity. Further, *habitus* is "poststructuralist," aiming to transcend "antinomies . . . of determinism and freedom, conditioning and creativity, consciousness and the unconscious, or the individual and society" (ibid., p. 55).

For Bourdieu, *habitus* operates along lines of cultural and social class groups (including generational distinctions) manifest as "capital." There are three interrelating forms: economic, cultural, and symbolic. Differentiated capital possessed by different groups produces in Bourdieu's words "classifiable practices and products . . . [as well as] the judgements . . . which make these practices and works into a system of distinctive signs" (Bourdieu, 1984, p. 170). In his work on French culture, *Distinction,* Bourdieu relates that tastes are formed out of these systems. Within a culture(s), how "class" is conceived is also instructive, here defined as individuals possessing "identical or similar conditions of existence and conditionings" (Bourdieu 1980/1990, p. 59). Chief among these are economic conditions, and always operating in the Bourdieu schema is power. He writes, "[What is constituted for each person and each group is] a particular relationship to a particular universe of probabilities . . . a certain state of the chances objectively offered . . . by the social world. The relation to what is possible is a relation to power" (p. 64). Integral is symbolic power—specifically here in language and its interactions. For Bourdieu this is "a power of constituting the given through utterances, of making people see and believe, of confirming or transforming . . . [a] vision of the world, and thereby, action on the world" (Bourdieu, 1977/1991, p. 170).

Three points from Bourdieu's concepts tie directly to Heath's work: One is the importance of early experience; two is that *habitus* is internalized "beyond the limits of what has been directly learnt—of the necessity inherent in the learning conditions" (Bourdieu, 1979/1984, p. 170); and three is the significance of race. While "race" is not mentioned by Bourdieu in connection with *habitus,* in the American context at least, historical classes can be conceived in terms of race.

Heath's study is replete with racial implications of *habitus,* indeed positing "competing" sub-habitus as part of the larger societal formation. Interestingly, economics did not figure strongly in cultural distinctions as both racial groups were ostensibly "middle class." What did count was the historical situation of recent desegregation and disparate communication patterns surrounding "the rituals and routines of classroom life . . . and the information and skills acquired in the classroom" (p. 137). Heath demonstrates convincingly in this piece and the larger work, *Ways with Words: Language, Life, and Work in Communities and Classroom* (1983) significant differences between racial groups in expectations of and in practices themselves. What matters greatly, surely exemplifying differences in *habitus,* is "context of language use" (p. 138). Since Heath's study, context in education has become almost commonplace; however, Boudieu's elaboration reminds us again of its importance in educational research for reform.

REFERENCES

Bourdieu, P. (1977). *Outline of a theory of practice.* (R. Nice, Trans.). Cambridge, MA: Cambridge University Press. (Original work published 1972)

Bourdieu, P. (1984). *Distinction: A social critique of the judgment of taste* (R. Nice, Trans.). Cambridge: Harvard University Press. (Original work published 1979)

Bourdieu, P. (1990). *The logic of practice* (R. Nice, Trans,). Stanford, CT: Stanford University Press. (Original work published 1980)

Bourdieu, P. (1991). *Language and symbolic power* (G. Raymond & M. Adamson, Trans). Cambridge, MA: Harvard University Press. (Original work published 1977)

Bourdieu, P., & Passeron, J. C. (1990). *Reproduction in education, society, and culture* (R. Nice, Trans.). London and Newbury Park, CA: Sage, in association with *Theory, Culture & Society,* Teesside Polytecnic, Department of Administrative and Social Studies (Original work published 1965).

Heath, S. B. (1983). *Ways with words: Language, life, and work in communities and classrooms.* Cambridge, MA: Cambridge University Press.

CHAPTER 7

The Alexander Study

PERFORMING CULTURE IN THE CLASSROOM: AN INSTRUCTIONAL (AUTO)ETHNOGRAPHY

BRYANT KEITH ALEXANDER

The notion of performing culture in the classroom is both a paradigmatic description of a phenomenon as well as a theoretical position. This research is poised at the productive intersection of critical pedagogy and the increasing focus on autobiography and autoethnography in Performance Studies. The essay seeks to contribute to the development of education as well as performance theory.

KEYWORDS

Pedagogy	Performance
Identity	Autobiography

The practice of performing culture is an all encompassing aspect of our daily being, inclusive of rituals, customs, policies and procedures, as well as those performances of self related to sex, gender, class and race. It is a method of defining, redefining, and maintaining our cultural identities and social selves. The classroom as a specific cultural site is not immune to these performances. In particular, the nested contexts of race and gender become variables that dictate and mediate the pedagogical enterprise. The classroom is a site in which "dense particularities," lived and imagined, are engaged (Mohanty 13). The process of education itself is a quintessential site for cultural proliferation and acculturation. "Critical theorists see school as a form of cultural politics; schooling always represents an introduction to, preparation for, and legitimatization of particular forms of social life. It has always been implicated in relations of power, social practices and the favoring of forms and knowledge that support a specific vision of past, present and future" (McLaren 168). Critical pedagogy is concerned with revealing, interrogating, and challenging those legitimated social forms and opening the space for additional voices. "In the broadest terms, critical pedagogy is concerned with the political agendas that anchor, motivate and emerge through the cultural practice of education" (Pineau 5).

This essay takes as its primary object cultural performance in the classroom, using autobiography and autoethnography as critical praxis. As a part of a broader study, it seeks to address the issue of how Black male teachers and Black male students perform and negotiate culture in the classroom by bringing their articulated experiences to bear upon the project. In order to accomplish this I offer a theoretical frame for the methodology, followed by an autoethnographic analysis of my own lived experience as a Black male student and teacher. I then present an ethnographic analysis of the articulated experiences of the Black male teachers interviewed, followed by the experiences of the Black male students interviewed.

CONSTRUCTING AN INSTRUCTIONAL (AUTO)ETHNOGRAPHY

Within this project I braid three methodological procedures that are variations of the primary method of ethnography: the ethnographic interview, focus groups[1] and autoethnography to formulate an "instructional (auto)ethnography." I use the classroom as a cultural site. In the process I deliberately reject the notion of an objectivistic ethnography that may deny or mask my lived experience and my membership within the

Alexander, B. K. (1999). *Performing culture in the classroom: An instructional (auto)ethnography.* Text and Performance Quarterly, *19(4), 307–331. Used by permission of the National Communication Association.*

cultural community of Black male teachers and students. Rather, like Goodall, I seek "to establish non-hierarchial connections to encourage lateral relations: instead of living within the bounds created by a linear view of history and society, we [my co-researchers and myself] become free to interact on an equal footing with all the traditions that determine our present predicament" (7).

The braiding of these methods yields a wealth of articulated knowledge. Writing about the ethnographic interview, Spradley says that "[t]he essential core of this activity aims to understand another way of life from the native point of view" (iii). This method is particularly appropriate for investigations into classroom culture. In *Schooling as a Ritual Performance: Towards a Political Economy of Educational Symbols and Gestures,* McLaren states that "a growing interest among educational researchers in qualitative research methodology and ethnographic portrayals of classroom life has sparked a developing awareness of the value of anthropological theory used in an educational context" (24). His own ethnography of a Canadian catholic school has contributed greatly to linking educational theories with theories of cultural performance, unearthing and formulating theories of cultural politics that operate within the educational system.[2]

A special issue of *Communication Education* entitled "When Teaching 'Works': Stories of Communication in Education" was dedicated to the emerging use of story in education. In the Foreword, Walter Fisher refers to Carter, saying: "Story has become more than a rhetorical device for expressing sentiments about teachers or candidates for teaching profession. It is now, rather, a central focus for conducting research in the field" (5). Hence the use of qualitative research methods like ethnographic interviews and narrative inquiry allows participants to articulate their stories in ways that are reflective of their lived experience within the specified context of the classroom. It moves towards the justification of autobiography as scholarship.[3] In *Autobiography, Politics and Sexuality: Essays in Curriculum Theory,* Pinar calls the use of autobiography in this context the gathering of "authentic educational experience in a thoroughly bureaucratized school establishment" (2). The link between narrative research and the use of autobiography is clear. The narrative form is the medium for articulating the lived experience found in autobiography.

In "Performing Theory/Embodied Writing," Madison uses autobiography as both process and product. Her explication of "the notion of theory" reinscribes the fundamental components of theory as a sense-making tool connected to memory and autobiography:

> You sense that theory is more than adoration or disdain. It is more than language, gatekeepers, belonging, respect,

or isolation. It is all and nothing more than recognition. You think you know something, but theory leads you to *know* it *again.* You were always aware of power, beauty, pain, language, race, and yourself. But theory circles you back to all of them, including yourself. Breaking the parts open, piece by piece, theory demands that you take notice—pay closer attention. You see again and greet anew. Things are more complicated, because things *are more.* Whether you agree with theory or not (even if you argue with it) it makes you feel and see differently. You speak differently and more. The recognition is not unrecognized. (109)

Autobiography, like theory, is a process of recreating, reviewing and making sense of the biographic past. Pinar states: "The biographic past exists presently, complexly contributive to the biographic present. While we say it cannot be held accountable for the present, the extent to which it is ignored is probably the extent it does account for what is present" (22). The critical move of making sense of the *autobiographic past* is the project of autoethnography.

In *Autobiographical Voices: Race, Gender, Self Portraiture,* Lionnet states that autoethnography is "the defining of one's subjective ethnicity as mediated through language, history, and ethnographical analysis; in short . . . a kind of 'figural anthropology' of the self." (99). The method is an explication of lived experience and encounters within a specified cultural context which combines the self-reflection of autobiography and the intense scrutiny of "other" as found in ethnography. In *Casing A Promise Land,* a primary example of autoethnographic work, Goodall explains the logic of this methodology.

> I personally believe that the sort of writing that I do is part autobiography and part cultural ethnography. It is not particularly different from the writing of an investigative reporter . . . What distinguishes it is not what makes it particularly different, but what makes it particular. For me, that is the authorial voice directed toward the experience of detection. (154)

Autoethnography positions me in my own study as what hooks calls an "indigenous ethnographer," one "who enters culture where they resemble the people they are studying and writing about" (126). This is not a new move for Black writers writing and theorizing on the Black experience. In describing the work of Zora Neale Hurston, Lionnet locates her in a "fundamental liminality—being at once a participant in and an observer of that culture" (99). The position places Hurston in the dilemma of constructing the cultural familiar as other. In reference to her own ethnographic work, Jones describes the construction of herself as other in this way:

The initial ethnographic experience is a collision with the self, an exercise in shifting the self from center to periphery. The ethnographer confronts the constructions of the other created prior to contact and the ways in which those constructions are intimately linked with the construction of the self. For me, a Pan-Africanist, African-American ethnographer doing fieldwork in Africa, the cultural collision derailed both constructions. (133)

Likewise, when faced with performing and negotiating culture with my Black male students, I ask myself what it means to them for me to be a Black male teacher. How does their construction of Black masculine identity "derail" my own construction and collide with my instructional role as teacher?

I implicate myself in this project as a member of the cultural community that I seek to explore and examine. In the process I join my voice with other Black male teachers and students in what Conquergood calls a "dialogic performance" where "different voices, world views, value systems, and beliefs . . . can have a conversation with one another" (9). Consequently, this project is dialogic in that it "brings self and other together so that they can question, debate, and challenge one another" (9). I seek to mark those points of intersection and divergence between what Lionnet calls the "individual (auto-) and the collective (ethno-) where the writing (-graphy) of singularity [can and] cannot be foreclosed" (108).

We all exist between the lines of our narrated lives, the stories we tell and the stories that are told about us. We all exist between the lines, the unsaid thoughts in the other's description. We also read between the lines, adding our hopes to the unspoken dreams and the dailiness of our shared existence. I approach ethnographic, autobiographic and autoethnographic research as a way of reading between the lines of my own lived experience and the experiences of cultural familiars—to come to a critical understanding of self and other and those places where we intersect and overlap.

FRAMING EXPERIENCE: ENTERING REFLECTION

Goodall states that "all the classic ethnographies that inspired [him began] with an account of cultural entry and surprise" (110). I use the same approach in constructing this project. I begin by describing how I entered a specified culture, a Center for Basic Skills-designated section of Interpersonal Communication, and how that entry

catapulted me on a journey. It is a story that I have told often, yet each telling allows me entry into new aspects of the experience.[4]

On the first day as a Graduate Teaching Assistant at Southern Illinois University, I walk into my Center for Basic Skills (CBS) section of Interpersonal Communication. I am immediately intrigued by the visual display of culture that presents itself. In my class are a handful of students whom I generically collectivize as White, a few that I initially describe as Hispanic, and a couple who are possibly Native American or East Indian. By far the largest percentage is Black. I introduce myself as Bryant Alexander and say that I will be their instructor. As I bend down to open my brief case I overhear a young Black man talking to another young Black man who says: "*Man, we got a brother for an instructor.*" They seem to experience some *comfort* in this acknowledged cultural familiar. I, too, experience a wonderful sense of personal acknowledgment. In that brief moment I remember what it felt like (those few times) when I had an instructor who was Black. I remember experiencing a positive appraisal in seeing my academic potential reflected and projected within the body and person of the instructor.

While defining and describing the class, I overhear the same young Black man talking to the same person: "*Maybe he's not a brother,*" then, he laughs slightly. I wonder what made him change his perception? Certainly the visual display of my race did not change. What did change was the assumed familiarity that came with racial identification. Within that short period of time my cultural performance came under scrutiny—my use of language and my overall communicative presentation, gesture, movement and behavior, redefined and (re)constituted me to him. My performance of "Black male" was evaluated by these Black male students as being inappropriate, incongruent or at least very different from their own cultural script.

I am reminded by Van Maanen that the limits and strengths of ethnography, and quite possibly this essay, might lie within the multiple roles I play as teacher and student, researcher and researched. Van Maanen suggests that "[e]thnographies are documents that pose questions at the margins between two cultures. They necessarily decode one culture while recording it for another culture" (4). Hence within the context of this instructional auto(ethnography) I critically describe and analyze my own lived experiences in the classroom, and that of others, in order to come to an understanding of where our experiences intersect while being acutely aware of my shifting and dual cultural membership and the shifting borders of my intention: self-reflection and research.

AUTOETHNOGRAPHY: REFLECTING B(L)ACK

In "Myths in the Making of a Teacher," Britzman states that teachers enter the classroom with an *institutional biography* that tells them how to navigate through the school structure and provides a foundation for the stock responses necessary to maintaining it. Additionally, implicit in these stock responses are particular images of the teacher, mythic images which tend to sustain and cloak the very structure which produces them (448). In this section I explore my experiences as a student and how those experiences translate and have affected my own cultural performances as a teacher in the classroom. I attempt to explore what have been "stock responses" and experiences within the classroom to gain new understanding of and exposure for the structures that produced them. In the autobiographical move, I acknowledge that time and distance have mediated my memory, but the felt experience of having Black teachers is written into my educational lifescript. It is that historical and yet somatically felt experience from which I draw.

In twenty-two years of schooling, from the first grade to the doctoral seminar, I can name the handful of Black teachers that I encountered in the classroom:

Mrs. Black, 1st Grade; Mrs. Babineaux, 5th-Grade History; Mrs. H. Landry, 6th-Grade Natural Sciences; Mrs. Mouton, 8th-Grade Chorus; Mrs. Dorsey, 9th-Foundations of Literature; Coach Johnson, 10th-Grade Physical Education; Mrs. Martin, 10–12th Grade Advanced Mixed Choir; Mrs. Shaw, 12th-Grade Medical Life Science; Professor Arceneaux, Freshman Year-Counseling & Orientation; Professor Braud, Sophomore Year-Introduction to Education; Professor Greer, Second Year Doctoral Study-Special Populations.

In my seven years of teaching as a full faculty member in predominately White educational systems, I have had no Black colleagues. In my border status as a graduate teaching assistant I had four Black colleagues who, as I did, negotiated the sometimes tenuous space of being both student and teacher in a predominately White university. Currently, as an Assistant Professor in an ethnically diverse educational institution, I have one Black female departmental colleague.[5] The presence of Black teachers in my educational past has made an indelible impact on my life as a student and consequently as a teacher. Their Black presence in the classroom was meaningful; it was a reflection of the familiar. My indoctrination into schooling as a first

grader and the culmination of my academic training as a graduate student is marked by the presence and absence of Black teachers. The name of my first grade teacher, Mrs. Black, and the title of my last course with a Black teacher on the doctoral level, appropriately and ironically describe Black teachers as a "special population."

I remember Mrs. Black, my first grade teacher, as I remember my mother's hot gumbo on a wet and rainy winter evening. From a six year old's perspective Mrs. Black was a huge Black woman, who nurtured her students as if they were her own children. Each morning I would leave the comfort and safety of my mother's arms to ride the school bus heading for Vermilion Elementary, a predominately Black elementary school nestled within the Black community of Lafayette, LA. Each morning Mrs. Black would wait for her students at the bus stop and, like a mother hen with little chicks, she would lead us to our classroom. Her maternal inclinations would extend to us in our joy and sadness. In celebration of academic accomplishment or the pain of playground skirmishes, she would kneel to our level and envelop us in her ample bosom, offering assurance and support.

The nostalgic memory of a thirty-five year-old man may romanticize that relationship. As I reflect, I remember both a childish oedipal fixation on Mrs. Black, as well as an awakening understanding of the sensuousness of human contact. Yet I romanticize that contact in terms of the intimacy of the teacher-student relationship. Her teaching was accompanied by a kind of "physical intimacy" that was more parental and less teacherly, though in my childhood the two seemed to be equated (Miller 159). More importantly, I acknowledge my conscious romantization of that relationship because it stems from my own desire to connect with students in ways that are meaningful, beyond the sometimes plebeian task of disseminating information and evaluating knowledge. My desire extends to what Simon calls establishing *unique pedagogical relationships* that reveal "the promise of pleasure in teaching/learning relationships" (95).

What also stands in my memory of Mrs. Black is a sense of comfort, of the familiar, of seeing my mother reflected in my teacher and knowing that the respect due my mother was translated in some literal way to Mrs. Black. Mrs. Black stood *in place of my parent* (mother).

My relationship with Mrs. Black was not a typical response to the power laden academic version of *in loco parentis* that operated at the time. The relationship was the kind of home grown cultural orientation that was a part of my childhood in the Black community. It served to extend rather than replace the parental and cultural influence in the lives of Black children. In the Black community *in loco parentis* was constructed to affirm community and family values. It attempted to build a bridge, not to create a wall of difference between that which was framed as academic (teaching and learning) and home values. The practice of *in loco parentis* that I experienced with my Black teachers within my childhood community was a form of cultural pedagogy. Black teachers never taught, per se, *about* culture as a formal part of the curriculum, as much as they taught *through* culture. In *Teaching to Transgress,* hooks says: "Though they did not define or articulate these practices in theoretical terms, my teachers were enacting a revolutionary pedagogy of resistance that was profoundly anti-colonial" (2). They used their shared cultural experiences, knowledge of Black children and of the surrounding Black community as a means of educating and nurturing the Black student.

Within the six years I spent at the university, from my undergraduate through my Master's degree, I had only two Black professors. Initially, I anticipated my relationship and orientation to the Black professors within that predominately White university would be similar to my previous experiences with Black teachers. Yet the notion of community had changed. The cultural performances that governed our relational orientation changed. I echo hooks when she says of her own educational transition:

> School changed utterly with racial integration. Gone was the messianic zeal to transform our minds and beings that had characterized teachers and their pedagogical practices in our all-black school. Knowledge was suddenly about information only. It had no relation to how one lived, behaved. It was no longer connected to antiracist struggle. (3)

I came to understand that what I had attributed to shared race and culture with my previous Black teachers was linked to a geographic community that shared a common approach to teaching and parenting Black children.

The notion of community, in this case, dealt more with the ideals, beliefs and values that people share within a geographic location and established relational dynamics than with a shared race. In the predominately White university the relationship between the Black professor and the surrounding Black cultural community may not be as clear. The Black professoriate, often transplanted and recruited from outside of the region, may not share the same cultural truths of the *folk* in the surrounding community. In "The Dilemma of the Black Intellectual" West identifies a tension between Black intellectuals in predominately White institutions and the surrounding Black community. He argues

that the dilemma is not based in the anti-intellectualism of the Black community, nor is it based in the

> arrogant and haughty disposition of intellectuals toward ordinary folk, but more importantly from the widespread refusal of Black intellectuals to remain, in some visible way, organically linked with Afro-American cultural life. The relatively high rates of exogamous marriage, the abandonment of Black institutions, and the preoccupations with Euro-American intellectual products are often perceived by the Black community as intentional efforts to escape the negative stigma of Blackness or viewed as symptoms of self-hatred. (134–135)

The relational dynamics with Black teachers in grade school that once seemed almost parental felt more like surveillance in the university. The sense of comfort that I had experienced with Black grade school teachers was not present with Black college professors. The extension of community in the classroom was not constructed with race and a perceived shared culture as a unifying link. In "The Race Question" Davis [cited in *Fires in the Mirror,* Smith] might suggest that my expectations may have limited my engagement with Black professors. Race is "an increasingly obsolete way of constructing community because it is based on unchangeable immutable biological facts in a very pseudo-scientific way" (30). Davis critiques the construction of race as a defining system of categorization and the accompanying false assumptions about a collective identity.

Davis' race question alludes to contemporary theories of race, two of which view race either as an "ideological construct" and false consciousness, or "race as an objective condition" linking it with biology and genetics (Omi & Winant 4–6). Yet, the sense of community that was built with Black grade school teachers did not acknowledge "race as a stable measurable deposit or category" (McCarthy & Crichlow xxi). Instead, it reflected Fine and Haskell's articulation of *communitas,* as a spirit and "vision of communal power that transcends [a] marginalized position in society" (13). "Race difference [was] understood as a subject position that can only be defined in what Bhabha calls 'performative terms'— that is, in terms of the effects of political struggles over social and economic exploitation, political disenfranchisement, and cultural and ideological repression" (cited in McCarthy & Crichlow xxi). Thus the Black teachers in my community "recognize[d] the value of each individual voice" and ultimately [made] a space for those voices" in the classroom (hooks 40).

In the presence of Black teachers I felt that somehow I was being held accountable to prove myself not to be a stereotype, to prove my worth as a student and my worthiness for being in school. I suspected that my own perceptions were somehow projections of struggles that the Black teacher was experiencing for himself/herself in the academy. The rhetoric of hiring, enrollment quotas, and Affirmative Action permeate the minds of even those who benefit from such systems. In that sense we were all involved in a collective struggle of performing legitimacy in which our co-presence reinforced and challenged the other. If we are to follow Boyd and Allen's notion that brotherhood, and consequently community, is built in collective struggle, then the Black teacher and Black student in the predominately White university are involved in a form of covert community building.

In many ways I felt that we were battling a dual and reciprocal issue of Black academic representation. The model Black teacher and the model Black student each served as a reflecting mirror for the other in the dominate White system that rewarded such "good" behavior. Each was performing for the other under the gaze of some larger on-looker, Big Brother. These cultural performances were engaged to signify and maintain cultural membership. Yet in this case it was not a presumed shared cultural membership in the Black community, but the academic community of the White university. As MacAloon suggests, cultural performances reflect upon and define individual selves, while dramatizing our collective reality within specified communities and contexts (1).

These cultural performances exchanged between me and my Black professors were performances of civility, of raising hands and silent glances. They were performances of controlled interactions, restrained passion and focused energy. They were performances of regulated bodies, sitting tall and walking straight. They were linguistic performances of choice words and sanitized phrases. They were performances of covert community building in which a formal public respect was engaged in the classroom and a "let's be real" attitude prevailed in private space away from any on-lookers.

The private conversations with Black male professors often began with a racial acknowledgment like, "Come in brother," or "How are you doing man?" This was followed by, "How are you doing in the class? Are you all right?" The questions were offered as a status report of comprehension, but also as a relational checkup. The professor seemed to be checking not only if "I" was all right, but if "we" were all right. Often they would recall and compliment me on some classroom contribution or request to hear my voice more often. While these engagements were validating, they were also covert, relegated to the office. These interactions seemed to

operationalize (make active and known) the performative dissimilarity between how we engaged each other in the "public" classroom versus the "private" office. My Black teachers and I defined ourselves to and for each other within the larger context of the predominately White university. Our public social interactions are viewed by multiple spectators within the classroom and the larger academic environment. Hence, what appears to be a practiced avoidance of racial affiliation ensues. Yet, in the privacy of an office space the shared racial and presumed cultural affinity might come to inform the educational relationship.

In saying this, I also understand that issues of representation are also intertwined with a struggle for authority and respect. Karamcheti acknowledges this concern of minority teachers when she says that "the more elusive issue for the minority teacher is the establishment of authority, of objectivity, of impartiality—that is, of those attributes traditionally associated with the performance of teaching" (138–39). Recently, a young Black male student disgruntled with his final grade offered me a reality check that brought the concern of my Black professors to bear upon my understanding of their (my) positionality as a Black male teacher.

The Black male student who, when not sleeping, participated vigorously in class, often brought rich examples of lived experience to the discussion. Yet, his aggressive and sometimes assaultive tone and admonishments of White students and White people in general often required me to temper his contributions by either paraphrasing his words, or by reminding the collective class of our social contract of respect. After receiving what he deemed an unsatisfactory grade at the end of the class, he angrily approached me. In an accusatory tone he said, "You gave a *brother* a C?" His tone did not suggest that he questioned the "C" as an assessment of his work. Disturbingly, the inquiry was somehow suggestive that his final grade was *not,* but should have been, predicated on his "brother status," and our common racial membership.

He refused to review his final examination and his grades. I invited him to sit, but he chose to remain standing. Acknowledging the presence of several of my White colleagues, he then began to engage in a cultural performance of "loud capping."[6] In a loud, animated voice, punctuated with flailing arms, he intimated that, throughout the class, my grading was unfair. Enraged, he hovered over my seated unflinching body suggesting that I showed favoritism to other students (White students). He was one of two Black students in the class, and the only Black male. He announced to the room that he was going to appeal the grade. In denunciatory terms he exited the room with a final pronouncement that he framed as "Before I leave I need to say that you are no kind of teacher. If you were a professor or something I could understand, but you are no kind of teacher!"

Within that moment I immediately questioned if this performance was a result of my status as a graduate teaching assistant or my status as a Black male teacher, a "brother" who had assigned a grade that another "brother," found displeasing. I then linked that experience with what I perceived as the distantiated positionality of my own Black male teachers. I was moved to rethink our relationships. Were they trying to avoid this kind of scene? How often were they the target for this kind of culturally imbued academic invective in which they were challenged both as teacher and as a Black man, knowing and not knowing which was being foregrounded? Were they trying to avoid students who played the "race card" as if it were some "ace in the hole" that carried special privilege or power? Surely the visibly racialized body of the Black student and the Black teacher are always and already "in play." In *Thirteen Ways of Looking at a Black Man,* Gates echoes Angela Davis in reference to the O.J. Simpson trial when she says, "Race is not a card . . . the whole case [education] was [is] pervaded with issues of race (111)." How many times were my Black male teachers expected to be a "brother" in the classroom, in which brotherhood was constructed as an unyielding and unearned support constituted in opposition to their role as teachers?

After nearly twenty-two years of schooling, I can count the number of Black teachers that I have had over the years, from the first grade to the graduate seminar. My *institutional biography* is informed by my experiences with them, but not as "a foundation [of] stock responses" in the sense of unreflected and standardized phrases used to deal with the moment (Britzman 448). These stock responses are really a reservoir of experiences that can be drawn upon for guidance and reflection.

ETHNOGRAPHY: ARTICULATED LIVED EXPERIENCES IN THE CLASSROOM

Teachers: Voices of Experience

The morning of each interview with a Black male teacher began with me hearing a sound: "the kind of sound that a clock makes when enveloped in cotton" (Poe). It was a sound both inside and outside of my own realm of existence. It was a sound that was emanating from me and yet rapidly approaching me, as if from outside my body. On each of the five days of individually scheduled interviews with Black male teachers, I awoke to, or was awakened by the same sound of my heart beating. The rapidly racing

pulse was not the regular rhythmic beat that comes in concentrated focus when listening to oneself. It was literally a sound; the kind of pounding that comes when someone wants in or something wants out. The kind of Edgar Allen Poe heart pounding sound that tells the tale: a pounding on the door of opportunity, or when "they" come to make you accountable for your crimes. They, the symbolic "they," the gatekeepers, the promise keepers, those who are your elders, those placed in authority, those who helped shape and dictate your existence, those who say: "well done little brother" or "you got it all wrong man."

This is how my mind and body anticipated each interview, with the pounding of my heart signaling the excitement of an ethnographer entering the field and the fervor of colleagues entering into a conversation. I experienced a kind of culture shock as I crossed in and out of real and imagined spaces, spaces in the here and now, spaces in the there and then of my own border identity of teacher/student and researcher/subject. The sound of my heart marked both anticipation and challenge. It was a recollection of me bracing myself when entering a classroom with a Black male teacher or having Black male students entering my own classes. The excitement was tempered with the anticipation of challenge that only Black men can offer each other. When these anticipated encounters are complicated by differences in age, authority, and institutional status, the challenge becomes more meaningful. It is parental in nature, affirming and disconfirming, an extension of the Black family, the Black community. I found myself having to negotiate whether I was seeking the advice and assistance of a cultural brother or BIG BROTHER—or both. The relational dynamics of these "brotherhoods" are often the same.

All of the interviews were conducted in the teachers' respective offices—some with bright lights and big windows, others located in the bowels of buildings. Were those perceived as private or hated as hidden? I could not tell. Each encounter was marked by what I experienced as a reading, a moment of detection. The interviews were initially facilitated through a cover letter outlining the scope of the project and an invitation to participate. The appointments were then arranged over the telephone. In the case of three of the five Black male teachers interviewed, the instance of the interview was our first face-to-face encounter. In each case I arrived early and waited for the arrival of the professor. Lingering in tight hallways I anticipated the encounter, wondering what he would look like, wondering if I would recognize him. The nature of the interview pool—Black male professors at a predominately White university—limited the possibilities. I told myself I was looking for a Black man, probably older, whose status as a faculty member would be self-evident. I was not quite sure what the "evidence" would be. I suspected that the Black professor also would have his anticipatory images of me—surely he would assume that I was a Black male, though that description had never been used in reference to myself, but only to the population that I was studying. The assumption is based in my own concerns about ethnographic work by researchers outside of the specified cultural community being studied. I extend my own concerns about researcher bias and a sanitizing objectivity that reduces the significance of cultural experiences to the other. I question whether I would participate in a study of this nature being conducted by a non-Black researcher.

Based on the limited number of Black males walking through the hallways of a predominately White universities, the possibility of us identifying each other was great. When I met each of the Black male teachers I was immediately pegged as the interviewer, either simply because I was the only other Black man in the hall or because of my studious preparedness for the interview: standing tall, dressed conservatively, with notepad and tape recorder in hand. In all but one case I also successfully detected who was the interviewee. My failure to identify one participant was not due to a misreading of Blackness, as much as it was a misreading of age: the professor was youthful and extremely casual in dress. He identified me first. In that moment, as in each of the encounters, I had to adjust my formal notions of the meeting and the interview protocols that I had been practicing.

Each encounter began with a ritual greeting of brotherman. I do not mean the articulated phrase, but the felt recognition—a look, a visual reading, a handshake, and a nodding approval that said: "You are welcomed here." "I support your efforts." But within the exchange there was also an intense Black male gaze, an intense focus on both the physical characteristics and racial character of the other. It was a reading of worth, value and substance. It was that "first impression" that social scientists talk about which sets a tone for the relational exchange. It was an immediate evaluation of masculinity, of sexuality, of "cool."[7] Within those moments, language, tone, attitudes and bodies were being negotiated, a sort of pre-interview protocol/performative assessment in which each of us engaged as prelude to the interview.

Each informal conversation began with a respectful "thank you for your time" from the junior to the senior, followed by a holistic overview of the project requested by the senior of the junior. This request served both as a reminder of the assignment and a character assessment—an opportunity to know someone through talk. I offered an abbreviated

version of the project, focusing specifically on the individual's contribution and the task at hand. In the process I emphasized my perceived value of the work and how we as Black male teachers and Black male students are all implicated in research that looks at cultural performance in the classroom. Abram, a Black male professor interviewed, echoed a similar sentiment:

> This work is important because relationships between young Black men and older Black men are valued within the Black community and also within the larger academic community. Though it is recognized and it is valued by the larger academic community, it is not always rewarded. The rewards within the Black community are spiritual rewards of a very different nature. [Abram]

His notion of the spiritual does not exclusively refer to a religious belief system. He refers to spiritual as in *esprit de corps;* that spirit of devotion and enthusiasm among members of a group for one another, their group, its purposes and common struggles. Inevitably, this form of community building becomes interwoven into a religious ethic espoused in the Black church.

The interviews began by starting the tape recorder. What followed often seemed like what Abram called "cultural languaging" which was engaged through a series of calls and responses. These calls and responses did not always resemble questions and answers, so much as a bifurcated monologue. It seemed that we were both involved in narrating the same story. The answers to questions were often given before the question was completed. The anticipatory response was signaled by the nodding of a head, a hand waving in the air, a smile accompanied by such affirming phrases as: "Yes, Lord." "You better know it!" or "Yes, yes that happened to me just the other day."

The planned interviews gave way to vigorous and animated conversations that were loosely structured with questions. The content of each conversation thus became a free flowing pattern of infused knowledge and experience. Within those moments were affirmations of felt cultural experiences that extended the interview beyond the parameters of the protocol. I offer a sample of their responses.

Sample Teacher Voices

> There are times when my Black male students ask me to repeat something that I have said in class. Often this is not because they didn't hear me the first time, but often I suspect that they want me to translate it in different terms. This could be considered paraphrasing, but I suspect that they want me to sort of re-code my message in Black English or at least with cultural references that

they can relate to. This is not a problem when I think that it is sincere, but sometimes it comes as a sort of challenge to see if I can "talk the talk." [Joseph]

Black students when I talk to them . . . we have shared values, shared beliefs, from a shared culture—it is recognizable. What social scientists call "empirical reference." We can always refer back to past experiences, especially if they are in their 20's or 30 something age group. There is definitely a relationship there. We talk the same language and sometimes that allows me to joke and tease with them in ways that are both playful and culturally significant in terms of driving home a point. [Malcolm]

As a Black male teacher I think that it is ultimately my responsibility to offer the young Black men in my class a reality check. It was certainly done for me in my own education, both in the Black community and by Black male teachers in the predominately White institutions that I attend. [Joseph]

They are going to polarize you [the Black teacher]. They want to know from day one, 'which one are you going to fall into.' I think that it is important that you convey that, 'I am not a sell out and that's for sure' and I would rather have them know that I am committed to culture. I do understand where I am coming from and I want them to be as committed to culture as I am. [Malcolm]

I think that within every relationship there is a common ground and there is a quake of difference that can become a point of conflict and also a moment of urgency. I think that the common ground when understood by both persons is an open door possibility for better communication in that relationship. I think that common ground when it is understood well is what should allow you a moment of essentialism, to come in and talk to this Black male student and say, 'We both know—in essence before we even talk. We know what's up. We understand what's coming down here.' Then we start talking, in the middle of the conversation. [James]

Each of my conversations with the Black male teachers was an adventure and an affirmation. It was an adventure into the articulated lived experiences of other Black male teachers. It was an affirmation of similarly felt desires, pains and challenges in teaching, mentoring and orienting to Black male students in ways that facilitate their growth as students and as men. The desires of these Black male teachers to share specified academic knowledge as well as cultural unification were intricately intertwined. Each manifested a culturally imbued pedagogy of desire in which

cultural affinity is used as a strategy for understanding and connecting with Black male students.

In relating to Black male students, the Black male teachers interviewed characterized their own positionality in shifting metaphors. These included Black male teacher as mentor, Black male teacher as Big Brother, Black male teacher as uncle, and Black male teacher as father. James said it best: "I think that when you are dealing with Black male students you have to be prepared to wear many hats." These "multiple hats" correspond to the shifting roles and relational orientations that must be negotiated. These all have accompanying responsibilities: to nurture, to foster, to care, to harbor, to understand, to empathize, to know and to admonish. All of these are traditional mandates of teachers and are part of the socializing process of young Black men, but they are magnified within the context of a shared minority status within the predominately White university.

In reflecting back on these conversations, I also wish to note an additional underlying theme that seems to have been a part of the discussions. The Black male teachers articulated an ethic of care, not only for Black students, but a desire to be fair. Their passion and empathic connection was clearly directed towards Black male students. Each acknowledged and claimed stakes in the education of young Black men. The stakes are reflected in the increased numbers of young Black men in prisons and those lost to drugs and disease. The stakes are felt in the larger Black community as violence, discontinuity of family living, and the disintegration of culture. The stakes are positively affirmed in the increased number of young Black men entering and graduating from colleges and universities. The stakes are reflected in the young men's increased self-esteem and their upward and forward gaze toward a positive future. Yet, in the midst of their impassioned pronouncements and fervently articulated commitments, Black male teachers also offered what may be considered *apologia*.

Many of their phrases articulated the desire to be fair to all students, Black and White. Their hope was that, in their "authentic" displays of self, they are consistently aware of the needs of all students, and that all students perceive them in that way. They also acknowledged that White students are challenged in different ways by the presence of the Black male teacher. Within that relationship is not only the challenge of negotiating information, but negotiating and evaluating a source of information. White students are challenged to reflect upon their own racial and cultural biases. They are challenged to make the empathic leap, to understand what it may be like for Black and other minority students not to see themselves consistently reflected within the faces, persons, rhetoric, language and ideology of their teachers. It becomes their challenge to understand how Blacks and other minority students negotiate the chasm that sometimes exists between racial and cultural knowing and the sometimes sanitizing space of academia.

In their desire to empower Black students, the Black male teachers interviewed also strongly expressed the desire not to dis-empower White students within their classrooms. They clearly acknowledge that White students in the predominately White university enter the system with an unearned empowerment that comes from being in the majority. Yet, they also made clear that the classroom where the Black male teacher is present is not a site of "turn about," but a site in which White students will be challenged in ways that expand their notions of education, culture, voice and privilege.

Taken collectively, the interviews spoke profoundly of the recognition that occurs when Black male teachers and Black male students encounter each other in the classroom. The encounter is a recognition of sameness as well as of difference. It is never static, always shifting. Hence, the notion of negotiating culture in the classroom is actually an issue of negotiating sameness and differences—all grounded in a shared racially gendered history, and against the backdrop of the Black community.

Students: Voices of Desire

Before each interview with a Black male student I had a moment of pause. This pause was the absence of sound or movement in which my progress was interrupted, reflected upon and anticipated before moving into the interviews. As I had paused before each conversation with Black male teachers, I paused now wondering if and how my own articulated experience as a Black male student would be reflected in narratives I was preparing to collect. I was torn in the tensiveness that exists between my own experiences as a student and my experiences as a teacher, not sure which I wanted to be validated in the pending interview. The parameters of my border identity seemed more problematized as I entered interviews with students than when I entered the interviews with teachers. Moments of confirmation and disconfirmation always seem heightened when experienced with students. In this moment of pause I feared that students might perceive me more as a double agent; teacher in the guise of student, Caliban[8] rather than student-teacher. Before each interview I paused and, in that stultifying moment of reflection and anticipation, confusion and clarity, I shifted the focus from me to them and wondered about their desires.

What would these young Black men get or what did they want to get out of this experience? I reflected on those who had agreed to be interviewed and those who did not, such as those members of Black fraternities who never returned my calls or letters. I was reminded of those "recommended brothas," who agreed to meet with me, but did not show. I wondered about those brothers who responded to my description of the project with: "I am busy" or "I'm not interested in talking about that." I wondered about *those* brothers as I thought about the desires of *these* brothers. What motivations framed these responses? What concerns did those who chose not to participate see in the project? Was their lack of participation an issue of time management or apathy? Did they see the project as divisive: *Caliban providing information to Prospero so that he can rule?* Did they see the project as a means to negatively critique Black male teachers? Was their lack of participation a means of protecting Black male teachers? Should I evaluate their absence as worth, a desire not to offer disparaging information about Black teachers? If so, what did they think of me? Was their lack of participation a disconfirmation of me (i.e., What kind of self-respecting brother would be asking these questions?) I began to wonder about my own desire, not the desire that motivates this research, but the desire for validation by these young men. I reflected back to that first day of class, being confirmed and disconfirmed, as if my role as teacher-now-researcher makes suspect my brother status.

For those who did participate I read their desire in relation to those who did not. I read their desire as a celebration of community, celebration as critique. The performance of culture in any community is not only an act of establishing membership and reflecting traditions, it is also being an agent of commentary and change. Turner's notion of "performative reflexivity" captures this element of any cultural community when its members turn inward to critique, and criticism thus becomes a part of the cultural struggle.[9] For the young men who participated, I also read their desire as protection, which comes from nurturing something that is rare and delicate. I read their desire to participate as a confirmation of the significance of Black male teachers in the predominately White university and of me as a Black male teacher-student-scholar interested in exploring these issues. *After the pause I engaged the process.*

I interviewed a total of 10 Black male students, nine of these were undergraduates and one was a first year Masters level graduate student on Fellowship. Their varying levels of experience with Black male teachers in the predominately White university ranged from having had from one to four such teachers within their four years of higher education. In all but one case, the students had actually sought out the Black male teacher, or assumed that the nature of the course—Black Studies, Black Literature, Black Musical

Traditions—would dictate the instructor's race. Of the undergraduate students, two were first year, three were juniors and four were seniors. All were in same age bracket of 19–23. Five interviews were conducted individually. The Masters student was included in a focus group that consisted of three seniors and one junior. All interviews were conducted in a classroom at the convenience of the student. Pseudonyms have been used in place of the real names of the participants. I use the following names as references in the individual interviews: Wendel, Martin, Jesse, Frederick and Marcus. In the focus group discussion I use the names Paul, Jerome, Kendel, Patrick and Donald.

As I review the interview tapes I see, hear, and feel a bleeding of my border identity as teacher-student-researcher. It is in phrases that move from the "we" of students to the "they" of teachers, and the "I" of both teacher and student. It is in the inquiring "you" of the researcher-interviewer and the collective "us" of Black men. I was often confused as to which role should be foregrounded in the moment. Was it the student role, the doctoral candidate asking questions of another student? Or was it the teacher asking questions of a student, or a brother asking questions of another brother? There had been many variations as we negotiated our multifaceted selves in the interviews. I found that in the interview moments I often shifted positions from the teacher-researcher who asked the questions to the student-researcher who received and responded to the answers. I realized that this dual positionality was also present during my interviews with Black teachers but, maybe because I associated myself more with a teacher-researcher than a student, my orientation to them in the interviews was not as encumbered by the slippage in my border identity.

While engaged in conversation with these students I used multiple and varied means of responding to them. I responded through my lived experience as a student and often shared narratives. I responded as a researcher gathering information and clarifying my understanding; I weighed and measured words. On another level I responded as a Black male teacher, the distantiated object of their critique. On that level I used their words as a yardstick to measure my own performances in the classroom. At no point within the interviews could I clearly establish how these levels of understanding and roles were ordered: student, researcher, or teacher.

While listening to their responses I moved from assessing my worth as a teacher to my shared experiences as a student and my expectations as a researcher. It was in these moments that I fully engaged Arnowitz and Giroux's notion of *border pedagogy*. I crossed into varying realms of understanding by allowing the parameters of my identity to shift

and inform the moment. My shifting roles allowed me to negotiate my roles as teacher-researcher and engage in a meaningful dialogue as a student and co-researcher. When transcribing the interviews, I came to realize that the multiple levels of my empathic response allowed me to better understand their articulated experiences and desires.

Yet, Arnowitz and Giroux's conception of border pedagogy provides a political charge, a shock and a directive that is at the heart of my research, in which the focus is on the student experience and not my shifting border identity. "Border pedagogy confirms and critically engages the knowledge and experience through which students author their own voice and construct social identities" (128–29). For purposes of this study, border pedagogy engages students in the active process of articulating their experiences with Black male teachers and other factors that affect their educational experience in the predominantly White university.

By engaging the students' voices in this study I place their articulated experiences in dialogue with teachers in order to equalize these voices and validate their experiences. "At issue here is the development of a pedagogy that replaces the authoritative language of recitation with an approach that allows students to speak from their own histories, collective memories, and voices while simultaneously challenging the grounds on which knowledge and power are constructed and legitimated" (Arnowitz & Giroux 129). At the same time, border pedagogy demands that student knowledge and cultural power also must be critiqued to unearth logics that are unreflectively promoted and advocated as fact.

The overarching nature of this study is an attempt to engage a border pedagogy that offers both Black male teachers and students an opportunity to critically reflect on the variables and conditions that affect their experiences within the predominately White university. Like Turner's notion of *performance reflexivity*, a border pedagogy "also involves engaging collectively with others within a pedagogical framework that helps to reterritorialize and rewrite the complex narrative that make up one's life" (Arnowitz & Giroux 131).

Sample Student Voices:

Well my experiences with Black teachers is different from my experiences with White teachers because I relate more to the Black teacher—some of the lingo, the terminology. I might say something in a White classroom setting and the White teacher may not pick it up as quickly. [Wendel]

In the Black classroom . . . there seems to be better communication between me and him. He can ask me a question and I can answer it in a way that's easy for me and he usually understands. But, I have also found with Black male teachers that they may understand me, but they are going to force me to say it in a different way that maybe non-Black students can understand. And that's all right because I know that he understands me, but now he's going to challenge me to say it better or proper—which is his job, and that's cool. [Marcus]

I have always felt that some Black male professors have been excessively hard on me. They seem to judge me by a higher standard. Sometimes I am *down* with that because I think that they are trying to make me tough, or they are trying to challenge me academically. But other times that seems to be more personal then academic . . . Maybe they are trying to pull that parental thing on me and that's cool, but with my parents I always know what the intent is—and it's not to break me down, but lift me up—I just need to know. [Marcus]

You need to understand that regardless of who you think I am, I am going to be one of the best students that you have in this class . . . because that is what I expect out of myself. So, you don't have to like try to present any more obstacles for me. I understand that other students might come in with that attitude, but until you find out what kind of personality I have, don't judge me. That is my biggest problem when I have some Black professors, men and women. Give me a chance to see what kind of brother I am first before you start to jump to conclusions. [Frederick]

Now I know that we are not all going to have the same experience in the White university. 'But, I expect you to support me and encourage me because you are older than me and I am younger than you. You know more.' I respect my elders. I expect them to help me. 'I don't need you doggin' me and you don't try to get to know me. You are just reading some stereotype and projecting it on me.' So I just said fuck you. It hurts. This is a Black man. This is someone I admire and someone who has gotten to a level that I want to go. But I don't need you to do that to me. [Patrick]

While I was engaged in these interview discussions I found myself thinking about the novel *Waiting to Exhale* by Terri McMillan, and the 1997 movie by the same name. In this piece of fiction the metaphor "waiting to exhale" becomes symbolic of something held back, and the subsequent force of released resistance. The interviews with Black male students were moments of release. They were moments when ten young Black men had an opportunity to express their desire, disdain and pain at their educational experiences.

These young men spoke of how cultural expectations were both positive and negative. They spoke of their desire for validation of their worth, knowledge, language skills, and intellect. They spoke to the perceived teacher expectations of the Black male student, many grounded in academic rigor and hard work, but also grounded in a presumed understanding of their authentic character. All of the young men interviewed spoke with passion and reverence, not only about Black male teachers, but about the process of education. Their talk was centered in the socio-cultural politics of the predominantly White university. Through their dialogue they suggested that the minority status of Black teachers and students necessitates bonds of recognition and support. Within this description they also included other "minority faculty" as sources of recognition and affinity seeking. Yet, in the midst of saying that "race matters," Frederick attempted to clarify the significance of difference in ways that did not mark or marginalize.

The question is not if race matters. It does matter. You recognize it the same way that you recognize someone's height, weight, anything that is a part of their physical characteristics. The question I think is how much do you allow that to matter? I have had some beautiful relationships with some White teachers, but Black teachers and I have an immediate link . . . but it is in those unseen things, those subtle things, those things that can enhance. They don't enhance my educational quality, but they can make the learning environment better, they can also make it more difficult. [Frederick]

Race matters as a bridge to understanding and lived experience; it can be both facilitating and debilitating.

Reflections

In "Black Studies, Cultural Studies, Performative Acts," Diawara reconstructs the project of Black Studies as Black Performance Studies. He explains that Black Performance Studies

would mean study of ways in which black people, through communicative action, created and continue to create themselves within the American experience. Such an approach would contain several interrelated notions, among them that 'performance' involves an individual or group of people interpreting an existing tradition—reinventing themselves—in front of an audience, or public. (265)

My status as a Black male signals a membership in both a racial and a gender population that bears a distinct history. My role as a teacher also signals a membership in both a professional and a political institution that has particular goals and objectives. In this sense I am always and already a participant in my field of study in which my performances of Black male teacher and student comes under scrutiny.

In many ways I celebrate the disposition of embodying these multifaceted roles, but they have also offered challenges. First, in this study there has been the challenge of orienting to the other. Who is the "other" in this case? Ethnography is always interested in coming to know and understand otherness. Yet otherness is a problematic determination, for in essence it marks difference in ways that are often pathologizing. In my ethnographic venture I claimed membership in my field of study, not as a schizophrenic participant-observer interested in engagement and subsequent critique, but as one who is experientially connected and involved in the community in an embodied way.

Second, my position as ethnographer places me in the dilemma of constructing the cultural familiar as other. This, in turn, forces me to understand otherness not as a construction of pathology using oneself as the standard, but as differences in human experience and how they exist within racial and cultural communities. Otherness is difference identified; I have come to understand otherness as dialects of difference within one speech community, shades of difference in a color palette or the performative variations in a tapestry of heritage.

Third, ethnography is always interested in reporting. Reporting can be a means of articulating knowledge; a means of translating embodied knowledge into a scholarly presentation. As a member of the *studied culture* as well as the *academic culture of study* I find myself torn within the process of articulating knowledge. I am cognizant of being Caliban. In reporting my findings I struggle between my allegiance to my primary cultural group, those Black male teachers and students who have trusted me with their narratives, and the academic cultural community in which this study is articulated. To what degree do I want to play "native informant" and what is my obligation to the "natives" and to those whom I "inform?" Yet, if the goal of ethnography is to provide descriptive understanding of a culture using lived and embodied experience, articulated in the words of indigenous cultural members, then my position as a native informant has enhanced the ethnographic description. These descriptions often clustered around sharing tropes and figures of language, which are the expressive components of a shared cultural dialect. Thus cultural performance has been shown to establish situated communities across borders and contexts.

The Black male teachers and students who functioned as co-researchers spoke about invoking a shared history, knowledge and struggle as a means of establishing a common ground in the classroom. They spoke about intuitive knowledge based on cultural familiarity and the shared lived experience of being both Black and male. The cultural performance in this construction is a combination of the knowing and the accompanying response to that knowledge. They ultimately described cultural performance as the collectively unthought actions that establish and recreate community in the classroom. Cultural performance, then, is the collective expectations of cultural members and the attempts to respond to those expectations in meaningful ways.

The Black male students interviewed placed a strong focus on language as a cultural performance. Their focus was not on language solely as a linguistic construction, but the active process of cultural languaging. *Cultural languaging* is thus defined as an overt attempt to use the tropes and figures of Black dialect coupled with allusions to Black cultural life, as a method of performing culture and signaling group membership within the classroom of the predominately White institution. In the following segment Frederick offers a specific example of a seemingly mundane cultural connection of food and family tradition. He then theorizes on its significance in the classroom:

> If I just come back from the Christmas break and say, 'We had some good greens and corn bread, Black eye peas.' A Black teacher can relate and say, 'We did the same thing. We had some chitlins too.' You know, those are the types of things that I think are important to an education that is often overlooked. You know we get caught up in textbooks and curriculum, but what binds those things together? [Frederick]

The question of what binds textbooks and curriculum is a serious theoretical issue that underscores the importance of establishing a link between schooling and the lived experiences, the "enfleshed knowledge" (McLaren 206) of students and teachers. Frederick offers an incisive analogy:

> You know it is similar to the way you look at a house. A house, you can have all of the materials to build a house, the bricks, the concrete the wood and everything, but if you don't have a quality construction person to put those things together and make that house a reality then those objects, those pieces of material are just that, pieces of material that have not come together to make anything that is useful for you. [Frederick]

Frederick says that only a teacher who is a "quality construction person" has the skills and understanding to translate the raw materials of curriculum and the classroom into a house of teaching and learning. Certainly all talk is grounded in specified cultural traditions and his analogy could be applied to all teaching. The teacher whom he describes as "a quality construction person," regardless of ethnicity, uses all the available means of reaching students. In this instance, the teacher uses cultural talk as means of bridging lived experiences and closing gaps of difference.

Jesse reinforces a kind of talk that is based in felt affinity, not necessarily in shared cultural traditions, but in a common struggle and difference that crosses lines of ethnicity:

> I think that it is easier for me to get closer with minority teachers, because I feel I can talk to them and they will understand me better or at least they seem to try more. I talk to them more, even the ones with foreign accents, because it seems that we are both struggling to understand each other, not just words, but really to understand. So I talk to them a little before and after class, that helps and motivates me to participate more in the class. Because I feel that they are interested in getting to know me and we are entering a relationship that is not just teacher-student, but something more. [Jesse]

Jesse moves from construction of talk that is linked to recognizable cultural expressions and cultural affinity, to talk in the sense of class participation and voice. He links the three together to suggest that his full class participation is contingent upon a felt connection with the teacher and a perception that his voice is going to be valued. Martin offers a similar sentiment: "You participate more in the class with a Black teacher. Not, that they are pushing me more—but because you are a little more close to them—you can talk to them about things" [Martin]. It is noteworthy that within his response he uses "you" as both a second person reference to himself, as well as in a collective sense of including me and other Black male students in his response.

Marcus uses the same technique of shifting personal pronouns as he speaks, not only in terms of comfort, but as a form of demand and challenge from the Black male teacher for him to participate. He shifts from a second person "you" to the singular individualized "me" to the collective "us" as references. In his use of "you," I felt the unification of my border identity, the "you" which referred to my role as student and as teacher. In his use of "me" as a personal identifier, he reclaims the subject position of his own narrative. In his use of "us," he recognizes the cultural community of Black male students in which we both maintain membership:

> *You* tend to participate more in the class with the Black male teacher. On one hand that is because *you* feel more comfortable and can talk the talk, but on the other hand Black teachers and more so Black men seem to demand more of *you, me.* They seem to require full participation from their Black students. They kind of want *us* to talk

back, not talk back as in being sassy, but like in church when you respond to The Word. I feel that they literally call on us more in class [emphasis added]. [Marcus]

Marcus alludes to challenge not as a contest of wills, but as a strong encouragement where there might be resistance or hesitancy. It is a culturally coded challenge; talk is negotiation in which the student negotiates his voice in the class as well as the cultural power that he is afforded in the presence of the Black male teacher.

Marcus' sense of comfort in the classroom with a Black male teacher, like that of other Black students, should be equated with the notion of feeling *safe* for the classroom is always a place of challenge. The construction of comfort is equated more with a sense of possibility. "The experience of professors who educate for critical consciousness indicates that many students, especially students of color, may not feel 'safe' in what appears to be a neutral setting. It is the absence of a feeling of safety that often promotes prolonged silence or lack of student engagement" (hooks 38).

Their descriptions of cultural performance acknowledged both the celebratory notions of culture, and those structures that create dialects of power and control. They spoke of challenge as an element of cultural performance: the challenge of knowledge, intellect, language and authority either as a rite of passage or a verification of qualifications, qualifications to teach and the performative qualification of a cultural membership. The Black students spoke about defending Black male teachers from questions of competency. The Black teachers spoke about providing all the available means of support to their Black students. In both cases their efforts are constructed as a form of maintaining community and encouraging personal growth and development.

In the midst of all the complexities of cultural performance that appeared in the interviews, the notion of authenticity emerged as central to how Black male teachers and students negotiate culture in the classroom. Professor James' thoughts on this issue are worth quoting at length.

> First of all. Negotiating, and by negotiating here I can use the slash negotiating and establishing myself. That is the first step I think. When I am negotiating and establishing myself, I AM CULTURE and especially when dealing with Black students, I AM AFRICAN-AMERICAN CULTURE in its most diverse sense. So, first of all, if you want other people to appreciate and be sensitive to and respect issues of otherness, then you have to establish yourself as an issue of otherness. You allow people to interpellate you as a kind of hybrid, as a kind of redefining entity, as something that is liberating, creating new spaces, new sights—and you allow yourself to be interpellated as that thing. You become a kind

of blind spot—that is, you turn your back to everything else and you say, 'You don't know for sure what you are, but you do know what you are not.' You present that in ideology in the classroom and I think that this is the first thing that you have to do. It is true that you have to revolutionize yourself before you can revolutionize the classroom. [James]

James offers a conflation of self and culture that is not meant as a reduction so much as a conjoining. He links the expressive forms of culture—the unique interpretive moves, difference, individuality and divergence—with a project for the individual self. To negotiate self within culture is to reveal the struggle for individuation outside of culture, to maintain an organic sense of self that resists a delimiting essentialism. In that sense, as a Black male teacher in the predominantly White university, encountering Black male students, he embraces self as other and self as spectacle.

Spectacle is not introduced here as a new concept, but as it relates back to the double-bind of representation for the Black male teacher which both resists and "claims moments of essentialism" as points of entry with Black students. Performative displays and ways of being can be recognized, associated with and moves toward establishing affiliative bonds.

I make it start with me. What I know is that wherever I go I am always and already again spectacle. As spectacle I am up for interpretation. I am that thing. I am Michael Jackson on stage. I can scream. I can dance and grab my crotch. I can wear whatever I do. It begins to define for the people watching me what I feel about culture. It helps to define what culture I am representing and what our talents are and the expanse of my boundaries. Maybe they also see the fact that my boundaries are unlimited, which is what I would prefer. [James]

He speaks of the paradox of representation, of being "both/and," of representing a racial or cultural group through recognizable cultural performances, but at the same time being a marker of difference. In this move he uses the individual self as an agent of social change. By dramatizing the individual self, he foregrounds the collective, which demands not only revisioning of cultural membership but broadens the perspective of cultural performance:

That is a way. I gave you an example of spectacle, but it has to be sincere spectacle, in a way that you walk out and look at a tree. You say that you know that is a tree and that it exists, and you never doubt its existence; everything seems real to you. I think that is the way that we have to be viewed by our students. We have to be viewed as real as a tree. [James]

James offers a beautiful analogy that deconstructs the binaries of essentialism and individuality and the relationship between authenticity and spectacle. Hence the negotiation of culture meets at an intersection between *the real* and the systems of power that are inherent in the performative assessment of *the real*. "Genetic authenticity is ultimately always on a sliding scale of greater and lesser degrees of raciality: a slippery scale of more colored than thou" (Karamcheti 141). So what James seems to suggest is that "essentialism" and authenticity, as they relate to this study and Black male students, are linked with sincerity. Sincerity becomes a presentation of the self that both reflects and refracts otherness.

Ultimately, the classroom is always a site of intercultural communication. It is a border crossing where the culturally and racially lived experiences of teachers and students become tender for negotiation. They meet as a confluence of rivers that wash and flow over each other. Surely the two can meet in ways that enrich the other. I am reminded of my father's words:

So when you're sitting in your college classes or teaching your college classes, remember what you learned in school and what you have learned at home. Know the difference. It's all right to talk like a teacher, but remember that you're a Black man. Talk like a Black man teacher.

Simple yet prophetic, he speaks to the paradox of "authentic spectacle," and the potential for dualism without contradiction. To teach as Black man is to negotiate and mediate the borders of the educational institutions in which I learn and teach, and the primary racial and cultural communities in which I claim membership.

So within my work I am seeking to read between the lines—searching for myself and others and the times when I am other within the company of cultural familiars. I seek to find that which is felt and translate it into that which is said, knowing that I can't really capture it. Knowing that the beauty is in the effort, but still hoping that others will read between the lines and know what I mean.

ABOUT THE AUTHOR

Bryant Keith Alexander is an Assistant Professor in the Department of Communication Studies at California State University, Los Angeles. A version of this paper was originally presented at the National Communication Association Convention, November 1998.

NOTES

1. In *Focus Groups: Theory and Practice,* Stewart and Sharndasani suggest that "amongst the most widely

used research tools in the social sciences are group in-depth interviews, or focus groups" (9). The method combines the benefits of small group decision making with the in-depth and focused probing of the ethnographic interview. Focus groups bring a group of people from a targeted population into a specified place in order to engage a topic or shared experience. In addition, according to Frey and Fontant, "group interview would avail the researcher of the opinions of a large number of subjects in a relatively easy-to access fashion; it thus would complement any other method being used" (24). The method has the benefit of generating a large amount of data within a specified site. Each focus group member is, in essence, an interview subject. The moderator serves as the interviewer who asks specific questions and encourages group discussion. The results of the focus group can be correlated with the findings of separate interviews, with the added benefit of data generated through the social influence of a small group. "This synergistic effect of the group setting may result in the production of data or ideas that might not have been uncovered in individual interviews" (16).

2. There is an increasing body of work that uses ethnographic and other narrative-centered qualitative methods to explore a range of cultural phenomena in the classroom. For example, McEwan and Egan focus on narrative in teaching, learning and research. Carter explores the use of story in teacher education programs. Marshall, Egan and Munby focus on the use of metaphors in teaching. Hesford examines how storytelling was used in feminist teaching, while El-baz and Cockran-Smith/Lytle focus on teacher's knowledge and the evolution of discourse.

3. The significance of autobiography as scholarship has been explored by many, including the work of Bell and Yalom who explore gender through the lens of autobiography and biography, McLaughlin and Tierney who explore the voices of those who have been traditionally left out of educational discourse, Thompson and Tyagi on autobiography and racial identity and Graham's work on writing the self in education.

4. My initial telling of this story occurred in multiple classes at SIU focusing on issues of the performance of gender, phenomenology, and critical pedagogy. In "public" the first telling was in 1997 at the Otis J. Aggertt Festival at Indiana State University. Subsequently, the first telling in "print" is in *The Future of Performance Studies: Visions and Revisions,* under the title "Performing Culture in the Classroom: Excerpts from an Instructional Diary."

5. According to a December 1998 fact sheet prepared by the Offices of Publications/Public Affairs and Analytical Studies at Cal State LA, the student "headcount by race/ethnic group" is as follows: 50.3% Latino, 23.5% Asian-American, 16.7% White Non-Hispanic, 9.1% African-American, and 0.5% American Indian. My colleague Kelly Madison teaches courses in mass media, critical race theory, and cultural studies.

6. In *Black Talk* Smitherman defines the synonym, loud talking, as follows: "to talk in such a way as to confront or embarrass someone publicly"   (156).

7. Majors and Billson in *Cool Pose: The Dilemma of Black Manhood in America* refer to "cool" in performance terms that entail behavioral scripts and impression management for the larger social communities in which they operate and towards other Black men.

8. In "Caliban in the Classroom," Karamcheti uses the metaphor of Caliban to describe the minority teacher. Following her lead I may enter the classroom, and consequently this study, as Caliban from Shakespeare's *The Tempest*-. In such case I serve as "a kind of native informant, lurching about the island and showing Prospero its sweet and secret places, serving to provide data with which Prospero can then rule" (142). As I write and theorize on my own experiences as a Black male teacher writing for and to a specifically academic and dominant (sometimes dominating) White cultural audience, I am especially cognizant of being Caliban. I am also aware of my constant negotiation and performance of narrative resistance. I am torn between the "native intellectual having an identity crisis . . . seeking to mediate and achieve synthesis between the [tales] of the exploiter and [the lived experience] of [the] exploited" (143). I become a tentative border spanner. I am caught "betwixt and between," but this is not a transitional space. It is clearly defined as a geographic and political positionality centered in the lived experience of the minority teacher, the Black intellectual—a space honed out of the negotiation of self and other, and the negotiation of self as other.

9. Turner's thesis in *The Anthropology of Performance* suggests a more complex relationship between society and its performative practices. "[The] relationship is not unidirectional and "positive"—in the sense that the performative genre merely "reflects" or "expresses" the social system or the cultural configuration, or at

any rate their key relationships—but . . . it is reciprocal and reflexive—in the sense that performance is
often a critique, direct or veiled, of the social life it
grows out of, an evaluation (with lively possibilities
of rejection) of the way society handles history
(21–22). Turner argues that "cultural performances
are active agencies of social change, representing the
eye by which culture sees itself and the drawing
board on which creative actors sketch out what they
believe to be more effective or ethical 'designs for
living'" (24).

REFERENCES

Alexander, B. (1998). Performing culture in the classroom: Excerpts from an instructional diary. In S. J. Dailey. (Ed.), *The
future of performance studies: Visions and revisions*. Annan-
dale: NCA.

Arnowitz, S. & Giroux, H. (1991). *Postmodern education: politics, culture & social criticism*. Minneapolis, MN: U of Minnesota P.

Bell, S. G. & Yalom, M. (Eds.) (1990). *Revealing lives: Autobiography, biography, and gender*. Ithaca, CT: SUNY P.

Boyd, H. & Allen, R. L. (Eds.) (1996). *Brotherman: The odyssey
of black men in America—an anthology*. New York: Ballantine
Books.

Britzman, D. P. (1986). Cultural myths in the making of a
teacher: Biography and social structure in teacher education. *Harvard Educational Review* 56(4) 442–55.

Carter, K. (1993). The place of story in the study of teaching
and teacher education. *Educational Researcher* 22(1) 5–12.

Cochran-Smith, M. & Lytle, S. L. (1993). *Inside/outside: teacher
research and knowledge*. New York: Teacher's College P.

Conquergood, D. (1986). Between experience and meaning:
Performance as a paradigm for meaningful action. In Ted
Colson (Ed.). *Renewal and revision: The future of interpreta-
tion*, Texas: Omega. 26–59.

Conquergood, D. (1985). Performing as a moral act: Ethical
dimensions of the ethnography of performance. *Literature
in Performance, 5.1.* 1–13.

Diawara, M. (1993). Black studies, cultural studies: Performative acts. In C. McCarthy & W. Crichlow (Eds.), *Race, identity and representation in education* 262–67. New York:
Routledge.

Egan, K. (1988). Metaphors in collision: Objectives, assembly
lines, and stories. *Curriculum Inquiry* 18: 63–86.

Fine, E. C. & Haskell Speer, J. (Eds.) (1992). *Performance, culture and identity*. West Port, CT: Praeger Publishing.

Frey, J. H., & Fontant, A. (1993). The group interview in social research. In D. L. Morgan (Ed.), *Successful focus Groups:
advancing the state of the art*. Newbury Park, CA: Sage.
20–34.

Goodall, H.L., Jr. (1994). *Casing a promised land: The autobiography of an organizational detective as cultural ethnographer*.
Carbondale, IL: SIU P.

Graham, R. (1991). *Reading and writing the self: Autobiography
in education and the curriculum*. Teacher's College P.

hooks, bell. (1994). *Teaching to transgress: Education as the practice of freedom*. New York: Routledge.

Jones, J. (1996). The self as other: Creating the role of Joni the
ethnographer for *Broken circles, Text and Performance Quarterly, 16.2:* 131–45.

Karamcheti, I. (1995).Caliban in the classroom. In Jane Gallop, (Ed.), *Pedagogy: The question of impersonation* 138–46.
Bloomington: Indiana UP.

Lionnet, F. (1989). *Autobiographical voices: Race, gender, self-
portraiture*. Ithaca, New York: Cornell UP.

MacAloon, J. (Ed.) (1989). *Rites, dramas, festival, spectacle: Re-
hearsals toward a theory of cultural performance*. Philadelphia: Institute for the Study of Human Issues.

Madison, D. S. (1999). Performing theory/embodied
writing.*Text and Performance Quarterly, 19.2,* 107–24.

Marshall, H. H. (1988). Work or learning: Implications of
classroom metaphors. *Educational Researcher 17,* 9–16.

McCarthy, C. & Crichlow, W. (Eds.) (1993). *Race, identity and
representation in education*. New York: Routledge.

McEwan, H. & Egan, K. (1995). *Narrative in teaching, learning,
and research*. New York: Teacher's College P.

McLaren, P. (1993). *Schooling as a ritual performance: Towards a
political economy of educational symbols & gestures*. New
York: Routledge.

McLaughin, D. & Tierney, W. G. (Eds.) (1993). *Naming silenced
lives: Personal narratives and the process of educational change,*
New York: Routledge. 29–51.

Miller, S. (1995). In loco parentis: Addressing (the) class. In
Jane Gallop (Ed.), *Pedagogy: The question of impersonation*.
Bloomington: Indian UP. 155–64.

Mohanty, S. P. (1989). Us and them: On the philosophical bases
of political criticism, *Yale Journal of Criticism, 2.2:* 1–31.

Munby, H. (1986). Metaphor in the thinking of teachers: An
exploratory study. *Journal of Curriculum Studies, 18(2):*
197–209.

Omi, M. & Winant, H. (1993). On the Theoretical Concept of
Race. In C. McCarthy, & W. Crichlow (Eds.), *Race, identity
and representation in education* (pp. 3–10). New York: Routledge.

Pineau, E. L. (1995). Critical performative pedagogy: Fleshing
out the language of liberatory education. Paper presented
at the Conference for the Pedagogy of the Oppressed, University of Nebraska, Omaha.

Singer, M. (1992). *When a great tradition modernizes: An anthropological approach to Indian civilization*. New York:
Praeger Publishing.

Smith, A. (1993). *Fires in the mirrow*. New York: Anchor Books.

Smith, A. J. (1993). *Examining the African self-consciousness of
African American students in a predominantly Black University*

and a predominantly White University: A comparative analysis. Unpublished thesis at Southern Illinois University.

Smitherman, G. (1994). *Black talk: Words and phrases from the hood to amen corner.* Boston: Houghton Mifflin.

Stewart, D. W. &Shamdasani, P. N. (1990). *Focus groups: Theory and practice.* Applied Social Research Methods Series 20, Newbury Park: Sage Publications.

Thompson, B. & Tyagi, S. (1996). *Names we call home: Autobiography on racial identity.* New York: Routledge.

Turner, V. (1988). Images and reflections: Ritual, drama, carnival, film, and spectacle in cultural performance. In V. Turner, (Ed.). *The anthropology of performance* (pp. 65–84). New York: PAJ Publications.

Van Maanen, J. (1988). *Tales of the field: On writing ethnography.* Chicago: U of Chicago P.

West, C. (1991). The dilemma of the Black intellectual. In b. hooks, b. & C. West (Eds.), *Breaking bread: Insurgent Black intellectual life.* Boston: South End. 131–46.

PERSPECTIVE 1: POSTPOSITIVISM ON THE ALEXANDER STUDY

D. C. PHILLIPS   *Stanford University*

My response to this paper is similar to my responses to the papers by Ellis (Chapter 9) and Sullivan (Chapter 10): No knowledge claims are put forward here, and indeed it is not absolutely clear what the author's aim was in writing the paper—it does not represent careful inquiry in the narrower or more "technical" sense that I discussed in my response to Sullivan. In the "Abstract" it is stated somewhat vaguely that the paper "seeks to contribute to the development of education and to performance theory" (p. 171), but no careful analysis is offered of that theory and the lacunae or problems within it are not laid out for our inspection, so it is not obvious how we are to judge whether (and in what way) the paper makes this contribution. (An inquiry that purports to make a theoretical contribution rather than an empirical one is still under an obligation to be clear and to be precise about what that contribution consists of, otherwise we will not be in a position to evaluate it. And an inquiry that cannot be evaluated is a defective inquiry.) A somewhat different aim is expressed in the second paragraph, where it is stated (still too generally) that the paper "seeks to address the issue of how Black male teachers and Black male students perform culture in the classroom . . . " (p. 171), but as an inquiry into this interesting though still vague topic the paper has important weaknesses.

The study as described here relies entirely on self report—self report of the author (made to seem more intellectually respectable or "scientific" or solidly based in a traditional genre of inquiry by being given the problematic label "autoethnography"), and self report of the individuals who were interviewed. But this kind of material is of notoriously slippery trustworthiness; and what things are told to an interviewer, the accuracy with which they are reported, and the language in which they are told, all can be influenced by many contextual factors and by the manner in which the interview is conducted and also by whom it is conducted. Added to which, self reports are often inaccurate, for people are not always good judges of their own behaviors, and sometimes what they report is not a description of their own behavior or an explanation for it, but an idealization of it or even a justification for it! Consider the case of Jesse, reported in the "Reflections" section of the paper; Alexander reports that Jesse said "his full class participation is contingent upon a felt connection with the teacher and a perception that his voice is going to be valued." Can we take this at face value? What, apart from what Jesse says, do we know about his participation in class and the factors that influence it? Perhaps he does not participate because he does not do his homework—we just do not know.

Traditional ethnographies, of course, do rely *to some degree* on information and insights gleaned from "informants," but no ethnographer worth his or her salt stops short at interviews; detailed observations are made, that often necessitate further interviews, the whole process being a dialectical one—a matter I commented upon briefly in my response to the ethnography by Shirley Brice Heath (Chapter 6). The present paper reports little if any traditional ethnographic data; what we are presented with are reminiscences of the interviewees, and the reflections of the interviewer on such matters as the emotions he recalled having during or immediately prior to the interviews (which I found interesting but generally of unclear relevance to the matter that I thought was at hand). I wanted to see descriptions (and analyses) of the students and faculty members interacting in the classroom, examples of the language the teachers used with students of different ethnic backgrounds, and examples of the questions the teachers asked and the answers that students gave—and examples of teacher feedback on those answers. In short, I wanted to see the kind of data and examples, and careful analysis of these, that Heath presented in her ethnography of Trackton that led to her insights about the lack of cultural congruence displayed in the use of language in its schools. Presenting us with this detailed material seems to be essential if Alexander is serious that his aim is to "address the issue of how Black male teachers and Black male students perform and negotiate culture in the classroom . . . " (p. 171); without it, what we have is not a study of the actual "performances" but rather a report about what on one occasion the "informants" choose to tell the researcher about their classroom experiences— reminiscences that could well change in form and substance if they were elicited under different conditions, and which we are in no position to evaluate.

The inquiry also would have been more rigorous if relevant demographic and contextual information had been collected and reported—such things as the social class of the students and teachers (class differences are often as important a source of alienation and difficulty in communication as are ethnic differences, and commonality of social class can reduce alienation and communication difficulties), what subjects the faculty members were teaching, and what academic classes the students were drawing their personal examples from. (I am presuming here—no data is presented—that interactions in a physics or calculus class are of a different order from interactions in a literature or ethnic studies class.) Furthermore, the way students react to teachers (and vice versa) also is often shaped by how well the students are doing in their classes, and again we are not presented with the relevant information. (For example, one of the students reported feeling his Black teachers "have been excessively hard" on him, but was this because he was lazy, or doing badly in the class, or what? Was it in fact true that the teachers treated him differently to the way they treated other students?) Another way to put all this is that interaction between students and instructors are influenced by many factors other than ethnicity, and these factors needed to be disambiguated if we are going to be able to draw any specific conclusions.

Another logically important aspect of a study of the interaction between Black faculty and students, where cultural similarity is a key explanatory feature, is that "baseline" data needs to be presented on interactions between Black teachers and non-Black students, and between Black students and non-Black faculty. Without this, there is no way of telling if the interactions between Black faculty and students are at all different from these other interactions.

The bottom-line here is that talking to people, and then writing up excerpts from these conversations, is too ill-disciplined to be worthwhile as research. Adding some snippets of theory is not much by way of improvement. If the topic of interest is worthwhile investigating—and, though it is not precisely formulated, Alexander's topic is worthwhile—then it is worth investigating *rigorously.* Otherwise we are missing out on an opportunity to add to our warranted knowledge.

PERSPECTIVE 2: PRAGMATISM ON THE ALEXANDER STUDY

NEL NODDINGS   *Stanford University*

What sort of research is this? The author tells us that it consists of ethnographic interviews and analysis. Our first question, then, might be how an ethnographic interview differs from other interviews. On page 172, the author cites Spradley's definition: "the essential core of this activity aims to understand another way of life from the native point of view." In anthropology, where ethnographic methods had their origin, researchers have usually studied cultures different from their own, and the purpose has been to recreate for readers a full picture of this other way of life.

In educational research, where ethnographic methods have now become popular, researchers often study a culture familiar to them—sometimes even a culture to which they themselves belong. Indeed, some researchers insist that the researcher should ideally belong to the culture under study. Alexander takes this position. He expresses "concerns about ethnographic work by researchers outside of the specified cultural community being studied" (p. 172). He may well be right that some Black professors and students would be reluctant to participate in a study conducted by a non-Black researcher, but issues of bias arise when the researcher is a member (and a "performing" one) of the culture under study.

Anthropologists have long argued over the merits of using an emic or etic approach. The *emic* approach uses cultural categories suggested by the experience of those being studied; the *etic* approach brings the analytic categories of the researcher to bear on the different culture. Both approaches offer advantages and disadvantages. The emic seems to be fairer to participants; it captures their culture as they see it. However, it can be too subjective. It can fail, in a given culture, to discover weaknesses and even moral evils that are simply not so categorized by its own system of classification. The etic approach offers the advantage of seeing the subject-culture with new, perhaps unclouded, vision. Its disadvantage is a tendency to impose categories that may be meaningless to those studied. Further, an outsider's view may misinterpret what is seen. In the wake of strong attacks against colonization, political hegemony, and the arrogance of western epistemology (Flinders & Mills, 1993; Goetz & LeCompte, 1984), anthropologists (like sociologists) have begun to argue over what methods and practices define their field. We could, then, find anthropologists who would defend Alexander's choice of an insider to study Black academic culture, and we could also find those who would raise objections to his choice.

There are issues more important to a pragmatist critic. What have we learned from this study? What might we have expected to learn? To this second question we might respond that a full description of Black academic culture is a reasonable expectation for a study purporting to be an ethnography. That expectation is certainly not met. There is very little discussion of categories associated with academic (professorial) work: committee work, publishing, lecturing, acquiring tenure, creating syllabi, choosing texts, evaluating student work, advising students, participation in professional societies, mentoring new professors, interacting with administrators, and so on. Now and then a professor's response includes a brief comment on one of these categories, but there is no systematic treatment of any of them. Similarly, we get only a sketchy sense of the corresponding student culture.

How nearly does Alexander's work approximate ethnography? It did not require "living with" his subjects for an extended period of time. As an insider to Black culture, he might have thought this unnecessary. But he did not observe them closely either. Instead he depended heavily on reflections on his own experience. This is a new form of ethnography—"autoethnography"—and one that will predictably raise objections. In devoting so little time to his participants, in failing to observe them in their classrooms, in referring so often to his own experience, he sacrificed the possibility of generating strong generalizations. Indeed, his description of his own encounters with Black elementary teachers stands in stark contrast to the description Jean Anyon has given of the interactions between some Black teachers and students in Newark, NJ (Anyon, 1997). We do not know whether the Black students he interviewed had elementary school experiences like his or more like some of the dreadful ones reported by Anyon.

If we return to the abstract introducing the article, we see that it may be unfair to judge this article by the criteria of ethnography. Alexander has restricted his study to "performing culture." He wants to show how Black culture is "performed" or demonstrated in college classrooms. We might still think that his purpose would have been better served by using familiar academic categories and describing cultural performance within each of them. But what can we learn from the report he has given us?

It is clear that Black professors experience considerable conflict as they perform Black culture in academic classrooms. Wanting to encourage their Black male students (there is no mention of Black females), they are torn between meeting them as Black-to-Black and meeting them as teacher to student. Some students make outrageous demands, expecting to receive good grades simply because both student and teacher are Black. Some identify common professorial methods as "White," and Black professors worry about losing credibility in the Black community. On balance, encounters between Black teachers and students seem to be highly valued, but the negotiation of culture is ceaseless.

Because of the emphasis on their Blackness, we get little sense of the professors as either individuals or professors. And we have to wonder whether Black culture is as uniform as it is portrayed here. Do all Black professors and students eat the same foods on holidays (p. 183)? Might a professor make a bad mistake in assuming that his Black students enjoy "black eye peas and chitlins"? Would the mistake be more troubling if it were committed by a White professor?

We don't get to know the Black students well either. They express some appreciation for the presence of Black teachers—better communication, enhanced feelings of safety, satisfaction of the need for role models. We are told that their "cultural expectations were both positive and negative" (p. 183) but, in the absence of life stories and aspirations, we do not know how to assess the sample comments. Why is Patrick so angry? What happened to cause this? Why does Frederick fear (and even expect) prejudgment on the part of Black professors? Marcus, too, says that "some Black professors have been excessively hard on me" (p. 183). Yet Alexander offers no analysis of this repeated concern. We need a fuller description of the participants and their experience.

Finally, a pragmatist would have to be concerned about the effects of such great emphasis on Blackness as identity. Assuredly, there are times when a Black professional (or role occupant of any kind) must speak *as a Black*. There are certainly times when I must speak as a White woman; but there are also times when other parts of my identity are more salient. The worry about race-gender-ethnicity identification is intensified when we reflect on western history and literature. How many fathers have said to their sons, "Never forget you are an Englishman!" and we now read these exhortations with some regret and embarrassment. It might have been better for everyone if these young men had at times relaxed their English identities and entered the world as polo players, poets, lovers, friends, physicians, carpenters, etc. (Read or re-read E. M. Forster, *A Passage to India* for a dramatic set of examples.) If we had fuller descriptions of the men in Alexander's study, we might have learned that they do in fact share their multiple identities in reciprocally valuable ways. We can hope that a future study will tell us more.

REFERENCES

Anyon, J. (1997). *Ghetto schooling: A political economy of urban educational reform.* New York: Teachers College Press.

Flinders, D. J., & Mills, G. E. (Eds.). (1993). *Theory and concepts in qualitative Research.* New York: Teachers College Press.

Goetz, J. P., & LeCompte, M. D. (1984). *Ethnography and qualitative design in educational research.* Orlando, FL: Academic Press.

PERSPECTIVE 3: CONSTRUCTIVISM ON THE ALEXANDER STUDY

YVONNA S. LINCOLN   *Texas A&M University*

Alexander's "Performing Culture" is not so much a performance—as are many experimental pieces appearing in the various social sciences literatures—as it is about the ways in which culture among Black men, teachers and students, is performed in learning environments. Performance and autoethnography stand at the far end of interpretive inquiry: the first as a public and interactional creation in some social and dramatic context, the second in the public exposure of some private event to a largely private and solitary audience. This piece stands at the crossroads of the two: an autobiographical rumination (from a larger journal on instruction) framed by ethnographic interviews and focus groups, circulating around the issue of culture as a performed ritual in the classroom. It is framed largely by the twin themes of culture as a classroom performance first articulated in McLaren's (1993) *Schooling as a Ritual Performance* and the experiences of Black men in learning environments (sometimes K–12 public schools, sometimes an institution of higher education).

Alexander's performative stage is both a real one—the college classroom—and an invisible one—memory. Memories serve to collect and illuminate a cultural experience in which Black teachers served as surrogate parents, extending the community beyond the family into the school experience. The college classroom serves as a counter to those memories, by virtue of the rare appearance of minority teachers, the absence of forms of comfort and loving found in largely Black classrooms with Black teachers, and the ritual necessity to sort efforts at testing of Black teachers by young Black men.

Alexander concludes, despite the testing, that there is a kind of affinity which exists by the simple virtue of color. While "black" is nothing more than a "genetic marker," like height, weight, or hair color, it nevertheless provides a starting point for what Alexander, following Conquergood, calls a "dialogic performance"—a conversation across difference which seeks challenge, alternative constructions, the search for likeness, and the collision of difference. The dialogic performance is, Alexander argues, far more powerful, immediate, and arresting for Black men—teachers and students—than it is for Whites, simply because it is heavily implicated in the larger context of gender identity, pervasive racism, and the negotiation of cultural identity.

If Turner (1988; whom Alexander cites) is correct that "cultural performances are active agencies of social change" and that "performance is often a critique, direct or veiled, of the social life it grows out of, an evaluation . . . of the way society handles history" (pp. 21–22) or, as

Conquergood (1985) puts it, performance is "a moral act," then we can begin to see Alexander's work in a stream of critical social theory which has as its central focus the challenge to existing social arrangements, and a set of negotiations toward new social arrangements. The possibilities for social critique, social change, rest with a set of lively interactions between performing current social arrangements and creating new scripts for different social arrangements.

Where Alexander's work is less clear is in how critique occurs in performance, and how the critique(s) ultimately creates different social arrangements. We are not certain from this piece how to move forward, how to enact the critique into a new order. Alexander is also less clear about what those who are not African American or Black, but who dearly wish for different and more just social arrangements, can do. How do self and other come together for this dialogical project when institutional racism, pedagogic racism, epistemological racism, and individual racism (Scheurich & Young, 1997) intervene to reinforce, if not continuously reinvent, existing social relations? There is a growing body of research, some of it autoethnographic (see the corpus of bell hooks's work, for instance), which provides an ongoing examination of race relations, analyses of cultural identity formation, and critiques of racist social arrangements. There is little, however, which explores how dialogic performances are revisioned, or rescripted, to support authentic cultural identity formation, while supporting and enlarging social justice. Alexander's piece is silent on this point, and readers are left to wonder what is happening between and among the White students in Alexander's classroom as identities are performed within Blackness.

REFERENCES

Conquergood, D. (1985). Performing as a moral act: Ethical dimensions of the ethnography of performance. *Literature in Performance, 5* (1), 1–13.

McLaren, P. (1993). *Schooling as a ritual performance: Towards a political economy of educational symbols & gestures.* New York: Routledge.

Scheurich, J. J., & Young, M. D. (1997). Coloring epistemologies: Are our research epistemologies racially biased? *Educational Researcher, 26* (4), 4–16.

Turner, V. (1988). Images and reflections: Ritual, drama, carnival, film, and spectacle in cultural performance. In V. Turner, (Ed.), *The anthropology of performance* (pp. 65–84). New York: PAJ Publications.

PERSPECTIVE 4: INTERPRETIVE AND NARRATIVE ON THE ALEXANDER STUDY

ARTHUR P. BOCHNER   *University of South Florida*

The educational research community is a plural and open society within which tradition and innovation co-exist. To maintain a sense of community, each educational researcher struggles to affirm what he or she has in common with other researchers without disconfirming or erasing the differences between them. What unites the community of educational research is a passionate commitment to explore and understand education; what differentiates members within the community are the terms we use to understand and express our diverse goals. The ideal for an academic community such as ours is respect for multiplicity, pluralism, tolerance, and dialogue. To achieve this ideal, it is necessary to resist the temptation to fall back on a single, familiar standard for judging the value of all research studies. Instead, we need an epistemological openness under which a plurality of research perspectives can flourish and be appreciated.

Bryant Alexander's monograph, "Performing Culture in the Classroom," represents a radical departure from traditional research and writing practices. Alexander is drawn to autoethnography and narrative inquiry out of a desire to discover or create new and better ways of living as a Black male professor who teachers and mentors Black male students. His research agenda is as much about the possible as it is about the actual. Prepared by his own lived experience to understand how the traditional research agenda that emphasized neutrality, objectivity, and scientific detachment could become a tool of oppression and domination, Alexander wants to radically democratize the research process, minimizing the power differential between researchers and participants, and placing greater emphasis on activism and social change. He is one of a new generation of researchers who want to move social research beyond the boundaries of received traditions, away from facts (pure and simple) and toward meanings (ambiguous and complicated); away from prediction and control and toward understanding and social criticism; away from generalizing theories (master narratives) and toward local stories; away from objectified variables and toward situated meanings; away from idolizing intellectualized abstractions and toward embracing emotionality, contingency, and activism; away from assuming the stance of the disinterested spectator and toward positioning oneself as a feeling, embodied, and vulnerable observer; away from writing essays and toward writing stories.

I recall a sign in the dean's office at Yale University that read "NEVER ASSUME." The sign was the dean's way of reminding visitors to his office that something always is assumed and an assumption is not a fact. All of us take something for granted. But what we take for granted is not taken for granted by everyone; nor is everything we take for granted necessarily true.

I was educated as an empiricist in the positivist tradition. In graduate school, I was taught that research was an activity in which one tested hypotheses, assigned subjects to experimental conditions, eliminated observer biases, controlled and manipulated variables, analyzed data statistically, and presented the (factual) results. By the time I had completed my doctoral work, I had internalized an empiricist conception of research. If someone handed me a research study to read, I would look immediately for the hypotheses, the data analysis, and evidence of objectivity. I didn't understand that my assumptions were relative to what I had been taught; nor did I consider that there might be useful alternatives to the kind of research that I knew and took for granted—goals other than prediction and control, concerns other than observer bias and objectivity, and ethical commitments other than debriefing.

In retrospect, I see now that my education as a researcher, sound as it may have been, was insular and narrow. Taking for granted an empiricist conception of research restricted my appreciation of different ways of knowing and different modes of representing the multiple realities and perplexities of social life; it constrained the range of topics that I could usefully investigate, making taboo or inaccessible many important areas of research such as child sexuality, spirituality, murder, and violence toward women; and it limited who could be reached by my research—who I spoke about, who I spoke for, and who I spoke to. By the standards of my conventional research education, I would have to ask Bryant Alexander, "Where are your hypotheses? Where is your data analysis? What are your findings?" Wouldn't those questions sound silly? Wouldn't that response miss the point?

When we assume, we take for granted. If we never have an experience that calls our assumptions into question, then we keep taking them for granted. Alexander's monograph draws attention to the taken-for-granted. By comparing his study to the others we have discussed thus far, we can begin to understand that there is no one right way to do research, one common purpose for research, one correct form in which to represent research, nor one universal standard to judge research. Every decision made in the process of formulating, conducting, and reporting research is a choice among alternatives. These choices one makes need to be guided by ethical as well as pragmatic issues.

Alexander's monograph draws our attention to questions such as these: What kind of relationship should exist between the researcher and the researcher participants? Should we consider the people we study to be "subjects" or "co-collaborators"? What does it mean to treat them as collaborators? What are our ethical obligations to them? How should their experiences and their voices be represented in the research story we write? How should the experiences and voice(s) of the researcher(s) be represented? For whom is the research being conducted and/or written? Whose interests are served by the research? In what form(s) should the research story be presented?

The main goal of Alexander's research is to show "how Black male teachers and Black male students perform and negotiate culture in the classroom" (p. 171). In contrast to the previous authors whose work we have examined, Alexander rejects the objectivist assumptions of neutrality and disinterest. Instead, he adopts the premises of what Michael Jackson calls "radical empiricism" in which it is assumed that "our understanding of others can only proceed from within our own experience . . . " (Jackson, 1989, p. 17). Alexander makes it obvious that he is invested in this topic, that his interests in the experiences of Black male professors and their students are rooted in his own lived history—his autobiography—and that his understanding and knowledge of the people he studies and represents must evolve not by observing them from a distance but by participating with them face-to-face, and putting their thoughts, feelings, and values on a par with his own. As a Black male professor/graduate student himself, Alexander does not stand apart from but rather becomes part of what he is studying. While important differences exist between Alexander and his research participants, they also share a common ground that becomes a useful position from which to explore their similarities and differences.

Alexander treats himself as a research participant, submitting his own experiences as primary data for empirical scrutiny, dissolving the distance between himself and the others he studies, refusing the pretensions of a distanced, superior investigator. In short, he puts himself on the line. You know where he's coming from. When he expresses how disconfirmed he felt when some students didn't show for their interviews and others flatly rejected the opportunity he gave them to discuss their experiences of male Black professors, he puts me in touch with his vulnerability and increases the level of trust I have in his observations and reflections. He becomes a vulnerable observer (Behar, 1996)—not a distanced author but a real, embodied, caring person. Similarly, when Alexander expresses how nervous he felt before he started each interview with a Black male professor, you get a sense of how much is risked when researchers narrow the distance and minimize the differences between themselves and their participants. It is difficult and demanding to be present and available to the others we study. Of course, the other side of risk is reward. Alexander sees himself in the other men he interviews. To know them more deeply is to understand himself more fully. To get closer to them is to get more in touch with himself. Anticipating this closeness quickens his pulse, but like the adrenalin that rouses an athlete to peak performance, this rush of passion kindles the flames of Alexander's desire to achieve a more authentic connection to Black male students.

Alexander raises important issues related to the ethics of research and writing practices when he says, "I find myself torn within the process of articulating knowledge." He feels a conflict between what he owes the men who participated in his research and his obligations to the academic audience to whom his writing is addressed. He wants to find a voice that can represent truthfully the experiences of these men, as well as his own experiences, without selling out to the dominant rules of academic discourse. He has a burning desire to write something that matters, something that is truthful, and something that is useful. I sense that he is struggling to write from the source of his own experience—to write subjectively and introspectively. Yet the ways he expresses himself on the page continue to hold to certain academic conventions that maintain the illusion of the author as an impersonal translator who reports "findings" as if he were not there. I got the impression that Alexander would like to write more freely, be less constrained by the conventions of academic writing, express events more imaginatively, less abstractly, and more in the mode of a storyteller than an academic reporter. But these desires are eroded by the tide of academic orthodoxy.

Notwithstanding Alexander's commitment to give voice to his participants and to empower them, he is unable to resist the pull of conventional standards of academic writing. Repeatedly, he interrupts his stories with references to the work of other researchers, giving long quotations from other sources, reviewing the literature, engaging in esoteric methodological discussions, using arcane jargon, and presenting his own analysis of what these men's experiences mean—not what the men say they mean but what Alexander interprets them to mean. As a result, the text loses its friendliness to readers. Generally, we are not invited into the experiences of these men. They are not developed as characters. The plot line is thin. We don't feel the power or tension of a drama. We get snippets rather than stories. Alexander tells but he does not show; experiences of these men are reported but, on the whole, they are not performed. Thus, the writing generally appeals more to the head than to the heart. A notable exception occurs when Alexander is writing about his own experiences—his life in school and his raw feelings of apprehension about interviewing these men. At these moments, I feel as if I share in his emotional experience in a way I never feel invited into the participants' experiences. When Alexander refers to his nurturing first-grade teacher, Mrs. Black, and the separation anxiety he felt when he left the comforting arms of his mother to ride the bus to school, I recall my own similar anxieties and the teachers who alleviated them.

This is what effective autoethnography does. It moves the reader back and forth from the author's stories of what was felt and experienced to what the reader feels and connects to and back again (Bochner & Ellis, 2002; Bochner, 2001). The authority of the story is measured by its capacity to evoke emotional response, by the identification and empathy that evolves between writer and reader, and by the connections the reader makes between the writer's feelings and his or her own (Bochner & Ellis, 2002; Denzin, 1997; Jones, 2002).

Both Alexander and Heath (Chapter 6) focus on the experience of life in school for differing populations of Black students. Each emphasizes the importance of teachers learning how to communicate effectively with these children. Whereas Heath treats the Black children as a social group, referring to them as the Trackton children, Alexander shows us some differences within the populations of Black male teachers and Black male children. Heath develops close relationships to the children, parents, and teachers over a period of 5 years; Alexander engages in a single conversation with willing participants. Both refer to themselves as ethnographers. Alexander positions himself squarely within his text; he writes in the first person; he is a co-collaborator and a participant; his observations originate from the source of his own experience; we know what is at stake for him; he recognizes but does not apologize for or defend his subjectivity; he engages his topic and his participants emotionally as well as intellectually; the stories he tells show the messiness of the participants' lives in school; he is a vulnerable observer.

On the whole, Heath keeps herself outside her text; she writes in the third-person; hers is a cerebral account; we don't know what is at stake for her or what life experiences provoked her interest in the difficulties of poor Black children; the account she gives is relatively unproblematic, cleansed of conflicts, racism, and emotional vulnerability. She is not a vulnerable observer. Both Alexander and Heath have something important to teach us. They teach us differently. Looking at their work side-by-side, we can see that the community of educational researchers is a plural and open society within which tradition and innovation co-exist.

REFERENCES

Behar, R. (1996). *The vulnerable observer: Anthropology that breaks your heart.* Boston: Beacon Press.

Bochner, A. & Ellis, C. (2001). Narrative's virtues. *Qualitative Inquiry, 7,* (131–157).

Bochner, A. & Ellis, C. (2002) Ethnographically speaking: Autoethnography, literature, and aesthetics. Walnut Creek, CA: AltaMira.

Denzin, N. (1997). *Interpretive ethnography: Ethnographic practices for the 21st century.* Thousand Oaks: Sage Publications.

Jackson, M. (1989). *Paths toward a clearing: Radical empiricism and ethnographic inquiry.* Bloomington, IN: Indiana University Press.

Jones, S. H. (2002). The way we were, are, and might be: Torch singing as autoethnography. *Ethnographically speaking: Autoethnography, literature, and aesthetics.* Walnut Creek, CA: AltaMira. (44–56).

PERSPECTIVE 6: RACE, ETHNICITY, AND GENDER ON THE ALEXANDER STUDY

BETH HARRY   *University of Miami*

Alexander's use of autoethnography presents a mix between the first person narrative used by Ellis (Chapter 9) and the outsider perspective of Heath (Chapter 6). In my commentary on the Ellis article, I note that the narrative works very well as long as the author focuses faithfully on her own internal experience. When she shifts her gaze to the behavior and, most importantly, to the motives of others, the memoir loses its claim to authenticity, and the reader becomes aware that there is now another point of view to be taken into account—a point of view that is assumed rather than sought by the author. The point is that the introspective narrator can presume to know his or her own motives but not those of others.

Ethnography, on the other hand, deliberately focuses on others rather than the self, and seeks the meanings of others' behavior through their actions and explanations. The traditional product of ethnography is the "realist tale" (Van Maanen, 1988) which, by documenting both observations and native explanations, can move toward a multifaceted theory of some aspect of a group's behavior. I believe Heath's study is an excellent exemplar of that genre.

In autoethnography the researcher has the best of both worlds because the genre demands the inclusion of multiple perspectives. As Alexander skillfully demonstrates, he can describe and analyze his own internal actions, observe and inquire about the meanings of the actions of others, and put these together to explain how Black male teachers and Black male students "perform and negotiate culture in the classroom" (p. 173). In this mode, the author "directly reject[s] the notion of objectivistic ethnography" (p. 173), and, as an "indigenous ethnographer," begins his exploration in the territory he knows best—the self. But the notion of indigenous status is challenged by the nuances of what Blackness means to his students, and the challenge of whether or not they will perceive him to be, truly, "a brother." So to understand this challenge better, he seeks others' definitions of the relationship between Black male students and their Black male teachers. He finds among teachers and students alike a strong consciousness of the need to "establish and recreate community in the classroom" (p. 176), and the portraits that emerge from his explorations show the challenge of creating a pedagogy that crosses the borders of student and teacher personas as well as the borders of ethnicity. Black male teachers must establish a community that covertly confirms and nurtures ethnic bonds without excluding White students.

While gender no doubt alters the nuances of this experience, I believe that the "culturally coded challenge" that ensues is immediately recognizable to any Black professor, regardless of gender, in the White academy. For myself, as a Black female in the academy, I am comforted by my immediate recognition of my own experience in this autoethnography. I am challenged too, because the voices of the students speak to the fact that when I am excessively hard on my Black students (which I often am), it is in an instinctive effort to protect them from anything in themselves that might place them in the shadow of the stereotype. However, according to Marcus, Patrick, and Frederick, in doing so I am already "reading some stereotype and projecting it onto [them]." The dilemmas so vividly portrayed by Alexander echo the arguments of many who have pointed to the complexity of race/ethnicity and the impossibility of essentializing ethnic identity.

At the end of the piece, there is one view that is still missing—the author's own students' views of him. I was somewhat disconcerted by the fact that the only two specific examples he gives of experiences with his own Black male students reveal that he himself is being "read" stereotypically by those students. In one case, something about his personal presentation causes a student to doubt his authenticity as "a brother." In the other, the expectation of undue privilege drives a student to see him as a traitor. The latter is an example of what West (1994) has called "racial reasoning," whereby the student seemed to define racial authenticity in terms of a kind of "closing ranks" process that should ensure that a brother would not "give a brother a C." Alexander locates his work at the borders of ethnic and professional identities, but the one border he does not attempt to cross is that between himself and those whom *he* actually teaches. To do this would be to face the ultimate challenge in negotiating identity within the classroom—the challenge of crossing the borders of power and authority—of asking "how do *you* see *me*?" as contrasted with "How do *you* see *others*?" In his border research, Alexander still locates himself just slightly off center.

REFERENCES

Van Maanen, J. (1988). *Tales of the field: On writing ethnography.* Chicago: University of Chicago Press.

West, C. (1994) *Race Matters.* New York: Vintage Books.

PERSPECTIVE 7: CRITICAL THEORY ON THE ALEXANDER STUDY

GEORGE NOBLIT   *University of North Carolina*

Bryant Keith Alexander provides a good example of how a critical study is different from interpretive studies. He has written a study that is an autoethnography like those of Ellis (Chapter 9) and Sullivan (Chapter 10) as well as a piece of qualitative research like that of Heath (Chapter 6) and Sullivan. It addresses issues of race like that of Heath, shares the intent of Carr et al. (Chapter 5) and Heath to improve the lives of the disadvantaged, and is actively promoting more rigorous and expansive definitions of education as does Heath, Sullivan, and Raudenbush et al. (Chapter 8). Yet what distinguishes Alexander is his critical theoretical frame and his use of it to move beyond understanding and towards emancipation (Carspecken, 1996). Moreover, it is clear that Alexander understands that this research is not only about changing the disciplines of knowledge, although he shares this interest with many of the above authors. This research is about racial identity and what he brings to it is both qualitative data and an impassioned subjectivity: ". . . I am always and already a participant in my field of studying which my performances of Black male teacher and student comes under scrutiny" (p. 183). In this statement, Alexander shows the depth of his understanding of critical research. One must be able to critique oneself even as one proceeds to use one's perspective to understand more than oneself.

Alexander is approaching his study with a particular theoretical lens. His perspective is critical but his analysis and critique is based in performance theory (Conquergood, 1983). This theory has been popular in both communication studies and anthropology. It begins with the realization that even though culture structures how we behave, we are all actively performing that culture. That is, we make decisions about how to represent and embody our culture: "It is a method of defining, redefining, and maintaining our cultural identities and social selves" (p. 171). In this there is a form of agency that is not acknowledged in more traditional and more passive conceptions of culture as ways of doing and believing. For Alexander, however, this agency is insufficient. Performances are also imbued with political agendas that must be revealed and interrogated. Autoethnography then is transformed from the interpretive study of self into a form of "critical praxis". It moves beyond the empathy which was so important to Ellis, Sullivan, and Heath ". . . to come to a critical understanding of self and other and those places where we intersect and overlap" (p. 173). This move expands the study of the self into a study of the social and collective. It also problematizes the distinction drawn in ethnography between self and other. Here they are each implicated in the other. As Alexander states, "I join my voice with other Black male teachers and students" (p. 173) in what he sees as a dialogic performance. That is, he not only conjoins self and other, he understands his own analysis and critique as a cultural performance as well. He explains: ". . . I critically describe and analyze my own lived experiences in the classroom, and that of others, in order to come to an understanding of where our experiences intersect while being acutely aware of my shifting and dual cultural membership and shifting borders of my intention: self-reflection and research" (p. 173). In this, we can see the demanding nature of critical inquiry, especially when couched within a performance ethnography.

Alexander pursues his study through autoethnography and ethnography. Yet because he is the researcher in the latter and because the people he studies share key elements of his biography (being Black male students and teachers), the two studies blend smoothly into the other. He starts by reflecting on his "institutional biography" (p. 174) in schools. He is careful to acknowledge that this account is recreated but nevertheless is real to him as he lives his life today. It is a narrative he uses to construct his identity. He notes that he had only a "handful of Black teachers" (p. 174) in 22 years of schooling. He has also had few Black colleagues in his years as a teacher in predominately White institutions. As he recounts the story of his first Black teacher, he admits to "romantization" (p. 174) of the relationship but also sees that as pointing to the nature of the relationship as being "more parental and less teacherly" (p. 174) that he too seeks to have with his students. This parental relationship did not replace his family but rather was more of an extension that ". . . was constructed to affirm community and family values" and was an attempt ". . . to build a bridge, not to create a wall of difference between that which was framed as academic (teaching and learning) and home values" (pp. 174–175). He now interprets this effort as "enacting a revolutionary pedagogy of resistance that was profoundly anti-colonial" (p. 175). It is here we begin to see that his analysis recontextualizes what could be seen by whites as an unremarkable relationship akin to parenthood, but when enacted by Black teachers for Black students in White dominated schools it had a entirely different and political meaning. As he moved to the university, however, he came to realize that this relationship and the pedagogy that it represented was tied to a specific community with shared values about how to educate and raise Black children. At university, the Black professors are often not of that community (Shujaa, 1993). Thus the Black professor and Black student are "involved in a form of covert community building" (p. 176). His critical approach has led him to discern the differences in the two teaching relationships. The latter relationship was being played out in the context of "the academic community of the White university" (p. 176) not in the context of an existing Black community. The Black professor and Black student then were engaged in a complex cultural performance: "They were performances of covert community building in which a formal public respect was engaged in the classroom and a 'let's be real' attitude prevailed in private space away from any onlookers" (p. 176). The relationship also was in part "a struggle for authority and respect" (p. 176) as well, since this is a required attribute of the teaching role, even though Black students sometimes called for Black teachers to "an unyielding and unearned support constituted in opposition to their role as teachers" (p. 176).

Alexander's ethnography is divided into his investigations of Black male teachers and Black male students. His encounters with the former were filled with "excitement . . . tempered with the anticipation of challenge that only Black men can offer each other" (p. 177). As a critical performance enthnographer, Alexander understood his interviews in ways most interpretivists do not. These interviews were not just cultural artifacts but active cultural performances. Both parties that began with a "ritual greeting of brotherhood" coupled with "a reading of worth, value, and substance" (p. 178). This "performative assessment" (p. 178) was followed by "cultural languaging" in the form of call and response that "gave way to vigorous and animated conversations that were loosely structured with questions" and "affirmations of felt cultural experiences" (p. 178). He learned that Black professors desired "to share specified academic knowledge as well as cultural unification" (p. 179). Their "culturally embued pedagogy of desire" used cultural affinity "as a strategy for understanding and connecting with Black male students" (p. 179). These teachers desired to both care for Black students but also "to be fair to all students." They challenged White students "to reflect upon their own racial and cultural biases" and "to understand what it may be like for Black and other minority students" as they "negotiate the chasm that sometimes exists between racial and cultural knowing and the sometimes sanitizing space of academia" (p. 180). Alexander concludes that for Black professors and students "negotiating culture in the classroom is actually an issue of negotiating sameness and differences—all grounded in a shared racially gendered history, and against the backdrop of the Black community" (p. 180). Clearly Alexander's critical perspective finds classroom culture to be much more complex than Heath (Chapter 6) represented in her study.

His study of Black male students was also understood as a set of cultural performances, including declining to participate in the study. Those who desired to participate, he argues, did so as a "celebration of community, celebration of critique" (p. 180). Alexander recognizes that all cultural performances involve "establishing membership and reflecting traditions" and "being an agent of commentary and change" (p. 180). Here Alexander critiques his initial understandings of the interviews with both Black professors and students. He realized that he was moving between identities as researcher and Black male as the interviews progressed and that this "dual positionality was also present during my interviews with Black teachers . . . " (p. 180). He was using a "border pedagogy" (p. 181) that allowed him to shift roles and engage "students in the active process of articulating their experiences . . . " (p. 181). Yet "border pedagogy demands that student knowledge and cultural power also must be critiqued to unearth logics that are unreflectively promoted and advocated as fact" (p. 181). In this, Alexander signals his understanding that even what he has learned should not be reified as fact, but considered and critiqued as possible political and ideological stances. The student interviews had moments of "released resistance" and "passion and reverence" (p. 182) for Black male teachers and education itself. Alexander concludes that race does matter in education but not in simple ways: "Race matters as a bridge to understanding and lived experience; it can be both facilitating and debilitating" (p. 182).

As a critical researcher, Alexander ends his article in ways that both explains what he has found and reconsiders it as well. He begins by problematizing his methodology, acknowledging that he was a "participant in my field of study" (p. 183). This in turn means his ethnography cannot be understood as a study of the other as he is also of the other. "Otherness is difference identified" (p. 183) and not a preexisting, presumed category. Finally, his representation is problematic in that he finds himself struggling with his "allegiance to my primary cultural group . . . and the academic community in which this study is articulated" (p. 184). Yet to the extent that ethnography is to yield detailed descriptions of lived experience "then my position as a native informant has enhanced the ethnographic description" (p. 184). It this same "cultural affinity" (p. 184) that the Black male students desired in Black teachers. Yet this affinity is itself a cultural performance. In this performance, Black male students and teachers face "the paradox of representation, of being 'both/and,' of representing a racial or cultural group through recognizable cultural performances, but at the same time being a marker of difference" (p. 185). That is, cultural affinity among Blacks also signals to Whites that Blacks are not like them. In the end, Alexander offers not a definitive understanding but rather a critical perspective that reveals that culture must be negotiated by Blacks in education in ways not required of Whites. Given the existing power of Whites over education, Blacks cannot hope for simple prescriptions or instructional strategies to make education work for them. As Alexander concludes: "To teach as Black man is to negotiate and mediate the borders of the educational institutions in which I learn and teach, and the primary racial and cultural communities in which I claim membership" (p. 185).

REFERENCES

Carspecken, P. F. (1996). *Critical ethnography in educational research: A theoretical and practical guide.* New York: Routledge.

Conquergood, D. (1983). Performing as a moral act: Ethical dimenions of the ethnography of performance. *Literature in Performance,* 5:1, 1–13.

Shujaa, M. J. (1993). *Too much schooling, too little education: A paradox of black life in white societies.* Trenton, N.J.: Africa World Press.

PERSPECTIVE 8: ETHICS, METHODOLOGY, AND DEMOCRACY, ON THE ALEXANDER STUDY

KENNETH R. HOWE   *University of Colorado at Boulder*

At the end of an episode in the long running TV series *Law & Order,* Stone (a White man) says to Robinet (a Black man), "The question you have to ask yourself is whether you are a Black lawyer or a lawyer who happens to be Black." This question followed Stone and Robinet's failure to convict a Black man in a racially charged case, an outcome about which Robinet should have been disappointed but was ambivalent. Stone's question troubled Robinet and he gave no answer.

Robinet returned in a later episode, having left his position in the district attorney's office, (where Stone had been his superior) and having become a defense attorney. He now had an answer to Stone's question: he was a Black lawyer.

As I read Alexander's study I couldn't help being reminded of how Robinet had come to believe that there was no way he could separate his racial position from his professional life. This actually runs deeper in Alexander. Race isn't merely an unavoidable consideration for him—a source of oppression that explains and mitigates hostility and that can be understood in terms of some generalized motivational structure that applies to all people (the view I attribute to Robinet). Different motivational structures operate that cannot be divorced from social history and positioning, and that can only be understood from the *inside*. As I understand Alexander, the implication is not necessarily balkanization. Once cultural practices (or "performances") are described from the inside, the hope is that others may come to better appreciate them and avoid distorting the nature of lives different from their own, and that "border crossing" may be facilitated.

More than the other authors I critique in this text (Carr et al., Raudenbush et al., Ellis, and Heath), Alexander is explicit about the moral-political aims of his research. He grounds it in critical pedagogy, which he characterizes as being concerned with "revealing, interrogating, and challenging . . . legitimated social forms and opening the space of additional voices" (p. 171). The study seems mostly confined to "revealing" and "interrogating," perhaps because, as Alexander notes, it is only a part of a broader study. In any case, his portrayal of Black male students and faculty in a predominantly White university can certainly inform the political projects of those committed to racial justice.

Like most "qualitative" research, however, the audience must take responsibility for sharing in the interpretation of results and drawing conclusions about what actions are needed. The standard of validity is not how well Alexander's finding *generalize* in the statistical sense, but how well they inform and *resonate* with readers in particular situations.

Alexander's study is not an ethnography as traditionally conceived; it is an "autoethnography." In its simplest terms, I understand this to mean that Alexander includes much of himself in his research. He is therefore liable of being charged from certain quarters with being subjective, biased, unscientific, and doing a biography *instead of* research, etc. (Such charged may also be advanced against Ellis's study (Chapter 9), and with more warrant, in my view. See my commentary on Ellis (p. 279).) In the extreme, Alexander might also be charged with being irresponsible—and therefore unethical—in his role as an educational researcher.

I don't want to pooh-pooh the importance of methodological rigor nor suggest that it may be disentangled from ethical obligations, but I do resist Procustean standards that serve to do little more than regiment researchers. Though I can't say whether Alexander would agree, one way to look at his research is as basically an ethnography, or, perhaps more accurately, as a critical ethnography (both of which I trust have the methodological seal of approval) in which he is one of the major informants. It is difficult to imagine Alexander's study being nearly as rich and informative if he hadn't so extensively included himself. Perhaps we should be more skeptical of his perceptions than those of the other Black men, but why? What are concrete examples of things he says that should prompt suspicion?

What Alexander's study illustrates is the artificiality of the distinction between personal ethics and professional ethics, especially for Black educational researchers (as well as other historically excluded groups, to be sure). Race is an inescapable part of how their lives unfold, in every walk. Thus we see Alexander being called upon by other Black men to be a "brother" and to avoid shedding his identity as he negotiates a White dominated university. As his father says, "It's alright to talk like a teacher, but remember you're a Black man. Talk like a Black man teacher." (p. 185). His study exemplifies his role as a *Black educational researcher* rather than an educational researcher who happens to be a Black.

In addition to helping others understand the boundaries within which Black male academics must operate—boundaries laid down by both Whites and Blacks—Alexander's study also helps drive home the ethical obligations of the educational research community regarding its membership. Although there are no general rules about whether and when the cultural membership of researchers and research participants must match (for example, Heath's study was an effective one in the absence of such a match), educational researchers are not interchangeable in the contributions they can make. Blacks, in addition to White women, Asians, and numerous other groups, bring certain "standpoints" to educational research unique to their social histories and positions and from which they can better understand and depict oppressive social arrangements. Alexander's study illustrates this point especially well by employing autoethnography. But the point is a general one, not necessarily tied to this or that research methodology. An educational research community that includes a diversity of standpoints better measures up to the requirements of a deliberative democracy than one that does not.

PERSPECTIVE 9: POSTSTRUCTURALISM ON THE ALEXANDER STUDY

LYNDA STONE   *University of North Carolina at Chapel Hill*

Michel Foucault (1926–1984) is arguably the most recognized of the French post-structuralists. He was born in Poitiers France, educated both at local and Parisian schools, and completed advanced degrees in philosophy and psychology. He was a cultural representative and instructor in Europe and North Africa and held several French university posts until he was elected to the Collège de France. Most notable in the United States was his connection to the University of California, Berkeley. His studies were often histories of those marginalized as he more generally looked for breaks and ruptures in western thought. During his last years, he was a political activist for prisoner and gay rights until his untimely death.

Bryant Keith Alexander contributes an important piece to growing literatures in "single sex" education, to methodologies in qualitative research, and to the significant tradition of critical theory and critical pedagogy in higher education. In the piece, he draws on a broad set of sources for analysis whose general purpose is to educationally empower a minority group, that of Black males. Such an aim is surely laudatory and necessary in an era in which there still is no level playing field in schooling for specific minority groups. In this study, as a black male professor, he uses his own educational background in an autobiographic interplay with interview data from teachers and students who share his culture.

Alexander's study joins others of a significant contemporary "critical" tradition in which social and particularly educational reform is predicated on identity: who one is matters especially for those marginalized, silenced, invisibilized in a "mainstream."[1] His language is part of a newer discourse of opportunity than that traditionally humanist—and it arises from origins in sociological structuralism. In addition to identity, "cultural politics" is central through such terms as voice, positionality, representation, and performance. Writings are meant to assert agency and power. In Alexander's words, he and others are involved in a "[collective] struggle for authority and respect . . . [through] performing legitimacy. . . . Black teachers . . . [and students] defined ourselves to and for each other within the larger context of the predominately White university (p. 178).

It is precisely a humanist/critical tradition from Alexander that Michael Foucault writes against. Two ironies are manifest in bringing forth this lens. First Foucault, it appears in his biographies, spent considerable time establishing his identity amid his own difficulties in schooling in which teachers and students were not like him. But second, unlike Alexander, he writes that his own writing is to "get free of oneself" (Foucault, 1990, p. 8). Overall Foucault's work undermines traditional and critical notions of the self, consciousness, rationality, and agency. In his words, his own project is to write something else: "to create a history of the different modes by which . . . human beings are made subjects" (Foucault, 1983, p. 208). In this critique, two of his concepts are instructive, theorizing on the author and on power. Both raise a central question for the efficacy and enactment of Alexander's autoethnography, returned to at the close.

From the overview on poststructuralisms to begin: Foucault works through language to explore relations, of discursive and related non-discursive practices. For him, further, the aesthetic functions in two ways, in his turning to and use of literary and many other forms of text and in the unique aesthetic that his own writings entail. Moreover, for him the aesthetic aspect of human life operates in how subjects are made. Subjectivity functions through forces of relation including some of "self-formation."[2]

As foundation for his own treatment, Foucault follows his friend and structuralist forebear Roland Barthes in proclaiming "the death of the author" in modern writing. Barthes begins that "writing is that neuter, that composite, that obliquity into which . . . [a] subject flees, the black-and-white where all identity is lost, beginning with the very identity of the body that writes" (Barthes, 1989 p. 49). For Barthes, what is lost is collected in the reader, but he too is not personal: "the reader is a man without history, without biography, without psychology" (p. 54). Foucault extends the death of the author into a more comprehensive account of discursive practice as the "author function." A reversal, itself unsatisfactory in Barthes, is undermined in textual operations. Foucault writes that these connect and disconnect, include and exclude. Indeed the author function is carried out in the "scission" between a real writer and a text that only minimally refers "to several selves, to several subjects—positions that can be occupied by different classes of individuals" (Foucault, 1984, pp. 112, 113). Texts, as authors and subjects in Foucault's idiom, "come to be constituted" (are made) in ever-fluid relations; traditional agency is denied. Significantly such relations, as all others, entail power. But here too, "power" takes on new meaning.

Significantly, Foucault writes against a traditional western notion of power. The general idea is that the power of empowerment is not easily locatable. Moreover there is implicit warning against illusion of such direct power. For Foucault, power is not something a person or group possesses as "sovereign." Here is his famous statement:

> Power is everywhere; not because it embraces everything, but because it comes from everywhere. And "Power," insofar as it is permanent, repetitious, inert, and self-reproducing, is simply the over-

all effect that emerges from all these mobilities, the concatenation that rests on each of them and seeks in turn to arrest their movement. One needs to be nominalistic, no doubt; power is not an institution, and not a structure; neither is it a certain strength we are endowed with; it is the name that one attributes to a complex strategical situation in a particular society. (Foucault, 1990, p. 93)

Several subpoints are instructive: power is productive; it is capillarial and it exists alongside resistance. Be careful here! For Foucault resistance is the irreducible opposite of power but it is no more or less sovereign, agentive, or enacted with any degree of achievement. And it surely is not a tactic toward a transcendental emancipatory aim. He writes (and one notes in the plural),

[Resistances are] points, knots, or focuses . . . spread over time and space and at varying densities. . . . [They produce] cleavages in a society that shift about, fracturing unities and effecting regroupings, furrowing across individuals themselves, cutting them up and remolding them, marking off irreducible regions in them, in their bodies and minds. (p. 96)

What does a Foucauldian rendering of "author-ity" and power leave for Alexander and his project? This is the central question. Of course this author (and all of *us*) must act in the world just as Foucault believes. He is political but he—and any others—cannot claim "the individual self as an agent of social change" (p. 185). This assertion of agency is too simplistic much as one might desire it; it is too facile an ascription to individuals and groups in a complex world. No wonder, one thinks, change seems so difficult and "advances" so transitory! But intervene one must, to disrupt discursive, institutional relations and practices in which invidious power prevails. Foucault's own politics provides an all-too-brief model: he took part in strategic collective planning; he passed out leaflets; he marched; he acted for political change in everyday senses. To close, having applied Foucault conceptually to Alexander's own theoretical framework, the study is yet an intervention; it deserves attention. Its implications for change—at the borders of educational institutions that he describes—deserve support and enactment.

NOTES

1. I interpret Alexander's "critical" tradition as a kind of generic hybrid prominent today in Anglo-American educational research. It is Marxist inspired.
2. This process of self-formation, tied to an important methodological break, Foucault names as ethics. For him a response to limiting/disciplining regimes of truth as power/ knowledge/subject is politics.

REFERENCES

Barthes, R. (1989). The death of the author. In *The rustle of language* (R. Howard, Trans., pp. 49–55). Berkeley, CA: University of California Press. (Original work published 1968)

Foucault, M. (1983). The subject and power. In H. Dreyfus & P. Rabinow (Eds.),*Michel Foucault: Beyond structuralism and hermeneutics* (pp. 208–226). Chicago: The University of Chicago Press.

Foucault, M. (1984). What is an author? In *The Foucault reader* (P. Rabinow, Ed., J. Harari, Trans, pp. 101–120). New York: Pantheon. (Original work published 1969)

Foucault, M. (1990). *An introduction: The history of sexuality, Vol. 1* (R. Hurley, Trans). New York: Vintage. (Original work published 1976)

Foucault, M. (1990). *The use of pleasure: The history of sexuality, Vol. 2* (R. Hurley, Trans). New York: Vintage. (Original work published 1984)

CHAPTER 8

The Raudenbush et al. Study

HIGHER ORDER INSTRUCTIONAL GOALS IN SECONDARY SCHOOLS: CLASS, TEACHER, AND SCHOOL INFLUENCES

STEPHEN W. RAUDENBUSH, BRIAN ROWAN, YUK FAI CHEONG

Michigan State University, University of Michigan and Michigan State University

We consider three explanations for variation in emphasis on teaching for higher order thinking in U.S. secondary classrooms: (a) current conceptions of learning encourage pursuit of higher order objectives primarily for high-track students in advanced courses; (b) many teachers lack adequate preparation to teach for higher order thinking; and (c) organizational norms discourage pursuit of higher order objectives. We asked secondary teachers in 16 schools to identify their instructional goals for each of their classes and constructed scales to capture higher order emphasis in math, science, social studies, and English. A three-level hierarchical regression analysis revealed powerful effects of track on higher order objectives in all disciplines, especially math and science. Effects of teacher preparation and organizational norms were manifest in English and social studies, but not in math or science. Differentiation of instructional objectives based on academic track is apparently deeply institutionalized, particularly in math and science.

Over the past decade, research on teaching has undergone an important transformation as researchers have turned their attention from instruction for basic skills toward teaching for higher-order thinking (Bereiter & Scardamalia, 1987; Peterson, 1988; Prawat, 1989; Newmann, 1990). This change results from a widespread perception that U.S. schools are comparatively ineffective in cultivating conceptual understanding of academic subjects. For example, recent large-scale assessments demonstrate that although U.S. students perform adequately on tests of basic skills, they perform comparatively poorly on tasks that involve problem solving, critical analysis, and flexible understanding of subject matter (U.S. Department of Education, 1991, pp. 32–41). In this light, teaching for higher-order thinking

is increasingly accepted as a goal toward which the education profession should strive.

Recent commentary and research also emphasize that teaching for higher-order thinking is important for the learning of *all* students in *all* academic subjects. For example, Peterson (1988) cites research suggesting

> the need for an increased instructional focus on teaching higher-level skills in mathematics to all students. Such an increased focus might be particularly important for lower-achieving students, who have more difficulty than their peers in learning these higher-order skills on their own. (p. 2)

With respect to secondary social studies, Newmann (1990) proposes that teaching for higher-order thinking is important for all learners:

> Any person, young or old, regardless, of experience, can participate in higher-order thought. Students will differ in the kinds of challenges they are able to master, but all are capable of confronting a challenge in the interpretation, analysis, and manipulation of knowledge. (p. 48)

Doyle (1983) also reviews research indicating that teaching cognitive processes and knowledge structures can be of special benefit to lower-achieving students.

Despite the emerging consensus on the importance of teaching for higher-order thinking, research (reviewed

Raudenbush, S. W., Rowan, B., & Cheong, Y. F. (1993). *Higher order instructional goals in secondary schools: Class, teacher, and school influences.* American Educational Research Journal, 30(3), 522–553. *Copyright 1993 by the American Educational Research Association. Reprinted by permission of the publisher.*

subsequently) generally finds that classroom instruction in high schools is focused on basic skills (Goodlad, 1984; Powell, Farrar, & Cohen, 1985). To the extent that teaching for higher-order thinking is manifest, evidence suggests that it occurs far more often in high-track than in low-track classes (Metz, 1978; Oakes, 1985; Page, 1990). Thus, at the high-school level in the United States, a sharp contrast exists between current visions of educational excellence and currently institutionalized patterns of educational practice.

In this article, we consider and test several explanations for variation across U.S. secondary classrooms in teaching for higher-order thinking. The first explanation holds that hierarchical conceptions of teaching and learning are deeply embedded in the high-school curriculum and that these conceptions discourage teachers from embracing higher-order instructional goals except when teaching the most advanced students in the most advanced subjects. If this explanation is credible, we should expect instructional goals to vary *within* teachers. That is, when the several classes taught by a given high school teacher vary in terms of the presumed academic ability of their students or the level of subject matter to be taught, that teacher should place more emphasis on teaching for higher-order thinking when teaching high-track students and when teaching more advanced subjects. Moreover, this tendency of a teacher to differentiate instructional goals across classes should be most pronounced in those academic disciplines that are most clearly differentiated on the basis of student ability and level of course difficulty.

A second explanation emphasizes differences among teachers rather than differences within teachers. According to this view, variations in teachers' subject-matter knowledge and pedagogical expertise are critical in understanding differences among teachers in instructional goals (Shulman, 1987). We hypothesize that more highly educated and experienced teachers, who are presumably more knowledgeable about their discipline and have acquired more pedagogical expertise, will embrace higher-order instructional goals with higher frequency than will less educated or less experienced teachers.

Rather than viewing teacher preparation as a global teacher characteristic, one might view it as varying from class to class for each teacher. We also investigate the effect of preparation to teach the specific content of each class to which the teacher is assigned. We hypothesize that when teacher preparation matches the content, the teacher will be more likely to pursue higher-order instructional goals than when preparation and content match poorly. The

adequacy of the match will depend both on the teacher's overall preparation and on the process used to assign teachers to courses.

A third explanation focuses on the organizational environments in which teachers work. Recent work on school restructuring, for example, suggests that bureaucratic rules that closely regulate or routinize teachers' work will discourage the pursuit of higher-order instructional goals, whereas organizational environments characterized by supportive administrative leadership, high levels of teacher collaboration, and strong teacher control over instruction will facilitate the pursuit of such instructional goals.

Using teachers' self-reported emphasis on teaching for higher-order goals in each of the classes they teach, we examined emphasis on teaching for higher-order thinking in a sample of 1,205 classes taught by 303 academic teachers in 16 diverse high schools in California and Michigan. The three explanations we consider imply that teachers' goals would vary at each of three levels: within teachers as a function of characteristics of the classes a teacher encounters; between the teachers working in a particular school; and across schools. Accordingly, we employed a three-level hierarchical linear model that enabled us to decompose variation in instructional goals into these three components. We then employed predictor variables measured at the class and teacher levels in an attempt to account for the manifest variation at each level. This procedure was replicated for each of four major academic disciplines: mathematics, science, social studies, and English.

We begin by reviewing the logic underlying the three explanations for variation in higher-order instructional goals. We then describe in detail the methods we used to test these explanations, including the scales used to measure emphasis on higher-order instructional goals in each discipline. Finally, we turn to the results and implications for research on teaching and school reform.

ALTERNATIVE EXPLANATIONS AND HYPOTHESES

Conceptions of Learning Rooted in the Secondary School Curriculum

A number of studies have reported that classes serving high-achieving students are substantially more likely to emphasize higher-order thinking processes than classes serving low-achieving students (Hargreaves, 1967; Metz, 1978;

Oakes, 1985, 1990; Page, 1990). A picture emerging from qualitative accounts is that educators commonly presume less able students to be capable primarily of rote memorization and procedural knowledge. In this view, more able students can apply knowledge and analyze problems as a prelude to thinking about alternative solutions. However, only the most able students can synthesize contrasting points of view to develop new theoretical formulations, to propose and defend alternative solutions to problems, or to evaluate critically alternative courses of action.

Several explanations might be offered to account for the disparity between high- and low-achieving classes in the instructional goals teachers have been found to pursue. Metz (1978) has argued that teachers resort to basic skills instruction in classes serving low-achieving students as a classroom management strategy. In this view, the routine tasks and slow pace of work that accompany much basic skills instruction keep low-achieving students busy while accommodating their preferences for easy work.

Neo-Marxists and critical theorists, on the other hand, see the disparity in instruction across academic tracks as flowing from the educational system's role in reproducing social inequality. In this view, tracking and ability grouping sort students on the basis of social class and ethnic background and then provide them instruction consistent with their future occupational destinies. The notion that low-track students are incapable of critical reasoning prepares these students to accept subordinate social roles, whereas the presumed superior cognitive powers of the high-track students justify the more prestigious and powerful social roles they will later occupy (Bowles & Gintis, 1976).

The pervasive influence of behaviorism in curriculum and instruction provides a final potential explanation for the link between academic track and the pursuit of higher-order instructional goals. As Shepard (1991) demonstrates, behaviorist theories imply that students learn best when complex learning tasks are broken down into smaller parts that are learned sequentially. Only when the earlier, simple steps are mastered is the learner ready for more complex tasks requiring analysis, hypothesis testing, and critical evaluation. This view of learning may help account for the differentiation of teaching objectives by student ability. Low-achieving students may chronically experience lower-order instructional emphasis because educators view these students as "stuck" in the early phases of the learning process. In contrast, the higher-achieving students, having mastered the basic skills, may be viewed as prepared to handle more complex learning tasks.

Indeed, Peterson (1988, p. 7) criticizes the traditional elementary school mathematics curriculum "as based on the assumption that computational skills must be learned before children are taught to solve even simple word problems." At the secondary level, the curriculum also reflects this sequential notion. For example, in mathematics, U.S. students commonly take pre-algebra, then algebra, then geometry. It is common to view higher-order objectives as more appropriate later in the sequence: Proofs are expected in geometry, but not algebra; mathematical reasoning is more appropriate in algebra than pre-algebra. As students progress through the grades, only the more able students appear to keep up with the academic mathematics curriculum, so that most will fall away before they encounter truly higher-order instructional objectives.

The interpretations we have described are not mutually exclusive. Teachers might emphasize low-level objectives in low-track classes as a classroom management strategy even if the larger educational system functioned to reproduce inequality in adult status. And neither of these views precludes the possibility that the curriculum has been constructed to facilitate a behaviorist conception of learning in which mastering basic skills is a necessary prelude to higher-order reasoning. These perspectives, taken together, suggested two hypotheses:

> *H1.* The higher the academic track of a class, the more likely a teacher will be to report an emphasis on teaching for higher-order thinking in that class; and
>
> *H2.* The higher the grade level of a class, the more likely a teacher will be to report an emphasis on higher-order thinking in that class.

These effects of track and grade may not operate similarly in each of the major academic disciplines. As Stodolsky (1988) points out, disciplinary specializations in the U.S. are founded on different epistemological bases. Therefore, there may be real differences in the degree of hierarchical curricular organization across the disciplines, with the result that the effects of track and grade will also vary. For example, the U.S. mathematics curriculum tends to be sharply differentiated by track. College-bound students take a markedly different sequence of courses than do vocational or general track students. Honors students often take yet a different sequence. Moreover, the prescribed sequence of courses tends to be especially rigid in math (e.g., algebra before geometry before trigonometry). The science curriculum is similarly quite differentiated by academic track, and the prescribed sequence of courses fairly standardized (though not as standardized as in math) with biology preceding chemistry preceding physics. On the other hand, the social studies and English curricula appear less differentiated in both ways. Courses more often have the same labels for college-bound and non-college-bound students, and the sequence of courses is more flexible.[1] These differences may be related to the different social functions served by the several disciplines. For example, it is common to view math as critical in gate-keeping decisions determining later occupational attainment, whereas social studies is essential in promoting political socialization. It would perhaps be functional for the math curriculum to be highly differentiated by ability and age but dysfunctional for the social studies curriculum to be similarly differentiated.

The notion that the disciplines differ in their degree of hierarchical organization led us to a third hypothesis:

H3. The effects of track and grade level on teaching for higher-order thinking should be greater in math and science than in English and Social Studies.

In summary, our discussion has focused on within-teacher variation in teaching for higher order thinking. We have conjectured that a given teacher intentionally differentiates instructional goals across the various classes he or she teaches and that, when teaching younger students or students in lower academic tracks, a teacher tends to place less emphasis on higher-order instructional objectives. If such within-teacher decision processes were the only source of variation in teaching for higher-order thinking, then variation between teachers would arise only to the extent that some teachers were assigned to teach more high-track or high-grade classes than were other teachers. We would then conclude that the effects of track and grade are deeply institutionalized in conceptions of teaching and learning that are essentially invariant across teachers and organizational environments.

Teacher Background and Training

An exclusive focus on intrateacher processes neglects effects of relatively stable differences in the background and preparation of teachers on teaching for higher-order thinking. Yet these differences might be important in understanding the variation in instructional objectives that students encounter. There has been considerable commentary on the kinds of preparation and knowledge teachers need to teach effectively for higher-order thinking. Talbert, McLaughlin, and Rowan (in press) extensively reviewed this literature, focusing on two types of knowledge: in-depth knowledge of subject matter and "pedagogical content knowledge" (Shulman, 1987), that is, in-depth knowledge of how to teach the subject matter. Teachers who lack the required knowledge apparently resort to "teaching the facts." An emphasis on transmitting procedural and factual information allows

teachers to control the flow of classroom interaction, thereby avoiding challenging discourse or responding to student questions that require a deep understanding of the subject matter being taught.

In this inquiry, we indexed teachers' broad subject-matter knowledge by reference to teachers' level of education, and we indexed broad pedagogical knowledge by reference to years of teaching experience, under the assumption that more highly educated and experienced teachers know their subject areas better and have acquired more pedagogical expertise. This reasoning generated two hypotheses:

H4. The higher a teacher's level of education, the greater the likelihood that the teacher will emphasize teaching for higher-order thinking; and

H5. The more years of teaching experience possessed by a teacher, the greater the likelihood that the teacher will emphasize teaching for higher-order thinking.

These hypotheses relate teacher background to a broad predisposition to teach for higher-order thinking. However, the knowledge required to teach for higher-order thinking is undoubtedly highly specific. For example, Talbert et al. (in press) discuss situations in which teachers who are generally capable of teaching for higher-order thinking do not teach in this way because of a mismatch between their knowledge and the particular content of the course or lesson they are assigned to teach. In fact, Talbert et al. (in press) argue that "cross-over" teaching—teaching out of one's subject area—encourages a "transmission" style instruction that omits teaching for understanding. In this study, we indexed the specific preparation of teachers by their reports of the degree to which they felt prepared to teach each of the courses to which they were assigned, suggesting the following hypothesis:

H6. The more prepared a teacher feels to teach a particular course, the more likely that teacher will be to emphasize teaching for higher-order thinking in that course.

Our hypotheses regarding effects of teacher education and experience (H4 and H5) are hypotheses about predictors of *between-teacher* variation in instructional objectives. In contrast, the hypothesized effects of the match between a teacher's preparation and the content to be taught in a particular class are, in part, *within-teacher* effects. To the extent a teacher feels differentially well-prepared to teach in the several classes assigned, that teacher's instructional goals are expected to vary across those classes. Of course, it might be that some teachers are, on average, better-prepared to teach their classes than are other teachers, contributing to between-teacher variation in instructional goals.

Schools as Formal Organizations

Finally, recent research asserts a relationship between the formal organization of schools and the distribution of teaching for higher-order thinking. For example, Darling-Hammond and Wise (1985) argue that the work of teachers is becoming more routinized and regulated as state education agencies and local school systems increasingly implement standardized curricula and use standardized tests to assess the performance of students, teachers, and schools.

Available evidence suggests that teachers alter their instructional practices in response to these policies (Bullough, Gitlin, & Goldstein, 1984; Darling-Hammond & Wise, 1985; Rosenholz, 1985; for a review, see Rowan, 1990). Because available texts and tests tend to stress "low-level" cognitive skills, instruction is allegedly becoming more highly focused on basic skills with a stress on content coverage over depth, a practice that Newmann (1990) has argued is incompatible with teaching for higher-order thinking.

These ideas suggested that two organizational features of schools would have direct effects on teachers' emphasis on higher-order thinking: the extent to which achievement tests are used to judge the quality of teaching and the extent to which teachers feel obligated to "cover the curriculum." In our view, these organizational features will produce variation at two levels of our model. To some extent, norms favoring accountability and curriculum coverage operate at the school level and should produce between-school differences in teaching objectives. However, previous research demonstrates that not all teachers will embrace these norms equally (Rowan, Raudenbush, & Kang, 1991). Teachers who inhabit different locations within the organization of the school may perceive organizational norms differently and may respond to them differently.

Our data include no direct measure of organizational emphasis on standardized testing to evaluate teaching. We reasoned, however, that if such an emphasis affected teachers' instructional goals, it would do so by influencing teachers' perceptions of how they are judged. We therefore tested the following hypotheses:

> H7. To the extent a teacher feels that the quality of his or her teaching is judged on the basis of achievement gains, that teacher will be less likely to teach for higher-order thinking; and

> H8. To the extent that a teacher expresses a need to "cover the curriculum," that teacher will be less likely to teach for higher-order thinking.

As we have seen, much of the debate about organizational influences on teaching for higher-order thinking has centered around the negative effects of school bureaucratization. However, an equally important line of work has emphasized the importance of school restructuring to promote teaching for higher-order thinking. In this argument, such teaching will require the development of a collegial "learning community" among teachers, supportive leadership from school administrators, and more control by teachers over the kinds of instructional policies and procedures that currently encourage a focus on low-level cognitive skills. As with bureaucratic controls, we expected that schools might systematically differ on these dimensions, but there was also strong evidence that teachers within the same school vary in the extent to which they receive administrative support, join other teachers in collaborative relations, and obtain control over important instructional policies (Rowan, et al., 1991). Thus, we added hypotheses about these organizational factors to predict between-teacher variation:

> H9. The more a teacher receives support from school administrators, participates in collaborative relations with other teachers, and exercises control over key policies in the areas of curriculum and instruction, the more likely that teacher will be to emphasize teaching for higher-order thinking.

DATA

Data for the study were collected in 16 high schools in California and Michigan. The 16 schools were chosen purposefully to guarantee diversity in secondary-school teaching contexts in terms of state policies, district resources, school organization, and student composition. In the spring of 1990, questionnaires were administered to all teachers in these schools. Response rates varied from a low of 50% to a high of 100% with a median response rate of 75%. Mathematics, science, social studies, and English teachers were administered a specifically tailored, subject-specific questionnaire that asked them to report information on each of the classes they were teaching. This procedure yielded complete data on 1,205 classes taught by 303 academic teachers.

Characteristics of the Classes

Table 1 presents descriptive statistics on characteristics of these 1,205 classes. The average class size was 25.69 students

(SD = 6.47). Grade levels ranged from 1 = freshman to 4 = senior (M = 2.34; SD = 1.00). In the analyses below, we included class size as a control variable.

For each class, academic teachers were asked to classify the academic track of the class according to the following coding scheme: vocational, general, college-bound (nonhonors), honors, and mixed. In this sample, only 4% of the classes were described as mixed, implying that teachers had little difficulty in classifying their classes according to track. Mixed classes were dropped from the analysis. For purposes of the analysis, two indicator variables were created: an "honors" indicator took on a value of one for honors classes, zero otherwise; and an "academic" indicator took on a value of one for college-bound (nonhonors) classes, zero otherwise. The classes having values of zero on both indicators were the vocational and general track (noncollege) classes.[2] Table 1 shows that of the 1,205 classes, 192 (16%) were honors classes, 506 (42%) were academic but not honors, and the remaining 507 classes (42%) were either general or vocational track classes.

Teachers were also asked to report their specific level of preparation to teach each class. This variable was recoded as an indicator variable that took on a value of one if a teacher felt "very well prepared" for that class, zero otherwise. In 61% of the classes, the teachers felt very well prepared.

Table 1 also reports zero-order correlations among the class-level predictor variables. The correlations tend to be weak. There was evidence that honors classes were smaller than nonhonors classes, r = −.13, and that honors classes tended to serve higher grade levels, r = .16.

Characteristics of Teachers and School Organization

Table 2 presents descriptive statistics for variables measured at the teacher level. The first set of variables describes the education and experience of teachers. Teachers in this sample were both highly experienced, with mean years of experiences = 20.02 (SD = 9.15), and highly educated (70% with masters degrees). We also collected data on sex and ethnic background: 91% were white, and 61% were male.

Five measures were constructed to indicate aspects of the organizational environments in which teachers worked. As discussed above, we view these as teacher-level variables, in part because responses reflect teacher perceptions of characteristics of their schools; and in part because previous research had found that these measures vary within schools in response to teacher locations within the academic division of labor (Rowan et al., 1991). We note that global differences in school organization not measured here, as well

as differences among schools in student composition and academic mission, were taken into account by including in the model a school-level variance component.

Emphasis on producing achievement gains and covering the curriculum was measured by Likert-type items with response options recorded on a six-point scale ranging from 1 = "none" to 6 = "a great deal." The first item asked teachers about the extent to which colleagues "judge the quality of my teaching on the basis of my students' achievement gains" (M = 3.97, SD = 1.27). The second asked teachers the degree to which it was important to "cover the curriculum" (M = 4.51, SD = 1.15).

Aspects of school organization hypothesized to promote teaching for higher-order thinking were measured by scales used in previous research (Pallas, 1988, Rowan et al., 1991). Supportive principal leadership was measured by a 13-item scale composed of assertions; for example, that the principal effectively copes with outside pressures, sets priorities, recognizes, encourages, and supports staff, and involves staff in decision making. Response options for each item ranged from 1 = "strongly disagree" to 6 = "strongly agree." Internal consistency was .92. The extent of staff cooperation and collegiality was measured by a six-item scale composed of assertions that staff members help each other in diverse duties, share beliefs and values about the central mission of the school, maintain uniformly high standards of performance for themselves, and seek new ideas. Response options again ranged from 1 = "strongly disagree" to 6 = "strongly agree." Internal consistency was .86. Teacher control was a nine-item scale indicating teacher control over school policy issues such as student behavior codes, content of inservice programs, student grouping, school curriculum, and text selection; and control over classroom issues such as teaching content and techniques, and amount of homework assigned. Response options were again on a six-point scale (1 = "no control" to 6 = "a great deal of control" for school policy items; 1 = "no control" to 6 = "complete control" for classroom items). Internal consistency was .75. Taken together, these measures show a close correspondence to ideas presented by Rosenholz (1985) and Little (1982) about the characteristics of effective school organization.

Table 2 also provides zero-order correlations among the teacher-level variables. Notable are the moderately large correlations between measures of teacher control, staff collaboration, and principal leadership.

MEASURES OF TEACHING FOR HIGHER ORDER THINKING

The outcome of interest in this article is the emphasis teachers place on higher-order thinking in formulating

Table 1
Descriptive Statistics for Class-Level Variables

Variables	Coding and range	M	SD
1. Class size[a]	(2, 38)	25.69	6.47
2. Student grade level[a]	(1, 4)	2.34	1.00
3. Honors track vs. nonhonor track	0 = nonhonors track 1 = advanced or honors	.16	.37
4. Academic track vs. nonacademic track	0 = nonacademic track 1 = academic track	.42	.49
5. Level of preparation	0 = not very well-prepared 1 = very well-prepared	.61	.49
6. Emphasis on high literacy in English classes 5 items[b] Reliability = .84	(16.43, 60.97)	50.87	9.49
7. Emphasis on writing in English classes 2 items[b] Reliability = .60	(15.71, 59.46)	50.79	9.44
8. Emphasis on higher order thinking in social studies 4 items[c] Reliability = .76	(29.22, 66.60)	49.53	9.90
9. Emphasis on higher order thinking in mathematics 4 items[d] Reliability = .75	(26.93, 63.89)	49.68	9.72
10. Emphasis on higher order thinking in science 5 items[e] Reliability = .79	(22.91, 65.60)	50.05	9.95

	Correlations			
	Academic track	Honors track	Level of preparation	Grade
Class size	.02	−.13	.02	−.05
Academic track		−.37	.00	.06
Honors track			−.03	.16
Level of preparation				.00

[a]Centered around the grand mean in the HLM analysis. [b]There are 89 English teachers and 323 English classes. [c]There are 65 social studies teachers and 272 social studies classes. [d]There are 74 mathematics teachers and 304 mathematics classes. [e]There are 75 science teachers and 306 classes.

Table 2
Descriptive Statistics for Teacher-Level Variables

Variables	Coding and range	M	SD
1. Years of experience[a]	(1, 40)	20.02	9.15
2. Level of education	0 = no master's degree 1 = has master's degree	.70	.46
3. Race	0 = others 1 = whites	.91	.29
4. Sex	0 = female 1 = male	.61	.49

5. Staff cooperation[a]
  6 items
  Reliability = .86
	(−2.51, 1.49)	−.04	.74

6. Teacher control[a]
  9 items
  Reliability = .75
	(−2.02, 1.22)	−.02	.58

7. Principal leadership[a]
  13 items
  Reliability = .92
	(−2.33, 1.34)	−.02	.71

8. Importance of covering the curriculum	(1, 6)	4.51	1.15
9. Achievement gains basis for judging teaching	(1, 6)	3.97	1.27

Correlations

	Race	Level of Ed.	Exper-ience	Staff coop.	Teach. cont.	Prin. lead.	Judge by ach. gains	Importance of curric. coverage
Sex	.02	.15	.00	−.12	−.21	−.20	−.12	−.11
Race		.03	−.04	.03	.08	−.04	−.07	.02
Level of education			.34	−.06	−.11	−.09	.07	.00
Experience				−.07	−.11	−.06	.16	.00
Staff cooperation					.41	.53	.05	.11
Teacher control						.46	.01	.08
Principal leadership							.15	.14
Judge by achievement gains								.25

[a]Centered around the grand mean in the HLM analysis.

instructional goals for each of the classes they teach. The term higher-order thinking has multiple intellectual roots, but in current usage it has come to denote a form of cognitive understanding constituted by knowing the general patterns and principles in a particular knowledge domain and by comprehending the relationships among these patterns and principles. Moreover, higher-order thinking has come to denote the application of such knowledge in problem-solving and conducting inquiry (Cole, 1990).

Although higher-order thinking undoubtedly shares common features across disciplines, we decided to treat the phenomenon as discipline-specific rather than generic. We therefore developed separate measures of teaching for higher-order thinking for mathematics, science, social studies, and English. In science and math, we used items developed as part of the NELS 90 survey, administered by the National Center for Education Statistics. By contrast, items for social studies and English are original in the current study.

In each of the four questionnaires, we used a set of eight discipline-specific items that asked teachers to rate the degree of emphasis they placed on particular learning objectives for each of the classes they taught. Degree of emphasis on an objective was indicated by a four-point Likert scale including the choices "none," "a little," "moderate," and "heavy" emphasis.

The scale for each discipline included items intended to indicate both "higher-order" and "lower-order" objectives, where the latter involve tasks requiring memorization or the development of procedural skills. We expected that responses to "higher-order" items would be positively intercorrelated and that the responses to the "lower-order" items would be positively intercorrelated. However, we expected that the "higher-order" items would be correlated negatively with to the lower-order items. To assess the tenability of these expectations, we performed separate factor analyses on the discipline-specific item sets using classes as the unit of analysis.[3] In math, science, and social studies areas we found that the factor analyses yielded two separate factors, one for higher-order objectives and a second, weakly reliable factor dominated by lower-order items (the results for English are described below). The implication was that embracing higher-order objectives in math, science, and social studies classes did not preclude also emphasizing lower-order objectives.

Because the higher- and lower-order items failed to form a single scale, we created separate higher- and lower-order scales for each subject and assessed the reliabilities of these scales.[4] This analysis indicated that the item sets tapping lower-order objectives in the three disciplines formed scales

with rather weak internal consistency (from .28 to .51). In contrast, the items sets tapping higher-order objectives formed quite reliable scales (internal consistencies from .60 to .84). Our subsequent analyses focus on these higher-order scales, though we briefly consider results for lower-order items in the discussion.

Math

For math, the scale had four items. Items in the scale were standardized separately and then averaged to form a scale score. To ease interpretation, this initial score was then rescaled to have a mean of 50 and a standard deviation of 10. The resulting scale had an internal consistency of .75 ($M = 49.68$, $SD = 9.72$). The items in the scale were: (a) understanding the logical structure of mathematics; (b) understanding the nature of proof; (c) knowing mathematical principles and algorithms; and (d) thinking about what a problem means and ways it might be solved.

Science

The science scale consisted of five items that tended to place heavy emphasis on scientific problem-solving and inquiry. The procedure for deriving the overall score for this scale was the same as for the math. The science scale had an internal consistency of .79 ($M = 50.05$, $SD = 9.95$). The five items were: (a) prepare students to evaluate arguments based on scientific evidence; (b) teach scientific methods; (c) develop problem-solving/inquiry skills; (d) develop scientific writing skills; and (e) develop skills in lab techniques.

Social Studies

The social studies scale developed here mirrors Newmann's (1990) discussion of higher-order thinking in high-school social studies classes. In addition to understanding key concepts and principles in a discipline, Newmann placed emphasis on engaging students in challenging problems and having students manipulate information to solve these problems. Again, the overall scale score was derived in a manner similar to the derivation of the math and science scale scores, resulting in a four-item scale ($M = 49.53$, $SD = 9.90$) having internal consistency .76. The four items were: (a) formulating and presenting arguments to a group; (b) critically evaluating historical accounts or arguments; (c) analyzing historical and social science theories; and (d) using historical concepts to interpret current social issues.

English

The factor analysis of items for the English scale yielded results different from the results for the other disciplines. In part, the difference reflects the different approach to higher-order thinking developed by specialists in this area. Bereiter and Scardamalia (1987) present a discussion of higher-order thinking in the areas of reading and writing that builds on Resnick and Resnick's (1977) conception *high literacy*. Bereiter and Scardamalia argue that higher-order thinking in reading and writing involves going beyond the extraction of meaning from simple texts (i.e., *lower literacy*). Instead, students are seen to be engaged in *high literacy* when they read literacy classics, make inferences about these texts through writing and discussion, and when they attempt to gain personal meaning from the literature they are reading.

The factor analysis of items for the English scale yielded two separate factors, both of which are included in this study. An initial factor appears to denote a concept of *high literacy* as it applies to reading. This five-item scale ($M = 50.87$, $SD = 9.49$) had an internal consistency of .84. The items were: (a) writing about literature in a variety of forms (freewrite, formal essays, etc.); (b) comprehending plot and basic meaning of assigned literature; (c) defining literary terms; (d) engaging in literary analysis; and (e) exploring personal responses to a variety of literature. A second factor is specific to writing. This two-item scale ($M = 50.79$, $SD = 9.44$) had an internal consistency of .60. The two items in the scale were: (a) writing about literature in a variety of forms; and (b) learning to prewrite, draft, revise, and edit. Note that the first item in the reading and writing scales are the same.

Lower Order Scales

As mentioned, our supposition that higher-order and lower-order items would correlate negatively was not confirmed. Instead, separate weakly reliable "lower-order" factors tended to emerge in each discipline. In math, the items intended to tap lower-order objectives included (a) memorizing facts, rules, and steps; (b) performing computations with speed and accuracy; and (c) developing an awareness of the importance of math in everyday life. In science, the lower-order items included (a) teaching scientific facts; and (b) increasing the awareness of science in everyday life. In social studies the items were (a) knowing important dates, events, places, and people; (b) being aware of current events; and (c) learning how to outline the material in a chapter. In English the intended lower-order items were (a) developing basic literacy skills; and (b) mastering grammar and mechanics. Internal consistencies of these scales were low, ranging from .28 for science to .51 for math.[5] The poor reliabilities precluded firm inferences about the correlates of lower-order objectives, though we conducted a

series of exploratory analyses that we summarize briefly in the "Discussion" section.

PARTITIONING VARIATION AMONG CLASSES, AMONG TEACHERS, AND AMONG SCHOOLS

The measurement analysis indicated that, for each of the four disciplines studied, there was reliable class-to-class variation in the extent to which readers emphasized higher-order learning objectives. We know that the 1,205 classes under study varied in this way because only if such variation existed could the scales that measure such instructional objectives achieve reasonably high internal consistencies with modest numbers of items per scale. However, this reliable class-to-class variation could arise for three very different reasons, each having fundamentally different implications for understanding how teachers develop instructional goals.

First, classes could vary reliably because the same teacher differentiates her objectives across the different classes to which she is assigned. We call this reliable *within-teacher* variation. Notice that it would be absurd to label teachers "higher-order teachers" or "lower-order teachers" if the main source of reliable variation among classes were within teachers. Rather, it would be crucial to understand the characteristics of classes that elicit higher-order objectives and to understand the basis of a teacher's differential judgments across classes regarding the appropriate objectives.

Second, there could be reliable variation across classes because there are important differences between teachers within a school in emphasis on higher-order objectives. We call this reliable *between-teacher* variation. In the extreme case, there would be no variation within teachers; that is, a teacher would pursue exactly the same objectives in each of her classes. In this instance, we should waste no time studying how characteristics of the different classes to which a teacher is assigned influence that teacher's choice of objectives because the choice never varies. Rather, we should focus on differences between teachers (within a school) that predict their pursuit of different objectives.

Third, it might be that reliable variation between classes arises because schools vary substantially in the objectives pursued by their teachers. We call this reliable *between-school* variation. In the extreme case, the extent to which teachers pursue higher-order objectives would be identical in every class within a given school. In this instance it would be futile to study either class differences or teacher differences that predict variation within a school. Rather, one should concentrate on uncovering how different schools shape the objectives of each teacher within them.

Using a three-level hierarchical linear model as described by Raudenbush, Rowan, and Kang (1991), we first decomposed the variance in the outcome measures into the three components described above.[6] Based on the variance decomposition from the baseline model, we estimated the reliability of between-teacher and between-school differences in instructional objectives and obtained a rough picture of the reliability of within-teacher differences from this model. Having identified the components of variation in the outcome, we then used a three-level regression model in an attempt to predict the variation at each level. The results varied substantially across the four disciplines.

Decomposing the Variation Among Math Classes

Table 3 shows that the within-teacher variance in higher-order math objectives was estimated at 60.11, the between-teacher variance at 33.60, and the between-school variance at .09. Hence, 64.1% of the variance in higher-order objectives was within teachers, 35.8% between teachers within

schools, with a trivial proportion of the variance between schools. Two other statistics are helpful in interpreting these variance components. First, the table presents chi-square tests of the null hypothesis that the true variance between teachers within schools was null, in which case the estimated variance of 33.60 was an artifact of chance. This hypothesis was easily rejected because the observed chi-square of 224.17 far surpassed the critical value at the .001 level based on 60 degrees of freedom. Similarly, we tested the null hypothesis that the true variance between schools was null. In this case we could not reject the null hypothesis because values of an estimated variance near ours (.09) are highly plausible when the null hypothesis is true.

The table also provides information about the reliability of estimates at the teacher and school levels. The reliability for discriminating between teachers within a school was estimated to be .68, whereas the reliability for discriminating between schools was estimated to be a trivial .04. The three-level program does not produce estimates of the reliability of within-teacher differences. However, we know that the internal consistency of the scale score for math classes was .75 (see Table 1), implying that about 25% of the total variance in the scale scores was attributable to measurement

Table 3

Decomposition of Variance (No Predictors Specified)

Variance	Math	Science	Social studies	Literature	Writing
Within-teacher	60.11	38.71	19.24	49.24	33.84
Between-teacher	33.60	59.50	63.71	34.46	44.62
Between-school	0.09	1.37	11.43	13.29	17.16
Reliability estimates					
Between-teacher	0.68	0.84	0.92	0.69	0.81
Between-school	0.13	0.20	0.29	0.54	0.57
Components of variance tests					
Between-teacher					
Chi-square statistic	224.17	409.28	576.04	267.02	373.09
df	60	60	50	73	73
p-value	0.00	0.00	0.00	0.00	0.00
Between-school					
Chi-square statistic	10.02	16.45	25.04	28.42	34.71
df	13	14	14	15	15
p-value	< .500	0.29	0.03	0.02	0.00

error. This represents a variance of about 23.6; when compared to the within-teacher variance estimate of 60.1, we see that about (60.1 − 23.6)/60.1 or 61% of the within-teacher variance was reliable.

In sum, the majority of the variance on the math scale was within-teacher variance with nearly all of the remaining variance lying between teachers within schools. These results encourage a search for differences across the classes to which a teacher is assigned that might predict the large component of within-teacher variation. The data also show potential for using teacher differences to predict teacher variation within schools. The data provide little hope for a search for school effects on the math scale.

Decomposing the Variation Between Science Classes

The results for science are listed in the second column of Table 3. The estimated within-teacher variance was 38.71; the estimated between-teacher variance was 59.50; and the estimated between-school variance was 1.37. Thus we estimate that 38.9% of the total variance to be within-teacher variance, 59.8% was between-teacher variance, and only 1.4% was between-school variance. Thus, the results differ from the math results in that the majority of variation was at the teacher level, with a substantial fraction within teachers. The results were like the math results in that little of the variation was between schools. Once again, the hypothesis that teachers within schools do not vary was easily rejected whereas the hypothesis that schools do not vary was readily retained.

The reliability for discriminating among teachers within schools was .84. The within-teacher variance clearly had a reliable component because the estimated within-teacher variance of 38.71 was nearly double the estimated measurement error variance component of 20.8.

Decomposing the Variation Among Social Studies Classes

The results for social studies are listed in the third column of Table 3. The estimated within-teacher variance was 19.24; the estimated between-teacher variance was 63.71; and the estimated between-school variance was 11.43. Thus, about 20.4% of the variance was within teachers, 67.5% was between teachers within schools, and 12.1% was between schools. Thus, the majority of variation was at the teacher level, and, not surprisingly, the hypothesis that teachers within schools do not vary was easily rejected. In this case, the hypothesis that schools do not vary was

rejected at the marginal significance level of $p = .03$. Thus, in contrast to the math and science results, there was some evidence of school-to-school variance for social studies.

Because of the large component of between-teacher variance, the reliability for discriminating between teachers within schools was .92. The school-level reliability was estimated to be .29. The within-teacher variance showed less evidence of having a reliable component than for math and science because the within-teacher variance estimate was about the same as the estimated measurement error variance component.

Decomposing the Variation Among English Classes

Recall that, for English, two scales emerged; one for literary emphasis and one for emphasis on writing. We consider each below.

Literary Emphasis

The fourth column of Table 3 lists the variance estimates, hypothesis tests, and reliabilities for literary emphasis. In sum, we found that 50.8% of the variance was within teachers; 35.5% between teachers within schools, and 13.7% between schools. Both the between-teacher and between-school variances were significantly greater than zero. Strong evidence existed that a reliable component of variation existed within teachers.

Writing Emphasis

We found that 35.4% of the variation was within teachers, 46.7% was between teachers within schools, and 17.9% was between schools. Both the between-teacher between-school variances were significantly greater than zero. Evidence of reliable within-teacher variance was weak.

Summary

Decomposition of variance in these scales is important because it has strong implications for where one might look to explain why classes varied in terms of the instructional objectives teachers pursue. In this regard, we discovered important disciplinary differences. There was little evidence of between-school variance in math or science objectives, while evidence of between-school variance was manifest for both social studies and English objectives. Large and reliable components of within-teacher variance were found for math and science, while between-teacher variance was more important in social studies. In English the results were a bit more complicated, with most variation in literary objectives found to lie within teachers and most of the variation in writing objectives found to lie between teachers. Having identified the components of variance in each discipline, the next task of the analysis was to employ a three-level regression model to predict this variation.

CORRELATES OF TEACHING FOR HIGHER ORDER THINKING

Approach

For each discipline, multilevel regression models were fitted in three stages. First, predictors that varied within teachers were specified in a *within-teacher* prediction model. These included the two indicators for student track (the academic and honors indicators), student grade, and teacher preparation.[7] The analysis also controlled for class size. Specifying the within-teacher predictors enabled us to estimate the adjusted within-teacher and between-teacher variance, that is, the amount of variance within and between teachers after controlling for the effects of the classes to which they were assigned.

In the next stage, teacher background variables, including years of experience, sex, and race, were added and their effects estimated in an initial *between-teacher* model. Control for such background characteristics is important to insure that estimates of hypothesized effects were not biased by uncontrolled background characteristics. Predictors with coefficients less than 1.5 times their estimated standard errors were tentatively dropped from the model.

At the third stage, the between-teacher predictors hypothesized to influence instructional objectives were added. These included teachers' level of education, emphasis on covering the curriculum, emphasis on achievement test gains, and perceptions of principal leadership, staff collaboration, and teacher control. Predictors with coefficients found to be less than 1.5 times their estimated standard errors were dropped and the model re-estimated. To guarantee that no predictor, including teacher background characteristics, could have been mistakenly dropped from the model, residuals were regressed on variables excluded from the model. If the approximate "t-to-enter" (see Raudenbush, Bryk, Seltzer, & Congdon, 1990) exceeded 1.5, that predictor was re-entered into the analysis. Hence, for each outcome we arrived at a final model including predictors related to the outcome and excluding predictors unrelated to the outcome. We used the relatively liberal criterion of $t = 1.5$ because we worried more about the bias that might arise from failing to specify a predictor than about the lack of efficiency that arises when the model is slightly overfit.

After estimating the final model for each outcome, we assessed the amount of between-teacher variance explained. This is the difference between the adjusted between-teacher variance (based on the within-teacher model) and the residual between-teacher variance (based on the final model) divided by the adjusted between-teacher variance.

With only 16 schools, the sample offered only limited opportunities to model the variation among schools in that identifying and controlling for relevant covariates and theoretically important predictors would be of questionable validity with only 15 degrees of freedom. This shortcoming was unimportant in the case of mathematics and science given lack of evidence that schools varied on the outcome.

The results for the final models in each discipline are presented in Table 4. Potential predictors are listed in the first column. Columns 2–6 provide results for math, science, social studies, literature, and writing. If a predictor was not related to an outcome, the table leaves that entry blank. The results for math and science were quite different from the results for social studies and English (literature and writing). We therefore describe these two sets of results separately.

Results for Mathematics and Science

Effects of Track and Grade

The crucial results for mathematics and science were the large effects of track. In math, the degree of emphasis on higher-order objectives was, on average, 10.50 points higher for academic classes than for nonacademic classes, $b = 10.50$, $t = 11.29$.[8] The gap between honors classes and nonacademic classes was 17.44 points, $b = 17.44$, $t = 14.52$. Recalling that the standard deviation of the math higher-order teaching scale was slightly less than 10 points, we see that the academic–nonacademic gap exceeded a standard deviation in magnitude, and the gap between honors and nonacademic classes exceeded 1.7 standard deviation units.

Large track effects appeared in science as well. The academic–nonacademic gap was $b = 10.25$, $t = 11.30$, though in this case the honors-nonacademic gap was similar at $b = 12.53$, $t = 10.10$.

There were some differences between the math and sciences results. In math, a significant effect of grade appeared, $b = 1.38$, $t = 3.41$. This result implies, for example, that the degree of emphasis on higher-order objectives would be $3 \times 1.38 = 4.14$ points higher for seniors than for freshman, an effect slightly in excess of .41 standard deviation units. The grade effect in science was in the same direction, but was smaller and of marginal statistical significance, $b = .78$, $t = 1.66$, implying an expected gap between seniors and freshman just exceeding .23 standard deviation units.

Teacher Preparation and Organizational Effects

Results for the two outcomes are quite similar with regard to teacher preparation and organizational effects.

Table 4
Predictors of Emphasis on Higher Order Objectives

Regression coefficient estimates (with standard error estimates in parentheses)					
Predictors	Math	Science	Social studies	Literature	Writing
Teacher-level					
Intercept	43.09 (1.91)	44.42 (1.32)	47.67 (1.33)	44.71 (1.57)	46.15 (1.56)
Experience			−0.22 (0.11)		
Education	−4.06 (1.85)				
Judge by Ach. gains			2.46 (0.79)		
Coverage	1.22 (0.75)			2.30 (0.52)	
T. control			3.91 (1.71)		
Staff coop. Prin. lead				1.52 (0.89)	3.14 (1.11)
Class-level					
Class size	0.14 (0.07)	0.02 (0.06)	0.04 (0.06)	0.23 (0.08)	0.11 (0.07)
Grade	1.38 (0.41)	0.78 (0.47)	0.46 (0.44)	−0.80 (0.44)	−1.10 (0.40)
Academic	10.50 (0.93)	10.25 (0.91)	3.56 (1.15)	5.27 (1.20)	4.26 (1.23)
Honors	17.44 (1.20)	12.53 (1.24)	9.07 (1.13)	8.95 (1.23)	8.69 (1.16)
Level of preparation	1.78 (1.17)	−0.87 (1.05)	2.74 (0.91)	3.57 (1.05)	−0.15 (1.06)

Variance components estimates					
Variance	Math	Science	Social studies	Literature	Writing
Within-teacher	24.29	20.27	14.14	41.81	27.19
Between-teacher	35.35	64.65	43.88	13.75	38.54
Between-school	0.13	2.56	7.31	17.30	23.40

No effect of level preparation was manifest for either outcome, and in science, no education effect appeared. In math, the education effect was in a direction opposite to that predicted, $b = -4.06$, $t = -2.19$. No organizational effects appeared in science. In math, a small tendency for teachers emphasizing curriculum coverage to also emphasize higher-order objectives appeared, but failed to achieve conventional levels of significance, $b = 1.22$, $t = 1.62$, $p > .10$. In sum, the analysis revealed no support for the explanations based on teacher preparation and organizational effects for mathematics or science.

Explanatory Power of the Model

The model accounted for an impressive 59.7% of the within-teacher variance for math and 47.6% for science (Table 5). Given the level of measurement error variance discussed earlier, these statistics quite substantially under-report the explanatory power of the model at this level.

Neither model explained substantial between-teacher variance. For science, none of the variance was explained because no teacher-level predictors were significantly related to the outcome. For math, the model accounted for 10.4% of the between-teacher variance.

Results for Social Studies and English

Effects of Track and Grade

Substantial track effects appeared in all three areas (social studies, literature, and writing), but the effects were not as large as in math and science. For example, in social studies, the gap between academic and nonacademic classes in higher-order emphasis was $b = 3.56$ points, $t = 3.10$, and the gap between honors and nonacademic classes was $b = 9.07$ points, $t = 8.06$. Again the standard deviation was slightly below 10 points, so these effects can be interpreted as just exceeding .36 and .91 standard deviation units, respectively. Patterns for writing and literature were quite similar. No positive effect of grade appeared in any area; though, unexpectedly, negative effects of grade appeared in the two English subjects.

Effects of Teacher Preparation and Education

Significantly positive effects of teacher level of preparation appeared for social studies ($b = 2.74$, $t = 3.01$) and for literature ($b = 3.57$, $t = 3.40$). These represented expected gaps in higher-order emphasis between classes for which teachers felt "very well prepared" and other classes. No such effect appeared for writing. No effects of the overall level of teacher

Table 5

Variances and Variance Accounted for at the Class and Teacher Levels

	Variance estimates			
	No predictors (from Table 3)	Class-level predictors only	Class-level & teacher-level predictors (from Table 4)	Percentage of variance accounted for[a]
Math				
Within-teacher	60.11	24.30	24.29	59.7%
Between-teacher	33.60	39.47	35.35	10.4%
Between-school	0.09	0.14	0.13	
Science				
Within-teacher	38.71	20.27	20.27	47.6%
Between-teacher	59.50	64.65	64.65	0.0%
Between-school	1.37	2.56	2.56	
Social studies				
Within-teacher	19.24	14.16	14.14	26.5%
Between-teacher	63.71	58.76	43.88	25.3%
Between-school	11.43	10.36	7.31	
Literature				
Within-teacher	49.24	41.61	41.81	15.1%
Between-teacher	34.46	23.15	13.75	40.6%
Between-school	13.29	14.53	17.30	
Writing				
Within-teacher	33.84	27.12	27.19	19.7%
Between-teacher	44.62	44.56	38.54	13.5%
Between-school	17.16	19.97	23.40	

[a]Percentage of within-teacher variance accounted for = (Variance with no predictors − variance with all predictors) divided by the variance with no predictors. Percentage of between-teacher variance accounted for = (Variance with class-level predictors − variance with all predictors) divided by the variance with class-level predictors.

education appeared in any of the areas, implying that no effect of having earned a master's degree was present.

Effects of Organizational Norms

Favorable effects of supportive principal leadership appeared in the two English subjects ($b = 1.52$, $t = 1.71$ in literature; $b = 3.14$, $t = 2.83$ in writing) but not in social studies. A favorable teacher control effect appeared in social studies ($b = 3.91$, $t = 2.29$), but not English. To gauge the magnitudes of these effects, standardized coefficients ("betas") may be computed as beta $= bS_x/S_y$, where S_x and S_y are the standard deviations of predictor and outcome given in Tables 1 and 2. Applying these formulas leads, for example, to standardized estimates of .24 for the effect of principal leadership in writing and .23 for the effect of teacher control in social studies. No effect of staff collaboration was found in any subject area.

Recall that we had hypothesized that emphases on curriculum coverage and evaluating teaching in terms of achievement gains would be linked to a decreased emphasis on higher-order objectives. No evidence emerged to support these hypotheses. In fact, an emphasis on achievement gains was positively associated with teaching for higher-order thinking in social studies ($b = 2.46$, $t = 3.09$); and an emphasis on curriculum coverage was positively related to such teaching for higher-order thinking in literature ($b = 2.30$, $t = 4.39$).

Explanatory Power of the Models

As compared to math and science, the models for social studies, literature, and writing were less powerful in explaining within-teacher variance and more powerful in explaining between-teacher variance (Table 5). This is not surprising. Track effects were not as large in the three humanities as they were in math and science, whereas teacher and organizational predictors were more helpful in the humanities than in math or science.

Percentages of within-teacher variance explained were 26.5, 15.1, and 19.7 for social studies, literature, and writing, respectively. The corresponding percentages of between-teacher variance explained were 25.3, 40.6, and 13.5.

DISCUSSION

A fundamental contradiction between current educational theory and practice provides the motivation for the present inquiry. On the one hand, an emerging consensus among educational theorists is that fostering higher-order thinking ought to be a principal goal of instruction in all academic subjects for all students. In contrast, field workers observing teaching practice in the U.S., both at the primary and

secondary levels, have described teacher-student interactions that focus primarily on empirical and procedural issues and only rarely on higher-order thinking, including the analysis of theories, the critical evaluation of arguments, and the conduct of inquiry and problem-solving. Field research cited earlier suggests that teaching for higher-order thinking, when it does occur, is far more likely to occur in high-ability classes than in low-ability classes, though theorists claim that the pursuit of such objectives is particularly important for students with limited academic background.

Measuring Emphasis on Higher Order Objectives

We sought to evaluate plausible alternative explanations for variation in the pursuit of higher-order instructional objectives. This evaluation required, first, accurate measurement of the degree of emphasis on higher-order objectives in each of four subject areas. What we learned about this measurement problem may be of value to future inquiry on this important topic. The items designed to tap emphasis on higher-order objectives, adapted from the National Educational Longitudinal Survey of 1990 (National Center for Educational Statistics, 1990), proved highly useful. A typical result is that a scale consisting of just four items achieved an internal consistency of about .75 across all classes. On the other hand, items designed to tap lower-order emphases, including memorization of facts and practice on procedures, were less useful. Rather than loading negatively on the higher-order scale, they constituted a second, weakly reliable factor. This pattern was remarkably convergent across the four disciplines. Apparently, emphasis on lower-order objectives does not preclude the simultaneous pursuit of higher-order objectives.

The implications for future measurement efforts seem clear. It would be wise to write more items tapping the higher-order dimension for each subject area. Using variance component estimates from internal consistency analysis, we can estimate the expected internal consistency of each scale as a function of the number of items in that scale. For example, if the math scale consisted of 10 items rather than four, we estimate that the internal consistency of the scale would rise from .75 to around .88; a 15-item scale ought to produce an internal consistency of about .92. Having more items might also enable the measurement of interesting subdimensions of teaching for higher-order thinking, including, for example, a subscale that taps emphasis on higher-order cognitive content and a subscale that emphasizes classroom interactions that facilitate higher-order discourse.

Evaluating Alternative Explanations

We considered three explanations for the underemphasis on teaching for higher-order thinking. First, we reasoned that conceptions of teaching and learning rooted in the secondary curriculum may encourage teaching for higher-order thinking only in high-track classes and more advanced courses in a hierarchically ordered sequence. We predicted that these effects would vary across disciplines because the curricula in these disciplines vary in the degree to which they are hierarchically organized according to track and grade. Second, we argued that inadequate teacher preparation might prompt a "transmission style" of teaching that avoids challenging teacher-student interactions. Such inadequate preparation could arise because the overall levels of teacher education and experience are inadequate or because of a poor match between teacher background and particular class assignments. Third, we hypothesized that organizational norms might affect instructional emphasis. A perceived need to produce achievement gains and to cover the curriculum might suppress teachers' adoption of higher-order objectives. On the other hand, organizational environments characterized by supportive administrative leadership, staff collaboration, and teacher control over the conditions of instruction were hypothesized to facilitate the pursuit of higher-order instructional goals.

The most prominent result of our study was the powerful link between track and emphasis on higher-order objectives. This link was strong and highly significant statistically in every discipline, but was especially pronounced in math and science. To convey a clearer sense of the practical significance of this effect, Figure 1 displays for each discipline the expected emphasis on higher-order thinking (controlling for the other effects in the model) in terms of the original scale. For example, one can see that in math, the expected emphasis on higher-order objectives is midway between "a little" and "moderate" in noncollege classes. For honors classes, the expected emphasis is midway between moderate and heavy. As mentioned earlier, this gap represents 1.7 standard deviation units. Track effects were smaller in English and social studies than in math and science.

The second central result was that the correlates of teaching for higher-order thinking did depend upon the discipline. Hypothesized effects of grade appeared only in math $(d = .41)$ and science $(d = .23)$.[9] No hypothesized effects of teacher preparation appeared in math and science, but important positive effects of teacher preparation did appear in social studies $(d = .28)$ and literature $(d = .38)$.[10] No effects of organizational norms appeared in math and science, but some evidence of such effects was manifest in social science and on both English scales (writing and literature).

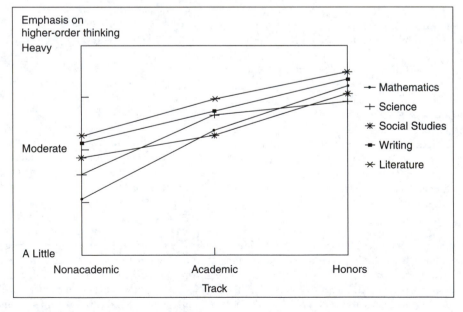

Figure 1
Track and emphasis on higher order thinking.

The teacher preparation effects arising in social studies and literature were effects of the teacher's self-reported preparation to teach a particular class. They were not effects of the overall level of education or experience. Our results provided no evidence that simply having obtained a master's degree or having extensive teaching experience predisposed a teacher to pursue higher-order objectives. Rather, the match between the teacher's preparation and the subject matter of a particular class appeared to be linked to higher-order emphasis.

The organizational effects were more complicated than anticipated. Some evidence of positive effects of supportive leadership and teacher control appeared; supportive principal leadership predicted an emphasis on higher-order objectives in writing (beta = .11) and literature (beta = .24), and teacher control over the conditions of instruction predicted higher-order objectives in social studies (beta = .23). However, neither the emphasis on curriculum coverage nor the need to produce achievement gains related to instructional objectives as hypothesized. In fact, rather than predicting low emphasis on higher-order objectives, emphasis on curriculum coverage predicted a higher-order emphasis in literature, and concern with achievement gains predicted a higher-order emphasis in social studies.

Implications for Policy and Future Research

Mathematics and Science

The findings suggest that differentiated instructional objectives are strongly institutionalized in the secondary mathematics and science curricula. In those disciplines, the typical teacher sets very different objectives for noncollege and college classes, and there is evidence, especially in mathematics but also suggested in science, that such a teacher sets higher-order objectives for courses taken later in a prescribed sequence. The appearance of the grade effect in mathematics may reflect the character of the secondary math curriculum, which is different from the other curricula in that the sequence of courses is to a larger extent hierarchical; certain courses (e.g., calculus) cannot be taken before certain other courses (e.g., algebra).

Commentary cited at the beginning of this article rejects the contention that higher-order objectives are less appropriate for low-track classes or more elementary classes than for high-track classes or more advanced classes. However, our study provides quite strong evidence that a diverse set of secondary math and science teachers disagree. If promoting higher-order thinking in secondary math and science is an important goal for educational policy, the advocates of such a policy must recognize that formidable institutional obstacles confront them. Our results provide little reason to believe that formulas like providing more preservice teacher education, improving the match between teacher knowledge and teaching assignment, deemphasizing standardized tests, or implementing school organizational reforms are by themselves likely to raise the conceptual level of discourse in the secondary math and science classes we studied. This does not mean that reforms of preservice education or school organization cannot be helpful. But to promote higher-order instruction for all students, such reforms must apparently challenge widely held conceptions of teaching and learning rooted in a curriculum that seems to have invariant characteristics across diverse secondary schools.

One might challenge these findings by criticizing the measures of teacher preparation and organizational environment employed in this study. One might especially challenge the absence of a large sample of schools that would have facilitated an exploration of school-to-school differences. Although we certainly encourage researchers to work on improved teacher and school measures, our findings for math and science are strengthened by results of our variance decomposition. In both math and science, large components of variation are *within-teachers*. Such variation cannot be accounted for by the main effects of teacher-level characteristics, no matter how well measured. Moreover, substantial proportions of this large within-teacher variance are accounted for by track. So our finding regarding track cannot be challenged by studies that improve measurement of teacher characteristics.

Moreover, no evidence emerged of important school-to-school differences in higher-order emphasis in math and science. So careful measurement of school-level characteristics, though certainly a laudable goal, would not likely be of much assistance in understanding the differentiation of objectives in these data. A critic might argue that idiosyncrasies in our sample or instruments may have worked against finding school differences. However, we were able to find evidence of significant school differences in the other disciplines. The school-to-school invariance we report is specific to math and science. This discipline-specificity of findings is in itself an important result requiring further exploration.

Social Studies and English

Important track effects appear in these disciplines as well; though they are not as powerful as in math and science. As in the case of math and science, this finding should encourage reformers to consider the institutional bases of the differentiation of instructional objectives across classes. Widespread conceptions about the relevance of higher-order objectives for different kinds of students, arguably rooted in the secondary curriculum, should not be ignored.

However, the appearance of teacher preparation effects and school organization effects provides some hope to policy-makers seeking to increase the prevalence of higher-order instruction through reforms of preservice education and school organization alone. The disposition of a teacher to strive for higher-order objectives in each class appears to be undermined by mismatches between prior training or interest and specific class assignments. And these findings encourage further exploration of how supportive organizational environments might raise the level of discourse.

Critics might again argue that better measurement of teacher characteristics would shed more light on how improved teacher preparation, selection, and assignment might increase teaching for higher-order thinking; and that improved measurement of organizational characteristics might uncover important insights about the likely effects of organizational reform. In the case of social studies and English, we would agree. Our results show large components of between-teacher and between-school variation in these subjects. Though these findings do not undermine the importance of track, they do encourage the specification of better theories and measures to understand how teacher and school differences influence the pursuit of teaching for higher-order thinking in social studies and English.

Interpretation of Track Effects

Oakes (1990, p. x) found that teachers in low-ability classes not only placed little emphasis on problem-solving and inquiry but that such classes "were the object of less teacher emphasis on nearly the entire range of curricular goals." To explore this possibility in our data, we replicated the analyses already described, this time with the lower-order scales as outcomes. We found some evidence to support Oakes's view. Space limitations preclude a full description of these results. However, significant *positive* effects of college-bound track appeared in math, science, and social studies. The effects were uniformly much smaller than the track effects on higher-order objectives and ranged from 0.29 SD units in social studies to 0.43 SD units in math. These findings of small effects must be viewed with caution in light of the comparatively weak reliability of the lower-order scales. Our working hypothesis would be that track effects on lower-order objectives are educationally significant, though less pronounced than track effects on higher-order objectives.

Further research using a multilevel methodology and aimed at specifying such effects across a wide range of objectives would clearly be illuminating.

Interpretation of Self-Report Data

Self-report data are limiting in that they do not provide direct evidence of teaching practice. However, they are appropriate in reflecting a teacher's *intended emphasis*. To the extent teachers do not intend to employ higher-order objectives, it would be surprising if such objectives emerged as prominent in a direct observation of practice. Of course, self-report data are subject to social-desirability bias. The likely effect of such bias would be to elevate the mean response to questions about higher-order objectives. Such bias would be more likely to blur rather than to exaggerate the effects found here, and so the possibility of such bias does not plausibly challenge the basic findings regarding the correlates of higher-order emphasis. Nevertheless, further research that combines self-report and observation data could be illuminating.

The Contribution of Analytic Methods to Interpretation

We urge other investigators of track effects in secondary schools to attend carefully to variation *within* and *between* teachers. It is possible that track effects result from the assignment of particular types of teachers to particular types of classes. However, our results show powerful *within-teacher* effects of track, especially in math and science. These findings undermine the validity of labeling teachers as "higher-order" versus "lower-order" teachers and encourage instead a search for understanding how and why teachers differentiate their objectives as a function of differences between the classes they are assigned to teach. A multilevel analytic strategy is important precisely because the contributions to variation at different levels (classes, teachers, schools) have different implications for interpretation and policy.

ABOUT THE AUTHOR

Stephen W. Raudenbush is a Professor in the College of Education at Michigan State University, 461 Erickson Hall, East Lansing, MI 48824. His specialization is statistical models for individual change and social context.

Brian Rowan is a Professor in the School of Education at 4112 School of Education, The University of Michigan, 610 E. University, Ann Arbor, MI 48109. His specialization is organization theory and research.

Yuk Fai Cheong is a doctoral candidate in the College of Education at Michigan State University, 401 B Erickson Hall, East Lansing, MI 48824. His specialization is hierarchical linear models in classroom and school effects research.

NOTES

Research reported here was conducted under the auspices of the Center for Research on the Context of Secondary School Teaching with funding from the Office of Educational Research and Improvement, U.S. Department of Education, Cooperative Agreement #OERI-G0087C235. We wish to thank our colleagues Milbrey McLaughlin and Joan Talbert for their crucial contribution in developing the questionnaire used in our study and Marian Eaton for her careful preparation of the data.

1. A preliminary analysis of the data used in this study confirmed these ideas. We examined course titles by track designation, course titles by grade level, and the amount of ability grouping by subject area. These analyses lent support to the notion that math and science tend to be more rigidly sequenced and tracked than do social studies and English.

2. By "track" we refer specifically to the designation of the class and not to a designation of students that might apply across subject areas or over time.

3. Two types of factor analyses were computed. First, principal axis factoring using varimax rotation produced an orthogonal solution. The number of factors was determined by the number of principal components having eigenvalues greater than unity. The second factor analysis used a direct oblimin rotation to achieve an oblique solution. For all five higher-order scales reported above, factor loadings on every item exceeded .40, though they tended to be considerably higher. The extent to which the ostensibly "lower-order" scales factored varied across subjects and was more sensitive to the method of rotation. Correlations between higher- and lower-order scales using the oblique rotation were near zero for English, .21 for science, .29 for social studies, and .43 for math. These must be viewed with caution in light of the questionable interpretability of the lower-order factors.

4. Items were weighted equally in constructing the scales. The purpose of the factor analysis was to check a priori conceptualization against the data rather than to compute weights for factor scores.

5. Low internal consistencies reflect both the small number of items per scale and the modest intercorrelations among the items.

6. This analysis was based on the computer program HLM3 (Raudenbush, Bryk, Seltzer, & Congdon, 1990) which produces maximum likelihood estimates of variance components and regression coefficients based on unbalanced data.

7. Recall that teacher preparation varied from class to class because we asked each teacher to report her level of preparation to teach the particular subject matter in each class.

8. Here, as in standard regression, $t = b/se$ where se is the estimated standard error of the estimated regression coefficient b. For example, in Table 4 we see that for the math outcome, the coefficient for academic classes is $b = 10.50$, $se = 0.93$; so $t = 10.50/0.93 = 11.29$.

9. Here d is the standardized mean differences between senior and freshman classes in emphasis on higher-order objectives, controlling for other predictors.

10. Here d is the standardized mean difference between "very well-prepared" teachers and other teachers in emphasis on higher-order objectives.

REFERENCES

Bereiter, C., & Scardamalia, M. (1987). An attainable version of high literacy: Approaches to teaching higher-order thinking skills in reading and writing. *Curriculum Inquiry, 17,* 9–30.

Bowles, S., & Gintis, H. (1976). *Schooling in capitalist America: Educational reform and the contradictions of economic life.* New York: Basic Books.

Bullough, R. V., Gitlin, A. D., & Goldstein, S. L. (1984). Ideology, teacher role, and resistance. *Teachers College Record, 86,* 339–358.

Cole, N. S. (1990). Conceptions of educational achievement. *Educational Researcher, 19*(3), 2–7.

Darling-Hammond, L., & Wise, A. E. (1985). Beyond standardization: State standards and school improvement. *Elementary School Journal, 85,* 315–335.

Doyle, K. (1983). *Evaluating teaching.* Lexington, MA: Lexington Books.

Goodlad, J. L. (1984). *A place called school.* New York: McGraw-Hill.

Hargreaves, D. H. (1967). *Social relations in a secondary school.* New York: Humanities Press.

Little, J. W. (1982). Norms of collegiality and experimentation: Workplace conditions of school success. *American Educational Research Journal, 19,* 325–340.

Metz, M. H. (1978). *Classrooms and corridors: The crisis of authority in desegregated secondary schools.* Berkeley: University of California Press.

Newmann, F. M. (1990). Higher-order thinking in teaching social studies: A rationale for the assessment of classroom thoughtfulness. *Journal of Curriculum Studies, 22*(1), 41–56.

Oakes, J. (1985). *Keeping track: How schools structure inequality.* New Haven, CT: Yale University Press.

Oakes, J. (1990). *Multiplying inequalities: The effects of race, social class, and tracking on opportunities to learn math and science*. Santa Monica, CA: The Rand Corporation.

Page, R. N. (1990). The lower track curriculum in a college-preparatory high school. *Curriculum Inquiry, 20,* 249–282.

Pallas, A. M. (1988). School climate in American high Schools. *Teachers College Record, 89*(4), 541–554.

Peterson, P. L. (1988). Teaching for higher-order thinking in mathematics: The challenge for the next decade. *Perspectives on research on effective mathematics teaching:* (Vol. 1. pp. 2–26). Reston, VA: Lawrence Earlbaum Associates.

Powell, A. G., Farrar, A. E., & Cohen, D. K. (1985). *The shopping mall high school: Winners and losers in the educational marketplace*. Boston: Houghton Mifflin.

Prawat, R. S. (1989). Teaching for understanding: Three key attributes. *Teaching and Teacher Education, 5,* 315–328.

Raudenbush, S. W., Bryk, A. S., Seltzer, M., & Congdon, R. (1990). *HLM 3.0: Computer program and users manual.* [Unpublished computer program manual]. East Lansing, MI: College of Education, Michigan State University.

Raudenbush, S. W., Rowan, B., & Kang, S. J. (1991). A multilevel, multivariate model for studying school climate in secondary schools with estimation via the EM algorithm. *Journal of Educational Statistics, 16*(4), 295–330.

Resnick, D. P., & Resnick, L. B. (1977). The nature of literacy: An historical explanation. *Harvard Educational Review, 47,* 370–385.

Rosenholz, S. J. (1985). Effective schools: Interpreting the evidence. *American Journal of Education, 93,* 352–388.

Rowan, B. (1990). Applying conceptions of teaching to organizational reform. In R. F. Elmore and Associates (Eds.), *Restructuring schools: The next generation of educational reform* (pp. 31–58). San Francisco: Jossey Bass.

Rowan, B., Raudenbush, S. W., & Kang, S. J. K. (1991). Organization design in high schools: A multilevel analysis. *American Journal of Education, 99*(2), 238–266.

Shepard, L. (1991). Psychometricians' beliefs about learning. *Educational Researcher, 20*(7), 2–9.

Shulman, L. S. (1987). Knowledge and teaching: Foundations of the new reform. *Harvard Educational Review, 57*(1), 1–21.

Stodolsky, S. (1988). *The subject matters: Classroom activity in math and social studies.* Chicago: University of Chicago Press.

Talbert, J. E., McLaughlin, M. W., & Rowan, B. (in press). Understanding context effects on secondary school teaching. *Teachers College Record.*

U.S. Department of Education, National Center for Education Statistics (1990). *The Condition of Education, 1991, Vol. I: Elementary and Secondary Education.* Washington, DC: Author.

Manuscript received June 5, 1992
Revision received December 2, 1992
Accepted January 8, 1993
Final revision received February 10, 1993

PERSPECTIVE 1: POSTPOSITIVISM ON THE RAUDENBUSH ET AL. STUDY

D. C. PHILLIPS   *Stanford University*

This paper represents a solid piece of educational inquiry, which does not mean that it is perfect, without blemishes. All research, from the postpositivist perspective, is criticizable and is prone to be superceded over time by further and better work. Apart from the facts that other researchers might be armed with stronger theoretical or methodological tools, or have more complete or accurate background knowledge, it is always the case that in doing specific pieces of work all researchers have to make choices; they cannot do all the things that might have been done in pursuit of a particular topic, for they are constrained by limited funds and limited time—in the quest for knowledge we do not have infinite resources. This always keeps open the possibility, then, that other choices about how to spend these finite resources might have been made—the choices that a researcher makes need to be intelligent ones, supported by a credible rationale, but rarely are they unassailable! The key issue is whether or not the resulting piece of inquiry advances our knowledge—does it produce findings or insights that are trustworthy and which advance our thinking about some problem domain, or does it provide a point from which we can launch new studies that will push our understanding further (or deeper)? In my view the paper by Raudenbush and his colleagues meets this general test. It does not make as exciting reading as one or two of the other papers that are used as examples in this book, but research—*qua* research—is not to be judged by its quality as entertainment or its ability to engage our emotions; inquiry that is to count as research is expected to be pursued with enough epistemological competence to produce results that we are warranted in accepting as likely to be true.

There are several points about careful or rigorous scientific inquiry that can be illustrated by reference to the study reported here; clearly I am not putting these forward as being a kind of template or algorithm for doing scientific work—for there is *no* possibility of finding such an algorithm!

1. From the perspective of many postpositivists, research is to be regarded as an attempt to answer or resolve a *problem*. Sometimes the problem is known—and is clearly and unambiguously stated—prior to the start of the research, but sometimes the problem emerges with clarity only during the course of the research; like our knowledge, our identification of problems is likely to be refined or recast as we move forward. But if there is no problem (or the inkling of one), there can hardly be any research or inquiry—do we inquire into matters that are regarded as *unproblematic?* (One of the great early figures in the history of pragmatism, the logician Charles Sanders Peirce, remarked that thought is stimulated by what he termed "the irritation of doubt.") All this is preamble to the fact that in this case, the problem was carefully delineated, and various possibilities with respect to it were teased apart. In brief: Currently in the realm of education, the fostering of higher order thinking is of importance as an instructional aim in many disciplines, yet much teaching of high school subjects appears to be focused only on imparting basic skills, and when higher order thinking is encouraged it is by-and-large found in "higher track" classes. Why is this? Which of several possible factors is at work here? This general problem is not only interesting to educationists, but resolving it might allow educational intervention to be effective—if we understand the factors that produce this phenomenon, we might (depending upon what they turn out to be) be in a position to intervene and increase the frequency with which higher order thinking takes place in lower track classes (if that indeed is what we wish to achieve).

2. In order to further refine the problem and make it researchable, Raudenbush et al., drawing on their background an understanding of how schools and classrooms operate and also on their knowledge of the research literature, formulated three likely rival explanations for the phenomenon of interest—basically, (i) that teachers have acquired the conception that higher order thinking is appropriate only for the best students in the most advanced courses and act accordingly only when teaching such students, (ii) that only teachers with relevant subject-matter expertise and experience are willing and able to pursue certain pedagogical goals such as the development of higher order thinking in a domain, and (iii) that institutional factors such as level of school bureaucracy or supportiveness of the administration might discourage or foster the pursuit of higher order instructional goals. The researchers then, in each case, went on to draw out quite specific hypotheses that would be true if that particular explanation were true, ending up with nine in all—the idea, of course, being to come up with propositions that are precise enough to be tested. Thus, for example, we can see that the second possible explanation leads (among others) to a specific hypothesis (H6) that "the more prepared a teacher feels to teach a particular course, the more likely that teacher will be to emphasize teaching for higher-order thinking in that course (p. 437)." Thus, if many teachers are found who feel well-prepared but who do not emphasize higher order goals in their teaching, H6 plus the explanation from which it was drawn would be in trouble! These would also be in trouble if numerous teachers who felt under-prepared nevertheless attempted to foster higher order thinking in those domains.

The point I am laboring here is that if questions or problems are vaguely or ambiguously formulated, any evidence that is collected will not be able to resolve them (for, to put it crudely, there is no "them" there!). It is always good to ask, if evidence or data is to be collected, "Why am I doing this? How *precisely* is this material going to be relevant to the *specific* questions I am concerned to answer?" This approach makes for competent inquiry; in this respect the study by Raudenbush and colleagues fares well.

3. It is worth laboring another point. The phenomenon of interest here—the relative low frequency of occurrence of higher order thinking in secondary school classrooms—is one about which many experienced educators and educational theorists might have strong beliefs or hunches, and so it might be thought that research is hardly necessary. But beliefs and hunches are not knowledge; some of our strongly held beliefs turn out upon investigation to be true, but many also turn out to be mistaken. (Recall that most people a little over five hundred years ago held, very strongly, the belief that the Earth was flat.) We need to have warrants for our beliefs or hunches—we need to turn them from beliefs into knowledge, especially if action or policy is to be based on them. It does not seem responsible to formulate policy or to allocate resources on the basis of beliefs or hunches, no matter how fervently held, unless there is no reliable, better warranted basis available.

4. Was the research design a competent one, able to provide trustworthy answers to the questions that had been formulated? It seems to me that it was. Sixteen schools in two states agreed to participate, in which there was a diversity of students and mode of school organization; 303 teachers working in 1205 classes of diverse types (honors level, college bound, vocational, and the like) were asked to fill in a relatively lengthy questionnaire in which they were asked to rate themselves with respect to their level of experience and preparedness, and they were also asked to judge the degree to which they emphasized higher or lower level thinking in their teaching. As the form that higher order thinking takes can vary across school subjects, the questionnaire had specific items crafted for mathematics, science, social studies, and English. Appropriate statistical analyses were performed to determine the degree of association between such factors as felt level of preparedness in a subject and felt level of emphasis on higher level thinking in teaching, and all the results were reported clearly and fully. The researchers reported some results that surprised them, and in places they addressed challenges that might be made to their work. In sum, the work was reported clearly and with openness—a reader can (with a little effort) understand precisely what data the researchers collected, how they analyzed it, and what they found. If we wished to replicate the study, we could do so. We cannot say that the findings are absolutely certain, but the study gives us good reason to accept the findings until such time as further work causes us to revise our opinion!

Personally I am not strongly enamored of self-report data; a teacher might report—and even believe—that he or she often does one thing while teaching when in fact something quite different is frequently done (it is very easy for any of us to misjudge the frequency of an aspect of our own behavior). Thus I would criticize the study for relying so centrally on this kind of data, and if the study were to be repeated I would argue strongly that this self-report material needs to be supplemented by a number of observational studies where researchers visit classrooms to observe whether or not teachers are doing the sorts of things they report doing. (However, it is notorious that such studies are extremely expensive, both in terms of money and time, and to do this with 303 teachers would be quite out of the question. I can understand why Raudenbush and his co-workers were not able to pursue this option, and decided instead to survey a large number of individuals working in a large number of different classrooms—a much quicker and cheaper alternative, although still one that required a great deal of effort.)

What I find quite impressive, and indicative of the solid scientific spirit exemplified in this study, is the fact that the authors actually addressed this issue, openly and non-defensively, in the final page or so of their paper. They make a brief but sensible case in defense of their decision to use this data; but they also acknowledge that "nevertheless, further research that combines self-report and observation data could be illuminating" (p. 458).

PERSPECTIVE 2: PRAGMATISM ON THE RAUDENBUSH ET AL. STUDY

NEL NODDINGS   *Stanford University*

In a study of this sort, characterized by systematic statistical procedures, a pragmatic critique could concentrate on the statistical methods and their effects or on the underlying assumptions and questionable definitions. One could do both, of course, but the second effort seems more important. High-powered statistical methods may be employed in ill-conceived studies, and hypothesis testing may distract us from an examination of the assumptions that gave rise to the hypotheses.

The first assumption we meet in this study is that higher order thinking is good. Does one dare to challenge this assumption? We can think of many situations in which higher order thinking is unnecessary and some in which it is counter-productive: cooking a familiar dish, listening to a student's problems (avoiding premature analysis), explaining a process that can be handled routinely, practicing scales or other piano exercises, riding a bicycle or horse, memorizing a verse, catching fly balls, completing a timed test in computation or typing. Readers can supply many more examples. The assumption that higher order thinking is good should yield to analysis that describes the purposes for which it is good, and the situations in which it is properly applied.

The second assumption we might challenge is one claiming that everyone is capable of higher order thinking. (See the Newmann (1990) quote, p. 206.) Does anyone really believe this? Surely, if we consider the three participants in the study of Carr et al. (the men with IQ scores of 30, 28, and 12), we would have to modify the claim, saying perhaps that "all normal people" are capable of higher order thinking. But is this even true? First, we face the problem of defining "normal" and, second, we have to say what we mean by higher order thinking. This is no easy task.

It is not unreasonable to entertain the possibility that many people are incapable of some forms of higher order thinking. Some years ago, studies of historical thinking suggested that a considerable number of high school students were unable to think using hypotheticals. Asked to speculate on what might have happened if the Japanese had not bombed Pearl Harbor, such students would answer, "That's silly! They did!" To make matters worse, this cast of mind seems resistant to teaching. Concrete thinkers cannot see the point of exploring counter-factuals. Is it important that they learn how to do so? One who answers yes to this must be ready to say why it is important.

As the authors of this article note, the problem of defining higher order thinking may be subject-dependent; that is, there may be little that can be said about higher order thinking in the generic sense. Higher order thinking in mathematics may be very different from higher order thinking in social studies (or it may not be). These researchers identify four learning objectives associated with higher order thinking in mathematics:

1. Understanding the logical structure of mathematics
2. Understanding the nature of proof
3. Knowing math principles and algorithms
4. Thinking about what a problem means and ways it might be solved

Most well prepared and highly experienced math teachers might evaluate only learning objective 4 as a higher order thinking objective suitable for all students. For example, I have a master's degree in math and 12 years of secondary school experience ranging over all the subjects usually taught in the math curriculum, but I certainly would not expect most students to master objectives 1 or 2—not even most students in an academic track. And why should they? What does such understanding contribute to the lives of people outside math or a few related professions?

Even number 3 is doubtful as an objective. If one means by it developing competence in the basic algorithms and knowing that addition and multiplication of real numbers are commutative, why call the objective "higher order"? Such understanding is elementary. However, if one aims at understanding commutativity at the level of abstract sets and invented operations, the objections raised against numbers 1 and 2 may be applied to this objective as well. Most people simply do not need this knowledge, and most are not interested. But such understanding is important—and fascinating—for math majors.

Number 4, however, is essential for everyone who can handle any math at all. A teacher who does not steer students toward this objective is depriving her students of an opportunity to develop real competence. *This* higher order objective applies realistically to all students, but the problems posed for different students or identified by them will vary greatly. My guess is that the best teachers know this. They do not reject higher order thinking for their general math students, but they do not describe "higher order" entirely in terms of "higher" content. They describe it in terms of their students' needs and interests. If I am right on this, the notion of higher order thinking needs much more analysis.

The researchers also are probably mistaken in positing a higher degree as an indication of subject matter knowledge. A teacher may have a master's in education that required little or no work on the subject she teaches. Moreover, she may not have studied her subject in depth at any level of her education. Such a teacher might "feel prepared," but her comfort might be tightly tied to teaching in a routine way. A better criterion of knowledge might be the number of courses a teacher has completed in her subject or the variety of high school courses in her subject that she has already taught. It is unfortunate that a methodologically sophisticated study should come to the conclusion that teacher preparedness has little to do with the pursuit of higher order learning objectives. Not only is this counter-intuitive; it could also be damaging to students and to the programs constructed by teacher educators.

Similarly, the use of years of experience as an indicator of pedagogical content knowledge is almost certainly an error. Studies have suggested that pedagogical knowledge gained from experience probably peaks at about 5 years. Teachers who do nothing (outside their own classroom work) to acquire new ideas may even lose ground after 10 or so years. A careful, thorough study would use something like videotapes or portfolios to evaluate pedagogical content knowledge.

Readers might profitably re-read every hypothesis suggested in this study and ask not how it arose (the authors are clear and generous on this) but what might be the effects of accepting it.

Remember that this is the crucial difference between pragmatism and foundational philosophies. We are not so concerned with the derivation of hypotheses from theories or data as we are with the consequences of posing and accepting them. In addition to asking about the effects, one might ask whether a given hypothesis should be broken into two or three. What would be the effect of such separation? For example, H9 includes three factors thought likely to promote the inclusion of higher order thinking aims. Many experienced teachers might find only one of these important— "exercises control over key policies in the areas of curriculum and instruction" (p. 208). One might also ask whether having such control actually implies a form of administrative support (at least implicit)—the sort that hands over appropriate pedagogical control to teachers.

There are several angles from which a pragmatist might critique the present study. I have examined some of the assumptions and definitions central to the study, and my purpose has been to analyze how these affected what the researchers did and what they concluded. We could extend the analysis of effects by asking, If well-prepared teachers really do reject higher order objectives for some of their students, what does this suggest by way of policies? Surely, it doesn't mean that we should prepare teachers less well. Does it mean that even our best-prepared teachers need further work on how to teach for higher order thinking? Does it mean that we should revise our expectations on such aims? Does it mean that we need more work on the analysis and definition of higher order thinking? Similarly, if it were to be shown that substantial numbers of students are incapable of some forms of higher order thinking, what should we do? Never accept such a conclusion? Ask what forms they are capable of? Undertake a serious study that attempts to separate forms that are important for all students from those important for only those with specialized interests? Readers are invited to add to my list of questions. One might even want to ask why tracking is considered so bad (think of the documented effects) and what might be done to make it a sound educational policy. Might we retain a form of tracking and remove the pernicious effects or must tracking be abandoned?

PERSPECTIVE 3: CONSTRUCTIVISM ON THE RADENBUSH ET AL. STUDY

YVONNA S. LINCOLN   *Texas A&M University*

Criticism of the Raudenbush et al. study might fall into two classes from a constructivist viewpoint: technocratic issues and moral-political issues. A third issue might be thrown in for good measure, that being the lack of connection to earlier research. Each of these merits some attention, because they go a long way toward explaining why teachers—the greatest focus by far of the Raudenbush et al. study—school administrators, and other practitioners routinely ignore educational research (broadly speaking).

In terms of the technocratic approach of this piece, three arguments might be made for why the piece does represent, to some extent, the technology of control. The first argument would point to the fact that the survey instrument itself is "ungrounded"; that is, it is not represented and (likely is not) grounded in anything other than researcher perspectives on what the appropriate, or right, or best, questions might be. It is little wonder that in several schools, the response rate was extremely low. Teachers, in my experience, often look over such instruments, and, in worse-case scenarios, allow that "This makes no sense to me" opinion. The worlds of academic researchers and classroom teachers are, to paraphrase Samuel Clemons, so far apart as to be said not to exist in the same world. Frequently, even the form of such questions appears to fly in the face of common sense.

Second, it represents a certain technocratic view (which concomitantly happens to be positivist, although that is not, as Howe points out, absolutely necessary) because it assumes a certain "managerial" purpose to the research enterprise. A foundational assumption to this piece of research is that researchers will find the answers, and subsequently pass it along to administrators (the "middle managers" of the schooling effort), who will then see to it that line workers (classroom teachers) carry out policy directives.

In fairness, this inquiry effort at least seeks to understand why teachers do what they do, and carefully considers the hypothesis that teachers do not routinely teach higher order thinking—even when perfectly capable and competent to do so—because of organizational imperatives (which one might assume to include feeling that they must "teach to the test," adhere rigidly to a state-mandated curriculum, or be responsive to state assessment requirements, or the like). Even so, fulfilling the imperatives of a research community far removed from the daily practices of classroom life is not much different from responding to the mandates of state-legislated assessment initiatives, or regulations imposed regarding school achievement scores and their link to state funding for schools. This is not merely the absence of consultation with stakeholders, although ignoring stakeholders is a serious epistemological breach, for what they can tell us of the constitutive practices of classrooms. It is also an hierarchical assumptional base regarding where the "best" knowledge comes from, and its corollary, viz., that the best knowledge cannot, or does not, derive from those with the most experience.

Third and finally, the work tends to be technocratic because it is built on a series of assumptions regarding how to obtain more precise data. The authors say, "For example, if the math scale consisted of 10 items rather than four, we estimate that the internal consistency of the scale would rise from .75 to around .88; a 15-item scale ought to produce an internal consistency of about .92" (p. 219). While statistically speaking, they are absolutely correct—that is, it is axiomatic within statistical models that a greater number of items will produce larger reliability estimates—this proposal for larger estimates of "internal consistency" represents a somewhat quixotic search for more certainty, more precision, more warrant for the claims or findings of the research. This desire for the reduction of uncertainty and the infusion of greater precision in estimating results is a form of technocratic reasoning: if consistency is higher, then uncertainty is reduced, and decision making can proceed with fewer and fewer qualms about the right and proper course. As this reasoning gropes toward its logical conclusion, it moves farther and farther away from the very real caution that the numbers—the regression analyses—are already far removed from classroom practices. The numbers are neither the actual experiences, nor are they direct experiences (observations) of those classroom practices; rather, they are artifacts in a system largely created, maintained and manipulated at some distance from the practices they purport to represent. They are proxies for the experiences in the 16 schools they represent, and we have no reliability estimates as to whether they are good proxies or not (although a rigorous critique of positivism would lend credence to the estimate that they are not).

An examination of the moral-political issues would lead one to conclude that, in traditional form, this work has done little to connect itself to values, moral issues, or political issues in any explicit way. First, the goal of "higher order thinking" teaching remains uncritically proposed. If higher order thinking, as a practice, were connected in some manner to the requisites for civic participation (which it often is, in the liberal literature on school reform), the warrant for this study would be clearer. That connection, however, is never made. Rather, higher order thinking is simply regarded as a social good, a political taken-for-granted. The possibility that other goals might be equally important, or even more important, is not considered. Rather, having determined what is important, the authors then undertake to investigate why it is not being done, or why it is being done differentially between classes and classrooms.

A second issue in this realm is the question of whether or not all three factors together might not impede the uniform teaching of higher order thinking, and whether, in fact, differential emphasis on teaching for higher order thinking might not be a function of a larger structural problem with schools and schooling in the first instance. A constructivist might argue that each of the hypothesized reasons for failure to teach higher order thinking uniformly throughout schools is responsible, and that each interacts with the other in ways which cannot necessarily be separated into neat hypotheses. Said another way, the root causes for failure to teach higher order thinking might consist of within-teacher, between-teacher, and organizational effects, taken together as mutually influencing variables which owe their power to structural features which inhere in the way schooling is organized.

A third issue, both moral and political, is the unexamined extent to which differential offering of higher order thinking might be complicit with the social reproduction (within schools) of inequality and class differences. The authors themselves provide powerful evidence that honors (and high achieving?) students are routinely offered courses which provide intensive practice in higher order thinking, while students of perceived lower (non-college track) achievement levels are offered such teaching far less. The net effect of such differentiated teaching is to reproduce class differences, class after class. In undertaking some interpretation of the results, why is this literature never mentioned, or this interpretive possibility explored?

Finally, a close reading of this piece suggests that one explanation (interpretation) for these data is that the teachers surveyed are acting out, within their classrooms, a rather classical psychological study: the self-fulfilling prophecy. They do not teach higher order thinking skills to certain classes because they may assume that such thoughtful teaching would be wasted on the non-college-bound. In their failure to teach for these skills, they create (construct?) the very reality which they assumed to exist initially. I wonder, as a critic asked to provide specific criticisms of this piece, whether the authors simply consider the research on self-fulfilling prophecies to be too unsophisticated to reference, or whether they consider it irrelevant to their own interpretations. It seems compelling to me, in light of their own evidence, and in light of the rather large within-teacher effects on which they report.

The technocratic foundations of this research might well be overlooked if the interpretive aspects of the inquiry had been well-attended to. The authors, however, write as though there were no critical theorist research, no psychological research, virtually no earlier research to which this work might be usefully joined. Two decades earlier, ignoring—or even being unaware of—critical theorist work, or constructivist work, or micro-ethnographic work in schools would have been not only forgivable, but understandable. The explosion of such work, however, has created a visibility which makes it difficult to ignore, impossible to dismiss, and urgently necessary to aid in interpreting many strands, forms or paradigms of research. Why the authors chose to interpret their own research without reference to the multiple hypotheses circulating regarding why children are offered different educations which appear to be highly correlated with their social class is difficult to understand.

PERSPECTIVE 4: INTERPRETIVE AND NARRATIVE ON THE RAUDENBUSH ET AL. STUDY

ARTHUR P. BOCHNER   *University of South Florida*

As an interpretive social scientist, I believe that interpretation saturates every moment of scientific inquiry. Scientific method, no matter how rigorously it is applied, cannot produce descriptions that are completely free of the influence of the describer. More than a century ago, a school of philosophy referred to as positivism began using the terms "objectivity," "rigor," and "method," to distinguish science from other forms of inquiry. Positivists believed that scientific truth could be found by applying rigorous methods that would enable scientists to observe nature in its own terms and thus produce descriptions of the world that correspond with reality. But their idea of "positive" knowledge hinged on the development of a neutral medium of communication, a language that could represent nature as nature would describe itself if it could (Rorty, 1982). Unfortunately, the theory of language on which positivism was grounded turned out to be problematic. From Dithey's hermeneutics to that of Heidegger and his student Gadamer through to Wittgenstein's idea of language games, and subsequently to speech act theory, semiotics, and the deconstructive paradigm of Derrida, philosophers of language have opposed the innocence of the positivists' conception of language as a neutral medium of communication. In different ways, these philosophers showed that language cannot function as a simple, neutral tool for mirroring reality, because it is a constitutive part of that very reality (Bochner & Waugh, 1995).

From the point of view of science, what is out there in the world must be clearly distinguishable from what is in the mind of the scientific observer. When we teach methodology to students of scientific method, we usually refer to scientific criteria such as reliability, validity, control groups, and significance tests, leaving the impression that there are sources outside of ourselves that determine which descriptions of the world will be considered true and which false. We make it seem as if "truth" is something decided by the external world and not by us (the observers). But as Rorty (1989) says, "where there are no sentences, there is no truth" (p. 5). The world cannot make descriptions of itself; only the human observer of the world can. The scientist eventually has to make descriptions (in the form of sentences) that fit his or her observations of the world. It is not the world describing itself; it is the scientist describing the world. The point is that scientific method per se does not make it possible for the mind to transcend the skin (Fiske & Schweder, 1986). As Thomas Kuhn (1962) showed convincingly, the history of science offers no warrant for thinking it is possible to distinguish unequivocally between what is in our minds and what is out there in the world.

The article written by Raudenbush and his colleagues is a prime example of the sort of research and writing that is promoted by a reverence for scientific method. Raudenbush and his colleagues tirelessly emphasize their allegiance to sound and rigorous methodology, repeatedly drawing attention to their measurement strategies and modes of analysis. The subtext is clear: one must first and foremost be true to the practices of science; good research is measured against standards of technical proficiency not imagination or creativity. Thus, as "scientists," Raudenbush and his colleagues adhere to conventions of scientific discourse that create distance and give the impression of neutrality. They assume the position of spectators, adopting the voices of detached observers using neutral language to produce an unmediated mirroring of reality. They give the impression that they only "receive" knowledge; they don't participate in it in a way that might unduly influence reception. What they "discover" in their research is presented to us as a reality that is independent of the researchers' participation in it. They do not reveal their own interests or investments in "higher order" teaching goals. Instead, they speak in the cool and detached terms of abstract concepts and categories. They go to great lengths to fit the topic of teaching higher order thinking to a research model that would be viewed as scientifically credible. Indeed, they repeatedly defend the reliability of their measures and the validity of their statistical model, pushing into the background the central issue of how to account for the cleavage between the goals teachers say they should seek and their "actual" teaching practices. Ultimately, they seem more obliged to show that their research meets the rigorous standards for good empirical research—measuring, predicting, rating, mathematically modeling—than that they have gained a thorough understanding about a complicated question about teaching philosophy and practice.

Ironically, these researchers subscribe to the importance of teaching and learning analytical thinking, yet they do not think critically about the core issue to which their research is directed. They present findings of previous research but provide no analysis of the contexts within which those results were produced. Nor do they interrogate the possibly robust meanings of terms that are central to understanding the research problem. For instance, one possible explanation for the apparent contradiction between the "consensus" on the importance of teaching higher order thinking and the apparent absence of this kind of teaching in certain tracks and institutions is that the consensus is false. But Raudenbush and his colleagues do not contemplate the various meanings of "consensus" or the conditions under which consensus either is reached or assumed. What does it mean to have a consensus? Under what conditions do groups and institutions reach consensus? What are the standards for judging when a consensus is more a matter of convenience, or the outcome of structures of power, than a valid reflection of a group, or institution, or discipline's viewpoint?

Nor do these researchers sufficiently emphasize that the goal of teaching higher order thinking is not a singular one intended to replace all other goals, but rather exists in tandem with other teaching objectives and strategies. In my view, the contrast between "higher order" and "lower order" seems overly simplistic as a representation of a broad array of teaching objectives. Where would one place emotional, ethical, aesthetic, political, or ideological objectives on such a bipolar continuum? Which are higher? Which are lower? The distinction between "teaching the facts" and getting students "to think" appears to leave out many of the emotional, creative, and psychological goals of instruction that are crucial to the education of the whole person.

Raudensbusch and his colleagues repeatedly defend the reliability of their measures and their measurement strategies. In comparison to this concern for scientific credibility, they show much less interest in the experience of teaching, of what the practices of teaching and learning mean to these teachers and to their students. They do not feel it necessary to observe a class in session, come into communicative contact with teachers and students, feel the emotional demands of a day at school, in classrooms, staff meetings, before and after school, and over the course of a whole day, week, or month. They keep themselves at a distance from the experience of teaching, relying instead on the efficiency of self-reported questionnaires that measure not what happens but what is intended to happen, not teaching per se but expectations about teaching, not issues that are demonstratively relevant and meaningful to the research participants but rather issues the researchers think the participants would (or should) regard as relevant and meaningful. The use of these self-reported questionnaires, while undoubtedly efficient for the kind of statistical analysis these researchers prefer to perform, leaves open to question the connection that is assumed between the rating items on these scales and the intellectual, emotional, sensual, embodied, and performed experience of teaching. Moreover, the research strategy focuses exclusively on the teachers and entirely omits the experience of students, as if teaching did not involve a dynamic, interpersonal process of engagement among teachers and students. Is not teaching a relational activity that centrally focuses our attention as teachers on ways of being with others, i.e., students?

When teaching "higher-order" thinking requires teachers to argue, challenge, criticize, and debate with students, the teachers performing these actions may find it increasingly difficult to maintain a positive and facilitative interpersonal, psychological, and emotional environment in the classroom. This may have little to do with how much "content" education or teaching experience teachers have acquired. Rather, a teacher's attraction to analytical teaching and her ability to do it well may be a function of how comfortable she is with herself, how much she accepts her own vulnerability in the classroom, how effectively she can express a wide range of emotions, and her capacity to deal with students' emotional reactions to criticism, challenge, and conflict. In my view, we need to consider thoroughly the emotional consequences for teachers and for students of the sort of "challenging teacher-student interactions" that Raudenbush and his colleagues point to so admiringly, but many teachers may find detrimental to maintaining an affirming psychological climate in the classroom.

The issues on which I have focused and, for the most part, Raudenbush and his colleagues have not, reflect our differing perspectives on inquiry. As a social science text, their article was shaped by the prevailing conventions of discourse within which they work. It is not so much what these authors left out of their analysis as it is the conventions that promote these omissions that trouble me the most.

Academic life involves reading, observing, and writing. We learn to conduct research and write monographs by reading and studying the work of our predecessors and mentors (Rose, 1993). Thus, the norms of what will count as legitimate research and publishable writing are carefully controlled by our disciplines through instrumental contacts with peers, professors, articles, monographs, and books. Methods of documentation and writing are formulated within the constraints of accepted practices of inquiry and recognized modes of representation. Regardless of the subject matter, these conventionalized practices confine inquiry to a limited range of researchable experiences represented in a narrow domain of recognizable texts (Rose, 1993). We are groomed to engage in certain types of research experiences and compose texts that satisfy the expectations of our discipline's norms. If our professional socialization takes, we learn to write effectively in the largely standardized genres of writing that are accepted as legitimate in our discipline (Rose, 1993). In short, what we learn is a great deal of conformity (Krieger, 1991). Moreover, our disciplines exert a means of social control over us by promoting norms that discourage innovative or creative modes of writing that deviate from legitimated genres.

The article by Raudenbush and his colleagues conforms to accepted practices of social science discourse—review the literature, state the problem, formulate the hypotheses, present the method, analyze the data, show the results. It is not artful, poetic, or innovative, nor did they intend it to be. For someone outside the small community of scholars to which it is addressed, this article could be torturous to read. Some of you probably were bored, perhaps even alienated. You may have found it long, redundant, and rather defensive. You may have even asked yourself, "What's wrong with me? Why did I feel this way?" If so, perhaps you can take comfort in sociologist Laurel Richardson's (1994) observation that social science writing is an impoverished form of discourse. Richardson grieves over how boring our undergraduates find the research articles they are assigned to read; how dry, inaccessible, and overly abstract they seem to graduate students; and how, even she, a seasoned scholar, must confess that she doesn't finish reading half of the articles in the journals to which she subscribes.

I suspect many of you will agree that orthodox social science writing is not very user-friendly. The authors of this article, to take one example, are very concerned about the validity of their descriptions but they don't make a special effort to communicate or relate to us as readers. Indeed, as a form of writing, articles such as this one tacitly promote an hierarchical structure that divides those in the know from those in the dark. There is a clear division here between the haves and the have-nots. Shrouded in mysterious language—academic jargon (e.g., hierarchical linear model, three-level regression model, intra-teacher variation, substantial fraction, components of variance, effects sizes, tracks, lower order scales, decomposition of variance) the research story is told in a fashion that fosters division. The rub is that writers must depend on our willingness to accept our lower position to achieve their self-authentication.

As a professor of communication studies, I frequently concern myself with the question of the connection between a writer and his or her readers, or a speaker and his or her listeners. Since I regard all action conducted in the everyday world as social and writing is a form of action, I see writing as a relational activity; it fosters a connection between communicators and their audiences. Writing can create distance or encourage closeness; it can alienate or it can heal; it can be devoid of feeling or it can arouse passions; it can be intellectually brilliant but lack soul, or be simple but heart-felt; it can be heady or it can emanate from one's gut. Of course, none of these are necessary oppositions. From my perspective, the ideal is writing in which the heart and head go hand in hand.

On the whole, the conventions of social science writing promote forms of writing that do not touch readers but rather keep them at a distance. These conventions also promote a defensive style of communication in which the writer is compelled to rule out all explanations or perspectives other than his or her own, as if the goal is to arrive at a single, unquestioned, unmediated, universal truth about the subject matter. The goal is to win approval for one's point of view. Usually this means one must establish the viability of one's perspective, an abstraction in the form of a theory that explains or accounts for one's observations. Concrete events dissolve into solutions of abstract analysis. To use Edith Turner's (1993) apt analogy, the reader is left to look through a stained glass window, seeing only murky and featureless profiles. The concrete details of sensual, emotional, embodied experience are replaced by typologies and abstractions that remove events from their context, distancing readers from the actions and feelings of particular human beings engaged in joint action, e.g., teaching and learning as a concrete event or activity. Is this what we want from social science?

REFERENCES

Bochner, A., & Waugh, J. B. (1995). Talking-with as a model for writing-about: Implications of Rortyean pragmatism. In L. Langsdorf & A. R. Smith (Eds.), *Recovering pragmatism's voice: The classical tradition, Rorty, and the philosophy of communication*. Albany: State University of New York Press. (211–233).

Fiske, D. J., & Schweder, R. A. (1986). *Metatheory in social science*. Chicago: University of Chicago Press.

Krieger, S. (1991). *Social science and the self: Personal essays on an art form*. New Brunswick, NJ Rutgers University Press.

Kuhn, T. (1962). *The structure of scientific revolutions*. Chicago: University of Chicago Press.

Richardson, L. (1994). Nine poems: Marriage and the family. *Journal of Contemporary Ethnography,* 23, 3–14.

Rorty, R. (1982). *Consequences of pragmatism: Essays 1972–1980.* Minneapolis: University of Minnesota Press.

Rorty, R. (1989). *Contingency, irony, and solidarity.* New York: Cambridge University Press.

Rose, D. (1993). Ethnography as a form of life: The written word and the work of the world. In P. Benson (Ed.), *Anthropology and literature.* Urbana: University of Illinois Press.

Turner, E. (1993). Experience and poetics in anthropological writing, In P. Benson (Ed.), *Anthropology and literature* (pp. 27–47) Urbana: University of Illinois press.

PERSPECTIVE 6: RACE, ETHNICITY, AND GENDER ON THE RAUDENBUSH ET AL. STUDY

BETH HARRY   *University of Miami*

The missing piece in this otherwise excellent study is readily evident—the race, ethnicity, and gender of the students. The research cited by the authors regarding differential instruction according to tracks (Oakes, 1985; Anyon, 1981) implicate both race and socioeconomic status in dramatic portraits of schooling as social reproduction (Bowles & Gintis, 1976). Raudenbush et al. focus on track placement without including any information on who comprise those classes. Without an examination of the characteristics of the students, this research is incomplete.

First, we should know the ethnic and gender composition of the student body as a whole, and also that of the vocational versus the academic programs. We should know also whether teacher ethnicity and gender correlated with those of their students. This is not to assume that we would need to see a mismatch between teacher and student ethnicity in order for race- and class-based discrimination to be documented. Indeed, there is good reason to believe that teachers who are members of minority groups can be as influenced by the stereotypical expectations of their profession and by detrimental institutionalized practices as are members of the majority group. In Rist's (1970) classic study of within-class tracking, for example, the teacher who sorted Black children according to apparent social class features was African American.

To know the composition of the student body would allow us to attend to that most recalcitrant of American evils—racism, and to the most invisible—classism. To ignore these is, implicitly, to place the entire burden on the skills level of the students. It is, really, to leave open the possibility that the students in the lower tracks have earned this place by virtue of a meritocracy. The portrait is truly incomplete without an understanding of the correlations between ethnicity, gender, socioeconomic status, and track placement.

The fact that the study finds the strongest evidence of differential use of higher order questioning in the within-teacher dimension is particularly provocative. That teachers hold differential expectations of students according to their track placement is not surprising, but that individual teachers' practice varies so greatly points to the power of negative stereotypes to affect even excellent teachers. This has serious implications for teacher preparation programs since, once more, if students' race/ethnicity is a factor in differential instruction, direct attention must be paid to teachers' beliefs about the abilities of children from poor and minority communities. Teaching is not a generic set of skills that, once learned and demonstrated in one context, will necessarily transfer to another. The study did find that a mismatch between teachers' prior training or interests and their class assignments was correlated with decreased use of higher order objectives.

The "mismatch" finding leads us to the issue of self-efficacy (Bandura, 1997), which may differ somewhat from a simple consideration of whether or not teachers are assigned to classes for which they are adequately prepared. According to the theory, self efficacy is shaped by mastery experience, vicarious experience, verbal persuasion, and physiological and affective responses. Tschannen-Moran, Woolfolk, and Hoy (1998) argue that while these factors shape teachers' efficacy, it is further influenced by the content and context of the instructional situation. A recent study by Spero (2000) takes the theory further, showing how White student teachers' sense of efficacy was destabilized by their experience in a Black community education project as they came face to face with community practices and values that were foreign to them. Their "hegemonic lens"—the set of beliefs and values through which their perceptions of Blacks were filtered—undermined these teachers' sense of efficacy. The research also had implications for how efficacy is measured, since the researcher noted that the student-teachers' efficacy showed an increase when measured by traditional efficacy instruments that took no account of content or context. Qualitative investigation, however, revealed just the opposite, that when content and context were specified, the study participants reported that their sense of efficacy had actually decreased.

The hegemonic lens of teachers are, like culture, so integral to the individual's identity that awareness of it comes with difficulty. A few years ago, I would have said that these lens are analogous more to wearing contact lenses than spectacles, since they are almost integral to the eye. These days we have a far more accurate analogy if we think of the power of hegemonic perceptions as a kind of laser eye surgery, by which the actual structures of the eye are altered to ensure accurate perception. The inculcation of cultural beliefs, particularly from the hegemonic perspective, is no less powerful. Research examining how teachers alter their pedagogical practices according to their expectations of students' capabilities cannot afford to ignore who those students are.

REFERENCES

Anyon, J. (1981). Social class and school knowledge. *Curriculum Inquiry, 11*(1), 3–42.

Bandura, A. (1997). *Self-efficacy: The exercise of control.* New York: W.H. Freeman & Co.

Bowles, S. & Gintis, H. (1976). *Democracy and capitalism: Property, community, and the contradictions of modern social thought.* New York: Basic Books.

Oakes, J. (1985). *Keeping track: How schools structure inequality.* New Haven, CT: The Rand Corporation.

Rist, R. (1970). Student social class and teacher expectations: The self-fulfilling prophecy in ghetto education. *Harvard Education Review. 40* (3) 411–451.

Spero, R.B. (2000). *Toward a model of "civitas" through an ethic of care. A qualitative study of preservice teachers' perceptions about learning to teach diverse populations.* Paper presented at the Annual Conference of the American Educational Research Association, New Orleans.

Tschannen-Moran, M., Woolfolk, A., & Hoy, W. (1998). *Teacher efficacy: Its meaning and measure.*

PERSPECTIVE 7: CRITICAL THEORY ON THE RAUDENBUSH ET AL. STUDY

GEORGE NOBLIT   *University of North Carolina*

I personally am intrigued by many of the arguments offered by those who are elaborating the "institutional" school of thought in education and sociology that is employed in this article. Their analysis offers intriguing possibilities about how the wider society works to structure schools even more than the internal organization of schools itself. These insights are provocative for critical researchers who argue that schools reproduce societal patterns of social relations. This article is a sophisticated analysis that examines and critiques competing theoretical explanations of why teachers teach or do not teach higher order skills to students. It employs rigorous statistical analyses and offers a thorough use of the data. It is a good article and worthy of our consideration. Moreover, it is also an article that demonstrates the difference between positivistic and critical research.

Critical researchers often focus on the conditions or structures in society that impede the development of communicative competence. Indeed, a key argument is that power systemically distorts communication (Habermas, 1970). That is, only in the absence of power and ideology is it possible to have genuine and authentic communication. In the presence of power and ideology, the less powerful cannot communicate authentically because their real interests would threaten the powerful and consequently authentic beliefs are dangerous to express. Their genuine beliefs and communications are kept private in what Scott (1990) terms "hidden transcripts." When these hidden transcripts are revealed to the more powerful, the less powerful are threatened, coerced, or exiled. Further, critical researchers understand the ubiquity of power in modern societies and have documented how power differentially affects students, teachers, administrators, women, people of color, gays and lesbians, and others. That is, as Foucault (1980) argued, power is infused in all the relations of society and thus is difficult to recognize. Indeed, this is the driving purpose of critical research: to reveal the dynamics of power and ideology in social relations. Yet it is clear that some people are prepared to use and understand the use of power and this is the not so hidden mission of elite educational institutions. Power and knowledge are deeply interpenetrated (Foucault, 1980). They may not be synonymous but each serves the interests of the other. Thus the elite are given the knowledge to develop and wield power and the poor are given knowledge to keep them subjects of the more powerful. Yet this is too simplistic as well. Power and knowledge are stratified so that at each level people have the knowledge necessary to fulfill their roles and the power to compel compliance. The system itself is not deterministic. Rather knowledge and power must be reproduced by the actors within the system. That is, individuals and groups take the culture and resources available to them and actively recreate the system. This means that the system is not total; each generation of actors change it as they reproduce it. Moreover, those with less power also are not fully dependent on those over them for their power and knowledge. The fact that they have hidden transcripts reveal that each level has understandings that come from their own histories and experiences as well from observing others including those with more power. However, the raison d'etre of critical research is that the structures of power and knowledge are reproduced and that breaking this cycle requires revealing the ideologies that justify differential power, revealing how knowledge is stratified, and engaging the less powerful as participants in the decisions about what is to be maintained and what is to be changed (Bowers, 1984).

The article by Raudenbush, Rowan, and Cheong invited the above introduction because their research reveals the stratification of knowledge in high schools in spite of calls for teaching all students the same curriculum of higher order thinking skills. The article documents these calls and investigates the explanations for the persistence of stratification in instruction. The explanations they investigated were three: (1) "that hierarchical conceptions of teaching and learning are deeply embedded" (p. 207) in the curriculum of the high school and discourage teachers from teaching higher order skills to less advanced students; (2) that "variations in teachers' subject matter knowledge and pedagogical experience" (p. 207) lead the less knowledgeable and experienced teachers to not teach higher order skills as much; and (3) that "organizational environments characterized by supportive administrative leadership, high levels of teacher collaboration, and strong teacher control over instruction" (p. 207) will lead to more teaching of higher order skills.

The research design was positivistic, specifying nine hypotheses that take into account the complexity of the variables and relationships being investigated. While this study is an excellent example of the statistical analysis of survey data, critical researchers would point out that positivistic studies serve technical interests rather than practical or emancipatory interests. The focus on variables transforms the complexity of human life into distributions and the interrelatedness of conditions, structures, and interpretations into discrete variable and measures. Studies such as this focus on the control of variables which in themselves are created by researchers so that the technology of their methodology may proceed. Statistical control relates variables as integers rather than as the real interpretations or lived experiences of those surveyed. That is, this study, like others of its ilk, first reduce human experience and then create knowledge from such reductions. Moreover, such studies then imply that if real life is altered in terms of what is learned from these reductions that it may be possible to improve the human condition. Studies like this then demonstrate how positivistic control requires life to be altered to fit its necessities.

Second, even good positivistic studies such as this one reveal that the construction of the needed hypotheses is itself a process of reduction. One must reduce knowledge that is complex and uncertain to the set of variables, which can then be related statistically. The variables employed are in fact rather far removed from the theoretical explanations they will be used to represent. In this study, the data appear to be self-reported by teachers. The theoretical explanations being examined, however, posit many phenomena that exist in the wider culture of schools such as "hierarchical conceptions of teaching and learning" (p. 207) or "organizational environments" (p. 207). Indeed, the theoretical explanations examined come close to giving these conceptions an objective existence even though they are measured using teacher self-reports. The inferences from the tested hypotheses to the theoretical explanations thus represent problematic inferences. Most importantly, the dependent variable is the "teachers' self-reported emphasis on teaching higher-order goals" (p. 207). The key finding that this emphasis is stronger in more advanced classes could possibly reflect that teachers believe they should *say* that they do more in higher level classes, thus converting the analysis into a study of what affects how teachers speak about their different classes. It may be that there is little correlation between what they report and what they do. This critique, however, is not really the important point from the perspective of critical researchers. Instead, the key point is that positivism serves the interests of technical rationality. By reducing the complexity of schooling and stratification and positing a reality that can be objectively known, the knowledge gained from positivistic studies can be used to justify the imposition of this reduced and singular perspective of reality. By acting upon the truth that positivism posits, other perspectives are denied and a hierarchical view of the world is reproduced. This is to say that while the variables can be correlated and the hypotheses can be tested, their validity is low. The variables and hypotheses only indirectly represent the theoretical explanations Raudenbush, Rowan, and Cheong wish to examine. More importantly the variables, hypotheses, and theoretical explanations as well are gross simplifications. Teachers have a range of perspectives on, and vested interests in, the teaching of higher order thinking skills. Teacher preparation is but one variable that affects teaching; others include the preexisting beliefs of teachers and the beliefs of others in the school and community. All three of these are not variables in the sense used in survey research. Each represents a collection of various perspectives and political arrangements that are not independent of the others. Finally, organizational norms as measured here misspecify the multiplicity of beliefs and practices within a school as well as their substantive meaning. Leaders support some teachers and not others, teachers collaborate in small groups and represent various interests, and teacher control may well mean that some teachers dominate others. Supportive leadership, teacher collaboration, and teacher control can all serve to reinforce stratification of knowledge in schools as well as discourage it. As discussed earlier, though, the measures used in this study are in fact rather far from these theoretical arguments, and thus not only is political complexity and multiplicity of perspectives ignored but the measures are rather poor approximations of the theoretical explanations being examined by these authors.

The data are interesting from a critical perspective as well. The teachers sampled are highly experienced and educated and very white (91%). The first two facts mean that the second explanation involving experience and knowledge has little variation to affect teacher self-reports of emphasis on teaching higher order skills. The last implies that we should limit the inferences of the data to white teachers. Other groups of teachers may well have rather different results. Further, the fact that the lower order skill and higher order skill scales did not correlate positively suggests that our current understanding of the teaching of these skills itself is faulty. Since one does not replace the other, the popular notion that these sets of skills are in competition in classrooms is suspect. In this study, this is important in that the competition construct was presupposed by the authors and by the theoretical explanations they hoped to test. Again the data and the theoretical arguments seem to be some distance apart. What is relevant is that the authors did not examine the theoretical significance of this, even thought they note that there were "strong *within-teacher* effects" and in turn "encourage instead a search for understanding how and why teachers differentiate their objectives" (p. 224). A critical researcher would conclude that what is missing is a sufficiently complex understanding of teaching and thus would have concerns about the significance of this study.

Nevertheless, the authors do find that the "results varied substantially across the four disciplines" (p. 216). Critical researchers would find that the differences reflect the differences in the relative statuses of the disciplines (i.e., mathematics and science are regarded as more difficult and consequently are more highly valued) and thus may reflect a stratification that reproduces the power of some ideas and some people over the others. However, a critical researcher would also ask if the findings could reflect a conception of higher order skills that is biased towards science and math. This concern is heightened by the fact that lower order skills and higher order skills were not negatively correlated and the concern that teaching itself may have been inadequately understood. The authors acknowledge this in part but are remarkably atheoretical. They posit the need for better measures but do not consider that it may be that the conceptions of higher order skills are biased towards science and math or that the conception of teaching is insufficient.

Moreover, their argument that the "underemphasis on teaching higher-order thinking" (p. 222) is due to the fact that "differentiated instructional objectives are strongly institutionalized in the secondary mathematics and science curricula" (p. 223) is a case of ad hoc theorizing. That is, they did not test this explanation directly but rather came to this explanation after their data showed that the track of the class taught was the most important variable in explaining the results—not one of the three explanations that were directly tested. For the authors, this pattern of results "suggest," p. 223) that an institutional analysis is appropriate. However, the authors do not elaborate what an institutional analysis itself would suggest. Instead they move to a discussion of the implications of the results discounting reform efforts in science and mathematics and encouraging reform efforts in social studies and language arts. A critical researcher would ask for more detail in their ad hoc theorizing so as to evaluate the reasoning of the authors and for a comparison of an alternative explanation that fit the pattern of results. Presumably the general argument, following the institutional school of thought, is that there are strong cultural beliefs external to the school which structure practices internal to the school more than variables within the school and profession of teaching. However, a critical researcher would offer at least one competing explanation (assuming that the data are valid for the moment). A critical researcher would no doubt agree that there are powerful cultural beliefs that structure schools and promote tracking. However, a critical researcher would also argue that the data demonstrates that there is an internal variable in the school organization that does explain the results. Tracking itself is an educational structure that reproduces inequality in school and society. Moreover, the fact that the effects of tracking vary across disciplines reveals that tracking reproduces the hierarchy of science and mathematics over the other disciplines as well. A critical analysis is also consistent with the findings that there are strong "*within-teacher* effects" especially in math and science. That is, it is the track that determines what is taught in high status disciplines, not the predelictions of the teacher himself or herself. For social studies and English, tracking has powerful effects even when teachers have prior training that contradicts the practice of tracking. Again, however, the internal school variable of tracking is the most important: "The disposition of a teacher to strive for higher-order objectives in each class appears to be undermined by mismatches between prior training or interest and specific class assignments" (p. 224).

In summary, then, this article reflects sophisticated statistical analyses and tests important explanations for a deemphasis on teaching higher-order thinking skills. It offers much to those concerned with the reform of education. To a critical researcher, however, the article needs theoretical development in the conception of teaching that it employs—the linkages between the theoretical explanations, the hypotheses offered, the variables measured, and the ad hoc theorizing that is said to fit the data. A critical researcher would see the data as indicating that schools use tracking to stratify who has what knowledge and in doing so reproduces a hierarchical society. Those taught higher-order thinking will be better able to analyze and critique ways of thinking and thus can participate more effectively in organizing the world in ways that benefit themselves. Those without these skills are less able to participate effectively and are more subject to dominance. In this case, we can see the conjunction of power and knowledge directly. Those with higher order skills will be better able to succeed in higher education and in the information economy that is so powerful. They will be better able to analyze situations and to direct the activities of others. This theoretical approach is more robust than that offered by Raudenbush, Rowan, and Cheong.

REFERENCES

Bowers, C. A. (1984). *The promise of theory: Education and the politics of cultural change*. New York: Longman.

Foucault, M. (1980). *Power and knowledge*. (C. Gordon, Ed.) New York: Pantheon Books.

Gramsci, A. (1971). *Selections from the prison notebooks*. New York: International Publishers.

Habermas, J. (1970). Toward a theory of communicative competence. In H.P. Dreitzel (Ed.) *Recent sociology no.2: Patterns of communicative behavior*. Basingstoke: Macmillan. (115–148).

Habermas, J. (1971). *Knowledge and human interests*. Boston: Beacon Press.

Noblit, G., & Dempsey, V. (1996). *The social construction of virtue: The moral life of schools*. Albany: State University of New York Press.

Noddings, N. (1984). *Caring: A feminine approach to ethics and moral education*. Berkeley: University of California Press.

Scott, J. (1990) *Domination and the arts of resistance*. New Haven: Yale University Press.

PERSPECTIVE 8: ETHICS, METHODOLOGY, AND DEMOCRACY ON THE RAUDENBUSH ET AL. STUDY

KENNETH R. HOWE   *University of Colorado at Boulder*

Raudenbush et al.'s study is markedly "quantitative" in its methods. It is like Carr et al.'s study in this respect, but even more so. But unlike Carr et al.'s study, it investigates ways of advancing what it conceives (implicitly) to be a positive behavior—"higher order thinking skills"—rather than ways of mitigating or eliminating what it conceives to be a negative one—"problem behavior." It is also unlike Carr et al.'s study in being correlational rather than experimental. That is, it is not a trial of a given intervention vis à vis the teaching of higher order thinking skills, but an investigation of the factors associated with teaching higher order thinking skills as things stand (or stood in 1993) in U.S. schools.

Simply by virtue of its heavy reliance on quantitative methods, Raudenbush et al.'s study is likely to be charged with being "technocratic" (or "positivistic"). But, as in the case of Carr et al., such a charge is too simplistic. I probably can't emphasize too much that the use of quantitative methods does not per se equate with positivism and the technical control that goes with it (e.g., Howe, 1985; 1988; 2003). Otherwise, any appeal to statistical patterns of inequality in, say, income or achievement, in a critique of schooling would render it positivistic. But such statistical patterns are commonly the starting point for the *anti*-positivist critiques provided by critical theorists.

To say that Raudenbush et al.'s study is not positivistic simply in virtue of employing quantitative methods, is not to say that it is not positivistic for other, more fundamental reasons. Three features of their study deserve examination in this regard: (1) their framing of the study in terms of the technical (or *etic*) notion of "higher order thinking;" (2) their failure to engage in dialogue with "stakeholders"; and (3) their marked silence on the moral-political dimensions of their research.

"Higher order thinking" is implicitly taken to be a goal by Raudenbush et al. to which schooling should aspire, for all children. The problem here is that it may very well be a biased conception of what good, intelligent, etc., thinking is. Given the emphasis on "problem solving," it might be an inherently *instrumentalist* conception, which teaches children not to question *ends* but only to find clever *means* for reaching them. Related to this problem, "higher order thinking" might be biased toward a western male perspective. For example, some researchers have argued that girls and women tend toward "connected knowing" in contrast to the "separate knowing" exemplified by boys and men (e.g., Belenky et al., 1986). Others have argued that various cultural groups may be distinguished in similar ways (e.g., as Heath does in the study that is the focus of my next commentary). What is "higher" versus "lower" is thus debatable.

Whether, or the degree to which, "higher order thinking" is indeed biased I cannot pursue further here. It is a potential threat, however, to Raudenbush et al.'s study, one that finds its roots in the positivistic practice of applying a technical—but inherently value-laden—language to social practices without checking it against the language of social reality embedded in such practices. This potential threat could have been reduced if Raudenbush et al. had engaged in dialogue with the multiple "stakeholders." But they didn't do this. They limited their interaction to the kind of "passive inclusion" (described in my general remarks) associated with researcher-designed survey instruments.

These features of Raudenbush et al.'s study are certainly limitations, and perhaps they should have been acknowledged as such in some way. But these features are far from what is required, however, to condemn this research as just one more instance of technocratic hegemony. "Higher order thinking" might very well be a biased, perhaps dangerous, notion. But it is still preferable to an exclusive focus on the "basics" and the associated curriculum and instructional methods that go with this.

Furthermore, Raudenbush et al. join a general conversation about stratification of various kinds in public education and examine some of its most important elements. Their finding that things such as curricular arrangements and tracking schemes prompt teachers to attend to higher order thinking skills much more than teacher training or experience do is certainly an important one. This suggests that it is the structure of schools that must be changed, more than teacher training. Such a finding with which critical theorists, for example, should nod in agreement. Their finding that testing/accountability schemes do not compromise teacher attention to higher order thinking skills, but increase it, is another important finding. Critical theorists might very well nod in agreement with this finding as well. It can be interpreted to mean that "higher order thinking skills" have found their way into testing/accountability schemes merely to put teachers under the thumb of technical control in another way.

My general point here is that Raudenbush et al.'s study cannot be pigeon holed as "technocratic-positivistic." Any research is going to have limitations, including presupposing certain values and value-laden concepts without the input of "stakeholders." This is especially true of the kind of wide-ranging policy research of which Raudenbush et al.'s study is an instance. But there is a "looseness of fit" between research methodology and larger research aims (Howe, 2003). Although not an example of the "democratic" approach to educational research in it's conduct, Raudenbush et al.'s study provides grist for democratic deliberation about schooling in the larger conversation.

This brings me to the third important feature of Raudenbush et al.'s study: its marked silence on moral-political issues and apparent embrace of the positivistic fact/value dichotomy. Raudenbush et al. clearly seem to be committed to the goodness of "higher order thinking" as well as the badness of reserving them for higher track students. But they don't explicitly express these value commitments anywhere.

There are at least two reasons Raudenbush et al. might have for this reticence. The first is *moral-epistemological*. This reason is associated with positivism's *non-cognitivist* view of values, the view that values are not subject to rational examination, are wholly "subjective," etc. Values are taken off of the table in educational research as beyond its purview. Educational research must therefore be wholly "technocratic." This is a view I dismissed in my general remarks, and have nothing to add here.

The second reason for reticence is *strategic*. Here educational researchers mute the moral and political dimensions of research not because they are positivists, but because they believe this is the best way to have an influence, including avoiding the charge of "bias." Raudenbush et al.'s reason for silence might very well be strategic. In the absence of evidence to the contrary, this is the interpretation of their view that the "principle of charity" demands.

However much the need to participate in strategic calculation amounts to playing by the rules of a corrupt game, and however much it might be used to rationalize away the need to confront difficult situations, it is a problem that educational researchers operating in the real world must face. It is a version of the fundamental question for educational researchers of how they ought to conduct themselves, ethically, in their role as educational researchers. It is altogether possible that it might be answered differently—and defensibly so—by different researchers.

REFERENCES

Belenky, M. F., Clinchy, B., Goldberger, N. R., & Tarule, J. M. (1986). *Women's ways of knowing.* New York: Basic Books.

Howe, K. (1985). Two dogmas of educational research. *Educational Researcher, 14*(8), 10–18.

Howe, K. (1988). Against the quantitative-qualitative incompatibility thesis (or dogmas die hard). *Educational Researcher, 17*(8), 10–16.

Howe, K. (2003). *Closing methodological divides: Toward democratic educational research.* Dordrecht, The Netherlands: Kluwer.

PERSPECTIVE 9: POSTSTRUCTURALISM ON THE RAUDENBUSH ET AL. STUDY

LYNDA STONE   *University of North Carolina at Chapel Hill*

Jean-François Lyotard (1924–1998). Relatively recently deceased, Lyotard was a philosopher known for his political activism and writing, and for extending the written form and content of philosophy. He began a life of engaged politics early on and later concentrated on scholarly work. In the English-speaking world he is best known for describing the postmodern condition; less known are his important writings on arts and ethics. Playing a key role in the 1968 revolt, he taught at Nanterre and for a lengthy period at the University of Paris VIII at Vincenne/Saint-Denis. He was associated with several American universities, most notably the University of California, Urvine.

The extensive, multivariate study of teachers' higher order instructional goals from Raudenbush, Rowan, and Cheong presents the best of contemporary yet traditional educational science. This carefully crafted study of secondary teachers in math, science, social studies, and English in 16 schools reveals the powerful effects of tracking as well as teacher preparation and organizational norms. One believes the study results and, even with some categorical variation, that they are generalizable. Moreover, the authors reveal harm: a premise of the study "rejects the contention that higher-order objectives are less appropriate for low-track classes or more elementary classes than for high-track classes or more advanced classes. However . . . [the study] provides quite strong evidence that a diverse set of secondary . . . teachers disagree" (p. 223). The authors conclude from their research: "to promote higher-order instruction for all students . . . reforms must apparently challenge widely held conceptions of teaching and learning" (p. 224). The study, one notes, is itself based in alternative explanations for the present state of tracked secondary classrooms that include insights from critical theorists and behaviorists and, as well, incorporates a self-critique internal to research processes and results.

Overall, given today's wide acceptance of the normative character of education and of research for reform, Raudenbush, Rowan, and Cheong make an important contribution. Indeed, an initiating point is that the authors use "modern science" for laudable aims and are to be congratulated. However, modern science is itself questionable from a postmodern perspective. Jean-François Lyotard's work presents a significant poststructuralist viewpoint from which to pose such critique. Initially an activist, Lyotard's project always has political and ethical aims. It also takes up aesthetics as a principal focus in writings although this focus is not generally familiar to educational theorists (see treatments of Lyotard in Dhillon and Standish [2000] and therein Stone [2000]). That domain, as others of sense-making, becomes manifest for Lyotard as "discursive form"; one central aesthetic characteristic is the sublime. As well, an unpresentable relation always operates.

Lyotard's famous *Postmodern Condition* (1979/1984) begins by distinguishing "modern" and "postmodern." He writes,

> I will use the term *modern* to designate any science that legitimates itself with reference to a metadiscourse . . . [making] an explicit appeal to some grand narrative. . . . For example, the rule of consensus between sender and addressee of a statement of truth-value is deemed acceptable if it is cast in terms of a possible unanimity between rational minds: this is the Enlightenment narrative, in which the hero of knowledge works toward a good ethico-political end. . . . Simplifying to the extreme, I define *postmodern* as incredulity toward metanarratives. (pp. xxiii–xxiv)

Science, for Lyotard (1985/1993), is an exemplar but the postmodern extends to all forms of social life, to all "expressions of thought: in art, in literature, philosophy, politics" (p. 79). It is a "condition": "The perspective then opens onto a vast landscape, in the sense that there is no longer any horizon of universality, universalization, or general emancipation" (p. 76). It is a rupture, an opposing movement (p. 77).

Following the linguistic turn, Lyotard (1979/1984) posits that "scientific knowledge is a kind of discourse" (p. 3). Indeed a specific discursive form is manifest in rhetorical presentation from Raudenbush, Rowan, and Cheong: publication in a most reputable journal, structure of argument that includes previous research, as well as explanations and hypotheses, research design and descriptive characteristics of data, statistical treatments and effects, discussion, and implications.

Adapting the idea of a "language game" from Wittgenstein, Lyotard locates modern science as a kind of knowledge and learning, as one game only. For him, "knowledge in general cannot be reduced to science, not even to learning" (Lyotard, 1979/1984, p. 18). It is more than learning; that is in declaring a "set of statements which . . . denote or describe objects and may be declared true or false" (p. 18). Knowledge relates to competence in performance. Here is Lyotard again: "[Knowledge] makes 'good' performances in relation to a variety of objects . . . to be decided upon, evaluated, transformed" (ibid.). Good performance conforms to what is accepted in the "social circle" of the knower. Here the circle is vast: modern, western, based in metaphysics, and in sought after metanarratives.

Thus far in a Lyotardian idiom, science is a discourse, a language game of rules for the good performance of statements about objects that, along with knowers, are in the world. However a problem exists that Lyotard names as "legitimation." His position is that embedded in the post-modern condition, with its distrust of the historical relations of knowledge and power and with them philosophy itself, science needs new legitimation. Educational philosopher Michael Peters (1995) explains that the distrust is of inquiry that "[purports] to justify certain practices or institutions by grounding them upon a set of transcendental, ahistorical, or universal principles" (p. 29). To be clear here, the problem is that modern science is not legitimate unless it can base its "generalizable" claims on a separate narrative—the "absolutes" of nature, God, mathematics, and the like. The question for science is this: "How do we know this to be true for all (most, similar) objects, entities, states of affairs?"

The "conclusion" within late and postmodern science is that there is no base, no external framework, no such justification. From philosophy this is primarily from calling into question a correspondence theory of truth: there is no way to guarantee that appearance is reality, that scientific results map onto an actual identical world. Initiating ideas have been theoryladenness of observation from N. R. Hanson; denial of the fact-value distinction from Willard Quine; and of course documentation of historic paradigm shifts from Thomas Kuhn (see Hanson, 1958; Quine, 1961; Kuhn, 1970).

Lyotard's description of the postmodern condition has significant implication for today's educational science. This comes in his theory of how postmodern language works. Giving up large narratives, there are only little, local ones whose rules and utterances are always moving and changing. These narratives are analogous to language games. Of them, commentator Bill Readings (1991) writes that they are "singular," and as such "each language-act carries with it a series of pragmatic utterances . . . [and implied rules] that evokes indeterminate judgment" (p. xxxii). This means that science and by extension social science is indeterminate. Lyotard (1979/1984) writes, "social pragmatics . . . is a monster formed by the interweaving of various networks of heteromorphous classes of utterances" (p. 65). Social science, and educational science, can neither determine "metaprescriptives" across language games nor form consensus within a community of inquirers. From Lyotard, the study from Raudenbush and colleagues is useful but its utility, as all inquiry is local, is particular and short-lived.

REFERENCES

Dhillon, P., & Standish, P. (Ed.). (2000). *Lyotard: Just education.* London: Routledge.

Hanson, N. (1958). *Patterns of discovery: An inquiry into the conceptual foundations of science.* Cambridge: University Press.

Kuhn, T. (1970). *The structure of scientific revolutions* (2nd ed.). Chicago: The University of Chicago Press.

Lyotard, J. (1984). *The postmodern condition: A report on knowledge* (G. Bennington & B. Masumi, Trans.). Minneapolis: University of Minnesota Press. (Original work published in 1979)

Lyotard, J. (1993). *The postmodern explained: Correspondence 1982–1985* (D. Barry, B. Maher, J. Pefanis, V. Spate, & M. Thomas, Trans). Minneapolis: University of Minnesota Press. (Original work published 1985)

Peters, M. (1995). Legitimation problems: Knowledge and education in the postmodern condition. In M. Peters (Ed.), *Education and the postmodern condition*, (pp. 21–39). Westport, CT: Bergin & Garvey.

Quine, W. (1961). *From a logical point of view: Nine logico-philosophical essays* (2nd ed.). Cambridge: Harvard University Press.

Readings, B. (1991). *Introducing Lyotard: Art and politics.* London: Routledge.

Stone, L. (2000). Exploring "Lyotard's Women": The unpresentable, ambivalence, and feminist possibility. In P. Dhillon and P. Standish (Eds.). *Lyotard: Just education* (pp. 177–193). London: Routledge.

CHAPTER 9

The Ellis Study

"THERE ARE SURVIVORS": TELLING A STORY OF SUDDEN DEATH

CAROLYN ELLIS

University of South Florida

This article is a personal narrative of a family drama enacted in the aftermath of my brother's death in an airplane crash. "True" stories such as this fit in the space between fiction and social science, joining ethnographic and literary writing, and autobiographical and sociological understanding. My goal is to reposition readers vis a vis authors of texts of social science by acknowledging potential for optional readings and encouraging readers to "experience an experience" that can reveal not only how it was for me, but how it could be or once was for them. This experimental form permits researchers and readers to acknowledge and give voice to their own emotional experiences and encourages ethnographic subjects (co-authors) to reclaim and write their own lives.

I grew up in a small town of three thousand people located in the foothills of Virginia, the same place my parents were born and raised. After attending elementary school in one-room school houses, both parents took wage-labor jobs. My mother sewed pockets on pants; my father worked on a farm and then pumped gas. After marriage, my father started a small construction business. Although he never grasped the "abstractions" of a calculator, he could intuitively figure out how much a new house or an addition would cost instantly. As the office manager, my mother organized the business and kept the books, although she never fully understood how taxes worked or how spread sheets were balanced. By the end of the booming 1960s, their construction business was considered the best in the area, and we went from near poverty level to being able to afford many of the luxuries of life. Still we lived similarly to

the working-class families that surrounded us—we bought the same things, only more and newer models, and our talk and stories were about close-to-home events, day-to-day joys, and real-life tragedies.

Art, my oldest sibling, was born in 1937. Thirteen years older than I, he was more like a caring and dependable uncle than a brother. Judy weighed only three pounds when she was born in 1948. She seemed fragile as a child and was easily moved to tears. I saw her sensitivity as both her most outstanding characteristic and her most problematic one. She and I slept in the same room and argued constantly about when to turn out the light, who had worn the other's clothes without asking, and whose turn it was to dry the dishes. Coping with a younger, competitive, and less sensitive sister who made top grades and was a better athlete than she could not have been easy. I was born in 1950, then Rex in 1952.

Rex and I had an intense and complex relationship as children. He and I fought almost everyday, but in contrast to my constant verbal irritation with my sister, our fights were physical and short-lived. I sat on top of him, holding his arms spread-eagle above his head. He squirmed as my face drew nearer and I threatened him with spittle dangling from my lips, sucking it in just before it escaped. Although he threatened all kinds of retribution, we ended most episodes laughing. He could have gotten me back during adolescence. But he didn't. All he ever did was win in arm wrestling a few times, just to show me.

Then I tried to outwit him. Often, I "borrowed" his bike when he wasn't looking. My parents didn't think a girl needed to have one. Finally, in exasperation, Rex secured his bike with a lock. That worked fine, until I discovered the lock not completely fastened one day, and I rode off for the afternoon. I convinced Rex I had picked the lock, and he never used it again. When he offered to let me borrow the bike occasionally after that, I stopped stealing it.

I had more academic smarts than Rex, but it never seemed to bother him. Although he followed me by two years in school, he managed to stand out, sometimes as an athlete, a jokester, or musician. People loved his common-sense approach to life, his charm, good nature, and seemingly unselfconscious ability to have fun no matter what.

Rex cared about me. I knew because I tested him. I used to wash my hair over a wash basin in the bathroom. Once when he came into the room, I held perfectly still, my head listlessly in the water, and didn't respond to his conversation. When he peered under my hair to see if I was breathing, I opened my eyes and said, "Boo." I never let on I knew he thought I was dead. I felt sorry when I saw his worried expression and never did anything like that again.

I remember when Rex accidentally blackened my eye with a baseball bat. He cried when he saw he had hurt me. I knew I cared about him then too, because I made sure my mother understood it had been an accident so she wouldn't punish him, and I felt worse about his crying about hurting me than I did about my black eye.

Once I even risked a spanking for refusing to find a switch for my father who, in a moment of anguish, wanted to spank Rex for swimming in a pond in the middle of winter. Rex and I could count on protection from each other.

THE CRASH

In 1982, at the age of 29, Rex was killed on his way to visit me in Florida. He was a passenger on board the Air Florida plane that crashed into the Potomac River on take off from Washington National Airport. The story I tell here describes the aftermath of the crash as my family and friends in Luray, the town where I was born and where Rex lived, react to and cope with this unanticipated tragedy.

· · · · · · ·

As adults, Rex and I had become great friends. The last time I had seen him, at my parents' home at Christmas a few

weeks before, he and I had spent only a few minutes together settling up for my parents' gifts and planning his trip to Tampa.

"I like it when you pick out the gifts," he had said. "Let's do this again next year. I can't wait to see you in Tampa."

"Yeah," I replied. "I'll get your airplane ticket. I know how to get the best rates."

"I tell all my friends you're a professor," Rex said proudly. "It'll be fun to come to your class." Suddenly, I feel nervous about being evaluated by my brother.

Rex was scheduled to arrive today, Friday, January 13, 1982. Although I was supposed to meet him at 4:30, his plane was just ready for take off from Washington when I called the airline at 3:45. Since I had invited several friends to dinner, I was glad for the extra time.

"Hey, what you doing?" my older brother, Art, asks when I pick up the ringing phone. I am surprised to hear from him, and, in spite of the lightness of his words, detect worry in his voice. Rather quickly, he asks, "Has Rex gotten there yet?"

"No, his plane has been delayed. Why?" Already I feel alarmed.

"Oh, someone called Mom and said a plane had crashed, and she thought they said something about Tampa. I just want to reassure her that Rex is okay. You know how she worries."

Although he says this nonchalantly, I tense up because I feel how hard he is working to normalize this conversation. Then I speak from inside a numb fog, "Where did they say the plane was headed?"

"Well, she thought they said it was coming from Tampa to Washington."

"Then that can't be it," I respond too quickly, adrenalin now starting to pump. We breathe.

Into the silence my brother says, "But there was confusion because they said it was Flight 90."

"That's his flight number, but Mom probably just got the number wrong." Yes, that's the explanation, I assure myself.

"No," he says. "I just heard the number myself on the radio."

"Did they say Air Florida?"

"I don't know, just that it had crashed into the Potomac."

"Oh, God, I'll call the airline and call you right back."

Flashes of lightening go off behind my eyes. My breathing speeds up, yet I am suffocating. As I dial, my hands shake, and I say aloud over and over, "No, please, God." Struck by the triviality of my everyday concerns, I remember how rushed I had felt getting ready for Rex's arrival and how important that had seemed. Now, if he is only alive, nothing else will matter. Of course he is, I admonish myself. Calm down. Mom has this all messed up. But then how did Art hear the same flight number?

I get a busy signal a couple of times before an Air Florida agent responds, "Air Florida, may I help you?"

The familiar greeting comforts me. See, there's nothing wrong, I reassure myself. "Yes, I want information on an arrival time."

"Certainly. What is the flight number?" he asks cheerfully.

"Flight 90."

Now his voice takes on a business-like quality as he quickly replies, "We cannot give out information on that flight."

"What do you mean you can't give out information on that flight?"

"We can't give out information on that flight," he repeats.

My heart pounds, as I calmly ask, "Did an Air Florida plane crash today?"

"Yes."

"Was it going from Washington to Tampa?"

"Yes," he says, seeming relieved to answer my questions.

"How many flights do you have going from Washington to Tampa today?"

"Two."

"When were they scheduled?"

"One this morning. One this afternoon."

"Did the one this morning make it?"

"Yes."

"Thank you very much," I say softly and hang up the phone, my heart pounding.

Art answers on the first ring. "There was a crash," I say. "And it sounds like it was Rex's plane."

"They are saying now there are survivors," says my brother, and I feel hope. He continues, "I'm going to Mom and Dad's. They're pretty upset. They're going to be more upset."

"Okay, yes, go. We'll keep in touch."

Now I am alone, in shock, adrenalin rushing through my body. Numb on the outside, my insides are over-stimulated. I tumble slowly through blank space. "Please, God, no," I hear myself moaning deeply from my gut. I move quickly to turn on the television. "Flight 90 crashes," it rings in my ears. "There are survivors in the water being rescued. Look, another head." This is not a movie, or an instant replay. I sit, my arms wrapped around my body, and sway back and forth twelve inches from the TV, breathing deeply and groaning. My eyes are glued to the rescue of the victims from the Potomac, and I search frantically for Rex. "He has to be there," I say out loud. In a daze, I am conscious of myself

watching the TV as part of the scene. Reality becomes hazy, and more multi-layered and boundary-less than usual.

A car approaches and I know from the familiar sound that it is Gene, my partner, and Beth, his daughter, home from shopping. When I rush to the door, the fog lifts suddenly and the slow motion scene I am in slips into fast forward. "What's wrong, honey?" Gene asks as he steps through the door, drops his packages to the floor, and embraces me.

Quietly and desperately, I say, "My brother's plane crashed."

"Oh, my God," he says calmly. Do something, I want to yell. Make it okay. But I say nothing. His body quivers; his embrace tightens. It feels good to be held and to have told someone. Not just someone. Gene, my anchor. He will know what to do and how to think about what has happened. My body slumps against his. "Oh, my God," he says again.

"It doesn't seem real," I say.

"Death never does," he replies. "But it is." Death? Why is he talking about death? It's just a crash. I cry quietly.

Then like a shot, I remember, "The TV. I've got to get back to the TV. There are survivors," and I break free from his embrace. That's right, he doesn't know there are survivors. That's why he's talking about death. "I'll see Rex being pulled from the river," I say loudly, fists clinched in the air. "Then I'll know he's all right. He had to make it. He's tough. There are survivors," I repeat.

Beth and Gene don't watch the instant replays of the people floundering in the icy water. Why do they sit silently at the kitchen table? They should be helping me look for Rex. They must not believe me. But they don't know him like I do. He can get himself out of anything. Any minute his head will appear. I continue rocking back and forth with my hands clasped together, periodically putting my face against the television screen to get a closer view. But I cannot find my brother in the Monet-like dots and lines. Hope and desperation alternate—hope when a new survivor is sighted, desperation when it is not Rex. There must be more survivors. "Rex, pop up out of the fucking water," I scream.

The announcers talk about the hero who just died saving others. "That must be Rex," I say, feeling proud. "He would do that. That's what he was like." Was? Why am I using the past tense. "He's not dead," I say. "I know he isn't." But if he has to be dead, I want him to be the hero. But then I will be angry that he could have saved himself and didn't. Why aren't Gene and Beth responding to me? They sit, silent, sad, watching me. He's not dead. Quit acting like he's dead. Of course, he's not dead. Not my brother.

Nancy, a friend who was coming to dinner, has heard about the plane crash and calls to give me up-to-date newscasts from her cable channels. Her calls distract me from watching what are now the same instant replays of the same people being pulled out of the same river. Twelve people have survived. Then they announce seven. Then there are five. And one dead hero.

Even I can see that there is no reason now to chain myself to the TV. Instead, I pace and chatter, "Okay, let's see. He has five chances out of seventy-nine, the number of people on the plane. That's about 1/16th possibility that he survived. Not much. But they think all the survivors were sitting in the tail section. He was, I mean is, a smoker. So he was probably in the rear, which makes his chances even greater. But then they think one of the survivors was a stewardess, so his chances are four out of seventy-eight." When all else fails, try probability. Gene and Beth stare at me, still without speaking. When I break down, Gene comes to hold me. But soon I am up, moving around, calculating frantically, like a mad woman.

It is announced on TV that relatives who are waiting at Tampa International Airport have been taken to a special room. They suggest that other relatives come there for up-to-date information and counseling. "Do you want to go?" asks Gene. "I'll take you."

My impulse to go is short-lived. "No, what good will it do? We're getting current information here. Why do I want to be around other upset people I don't know? What can counseling do? I want to be here with you, and where I can talk to Art."

Every half hour, I am on the phone with Art. It takes at least 10 attempts to get through the busy circuits. The Tampa-Virginia lines are being overworked by all the grieving people soothing each other, seeking information, and refusing to believe their worst fears are true. Just like us.

Art is with our parents, who, he says, "are a disaster." The news is spreading through Luray, and the phone is constantly busy with people who want to know "Is it true?" and "What's the latest?"

My brother and I do not break down as we share information, of which there is practically none, and what is available keeps getting worse. And worse. Our spirits drop every time we talk, "but I still have hope," I say. "I know he's alive."

Art replies, "It doesn't look good, Susie (his pet name for me)." Not him too. It's not like him to give up. I hide my anger, and an inner voice says, He's probably right. Get yourself ready for this. No, no, other voices scream, and I listen to them instead.

Sometimes I feel like laughing when I survey this horrible, surreal scene, that plays as a TV suspense show. Then I

switch from being an observer to being a participant in the tragedy, and I sob.

"Call the people we have invited to dinner and cancel," I instruct Gene, who wants to help. "I don't want to talk to anyone."

Each time I hear him say, "Carolyn's brother's plane has crashed. It doesn't look good," I cry anew. Glad for the felt sympathy, I also am distressed when Gene's words give reality to the experience.

When I finally plop down, exhausted, at the table with Gene and Beth, we stare silently, and nervous giggles alternate with my sobs and Gene's comforting touches. "Eat something," Gene commands. "You must eat." Is he kidding? I will throw up if I eat, but suddenly I have a craving for the warm, strong taste of Scotch, which I seldom drink. From that day on, every time I experience severe stress I will want Scotch.

"I feel like getting out, going to the mall," Beth says. "I'm not doing anything useful. But I'll stay if you want me to."

"No, go have a good time," I respond, appreciating her concern. Feeling closer to Gene when we are alone, I tell him I am glad he is with me.

Gene takes a rational approach, "What can you do? It's done now."

"I just know he's alive," I insist.

I speak of my parents and the agony they must be going through. I think of the difficulty of Art's position. "I am glad I'm not there. But I feel I ought to be there. I wish I were there." My confused thoughts mix with each other in slow motion. Finally I put the big pot of Mexican stew I have made into the freezer. A few weeks later, I will throw it out.

Beth brings us two cat humor books. "We need some laughter," she explains. When she and Gene read aloud and laugh, I smile but don't hear.

"We are sitting around looking at each other, too," Art says when he calls at 10 p. m. "The airline will let me know when it's official."

"Why are you assuming he's dead?" I ask.

"Because Bev [our cousin] went to the Marriott Hotel in Washington where they announced the list of survivors. He wasn't on there, Susie," he says reverently. Did I hear him right? It is hard to hear from inside the fog, with my heart beating so loudly.

"I don't care," I say after a pause, defiantly. "I won't give up hope."

"I don't think there's any hope left," Art says even more softly, and this time I know he's right. I feel closer to him than ever in my life, and understand that he needs me to face reality and help him carry the burden.

I try. "Yeah, I guess you're right. What do we do now? Have you told Mom and Dad?"

"No. I want to wait until I get the official word." I wonder why. But I know. He wants to put it off as long as possible. And he hopes for a miracle, just like I do.

"Okay, I understand," I say, to be supportive of his decision.

Art and I talk several times the next few hours, and decide to call Judy, our sister, the next morning. "Why put her through a night of agony?" I rationalize, without acknowledging that I do not want to experience her shock of grief now, which will be raw and unmonitored. Art agrees quickly, and then we make other decisions together. We express our love for each other for the first time. Sharing our brother's death brings us closer and makes us aware of what we usually don't say.

I decide to wait a day before going home. "I need to be with you right now," I say to Gene. "When I get home I'll have to be together. I need to collapse and feel your love." In spite of Gene's chronic emphysema, he seems strong and glad to help me. When he offers to come with me, I say, "I'd love it, but it's too hard for you."

During the night, Gene's tight embrace and burly chest, barrel-shaped from the steroids he takes to combat his emphysema, comfort me each time I cry. We make love in the night, quietly, softly, for the attachment.

When the phone rings at three a. m., I jump, still hoping for good news. I am angry, feel sorry for myself, and cry again after I figure out that it is an obscene phone call.

Art calls early the next morning, and says Air Florida finally called at three a. m. to tell us officially that Rex was dead. "It's been horrible," he says. "I lay awake all night waiting for the call I knew would come. Mom and Dad were full of hope. At three, Dad came in and woke me—I must have dozed off—and said, 'It's the phone.' I had instructed the officials to talk to no one but me, and I couldn't believe I hadn't heard the phone. I answered knowing what they would say. Mom and Dad stood around me like little kids waiting for the news. They knew by my voice. Everyone started sobbing. Then Aunt Florence came into the room and said, 'He's dead, ain't he?' We all cried together."

Sorry not to have shared that moment, I crave attachment with my family, and even with the pain—I want to feel as much pain as I can. Rex is worth my suffering. At the same time, I am glad to be with Gene who comforts me.

I am relieved when Art says, "I called Judy." Does my relief come from not wanting to take care of her? From the lack of closeness that has characterized our relationship from early on? Or because I now do not have to be the bearer of such news?

"How did she take it?" What a ridiculous question.

"She started sobbing and couldn't talk. Her husband got on the phone."

"I'll call her now," I tell my brother. "We'll make plans to come to Luray tonight. I need today."

"I understand," he says.

"Hang in there, little brother," I say, using my pet name, and then realize that he is now my only living brother. "I'll be there soon. Then you can lean on me. I know you're holding everyone together." My words feel forced, and I am not sure I will have the strength.

"Thanks," he says. "It'll be good to have you here."

By the time I call my sister, I am numb. Interspersed with sobs is talk of her belief in God. I am glad she has it, but I don't want to hear it now. We make airline reservations for later that day, managing to connect on the same plane from Atlanta to Washington.

A newspaper reporter calls, identifying himself as a Washington correspondent. Thinking this is an official, I answer irrelevant questions: "When did you last see your brother?" "What was he like?" "He was wonderful, just wonderful." What else could I say? "I can't talk anymore." The reporter doesn't press. "How dare they," I say to Gene as I hang up, and then wish I had said more. Rex would have liked to be in the *Washington Post*.

When some of my colleagues arrive with food, I am still in my housecoat and have not combed my hair or brushed my teeth. Aware that my robe sometimes exposes the curve of my breast, I listlessly pull the sash tighter several times. Finally, I say, "Oh, what difference does it make anyway?" and let it hang. Nothing is sexual now. I have two Scotches, but I can't eat. No one speaks of my brother. I am glad they came.

Because of weather conditions, my plane is late taking off. My brother was just killed in this icy weather—I must be crazy to get on a plane. But I have no options. I take a deep breath and walk past the smiling stewardess. How could she be the same as always? On take-off, I pretend to be my brother and the plane is crashing and I imagine what it must have been like for him. Eyes closed, I feel the plane diving, then the smack as it hits the water. Then darkness. God, I hope he didn't know what was happening.

My sister's flight is even later than mine. When I get nervous waiting for her at the departure gate in Atlanta, I run to her gate and ask the arrival time. "It should be here in a few minutes," the woman says nonchalantly.

"My brother was killed on the Air Florida flight yesterday. I am connecting with my sister here to go home." Suddenly I have her attention.

"Oh, my, well, don't worry. If it doesn't come in a few minutes, we'll try to delay your departing flight." Hearing my words and seeing the attendant's concern make tears stream down my face. When people show compassion, I feel sorry for myself.

I am relieved to see my sister and her husband walk through the door. She is sobbing, and I am near tears as we embrace. Momentarily, my pain increases (or escapes) with hers. At the same time, I feel close to her, glad to be with family. We run to the departing flight, holding onto each other.

What will it be like to see my parents? I take a deep breath, my head swims, and I walk into the house. My Dad cries and holds on to me. Already in my caretaker role, I have no tears. My Mom's body is rigid in response to my hug. "It's going to be okay," I say. "We'll talk."

"It won't be okay," she says angrily. "He's dead. He's not coming back." I am silenced by the truth of her response.

I ignore the two local ministers I don't know and hug Barbara, my sister-in-law, who whispers into my ear, "They found his body."

"Thank God," I say, feeling great relief and then wonder why. "When?"

"They called an hour ago."

Art and I hug each other tightly. The atmosphere feels like death. When the town sheriff and the funeral director stop on their way to Washington to identify and bring back my brother's body, my mother sobs, "Bring my boy home." My grief for her then, and for myself, threatens to take me over. Afraid, I choke it down.

From Saturday evening until the funeral on Monday our house was filled with people. The only quiet time was at night when I would talk to Mom who lay on the couch in the living room. My father slept beside her in his lazy boy chair. Neither wanted to be in their separate bedrooms.

"Rex brought me a rose in a bud vase the week before he died," Mom says. "When I asked him what occasion it was for, he said, 'Because I love you.'"

Over and over, she describes the details of the last time she saw him. "He came in here, in this room, and asked me for a strap to tie around his suitcase. I can see him now kneeling on the floor and tying it on. Then he hugged me like he didn't want to let go. 'I don't know when I'll be back. Expect me when you see me,' he said."

"My life is over," she sobs, believing it and coming close to convincing me.

Every night I listened and asked the same questions so she could tell her story again. Besides, I liked picturing him

leaving on a trip and I wanted every detail of the last time she saw him. Maybe she would remember something new, provide a clue to Rex's death, something that would make it all make sense. Finally, when I venture, "I'm upset too," I get no comfort.

"A mother's pain is worse, the worst there is," she says bitterly, her self-absorption offering no place for my grief. In contrast, my father is warm and open in his sadness, receiving my love. We hug and cry silently together, feeling a lot but not saying much.

The only time I had for myself was when I showered. I love feeling the hot water run over my body. As I cried and relaxed, the pain would break through my numbness and a moan from deep in my being would escape. Amazed at the intensity of the pain, I pushed it down. I can't deal with you now. Would I ever be able to? I talked out loud to Rex, telling him how much I already missed him. "Rex, help me deal with this. Help me comfort Mom and Dad." It was a close, peaceful feeling.

"I am communicating with Rex," I tell my Mom, thinking she will like that I am being "religious," even though it doesn't fit into her Lutheran doctrine.

"What kind of religion do you have anyway? You can't talk to the dead," she replies, and I shrug.

The people came. Three to four hundred of them. They occupied my parents and validated for me how important Rex had been. I became the greeter, letting them in, hugging, listening to them marvel at how I had changed, and then directing them to my parents, who sat side-by-side in their lazy boy chairs. Offering their sympathies, men looked sad and stoically held my father's hand and kissed my mother. Women were more likely to cry openly with my mother and often with my father, sometimes falling in sobs into my parents' arms. Older people comforted, while the younger ones stammered about not knowing what to say. That would come with experience. My mother cried continually and my father wiped tears constantly. I was the dry-eyed director, who craved and feared collapsing into my parents' embrace.

Everyone came bearing food. The smell was sickening. Knowing exactly what to do, several community women took over our kitchen. They served big meals to whomever was there, ignoring that no one ate much. Later in the week, it would take hours to throw away all the uneaten food: green beans cooked with ham hock; whole Old Virginia hams—the real ones, salty, strong, and fat; green and red jell-o salads embedded with nuts and coconut, made in circular tins with globs of Miracle Whip filling the middle hole; apple pies made quickly from canned apples with dough crisscrossed on the top and too much cinnamon added; sweet pound cakes, chocolate layer cakes with chocolate icing, and yellow cakes with white frosting; big, fluffy white loaves of Wonder Bread; gallons of sweet tea in pickle jars that still tasted and smelled of pickles. Years later I would find containers of instant coffee—the family size—, Coffee Mate, and hundreds of plastic utensils still bundled in plastic wrappers in the cabinets.

Part of the role of greeter was to record who had brought what so that thank you cards could be sent. My sister and I took turns keeping records. Sometimes I wanted to scream, What a waste of time and energy. Other times I was glad for the task and respected the ritual of acknowledgment.

Mixed in with the mourners came the florists with the flowers we had requested not be sent. Donations for my parents' church also poured in. "What can we do?" everyone asked. Write some thank you notes, I wanted to say, but didn't. It was not their job. Then go help throw food away, I thought, but again, I said nothing. Proper etiquette dictated that you wait until people insisted—or, better yet, just did something. I had never been involved in a funeral before, but I intuitively knew the rules. They were an extension of the small-town etiquette that I had lived the first twenty-two years of my life.

I helped my mother make up a list of pallbearers. "They should be his best friends," she instructs. "It can't be relatives. They have to be men. There must be six." This is not the time to argue for women pallbearers. This is for my mother.

On Sunday I call the funeral director and ask to see Rex's body. Because the body had been in water and because Rex had a bad head injury, we wouldn't have an open casket funeral. "Do you want to go?" I hesitantly ask my mother.

"I just can't. But I wish I had his gold chain so you could put it on him. The one I gave him, that he always wore, that he was wearing the day he died."

"Why don't I put my gold chain around his neck? The one you gave me."

"Good," she says, smiling for the first time.

The funeral home. What a place. What a smell—intense flowers mixed with cologne, disinfectants, and just a hint of embalming fluid. It's the only context in which I hate the odor of flowers. I have trouble catching my breath as I enter. Yet I walk ahead of Art and Rex's ex-wife into the room containing the casket. I have to see him.

I stand close to the casket as the director opens it. I am not afraid of you. I love you. There he is. Is it him? I have to be sure. I know it is. I dare hope and know it is impossible that they have made a mistake. But it doesn't look like him.

His face is swollen and his nose, from being broken, is flatter and much bigger than usual. And that dead color doesn't help either. Then the huge gash on his forehead glares at me from underneath multi-layers of pasty make-up. I swallow, and it is MY head hitting the front seat as we crash.

He is shrouded in polyester, dead clothes complete with clip-on tie, an outfit that would have horrified him. I want to dress him in his own clothes. But my Mom has proudly announced she told the funeral director to put him in a new blue suit. No one else is going to see him. What difference does it make anyway?

Art stands frozen some distance behind me. In a short while, he leaves. Rex's ex-wife, who also is behind me, looks relieved when I ask if I can have time alone with Rex. I glide my hands over the hardness of his body, remembering his being and adding to my memory now his deadness. I caress his face lovingly and talk softly to him. "I'm going to miss you. I love you." Then I put my necklace around his neck and say, "This is for you. From Mom and me. We love you." And I walk away.

"Can you tell if he died in pain or fear?" I ask the funeral director.

"Not really," he replies. "When a person dies, the muscles relax." Later I realized he had to say that. Was he going to tell me that my brother had the look of utmost fear on his face?

"What is it like to bury friends?" I ask. My way of dealing now is to be the rational field worker. My brother's is to kid with the director as usual, even making dead people jokes.

Art and I felt as though we were in a conspiracy, directing this event, often from behind the scenes, to make sure things went as smoothly as possible. Whenever we could get away from rituals, we met in the hallway to plan and anticipate problems. I covered when Art was with the funeral director, or on the phone with callers—concerned friends, acquaintances, and business people who had heard the news and needed more information, and airlines officials. "The airlines are paying for the whole funeral," he tells me. "They told the funeral director to do whatever we wanted."

Even with the planning, we did not anticipate the effect seeing the flag-draped casket would have on my mother on Sunday night when our family went to the funeral home to receive friends. Silently, we walk through the bitter cold weather and into the funeral home. When my mother sees the casket, she screams, "My baby. Oh my baby is dead." She collapses to the floor, while the rest of us stand rooted to our spots. It is like a play rehearsal, and my mother has messed up her lines. In slow motion, we finally help her up and support her still sobbing to a chair. My once-powerful and imposing father looks helplessly on, confused, as someone approaches to remove his coat.

Several hundred people have come to pay respects. Art and I shake hands or hug each one, thank them for their expressions of sorrow, exchange light talk, smile, sometimes even laugh. "It is God's will." "God will look after him," they say to make us and themselves feel better. I nod. The same sentences are uttered over and over. It doesn't matter. There are no points for originality. We pass each person to the rest of the family seated behind us, the receivers of sympathy. Sometimes I want to be there too, to give in; other times I am glad for the numbing effects of being in control. There are hugs, quiet talk now, and sniffles. Sometimes sobs. Then they stare quickly at the closed casket, hands down and crossed in front, and sign the book. It is important to document that you came; the family should have a record, to know who and how many.

"How are you doing?" I ask Art, when there is a lull in the line. "Want a Valium? I had one. It helped. I feel calm and removed, like I am watching this on a movie screen." I want to be protected from my grief.

"No, I'm going to do it on my own," he responds, tightly under control and afraid to change anything.

I want this ritual to be over. Yet I want the people to keep coming, to share their grief with my parents, and to show their love for Rex. When it is done, Art and I say at the same time, "We made it through another one."

"The biggie is tomorrow," says my brother. No. The biggie comes after tomorrow when we both have to face the void of life without Rex.

The next day, Monday, is the funeral. We prepare a big lunch for the minister, relatives, and out-of-town guests. Again people eat little. The funeral parade leaves from our house. A town policeman, my eighth-grade boyfriend, holds up traffic so we can enter the main road. Now he stands, with rigid posture and hat held over his chest, crying openly. I wave and feel tears on my face and love for the small town in which I was raised. I take a deep breath and another Valium. Wonderful numbness settles over me. How I dread the funeral. The icy cold, windy weather seems appropriate now.

This time my brother holds onto my mother and I support my father as we enter the side door of the funeral home. My brother-in-law and sister take care of Aunt Florence, who has difficulty walking. The curtain is drawn before we approach the casket so that the crowd cannot see our grief. But it is impossible to keep it hidden. Mom screams when she sees the casket, and Art holds on tightly as she breaks

out into loud sobs. The rest of us cry softly, staring at the casket draped by the American flag, surrounded by the flowers that people weren't supposed to send. I am removed. This isn't what I want. I kiss the casket.

When the curtain is opened, I see that the funeral home is packed. I am glad that hundreds of people stand in the hall and outside in below zero weather, while others wait in their cars to go to the cemetery. Rex is here, watching with me, like Tom Sawyer. How he relishes all these people. You ham. You would have loved all the media coverage of your death. I smile. And just think, Rex, you lucky stiff, you will never have to suffer through the death of loved ones.

Although the music moves me, I shut it out. This is not the place to break down. My parents' minister makes some abstract statements about God's will and about Rex. I fight back the urge to stand up and ask the minister if I can please say something personal about my brother. I would say it like a Pentecostal minister and we'd all wail together. I want to get in touch with the spirit of my brother. Why is this minister who hardly knew Rex running the show? I sit silently, since I can't risk upsetting the ritual, or my parents. When the service is over, suddenly I jump from my seat and kiss two of Rex's close friends who are helping to remove the death flowers to the hearse. We cry openly then and I feel better.

The curtain is drawn again. The casket is removed by the six male pallbearers. The family is removed, led to their cars by the funeral director. Poof! Magically we will appear at the cemetery.

At the cemetery we are seated in front of the magic casket and the freshly-dug hole in the ground. When I see Rex's ex-wife standing near, I grab her hand, and bring her to sit with the family. I don't care if it is appropriate. Rex would want her here. My body shakes violently from the cold and wind, as she and I hold onto each other.

The service is brief, and meaningless. After the minister reads scripture, I kiss the casket. "I love you," I say, once again feeling tension between freedom of expression and ritualistic expectation. Even though I dread facing the silence at home, I want this to be over. When it is done, people chat as though they have just gotten out of a play.

Many people come home with us to have dinner. This time they eat heartily and talk, reaffirming kinship ties. I still have no appetite and I say little. As soon as they leave, my mother takes sick and does not have the strength to walk. We put her to bed on the couch and tip-toe around her. Next morning, when she can't stand up, the doctor puts her in the hospital, and says she is in severe shock.

My sister and I write hundreds of thank-you notes, and I am reminded of our childhood relationship when we argue once about who should do what. Then we try to make it better by both insisting on doing everything.

Rex's friends organize a party. "A better way to remember him," we say. But it isn't what we want either. We want Rex. Okay, the joke is over, Rex, come out of hiding. "If the boy would just send me a sign that he's okay, I would feel better," a friend says. "He left so suddenly." "Yeah, have a drink in Heaven and tell us how it is." But our gayness keeps switching back to serious talk. I have a Scotch, and my feeling breaks through, my sobs catching me by surprise. "I am tired of supporting everyone, including myself," I say to Rex's friends who gather around me. "I don't know why I feel I have to be so strong."

"You don't. Let go," I hear, and I feel a bond with the people who embrace me.

"Ah, help," my aunt Helen yells from the bedroom of Rex's house, where we have gone to check on his things. She points to the ripple of the bed, backs off, white, as though she has seen a ghost.

"It's okay. It's a water bed," I assure her. "See," I say, pushing down on the mattress. "It's not a ghost." The smile on my face feels alien.

We open some of Rex's drawers. What an invasion to be looking at another's personal items. "That's what Rex used to tickle his girlfriends," my brother says to my father, who is examining a dildo. My father smiles devilishly—I am glad the thought pleases him—and then he respectfully puts it back in its place. We close the drawers without disturbing anything else, pick up little mementos of Rex, and leave. I am relieved when Art says he will go through Rex's possessions later and sell everything at an auction.

During my last few days at home, I visited my mother often in the hospital. "I'm in shock," she says almost proudly from her quiet, withdrawn posture. Being sick showed how much Rex had meant to her; and for a while she didn't have to cope. "They say I can stay here as long as I want," she announces. "I don't want to go home and face what has happened. I feel safe in the hospital."

Now it would be happening, a few seconds after take off. There is the bridge it hit. Here is how his head snapped forward. Boom. I let my head fall into the seat in front of me. The vivid picture of the gash in Rex's head helps me reenact the scene.

When I see Gene at the Tampa airport, I fall into his arms, overwhelmed by my love and need for him. Then I shudder when I feel his frail body and hear his labored breathing, realizing that one day I will be experiencing his death, too. I hold onto him tightly. He and Rex have been the two most important people in my world.

Gene is totally devoted to me during the next few days and tries hard to ease my pain, but I can't cry or even talk about what I feel. "Let's go see *Ragtime* at the theater. It will get your mind off death," Gene says. When I see a casket in the movie, I recoil, and then cry until the end.

When I get home that night, I lie alone on the couch in the living room, unable to sleep. When I sense Rex's spirit, it scares me, and I retreat into the bedroom, clutching my pillow, to be with Gene.

That was the last time I would feel Rex's presence so strongly. I would always be sorry that I had not stayed on the couch that night. Maybe he had come to say good bye. Did that really happen?

• • • • • • •

I didn't dream about Rex until more than a year after he died. In the first of a series, we are children playing in my father's brown sand pile. Dump-truck mounds of fine, light-colored sand from waves at the points they blend into other heaps of the heavy, moist darker kind, better for building castles. All the neighborhood kids used to play "king of the mountain" in this basketball-court-sized playhouse. When we grew tired of that game, we played hide-and-go-seek, or "drove" our toy trucks that were filled with sand scooped with our pretend backhoes, fantasizing about my father's real trucks and loading equipment.

In the second dream, we are older. Although I don't remember the context—only a dark background highlighting the two of us—I am aware as I look at Rex that he is going to die. But he doesn't know it and acts as if nothing is wrong. I keep my awareness secret because I know Rex hates to be out of control.

In the third dream, I decide that there has been a mistake. Rex has not died. He just went away for a while. Now he is back and we are having a conversation. Overjoyed, I begin to tell him that I thought he had died. But I stop in mid-sentence because I feel confused, unsure of whether the accident happened or not. Then I decide the accident occurred, but Rex survived and has just been in the hospital for a while. Now he is well. Elated, I start to tell him again that I thought he died, and again I stop.

In the fourth dream, Rex is already dead, yet we are together. How can he be dead and not know it, I wonder. Maybe he isn't really dead. What am I going to do? I can't tell him. How can he possibly handle it? How can I? I begin to tell him how horrible I felt when I thought he had died in the crash. I wake up, realizing he is really dead.

Shortly after that, I finally tell Rex in a dream that he is dead. I awake screaming and crying, and I don't dream about him again for a long time. In my dreams, as in my life, there is no other ending.

BETWEEN FICTION AND SOCIAL SCIENCE

My "experimental ethnography" (Marcus and Fischer 1986) fits in the space between fiction and social science in the same fashion as other introspective, socioautobiographical (Zola 1982a) accounts of Broyard (1992), Butler and Rosenblum (1991), Ernaux (1991), Frank (1991), Haskell (1990), Lear (1980), Lerner (1978), Mairs (1989), Murphy (1987), Roth (1991), Yalom (1989), and Zola (1982a). "True" stories such as these join ethnographic and fictional writing, the personal and the social, autobiographical and sociological understanding, and literature and social science.

This story is an introspective case study in emotional sociology (Ellis 1991a; 1991b). Positioning myself reflexively as both narrator (author) and main character of the story, I assume that some experiences can be understood only when feelings are a significant part of the research process. This is true of epiphanies, like the one described here, that "leave marks on peoples' lives," and after which the person is never "quite the same" (Denzin 1989, p. 15).

In this article, I seek to connect lived experience to research in sociology of emotions, to engage readers in topics that usually are overlooked by social scientists, and to show a new form for representing these practices. I speak to those who have encountered emotionality associated with loss, and to those who would embrace a sociology that attempts to cope with emotional experiences that escape orthodox social science.

Although social scientists have written about disasters, their emphasis tends to be on the destruction of community (Bates, Fogelman, Parenton, Pittman, and Tracey 1963; Erikson 1976), community behavior during disasters (Dynes 1970, Wallace 1956), community social order (Wright, Rossi, Wright, and Weber-Burdin 1979), and community mental health crisis intervention (Frederick 1981; Tierney 1979). But in airplane crashes, unlike most natural disasters, there is no community for survivors or families of victims. Passengers are strangers who have come from many regions, and survivors disperse quickly after accidents (Frederick 1981).

Even where social scientists have studied response to this kind of anonymous sudden death, their emphasis has been on comparing fragments of experience, such as how families are notified (Caplan 1976), and on examining

generalized outcomes of experience between sudden and chronic death or between natural and violent deaths, such as the length and course of bereavement, or levels of emotional disturbance of survivors (Parkes and Weiss 1983). This work provides categorical knowledge of what takes place after families are informed of a sudden death, but readers learn little about how family dramas are enacted in the aftermath of such loss. Even work done on psychosocial effects of disaster tends to be based on coded interviews and quantitative data (Gleser, Green, and Winget 1981), with emphasis on "syndromes" and time-space models (Wallace 1956) instead of lived experience.

Research practices of orthodox social science do not encourage scholars to document these events in their own lives or even to talk about themselves (Krieger 1991). We are inhibited by the bias that WE study THEM, believing that somehow as sociologists we can escape the social processes that we so eagerly seek to categorize about others' lives (Ellis 1991b; Gouldner 1970). Thus few social scientists have dealt in their studies with the impact of death on their lives and work. An exception is Rosaldo's (1989) acknowledgment that in understanding his rage in response to his wife's sudden death he came to understand the rage expressed in the after-death ritual of Ilongot headhunting. Others such as Krieger (1991) mention that death of a family member inspired their studies.

As social scientists, we consider "after death" a sacred, private time when work and study are put aside, the emotional intensity of which is outside the purview of what we study (Ellis 1991b). We do not expect survivors to chronicle, reflect on, or analyze events as they occur in such epiphanies, nor to have an interpretive framework for making sense of their experiences (Denzin 1991). That they do try, however, is manifested in the private diaries and public memoirs that are written by people who have experienced death of loved ones. Mostly we learn about emotional reactions to death from these personal accounts (Lewis 1963; Lerner 1978), and from film (Sargent 1980), poetry and literature (Agee 1938). From these sources, it is clear that death is an event that changes the meaning of survivors' lives forever. Yet, it remains an experience about which social scientists do not know how to talk.

This article brings this kind of experience into the open, allowing us to converse about and try to understand it. As such it accomplishes what Rorty (1982) says we should expect from social scientists—"to act as interpreters for those with whom we are not sure how to talk" (see also Bourdieu and Wacquaint 1992, p. 206). This is, after all, what we. "hope for from our poets and dramatists and novelists" (Rorty 1982, p. 202). Shouldn't social scientists be able to address the problem so vividly described by C. S. Lewis (1963, p. 13) in his response to his wife's death?

> An odd by-product of my loss is that I'm aware of being an embarrassment to everyone I meet. At work, at the club, in the street, I see people, as they approach me, trying to make up their minds whether they'll 'say something about it' or not. I hate it if they do, and if they don't . . . Perhaps the bereaved ought to be isolated in special settlements like lepers.

WRITING AND READING THE STORY

> All autobiographic memory is true. It is up to the interpreter to discover in which sense, where, for which purpose.
>
> Passerini, quoted in Personal Narratives Group 1989

Writing this story is an attempt to see myself among others, as a case among cases, an instance that records a difficult passage of lived experience into verbal expressibility (Bochner and Ellis 1992; Geertz 1983; Scarry 1985). This project embodies what Jackson (1989) calls "radical empiricism" (after William James), a methodology in which "we make ourselves experimental subjects and treat our experiences as primary data" (p. 4).

My account of Rex's death tells a story that is possible, not one that is necessary. One way of knowing about others' intimate experiences is to reflect on our own. "We cannot live other people's lives," but we can "author" our own (Geertz 1986, p. 373). As social scientists, we will not know if others' intimate experiences are similar or different until we offer our own stories and pay attention to how others respond, just as we do in everyday life. The "truth" of this story then lies in the way it is told and the possibility that there are others in the world who resonate with this experience. Most likely, my story is unique enough to provide comparisons, yet universal enough to evoke identification.

As a thick description (Geertz 1973) of the lived experience of emotionality, this story includes dense and detailed narrative that shows what happened, and the intentions and meanings that unfold both during interaction and during my telling of the experience. To write it, I used a process of "emotional recall," similar to the "method" acting of Lee Strasberg at the Actors' Studio (Bruner 1986). To give a convincing and authentic performance, the actor relives in detail a situation in which she previously felt the emotion to be enacted. I placed myself back into situations, conjuring up details until I was immersed in the event emotionally. Because recall increases when the emotional content at the time of retrieval resembles that of the experience to be

retrieved (Bower 1981; Ellis and Weinstein 1986), this process stimulated the memory of more details. Since I wrote this story in 1985 soon after the death of my partner, Gene, when I was immersed again in the emotions of death, the emotional distance I had to travel to write was not extensive.

Although social scientists debate emotional (Isen 1984) and recall bias (Loftus, Smith, Klinger, and Fiedler 1992) in traditional social science, I do not see the need to be detached from this experience in order to convey its meanings nor do I distrust the vividness of my emotional memory. Although memory is fragmented, it seems to have "a simple order of succession . . . [which] "constitutes a kind of lasting chronicle, fixed in my memory, of the temporal course of my experience" (Crites 1971, p. 299).

When I put myself back into this emotional epiphany, I find most of the details of events experienced and words spoken nearly as clear as when I wrote them. Is what I describe here a partial account of the way this event "actually" happened? Or have my written words now taken on a reality greater than the event so that I cannot separate them from emotional recall or cognitive memory of what occurred? How much of what I write is interpreted from my present position? Since understanding is not embedded in the personal event as much as it is achieved through an ongoing and continuous "experiencing of the experience" (Ellis and Bochner 1992), perhaps it doesn't matter.

As an ethnographer I have worked from an "assumption of truth rather than an assumption of fiction" (Webster 1982), which means that I have not deliberately fabricated details and have limited myself to events I remember. Nevertheless, as a storyteller I am primarily concerned with evocation rather than "true representation" (Marcus 1986; Tyler 1986). In my text, "learning about" integrates emotional and cognitive dimensions, and emphasizes "participating with" rather than "describing for" the other (Bochner and Waugh, in press). Instead of privileging cognitive knowing and the "spectator theory of knowledge" in which knowing is equated exclusively with observing from a distance (Dewey 1980; Jackson 1989), this article incorporates feeling and participatory experience as dimensions of knowing.

I seek to reposition readers vis a vis the authors of texts of social science research, evoking feeling and identification as well as cognitive processing. As you read this story, some of you may have felt empathy with me, as you would in watching a "true-to-life" movie; some of you may have been reminded of parallels in your own lives, as in reading a good novel. Perhaps reading my work evoked in you emotional experience that you could then examine, or led to recall of other emotional situations in which you have participated.

Acknowledging a potential for optional readings gives readers license to take part in an experience that can reveal to them not only how it was for me (the author), but how it could be or once was for them (Ellis and Bochner 1992; Turner 1986).

I write this narrative as an example of a form that will permit researchers and readers to acknowledge and give voice to their own experiences. I also write it to motivate social scientists to encourage ethnographic subjects (co-authors) to reclaim and write their own lives as well, the ordinary and daily (see Zola 1982b) as well as the horrendous and tragic described here. As Richardson (1990, p. 65) says so eloquently:

> Narrative is the best way to understand the human experience, because it is the way humans understand their own lives. . . . If we wish to understand the deepest and most universal of human experiences, if we wish our work to be faithful to the lived experiences of people, if we wish for a union between poetics and science, if we wish to reach a variety of readers, or if we wish to use our privileges and skills to empower the people we study, then we need to *foreground*, not suppress, the narrative within the human sciences.

In writing their own stories, subjects may be able to reclaim their experience from the lifeless abstractions, typologies, and categories of social science, and give meaning to their own lives (Bertaux-Wiame 1981; Bruner 1986; Polkinghome 1988). Telling a story, as Crites (1971, p. 311) points out, "makes it possible to recover a living past, to believe again in the future, to perform acts that have significance for the person who acts."

Each writing and reading of my text has permitted me to relive my brother's death from an aesthetic distance (Scheff 1979), a place that allows me to experience the experience but with the awareness that I am not actually again *in* this situation, and thus I muster the courage to continue grieving. This process may not be attractive to everyone. Often it was painful for me, so painful that even now in 1992, ten years later, I experience intense emotions of loss when I read this story. Indeed, my emotional reactions over the years have been so pronounced that at times I have noted them as I edited. For example:

> As I write this in 1986, my gut churns and my hands shake. Nauseous, a lump forms in my throat. Over four years later Rex's death can have close to the same impact on me as the day it happened.

> Why am I doing this to myself? I ask in 1988. Each time I edit this, I sob. I have tapped into the unresolved pain. Can it ever be resolved?

In 1990 when I edit this, a voice says, Oh, no. I don't want to relive this. Surprised by the strength of my feeling, I am anxious, unwilling to read the words on the page. These are not yet "just data." Maybe they never will be. I refuse to relive that time, and try to read the sentences for style. I can't. But it's too late to turn back. I am committed to this project. My hands shake, and I am back in this scene calling the airlines.

In spite of my agony, my interaction with this text enriches my life by making available to me emotional intensity. Through feeling the pain of loss, I also feel the attachment to my brother and to my family. As Arthur Frank (1991, p. 41) says: "To grieve well is to value what you have lost. When you value even the feeling of loss, you value life itself, and you begin to live again." By writing about my brother, he again becomes a part of my world (see Ernaux 1991, p. 31).

Writing, reading, telling, and reflecting on my story help me understand better the position from which I live and speak now in this and all my academic work. As an educated person, I value the understanding that comes from abstract thought. Yet, I am still connected to my working-class roots where the meaning inherent in concrete experience, stories, and dialogue was privileged over the theoretical and general. In returning to that form now, I find a place to integrate my sociological and personal interests in community, ethnography, family, relationships, and emotions.

The sudden loss of my brother threatened, like nothing before, the meaning I had socially constructed for my life, which was that life was by definition meaningful. Connecting my life and my various scholarly interests in this story, showing how my biographical and sociological life and writing are mutually influenced (Zola 1983), and sharing the unity and wholeness of lived experience with others provides a way of reconstructing my life.

Writing our own stories creates a way in which we as authors can interact with and interpret our own lives (Parry 1991). In the process, we can make true a plot in which we play the part of, and become in the playing, actual "survivors."

ACKNOWLEDGMENTS

Thanks to Arthur Bochner and Laurel Richardson for encouraging me to write this piece. I appreciate their responses, and also the comments of Norman Denzin, Douglas Harper, Susan Krieger, and Michal McCall. I dedicate this story to Rex.

REFERENCES

Agee, J. (1938). *A death in the family.* Toronto: Bantam.

Bates, F. L., Fogelman, C. W., Parenton, V. J., Pittman, R. H., & Tracey, G. S. (1963). *The social and psychological consequences of a natural disaster: A longitudinal study of hurricane Audrey,* Pub. 1081. Washington: National Academy of Sciences.

Bertaux-Wiame, I. (1981). The life history approach to the study of internal migration. In D. Bertaux (Ed.), *Biography and society: The life history approach in the social sciences* (pp. 249–265). Beverly Hills: Sage.

Bochner, A. & Ellis, C. (1992). Personal narrative as a social approach to interpersonal Communication. *Communication Theory 2,* 165–172.

Bochner, A. & Waugh, J. (in press). Talking-with as a model for writing-about: Implications of rortian pragmatism for communication theory." In L. Langsdorf & A. Smith (Eds.), *Recovering, pragmatism's voice: The classical tradition, rorty and the philosophy of communication,* Albany: SUNY Press.

Bourdieu, P. & Wacquant, L. (1992). *An invitation to reflexive sociology.* Chicago: University of Chicago Press.

Bower, G. H. (1981). Mood and memory. *American Psychologist 36,* 129–148.

Broyard, A. (1992). *Intoxicated by my illness.* New York: Clarkson Potter.

Bruner, E. (1986). Experience and its expressions. In V. Turner & E. Bruner (Eds.), *The anthropology of experience* (pp. 3–30). Urbana: University of Illinois Press.

Butler, S. & Rosenblum, B. (1991). *Cancer in two voices.* San Francisco: Spinsters Book Co.

Caplan, G. (1976). Organization of support systems for civilian populations. In G. Caplan & M. Killilea (Eds.), *Support systems and mutual help* (pp. 273–315). New York: Grune and Stratton.

Crites, S. (1971). The narrative quality of experience. *Journal of the American Academy of Religion xx,* 291–311.

Denzin, N. (1989). *Interpretive interactionism.* Newbury Park, CA: Sage.

Denzin, N. (1991). Representing lived experiences in ethnographic texts. In *Studies in symbolic interaction, 12,* 59–70 Greenwich, CT: JAI.

Dewey, J. (1980). *The quest for certainty: A study of the relation of knowledge and action.* New York: Perigree Books.

Dynes, R. (1970). *Organized behavior in disaster.* Lexington, MA.: Heath Lexington Books.

Ellis, C. (1991a). Sociological introspection and emotional experience. *Symbolic Interaction* 14: 23–50.

Ellis, C. (1991b). Emotional sociology. In N. Denzin (Ed.), *Studies in symbolic interaction 12,* 123–145 Greenwich, CT: JAI.

Ellis, C. & Bochner, A. (1992). Telling and performing personal sdtories: The constraints of choice in abortion." In C. Ellis & M. Flaherty (Eds.), *Investigating subjectivity: Research on lived experience* (pp. 79–101). Newbury Park: Sage.

Ellis, C. & Weinstein, E. (1986). Jealousy and the social psychology of emotional experience. *Journal of Social and Personal Relationships 3,* 337–357.

Erikson, K. (1976). *Everything in its path: Destruction of community in the Buffalo Creek flood.* New York: Simon and Schuster.

Ernaux, A. (1991). *A woman's story,* translated by Tanya Leslie. New York: Ballentine.

Frank, A. (1991). *At the will of the body: Reflections on illness.* Boston: Houghton Mifflin.

Frederick, C. (Ed.) (1981). *Aircraft accidents: Emergency mental health problems.* DHHS Pub. # (ADM)81–956. Rockville, MD.: National Institute of Mental Health.

Geertz, C. (1973). *The interpretation of cultures: Selected essays.* New York: Basic Books.

Geertz, C. (1983). *Local knowledge: Further essays in interpretive anthropology.* New York: Basic Books.

Geertz, C. (1986). Making experiences, authoring selves. In V. Turner & E. Bruner (Eds.), *The anthropology of experience* (pp. 373–380). Urbana: University of Illinois Press.

Gleser, G., Green, B. & Winget, C. (1981). *Prolonged psychosocial effects of disaster: A study of Buffalo Creek.* New York: Academic Press.

Gouldner, A. (1970). *The coming crisis of western sociology.* New York: Avon Books.

Haskell, M. (1990). *Love and other infectious diseases: A memoir.* New York: William Morrow.

Isen, A. M. (1984). Toward an understanding of the role of affect in cognition. In R. S. Wyer, & T. K. Srull (Eds.), *Handbook of Social Cognition 3,* 179–236. Hillsdale, NJ: Erlbaum.

Jackson, M. (1989). *Paths toward a clearing: Radical empiricism and ethnographic inquiry.* Bloomington: Indiana University Press.

Krieger, S. (1991). *Social science and the self: Personal essays on an art form.* New Brunswick: Rutgers University Press.

Lear, M. (1980). *Heartsounds.* New York: Simon and Schuster.

Lerner, G. (1978). *A Death of one's own.* New York: Simon and Schuster.

Lewis, C. S. (1963). *A grief observed.* Greenwich, CT: Seabury Press.

Loftus, E., Smith, K., Klinger, M., & Fiedler, J. (1992). Memory and mismemory for health events. In J. Tanur. *Questions about questions: Inquiries into the cognitive bases of surveys* (pp. 102–107). New York: Russell Sage Foundation.

Mairs, N. (1989). *Remembering the bone house: An erotics of place and space.* New York: Harper and Row.

Marcus, G. (1986). Contemporary problems of ethnography in the modern world system. In J. Clifford, & G. Marcus (Eds.), *Writing Culture* (pp. 165–193). Berkeley: University of California Press.

Marcus, G. & Fischer, M. (1986). *Anthropology as cultural critique: An experimental moment in the human sciences.* Chicago: University of Chicago Press.

Murphy, R. (1987). *The body silent.* New York: Henry Holt.

Parkes, C. M. & Weiss, R. (1983). *Recovery from bereavement.* New York: Basic Books.

Parry, A. (1991). A universe of stories. *Family process 30:* 37–54.

Personal Narratives Group, (Eds.) (1989). *Interpreting women's lives: Feminist theory and personal narratives.* Bloomington: Indiana University Press.

Polkinghome, D. (1988). *Narrative knowing and the human sciences.* Albany: State University of New York Press.

Richardson, L. (1990). *Writing strategies: Reaching diverse audiences.* Newbury Park: Sage.

Rorty, R. (1982). *Consequences of pragmatism.* Minnesota: University of Minnesota Press.

Rosaldo, R. (1989). *Culture and truth: The remaking of social analysis.* Boston: Beacon Press.

Roth, P. (1991). *Patrimony: A true story.* New York: Simon and Schuster.

Sargent, A. (1980). *Ordinary people,* based on a book *Ordinary people* by Judith Guest. Hollywood, CA.: Paramount Home Video.

Scarry, E. (1985). *The body in pain: The making and unmaking of the world.* New York: Oxford University Press.

Scheff, T. (1979). *Catharsis in healing, ritual, and drama.* Berkeley: University of California Press.

Tierney, K. (1979). *Crisis intervention programs for disaster victims: A source book and manual for smaller communities.* DHEW # (ADM)79–675. Washington: National Institute of Mental Health.

Turner, V. (1986). *The anthropology of performance.* New York: PAJ Publications.

Tyler, S. (1986). Post-modern ethnography: From document of the occult to occult document. In J. Clifford, & G. Marcus (Eds.), *Writing culture* (pp. 122–140). Berkeley: University of California Press.

Wallace, A. (1956). *Tornado in worcester: An exploratory study of individual and community behavior in an extreme situation,* Pub. 392. Washington: National Academy of Sciences.

Webster, S. (1982). Dialogue and fiction in ethnography. *Dialectical anthropology 7:* 91–114.

Wright, J., Rossi, P. Wright, S., & Weber-Burdin, E. (1979). *After the clean-up: Long-range effects of natural disasters.* Beverly Hills: Sage.

Yalom, I. (1989). *Love's executioner: And other tales of psychotherapy.* New York: Basic Books.

Zola, I. (1982a). *Missing pieces.* Philadelphia: Temple University Press.

Zola, I. (Ed.) (1982b). *Ordinary lives: Voices of disability and disease.* Cambridge: Apple-wood Books.

Zola, I. (1983). *Socio-medical inquiries: Recollections, reflections, and reconsiderations.* Philadelphia: University of Temple Press.

PERSPECTIVE 1: POSTPOSITIVISM ON THE ELLIS STUDY

D. C. PHILLIPS   *Stanford University*

I was very moved by this paper, and it stimulated me to reflect on many things. Part of my reaction was shaped by the fact that my careful reading of it took place only a few days following the horrendous events in New York and Washington on September 11, 2001, and Carolyn Ellis's account of the loss of her brother in an airline crash gave me an inkling about what thousands of families were going through, which heightened my sense of tragedy.

That being said, however, I must state clearly that I do not regard this paper as an instance of disciplined inquiry of the kind that we could label as *educational research.* To my mind it is a piece of autobiography, or even of journalism. And this brings me to my first major point: *Not every valuable intellectual endeavor has to be cast in the form of research!* Far from it—on many occasions we have as much, or more, to learn from a piece of journalism or an autobiography, than we have to learn from a piece of research, and the authors writing in these genres have nothing to apologize for. But they should not try to disguise what they are doing; research is a specialized genre—no better or worse as a genre, just different from what Ellis is doing in her paper. (In my view it is a weakness that Ellis makes an effort to dress up the paper as a piece of "experimental ethnography," but I do not take this seriously and regard it as playing with words; the paper certainly has little in common with what are widely judged to be paradigmatic ethnographies.) To stress again, the issue here is not the value of work done in any particular genre;

rather it is a question of being clear about what the genres are, and what is the point of each of them (to put it rather crassly, as if genres always have clear "points"). Or, to use expressions from the philosopher Ludwig Wittgenstein, research and autobiography are different "*language games*" or "*forms of life,*" and problems arise when such games or forms are mistaken for each other.

Perhaps an analogy will help here; it is based on a piece of my own personal history. Recently I had a mercifully mild attack of vertigo that lasted about a week. If I were to write up my experiences during those 7 days, I would hardly expect the document to count as a piece of medical research (or, I hasten to add, as a piece of ethnography!)—the point of my description of this dizzying condition would not be the same as the point of medical research into it (which would be something like finding the cause or causes of the condition, unraveling its etiology, the making of accurate prognoses, and so forth). Nevertheless it might well be the case that my account could be used in the training of medical practitioners. My line of thought here is as follows: Doctors often would be better, in my lay opinion, if they actually had suffered from the diseases they purport to treat; but as it is unlikely that I could arrange for each doctor-in-training to suffer from all diseases, a compromise position might be that they should have access to accounts of what it actually is like to suffer from particular maladies. I can even imagine that a medical journal might make a regular feature of this and publish a first-hand account of a different disease in each issue. This, however, would still not make the first-hand, autobiographical descriptions, into pieces of research; they remain autobiographies, but ones that are extremely useful for training purposes!

My second point is, in essence, a brief answer to the questions "What is the central point of the 'form of life' known as research? Why doesn't the paper by Ellis qualify for this category?" The answer, I believe, is straightforward: Research has *epistemic goals*—it attempts to contribute to human knowledge by making discoveries, solving (or dissolving) problems, establishing regularities, ascertaining "facts" relevant to some problem or issue, refuting hypotheses, building and testing explanatory theories, and the like. It seems patently clear that Ellis did not have goals of this sort when she wrote her autobiographical study. According to the abstract that opens her paper,

> My goal is to reposition readers vis à vis authors of texts of social science by acknowledging potential for optional readings and encouraging readers to "experience an experience" that can reveal not only how it was for me, but how it could be or once was for them. (p. 250)

It should be apparent that, no matter how worthy they are as goals, "repositioning readers" and "encouraging" them are not the kinds of goals that are to be found as central in the form of life normally identified as research. There is no epistemic aim here, but rather an educational or even rhetorical or political one. Ellis is trying to "reposition"—change the attitude or perspective of—her readers; she wishes (as she also put it in the abstract) to stimulate readers "to acknowledge and give voice to their own emotional experiences." This is a novelist, or journalist, or autobiographer, or even a teacher talking—but it is not someone speaking the language of research!

Third, if Ellis *was* speaking the language of research, we would be justified in asking how the claims made in her paper could be tested—for if they are not testable, they are not the claims of a researcher. It is always legitimate to ask a researcher the following question: "Is there any conceivable evidence that would show the conclusions were wrong?" This question is close to the heart of the logic of testing; we seek to find evidence that would disconfirm a hypothesis, and if we *fail* to find it, this is an indication—but an indication only—that the hypothesis is sound. If we do not know what in principle would disconfirm the hypothesis, we ought to suspect that we are not dealing with scientific research (in the broad sense of "scientific" advocated by postpositivists).

It hardly needs stating that this is an extremely puzzling line of questioning to direct at Ellis, for two reasons. First, she has not advanced any hypotheses, so it is impossible to test them! Second, if we look at her project as a whole, how does one test an autobiography? Testing does not seem to be part of the genre (and I am far from advocating that it ought to become part of the genre). Of course we might try to show that events described in the autobiography did not happen, but this would be beside the point—for an autobiography is often a record of the perceptions and feelings of the author, and who is to say that the author did not have the feelings she describes, or did not see events the way she describes? (Jean Jacques Rousseau's *Confessions* is self-serving, and is almost certainly packed with half-truths, untruths, and exaggerations, yet it rightfully stands as one of the greatest autobiographies ever written—the desiderata for autobiographies are not the same as the desiderata for research!)

PERSPECTIVE 2: PRAGMATISM ON THE ELLIS STUDY

NEL NODDINGS   *Stanford University*

The first question that arises for a critical reader of this article might be "Is this sociology?" It is certainly a beautifully written and deeply touching story, but how does it differ from more familiar, journalistic/personal accounts? Why would a pragmatist ask these questions?

A pragmatist makes decisions and judgments according to consequences or effects. If we judge this article to be a valid piece of sociology, what effects can we predict? Many sociologists would reject the article, insisting that it is not sociology and that accepting it as sociology diminishes the field. The fact that the story is followed by "sociology talk" and an attempt to justify the work as sociology tells us that the writer is familiar with the discourse of sociology, but that does not make the study itself sociology. I have personally observed a fine (and very professional) sociologist "go ballistic" over an article similar to this one. "My field!" she cried. "If we allow this sort of thing, my field will be finished!" Such an effect—wrecking a field—is surely to be avoided.

But is this assessment of effects plausible? Other sociologists might predict an enrichment of the field, even a welcome expansion. The unhappy sociologist would not be comforted by talk of expansion and enrichment. The expanded field would simply be something else, not sociology. A newcomer to the field might protest that it *must* be sociology; after all, it has appeared in a journal of sociology. What else could it be? Such naïve acceptance obscures the battles going on behind the scenes. Our suffering sociologist might now predict that, even if the field survives, this particular journal will surely lose respectability if it does not mend its ways. And it might!

This is a problem with which every responsible editor struggles. On the one hand, good editors want to publish articles "on the cutting edge"; on the other, they do not want to subject their journals to possible ridicule, and they certainly do not want to contribute to the demise of their field. Whether the field is actually hurt or not depends greatly on who espouses this form of sociology. If very powerful sociologists back such efforts, the new methods are likely to be accepted.

When prominent sociologists disagree, however, the field is likely to enter a crisis (Gouldner, 1970; O'Neill, 1972).

What other effects should we look for? Were any of the research participants hurt? Since the research was directed primarily at the researcher herself, this does not seem likely. It is possible, however, that the researcher's mother could have been hurt by the account. Few of us would be pleased to see ourselves described as weak and self-centered. One wonders whether the mother was permitted to read the account and, if she did read it, how her reaction might be described. In much ethnographic research today, participants are asked for their views and, sometimes, dissenting accounts are included in the final publication. In this case, we hear only from one voice.

Ellis claims, rightly, that a new sociology described by Alvin Gouldner (1970) speaks against "the bias that WE study THEM," but Gouldner also warned against allowing personal accounts to pose as sociology. It is one thing to incorporate a personal account as part of an explanation for the interpretation that follows; it is quite another to offer a personal account as, in itself, a sociological study. What does this study tell us about a particular social group? It may be too idiosyncratic to contribute much to our knowledge of the suddenly bereaved and how they behave.

Ellis offers another justification for her work. Citing Richard Rorty, she endorses the idea that social scientists should "act as interpreters" for people with whom we cannot easily talk. But Rorty also says that this is what we expect from poets, dramatists, and novelists. If we can also expect this from social scientists, how should their interpretations be different and, if they need not be different, why should we call them social scientists? Ellis's mention of C. S. Lewis's treatment of his wife's death makes us wonder even more. Lewis (1964) did not claim to be doing philosophy in that work.

Pragmatists encounter another problem—troubling in its familiarity—in the quotation from Passerini: "All autobiographic memory is true." Most careful pragmatists would say that all autobiographic memory contains *meaning,* but they would avoid claims to truth. (This is reminiscent of the argument between Peirce and James.) Indeed, without the sort of triangulation that ethnographers usually use, we would be hard put to claim even warranted assertibility. The researcher can say (with some authority) that this is an account of what *she* went through, but we cannot say very much about how her experience fits that of others, because others are not consulted. We would feel better even about the account of her own experience if we heard the interpretations of others. Has she reported her own behavior accurately? Notice that Ellis does question whether her account can be universalized.

Finally, we might ask about the effects on readers. If this piece were published in a popular magazine or newspaper, we might expect that many readers would profit from the story. We all need to know more about how others handle suffering and unexpected loss. It is also true, as Ellis says in closing, that "writing our own stories creates a way in which we as authors can interact with and interpret our own lives" (p. 261). The problem is that ordinary people do not read journals of sociology, and writing our own stories does not usually qualify as social science. We are left with the important question: what does this contribute to sociology?

REFERENCES

Gouldner, A. W. (1970). *The coming crisis of western sociology.* New York: Basic Books.

Lewis, C. S. (1964). *The case for Christianity.* New York: Macmillian.

O'Neill, J. (1972). *Sociology as a skin trade.* London: Heinemann.

PERSPECTIVE 3: CONSTRUCTIVISM ON THE ELLIS STUDY

YVONNA S. LINCOLN   *Texas A&M University*

Carolyn Ellis has been one of the pioneers in autoethnographic interpretive inquiry, reclaiming ethnographic authority via re-situating herself as the *I,* rather than the *Other;* by drawing on the emotional rather than the distanced voice of traditional social science; and by enriching the narratives of lived experience. One of the main characteristics of the "new ethnography" (Goodall, 2000; Spickard, Landres, & McGuire, 2002) is "learn[ing] who you are as a fieldworker, as a writer, and as a self" (Goodall, 2000, p. 7). Ellis's work is a clear demonstration of this impetus to learn the self through the narratives of the self.

The focus on differences between conventional scientific inquiry and interpretive inquiry is not, as some have assumed and many others contradicted, the difference between qualitative and quantitative approaches. Qualitative inquirers have sometimes been quite positivistic in their intents, while some quantitative scholars have been seriously intent on engaging in phenomenological and interpretive work (utilizing quantitative data to demonstrate, in demographic terms, long-term historical and social trends which then become the fodder for interpretive and critical theorist critiques of social arrangements). It is, rather, the emphasis on the lived experience, the human capacity for and bent toward *storying* the events and situations of their lives, and the rhetorical strategies of narrative, which permits the parsing of conventional from interpretive inquiries. Ellis's work emphasizes all of these, embodying a reality construction which is claimed solely for herself, although authored and offered for its claims to embrace a wider human experience: the experience of the loss, sudden loss, of a loved one. In some sense, this story can be repeated 2,000 times in the tragedies of September 11, 2001, at the World Trade Center, at the Pentagon, and in the crash of Flight 99. The story Ellis tells reaches beyond our own borders, to war-torn regions, to areas of the world where sudden natural catastrophe claims lives, to the unheralded survivors of automobile accidents. It is a story to which all of us can relate, many far too closely. It is, in some senses, the vicarious experience of much of the world's population outside of the United States.

Its epistemology is neither male nor female; it is the experience of each human being who has lost someone dear abruptly and seemingly without reason. The story, however, displays a distinctly feminine "voice" in that it unashamedly connects experience to profound emotional content, the "lover" model of research and narrative spoke of by Shula Reinharz (1979) nearly 25 years ago. It is is a voice both emotional and embodied.

The methodological strategy for the piece is at once retrospective (like many standard and intensive interviews) and introspective ("What am I feeling? How did this feel? How does it feel now?"). In those senses, the work falls into something which might loosely be called "confessional tales," although it is hardly a confession, since it does not seek to reveal the "real" experiences of a fieldwork effort, but rather places into narrative form the firsthand experience of a grievous loss, unconnected to any realist narrative of an "othering" ethnography. It is, in terse terms, not at all remove from another experience reported on previously; it is close, peopled with real individuals whose identities are not hidden, neither a humorous, sly exposé, nor a post-tenure attempt to come to terms with the human side of ethnography. It is, rather, the consummate researcher-as-other/other-as-researcher, the vicarious account of the human side of social science.

If there are ethical issues in this work, they remain close to home. A reader might ask how the family members feel about having their grief appear in print. We know little, if anything, about Ellis's mother or father might feel, or have felt, about having their very private sorrows available for others to study. We don't, as readers, know this, although we assume that the persons involved at least knew of Ellis's intention to write about this experience.

What we do know is that this form of ethnographic writing is still sparse in the journals and books, although it is increasingly finding spaces in the various venues as a recognized form of narrativized meaning-making. While no one believes that such writing forms will eventually come to represent social science in its entirety, this kind of work is critical for its ability to open a dialogue about what social science is supposed to accomplish, and for its rich emotional context, recentered on ordinary human experience. Such writing creates space for other such work to inhabit. This kind of social science parallels closely the move in history to recreate the lives of "ordinary people," and to resist the writing of history as the history of "Great Men." It reconnects all of us to the lives of ordinary human experience, and in doing so, reminds us that no life is really that "ordinary."

REFERENCES

Goodall, H. L., Jr. (2000). *Writing the new ethnography.* Walnut Creek, CA: AltaMira Press.

Reinharz, S. (1979). *On becoming a social scientist.* San Francisco: Jossey-Bass:

Spickard, J. V., Landres, J. S., & McGuire, M. B. (2002). *Personal knowledge and beyond: Reshaping the ethnography of religion.* New York: New York University Press.

PERSPECTIVE 4: INTERPRETIVE AND NARRATIVE ON THE ELLIS STUDY

ARTHUR P. BOCHNER   *University of South Florida*

Carolyn Ellis and I have been partners for more than a decade. Shortly after we met in 1990, she sent me a draft copy of a book manuscript she had written entitled *Final Negotiations* (Ellis, 1995). The book described in detail the history of Carolyn's nine-year relationship with Gene Weinstein who died of emphysema in 1985 (Ellis, 1995). As I read through the chapter in which Carolyn told the story of her brother's death in an airplane crash, I felt as if all my senses were being pricked. I had never before read a social science article in which the researcher wrote from the source of her own grief, openly expressing what it felt like to be stricken so suddenly, refusing to gloss the layers of conflicting feelings, the exciting rush of adrenalin countered by the deadening fog of numbness, the waves of hope and despair, and, finally, the struggle first to choke down, then to grope toward an understanding of the meaning of her suffering and loss.

My immediate reaction was overwhelming sorrow. I felt the pressure squeezing in my chest when Carolyn told how her heart was racing when she asked the Air Florida agent for information on Rex's flight. I felt the tightness in my throat, holding back the swell of sadness inside me as Carolyn recounted the television replay—"Then they announce seven. Then there are five. And one dead hero" (p. 253). And I could no longer stifle my tears, which flowed freely down my cheeks, when Carolyn's mother sobbed, "Bring my boy home." I felt as if I had been swept into the experience of sudden loss. It wasn't a place I wanted to be, but the same can be said for Carolyn, her family, Rex's friends, or the people of Luray, Virginia. Carolyn's writing had a raw force that made me feel its truth in my stomach, so close to the bone of reality. The truth wasn't pretty—bad things happen to good people, the course of one's life can turn in a split second, the meanings one attaches to life are never completely secure, some people may never come back from such a blow—but it was something that had to be endured, worked through, and learned from. Others, those for whom one tells a story, need to feel it—the shock, the numbness, the exhaustion, the hope, the resolution, the sorrow—to know its truth. The writer—the teller of the story—needs to write it to work her way through the pain and be transformed by its truth.

As I contemplated all the feelings and thoughts that were running through me, I felt a rush of optimism about the future of social science inquiry. Yes! I shouted to myself. This is what social science is missing! This is what social science needs to become in order to make a difference in the world—daring, honest, intimate, personal, emotional, moral, embodied, and evocative. Here was a social scientist venturing beyond the realm of predictable events and rational actions, revealing life's particularities, bearing witness to the wreakage of human suffering, showing what it might mean to live well while afflicted by loss, inviting her readers to receive her testimony and become witnesses themselves, questioning the subject matter and methodologies of her discipline, refusing to hide behind academic jargon and citations, making us feel the truth of her story in our guts.

When Carolyn and I met to discuss her book, I advised her to take this chapter out of the book. "It's too powerful for the book," I said. "The story of Rex's death overwhelms the other story you are telling there. It is what most people will remember first when they finish the book. Besides, you should publish it in an academic journal where scholars can see an example of what social science could be if it embraced narrative, if it made the heart as important as the mind, if it encouraged the goal of empathizing with the sufferings of others, if it were written from inside experience, and if its authority came from the emotions it evokes in its readers as well as the lessons it teaches about human vulnerability, moral choice, and suffering." Although Carolyn felt Rex's death was a significant event in her relationship with Gene, she agreed with me. She took the chapter out of the book and published it in *The Sociological Quarterly*.

As a wounded storyteller, Carolyn offers her testimony as a witness to the pain and suffering of sudden death. She tells her story for your sake as well as for her own. She wants you to enter into dialogue with her and with her story, not to stand outside it as a detached critic but to step into it as if it were happening to you.

Try to put yourself in Carolyn Ellis' shoes. Your brother is coming to visit you. The two of you are close and loving siblings who don't get to see each other nearly as often as you'd like. You anticipate his visit eagerly, knowing it will be a relaxing and fun-filled holiday. You stock up on his favorite foods and buy presents you know he will adore. You chuckle when you realize that he will adore the gifts *because* they are from you. You picture his smiling face in your mind all day as you work furiously to finish projects you know won't get done while he is here. Then the phone rings. There's been a crash. The plane is in the water. Your brother may be dead.

Stop for a minute. Become aware of your body? How do you feel? Numb? Frightened? Sad? Is adrenalin rushing through you? Do you cry? Scream? Think what to do next? To whom do you want to talk? What do you say?

Return to the scene. Recall how you talked to your brother on the phone yesterday. How you thought about him all day, replaying some of the happiest moments of your childhood in your mind. He was alive then; he can't be dead now. He's too young, fresh, full of life. You had no warning, no sign that anything like this could happen. Neither did he. It doesn't feel real. It's too sudden—shocking. Feelings flood your consciousness, overwhelming you. You feel light-headed, as if you are falling from the edge of a cliff. You sense yourself descending into an abyss of despair. Nothing makes sense. You feel lost, unanchored, adrift in meaninglessness. Life feels so dangerous, death so arbitrary, knowledge so uncertain, loss so painful, the future so unpredictable. You wonder, how can I make sense of this? How can I go on with my life—feel safe and sane again? To whom or to what can I turn?

Take a minute to regain your composure. Return to the present. Recall that this is a book about different perspectives on research and how various seasoned scholars react to them. The editor of the book endorses the idea that many different approaches to research are legitimate. By selecting these six studies, he has invited you to contemplate the legitimacy of a wide range of methodologies and perspectives to which most students never get exposed. Normally, students are socialized into research by reading and studying the work of their predecessors and mentors. Through these instrumental contacts with peers, professors, articles, monographs, and books— classics in the field—the discipline of educational research establishes norms of what will count as legitimate research. Methods of gathering and accumulating documentation are formulated within the constraints of accepted practices of inquiry and recognized modes of representation. Regardless of the subject matter, these conventionalized practices normally confine inquiry to a limited range of researchable experiences represented in a narrow domain of recognizable texts (Rose, 1993). As a student you are groomed to engage in certain types of research experiences and to compose texts that represent those experiences in a form that meets the expectations of your discipline's standards (Richardson, 1994). In short, what we learn is a great deal of conformity (Krieger, 1991)! As Rose (1990) observes, "If you write a nonconforming text, then the rewards of the discipline may be withheld because the book does not read as a legitimated contribution to knowledge" (p. 14).

Although human experience may be abundantly diverse, the accepted canons for representing or expressing it within academic disciplines are highly conventionalized and restricted. When a researcher such as Carolyn Ellis wants to use novel, poetic, or creative modes of expressing herself, she may feel as if she is isolated in a forbidden zone in which she risks losing the credibility and support normally reserved for those who conform to conventional research and writing practices without resistance. If an author takes the risk of writing in ways that breach accepted conventions, her work may be rejected because it doesn't fit into accepted definitions of legitimate "research" and, as a result, she may feel as if she has been exiled from her discipline (Ellis & Bochner, 2001).

The question of what constitutes legitimate research is an unsettled and contested question. Fields of inquiry change over time and as they change so do our conceptions of what research is and what it should it do. As women, Blacks, and people from third-world countries gained increasing access to graduate programs, they revealed convincingly how a research model based on neutrality, objectivity, and scientific detachment could function as a tool of oppression and domination. Many of them insisted that their research projects should make sense in the context of their own lived experiences. They questioned not only what should be studied, but how and for what purposes. Wasn't research always political in some sense? Didn't social and educational research usually involve engagement in relationships? Wasn't it as much a product of interaction as of observation? Weren't the results always dependent in part on the embodied experiences, motives, and participation of the researcher? Shouldn't we worry as researchers about how we represent others, speak for them. Is it legitimate to write as if we play no part in the interpretations we make? After all, when we do research, there is always the investigator and the investigated.

When we write our results, how can we tell what enters from our side and what from theirs? The world can't describe itself, can it?

"THERE ARE SURVIVORS," is a work of self-narration, sometimes referred to as autoethnography, in which Carolyn Ellis uses her personal experience to display multiple levels of consciousness and emotionality, connecting and contrasting her own personal suffering, the ways in which members of her family cope with their loss, and the patterns of ritualized grieving she observes when she returns for her brother's funeral to the community in which she grew up. Focusing on her own feelings and thoughts while paying close attention to the concrete details of other people's reactions and emotions, Carolyn exposes both the inner world of a vulnerable, suffering, and searching self and the outer world of a grieving community of fellow sufferers coping as well as they can with tragic circumstances. The text she produces invites us to experience and reflect on how loss is written on and expressed by one's body, how it is lived through and coped with over time, and how cultural practices are used to restore a sense of order and continuity in the aftermath of tragedy.

As an academic monograph, Carolyn Ellis's text raises the question of what place narrative should occupy in social science inquiry. Should all social and educational research be driven by a search for general principles? Are the standard methodological practices of science useful when one wants to know what to do or how to act? To what sort of research can one turn for moral and political guidance? Is theory always to be preferred to story?

Richard Rorty (1989; 1991) strongly prefers narratives over theories: "The attempt to find laws of history or essences of cultures—to substitute theory for narrative as an aid to understanding ourselves, others, and the options which we present to each other—has been notoriously unfruitful" (1991, p. 66). He advises "that we should stay on the lookout . . . for the rise of new genres—genres which arise in reaction to, and as an alternative to, the attempt to *theorize*—about human affairs" (p. 73.) Using novelists such as Dickens and Kundera as his model, Rorty advocates a social science that pays attention to the concrete details of human suffering. Compared to theorists, Rorty observes what is important about storytellers is that they excel at details. In Rorty's ideal academic community, social science is continuous with literature, in part, because the social sciences have a moral importance, whether they accept it or not, and also because, as Rorty (1982) notes, "What we hope for from social scientists is that they will act as interpreters for those with whom we are not sure how to act . . . the same thing we hope for from our poets and dramatists and novelists" (p. 202).

Autoethnography is a species of narrative inquiry that has blossomed in reaction to the excesses and limitations of theory-driven, empiricist social science. Whereas empiricist social science fuels an appetite for abstraction, facts, and control, narrative social science feeds a hunger for details, meanings, and peace of mind. In some circles, narrative has become a rallying point for those who believe strongly that the human sciences need to become more human. We are supposed to be studying people, trying to understand their lives, and narratives come closer to representing the contexts and preserving the integrity of those lives than do questionnaires and graphs. But it would be a mistake to conclude that the enthusiasm for narrative is simply the reflection of a scholarly change of heart. It also is an expression of the desire to produce work that is personally meaningful for the researcher. Richardson (1992) describes her turn toward narrative as a longing for forms of expression that would turn sociology—her research field—into a non-alienating practice, where she wouldn't have to suppress her own subjectivity, where she could become more attuned to the subjectively felt experiences of others, where she would be free to reflect on the consequences of her work not only for others but also for herself, and where all parts of her self—emotional, spiritual, intellectual, and moral—could be voiced and integrated in her work. In short, narrative inquiry is a response to an existential crisis—a desire to do meaningful work and to lead meaningful lives. As Freeman (1998) says, "We need to understand lives and indeed to *live* lives differently if we are to avoid further fragmentation, isolation, and disconnection from each other" (p. 46). While some narrative research may make traditional knowledge claims, most narratives function ontologically, practically, and existentially. Jackson (1995) advises a shift in how we construe the purposes of research, suggesting that we should be less concerned with the question of how we can know and more concerned with the question of how we should live. This is the moral of stories—its ethical domain. When it comes to communicating ethical consciousness, as Fasching and Dechant (2001) advise, it is much more effective to tell a story than to give an abstract explanation.

Carolyn Ellis admits that her brother's death threatened the meaning of her life "like nothing before" (p. 261). Telling her story is a way of restoring meaning. She may not have been able to save Rex's life but she can save her own. She isn't seeking pity, nor is she portraying herself as pathetic, helpless, or downtrodden. Instead, she engages in an act of self-narration. She tries to make a life that is falling apart come together again, by picking up the pieces and molding them into a coherent story, shaping a view of the world from which she can envision a hopeful, promising future. For Carolyn this narrative challenge—to create meaning out of chaos—is a terrible and crucial struggle. The sense of unity in her life had been unceremoniously ruptured by Rex's sudden death. One decisive blow of fate erased any illusions Carolyn may have harbored of living a well-planned and orderly life. But it didn't erase the memory of Rex, of what he meant to her, of how frightened she felt to face her life without him in it—not to be able to hear his voice, to touch his breathing body, to share stories with him. Out of the incoherence and numbness of her painful loss, Carolyn struggles to create a story that will defend her against the prospect of a meaningless, fragmented, and isolated existence. At risk is the integrity and intelligibility of her selfhood, the story she uses to link birth to life to death as a continuous and sensible stream of experience. As a researcher, she understands that her experience per se is not the story but rather she must discover the story that is in her experience.

The story comes to a climax when Carolyn reveals a series of dreams she had about Rex more than a year after he died. The dreams appear to be about Rex, but they are just as much about Carolyn. They animate Carolyn's unconscious struggle to keep Rex alive. In the first dream, Carolyn and Rex are innocent children—curious, imaginative, playful. They live in the moment without fears, anxieties, or worries about the future. In the second dream, Carolyn and Rex have grown up. She knows he is going to die but keeps it a secret from him because "Rex hates to be out of control." Is she keeping what she knows from Rex or from herself? He won't have to deal with it if she keeps it secret. Nor will she. The dream suggests Carolyn wants to hide from the reality of Rex's death. She is no longer innocent. Now she must make a choice. Suppress the knowledge of Rex's death or admit it and deal with it. She is not ready to confront her loss. The third dream reveals the intricacies of denial. Carolyn is confused and uncertain. Did Rex die or didn't he? The unreality of his death reveals itself as if it were a dream. Though Rex appears to have survived, Carolyn still can't talk to him about what she knows or tell him that she thought he had died. Now it becomes evident that Rex and Carolyn are different parts of the same person. In the fourth dream, these parts begin to merge and integrate as Carolyn realizes that Rex is dead. She sees that it is not a question of how he will handle it, but how she will. After telling him he is dead, in her final dream, she has no need to dream about Rex again. She may never feel resolved about his death but she can go on with her life realizing that Rex lives on inside her. He stays alive in the stories she tells, the memories she clings to, and the emotions she feels when she thinks of him.

Carolyn refers to "THERE ARE SURVIVORS" as a story of sudden death. Certainly, the suddenness of Rex's death leaves a scar of sorrow that will never heal completely. For Carolyn's mother, it may never heal at all. But Carolyn's story is not only about loss and grief and sorrow. It's as much about life as it is about death. It's a story about memory and truth and connection. It's a story about recognizing what's important in life. It's a love story.

REFERENCES

Ellis, C. (1995). *Final negotiations: A story of love, loss, and chronic illness.* Philadelphia: Temple University Press.

Ellis, C., & Bochner, A. P. (2001). Narrative's virtues. *Qualitative Inquiry, 7,* 131–157.

Fasching, D. J., & Dechant, D. (2001). *Comparative religious ethics: A narrative approach.* Oxford, UK: Blackwell.

Freeman, M. (1998). Mythical time, historical time, and narrative fabric of self. *Narrative Inquiry, 8,* 27–50.

Jackson, M. (1995). *At home in the world.* Durham, NC: Duke University Press.

Krieger, S. (1991). *Social science and the self: Personal essays on an art form.* New Brunswick, N.J.: Rutgers University Press.

Richardson, L. (1992). The consequence of poetic representation: Writing the other, rewriting the self. In C. Ellis and M. Flaherty (Eds.), *Investigating subjectivity: Research on lived experience.* Newbury Park, CA: Sage. (125–137).

Richardson, L. (1994). Nine poems: Marriage and the family. *Journal of Contemporary Ethnography, 23,* 3–14.

Rorty, R. (1982). *Consequences of pragmatism: Essays 1972–1980.* Minneapolis: University of Minnesota Press.

Rorty, R. (1989). *Contingency, irony, and solidarity.* New York: Cambridge University Press.

Rorty, R. (1991). *Essays on Heidegger and others.* New York: Cambridge University Press.

Rose, D. (1990). *Living the ethnographic life.* Newbury Park, CA: Sage.

Rose, D. (1993). Ethnography as a form of life: The written word and the work of the world. In P. Benson (Ed.), *Anthropology and literature.* Urbana: University of Illinois Press.

PERSPECTIVE 6: RACE, ETHNICITY, AND GENDER ON THE ELLIS STUDY

BETH HARRY   *University of Miami*

I will offer a critique of this piece from two points of view: One, its success as a personal memoir whose purpose is to present the experience of grief through an intensely personal lens. On this level it succeeds with but one exception. Secondly, I will comment on the article's ability to go beyond the personal level to that of the group, to present contrasting views of personal grief versus collective mourning.

This memoir is about knowing. The knowledge that the narrator seeks to present is as incontrovertible as that of the measurements reported by the scientist who studies the rate of growth of a plant, meticulously documenting the conditions under which changes occur. The carefully introspective narrative is equally meticulous, and demonstrates that knowledge of the self can be understood and portrayed effectively without formal sociological analysis. What is known, however, can be defined only by the one who experiences it, and verified only by its ability to evoke in the reader an immediate recognition of its authenticity. The basis for such recognition lies in what has traditionally been described as the intuitive realm. But intuition is really a process based on lived experience (Polyani, 1966). This does not mean that a reader who has not experienced the death of a loved one cannot relate to the memoir, since there are other human experiences which may mirror many of the emotions detailed in the narrative. But the closer the reader's experience is to that being described, the more able is he or she to identify with the memoir and to verify its authenticity. Thus, the identity of the reader also becomes a salient aspect of the success of this memoir.

When I was 19, I read for the first time *Riders to the Sea,* by the Irish playwright Synge. Having never experienced the loss of a loved one, I had, at that point in time, no understanding of why the mothers of fishermen lost at sea could not rest until they had recovered, for the purposes of burial, some portion of their sons' clothing. Fifteen years later, when my own daughter died, the universality of the need for rituals of mourning and burial was suddenly brought painfully home to me. Since then, my understanding has deepened with the burials of my father, a dear friend, and a neighbor whose sudden and uncalled for death horrified our community. I came to see that the form of rituals surrounding death is a profound statement of a group's interpretation of the meaning of life and death, and of the the group's sanctioned ways of knowing and expressing feeling. Thus, my own reactions to Ellis' memoir are greatly influenced by my own knowledge and interpretation of grief.

The memoir offers three views of the grieving process: the internal processes experienced by the narrator, the individual expressions of grief by others, and the group norms that govern the collective expression of grief. In a formal sociological analysis the researcher would have examined the relationships between these three levels. In this piece, however, those relationships are revealed through the narrator's skillful juxtaposition of the responses of "I", "you," and "they". There is one important caveat: that the narrative must rely impeccably on the view available only to the narrator's introspective lens. The kind of knowing represented here is valid to the extent that it refuses to venture beyond the boundaries between self and others. When it attempts to cross those boundaries, the narrative falters.

The introspective view in this memoir connected immediately with my own experience. The author's intensely personal detailing of her most minute responses to each moment of the process of becoming aware of her brother's death and of the subsequent process of coping with her grief reveals the power of first person narrative and of introspection. Only the "I" of this narrative could know and describe the layers of feeling and rationalization at work in coming to terms with an unexpected death—the efforts to know and not know, to hope and to accept, to express and to restrain. Perhaps most clearly presented is the experience that those who have grieved know only too well—the sense of unreality that alienates one from oneself as the normal requirements of life continue, inducing a feeling of standing outside and watching grief take over. Only through experience can one know the sense of disbelief that the airline stewardess, who represents at that moment the totality of an unresponsive world, can still smile and act "the same as always."

At the level of individual others, the narrative works well up to a point. The clarity of the author's reactions is sharpened by the juxtaposition of the responses of key others who share the experience, as well as of others who are only peripherally involved. As the narrator interacts with these others, she must shift the intensity of her own expression of grief according to whom she is interacting with. As Ellis describes these shifts, there emerges a convincing portrait of the self in interaction with others. However, as she reveals her own reactions to the expressions of others, there are moments when she moves beyond the self's knowing of itself, and attempts to interpret the experience of others. At these points I become sharply aware of the impossibility of knowing whether she is accurately interpreting what others are feeling.

For me, no doubt by reason of my own history as a mother, this realization is most poignant in the narrator's descriptions of her mother's responses. There is a clear, though implicit tone of impatience with the egocentricity of her mother, who assumes the right to be the principal mourner and "almost proudly" withdraws into shock. The narrator's implicit interpretation is, momentarily, convincing, but it is clear that there is a history of mutual disagreement between the two, at least on the topic of religion. I am jogged into an awareness that, at this boundary of self and other, there is now another point of view to be taken into account. It is here that the author's attempt to offer the "truth" of the experience meets its main obstacle—at the boundary between "I" and "you." Just as her mother cannot imagine that anyone's grief could be as great as her own, so can the narrator not "know" the true meaning of her mother's seeming egocentricity. Mothers who have experienced the death of a child may well "know" that "a mother's pain is worse, the worst there is." I am, in turn, impatient with the narrator, because I know that she cannot know this truth. She has not experienced it.

Beyond "I" and "you," stand "they," and the narrator's contrasting portrait of individual and group needs reveals how individual grieving is converted to a ritualized group mourning process. The points at which private grief is superseded by collective mourning show how group practices serve to support as well as constrain the individual. There is safety in the "intuitive" knowledge of the social rules that attend the rituals of death and burial, yet this safety privileges the needs of the group over those of the individual. The narrator is at once "protected" and restrained by these rules and, despite some amount of resentment of them, is so committed to the need for personal restraint that she turns to medication to further ensure it.

It is at the level of the conflict between group and individual needs that the piece begins to lose me as the complete aficionado. I believe that this occurs because once the narrative moves from the personal to the group realm, the appeal of the piece no longer relies solely on the reader's intuitive grasp of the essential human experience of pain. Assumptions about group behavior now come to the foreground and an analytic and comparative mode of thinking come into play. The "small-town etiquette" to which the narrator refers is based on an unstated set of shared understandings regarding the appropriate expression of emotion. The analogy that her mother's hysteria has "messed up her lines" in this "play rehearsal" underscores the customary reliance of the group on ritualized forms of expression. The ritual broken, there ensues a sense of helplessness and confusion.

The reader whose scripts for mourning differ from those reflected here may now be alienated from the narrative. Where previously the intensely personal focus evoked a powerful sense of the universality of human emotion, the contrast between the personal and group experience evokes a new kind of emotion—a sense of disbelief, even anger, that group rituals should so negate the individual. For many ethnic minorities, there can be no sense in the statement, "Although the music moves me, I shut it out. This is not the place to break down"

(p. 225). The narrator's acknowledgment that in a "Pentecostal" tradition "we'd all wail together," offers a sociological awareness that, in a traditional piece of research, would form the basis of extended analysis. For me, as one who shares both the expressive and the restrained traditions, frustration with the latter surmounts and I find myself resenting the narrator's use of medicine to ensure her compliance with group norms.

I was fully immersed in this piece and moved by its power to show the ways in which we are all the same, the ways in which skin deep differences are of no importance. Cultural differences, however, shine through and beg another level of analysis—the why's and how's of human group mourning as contrasted with individual human grief.

REFERENCES

Polanyi, M. (1966). *The tacit dimension.* NY: Doubleday, & Co.

PERSPECTIVE 7: CRITICAL THEORY ON THE ELLIS STUDY

GEORGE NOBLIT   *University of North Carolina*

As positivism has lost its stranglehold on the social and educational research, the methodologies of research have both reached back to earlier methods that fell into disrepute under positivism and pushed ahead to elaborate theories of knowledge in ways not seen in history. These theories of knowledge use the historic methods to serve new purposes. Carolyn Ellis, in this study, has a theory of knowledge many would see as essentially interpretive. The purpose of interpretive research is to make sense of events, social scenes, cultural performances, and so on. Interpretive research does this by investigating the interpretations made by people in the scene studied as the author also interprets the meaning for herself and for the audience for whom she is writing. The reader in turn is expected to make an interpretation of what the layers of interpretation offered by the author mean for her or him. Unlike the article by Carr et al. where positivistic knowledge served technical interests, this article is a good example of how an interpretive theory of knowledge serves practical interests. For Habermas (1971), practical interests should not be confused with everyday uses of the word practice, which has the implication that one is applying skills learned through training. This definition is much too close to his understanding of technical. Whereas technical implies that things are well understood and have been proven to work with reasonable certainty, practical refers to a level of uncertainty and an expectation that things can be understood better by engaging in a course of action. The practical is grounded in everyday life, rejecting theory, idealism, and speculation.

Ellis, in her moving account, is serving practical interests by offering a narrative of personal tragedy with the expectation that it may evoke a set of understandings for readers (including empathy and parallel emotional experiences) that they "could then examine" (p. 260). I, for one, was entranced by the account and was called to reconsider the deaths of my parents, and to anticipate the horror should my wife and/or children die before me. It brought to me vivid recollections of similar feelings, scenes, and relationships. I came to understand that my personal experiences were in many ways shared by others, and concluded both that these terrible experiences were somehow inevitable and that I had and would survive other deaths and their aftermaths. I even resolved to not perpetuate the distancing from the emotions that often seem required, but as I write this I fear my resolve may not be up to the challenge. In any case, this study is an excellent example of an interpretive study even if it is all too personal and emotional for some social scientists.

My critique of this study is about what is hidden behind this account, what was not studied and what would be necessary to actually change the cultural practices that have come to structure sudden death. From a critical perspective, Ellis has enabled readers to interpret death in novel but important ways but has missed what might enable a transformation in our understanding. Since my critique is about that not studied, I will be able to only point to what might be important and will do so by moving through the article as it is presented. Moreover, I cannot offer a theory about how the various points might interact, if they do at all. This would take a new study with new data.

Ellis sets the stage for her study by focusing on relationships within her family. This works for her intentions but a critical ethnographer would note that later she recounts the significance of control over emotions. A critical researcher would recognize that control over emotions may be linked to the families working class origins and/or Appalachian culture. Clearly, Ellis is not offering a simple story of social class. Her family improved their economic and social standing over time. Yet "we lived similarly to the working-class families that surrounded us . . ." (p. 250). Ellis's narrative is also driven by her new social class and geographic mobility, coupled with Rex's staying near the family and his "common-sense approach to life . . ." (p. 251). Indeed, Rex would not have died in this way if not for Ellis's social class mobility. He was traveling to see her in the place where she was a professor. Thus there is a possible critique of how America has structured social class and class mobility. Indeed, it seems plausible to argue that social class mobility is often coupled to geographic mobility, and that another possible tragedy was how education and work is structured to leave Rex behind.

For me, the crash also invited an investigation of the airline industry. Rex died seemingly because a plane's wings were not appropriately de-iced. The critical possibilities here are legion. First, Air Florida itself could be investigated to explain how this could have happened. Were they cutting fiscal corners? Were they so interested in getting a plane out on time that they did not de-ice the plane appropriately? Was there a corporate culture that devalued passenger safety? Second, the airline industry as a whole could be investigated to see if this airline was an exception. If not, was the industry as whole in such poor shape that this was likely to happen to some plane sometime? What was the role of competition between airlines? Third, the Federal Aviation Authority might be implicated. Were their procedures such as to allow these problems? How did government regulations affect the airline, the airline industry, the airport, and the de-icing procedure? This accident took place after President Reagan replaced air traffic controllers for their collective bargaining efforts. Was this a factor? Fourth, the airport itself could be studied. National airport is well-known as a dated facility with excessive air traffic and this could have played a part. Were the ground crews overworked or pressed for time? Were airport procedures adequate? Did someone make a bad decision in this one case? Were the pilots informed as to the state of their plane? A critical researcher would have found these and other questions essential to explaining what happened and what must be done. Indeed, one could ask a set of questions about how families were treated in this instance by the airline industry and the media.

Gender roles and family dynamics also invite a critical perspective. Ellis and her partner share the understanding that he is to be supportive, not emotional: "Gene, my anchor" (p. 252). He does not share the emotional experience that Ellis wishes for her reader and this is somehow acceptable. What cultural assumptions guide this? Clearly, her male partner is allowed power and she emotion. While this may be explained by the fact that it is her brother who has died, her other brother, Art, also seems to share her partner's distancing from emotion even though the parents "are a disaster" (p. 253). Indeed, Ellis draws strength from these men who are the ones that declare that death has occurred even as Ellis wants to hope it has not. Ellis is allowed emotional distance only by being "numb" (p. 252) when she talks with her distraught sister.

The family dynamics are also intriguing to a critical researcher. Ellis and her brother, at a minimum, have to assume a "caretaker role" (p. 255) even as the mother aggressively asserts her status: "A mother's pain is worse . . . " (p. 255) and coldly rejects Ellis's emotions. The father is more emotional and, in the narrative, does not have the power of the mother. The parents had to be physically supported to the funeral. The mother screams her sorrow as the others "cry softly" (p. 257). Even the mother's being hospitalized claimed her superiority at least in grief. A critical researcher would interrogate the dimensions of power in gender and family dynamics. Ideology may explain why women and men behave differently but we see contradictions that invite analysis as well. Her father is different from the other men in the story in regard to emotions but has less power in the family and narrative. Is this the cultural cost of expressing emotions for men in this community? Men may gain and lose power via the management of emotions. Women may also, but seemingly in different ways.

While the narrative invites us to value emotions, it is the control over emotion that seems unnatural. From whence does this come? As above, it seems gender is implicated as are the different generations within the family. Yet control over emotion appears again and again in the narrative. The airlines and the media both display control over emotion. The funeral is a "conspiracy" between Ellis and her brother "to make sure things went as smoothly as possible" (p. 256). That is, it appears that some have to be strong while others are allowed the authenticity of grief:

> The same sentences are uttered over and over. It doesn't matter. There are no points for originality. We pass each person to the rest of the family seated behind us, the receivers of sympathy. Sometimes I want to be there too, to give in; other times I am glad for the numbing effects of being in control. (p. 257)

Art even refuses sedatives: "No, I'm going to do it on my own" (p. 257). At the service, Ellis concludes, "This is not the place to break down" (p. 257). Yet grief does relieve the sufferer as when she approaches two of her dead brother's friends and "we cry openly and I felt better" (p. 257). The juxtaposition of control and unreleaved grief made me doubt her assertion that weather caused her shakes: "My body shakes violently from the cold and wind . . . " (p. 257). A critical researcher would want to better understand whose interests are served by some being in control and others giving way to grief. The analysis would clearly be complex. The mother seems to gain power from grief while others do so from suppressing it. Further, what does this say about our society? Is grief feared because it defies power? Or when Ellis remembers Rex hated being "out of control" (p. 258), is she expressing an ideology that serves those in power? Is control desired because without it retribution might be sought, threatening the larger structures of domination in our society?

Finally, a critical researcher would see the closing sections as a way of seeking legitimacy for her narrative. Ironically, this legitimation argues for opening a new space within the disciplines. Taken literally, then, one could argue this is a way to control the narrative itself by making it serve sociology. Ellis frames some of her discussion in the classic sense of identifying a gap in the research that deserves study, undercutting any notion that social science itself would be transformed and emancipated from its strictures. This potential is identified in the final section where the possibility of a definitive truth is denied, the value of abstract thought is limited, and the subjects of research are invited to reclaim and write their own stories. Ellis, as an interpretivist, links this back to personal and emotional understanding where a critical researcher would link this to strategic actions to deny the power of the disciplines and to empower everyday people to not only narrate their lives but to redesign the place of emotions in their lives. Moreover, the critical researcher would want a more structural analysis of why and how all this occurred, and how it is that the family does not consider that Rex's death is not only the isolated tragedy of this family, but also the result of corporate and governmental actions and/or inactions. How is it that grief is socially constructed so that accountability is not demanded?

REFERENCES

Habermas, J. (1971). *Knowledge and human interests*. Boston: Beacon Press.

PERSPECTIVE 8: ETHICS, METHODOLOGY, AND DEMOCRACY ON THE ELLIS STUDY

KENNETH R. HOWE   *University of Colorado at Boulder*

Ellis's study is a lightning rod for thinkers who react against what they perceive to be the excesses of *postmodernist* social research. One charge is that it is not even an instance of social research. A second is that it is ethically aimless.

Included within the broad purview of educational research ethics is the shape it should take in the wake of the "interpretive turn." One of the general implications of the interpretive turn is that epistemology and ethics cannot be disentangled. The educational research community has responded to this development by dividing itself into three general camps (Howe, 1988).

The first camp, typically associated with positivism, pretty much ignores or dismisses the blurring of epistemology and ethics. It tenaciously hangs on to the fact/value dichotomy and the "technocratic" approach that goes with it (described in my general remarks pp. 79–83).

The second camp, typically associated with postmodernism, wholeheartedly embraces the merging of facts and values but construes facts (and knowledge, epistemology, rationality, etc.) as radically subjective, relative, and undecidable. Ironically, although fiercely antipositivist, it adopts the positivists' skepticism toward values.

Neither of the first two camps provides a good ethical basis for educational research. Indeed, they may be criticized for offering no ethical basis at all. However else they differ, they share a deep skepticism toward values generally (House & Howe, 1999). As intimated above, the postmodernist skepticism is simply more thoroughgoing. It applies not only to values, but to facts, epistemology, and rationality, as well.

The third camp, typically associated with critical theory and pragmatism (Howe, 1988), takes a different track. Like the postmodernist camp, it embraces the merging of epistemology and ethics. But rather than adopting the positivists' skepticism toward values and applying it across the fact/value divide, it moves in the other direction. It takes knowledge, rationality, and the like, and applies *them* across the fact/value divide, resulting in a view in which ethics falls within the purview of epistemology and in which it is the subject of rational investigation. Elsewhere (Howe, 1988), I have labeled the third camp "transformationist," and have argued that it is the only tenable response to the interpretive turn.

For her part, Ellis seems to embrace the position of the second, or postmodernist camp. (I use the term "postmodernist" for convenience, and I should note that the way I describe the second camp probably doesn't coincide, at least not neatly, with the views of all of the members of the diverse group of thinkers who embrace the idea of "postmodernism.") Ellis may very well eschew the kind skeptical, subjectivist premises associated with the second camp, but she provides little by way of argument that would permit her to avoid being characterized in this way.

Ellis' story of her brother's death is gripping, to be sure, and an insightful chronicling of the emotions and the norms of behavior that attend such events. But what are we to make of this vis à vis social research?

Ellis says that true stories such as hers are between fiction and sociological understanding, and help fill a gap in the sociological understanding of emotions. Perhaps these claims can be warranted, but she does little more than assert them. I am thus left wondering why, on the continuum, her method isn't much closer to fiction in its epistemological and ethical dimensions than it is to sociology.

Ellis's most crucial claim vis à vis ethics is that her method "encourages ethnographic subjects (co-authors) to reclaim and write their own lives" (p. 250). But how does it do this? And to what end?

Regarding the question of how, since it is the readers of sociological journals who are likely to have access to Ellis's work, is it only they who will be enabled to reclaim and write their own lives? Regarding question of ends, is Ellis *simply* offering her work to readers so they can reclaim and write their own lives, eschewing any judgments about what would be a good outcome of this? Or does she have some good outcome in mind, say, emancipation?

It is because Ellis fails to provide any clear guidance on how to answer either of these questions that she is vulnerable to the charge that her method is ethically aimless (perhaps even narcissistic).

The two charges against Ellis's study—that it is ethically aimless and not even an instance of social research—are serious, to be sure. And they have considerable merit, in my view, at least from a narrow perspective. From a broader perspective, however, Ellis provokes social researchers to examine the idea that autobiography has a place in social research. Such provocation fits nicely with what she explicitly describes as an "experimental" approach. Furthermore, we can see in (subsequent) studies such as Alexander's just how autobiography may be used in social research in thoroughly fruitful and defensible ways.

REFERENCES

House, E., & Howe, K. (1999). *Values in evaluation and social research.* Thousand Oaks, CA: Sage.

Howe, K. (1988). Against the quantitative-qualitative incompatibility thesis (or dogmas die hard). *Educational Researcher, 17*(8), 10–16.

PERSPECTIVE 9: POSTSTRUCTURALISM ON THE ELLIS STUDY

LYNDA STONE   *University of North Carolina at Chapel Hill*

Hélène Cixous (1937–) is known to English-speaking audiences as one of "the three French feminists," along with Kristeva and Luce Irigaray. Multi-lingual both literally and figuratively through her writing, Cixous is Algerian/Jewish by birth and culture. The death of her father at age 11 has had a lasting effect on her life, leading her first into the lives of women through her mid-wife mother, then into language and writing. Her thesis concerned the work of James Joyce. She taught at Nanterre and helped found the University of Paris VIII where she holds a chair in English literature. Since the late 1960s she has written as a poet, playwright, and academic essayist; prime themes are writing and subjectivity.

Published in the early 1990s; Carolyn Ellis's courageous sociological narrative of the sudden death of a loved one has added significance following September 11, 2001. Readers understand even more so the loss that she experienced over the airplane crash that took her brother's life. Ellis's own scholarly purpose is to extend what it means to do research in the social sciences. She writes, "'True' stories . . . fit in the space between fiction and social science, joining ethnographic and literary writing, and autobiographical and sociological understanding" (p. 250). Ellis's methodological exemplification is not directly related to education but it clearly joins a tradition over the last couple of decades of using narrative in educational research (e.g., Weiler, 1999; Fine, 1998).

Ellis's narrative is intensely personal in retelling of the days' events surrounding the plane crash. She writes as family member, as sister, daughter, and partner, as child and adult. Hers is an honorable and traditional role as "caretaker," putting her own pain aside to allow others theirs. Love and focus on others is freely given but carries personal consequences. She recounts, "'A mother's pain is worse, the worst there is' . . . [my mother] says bitterly, her self-absorption offering no place for my grief" (p. 255). As one caring (Noddings, 1984), Ellis's womanly responsibilities range from family planning to "greeting." The latter is a kind of behind-the-scene public duty to welcome mourners, to record all acts of sympathy, to feed everyone. There is mutual care especially between Ellis and her male partner and with her father and brother, but in traditional rituals surrounding death her wishes are never considered first. For example, feminist inclinations are banked when no women pallbearers are allowed (p. 256).

Ellis's epiphany recreates and reminds us of women's historical duty to support and sustain others. In this day and age, however, given her own comments of self-need and desire for alternative scholarly expression, the piece entails a certain irony: She never directly asserts herself as a woman, nor significantly names herself as a woman writer.[1] Enter French feminist theorist, Hélène Cixous, whose work contributes a particular feminist poststructuralist perspective. Relative to the overview, Cixous's project is very similar to that of Derrida with whom she shares among other ideas a critique of binaries. Language in terms of writing is central, establishing relations within text, among texts, and between text and, for her especially, writing practices of gender and sexuality. Further, subjectivity is tied to binaries of these practices and is "not directly" agentive. Again persons act—perhaps more importantly for Cixous—they desire. The "unknown" relation is the effect of desire on conscious, rational action. Finally an aesthetic of artistic, especially literary, evokes desire.

To overview Cixous, here is a comentator's statement:

> Cixous' name is most often associated with that of *écriture féminine*—"feminine writing." For Cixous such a writing is feminine in two senses. First while . . . [suggesting] that feminine writing is potentially the province of both sexes, she believes women are currently closer to a feminine economy than men. . . . [She] suggests that a feminine writing will bring into existence alternative forms of relation, perception, and expression. It is in this sense . . . [that] Cixous believes writing is revolutionary. (Sellers, 1994, p. xxix)

Cixous's notable introduction to English audiences in 1976 is her classic essay, "Laugh of the Medusa."

Influenced by Freud, and especially in what follows this critique by Derrida and Marcel Mauss, Cixous's idea of "feminine economy" ranges across sexual difference, otherness, and writing. At the outset she has much to say to Ellis about cultural binaries, about death of the son for the mother, about living life, about invisible strength. In the book, *The Newly Born Woman*, written with Catherine Clément, Cixous's essay "Sorties" sets out founding cultural binaries in this way:

> Where is she?
>
> Activity/passivity
>
> Sun/Moon
>
> Culture/Nature
>
> . . . .
>
> *Man*
>
> Woman
>
> Always the same metaphor: we follow it, it carries us, beneath all its figures, wherever discourse is organized. . . . Logocentrism subjects thought . . . to a binary system, related to "the" couple, man/woman. (Cixous, 1975/1994, pp. 37–38)

In this system, woman is always passive, invisible, subordinate. Cixous ironically continues, "Ultimately the world of 'being' can function while precluding the mother. No need for a mother, as long as there is some motherliness. . . . Either woman is passive or she does not exist. What is left of her is unthinkable, unthought" (p. 39).

For Cixous, transforming binaries occurs through recognition that categories of man and woman are themselves problematic and, as indicated earlier, that each person is constituted of the masculine and feminine. But there is distinction, difference: Historically "speaking," women actually have a positive rather than a negative position; they live with what Cixous names as a "bisexuality," recognizing both aspects in their own being as well as in being related to the other. Here is Cixous (1975/1994) again: "[I] am speaking here of femininity (a kind of living with the masculine and feminine) as keeping alive the other that is confided to her, that visits her, that she can love as other" (p. 42). In contrast to women, Cixous believes that for traditional men this "non-exclusion" is threatening and intolerable. One way to see this "sexual" difference is through Mauss's theory of the gift. Within a phallocentric order in which there is no "free" gift, the difference between men and women giving concerns the need and expectation of return. For men,

Cixous explains, the return is "more masculinity": virility, authority, power, money, pleasure (see p. 44). In contrast, women "do not make a monarchy" of their bodies, of desire. Again Cixous,

> [She] doesn't try to "recover" her expenses. She is able not to return to herself, never settling down, pouring out, going everywhere to the other. . . . [She] is how-far-being-reaches . . . She surprises herself at seeing, being, pleasuring in the gift of changeablity. (pp. 44–45)

For Cixous, the poststructuralist, while there is no essence of woman nor of *I,* there is—culminating—writing. From "Medusa," Cixous (1976) asserts, "I shall speak about women's writing: about *what it will do*" (p. 875). Commentator Mireille Calle-Gruber (1994) says this of her texts: "Inscribing the joys of writing . . . [presenting] a *moment* of . . . driving forces. . . . [Writing] *gives the gift* of the texts; the thrust of language, the happening of meaning. . . . It is the gift of the heuristic . . . where words speak and make marvels" (p. 208, emphasis in original).

For Ellis, writing as a woman thus can be more than the telling of a narrative in social science. It can be a celebration of the feminine but more so, of being a woman—and in the current vernacular, of having a voice. Ellis's contribution to sociological theory is important but, in the process of a being a "woman writing," she "escapes death" through education, through a telling that is more than the story.

NOTES

1. Given Ellis's familiar and societal culture, there was no place for expression of her own desire; this is precisely Cixous's point. Importantly, there is also no essentializing of ethical blame. As explicated in what follows this is because at the least all persons are made up of masculine and feminine aspects.

REFERENCES

Calle-Gruber, M. (1994). Afterward. *The Hélène Cixous reader* (pp. 207–220). London: Routledge.

Cixous, H. (1976). Laugh of the medusa. *Signs: Journal of Women in Culture and Society 1*(4): 875–893.

Cixous, H. (1994). The newly born woman. In *The Hélène Cixous reader* (pp. 37–45). London: Routledge. (Original Work Published 1975)

Fine, M. (1998). *The unknown city: Lives of poor and working class adults.* Boston: Beacon.

Noddings, N. (1984). *Caring: A feminine approach to ethics and moral education.* Berkeley: University of California Press.

Sellers, S. (1994). Introduction. *The Hélène Cixous reader* (pp. xxvi–xxxiv). London: Routledge.

Weiler, K. (1999). *Telling women's lives: Inquiries in the history of women's education.* Philadelphia: Open University Press.

CHAPTER 10

The Sullivan Study

VOICES INSIDE SCHOOLS:
NOTES FROM A MARINE BIOLOGIST'S DAUGHTER:
ON THE ART AND SCIENCE OF ATTENTION

ANNE McCRARY SULLIVAN

National-Louis University, Tampa, Florida

Through an autobiographical lens, Anne McCrary Sullivan explores the sensory and emotional aspects of attending and their implications for teaching, learning, and research. Her poetry and stanzaic prose attempt to awaken in the reader an artistic engagement with the various meanings of attention. Her use of this genre challenges traditional approaches to representing knowledge.

In an age of attention deficit disorder and of frequent teacher complaints that overentertained children do not want to pay attention, the issue of attention in educational settings is critical. John Dewey's early insistence that curriculum grow out of the interests of the child (Dewey, 1902) included the concept that students would, without coercion, give attention to matters and materials of immediate relevance to their lives. A strong contingency of educators and researchers continues to find this concept critical. More generally, the focus has been on how to get students to pay attention whether or not the curriculum has interest or relevance—how to trick, entertain, bribe, or coerce them to perform (Kohn, 1993). Historically, in the field of education, our concern with engaging and maintaining student attention has been consistent, but our investigations of the nature of attention and its development rather limited.

What exactly are teachers asking for when they say, "Pay attention"? What are the relationships between attention and intrinsic motivation? Is it possible to teach habits of attending? How can we enroll peripheral attention to the advantage of education? How can we know the long-term effects of attending?

In the realm of educational research, qualitative researchers call for learning about phenomena by giving them sustained attention. What is the nature of the researcher's attention? How do we learn to attend with keen eyes and fine sensibilities? How do we teach others to do it?

My autobiography is largely an autobiography of attention—learning it, teaching it, discovering its role in research. It's a story that began when I was very young.

I. An Autobiography of Attention (Part I)

Notes from a Marine Biologist's Daughter

> My mother loves the salty mud of estuaries,
> has no need of charts to know what time
> low tide will come. She lives
> by an arithmetic of moon,
> calculates emergences of mud,
>
> waits for all that crawls there, lays eggs,
> buries itself in the shallow edges

Sullivan, A.M. Notes from a Marine Biologist's Daughter: On the Art and Science of Attention: Harvard Educational Review, 70(2) 211–227. Copyright © 2000 by the President and Fellows of Harvard College. All rights reserved.

of streamlets and pools. She digs
for *chaetopterus,* yellow and orange
worms that look like lace.

She leads me where *renilla* bloom
purple and white colonial lives,
where brittle stars, like moss,
cling to stone. She knows
where the sea horse wraps its tail
and the unseen lives of plankton.

My mother walks and sinks into an ooze,
centuries of organisms ground
to pasty darkness. The sun
burns at her shoulders
in its slow passage across the sky.
Light waves like pincers
in her mud-dark hair.

Mother Collecting Marine Specimens

She poles the skiff from sunlight
into the drawbridge shadow, eases
against a piling, its muddy shapes
exposed by lowering tide.

In a cave-like cool, she nudges
grey clusters, crusty forms.
She scrapes, selects,
lays silty bits and clumps
in a bucket of clear water.

Intent, she peers and plucks.
A streak of blood appears on her thumb.
She doesn't notice. She never does.
I slide a finger over creosote blisters,
hear them pop, feel them flatten,
then stare into the realm of the underbridge—
great toothy gears, twisted cables.

Above our boat, the whirr of tires.
No one knows we're under here
or thinks of these barnacles,
their hair-like legs kicking
just below the water line.
Bells begin to clang, the hum
ceases, the bridge shudders,
its teeth begin to grind.

When we reenter brightness
and the ordinary pitch of traffic,
I lean to look in Mother's bucket:
green stones, yellow trees,
purple stars, an orange flame.

Herding Fiddler Crabs

The sun is high, beginning its downward arc.
Our pits, buckets buried in mud to their rims,
are ready. We encircle the herd, our arms
raised in mud-smeared curves, mimicking
the crabs' outspread pincers.
We stamp our feet, close in.
They flee like receding tide.

I remember the films shot from airplanes,
the estuary greens, blues, blacks
curving around each other's shapes,
and on the mud flats, herds
of indistinguishable bodies
making silent, amoebic migrations.

It's different down here. Listen.
Thousands of clicks,
the small collisions,
claws and carapaces,
finely jointed legs landing
in frantic succession
on mud. And there—
so many tiny fallings.

Mother in Water

"Did you see
how she stared and trembled?
If I ever get like that
I want you to row me
beyond the breakers,
push me over.
I mean it. Promise."

Sometimes I see us
in a small white boat.
At the bow, she sits,
back erect,
facing forward.
Her head jerks lightly.
I row. My arms ache,
eyes sting.
Behind us, land
flattens to a line.

Before she was twelve
she knew these waters,
poled alone
in a wooden skiff
through the winding maze
of slough and marsh,

channel and sandbar;
she'd beach the boat,
take off her shirt and swim.

Only water now. Water.
How easily, quietly
it opens. Just
beneath the surface
I see her gliding,
gills opening,
expanding like sponges,
waving like feathers.
A flash of silver
darts into the green.

How I Learned to Love Picasso

At nineteen, I knew nothing, wanted to know
everything,
including why those paintings hung in the Petit Palais,
why people lined up for blocks in the cold,
why I stood with them blowing clouds of breath.

Les Demoiselles D'Avignon. I stared
at fractured shapes and faces,
pondered all that flesh pink
and then one leg
where a thick blue line
plunged from thigh to calf.

I imagined that line gone.

Learning Blue

My mother taught me blue—
water under the boat,
shadow in the marsh,

blue flashing
at the sides of fish,

blue crabs waving
blue and white claws,

blue speck
at the clam's inner hinge,
just beside
where the soft body lies.

Now I learn blue again—
oyster bruise
at my inner thigh,

blue-black ink
of the squid's soft gland
deepening, spreading, tender.

Beware: The Poet Comes for Tea

She sits, rattles the ice in her glass,
laughs at small talk, but
she's looking under your skin.

She sees your bones, that fine crack
in the left radius; she hears the blood
rushing out of the heart, leaping

into its hopeful journey,
then limping back to the side door,
knocking lightly, pleading.

She feels that spark at the synapse,
flinches, just barely; you don't see.
Later, she goes to her room and writes

your life. She will mail you a poem
which disrupts breath, makes you weep
for all you thought hidden, interior, safe.

Dolphins

This evening, in diffuse light,
I learn from dolphins what I must know
of poems—how they break the surface
when least expected, make their arcs
in peripheral vision. Startled

at the first glimpse, I jerked to see
their fine motion, the dark lines
tracing their quiet way.
I had been walking, just walking
the curve of the shore, thinking of

who knows what. Who cares? It's gone,
replaced. Oh, grace! I turned
to follow their benedictions, my pace
matching the pace of one slow swimmer.
Each time it rose, it rose

beside me, until it turned
to deeper water. I saw
the last blip of its dark morse code,
then stood and stared,
watching and wanting.

Water and water and water.
Visions cannot be commanded.
The air grows chill now with pink
consolation. One line of light
lies on the nervous surface.

When I die

Write to my friends.

Tell them what time of day or night
I died and what the weather was.

Tell them the color of the walls
that last contained me.

Describe the quality of light in the room,
its brightness or its grayness. Did light
make a pattern on my face?

Tell them if I closed my eyes myself; or
give the name of the one who closed them for me.

Tell if there were flowers in the room,
or outside the window, or if there were any scent
that might be called the scent of death.

Tell them the sound of my silence.
Listen carefully for this.

Say who pulled the sheet over my head;
describe the shape of my body under it.

When had I last listened to music?
What was the sound of my last breath?

Was there any small ugliness?
A trail of saliva? A drooping?

Did anyone notice an insect in the room?

Write quickly; avoid nothing.
My friends are poets. They need details.

II. Poems in the Academy (Part 1)

Poems are an anomaly in educational journals. Many readers will be puzzled about the presence of these poems, unsure of their relation to educational inquiry and theory. I would suggest that the relations are multiple, subtle, and complex, and that these very characteristics are part of their potential value.

As a case study of a woman whose life has been grounded in attention, these poems collectively raise significant questions about the nature of attention: how it develops; whether a model of intense attention has power for teaching attention; how attention to external realities might facilitate awareness of internal realities; how focused attention to an immediate reality may engage memory and/or imagination. "The purpose of art," says novelist James Baldwin, "is to lay bare the questions which have been hidden by the answers" (1962, p. 17).

As a collection of forms that construct their organization from the web-like motions of the mind, rather than in the linear discursive patterns traditionally prescribed by the Western academy, these poems invite new ways of engaging with the problem of attention, new ways of investigating histories of attention, and complementary ways of mapping such investigations.

As representations of lived states of attention, they resonate with recent brain research related to attentional phenomena, including the roles of peripheral and focused attention (Caine & Caine, 1994; Lozanov, 1978), and the significance of emotion in engaging and sustaining attention (Csikszentmihalyi, 1991; Damasio, 1994; Sylwester, 1995).

Incorporating highly concrete observations, these poems exemplify a degree of concreteness and detail that has potential for enriching both the accuracy and power of traditional field notes, as qualitative researchers strive to evoke the worlds they represent.

As manifestations of a way of processing information and experience that differs from long-established, well-entrenched, but recently challenged academic norms (Barone & Eisner, 1997; Eisner, 1997), these poems, appearing in this particular place, constitute a political statement on behalf of the enfranchisement of artists, whose voices have been marginalized in the academy.

III. Aesthetic Vision: A Complex Attention

Aesthetic vision suggests a high level of consciousness about what one sees. It suggests an alertness, a "wide-awakeness" that Maxine Greene (1978, 1995) has urged educators and researchers to learn from artists.

Aesthetic vision engages a sensitivity to suggestion, to pattern, to that which is beneath the surface as well as to the surface itself. It requires a fine attention to detail and form: the perception of relations (tensions and harmonies); the perception of nuance (colors of meaning); and the perception of change (shifts and subtle motions). It dares to address the ineffable (Eisner, 1979).

Aesthetic vision adjusts the flow of time. It may seize a moment in order to stare at it and see more fully, more deeply, but aesthetic vision does not assume that what one sees in the moment is what one will always see. It perceives the potential for transformation within any apparent fixity—a block of wood, a piece of clay, a display of words, the configuration of a classroom, or the behavior of an individual child.

Aesthetic vision is always from a specific point of view, filtered by a specific consciousness. It is personal and situational. It includes emotion, imagination, and paradox. It embraces complexity.

Teachers who function with aesthetic vision perceive the dynamic nature of what is unfolding in front of them at any given moment. They know how to "read" students, respond quickly, and reshape the flow of events (Eisner, 1979, 1983). They do not accept that what they see is immutable. They have a finely tuned sense of how to move toward new pedagogical configurations (Greene, 1994).

Likewise, researchers with aesthetic vision perceive the dynamics of a situation and know how to "read" it. They look at details within their contexts, perceive relations among the parts and between the parts and the whole. They look for pattern within disorder, for unity beneath superficial disruption, and for disruption beneath superficial unity. They construct forms and suggest meanings.

IV. An Autobiography of Attention (Part 2)

My mother, the scientist, taught me to see. She taught me attention to the complexities of surface detail and also attention to what lies beneath those surfaces. She taught me the rhythms of tide and regeneration, and the syllables of the natural world rubbing against each other. In doing so, she made me a poet.

My mother, the teacher, held classes in mud and water and light. She taught with buckets and shovels and nets. Her students' tennis shoes, and hers, squished loudly as they worked, discovered, learned. I observed that my mother and her students were happy. I became a teacher.

My mother, the researcher, went into the field twice a day whatever the weather for years, methodically, with her plankton nets. Then she sat patiently at the microscope on the kitchen table, observing, noticing, discovering patterns, making sense. In that kitchen, I learned the patience of research.

My mother made order of the raggedness of the living world, and I was paying attention. But I didn't know at the time that I was, and I'm quite sure that she didn't think I was. I gave little overt attention to her work. She dragged me along on the mud flats, to the boat docks, under bridges. I went and entertained myself as best I could. While she focused intently on the organisms that grew on pilings, paying such acute attention that she didn't even notice the bleeding cut on her hand ("she never did"), I was distractedly popping creosote blisters.

And yet, there is another layer to this, because years later I remember with a vividness and an intensity that compel me to poetry. On some level, in some hidden and inarticulate way, I must have been attending and recording extremely well. I was learning, internalizing, without any direct instruction.

Mother did sometimes offer direct instruction, telling me the Latin names of organisms and placing them in their scientific categories. I remember very little of what she taught

me in this direct way. What I do remember is so deeply embedded in experience that it has entered my ways of thinking and perceiving, my very way of being, without the intermediary of language—at any rate, without language that addressed this learning directly.

What did physicality and emotion have to do with my learning and with sublingual attention? How important were the tactile impressions of sun on my skin, mud beneath my feet, the water's salt at my lip, the rockings of Mother's wooden boat? How did they matter, those lappings and squishings, the bubblings and "thousands of clicks, / the small collisions, / claws and carapaces?" What did I learn from surprise and delight at the laciness of the worms she dug up from mud, the "yellow trees, purple stars, an orange flame" suddenly in her bucket? What are the implications of this for education in a society that demands artificial attention and immediate testable results? What are the implications for researchers who are trying to make visible the invisible processes of cognition?

V. Poems in the Academy (Part 2)

Poems, born of attention, also invite attention. They rarely get it. As a society, we have not been taught how to attend to art, how to "read" it, how to process its content or its potential for generating useful questions. We are relatively illiterate in the arts, even those of us who are otherwise deeply and well educated, unless we have specifically sought those kinds of reading lessons. As a culture, our lessons in art have generally been indirect and have indicated that art is peripheral, an expendable extra. In short, to borrow a term from John Dewey, we have been *miseducated*.

Dewey understood and defended, sometimes a bit feistily, the role of art as a way of encoding knowledge about complex relations:

> To think effectively in terms of relations of qualities is as severe a demand upon thought as to think in terms of symbols, verbal and mathematical. . . . Production of a work of genuine art probably demands more intelligence than does most of the so called thinking that goes on among those who pride themselves on being "intellectual." (1980, p. 46)

Many in the academic community, not having been taught to read aesthetic forms, reject them as representations of knowledge. If, however, we are to become literate in a wider range of the forms in which knowledge may be encoded, we must give attention to these forms. We must stare at them, ponder them, arrive at an understanding not only of what the forms contain, but also of how form informs.

Walker Evans, the early twentieth-century photographer, an arts-based researcher long before the term became popular, advocated focused attention as a way of coming to know. He advised us, "Stare. It is the way to educate your eye, and more. Stare, pry, listen, eavesdrop. Die knowing something. You are not here long" (Thompson & Hill, 1982, p. 161).

Contemplating my own autobiography of attention, I become aware of the extent to which I have learned about visual art simply by staring at it, as in "How I Learned to Love Picasso." I stood in front of that large painting, *Les Demoiselles D'Avignon,* and stared, allowed my eye to move as it would among the details. I stared with a curious eye, an eye that didn't yet know how to understand, didn't yet know that art could teach me. For rather a long time I stood there, wondering what I was "supposed" to be seeing. Then I allowed imagination to guide my vision. When I imagined that blue line gone and suddenly felt in the painting a shift of energy and balance, a loss that I couldn't articulate but that I undeniably felt as loss, I realized for the first time that all of the parts of the composition mattered. Any alteration of the part would have an effect on the whole. Nothing was accidental. There was an ecology of the work of art. This was, for me, a revolutionary and long-lasting insight, as was the new understanding that I could learn about art by giving it focused attention.

How often do we teach children in school this kind of attention? How often in school were we ourselves encouraged to stare?

VI. Teaching Attention

How might we teach attention? I've been struggling with that question for over twenty years now. When I taught high school English and creative writing, I was always searching for ways to bring students into attention, the sort of deep attention that would elicit the capacity for poetry that I believed they all had in them. I would do things like take them out on the broad lawn in front of the school, have them spread out, each to sit alone and watch a small patch of grass, to observe and record "what happens there."

The wording, "what happens there," was important. Skepticism about this assignment was generally high among my students. "Just stare," I would say. "Stare at the grass until something happens." No one ever failed to see things happen. Small events became sources of excitement— an ant crawling up a blade of grass, a flutter of motion produced by a breeze, a shifting of light, the crossing of a cloud shadow.

In another homework assignment, I would ask them to "find a place where there's nothing going on. Sit there for ten minutes and record everything that happens." In response to this assignment, tenth grader Rhonda Rogers sat on her back porch and made the journal entries that led to this:

> Secluded
> and alone,
> I sit searching.
>
> The nightly cicadan chant
> converses with itself.
>
> A cricket's flat drone echoes,
> rattlingly hollow.
>
> Zephyrs shudder empty limbs.
> Detached leaves scuttle on pavement.
>
> A dog passes,
> his nails click, click, clicking
> on asphalt.
> In the distance, one lonely
> wails.
>
> Forlorn, questing cars
> slug into darkness.
>
> An isolated airplane
> dissolves into vacuous night.
>
> In houses nearby,
> occasional voices, indistinguishable,
> mumble.
>
> Somewhere, a door slams shut,
> closing someone in—
> or out.
> Self-trapped moths flutter,
> taunt lights
> until their muted thuds
> interrupt a clangorous quiet.
>
> My mind reaches . . .
> Through raucous recess,
> damns this solitude. (Rogers, 1984, p. 31)

Clearly, Rhonda had a gift for language that this assignment did not teach her. But with this and other assignments for attention, her capacity for subtle detail and fine distinctions increased, her work as an artist grew richer with particularity and concreteness. She was developing as an artist and, I would suggest, as a researcher in the world of her experience. As we consider her poem now, we may also find that it raises interesting questions about the researcher's positioning: the role of the subjective perspective in selecting and arranging details, and the inherently interpretive nature of reporting.

Attention, Empathy, and Research

When I left the world of teaching high school and entered a university context, I continued explorations in poetry and attention as they related to teaching and to research. Working with preservice teachers, for example, I gave the assignment: "Choose a student to observe over a period of three weeks. Select a student who is different from you, one you have trouble understanding, maybe one who drives you up the wall. Record the child's actions and re-actions, audible language and body language." It was a tra-ditional sort of case study assignment except for the product it required: "Construct a poem, from the point of view of the child you have observed, incorporating at least one fragment of that child's speech."

Students reported that this was a very difficult assign-ment, not because of the poetic form—I had taught them strategies that related data gathering to poetry and we had written poems—but because of the difficulty of getting in-side the skin of someone "so different from me." To get un-der the skin of the other, rather than to simply report observable externals, demanded a deeper sort of attention, an attention that required an imaginative penetration of bar-riers and that conjoined with empathy.

Shelley Scholl, one of my students, asked if she might modify that assignment a little. She wanted to write a short poem representing each of the students in the twelfth-grade English class in which she was interning, not actually speak-ing in first person but representing something of what she knew or imagined of the student's inner life. This is what her short poems looked like:

i.
Silent in the corner,
Luke Pennington
stares down at his boot toes,
out the window,
sketches vultures,
wishes he were
anybody else.

ii.
Karen holds her breath each night,
holds Clay in the swaying single-wide,
fingers her engagement ring
and prays for eighteen.

iii.
Stephen's left leg
juts a leaden semi-arabesque

into the aisle between the desks;
Cheek pressed against the unread text,
he dreams of his future. (Scholl, 1995)

When I read Shelley's collection of small poems, it was clear that she had focused a keen attention on these students and that her attention to exteriors had helped her go more deeply into awareness of complex interiors. The class she was teaching was, by many evidences, "difficult." It was a class that could and did try the patience of the supervising teacher as well as her intern. But Shelley reported that her patience grew as she focused attention on individuals and deepened her sensitivity to their contexts. Maxine Greene has proposed that engagement with great works of fine art may open the imagination's way into empathy (Greene 1995). Making art, "fine" or otherwise, also has this potential.

In the research realm, Elliot Eisner observes, "One job that scholars increasingly want done is engendering a sense of empathy . . . because we have begun to realize that hu-man feeling does not pollute understanding. In fact, un-derstanding others and the situations they face may well require it" (1997, p. 8).

VII. On Attention, Education, and Art

To deny the potential role of artistic attention and artistic rep-resentation in investigations of educational issues is to limit our approaches to knowledge. It is the researcher's essential role, Eisner contends, "to highlight, . . . to call to our attention . . . to deepen and broaden our experience . . . to help us un-derstand what we are looking at" (1991, p. 59). These are also essential roles of the artist. Lawrence Stenhouse maintains that "all good art is an inquiry and an experiment. It is by virtue of being an artist that the teacher is a researcher. . . . The artist is the researcher *par excellence*" (1988, p. 47).

The artist is a researcher with his or her whole organ-ism, inquiring, testing with the body as well as the mind, sensing and seeing, responding and retesting—a multitude of functions performed simultaneously—registering com-plexity, then sorting, finding pattern, making meaning. To the extent that the artist is a connoisseur (Eisner, 1991), to the extent that he or she has a rich repertoire of experiences against which or within the context of which to "test" (Schön, 1987), the artist becomes an astute researcher, ca-pable of illuminations and new meanings, new visions of possibility, new questions. We must not overlook the po-tential role of the artist, alongside that of the scientist and the traditional educational researcher, in our investigations of attention and other critical educational issues.

The poem "Notes from a Marine Biologist's Daughter" first appeared in *The Gettysburg Review,* volume 7, number 4, and is reprinted here with the acknowledgment of the editors.

Three other poems appeared previously in the following publications: "Mother Collecting Marine Specimens" and "Mother in Water," 1994, *Tar River Poetry, 33*(2); "Herding Fiddler Crabs," 1998, *Earth's Daughters, 51*(17).

REFERENCES

Baldwin, J. (1962). *Creative process.* New York: Ridge Press.

Barone, T., & Eisner, E. (1997). Arts-based educational research. In R. Jaeger (Ed.), *Complementary methods for research in education* (pp. 73–98). Washington, DC: American Educational Research Association.

Caine, R., & Caine, G. (1994). *Making connections: Teaching and the human brain.* New York: Addison-Wesley.

Csikszentmihalyi, M. (1991). *Flow: The psychology of optimal experience.* New York: Harper Perennial.

Damasio, A. R. (1994). *Descartes' error: Emotion, reason, and the human brain.* New York: Putnam.

Dewey, J. (1980). *Art as experience.* New York: Perigree. (Original work published 1934)

Dewey, J. (1990). *The child and the curriculum.* Chicago: University of Chicago. (Original work published 1902)

Eisner, E. (1979). *The educational imagination.* New York: Macmillan.

Eisner, E. (1983). The art and craft of teaching. *Educational Leadership, 40*(4), 4–13.

Eisner, E. (1991). *The enlightened eye: Qualitative inquiry and the enhancement of educational practice.* New York: Macmillan.

Eisner, E. (1997). The promise and perils of alternative forms of data representation. *Educational Researcher, 26*(6), 4–10.

Greene, M. (1978). Towards wide-awakeness: An argument for the arts and humanities in education. In *Landscapes in learning* (pp. 161–167). New York: Teachers College Press.

Greene, M. (1994). Carpe diem: The arts and school restructuring. *Teachers College Record, 95,* 494–507.

Greene, M. (1995). *Releasing the imagination: Essays on education, the arts, and social change.* San Francisco: Jossey-Bass.

Kohn, A. (1993). *Punished by rewards.* New York: Houghton Mifflin.

Lozanov, G. (1978). *Suggestology and suggestopedia—theory and practice.* Working document for United Nations Educational, Scientific, and Cultural Organization (UNESCO). (ED-78/WS/119)

Rogers, R. (1984). Secluded. In D. Houchins (Ed.), *Mindflight 4* (p. 31). Baytown, TX: Robert E. Lee High School.

Scholl, S. (1995, November). Untitled poems. In A. Sullivan (Ed.), *Poetry and passion in teacher education: Personalizing and internalizing knowledge.* Papers presented at the Annual Convention of National Council of Teachers of English, San Diego.

Schön, D. (1987). *Educating the reflective practitioner.* San Francisco: Jossey-Bass.

Stenhouse, L. (1988). Artistry and teaching: The teacher as focus of research and development. *Journal of Curriculum and Supervision, 4*(1), 43–51.

Sylwester, R. (1995). *A celebration of neurons: An educator's guide to the human brain.* Alexandria, VA: Association of Supervision and Curriculum Development.

Thompson, J., & Hill, J. T. (Eds.). (1982). *Walker Evans at work.* New York: Harper & Row.

PERSPECTIVE 1: POSTPOSITIVISM ON THE SULLIVAN STUDY

D. C. PHILLIPS   *Stanford University*

There is an ambiguity in the important term "inquiry" that is brought to the fore by this paper. In its more technical usage, the term is close in meaning to "scientific research," and clearly applies to investigations that have an *epistemic aim*. Thus, medical researchers are carrying out inquiries to determine if the operation of the HIV virus can be interfered with; anthropologists and others are trying to solve the riddle of human origins, and such related matters as the relationship between our own species and the Neanderthals; and various educational researchers are trying to pin down the precise effects of class size reduction. The FBI is "making inquiries" into the September disasters in New York and Washington, D.C., meaning that they are seeking to reach evidence-based conclusions about the truth of certain hypotheses about the cause of those dreadful incidents. On the other hand, there is a very general usage in which "inquiry" can refer to any relatively complex but cohesive activity that has the goal of reaching an informative conclusion or the making of a complex product. I believe that in my role as a philosopher I carry out inquiries in this sense—I go through a complex set of processes in order to reach conclusions about such matters as "Is Dewey's theory of knowledge valid?" and "Can social scientists possibly discover laws that are analogous to the laws of physics?" I have little doubt that poets and painters make numerous inquiries in the course of producing their respective verses and landscapes. But it is important to note just *how* general this second sense of the word is; essentially, "inquiry" here has a meaning close to "thinking," so all of us are often inquiring!

All this is by way of preamble to the following point: I see no reason to regard the paper by Sullivan as an inquiry in the narrower sense in which we expect pieces of educational research to be pieces of inquiry; it does not constitute an inquiry, with an epistemic aim, into the nature of attention. (No epistemic claims at all are made by the author.) Although the author calls the paper "a case study," and the "abstract" claims she "explores the sensory and emotional aspects of attending," it is not clear to me that she offers us either a "case" or an "exploration." The paper is hard to characterize in terms of traditional genres; it can be counted as a typical "academic exercise" if I can be so blunt, and so it is at best an inquiry in the loose sense of the term, although I shall suggest below that it is not even that!

It is important that we cling to common sense here—writing poems, and reading them, are not in any meaningful way *research* and are not in themselves inquiries in any but the broadest sense of being thoughtful activities. Writing a poem is a literary or artistic endeavor—and an important one, but it is not research although a poet might well at some stage engage in what we could loosely call "research"; reading a poem is an interpretive or appreciative or literary activity, again nothing like research or inquiry in any standard sense of these terms. On the other hand, *analyzing* a poem is an activity I would be happy to embrace as being, in the broad sense, a form of inquiry—but we do not get any analysis in this paper. (I hope it is unnecessary to stress that I am not denigrating the making or the reading of poetry; on the contrary, I value both activities highly and wish that personally I were better at both of them. Neither am I asserting that the reading and discussing of poems is not an important educational activity; these things simply are not educational research—they belong to a different "form of life," a notion I touched upon in my commentary on the paper by Carolyn Ellis.)

My general point here has merely been one about "truth in advertising." This acts as segue into the next point. The poems certainly could be *part* of a case study or of an exploration of the topic of attention, but a lot more would be required than we are offered here. If the poems were each accompanied by a detailed analysis or commentary, in which it was pointed out how the author had attended to certain things and how those things were represented, it would be getting close to being an inquiry. If, in addition, the analysis or discussion used the insights thus developed to make some general points about attention—points that were lacking in the wider literature on the topic, then I would not only say the paper represented an inquiry, I also would say that it would then have made an important contribution to the topic. But we get none of this; what we are faced with are a number of interesting poems, plus a very general and somewhat scattered discussion that makes no concerted effort to tie in with these poems. To point to merely one example of a lost opportunity: The author states, rather boldly, that "these poems invite new ways of engaging with the problem of attention, new ways of investigating histories of attention," but the reader is given no inkling of what these "new ways" are! And to illustrate how disconnected the "theoretical" part of the paper is from the poems that are supposed to be some kind of evidence or case that supports the theory or that are illuminated by it, consider the following passage:

> Teachers who function with aesthetic vision perceive the dynamic nature of what is unfolding in front of them at any given moment. They know how to "read" students, respond quickly, and re-shape the flow of events. . . . They do not accept that what they see is immutable. They have a finely tuned sense of how to move toward new pedagogical configurations. (pp. 287–288)

The bold (if not rash) generalizations in this passage may or may not be true; certainly the author offers no evidence either way. But the key question is "How are the points here related to the poems?" What justification do they offer for including the poems in the paper, or, to turn it the other way around, what justification do the poems provide for these assertions? Perhaps it is being suggested that teachers who read these poems will develop "aesthetic vision," but certainly there is no warrant for this to be found in the paper. Reluctantly I reach the conclusion that the paper is too disjointed, too illogically developed, to count as a clear inquiry into anything.

My final point is that I do not doubt that these poems were written by an individual who has paid close attention to certain phenomena, and I do not question that the fruit of her attention or explorations are *embodied* or *exemplified* in the poems (the author herself calls them "representations of attention"); and I would not question (for it strikes me as obvious) that it is also the case that a reader will not get much out of the poems unless he or she pays close attention to them. But none of this constitutes an "exploration" of "attention" in the sense of being a *rigorous inquiry* into the subject! And it seems close to being a truism that authors of *all* worthwhile works of literature, poetry, or art generally will have had to pay attention to the phenomena they are depicting or representing (for otherwise, why would we bother with these works, and why would we feel that it was worthwhile to spend time appreciating them?). Consider a different example: Shakespeare no doubt played very close attention to many things, and it is due to his resulting insight (in part) that his plays have survived the passage of the years. But *Hamlet,* to take a specific example, is not a "case study" of attention; rather, it exemplifies, or is the fruit of, the close attention that the author had paid to many human phenomena (which no doubt a literary theorist could write a long analytic essay about). The play itself is a case study (if it is a case study of anything), I would suggest, of a sensitive young man driven to the edge of madness by the murder of his father and the untimely remarriage of his mother. The play was so good it was worthy of publication, of course, but it is a serious confusion of genres to think that it ought to have been published in a journal of educational theory or research!

PERSPECTIVE 2: PRAGMATISM ON THE SULLIVAN STUDY

NEL NODDINGS   *Stanford University*

In what sense are visual art and poetry "research"? One does not have to be a positivist to question whether it is wise to blur the lines between poetry and research. Robert Frost said,

> Scholars and artists thrown together are often annoyed at the puzzle of where they differ. Both work from knowledge; but I suspect they differ most importantly in the way their knowledge is come by. Scholars get theirs with conscientious thoroughness along projected lines of logic; poets get theirs cavalierly and as it happens in and out of books. They stick to nothing deliberately, but let what will stick to them like burrs where they walk in the fields. (1949, p. viii)

Frost may have been guilty of overgeneralization here, for surely poets often perfect their poetry along projected lines of logic, and scholars frequently employ intuition, letting things come in as they will and sticking to them "like burrs." It seems right, however, to say that the enterprises are fundamentally different and that the skills required for proficiency in one area do not make one proficient in the other.

If Frost was basically right, then scholars and poets exercise their attention in very different ways. Both ways are valuable, but they are not identical. Moreover, there is little reason to suppose that the capacity to exercise attention in one domain can be used in a different domain. Great mathematicians are sometimes incapable of attending to human beings. The same can be said for great artists. Musicians may be hopeless at attending to mathematics. Scientists and economists may be oblivious to the ordinary world around them. And poets and artists rarely see things in a way that would win assent from scientists qua scientists.

The pragmatist must ask about the consequences of blurring the distinctions between fields such as research and art. Will both fields benefit? Will one or both be hurt? Clearly, human beings learn from research and from art, and problem solving is used in both, but these common features—important as they are—do not make research and art equivalent. Indeed, we sometimes say that a certain research study is "a work of art." By that, we mean that it has been executed so finely that it exhibits an aesthetic quality not usually found in research. Without that quality, however, it would still be research.

What would it mean to say that a work of art was well researched or that it is an impressive piece of research? A painting depicting an historical event can be accurate or inaccurate, but its reflection of historical facts has little to do with its acceptance as a work of art. If I deny that an artist is a researcher, have I taken anything away from the essence of her artistry?

We may admire Sullivan's poetry, be deeply touched by it, and even learn from it. Further, we may agree that education journals should publish poetry, humorous comments, letters, and illustrations in addition to research reports, position papers, reviews, and essays. There is no compelling reason to call all of these "research."

It may seem that I am trying to defend the integrity of research. That is true. But I would also like to preserve the identities of art, poetry, and prose literature. In the last few years, I have reviewed some dreadful poetry submitted as research on teaching. It seems unlikely that such poetry would be published by any respectable review of poetry. Calling it research does not improve its quality as poetry. Similarly, we rarely consider a research report "literature" (except in the trivial sense—the "literature" of the field). Once in a great while, a piece of legitimate research qualifies as literature but, when it does, that research has the qualities we usually associate with literature, and it is on this basis that we make our judgment. For example, it seems to me that William James's *Varieties of Religious Experience* is a work that qualifies as both philosophy and literature (and psychology, too).

Now let's set aside the question of whether a work of art should be considered research and ask what we can learn from this article. If we look at the poetry, the possibilities are endless; it evokes a full range of emotion, stirs memories, invites reflection, and generates ideas. The material on attention, in contrast, is very limited.

It may not be possible to "teach attention." Indeed, when we teachers exhort students to "pay attention," it is usually because their attention has already strayed from the object of our own attention. We can give students the time and space to "just look" (Noddings & Shore, 1984), and we can help them to see, if they are interested. But forced attention hardly qualifies as attention. Sullivan herself reports that her mother was so engrossed in her biology that she did not even notice a bleeding cut on her own hand. Meanwhile her young daughter was "popping creosote blisters." Mother and daughter, both "attending," saw very different things, interpreted what they saw differently, and used their perceptions to produce entirely different forms of work.

We probably do not learn "attention." We learn to attend to natural beauty, to the workings of mechanical devices, to the texture of baked goods, to sounds of distress, to musical themes, to dogs or cats, to people. Attention is of great importance in moral life, for example, but it would be a mistake to suppose that one who is superbly attentive to the needs of other human beings will also be attentive to the details of a painting. We do not learn something global called attention. Rather we learn to attend to *something*. Probably the key to this learning is living with or studying with someone who exercises the capacity to attend to particular objects or events and also attends *to us*. From such people we learn to see, but our seeing may still lead us on a path that diverges from that of our mentor.

The error of supposing that attention is something that can somehow be mastered in itself is widespread. Even such a fine thinker as Simone Weil made this error. Weil (1977) argued that attention to geometry could increase attention to God which, in turn, should increase our attention to human beings:

> Not only does the love of God have attention for its substance; the love of our neighbor, which we know to be the same love, is made of this same substance. Those who are unhappy have no need for anything in this world but people capable of giving them their attention. The capacity to give one's attention to a sufferer is a very rare and difficult thing; it is almost a miracle; it is a miracle. Nearly all those who think they have this capacity do not possess it. Warmth of heart, impulsiveness, pity are not enough. (p. 51)

Weil was right in claiming that the capacity to give sustained and loving attention to a particular sufferer is rare. So is the capacity for attention to poetry, or geometry, or insects, or paintings. But she was wrong in supposing that the modes of attention affect one another. There is no evidence for such a claim and much against it.

Sullivan laments the lack of attention to poetry. I do, too, but I think schooling bears considerable responsibility for this lack of interest and attention. Instead of inviting attention, we try to force it. Poetry holds the potential to provide lifelong pleasure, but we do not present it in school as something to enjoy. We present it as something to analyze. Students might come to love poetry if teachers were to give them opportunities to simply enjoy it. A teacher who, eyes shining with love, reads or recites a poem without forcing analysis, gives her students a special gift. She shows them a result of her own attention—delight—and attends sensitively to them in the way she invites their attention. Who knows what the effects will be? One child may come to love poetry, another to love the teacher, and still another may decide to become a marine biologist because she has seen how one's eyes can light up when she is willingly attentive to something she loves.

Clearly, the Sullivan article can induce positive effects. It offers delight and triggers reflection. To call it "research" does not do it justice.

REFERENCES

Frost, R. (1949). *Complete poems*. New York: Henry Holt.

Noddings, N., & Shore, P. (1984). *Awakening the inner eye: Intuition in education*. New York: Teachers College Press. (Reissued 1998, Troy, NY: Educator's International)

Weil, S. (1977). *Simone Weil reader* (G. Panichas, Ed.). Mt. Kisco: Meyer Bell.

PERSPECTIVE 3: CONSTRUCTIVISM ON THE SULLIVAN STUDY

YVONNA S. LINCOLN   *Texas A&M University*

To imagine forms of research as moving along a continuum, from positivist to phenomenological, from strictly quantitative to mixed methods to qualitative and open-ended, is the only way to place the Sullivan work in perspective. It falls well to the side of qualitative research, moves beyond interpretivism, and resides quietly in autoethnographic, narrative, and poetic approaches. It is *about* qualitative research, but it is also about a pervasive problem in learning—attention—and it is about research processes.

Thorp (2001) speaks of the role of a "patient elder" in gently drawing children into the bright and curious world of learning. Patient elders listen. They wait on children's discovery and surprise. They attend to facial expressions and the realization of possibility on a child's face. Primarily, however, they are *there* for children. The reader is struck by the figure in the background of this story: the author's mother, the marine biologist. Although the child of the story writes in recollection, as though she were simply brought along on these collection and study trips, in fact, she was in the presence of one of Thorp's patient elders. Sullivan's own patient elder—her mother—taught her time and tide and systematicity and rigor and the many moods of a natural, living system, the estuary where the mother's studies occurred. While Sullivan reports that she didn't pay much attention to her mother's work, in fact, in the presence of the quiet discipline of an inquiring mind, Sullivan learned the deep lessons of mindfulness, of absorption, of pure and unalloyed attention.

Now, in retrospect, the elegance and beauty of the marsh, the patient and unhurried work, the sheer sensual pleasure of sun and swimming and smells and sights come back, their lessons distilled into reflections on how children learn, on the role of profound attention in doing good qualitative research, and in poems which in their dazzling, gorgeous illumination blind the heart with moments of truth. This piece makes the link between oral and literary forms (for poetry is first and foremost an oral form), and the scientific enterprise of systematic observation, absolutely clear. It demonstrates, too, that the Enlightenment stricture of separating art from science, poetry from problems, and fiction from truth, as posed dichotomies has largely been proven foolish.

This particular work is perhaps one of the clearest examples of constructivist autobiography. It represents the present, but this present moment has been constructed via memory and reconstructed through poetry. Furthermore, the constructions and reconstructions move easily between the fluid learning styles of the very young and the "crystalline" learning styles of the adult, each drawing on the other to derive a mature aesthetics for both learning and qualitative research.

The argument for artistry and aesthetics is one increasingly seen in constructivist and interpretivist work, for the simple reason that artistry and aesthetics—and their amiable companions, rhetorical structure, narrative, oral history, performance ethnography, poetry, and ethnographic fiction—expand the range of what may be considered epistemologies, ways of coming to know, ways of relating between knower and known. There is, however, a larger, if somewhat implicit, argument to be made here. Sullivan does not address the point directly, but it is quite clear that if there are expanded epistemologies (those epistemologies well beyond the limited range of positivist thinking), there is also an expanding range of both methodologies—strategies for coming to know—and for representational styles. Methodological strategies Sullivan herself advocates are absorption—staring at the ground "until something happens"; staring at Piccasso's Les Demoiselles D'Avignon; Walker Evans's advice to "stare" so that one may "die knowing something"—and the provision of a certain physicality to learning processes—the opportunity to connect learning with an embodied, corporeal, palpable moment. (The latter strategy speaks strongly to the ill-advised policies of school districts around the country, where physical education—and its concomitant connection to the embodied, the outdoors, the physical, the sensuous—is being slowly abandoned.) Absorption and physicality are to learning as active listening, observation, and prolonged engagement are to qualitative research. There is no substitute for being there, and for paying attention while there.

Perhaps the most important point to be derived from Sullivan's work is yet another indirect, but powerful, implication. It is difficult, in the face of the "artificial attention" and distractions afforded to children to demand, or command, attention. Perhaps attention, like love, is ill-commanded. Like Sullivan herself, we may find that attention comes best when it is not bidden, but, like love, permitted room to grow, given space in the garden by a "patient elder," cherished when it flourishes, and playfully elicited as though it were laughter.

REFERENCES

Thorp, L. (2001). *Voices from the garden: An ethnographic study of a garden curriculum.* Unpublished dissertation, Texas A&M University, College Station, TX.

PERSPECTIVE 4: INTERPRETIVE AND NARRATIVE ON THE SULLIVAN STUDY

ARTHUR P. BOCHNER   *University of South Florida*

Ann McCrary Sullivan treats a teacher's concern for her students' attention as an analogue of a qualitative researcher's regard for using all of her senses to attend to the concrete details of observation. Drawing on her own autobiography, Sullivan composes a poetic portrait of how her mother, a scientist, taught her to observe details and patterns of relationship and "in doing so, she made me a poet" (p. 288). Ironically, she shows how the work of science is artistic and poetic, transgressing the boundaries that normally separate these two cultures of inquiry: "[Mother] taught me the *rhythms* of tide and regeneration, and the *syllables* of the natural world rubbing against each other" (p. 288). Instead of driving a wedge between science and art, Sullivan portrays an ecology of inquiry that joins them. In the process, she discredits crude stereotypes that depict science as sterile and uncreative and art as idiosyncratic and devoid of rigor.

Sullivan does not hide her political motives for writing this monograph. By publishing these poems in the *Harvard Educational Review,* an orthodox research journal, she defies the scientific domination of educational research. She doesn't hide her anger about the disempowerment and marginalization of artists and art based inquiry. When educational research shuns other ways of knowing—artistic, emotional, narrative—she suggests, it turns into a kind of imperialism that omits a whole world of significant and intriguing human action, feeling, imagination, and meaning. These other ways and forms of knowing threaten the monolithic authority of empiricism, calling into question the singular vision of the positivist's eye. Why is neutrality and detachment toward our subjects to be preferred over empathy and caring? Why is objective knowledge a higher goal than human solidarity? Is our capacity to feel less important than our ability to know? Does prediction and control give our lives meaning, free us from contingency and fate, or help us lead more passionate or moral lives? Why should we be more interested in what *is* than in what *could be?* Shouldn't these questions be asked when we contemplate the ideals of education and the goals of educational research?

Consider some of the differences between the following questions: (1) What does it *mean* to pay attention? (2) What do we want from students when we ask them to pay attention? (3) What are the predictors of the extent to which students pay attention? (4) Which students are more likely to pay attention? Questions 1 and 2 are of a different order than questions 3 and 4. They ask us to make sense of the experience of paying attention, to make it intelligible or meaningful. This is how I understand Sullivan's project. Hers is an autoethnographic study of sense making. She is trying to make sense of her childhood experiences with her mother. The sense she makes is achieved by placing her personal and interpersonal experiences in the frame or context of learning how to attend. Whereas her mother was a field marine biologist, she became a poet and a teacher. What could possibly link a marine biologist to a poet? What is the pattern that connects them?

The primary human mechanism for attaching meaning to human experiences, writes Harold Brody (1987), "is to tell stories about them" (p. 5). Elizabeth Stone reinforces this connection between meanings and stories when she observes (1988) that "our meanings are almost always inseparable from stories in all realms of life" (p. 244). Applying a narrative intelligibility, Sullivan tells stories about her mother, making her mother's humanity visible and showing us poetically how her mother—the scientist, teacher, and researcher—laid the groundwork for her daughter's development as a poet, a teacher, and a researcher. She reads new meanings into old memories, reaching for a fresh interpretation of her mother that accommodates her desire for self-understanding. Her poems recollect the meanings of her childhood experiences, disclosing to herself and to us—her readers—the truth in these experiences. Because her lived experiences are saturated with the possibilities of meaning, they have a poetic dimensionality. Thus she turns to poetry in order to represent the meanings of her experiences in a suitably edifying manner.

Sullivan writes about herself but not necessarily for herself. If she is the one, we are the many—the many in the one (Brady, 2001). She wants us to grasp the felt meaning of her experience and to use it for ourselves. Anchored in the empirical world, these poems are intended to stir up something in us. In this sense they are as much existential as they are academic. They ask us to contemplate what we see and feel, and how deeply we see and feel, when we teach and when we do research. How much patience do I have? How do I get inside or under the skin of my students? How acutely do I pay attention? What do I feel as I engage in the activity of teaching, reading, observing, analyzing, and/or writing? Sullivan's poems and what she says about them should inspire each of us to question the motives and consequences of our teaching and research. Are we just going through the motions or do we really care? Are we attending fully and patiently to what we are doing? Why is the research we do read by so few people? Why do undergraduates find most of what they are assigned to read boring and unimaginative? Why do graduate students say that most scholarship is dry and inaccessible? Why do even seasoned scholars admit that they don't finish half of what they start to read? Could it be because the forms we use to communicate what we mean do not allow readers to feel the truth of what we have to say or try to show? The passion is missing. We aren't moved or stirred. The language is esoteric, riddled with jargon, and elitist. To write like this can be self-alienating; to have to read it can be an exercise in despair.

When Sullivan says "attention must be paid," I am reminded of Heath's desire to make teachers adopt the practices of ethnography. As teachers we need to be aware of the culture of the classroom, we need to be able to penetrate deeply into the minds and under the skin of our students, and we need to see the patterns that connect them to each other as well as to us, intellectually, emotionally, and aesthetically. They are not only specimens for our fieldwork but also living, thinking, feeling individuals who want to be understood, cared about, attended to, and noticed. To be effective teachers, we have to grasp and seize their meanings—however contingent and perishable they may be. Teaching, in this sense, as Sullivan notes, is an artistic endeavor, a form of art based research. Sullivan's mother implicitly taught her to attend to details, to look for patterns, and to be patient. The lesson is that teaching is an interpersonal activity. Who we are, how we are personified, what we say and do in the classroom communicates much more than the content of our classes. Through the form(s) by which we teach, we inform our students, showing them how, how much, and to what we attend, contributing to the formation of their emotionality and ethics as well as their intellect.

In the aftermath of postmodernism, we understand that all attempts to speak for, write about, or represent other people's lives are partial, situated, and mediated. There is no such thing as an objective vocabulary. As Rorty (1982) concluded, "Objects are not 'more objectively' described in any vocabulary than in any other" (p. 203). Yet most people are still misled (or want) to believe that graphs are more objective than poems. They don't ask what is going on when a term is transformed into a variable, a variable into a measure, a measure into a number, and a number into an interpretation of a number. What values are being created? What meanings inscribed? After all, the world doesn't exist in the shape of the sentences we write when we theorize about it (Rorty, 1989). Writing is a process of turning life into language. Written reality always is a second-order reality. Whether we are empiricists, interpretivists, critics, statisticians, or poets, the symbols or language we use necessarily reshapes or remakes the events we describe.

When I read Sullivan's poem, "When I die," I thought about my mother, who died in September 2001. During the last 3 weeks of her life, she was unable to communicate, except to nod her head occasionally. Mother was 90 and had outlived most of her friends. Sometimes she would talk about them as if they were alive. Given the opportunity, she would have kidded with them, made them smile, found the humor in her situation. I knew all too well the sound of mom's silence. Near the end, it was deafening. How I wanted her to speak one more time—at least to tell me she understood how much she meant to me. But there were lessons in the silence. When our eyes made contact, we achieved a deeper intimacy. You don't have to speak to know you've been heard. Like so many mothers, mom didn't want her son to see her die. She waited until she knew I had let go and then she passed, while I was on my way to see her. When I arrived and saw her for the last time, there was no sheet over her head. I kissed her forehead and was shocked by how cold she felt. What was left was not mother but a thin, frail, hollow body. Where are you, mother?

Shelley Scholl's collection of small poems reveals her unusual capacity to grasp the inner life of her students. Responding as a teaching intern to Sullivan's request for a poetic depiction of her student's inner life, Scholl makes incisive connections between their outer appearances and their inner existence. Her evocative interpretations make it possible for me to sense the pain of Luke's self-hatred, the impatience of Karen's adolescent desire, and the listlessness of Steven's daydreams. Notwithstanding the evocative power of the images she created, Scholl's poems left some ethical questions unanswered. Should the students know how she sees them? Is it appropriate to disseminate these depictions to others without the students' consent? Did she share them with the students? Did they have an opportunity to react—to talk back—to how they were represented? Did she make it evident that this is how she saw them and not necessarily how they are?

What if every teacher were asked to do this—to put into language the images and impressions they have of each of their students? To take the project a step further, what if we asked our students to do the same for us—their teachers? Each of us—teachers and students alike—would be putting ourselves in each other's place. The consequence, I believe, would be the creation of a deeper, more engaged, and attentive interpersonal climate in the classroom. The focus would shift from control to empathy as teachers and students faced each other vulnerably and treated each other with compassion. Our teaching would become a moral and ethical endeavor addressed more to knowing how to live than to knowing how to know (Jackson, 1995). In teaching as well as in research, the pursuit of knowledge would be construed as a means of developing engaged and caring relationships with others rather than as a technical endeavor consisting of distancing ourselves from others in the name of objectivity.

In the process of defying academic norms, particularly the tacit rule of observer distance and objectivity, Sullivan encourages and promotes the project of narrative, artistic, emotional, and subjective understanding. Poetry and narrative can be used effectively—as Sullivan shows—as tools for reflexive knowledge, self-understanding, and turning the focus back to the observing self, who can never be completely extricated from the observed other. Her poems represent a mother's life seen through the daughter's eyes. The poems turn back on the daughter, giving her a self-understanding she presumably did not have before she wrote them. Thus, the poems are not only a mode of representation, but also a method of inquiry—poetic inquiry. Sullivan uses the poems to consider the boundaries between herself and her mother, her self and her work, science and art, data and aesthetics. She also uses her poetry to invite us into a conversation about what it means to be an intellectual, to attend closely, to really see, and feel, and touch, and be touched by others and by the concrete details of living; to break through the surface of things, recognizing that real learning often is attended by pain, struggle, loss, and conflict—experience that takes your breath away, "makes you weep for all you have thought hidden, interior, safe" (p. 286). When you finish reading Sullivan's poems and what she says about them you can return safely to the old questions—Is it true? Are they valid? How does she know? Or you can join a new conversation, tell your own stories, write poems, attend more closely, seek detail, feel deeply. Does everything we do have to start at the head? What good is social science and educational research if it has no heart and no moral center?

REFERENCES

Brady, I. (2001). Anthropological poetics. In N. Denzin & Y. Lincoln (Eds.), *Handbook of qualitative research,* 2nd edition. Thousands Oaks: Sage. (949–979).

Brody, H. (1987). *Stories of sickness.* New Haven: Yale University Press.

Jackson, M. (1995). *At home in the world.* Durham: Duke University Press.

Rorty, R. (1982). *Consequences of pragmatism: Essays 1972–1980.* Minneapolis: University of Minnesota Press.

Rorty, R. (1989). *Contingency, irony, and solidarity.* New York: Cambridge University Press.

Stone, E. (1988). *Black sheep and kissing cousins: How our family stories shape us.* New York: Penguin,

PERSPECTIVE 5: ARTS BASED EDUCATIONAL RESEARCH ON THE SULLIVAN STUDY

TOM BARONE   *Arizona State*

The article by Anne McCrary Sullivan, "Notes from a Marine Biologist's Daughter," begins with a set of autobiographical poems. These poems lie at the heart of the article and, in my judgment, achieve the status of literary art. But the article, taken as a whole, is not a work of art. It is expository and not entirely literary, insofar as the poems are followed (largely) by an essay consisting of prosaic, linear forms of discourse. Because its essay section further develops the themes embodied within the poetry, the article is an example of *arts based* educational research (ABER).

Indeed, I contend that the article provides a *good* example of this form of research. The article is good because it is useful: it serves an important educational purpose. The author succeeds in her attempt "to awaken in the reader an artistic engagement with the various meanings of attention" (p. 284). For this reader, the attempt is successful because the text manages to raise important questions about commonplace conceptions of attention in relation to teaching, learning, and research. It does so primarily through poetry but also through the linear exposition that follows the poetry.

Certain design elements help this article achieve that purpose. Three of these elements are referenced in the following questions. The first two questions relate primarily to the poetry sections of this article. The third refers to characteristics in both the poetry and the subsequent essay.

1. Does the educational researcher/author/artist create a carefully observed virtual world?

The author, Anne Sullivan, is masterful in her attention to autobiographical detail. Her work is, in fact, dedicated to acts of attentiveness which the author identifies as necessary for researching and writing good poetry. In her poem "When I Die," Sullivan implores those who will witness her death to search out the details of the event, to search again (re-search), and then to

> Write quickly; avoid nothing.
> My friends are poets. They need details. (p. 287)

The details in her own poems make her point about attention in a powerful manner. As a poet she provides the minutiae of experience that, taken together, create the carefully observed virtual world of her life as the daughter of a marine biologist who taught her the importance of detail. Indeed, Sullivan's article demonstrates the importance of attention to detail in life at large, in art and science, and in the processes of learning and researching.

The details enable us to experience the manner in which Sullivan the child, learned to attend to sensory qualities in the watery world of her mother and her own childhood. For example the specific images provided in "Learning Blue" (blue in the water, the sides of fish, clam shells, the "oyster bruise at my inner thigh, the blue-black ink of the squid's soft gland") trigger mental images that transport us imaginatively to Sullivan's early life under her mother's tutelage in tidal pools and estuaries. These details endow the virtual world with a degree of plausibility. They enable readers to accept the possibility that such a set of experiences might have actually occurred.

More details are found in the section "Teaching Attention," in which the adult Sullivan is seen teaching poetry, first as a high school teacher and then a university teacher of preservice education students. The contents of two of her students' poems serve to reinforce earlier points about the importance of attention in teaching poetry, but these poems do not achieve the creation of a detailed, credible virtual world to the extent that Sullivan's own poetry does.

Research traditionalists may easily misunderstand the point of the carefully observed details that are selected and combined in the Sullivan text. Those who have been professionally socialized to recognize only one of the two purposes identified by Rorty as central to human inquiry may demand of Sullivan's text the same sort of utility found in good examples of social science research. Some may still adhere to classical, formalist, and/or modernist notions that portray the arts (including the literary arts) as producing primarily formal, ethereal objects that are quite admirable but of no practical value. In this view, aesthetics are not to be confused with the affairs of everyday commerce, including educational practice. Things of beauty are seen as categorically different from things of use. Research, most traditionalists argue, happens only when the researcher is on a quest for certainty, not when the kind of utility the research offers is primarily heuristic in nature.

From that standpoint, traditionalists would demand the portrayal, not of a possible world, but of one that is conventionally "real." For them, the world portrayed must accurately correspond to one that is (or was) literally true. It must possess validity, approximating to a high degree that which it purports to represent.

Of course, validity (or the lack of it) may indeed be relevant when a reader in a position of power chooses to use an arts based research text to influence evaluative judgments about the fate of the persons portrayed in it (here, Sullivan and her mother). The purpose of the Sullivan article, however, is not to provide information to be used for evaluative purposes. Indeed, the vast majority of its readers will not be acquainted with the person who is the author, or with the actual setting described in her poetry. The text of this piece of arts based educational research does not aim reduce certainty in the minds of readers about the characters and events portrayed in the setting. A work of arts based research such as "Notes from a Marine Biologist's Daughter" aims, instead, to generate seldom asked questions. To that end, the text does not need to be literally true, or conventionally valid, but rather "true to life." It must resonate with the experiences of readers, in order to entice them into momentarily inhabiting a world that is believable and possible. This brings us to our second question to be asked of the Sullivan piece.

2. Is the virtual world sufficiently inviting to the reader?

The world that Sullivan creates through her autobiographical poetry is not merely believable. It is also compelling. As a reader I was drawn in to this world by the effective use of a host of literary devices. I will mention only two. First, the precision of the language is remarkable. In "Herding Fiddler Crabs" one can almost see and hear the creatures through the evocative language and textured characterizations:

> Thousands of click,
> the small collisions,
> claws and carapaces,
> finely jointed legs landing
> in frantic succession
> on mud. . . . (p. 285)

Moreover, the poems are sequenced in a manner that provides a kind of narrative drive, pulling the reader through a part of Sullivan's life story. The first few poems serve as an introduction to the manner of her mother's work. They then focus on Sullivan's own attentiveness to the details in paintings. The last poems address the attentiveness of the poet that she had become.

Finally, taken as a whole the poems cohere thematically, and the theme is indeed the nature of attention. The literary qualities of these poems compel the reader to attend. This is important if the criterion for good ABER suggested in our third question is to be achieved:

3. Does the recreated world of the text serve as an analogue that prompts questions about educational beliefs and values?

Traditional texts of social science research entice readers with the promise of truth that can be used to explain, predict, and sometimes control future events in places other than those studied. To that end, findings must be generalizable from a sample of subjects to an entire population. But no sampling occurred as a prelude to the research of the Sullivan article; indeed, there is no "population" apart from the characters who people the poems. This study simply does not aspire to generalize in the manner of traditional social science. "Notes from a Marine Biologist's Daughter" would indeed be misjudged if its content were expected to generalize in a conventional manner to people, events, and settings outside of the text. "Generalization," in this usual sense of that term, is not a hallmark of arts based research.

That fact, however, does not mean that the article is devoid of a potential to prompt readers to reach beyond its textual boundaries. Research of all sorts must escape from what has been called the "tyranny of the local" in order to achieve some broader utility for readers who live outside the world of the text. But in most ABER the nature of that "escape" is quite different, perhaps more subtle, than in traditional forms of research, and is, in fact, suggested in one of Sullivan's poems.

In "Beware: The Poet Comes for Tea," Sullivan describes the work of a poet who is so observant ("she's looking under your skin") that after "she goes to her room and writes your life" (p. 284):

> . . . She will mail you a poem
> which disrupts breath, makes you weep
> for all you thought hidden, interior, safe. (p. 286)

Readers of Sullivan's poetry may indeed find that it disrupts usual ways of seeing, startles them into new awareness of themselves and the world around them. It fosters in the mind of the reader a disequilibrium between the familiar and that which the poetry reveals. This disquieting imbalance can lead to an interrogation by the reader of that which has been previously taken for granted.

The authors of most arts based research texts never explicitly reveal the questions they wish to prompt. But Sullivan, early in her article, does:

> What exactly are teachers asking when they say "Pay attention"? What are the relationships between attention and intrinsic motivation? Is it possible to teach habits of attending? How can we enroll peripheral attention to the advantage of education? How can we know the long-term effects of attending? . . . What is the nature of the researcher's attention? How do we learn to attend with keen eyes and fine sensibilities? How do we teach others to do it? (p. 284).

These questions are first adumbrated in the poetic sections of the article. There a central metaphor emerges as notions of attentiveness are, not directly described, but rather embodied within the world created by Sullivan in her poems, and re-created by the reader in the act of reading. The metaphor may then be transferred by readers to their own life worlds, perhaps serving to problematize elements of those worlds, even disrupting that which was deemed "interior, hidden, safe."

The metaphor contributes to the article's central theme that does indeed relate to the various meanings of attention. But the theme that is first suggested in the poems is further developed in the theoretical discussions following it. The content of both the poems and the more linear discourse was carefully selected and arranged in accordance with the theme. This theme served as a controlling and structuring device, suggesting which content was to be included in the text and which was not, and how the content was to be organized.

Sullivan's theme is spelled out directly in later sections of the article and is connected to educational inquiry and theory. In denotative language, she describes how the meaning of attention in the poems relates to understandings within the academic community, as found in recent brain research (p. 572), to speculation about how attention may be taught in school, to the connection between attention and empathy, and so on. In much ABER, there is no such explication of the theme. Rather it remains tacit, while subtly pervading a literary-style text. In such cases, the research may be characterized as more artistic than arts based.

In both artistic and arts based research, however, *metaphor* and *theme* serve as vehicles for transporting the text from one specific location to another. They give the text its potential for focusing readers' attention simultaneously on life phenomena (including educational phenomena) embodied within the local world of the text and analogous phenomena outside of it. In this manner still unfamiliar to many in the educational research community, a text of educational research such as Sullivan's can transcend itself, as readers hear it demand attention to their own nearby worlds, and use it to reconsider entrenched beliefs and values.

Finally, this: Arts based forms of research are relatively new to the educational research scene. The application by critics (such as those in this book) of inappropriate criteria for judging their worth has often caused them to be dismissed as useless or even harmful. Traditionalists are often disconcerted by the fact that the research methods which they regard as the only legitimate ones are dysfunctional for the purposes of arts based researchers. The result has been continued, marginalization of the latter by the former. Indeed, those who do not honor the important research purpose ABER can serve sometimes insist that this is not research at all—a form of inquiry perhaps, but not research.

The result of this marginalization has been, in my view, harmful to education in general. The dismissal by some traditionalists of works such as Sullivan's as unworthy of the label of research is the result of an inability to see their unique potential for improving educational policy and practice. But what if educational policy is indeed influenced for the better as policymakers who read the Sullivan article are prompted to consider meanings of attention that are alternatives to more familiar ones? What if practitioners are encouraged to imagine new ways of teaching attention? What if some researchers find their narrow notions of research utility broadened? And what if other researchers are emboldened to engage in the production of their own arts-based research texts? These would, in my view, be useful outcomes indeed.

PERSPECTIVE 6: RACE, ETHNICITY, AND GENDER ON THE SULLIVAN STUDY

BETH HARRY   *University of Miami*

This article is about learning through human connectedness. The author focuses mainly on learning through total physical and sensual engagement, but to me, the poems speak primarily of the power of the human bond in a child's learning.

As the author outlines the apparent connections between these poems and contemporary study of the nature of attention, she refers to one line of research that captures my attention: "the significance of emotion in engaging and sustaining attention." The poems do, as the author points out, show how a child who "paid little overt attention" to her mother's work was, nonetheless, "attending . . . recording . . . learning, internalizing, without any direct instruction." The author goes on to ask what "physicality and emotion have to do with learning and sublingual attention." She asks about the importance of the tactile impressions of sun, mud, salt, and movement.

It is noticeable to me that the author does not ask, at least not explicitly, what her relationship with her mother had to do with this learning. On reading these poems, what stands out for me is the image of the poet's mother and her relationship with the child. This is what is in the foreground. In the first poem, "Notes from a Marine Biologist's Daughter," agency and action are in the hands of the mother: She "loves . . . charts . . . lives . . . calculates . . . waits . . . digs . . . leads . . . knows." As images of light and dark imprint this mother's actions on the mind's eye of the child, it is the mother who is the true focus of the poem. The same is true in "Mother Collecting Marine Specimens," where agency weaves between the mother, the child, and a very private "we" hidden from the world in the shadow of the drawbridge. In the third poem, "Herding Fiddler Crabs," the mother and child engage in a unified action, together circling the crabs, then "stamp our feet, close in," as the tiny creatures "flee like receding tide." In "Mother in Water" we gain a glimpse of the mother's view of life and death as she elicits from the young girl a promise beyond a child's comprehension but which reflects the mother's assumption that there is a permanent bond between the two. The poet gives us also a glimpse into her mother's history, her own childhood love of the water and its life forms. The poems "How I Learned to Love Picasso," "Beware, the Poet Comes for Tea," and "When I Die," take us to another era in the poet's life and learning. We see now the adult outcome of all that loving watching—the poet's eye that sees beyond surface appearances, that intuits the internal details of another's heart. The habit of looking beyond and of envisioning another level of reality now determines that "aesthetic vision" will be the outcome of the poet's attention.

Certainly, total physical and sensual engagement resonate throughout the poems and Sullivan's point that knowledge can be gained "in some hidden and inarticulate way" challenges the foundations of the teaching-learning paradigm into which teachers are inculcated. But it is the context of the parent-child bond that provides the cement for the child's learning. When I think of the messages we give student teachers about how to capture and keep children's attention, I find very little that can approximate this lesson. Indeed, how many teacher educators still maintain that teachers should not become "too involved" with their students; should not seek to know much of their lives outside the classroom, and should not seek to foster bonds beyond the parameters of this year's class assignments? Perhaps more important, how many teachers premise their teaching on the belief that to teach is to impart knowledge that exists as a body of facts untouched by human perception and response, or by the identities of those who teach and learn?

The power of relationship in children's learning brings us to the connection between learning and identity. These poems are not just by someone with an eye for detail. They are by "a marine biologist's daughter." One might say that she had the privilege of being in the loving company of one fully attuned to the natural world. When she says that her mother "taught [her] blue," she means that she learned the innumerable nuances of blue through the eyes and focus of her mother, and in so doing, became attuned to its myriad meanings. What a different conception of "learning blue" than is demonstrated by Lem's preschool teachers in Shirley Brice Heath's ethnograpy! Yet Lem's experiences in his community provided him with what Moll has called "funds of knowledge" on which his teachers could build. His fascination with the why's and wherefore's of fire trucks were fertile ground for learning the nuances of red, of speed, of urgency—a ground untapped by his teacher.

These poems challenge the belief that learning is a neutral, objective, and individual activity. To see the learner in his or her totality is to include all aspects of his or her identity. The portrait offered by these poems brings to mind bell hooks's (1994) concept of "engaged pedagogy." Hooks's account of the contrast between her pre- and post-segregation schooling underscores the point that the teacher student relationship creates the context for learning and that such contexts are never neutral. By making sure they knew the children's lives, hooks's Black teachers forged relationships with their students that transformed school into a place of "sheer joy." Both hooks and Siddle-Walker (1996) have shown how, for Black children growing up in segregated American schools, teaching and learning were an integral part of ethnic identity because Black children learned from their Black teachers that a "devotion to learning was a counter-hegemonic act, a fundamental way to resist every strategy of white racist colonization" (p. 2). In contrast to the "messianic zeal" of her Black teachers to nurture the talents of Black children, hooks's White teachers attempted to present teaching as an objective and compartmentalizing process that seemed to "denigrate the notion of wholeness and uphold the idea of a mind-body split" (p. 16). The attempt at neutrality was transparent, however, as hooks explains that, not only did her desegregated schooling rob the learning process of its "ecstasy, pleasure, and danger," but replaced them with the implicit warning that "too much eagerness to learn could easily be seen as a threat to white authority" (pp. 2–3). In segregated and desegregated schools alike, teaching and learning was a sociocultural activity that occurred on all three planes of experience—personal, interpersonal, and community (Rogoff & Chavajay, 1995).

Sullivan's poems remind us that learning is never neutral, if only because of the power it brings. Nor is learning an activity separate from identity and relationships. Nor is it a function only of the mind.

REFERENCES

hooks, b. (1994). *Teaching to transgress: Education as the practice of freedom.* New York: Routledge.

Rogoff, B., & Chavajay, P. (1995, Oct). What's become of research on the cultural basis of cognitive development? *American Psychologist,* (859–877).

Siddle-Walker, V. (1996). *Their highest potential: An African American school community in the segregated South.* Chapel Hill: University of North Carolina Press.

PERSPECTIVE 7: CRITICAL THEORY ON THE SULLIVAN STUDY

GEORGE NOBLIT   *University of North Carolina*

Anne McCrary Sullivan wants us to understand that the pursuit of a science of education is too simplistic. There are many ways to know, and each of these contribute to our understanding of learning and teaching. She shares how her life illuminates a key phenomenon in education, attention, that has been studied in all too limited ways. To demonstrate how other approaches to knowing can contribute to a better understanding of education, she offers an autobiography of attention, understood aesthetically via qualitative research. She juxtaposes one of the ways she came to understand attention, poetry, with theorizing aesthetics and with her lived life with her mother and later her own students. She covers a lot of territory and speaks in multiple ways. This all feeds her central thesis that aesthetics offer us valuable ways to understand complexity. We are with her and her mother as Sullivan witnesses her mother's attention to marine life. We follow her claims to how poetry can be "highly concrete" (p. 287) and detailed and how her mother taught her "attention to the complexities of surface detail and also to what lies beneath those surfaces" (p. 288). We see how she has applied what she learned with high school students and prospective teachers, using poetry to represent attention. She is a good artist. I was pulled along by the juxtapositions of detail and exegesis, of autobiography and academic argument, of poetry and postulation. I learned a lot about attention along the way, but I was left asking why is it that educational researchers have not paid attention to attention, so to speak, and especially in the ways Sullivan is offering. Why haven't we been taught to do what she does so ably here? This requires a critical approach that goes beyond the interpretive approach she elaborates here. I agree we need to prepare our people to have an "aesthetic vision" (p. 288) but while this article demonstrates what it could offer it does not demonstrate what would have to be changed for all of us to be able to have such capability. For this a critique of education and society is needed.

Sullivan has a host of moves in this article. I have identified some of them above, but I have not discussed that her key move is the literary device of analogy. Her analogies are many but include that between her mother and herself, between artist and researcher, between poetry and qualitative research, between attention and understanding among others. Analogy is an interesting literary device because it emphasizes similarities. One might push analogy to consider where it breaks down, but this is not Sullivan's approach here. Such an approach would call attention, so to speak, to even more complexity than addressed here. Moreover, there are other literary devices she might have employed. Irony for example is used to express the unity of opposites. Satire represents a disreputable analogy while farce undercuts reputability itself. My point is only that analogy is not the best literary device if one wants to understand why aesthetic vision is not available to the populace or to educational research. For this understanding, a literary device that pushes us to consider and explain contradictions would be better.

This said, I must admit that critical approaches have not always been hospitable to aesthetics. The classic case is the rejection of Walter Benjamin, the literary critic, by the Frankfort School of critical theory before World War II. In this case, his aesthetics seem to have challenged the rationalistic bent of the Frankfort School. More appreciation for the power of the arts and aesthetics can be seen in the recent work of critical researchers working in the area of cultural studies. Here the interest has been to better understand what has been regarded as pop culture as sites of resistance and cultural production. The approach in cultural studies has been to ask what is being socially constructed by art, even if some would consider it vernacular, rather than fine, art. This seems to be a useful way to reconsider Sullivan's work. Agreeing with her central point that aesthetics is undervalued in research, education, and life, I also ask what might her account be constructing as the reality of aesthetics.

Sullivan opens her article by establishing that attention has not been widely investigated, rather that "the focus has been on how to get students to pay attention" (p. 284). Sullivan, in saying this, points out that education and educational researchers have skipped over understanding the phenomena of attention and assumed the problem to be one of power. Students should attend, it is assumed, and thus what is needed are better ways to get students to comply with this assumption. Sullivan does not pursue this further leaving a critical researcher to consider what does this mean. On one level, there is a critique of education as a form of power that is to teach students that compliance is what is expected. The not so hidden curriculum is revealed even if we lack further data to pursue exactly what the substance of the curriculum of compliance actually entails. We also are lacking any historical perspective on the origins of education as a formal system and thus not only inculcating students into their culture (as would happen even if education was more informal socialization) but also having organizational needs as a formal system for discipline. On another level, there is critique of knowledge itself. In this case, it seems that research is geared to reinforce the power of the institution of education to the extent that it provides understandings of how to get students to comply. That is, educational research is essentially applied research not basic research. Sullivan is pursuing basic research even if she is working in the field with students, while the bulk of existing knowledge is limited to advancing the ability of the organization to coerce or cajole participants to be good organizational people. As is evident, a critical approach would push for an explanation of Sullivan's assertion. This, of course, implies a criticism of Sullivan's approach; even her research itself was seen as valuable. It could be argued that Sullivan has ignored key salient contexts that will likely affect the reception of what she has found. Indeed, by not addressing the interest of the institution of education in power, her knowledge has little power in itself.

This issue can be elaborated to reconsider how she has represented her knowledge. As above, I found her account informative but then critical researchers have some affinity for underdogs. Sullivan chooses to frame her account as an autobiography. Unfortunately, there is a hierarchy of research in education and, while the hierarchy is changing, positivistic knowledge still holds sway in many arenas including federally funded research and the psychological fields (educational psychology, school psychology, special education, etc.). Psychology is important here because attention has been conceptualized as a psychological affair. Sullivan's autobiography then is likely to be devalued by those who believe in positivism as being overly subjective, not generalizable and lacking empirical rigor. Given this, a critical researcher would have tried to address these issues directly and critiqued positivism as well as a psychological perspective. The former can be argued to serve technical interests as I have done in the critique of the article by Carr et al. The argument then would be that Sullivan's approach itself is essentially interpretive as I argued with the article by Ellis. It serves practical interests but is unlikely to uncouple the phenomena from the systems of power in which it is currently imbedded. A critical approach better serves these interests. The critique of the psychological perspective could start as above with the argument that attention is not psychological but organizational and institutional in nature. Thus what is needed is a social analysis that better understands the phenomena and the contexts in which people engage in, or require, attending. Further, the critique could consider in whose interests is it to frame attention as a psychological phenomenon. Attention as a psychological phenomenon allows educators and researchers to see inattention to be an individual attribute and thus the institution is not challenged to change. In schools, it also allows the power of the teacher to require it to be unquestioned. It is Johnny's problem and Johnny needs to change even if, as Sullivan argues, we do not even know much about that which we are requiring.

I am no poet or regular reader of poetry. Thus I will not engage her poetry as art but I will comment on what a critical researcher might wish to explore further in her poems. First, it is clear that attention is somehow linked to domination of the natural world. Her mother was about saving nature, I am sure. Yet she was attempting to save it by increasing human knowledge—assuming that humans would have dominion over marine life. Second, there is a tension between how Sullivan learned from watching her mother attend and the abstract knowledge that her mother used ("I remember the films shot from airplanes . . ." [p. 285]) and produced ("Then she sat patiently at the microscope on the kitchen table, observing, noticing, discovering patterns, making sense" [p.288]). Sullivan learned how to attend but linked it to art where others are invited to interpret. Her mother linked attention to positivism where definitive knowledge is the goal. This difference seems to invite a critical perspective on what her mother taught and what Sullivan learned. Third, Sullivan may have contradictory wishes for aesthetics and poetry. In "How I Learned to Love Picasso" she portrays aesthetics as giving access to high culture and possibly status even as she teaches us admirably how to engage a painting aesthetically. In "Beware: The Poet Comes for Tea," we see the linking of poetry to power. Here the poet is invasive and all knowing. These can then be juxtaposed to her opening, which complained that attention had not been understood because it had been confounded with power. Indeed, "When I Die" seeks power over the account of her own death! The critical researcher would delve more deeply into these issues than she has.

Of course, Sullivan is after the legitimation of poetry and aesthetics in educational research, arguing that what they offer is a way to embrace the real complexity of social life. I agree with her position but would also point out that she limits art by linking it to interpretivism. If art enables us to get behind that which is hidden by our assumptions as she asserts, then art may also be able to help us understand who and what is served by these assumptions. Poetry may be superior to field notes as a form of representation but representations hide as well as reveal. What is the poet doing and how does poetry serve whom? Even when Sullivan acknowledges politics, she reduces it to an assertion: "a political statement on behalf of the enfranchisement of artists, whose voices have been marginalized in the academy" (p. 288). This statement is not followed with attention to how and why artists have been marginalized and what types of political strategies may be necessary to center them in the academy. I suspect this is because Sullivan is employing analogy as her primary device in this article. Yet it is also in part because of her interpretive perspective on aesthetics. She asserts aesthetic vision sees "potential for transformation" (p. 288) but focuses more on what aesthetics allows one to see or "read" (p. 288). It may be that "physicality and emotion" (p. 288) have much to do with attention, but being dominated or feeling injustice seem to be missing.

Again I agree with her argument that aesthetics is not taught or valued in much of the academic community (although I would note that the arts are part of the academy), and I am taken with her use of observation and poetry as representation. Having preservice teachers observe and poetically represent students differently from themselves is especially provocative. The poems she offers demonstrate that empathy was achieved. Yet this is not enough for a critical researcher. The critical question remains: how could close observation and poetic (or aesthetic) representation be used to transform the life and school situations of those traditionally not well served by schools? Sullivan has constructed an aesthetics that can interpret but cannot critique the social value assigned to aesthetics in education, the academy, or the world. Aesthetics is a tool to understand but not transform our society.

PERSPECTIVE 8: ETHICS, METHODOLOGY, AND DEMOCRACY ON THE SULLIVAN STUDY

KENNETH R. HOWE   *University of Colorado at Boulder*

The ethical dimensions of McCrary Sullivan's study are quite subtle, at least in terms of the issues typically considered to be within the purview of research ethics. Getting at them requires interpreting ethics in its broadest meaning, the meaning contained in Socrates's question: How ought I live my life? This question includes regard for the good of oneself in addition to regard for the good of others. Regard for the good of others by itself is what morality is about (Williams, 1985) and, however central, morality makes up only a part of ethics more broadly conceived.

McCrary Sullivan encourages us to see the importance of aesthetics in the ethical life in the broad sense just described. This element is largely missing, she believes, not only from the lives of educational researchers qua researchers, but from educational institutions and contemporary society in general. Within this general terrain she focuses on how aesthetic activity—the appreciation and production of art—fosters "attending," a capacity that is required across a broad range of intellectual activities.

McCrary Sullivan anticipates the likely response that aesthetic activity is one thing, intellectual activity is quite another. The implication is that aesthetic activity—and the form of attending that goes with it—may and should be bracketed from the form of intellectual activity that counts as research. Against this dichotomous way of thinking, she quotes Stenhouse (1988): "The artist is the researcher *par excellence*" (p. 574). She also seeks support from Dewey (1963), who holds the view that the production of art requires an exceedingly high, perhaps the highest, level of intellectual activity.

Dewey is a good choice of an ally. He pervasively stalks the "dualisms" with which McCrary Sullivan must contend, and would surely deny that a rigid epistemological line may be drawn between aesthetics and research, much less between aesthetic activity and educative activity (Garrison, 1997). Moreover, aesthetic activity is a feature of the ethical on Dewey's view, as well as the ultimate foundation of democracy. Dewey (1963) argues that we can find no defense of democracy "that does not ultimately come down to the belief that democratic social arrangements promote a better quality of human experience . . . " (p. 34).

McCrary Sullivan is fighting an uphill battle that is not likely to be won any time soon. Even if she wins the point that aesthetic activity is a genuinely intellectual activity, she faces the additional problem of winning assent to the idea that it can also count as *research*. There is a deep-seated view in the educational research community—amounting to a prejudice—that for something to count as research, and thus worthy of serious consideration, it must be *empirical* in a rather crude sense. And not only are educational researchers who employ the arts marginalized by this prejudice, so are philosophers and curriculum theorists, to name the most obvious cases.

REFERENCES

Dewey, J. (1963). *Experience and education.* New York: Macmillan Publishing Company.

Garrison, J. (1997). *Dewey and eros.* New York: Teachers College Press.

Stenhouse, L. (1988). Artistry and teaching: The teacher as focus of research and development. *Journal of Curriculum and Supervision, 4*(1), 43–51.

Williams, B. (1985). *Ethics and the limits of philosophy.* Cambridge: Harvard University Press.

PERSPECTIVE 9: POSTSTRUCTURALISM ON THE SULLIVAN STUDY

LYNDA STONE   *University of North Carolina at Chapel Hill*

Julia Kristeva (1941–). Today a practicing psychoanalyst and professor, Kristeva was born in Bulgaria and has lived in Paris since the mid-1960s. She assumed a central role in French intellectual life through association with the journal Tel Quel. *Bringing the work of Bahktin to France, Kristeva studied with Todorov and Goldmann, worked for Lévi-Strauss, and attended Lacan's seminar. Her work includes philosophical analyses, essays on her psychoanalytic practice and on contemporary politics, and relatively recently, novels. She is professor at the University of Paris VII and associated with Columbia University.*

Anne McCrary Sullivan has produced an interesting autobiographic piece within arts based educational research. Her "research on attention" is situated in what has become a very respectable tradition in which the dichotomies of science and art, of the intellectual—objective—and the personal—subjective—have been transformed. The educational theorists who influence this author, Eisner, Greene, and Barone among them, have led the arts revolution. Sullivan's piece contributes well to the tradition.

Sullivan utilizes autobiographical poetry to teach about attention learned from her mother, manifest in poetry, and taught to others. The results are "more" than awareness: learning, transfer, knowledge. In prose explication, here is Sullivan:

[These] poems collectively raise significant questions about the nature of attention: how it develops; whether a model of intense attention has power for teaching attention; how attention to external realities might facilitate awareness of internal realities; how focused attention to an immediate reality may engage memory and/or imagination (p. 287).

Beyond "concreteness" and "detail" (p. 287), extension is to matters of aesthetic vision, and to the politics of the poetic in education. Sullivan puts her educational issue specifically, "What are the implications . . . for education in a society that demands artificial attention and immediate testable results?" (p. 289). This engaging piece provides one "answer."

The use of poetry opens up interpretation; Sullivan's writings offer other meanings. A set of topics pertinent to interpretation are located in the work of poststructuralist Julia Kristeva. For her, interpretation is "revolt" (Kristeva, 2000, p. 2). Revolt or politics arises out of a psychoanalytic framework. Herein relation is basic as the unknown in the psyche of an individual and its counterpart in a society. Related, too, is language with its own aesthetics, basic to the development of a subject, an individual. Kristeva does not write about education directly but her project for revolt has significant implications (see Stone, 2002).

To begin, Sullivan might applaud a poststructuralist approach but her own rendering is yet humanist and romantic: there is an essential self, and a relationship to mother that is active, up front—Sullivan's feelings are "self-evident." Indeed Sullivan's focus is women: all characters are women—mother, daughter, teachers, students. Only the theorists (save for Greene) are men. Given Sullivan's implicit dualism, Kristeva's intent differs as she seeks the feminine in both women and men. Her initial and significant contribution rereads Freud and challenges the work of psychoanalytic theorist, Jacques Lacan. A central concept is the semiotic.

Kristeva's theory of the semiotic is developed early in her work and remains central. The semiotic is a "space," based in drives, that occurs for the infant prior to language acquisition. As commentator Elizabth Grosz (1989) explains,

> the semiotic involves both the inscription of polymorphous impulses across the child's body; and the *return* of these infantile inscriptions in adult form. . . . [As Freud's repressed, they] form a site, a threshold from which the earliest vocalizations, and eventually naming and language, can develop (p. 44, emphasis in original).

From Plato, this "articulation" is named *chora*. Kristeva (1984) offers biological and linguistic explication. First, "genetic programmings are necessarily semiotic: they include the primary processes such as displacement and condensation, absorption and repulsion, rejection and stasis" (p. 29). Significantly, "drives involve pre-Oedipal semiotic functions . . . that connect and orient the body to the mother's body" (p. 29). Second, employing structuralist linguistics, the semiotic is neither signifier nor signified; it has no existence, it has no meaning; yet it is. The chora is thus the place where the subject is "generated" and "negated," where "unity succumbs before the charges and stases that produce him" (p. 28).

What is produced is a "subject," not an individual in the humanist sense but from Emil Benveniste, a split speaking subject of utterance and statement. For Kristeva (1984), there is always a fragmented "subject in process" (p. 37) that undermines the unity of the sign and the unified subject. Related is the symbolic in which Lacan theorizes the emergence of the ego, through the acquisition of language as entry into culture, as the law of the father. With modification Kristeva sums, "By symbolic, I mean . . . all the effects of meaning that appear from the moment linguistic signs are articulated into grammar, not only chronologically but logically as well" (p. 21). Thus the symbolic is lingustic, egoistic, paternal, and regulative; the semiotic is pre-linguistic, unconscious, maternal and disruptive. Opened up by Kristeva are significant ideas: a value in the unconscious, a reclaiming of the maternal and an emergence of the aesthetic.

The last two deserve brief attention—they are, afterall, the topic and method from Sullivan. For Kristeva, the feminine is an adult return to the semiotic, in language, capable of use by women and men. This is the aesthetic, literature, poetry rather than the analytic, philosophy, prose. It erupts from and breaks through the unconscious; given open form, 'something other' is said. Connecting women to writing, Kristeva (1996) asserts this:

> The fact that women can find their way into the world of intelligence seems to me to be great praise for femininity. But I do believe femininity is more a question of themes, of fantasies, imaginary experiences, a relation to the Other, the child, to one's mother and father, than it is a question of *écriture* (pp. 209–210; here Kristeva distinguishes herself from Cixous).

The stance of course is Freudian and related to Kristeva's theorizing on motherhood.

All too briefly: Recall that Freud posits separation of the infant from the mother and attachment to the father as well as differentiation between males and females in this process. In the psychoanalytic tradition, females "lack" both in having a penis and in entering culture. Separation begins when the infant is able to "conceive" of itself as different from its mirror image, when it becomes an object. Kristeva's contributions are to value the mother, to describe a separating father relation as well, and to name still another "entity," the abject and the process of abjection. Kristeva (1982) writes,

> to each ego its object, to each superego its abject. . . . Not me. Not that. But not nothing, either. A "something" that I do not recognize as a thing . . . and which crushes me. On the edge of nonexistence and hallucination, of a reality that, if I acknowledge it, annihilates me. There, abject and abjection are my safeguards. The primers of my culture (p. 2).

For her this is radical otherness—identified culturally with women, with motherhood. Recognition of abjection is part of life: vile bodily waste to be cleaned up, loathesome corpses to be tended. But, again, both women and men can be "dejects" (Kristeva, 1982, p. 8), the one who embraces abjection and becomes in Kristeva's words "a deviser of territories, languages, works. . . . [that] constantly question his solidity and impel him to start afresh" (p. ibid). A deject is a poet. A deject posits revolt and with it, change potentially for educational research and education. Indeed Sullivan is a poet and, from within a Kristevan interpretation, potentially a "revolutionary."

REFERENCES

Grosz, E. (1989). *Sexual subversions: Three French feminists.* Sydney: Allen & Unwin.

Kristeva, J. (1984). *Revolution in poetic language* (M. Waller, Trans.). New York: Columbia University Press. (Original work published 1974)

Kristeva, J. (1982). *Powers of horror: An essay on abjection* (L. Roudiez, Trans.). New York: Columbia University Press. (Original work published 1980)

Kristeva, J. (1996). A conversation with Julia Kristeva. In R. Guberman (Ed.), *Julia Kristeva interviews* (I. Lipkowitz & A. Loselle, Trans., pp. 18–34). New York: Columbia University Press. (Work originally published 1985)

Kristeva, J. (1996). Reading and writing. In R. Guberman (Ed.), *Julia Kristeva interviews* (pp. 204–210). (S. Gavronsky, Trans.). New York: Columbia University Press. (Work originally published 1987)

Kristeva, K. (2000). *Sense and non-sense of revolt* (J. Herman, Trans.). New York: Columbia University Press. (Work originally published 1996)

Stone, L. (2002, August). *Crisis of the educated subject: Insight from Kristeva for American education*. Paper presented at the eighth biennial meeting of the International Network of Philosophers of Education, Olso, Norway.

CHAPTER 11

Challenges Facing Researchers and Scholars in the 21st Century

James L. Paul

Throughout this text we have examined the nature of the research perspectives that guide the work of scholars and researchers and the implications of the perspectives for understanding different kinds of research. Perspectival differences have implications that extend far beyond considerations of the relative qualities of individual studies. They reach to the core of university culture and are reflected in the norms and enacted in the rituals that impact decisions about faculty and students. The resolution of differences, whether among colleagues at the table, through informal negotiations, or by policy fiat, have significant ethical and professional implications for students, faculty, the academy, and the profession. The research productivity of faculty in education and the social sciences and, ultimately, the quality of our work are influenced and shaped by the substantive justification and manner in which those differences are resolved. The following three vignettes suggest some of the specific kinds of perspectival and ethical issues that arise in the routine work of scholars.

Nancy Martin, an assistant professor in social foundations has applied for tenure and promotion to associate professor. Dr. Martin has six articles published in scholarly journals, which is usually considered a minimal expectation for tenure and promotion at her university. The tenure and promotion committee focuses on two problems that concern them. First, one criterion for promotion and tenure is that publications must be data based and Dr. Martin has only one data based article. Even though the other five were published in refereed scholarly journals and three of them were major addresses at the American Educational Research Association meeting, they are philosophical papers dealing mostly with hermeneutics and queer theory. The second concern is that she has been an outspoken critic of the research preparation program in the college that includes only statistics and research design courses. The committee votes to deny tenure. Dr. Martin acknowledges the criterion of data based articles, although she disagrees with it, but also believes that, her sexual orientation as well as the kind of research she intends to pursue entered in to the committee's decision.

Maria Alvarez is a fourth year doctoral student in science education. Her committee approved her study of supervision of the science curriculum in the local school system. The local school system approved the study and, although no one from the schools was on the committee, it was agreed that they would receive a copy of the study and Ms. Alvarez would make a presentation at a meeting of the science teachers in the spring. The study was conducted, but early in the analysis of her data, Ms. Alvarez and her chair called an urgent meeting of her doctoral committee. She had found serious problems of malfeasance in the supervisor's performance of *his duties and ethical problems in his interactions with several of the science teachers that, if revealed, would result in the supervisor and at least two members of his staff being fired. Ms. Alvarez was distraught because, not only had she uncovered some serious problems that she did not know how to handle, she believed the school administration would not be open to any of this information even if she chose to share it. Ms. Alvarez and her committee had to decide what to do with the study.*

The search committee reviewing applications for an assistant professor position in the Department of Educational Leadership considers whether or not to invite Robert Johnson for an interview. Unlike the other two candidates who will be invited, Dr. Johnson graduated from a university that emphasizes preparation in qualitative research methods. Like the professors with whom Dr. Johnson studied, his dissertation and the three articles he co-authored with his major professor are qualitative in nature. The committee finds little in his research preparation or interests expressed in his letter of application to suggest that he has any inclination to conduct quantitative research or even any particular competence in this area. The department is understaffed and has a rather large number of part-time doctoral students needing supervision for their dissertation research. All of the faculty members in the department have strong quantitative research interests and, although they do not reject qualitative research, they believe Dr. Johnson's views may be too extreme to make him a good colleague in the department.

As reflected in these three vignettes, perspectival differences and ethical issues reach into the politics of relationships among scholars. In addition to privileging different kinds of research, these differences have implications for the supervision of doctoral student research, criteria for employing and tenuring faculty, values with respect to gender and sexual orientation, and virtually every other area of academic culture. These differences extend beyond the ways scholars define and reason about research and inquiry to their identity in an academy deeply divided along philosophical lines, and the curriculum needed to prepare researchers and scholars for the future. These issues are taken up in this chapter.

CHALLENGES IN DEFINING RESEARCH

One of the challenges in agreeing on a definition of research involves finding a way to respect and include perspectives that are so fundamentally different, such as the nine perspectives described in this text. The prevailing view of research reflects the dominant perspective and, to the extent possible in a logically consistent and meaningful definition, concessions to other perspectives. For example, mainstream social scientists and educational researchers guided in their research by a positivist epistemology, began according some legitimacy to qualitative research methods in the late 1970s. What was accepted was the value of qualitative methods in generating more interesting hypotheses and helping in the discussion of findings. The positivist epistemology, however, was essentially unchanged.

The last quarter of the 20th century involved dramatic rhetorical struggles over what is and what is not research. Moreover substantial gains were made among scholars in accepting different views such as those discussed in this text. At the end of the century, however, and at the beginning of the 21st century, there was considerable evidence of some retrenchment as a more exclusive view of research was advanced with significant governmental support. The retrenchment, or shift to a more conservative and traditional view of research, reflected, among other things, changes in the political *zeitgeist* of the country at the turn of the century. The election of George Bush as president and a strong Republican Congress clearly signaled a shift to a more conservative government. Also, the tragic violence of September 11, 2001, created a strong consciousness of fear and the need to come together to meet security needs. As suggested by Kati Fowler, doctoral student at the University of South Florida, the enthusiasm for diverse voices in public policy and debate, and also the tolerance for all things relativist, was drained by the rise of a culture of uniformity—one nation, under one God, with one voice.

Three markers of perspectival changes at the beginning of the 21st century as they relate to research were described in Chapter 1. These include (1) the work of a distinguished panel on a definition of research, under the auspices of the National Research Council (NRC) of the National Academy of Sciences (NAS), published in *Scientific Research in Education* (2002); (2) the passage of the No Child Left Behind Act of 2002 that prescribes the kind of research to be used in supporting program decisions; and (3) the political storm in psychology at the end of the 20th century created by the publication of a study that met all of the criteria of good research, but was rejected because the findings were unacceptable on ethical grounds and questions were raised about the kinds of questions researchers have a right to ask. Defining research in public policy in a way that excludes some views as exemplified by the NRC report and the No Child Left Behind Act of 2002, and highlighting ethics as the final arbiter for knowledge, no matter how scientific, vividly illustrate conundrums created by the complex interface of the values and moral perspectives of society and the work of science.

A liberal political environment is more likely to support a pluralistic research philosophy while a conservative environment is more likely to support the canons of traditional science such as certainty about truth and methods of knowing it. Notwithstanding the NRC panel's successful attempt to rescue a radically regressive view of research that was being advanced by members of the Federal Congress, the panel's final report still caused concern among those with a more pluralistic view of research. The shift to a more conservative view of research, reflecting the current political environment, makes it more difficult to support alternative approaches to research and it may reduce the likelihood of a deep and meaningful rapprochement to sustain the pluralistic discourse on research generated during the last quarter of the 20th century. This has implications for how research will be defined and will have a profound impact on scholars and all institutions involved in conducting educational research. Lawrence Summers, for example, president of Harvard University, recently commented that Harvard faculty worry more about the "hard-soft" than the "left-right" spectrum as the "soft" is becoming "harder" with the modes of understanding now favoring analytic domains. Summers believes emphasis should be placed on knowing and having basic understanding of literature rather than what he calls the "current fashions in literary theory." (Traub, 2003, p. 45).

Obviously, the two spectra Summers mentions, "left-right" and "hard-soft" are conflated. Liberal scholars worry about what may be lost in a hard right turn and the idea that a "soft right" is the only option remaining. They are concerned about losing several decades of intellectual growth in thinking about knowledge and mind. The recent history of successfully building some bridges over the deep divide between the humanities and the social sciences is still fresh in the minds of scholars who want to protect those bridges and build more. Fear that those gains could be lost now fuels the debate about research philosophy. Is the shift as reflected in the three markers described here regressive, returning to the insularity of academic disciplines, and is the hegemony associated with privileging a single perspective gaining strength, or is it something else? Whatever else critics may suggest, the next decade of research and scholarship will not be simply an extension of the last decade. Philosophical and political changes at the beginning of the 21st century are reshaping the landscape of research and the engineers of the changes are a mixed group of scientists, humanists, and politicians with different kinds of interests and agendas. Hope for rapprochement that accords a meaningful scholarly space for multiple perspectives may be waning and humanists fear losing their voice in defining what counts as research. The challenge, perhaps now more than ever, is for researchers and scholars to be well prepared for their work and to be vigilant in protecting the place of criticism and sustaining a pluralistic view of knowledge and knowing.

THE WALL: COMING DOWN OR BEING REPAIRED?

Leadership in developing narrative, arts based, and race and gender based perspectives began primarily in the humanities. Leadership in developing postpositivist and pragmatic perspectives started in the social sciences. The extent to which these views can be considered useful to scholars in both the humanities and social sciences depends, in part, on the traditional barriers to interdisciplinary communication being overcome. Those barriers have been a formidable wall, each side reflecting different worldviews and values with respect to the nature and role of research. A great deal of gain was made during the latter part of the 20th century in breaking down parts of the wall but there is reason for concern now that some of those gains may be lost.

From Jericho to China to Berlin, a wall has played a powerful political role protecting what was considered to be valued interests. All of them eventually came down or deteriorated, becoming artifacts of history. Other political forms of protection, such as laws and policies governing jurisdictional boundaries, were created to protect the valued interests as they changed. A thick cultural and political wall separated the sciences and humanities in the academy from the middle of the 19th century until the later part of the 20th century when it started to deteriorate. Although most of the wall continues to stand with ideological reinforcements, some parts have broken down, permitting rhetorical and conceptual passage in both directions. The mutual migration of humanists and social scientists during the past half-century created exciting interdisciplinary and promising perspectival reforms in understandings of research and scholarship. This may be changing with uneven gains accompanied by a great deal of political turbulence, confusion, and incoherent debates. There is some evidence that changes in the national political *zeitgeist* and strong federal initiatives that specify a more traditional view of research, such as the *Leave No Child Behind* legislation, may be reinforcing the wall and deepening the divide.

Some of the most interesting breaks in the wall have been those being created by human scientists, i.e., those working in the social sciences, who are rethinking their work and attempting to bring depth and meaning to the human part of their research. The singular preoccupation of positivism with uncovering facts has been muted, if not replaced in some areas, by interests in epistemological issues and appreciation for the theory-ladenness and value-ladenness of facts. Many social scientists now are interested in ethical theory, hermeneutics, narrative, biography, and artistic forms for representing reality. They are using language differently and employing holistic metaphors in an attempt to bring coherence and meaning to their scholarship.

On the other side of the wall, humanists are creating openings as they look for ways to create more interesting accounts of life that resonate with experience and current research in the social sciences. They are interested in critiques of all forms of knowledge, especially the presumptive hegemony of traditional science's claim to have the only valid view of reality and truth. They have asked new and penetrating questions that bring statistically reliable and valid data, that is "good data" one can accept as true, under the lights of politics, meaning, and values. Humanists have brought gender, race, ethnicity, sexual orientation, and religion into discourses about knowledge as well as an appreciation of the layered complexity of all claims of truth.

The depth and power of scholarship have deepened and been enriched on both sides of the wall by the interpenetration of areas of the humanities and the social sciences. Many social scientists and humanists are finding new purposes in moving beyond their own disciplinary boundaries, finding the areas between disciplines more interesting and provocative than within their own disciplines. The cognitive revolution, with conceptual roots in the 1950s and 1960s, is an excellent example of the "border crossing" (Giroux, 1992) by social scientists and humanists that occurred during the last half century.

The cognitive revolution was a revolt against the positivist epistemology reflected in behaviorism and it was made possible by the deep collaboration of humanists and scientists. The neurosciences, developmental psychology, biography, linguistics, and philosophy were among the disciplines converging on the study of the mind and its work. Interest in cognition, then, and the revolutionary shift in thinking about the mind, became key points of leverage in opening the interdisciplinary conversation and, in the process, passages through the wall that had divided the humanities and the sciences.

The cognitive revolution, of course, is only one of many examples of intellectual initiatives that penetrated the wall and opened up meaningful communication between and among humanists and social scientists. Qualitative and interpretive research is another. The development of nonquantitative, i.e., nonpositivist, research methods created and reflected further passage through the wall. Successful rhetorical and political battles were fought to create a space for nonpositivist understandings of knowledge and ways of knowing on the education and social science side of the wall. Although there is not widespread acceptance of all the different forms of qualitative and interpretive inquiry, the proliferation of qualitative methods during the last two decades and current disinterest of qualitative researchers in the debate with quantitative science is a reflection of some success in breaking through the philosophical and political barriers. This is not to suggest that the two cultures characterized by C. P. Snow (1959) as "literary intellectuals" and "natural scientists" have become one. They have not. It is, however, to suggest that there is more diversity among perspectives and the wall, although it has not and will not come down, became less of a formidable barrier as new alliances and diverse scholarly communities were created.

CRITICAL PHILOSOPHICAL ISSUES DIVIDING SCHOLARS

In this text, leading scholars in education and the social sciences have critiqued exemplar studies from different methodological genres of inquiry including experimental, correlational, ethnographic, narrative, mixed method, and arts based. The critiques have been anchored explicitly in nine of the most common philosophical positions, i.e., postpositivism, constructivism, pragmatism, ethics, critical theory, narrative, race-ethnicity-gender, arts based, and poststructuralism.

Although there are few, if any, points of agreement about knowledge that would be shared across all of the perspectives represented in the text, there is some agreement about the critical issues that divide scholars. They are described here as a review of some of these issues raised throughout the text.

Nature of Knowledge

1. Researchers differ regarding the nature of knowledge, with some emphasizing objectivity and others emphasizing subjectivity and the relational and dynamic nature of knowledge.

2. Researchers differ regarding the location of knowledge, with some being clear that there is an external reality that is the object of research, while others believe that knowledge is in the mind, i.e., perceptions and constructions. The distinction is between truth as a reality external to, and relatively independent of, our perceptions versus truth as an inner reality, contained in our perceptions.

3. The Cartesian dualism, mind and matter, that anchored positivist epistemology, has been fiercely resisted by scholars interested in more holistic, connected, and systemic accounts of reality and truth.

4. There has been a revival of interest in the imaginative foundations of knowledge, including interest in the study of the mind, and the development of different epistemologies, including, for example, constructivism, arts based educational research, and narrative.

5. Many scholars are concerned about an apparent increase in acceptance of nihilism and relativism, views that are embraced by some postmodern theorists.

Method

6. Although better research methods increase our confidence in findings, the issue of how certain we can be that our findings are true varies with different traditions. Some view certainty as desirable and, to some extent, attainable. Others view it as a philosophical artifact of positivism and an unrealistic goal in the human sciences.

7. Many believe there has been an overemphasis on mechanics and right procedures and a mystification of method, especially of data analysis, that has substituted for thoughtful analysis of the epistemological nature and the social, political, and ethical meaning and implications of those data.

Lines and Boundaries

8. The rhetorical and paradigm-bound wall separating the humanities and the social sciences became the target of many on both sides of the wall during the last half of the 20th century and parts of it are breaking down.

9. The lines separating research, inquiry, evaluation, and scholarship have blurred.

10. The boundaries separating traditional disciplines have become less defined and more penetrable.

11. The separation of education researchers from the departments housing their disciplines is a challenge with respect to the fragmentation of knowledge and, in some instances, currency in perspective.

Sociology, and Politics

12. Scholars from different perspectives have emphasized the need for respecting intellectual diversity and loosening the grip of the traditional philosophy of science, i.e., positivism. Logical positivism, a dead philosophy of science, has been replaced by postpositivism as the

mainstream philosophy of science. It is more inclusive but, as expected, concerns about hegemony continue as they would with any "mainstream" view that is by definition exclusive.

13. There is a need to recognize the sociology of knowledge. An example is the nature and policy implications of data being collected on the disproportionate representation of African-American boys in special education.

14. There is increasing awareness of the politics of knowledge such as the destructive force of some debates in silencing voices of minorities. The politics also extend to issues of promotion and tenure, paneling research funding reviews, and publication criteria. The issues are not necessarily matters of good and bad quality, although they are represented as such, but rather different philosophies of research. Research is an activity with huge political meaning for participants, researchers, and for the corpus of "approved" knowledge.

Vocabularies

15. Vocabularies for addressing nonquantitative issues have been problematic because they come from so many different disciplines and do not have shared meanings. This has often created a discursive incoherence in the literature and in debates.

16. A radical linguistic ontology emerged, especially among French scholars, locating reality in language and advocating the deconstruction of language as the preferred method of scholarship. Knowledge of this view is important in reading some of the literature but it is not widely accepted among researchers.

Researcher, Scholar, Self

17. Many scholars consider where a researcher stands with respect to a study being planned and conducted or critiqued, that is, their epistemology, is a part of the study or critique and should be made explicit.

18. Many scholars recognize now the influence of the researcher's values, race, ethnicity, history, and worldview in all stages of the research process and the need, therefore, to know who the person is as well as the form and substance of his or her research.

19. Complete objectivity is, for most researchers, desirable but recognized as not possible. Researchers for whom it is desirable attempt to carefully specify the lack of objectivity. Many researchers, however, see objectivity as an epistemological ruse and attempt, rather, to become more deeply subjective.

Ethics and Accountability

20. Researchers are now more accountable for their conduct, methods, and research perspectives than ever before. In addition to human subjects review procedures, research is much more likely to be critiqued by scholars from different perspectives.

21. The complexity facing researchers is amplified by epistemological pluralism, i.e., different views of knowledge and knowing, and by the growing recognition of their perspective-laden and value-laden participation in their findings and how they represent their findings.

22. Researchers are much less likely now to be able to make decisions alone about their research participants, methods, procedures, and representation of their findings. In addition to more careful monitoring of research, researchers are encouraged to be more democratic and deliberative in planning, conducting, and disseminating the findings of their study.

EDUCATIONAL RESEARCHER'S IDENTITY IN THE ACADEMY

Ellen Condliffe Lagemann (2000), dean of the Harvard Graduate School of Education, wrote an insightful and useful analysis of the history of educational research. She begins with a reference to an article by Harvard philosopher, Josiah Royce that appeared in the first issue of the *Harvard Educational Review* in 1891. In his article, titled "Is There a Science of Education," Royce argued that teachers should have "scientific training," by which he meant, "opportunities to learn and reflect on their craft" (Lagemann, p. ix). Quoting Royce: "(there was) no universally valid science of pedagogy . . . capable of . . . complete formulation and . . . direct application to individual pupils and teachers" (Lagemann, p. ix).

Nevertheless, although the study of education became a part of the university curriculum at the end of the 19th century, as Lagemann points out, it never gained internal coherence as an area of scholarship. Emerging in the academy at a time when the wall separating science from the humanities was being reinforced, educational research was being profoundly influenced by several different fields of study, especially psychology.

Education researchers had to find a place in the academy, that is, they needed to fit somewhere in the humanities or the social sciences. Consistent with their mission in developing knowledge to support educational practices and the preparation of teachers, they also had to find a place with public schools. The issues in public schools included, for example, the special role of the school in a democracy, the role of teachers, the role of students, individual differences among students and teachers, the lack of a science of pedagogy, the lack of adequate teacher preparation, lack of specification—or specifiability—of educational outcomes, local variations of schooling, and the politics of the curriculum and pedagogy.

The issue of an identity for educational researchers in the academy at the beginning of the 20th century loomed large. With a strong liberal arts curriculum in the humanities on one hand and a rapidly emerging curriculum in the social sciences on the other, educational scholarship did not fit clearly in either place. Unfortunately, it was necessary to be aligned with either the humanities side, or the science side, of the academy. The lack of a clear identity with respect to where educational research belongs has been, and continues to be, a challenge for educational researchers and scholars. Lagemann (2000) comments that educational scholarship has been "reluctantly tolerated at the margins of the academy and rarely trusted by policy makers, practitioners, or members of the public at large" (p. x).

There are several disciplines with scholars who focus on educational issues in their research, e.g., educational sociologists, educational historians, philosophers of education, and educational anthropologists. Faculty most associated with research methods in colleges of education are in departments of educational psychology or statistics and measurement. Several disciplines have scholars who teach teachers, e.g., science, math, social studies, and English. These and other specializations are typically found in colleges of education. However, these faculty rarely have joint appointments or are actively involved in the department housing their discipline. Further, their own preparation, in most instances, was largely in colleges of education with some coursework in their discipline. Of course, this is not unique to education as some disciplines in the social sciences, such as psychology, have faculty specializing, for example, in history or ethics.

The point here is not to argue whether or not discipline-based educational specialists are necessary. They clearly are. The preparation of teachers, leaders, specialists, and researchers in education requires faculty who are dedicated to addressing the needs of students, schools, and policy makers and, thus, contributing to the viability of schools in a democracy. Difficulties do arise, however, out of the disconnection between the "specialists" in education and their disciplinary homes.

The problem of disconnection is much deeper than suggested by the distinction between educational specialists and their foundational discipline. It is more accurately a disconnection that has grown within the disciplines as specialization has increased. Specialization has become the new wall in the academy. Slife and Williams (1995), among others, have described the fragmentation and lack of an integrating theory in psychology. Clinical, social, experimental, educational, school, and neuropsychological specialists, for example, typically do not know the literature and current knowledge in fields other than their own and there is no framework that unites them. The nature of knowledge generated in experimental psychology, for example, is different than the knowledge generated by a policy scientist, which is different than knowledge generated by an autoethnographer. The assumptions, logics, and methods are different. The fragmentation of areas within as well as between the social sciences and the diversity of epistemologies are issues in the preparation of scholars and researchers (Paul & Marfo, 2001). Research preparation programs are challenged to avoid the dilemma described by Abraham Maslow when he suggested that giving one only a hammer predisposes him or her to treat everything like a nail.

These philosophical, political, and ethical issues face researchers and scholars in the present and foreseeable future. The curriculum for preparing researchers must include material and experiences that address these current realities.

PREPARING RESEARCHERS AND SCHOLARS FOR THE 21ST CENTURY

A great deal has been written about the preparation of researchers and scholars for the 21st century (Cizek 1999; Paul & Marfo 2001; Schoenfeld, 1999). Several issues in the curriculum to prepare researchers, as they relate to the critiques of perspectives on knowledge presented in this text, are highlighted below.

The intellectual climate for which researchers and scholars are being prepared is very different than the climate existing when the basic research preparation curriculum, consisting of courses in statistics and research design, was developed more than a half century ago. The statistical methods and designs have changed radically; however, the basic philosophies and structure of the curriculum remain generally the same. The emphasis on quantitative methods without attention to the philosophical foundations of those methods limits the student's understanding of the history and epistemological grounding of the methods and the political and ethical implications of every part of the research process. Learning about the philosophy and political nature of research should precede, or at least accompany learning how to do research. In the absence of attention to the nature(s) of knowledge and knowing, opening the curriculum door to nonquantitative approaches is problematic. Debates about knowledge that are limited to the level of method are incoherent. A deeper level of analysis is required to reach meaningful understandings about a broader research preparation curriculum. For example, new courses in qualitative research methods are being developed and taught in colleges of education. How are these courses to be evaluated in a manner that is philosophically sound? Although all methods must be evaluated with respect to a set of standards, it is generally inappropriate to use criteria for one genre of research, i.e. quantitative or qualitative, to evaluate another. Discussion of the logics and values that constitute the standards is the appropriate level at which to begin. At present, the kinds of qualitative courses being developed and taught in colleges of education depend on the interests and competencies of faculty on the scene. With the proliferation of qualitative and interpretive approaches, which Page (2000) termed the "inward turn," there is not the quality control that exists in the well-developed quantitative curriculum. This situation is serious because scholars and researchers poorly prepared in the non-quantitative philosophies and methods of inquiry will, ultimately, contribute to the incoherence of some of the debates about knowledge and produce less than quality work. Furthermore, they will be disadvantaged as young faculty attempting to produce publishable quality research.

One of the challenges in research preparation programs is that some faculty members now preparing researchers do not necessarily accept pluralistic views of knowledge or the paradigm shifts that have brought the social sciences and humanities closer together. Neither are they necessarily convinced research is as culturally and ethically complex as some scholars have argued. It is more difficult to effect changes in the research preparation curriculum where there is little appreciation of the need to do so.

One of the concerns to most research faculty is the extent of the changes that may be needed. Given the realities of time limitation for what can be required in the curriculum, each course must be a vital part of the curriculum. The decisions about how many quantitative and qualitative methods courses to require are difficult to make when one considers the need for coursework, for example, in philosophies of research, sociology and politics of knowledge, and ethics. There is a need, of course, to infuse ethical analysis into the entire research preparation program, not simply in one course. This not only involves issues typically addressed by institutional review boards, such as informed consent and confidentiality, it involves rethinking decisions made in the planning, conduct, analysis, representation, and presentation of the research in a democracy. Democratic deliberation is a conceptual framework and set of skills that need to be part of the research preparation curriculum.

The changes in the academic cultures—including worldviews, values, and methods—of social scientists and humanists have created a context within which the preparation of researchers and scholars needs rethinking. There is a need for curricula that go beyond methods to include understandings of the philosophy and history of science, criticism, ethics, and the sociology and politics of knowledge. Perhaps more than ever, those entrusted with building the knowledge bases for policies and practices in education and human service fields, need to have informed respect for different research and scholarly traditions and to learn methods of critique aimed at enriching the conversation about scholarship rather than politically silencing unfamiliar or even unwelcomed voices.

In the current academic environment, research preparation programs should promote interdisciplinary scholarship in contexts such as collaborative research groups. Border crossings, breaking down traditional disciplinary barriers, and changes in the culture of the academy should be reflected in the content and methods employed in preparing researchers and scholars. Failing to do so will prepare students for a world that no longer exists.

A CONCLUDING PERSPECTIVE

Researchers and scholars at the beginning of the 21st century enjoy the best of times with affordable rapid data processing, word processing, and data storage and retrieval capabilities that were not imagined three decades ago. Scholars now have extraordinary abilities to access libraries and national data sets, to exchange files, manipulate data, process data by knowing the concept of the analysis without having to be a statistician, and to participate in real-time video conferences and chat-room discussion groups with colleagues around the world. Technology has made our work portable; the *Encyclopaedia Britannica* and statistical and qualitative data analysis packages are contained on small disks and laptops that easily fit under the seat on an airplane. It is an exciting time to think and to discover or create new knowledge and understandings.

The electronic and digital advances have occurred in an environment in which the world has become much smaller; diversity is a much more profound human reality, and the need for ethical reasoning about all human affairs has never been greater. The valued western ways of knowing are institutionalized and still manage, in many quarters, to escape cultural, political, and ethical critique. This occurs although many scholars, as well as the children whom education research is supposed to serve, may not be of Western European decent.

The new world in which we live, the world that is changing daily, brings new questions about ourselves, families, relationships, institutions, and values that we were not forced to ask in earlier times. Our beliefs about what is real, true, and worthy are at the epicenter of our ability to cope in ways that are rewarding in the changing world in which we live and the tools with which we work. They also form the foundation for research and scholarship. Scholars frame their work with different perspectives of reality, truth, and values, and these perspectives shape and are shaped by the logics, forms for representation, and outcomes of the research process.

In this text, nine eminent scholars examined six approaches to research from different philosophical perspectives. The difference between this analysis and what one typically finds in the literature, or a debate, is that there are multiple accounts given and the positions are made explicit. Researchers and scholars prepared for the 21st century will be well served if they have an understanding of, and respect for, different accounts of knowledge and method. This text and the Instructor's Guide were prepared to help meet that need.

QUESTIONS

1. How can fundamental differences in research perspectives be respected?
2. To what degree should there be an interface between public policy and research agendas?
3. Is the shift as reflected in the three markers described in this text regressive, returning to the insularity of academic disciplines, and is the hegemony associated with privileging a single perspective gaining strength, or is it something else?
4. How do these new perspectives change the nature of data and the understanding of truthful claims?
5. Do these perspectives represent a shared set of values or a divided set of issues?
6. What ought to be the identity of educational researchers in the 21st century?
7. Why is a philosophical undergirding of educational research essential for the field?

REFERENCES

Cizek, G. J. (1999). The tale wagging the dog: Narrative and neopragmatism in teacher education and research. In J. D.Raths, & A. C. McAninch (Eds.), *What counts as knowledge in teacher education?* (pp. 47–69). Stamford, CT: Ablex Publishing Co.

Giroux, H. A. (1992). *Border crossings: Cultural workers and the politics of education.* New York: Routledge.

Lagemann, E. C. (2000). *An elusive science: The troubling history of education research.* Chicago: The University of Chicago Press.

Page, R. N. (2000). Future directions in qualitative research. *Harvard Educational Review, 70* (1).

Paul, J., & Marfo, K. (2001). Preparation of educational researchers in philosophical foundations of inquiry. *Review of Educational Research, 71,* 525–549.

Schoenfeld, A. H. (1999). The core, the canon, and the development of research skills: Issues in the preparation of education researchers. In E. C. Lagemann, & L. S. Shulman (Eds), *Issues in education research: Problems and possibilities.* (pp. 166–203). San Francisco: Jossey Bass Publishers.

Slife, B. D., & Williams, R. N. (1995). *What's behind the research? Discovering hidden assumptions in the behavioral sciences.* Thousand Oaks: Sage Publications.

Snow, C. P. (1959). *The two cultures.* Cambridge: Cambridge University Press.

Traub, J. (2003, August 24). Harvard radical. *The New York Times Magazine.*

Afterword

A Metacritique of the Text

This text, like all texts, came from somewhere. It came from my values and my belief that researchers need to have knowledge about different perspectives and to appreciate the potential of critiques from multiple perspectives. My metacritical comments here are limited to the following questions: What values did I bring to the development of this text? What choices did I make reflecting those values? And, to what extent were my choices critiqued by other scholars?

Regarding my own values, I believe finding knowledge, understanding, and meaning are different but essential products of research and inquiry. Different research epistemologies lead to different kinds of outcomes and no single approach to research necessarily leads to all three. I value different kinds of research because there are different kinds of needs. I believe systematic studies, whether statistical with large sample sizes, ethnographic, ethical, or other forms of research, are needed to generate the knowledge, understanding, and meaningful applications needed to improve all aspects of education.

What choices did I make in creating this text? I decided to create a text that included multiple perspectives and critiques of different approaches to research. My decision about which nine perspectives to include was based on my own reading of literature in the social sciences and the humanities and years of teaching doctoral students about the philosophical and ethical foundations of educational research. My selection of the scholars was based on my belief that each of these scholars is one of the most articulate and insightful thinkers and writers about the perspective I asked them to represent in the text. My selection of the studies was based on my belief that these are among the most common approaches and the ones I selected were exemplary and, at the same time, posed particular challenges. Other decisions could have been made—other perspectives, scholars, or studies—and the outcome would have been different. However, I believe the overall outcome in demonstrating the nature of perspectives and the value of criticism would have been essentially the same.

To what extent did other scholars critique my choices and, therefore, the text? In the beginning of the process of working on this text, I consulted numerous scholars in different fields, including education, anthropology, sociology, psychology, communications, and philosophy. Those discussions plus my own readings and experience led me to the decisions I made. After submitting the manuscript to the publisher, several outside reviewers were retained to read and comment on the text. Some of the advice was contradictory and that is not surprising since this is a book about perspectives and each reviewer reads the text from his or her own perspective. For example, one reviewer especially liked one of the perspectives not described widely in the research literature while another reviewer suggested it should be deleted. The reviews were sufficiently helpful that I reworked a great deal of the text, mostly to make it more accessible to students as several had suggested. Any decisions I would have made would have been consistent with some of the views of most of the critics and at odds with others. However, the reviewers' different as well as shared views of the material helped me gain perspective on my approach to the text. It was not my purpose to align my views with all of the views of the reviewers. That would not have been possible; neither would it have been sensible. Rather my purpose, and the publisher's purpose, was to have the text critiqued by informed scholars with different perspectives and to respond as prudently I as could within the context of my own values and perspective.

My hope is that each reader gained awareness of his or her own perspective while critically reading the material in this text. Some of the material likely resonated with your views and values; some did not. The purpose here was not to persuade you that one perspective was better than another or that the perspective you held before reading the text was wrong. Rather, it was to assist students in developing more informed and diverse critical perspectives.

Glossary

alterity   philosophical term for "other" or "otherness." Denotes the systematized construction of classes of people rather than a description of individual differences.

attached significance   meaning that is created or inscribed through interpretation.

axiology   the study of values. Also termed value theory, axiology is a branch of philosophy focused on the nature of value and the kinds of things that have value.

bricoleur   when applied to research, a bricoleur utilizes a variety of methodological tools, combining perspectives and adapting methods as needed. This approach involves understanding that research is interactive, and is influenced by the researcher's own history, social class, gender, and ethnicity.

communitarianism   rejects individualism and the notion of "basic" individual rights; asserts the rights of the collective that are independent of, and at times opposed to, the rights of the individuals.

contingent   those events that occur are dependent upon conditions or other occurrences that have not yet been established; once those other conditions or occurrences are established, it is not certain that their establishment is inevitable—it could have been something else.

care theory   asks researcher to consider the consequences of their work; used to guide ethical judgment.

constructivism   theoretical perspective; maintains that knowledge is a product of our social practices and institutions; an interpretive stance that attends to "meaning-making" activities of individuals and societies.

critical ethnography   a qualitative, interactive research methodology working from the theoretical frame that all societies have systematic inequalities; such inequalities are maintained by a complex culture.

critical theory   social theory that is concurrently self-reflexive, practical, normative, and explanatory. A critical researcher attempts to uncover the "dynamics of power and ideology" of institutions, texts, or relationships and promotes awareness and emancipation.

deliberative conception   alternative to the technocratic conception; maintains that values should be considered when conducting research.

dialogic approach   a research approach that dignifies the voice of the participants, seeking their input on important matters; it recognizes that how the participants see these matters is more significant than how the researcher sees them.

epistemology   the theory of knowledge; or, the study of the nature of knowledge. Important questions focus on the nature of knowledge, the place of experience in generating knowledge, and the place of reason in doing so; relationships between knowledge and certainty, and between

knowledge and error; and the changing forms of knowledge that arise from new conceptualizations of the world.

ethnicity   a social construct that divides people into smaller groups, based on traits such as language, behavioral patterns, history, ancestral geographical base, and shared sense of group membership. Ethnic classification is used for identification, rather than differentiation.

expert approach   a research approach that places the researcher's perspective above that of the participants; in so doing, a power imbalance is created and maintained.

fallibilism   doctrine that states that particular beliefs and propositions are inherently uncertain and possibly mistaken; according to Phillips, "all judgments of truth in matters pertaining to theories or abstract models of reality are fallible ones."

formative evaluation   evaluation most commonly used in ABER; rather than objectively appraising the work of art, this type of evaluation considers the potential of the work to persuade its audience to ask important questions.

gender   is the culturally specific set of characteristics that identifies the relations between women and men, and varies over time and across settings. (Gender is different than sex, which identifies the biological difference between men and women).

heuristic   a process, or method, that enables a person to learn something for themselves.

historicism   philosophical doctrine that maintains that texts, social structures, and events are better understood contextually, that is, within the context of their historical development.

ideology   consciously shared system of beliefs that echoes the interests of a group, nation, society, or political system. Ideology can help to explain or change how things are in a particular society, and underlie political action.

intelligible frames   (see also negotiated meaning) the coming together of our experiences, both old/new and direct/vicarious, that allows us to construct personal meaning; these frames are often formed out of our narratives.

knowledge claims   the statements a particular discipline or paradigm holds and makes that provide a foundation for thinking therein; things that the particular discipline is said to know.

linguistic turn   a recognition that the formation or reformation of language, or the deeper understanding of the language we use, is a better way to solve problems of a philosophy; a recognition that language does much more than relate events as they appear: language is a maker of meaning.

meaning-making activities   human beings construct meaning from their assorted and collected experiences; this idea posits that no two humans will share exactly the same experiences, so they will construct different meanings in this lives; meaning-making activities are contingent activities.

methodology or methodologies the general study of method in particular fields of inquiry; the branch of philosophy, closely related to epistemology, which explores methods used by science to arrive at posited truths concerning the world.

moral responsibility   the researcher must understand that the activities and explorations she undertakes create a value within the framework of interactions with her participants. Because she can never be detached from her work, her participants, or her inquiry, she must act with a framework that cares for and assumes responsibility for that, even after the work seems finished.

negotiated meaning (see also intelligible frames)   considers the practice of communication in its role of meaning-making. People are not spectators but participants in life, and their telling of the world to those with whom they interact gets performed and negotiated into the everyday world we all experience. This shifts the focus of inquiry from objects to meaning, from theories to stories.

ontology   a branch of metaphysics that focuses on what exists; a philosophical investigation of the nature, constitution, and structure of reality.

positivism   a philosophical movement that began in the 1920s through an outgrowth of British empiricism. Positivists maintained that assertions about the world could (and must) be verifiable through experience or observation.

postmodernism   a reasoned critique of many of the assumptions of the modern period; a reaction to modern philosophy, pondering in whose collective interest is scientific inquiry advanced; it is sometimes regarded as a complex cluster of categories of inquiry within a suspicion of grand and metanarratives, seeking to understand discrepancies between what we purport to know and what actions we take because of that belief.

self-reflexive   a way of looking back on the self and on inquiry that explores and demonstrates a situatedness and personal investment; to see the role of the self through probing the self for truthful insight.

sociology of knowledge   the exploration of and the idea that knowledge is generated socially, within contexts that are constructed over a period of time by people holding and being held by power structures; knowledge is constructed, questioned, refined, and encoded within those social entities.

subjects vs. participants   born, perhaps, of people-first thinking, this recognizes that the research relationship between the researcher and the research participants is more intimate and personal, even more collaborative, than once believed.

teleology   the philosophical doctrine that all of nature, or at least intentional agents, are goal directed or functionally organized.

verisimilitude   the appearance of being true or real; something that only appears to be true or real.

verstehen   German term for understanding.

warranted assertions/beliefs a non-static and non finalized correspondence between two separate orders, though one that is cognitively effective and successful. Dewey defined this term to replace the more common "truth" because he saw it as too limited and coercive.

Author Index

Agee, J., 259
Albee, G., 15
Anyon, J., 191, 238
Alexander, B. K., 171
Asby, R., 32

Bandura, A., 239
Baynes, K., 32
Bergmann, G., 37
Bernstein, R., 31
Blackburn, S., 27
Bochner, A., 196, 234, 270
Bohman, J., 32
Bourdieu, P., 168, 169
Bowers, C.A., 163, 240
Bowles, S., 238
Brady, I., 299
Bratman, M., 22
Brody, H., 298
Burbules, N., 33

Campbell, D.T., 126
Carlson, J.I., 92
Carr, E.G., 92, 128
Castel, R., 35
Chartier, R., 34
Chavajay, P., 161
Cheong, Y. F., 206
Cixous, H., 282, 283
Cizek, G.J., 323
Conquergood, D., 193
Cutrofello, A., 133

D'Amico, R., 34
Dechant, D., 272
Denzin, N., 196
Derrida, J., 30, 132, 133
Dewey, J., 8, 22, 311
Dhillon, P., 247

Ellis, C., 196, 250, 269, 270, 277, 278, 281

Fasching, D.J., 272
Flinders, D.J., 190
Foucault, M., 35, 240
Frazier, E.E., 160
Friedman, M., 2, 3

Garrison, J., 311
Gintis, H., 238
Giroux, H., 319
Goetz, J.P., 190
Goodall, H.L., Jr., 267
Gouldner, A., 266
Grosz, E., 312
Guba, E.G., 48

Habermas, J., 126, 163, 240, 276
Hacking, I., 26, 33
Hallum, A., 117
Hanson, N., 33
Heath, S.B., 135, 146
Hempel, C., 32
House, E., 279
Howe, K., 244, 245, 279
Huyssen, A., 29

Iggers, G., 34

Jackson, M., 124, 195, 300
Johnson, B., 133
Jones, H., 196

Kalyanpur, M., 161
Kaplan, A., 5–6
Keller, E., 31
Kemp, D.C., 92

Krieger, S., 236, 270
Kristeva, J., 312, 313
Kuhn, T., 126, 234, 248

Labov, W., 160
Lagemann, E.C., 322
Landres, J.S., 267
LeCompte, M.D., 190
Lewis, C.S., 266
Lincoln, Y.S., 118
Lyotard, J., 247, 248

Marfo, K., 323
Magnito McLaughlin, D., 92
McCarthy, T., 32
McConnachie, G., 92
McGuire, M.B., 267
McLaren, P., 193
Meinecke, F., 34
Mills, G.E., 190
Mills, W.W., 164

Newmann, F. M., 229
Newcombe, N.S., 15

Noddings, N., 128, 153, 295

O'Neill, J., 266
Oakes, J., 238
Oldroyd, D., 32

Page, R.N., 8, 9–10
Paul, J., 1, 3, 315, 323
Perry, J., 22
Peters, M., 248
Phillips, A., 124
Phillips, D., 2, 3, 4, 33
Polyanski, M., 274
Popper, K., 23, 31

Quine, W., 3, 248

Rajchman, J., 30
Raudenbush, S.W., 206, 247
Reinharz, S., 267
Richardson, L., 236, 261, 271
Rogoff, B., 161, 306
Rorty, R., 122, 234, 271, 299
Rose, D., 236, 270
Rowan, B., 206
Russell, B., 21

Sailor, W., 3
Scheurich, J. J., 193
Schoenfeld, A.H., 323
Scriven, M., 2
Scruton, R., 21, 27
Shand, J., 23, 24, 27, 28
Shields, L., 117

Shore, P., 295
Siddle-Walker, V., 306
Sleeter, C., 6
Slife, B.D., 323
Smith, C.E., 92
Smith, D.E., 153
Snow, C.P., 319
Sommers, T., 117
Spero, R.B., 239
Spickard, J.V., 267
Spivak, G., 132
Standish, P., 247
Stanley, J., 126
Stone, L., 312
Sullivan, A.M., 284

Taylor, C., 35, 36, 120
Thorp, L., 296

Toulmin, S., 22, 25, 27, 28, 33
Turner, E., 237
Turner, V., 192

Van Maanen, J., 197

Waugh, J.B., 234
Weil, S., 295
West, C., 30, 198
Wexler, 164
Williams, B., 310
Williams, R.N., 323
Wolker, R., 27

Young, M.D., 193

Subject Index

Absolute truths, 52, 54
Activities contingent on language, 65
Alexander study, 171–205
 constructivism on, 192–193
 critical theory on, 198–201
 ethics, methodology, and democracy on, 201–203
 interpretive and narrative on, 193–197
 postpositivism on, 188–189
 poststructuralism on, 203–207
 pragmatism on, 190–192
 race, ethnicity, and gender on, 197–198
Alterity, 329
Analytical philosophy, movement in, 22, 36
Annales Circle, 34
Archaeology of Knowledge, The, 38
Arts based educational research
 criteria for judging, 70–71
 epistemology of, 47
 heuristic approach, 70
 inquiry purposes, 69–70
 methodology of, 47
 ontology of, 47
 origins and growth, 68–69
 Sullivan study, in the, 301–305
 values of, 47
Attached significance, 329
Axiology, 60, 63, 329

Being and Time, 37
Bricoleur, 62, 329

Care theory, 59, 329
Carr et al. study, 92–134
 constructivism on, 118–120
 critical theory on, 126–130
 ethics, methodology, and democracy on, 130–131

interpretive and narrative on, 120–125
postpositivism on, 114–116
poststructuralism on, 132–134
pragmatism on, 116–118
race, ethnicity, and gender on, 125–126
Cartesian Revolution, 27
Causation, concept of, 54
Classical period, 24
Cognitive language, 37
Communicative language, 37
Communitarianism, 329
Comprehensive Multisituational Intervention for Problem Behavior in the Community: Long-Term Maintenance and Social Validation, 92–114
Conduct of Inquiry, The, 5
Constructed reality, 61
Constructions, 60
Constructivism, 44, 329
 axiology, 60, 63
 bricoleurs, 62
 constructed reality, 61
 enacted reality, 61
 epistemology of, 46, 60, 61–62
 methodology of, 46, 60, 62–63
 ontology of, 46, 60, 61
 physical/temporal reality, 61
 theoretical and interpretive stance, as a, 60–64
 values of, 46
 verstehen, 61
Constructivism on
 Alexander study, on the, 192–193
 Carr et al. study, on the, 118–120
 Ellis study, on the, 267–268
 Heath study, on the, 155–156

Raudenbush et al. study, on the, 231–233
Sullivan study, on the, 296–297
Contemporary analytic philosophy, 36
Continental tradition, parallel development in the, 33
Contingent, 329
Cosmopolis: The Hidden Agenda of Modernity, 25
Critical ethnography, 329
Critical perspective
 epistemology of, 47
 methodology, 47
 ontology of, 47
 values, 47
Critical theory, 44, 329
 Alexander study, on the, 198–201
 Carr et al. study, on the, 126–130
 Ellis study, on the, 276–279
 Heath study, on the, 162–166
 Raudenbush et al. study, on the, 240–244
 Sullivan study, on the, 307–310

Debates, role of, 9–10
Defining research, challenges in, 316–318
Deliberative conception, 329
Democratic deliberation, 45
Dialogic conception, 329
Différance, notion of, 38
Discursive theory, 37

Educational inquiry, 49
Educational researcher's identity in the academy, 322–323
Education science
 and the law, 13–14
 and public policy, 11–13

Ellis study, 250–283
  constructivism on, 267–268
  critical theory on, 276–279
  ethics, methodology, and
    democracy on, 279–280
  interpretive and narrative on,
    268–273
  postpositivism on, 263–265
  poststructuralism on, 281–283
  pragmatism on, 265–266
  race, ethnicity, and gender on,
    273–276
Empiricism, 26, 27
Empiricist epistemology, 51
Enacted reality, 61
Enlightenment movement, 27
Epistemology, 23–24, 46, 329
Error, detection and elimination
  of, 52
Ethics, 24, 45
  epistemology of, 46
  methodology of, 46
  ontology of, 46
  values of, 46
Ethics, methodology, and
  democracy
  Alexander study, on the,
    201–203
  Carr et al. study, on the,
    130–131
  Ellis study, on the, 279–280
  Heath study, on the, 166–167
  Raudenbush et al. study, on the,
    244–246
  Sullivan study, on the, 310–311
Ethnicity, 329
Expert approach, 329
Expressive language, 37

Fallibilism, 52, 54, 329
Formative evaluation, 329

Heath study, 135–170
  constructivism on, 155–156
  critical theory on, 162–166
  ethics, methodology, and
    democracy on, 166–167

interpretive and narrative on,
    156–160
  postpositivism on, 151–153
  poststructuralism on, 167–170
  pragmatism on, 153–154
  race, ethnicity, and gender on,
    160–162
Heuristic, 330
Higher Order Instructional Goals in
  Secondary Schools: Class Teacher,
  and School Influences, 206–226
Historicism, label of, 34, 330
Hypothetico-deductive method, 6

Idealism, 26, 27
Ideology, 330
Induction connection to
  positivism, 32
Intellectual occupation with
  science, 32
Intelligible frame, 66, 330
Interpetivism, 44, 47
Interpretive and narrative
  Alexander study, on the, 193–197
  Carr et al. study, on the,
    120–125
  Ellis study, on the, 268–273
  Heath study, on the, 156–160
  Raudenbush et al. study, on the,
    234–237
  Sullivan study, on the, 298–301
Interpretive perspectives, 65–67
Interpretive social science, 65, 66

Kant, Immanuel, significance of, 27
Knowledge as justified true
  belief, 30
Knowledge claims, 54, 330

Language, functions of, 37
Language and philosophy,
  36–38
Leadership in perspectives, role of,
  318–319
Linguistic philosophy, 36
Linguistic turn, 36, 330
Logical Investigations, 37

Logical positivism, 2, 6, 32, 36
Logic of Scientific Discovery, The, 3
Logics in use, 5–6
Logik der Forschung, 3
Logocentrism, origins of, 30

Margins, research from the, 6–7
Meaning-making activities,
  60, 330
Meditations on First Philosphy, 27
Metahistory: The Historical
  Imagination in Nineteenth-Century
  Europe, 35
Metaphysics, 23
Metaphysics as a foundation for
  philosophy, rejection of, 32
Methodology, 45, 46, 330
Modernity, role of, 24, 25–26
Modern period, 24
Modern philosophy, 25–26
Moral responsibility, 65, 330
Moral theory, 24
Multiple sciences, emergence
  of, 33

Naturalistic ideal, 51
Natural logic, concept of, 6
Negotiated meaning, 330
"New Historicism," emergence of,
  34, 35
No Child Left Behind (NCLB),
  13–14, 43

Objective Knowledge: An Evolutionary
  Approach, 31
Of Grammatology, 38
Ontology, 45, 46, 330
Order of Things, The, 33

Paradigm Dialog, 10
Performing Culture in the
  Classroom: An Instructional
  (Auto) Ethnography, 171–205
Perspectivalism, 43
Perspectives of knowledge,
  changing, 4–5
Perspectivism, 43
Phenomenology of Spirit, 35

Philosophia, 23
Philosophical Investigations, 37
Philosophical issues presented to
  scholars, 319–321
Philosophy and psychology,
  differentiation of, 24
Philosophy in educational research,
  23–24
Physical/temporal reality, 61
Politics and self-interest, role of, 8
Positivism, 330
  defeat of, 2–3
  remnants of, 3–4
Positivistic view of science, 51
Positivist legacy, 1–4
Post-analytic philosophy, 29, 36
Postmodern Condition, 29
Postmodernism, *29,* 330
Postmodern social theory, 8–9
Postmodern view, 51
Postpositivism, 44, 51, 53, 54, 55
  Alexander study, on the,
    188–189
  Carr et al. study, on the, 114–116
  Ellis study, on the, 263–265
  epistemology of, 46
  Heath study, on the, 151–153
  methodology, 46
  ontology of, 46
  Raudenbush et al. study, on the,
    226–229
  Sullivan study, on the, 292–294
  values of, 46
Poststructuralism, 44
  Alexander study, on the, 203–207
  Carr et al. study, on the, 132–134
  Ellis study, on the, 281–283
  epistemology of, 47
  Heath study, on the, 167–170
  methodology of, 47
  ontology of, 47
  Raudenbush et al. study, on the,
    246–251
  Sullivan study, on the, 311–313
  values of, 47
Pragmatism, 44
  Alexander study, on the, 190–192
  Carr et al. study, on the, 116–118

Ellis study, on the, 265–266
  epistemology of, 46
  Heath study, on the, 153–154
  methodology, 46
  ontology of, 46
  Raudenbush et al. study, on the,
    229–231
  Sullivan study, on the, 294–296
  use of, 57
  values of, 46
Preparation, contemporary,
  323–324
Principia Mathematica, 37
Priori, 28
Problems of Philosophy, The, 21

Quantitative-qualitative debate, 10
Questioning at Home and at School:
  A Comparative Study, 135–170

Race, ethnicity, and gender, 45
  Alexander study, on the,
    197–198
  Carr et al. study, on the, 125–126
  Ellis study, on, 273–276
  epistemology of, 47
  Heath study, on, 160
  methodology of, 47
  ontology of, 47
  Raudenbush et al. study, on the,
    238–239
  Sullivan study, on the,
    305–307
  values of, 47
Rapport, building, 97
Rationalism, 26, 27
Raudenbush et al. study, 206–249
  constructivism on, 231–233
  critical theory on, 240–244
  ethics, methodology, and
    democracy on, 244–246
  interpretive and narrative on,
    234–237
  postpositivism on, 226–229
  poststructuralism on, 246–251
  pragmatism on, 229–231
  race, ethnicity, and gender on,
    238–239

Reconstruction in Philosophy, 22
Researchers, challenges facing
  defining research, challenges in,
    316–318
  educational researcher's identity
    in the academy, 322–323
  leadership in perspectives, role of,
    318–319
  philosophical issues presented to
    scholars, 319–321
  preparation, contemporary,
    323–324
Research products, utility and
  application of, 7
Revolution in Poetic Language, 38

Scholastic period, 24
Science
  intellectual occupation
    with, 32
  interaction of science, public
    policy, and social values,
    interaction of, 16
  and social values, 14–16
"Science wars," 33
Scientific Research in Education, 11
Self-reflexive, 330
Sensa, 27
Social construction, 34
Social Construction of What?, 34
Social frame to inquiry, 22
Social theory, father of, 28
Social validity, 101
Sociology of knowledge, 58, 330
*Structure of Scientific Revolutions,
  The,* 33
Subjects *vs.* participants, 330
Sub-traditions, philosophical,
  26–28
Sullivan study, 284–314
  arts based educational reseach on,
    301–305
  constructivism on, 296–297
  critical theory on, 307–310
  ethics, methodology, and
    democracy on, 310–311
  interpretive and narrative on,
    298–301

Sullivan study, *(continued)*
  postpositivism on, 292–294
  poststructuralism on, 311–313
  pragmatism on, 294–296
  race, ethnicity, and gender on,
    305–307
Superordinate processes of
  argument, 26

Teachers and school organizations,
  characteristics of, 211

Teleology, 330
"There Are Survivors": Telling a
  Story of Sudden Death,
  250–283
Tractatus Logico-Philosophicus, 32
Truth and Method, 37
Two Dogmas of Empiricism, 3

Unified science, theory of, 33
Universal rationality, 6
Unwarranted beliefs, 50

Values, 46
Verification, 96
Verisimilitude, 330
Verstehen, 61, 65, 330
Voices Inside Schools, Notes from a
  Marine Biologist's Daughter: On
  the Art and Science of Attention,
  284–314

Warranted assertion, 58, 328
Warranted beliefs, 50